"Fascinating. A fresh, unpredictable story."
Kathleen M. Brown, *Journal of American History*

"The best kind of comparative history.... Readers will find witty and evocative writing, challenging ideas, an abundance of images and page-turning stories of individual lives.... This is a complex and thought-provoking book, one that takes the study of marriage—a subject both deeply political and powerfully intimate—to new and inspiring places."
Katherine Ellinghaus, *Australian Historical Studies*

"An accomplished example of contemporary historical scholarship.... [*Illicit Love* is] a book that amply realizes McGrath's long-standing ambition to 'write history that people want to read.'"
Mark McKenna, *Australian Book Review*

"The real drama in *Illicit Love* lies with the lovers, in relationships, not regulations. Love infuses McGrath's characters with power and presence. We cynics might call it strategy . . . but McGrath makes it clear that we miss something important when we do so. McGrath's 'love'—both for and between her characters—gives a depth to this fresh and sometimes dazzling book that must resonate with us all."
Lisa Ford, *American Historical Review*

"Combines warmth, compassion, meticulous scholarship, and wise observations.... This is a valuable and arresting work of scholarship."
Elaine Hatfield and Richard L. Rapson, *Pacific Historical Review*

"Superbly written.... From the opening line, 'We are waiting on a file' every historian will be hooked. But the moving stories [McGrath] tells of the radical valency of unguarded love will touch many readers' hearts, all with an entirely new appreciation of the shattering potential of the adage, love conquers all."
Liz Conor, *Aboriginal History*

"McGrath's intention 'to carve some space in the history books for feelings, for tenderness and tender emotions,' offers a fresh new perspective and compelling reading."
Susana D. Geliga and Margaret D. Jacobs, *Gender and History*

"Superbly researched and imaginatively presented, McGrath's reconstruction of stories of marriages and sexual intimacies across the lines of race and domination between settler-colonial and indigenous peoples in the United States and Australia is a remarkable instance of interweaving the two 'national' histories."
Dipesh Chakrabarty, Lawrence A. Kimpton Distinguished Service Professor of History at the University of Chicago and the author of *The Calling of History: Sir Jadunath Sarkar and His Empire of Truth*

"Read this book to explore both the direct and the twisted paths linking marriage and sovereignty, in richly detailed case studies spanning two disparate continents on both of which racial hierarchy characterized settler colonialism."
 Nancy F. Cott, Jonathan Trumbull Professor of American History, Harvard University

"Ann McGrath reminds us that 'weddings' have long mixed politics and intimate passions in the interests of family, tribe, and nation. Heart-wrenching stories and subtle distinctions are laid bare in fine prose, and we find the kinship between Australia and the United States even closer than we might have thought."
 James F. Brooks, author of *Captives and Cousins: Slavery, Kinship, and Community in the Southwest Borderlands*

"This is a convincing and lively analysis of how marriage helped create the modern nation. Using case studies from the Cherokee Nation and northern Australia, McGrath deftly makes the case for the key role played by marriage in settler colony histories. McGrath's moving account is transnational history at its best."
 Philippa Levine, author of *The British Empire: Sunrise to Sunset* and *Gender and Empire*

"Investigating marriages between the colonized and their colonizers, *Illicit Love* is an astonishing transnational history of transgression, revealing intertwined lives and irreconcilable ideas, courage and conflict, denial and defiance, secrets and surveillance, love and violence.... McGrath asks novel questions, tells untold stories, and writes a new history of empire. This innovative and inventive work will itself open up new worlds for its readers."
 Martha Hodes, author of *White Women, Black Men: Illicit Sex in the Nineteenth-Century South*

"This is a beautiful book, a tale of family, racial mixture, and identity in two settler colonial societies.... McGrath's stories of love and marriage across the color line, told in luminous prose, will delight.... *Illicit Love* ought to be a prizewinner."
 Paul Spickard, author of *Race in Mind*

"A powerful testament to the power of personal stories to complicate our understanding of larger historical processes."
 James Joseph Buss, *Western Historical Quarterly*

"*Illicit Love* is a stunning piece of comparative history. With the storytelling abilities of a novelist and the detective skills of the accomplished historian that she is, Ann McGrath reveals how interracial relationships stirred a myriad of emotions among nineteenth- and early twentieth-century Americans and Australians and raised what became enduring questions about the meaning of Cherokee and Aboriginal identities."
 Gregory Smithers, author of *Science, Sexuality, and Race in the United States and Australia, 1780s–1890s*

ILLICIT
LOVE

Borderlands and Transcultural Studies

SERIES EDITORS:
Pekka Hämäläinen
Paul Spickard

Illicit Love

Interracial Sex and Marriage in the United States and Australia

Ann McGrath

University of Nebraska Press
Lincoln and London

© 2015 by the Board of Regents of
the University of Nebraska

All rights reserved
Manufactured in the United States of America

Publication of this volume was assisted by
the Virginia Faulkner Fund, established in
memory of Virginia Faulkner, editor in chief
of the University of Nebraska Press.

Portions of this book previously appeared in
a different form in "Consent, Marriage, and
Colonialism: Indigenous Australian Women and
Colonizer Marriages," *Journal of Colonialism and
Colonial History* 6, no. 3 (2005); and "Naked Shame:
Nation, Science, and Indigenous Knowledge in
Walter Roth's Interventions into Frontier Sexualities,"
in *The Roth Family: Anthropology and Colonial
Administration*, ed. R. McDougall and I. Davidson
(Walnut Creek CA: Left Coast Press, 2008), chap. 13.

Library of Congress Cataloging-in-Publication Data

McGrath, Ann (Ann Margaret)
Illicit love: interracial sex and marriage in the
United States and Australia / Ann McGrath.
pages   cm.—(Borderlands and transcultural studies)
Includes bibliographical references and index.
ISBN 978-0-8032-3825-1 (hardback)
ISBN 978-1-4962-0384-7 (paper)
ISBN 978-0-8032-8541-5 (epub)
ISBN 978-0-8032-8542-2 (mobi)
ISBN 978-0-8032-8543-9 (pdf)
1. Interracial marriage—United States—History.
2. Interracial marriage—Australia—History.
3. Miscegenation—United States—History.
4. Miscegenation—Australia—History.
5. Indigenous people—United States—History.
6. Indigenous people—Australia—History. I. Title.
HQ1031.M3946 2015
306.84'6—dc23
2015023634

Set in Garamond Premier by M. Scheer.
Designed by N. Putens.

For my family—past, present, and future

CONTENTS

List of Illustrations ... ix

Preface: Flowers for the Bride ... xiii

Acknowledgments ... xxvii

Introduction: A Perfect Marriage? ... 1

Part 1. Secrets of New Nations

1. Harriett Gold and Elias Boudinot: Against History? ... 35
2. Ernest Gribble and Jeannie ... 87

Part 2. Marriage and Modernity among the Cherokees

3. Socrates, Cherokee Sovereignty, and the Regulation of White Men ... 147
4. John Ross and Mary Bryan Stapler ... 193

Part 3. Queensland's Marital Middle Ground

5. Husbands under Surveillance   251

6. Consent and Aboriginal Wives   293

Part 4. Embodying New Worlds

7. Polygamy's New Worlds   325

8. Entwined Sovereignties and the Great Unwedding   349

Epilogue: Transnational Families   369

Notes   395

Bibliography   457

Index   489

ILLUSTRATIONS

Figures

1.	Flowers from the wedding of John Ross and Mary B. Stapler	xvi
2.	John Ross and Mary B. Stapler's marriage certificate	xvii
3.	Dolley Madison portrait	xviii
4.	Dolley Madison cartoon	xix
5.	Clara Sue Kidwell at the Cherokee Female Seminary, Tahlequah, Oklahoma	xx
6.	Alfred Jacob Miller, *The Trapper's Bride*	xxi
7.	Harriett Gold	36
8.	Elias C. Boudinot	37
9.	Major Ridge	42
10.	John Ridge	43
11.	Catharine Brown	54
12.	Elias Boudinot IV	64
13.	Boudinot IV's home in Burlington, New Jersey	65
14.	Wedding of Mathilda and Cuthbert Simpson, 1926	88
15.	Yarrabah beach	89
16.	Yarrabah shipwreck	90
17.	Multigenerational family group in traditional housing	92
18.	Men carrying *woomeras*, spears, and decorated shields	93
19.	Ernest Gribble in a Yarrabah classroom, ca. 1900	96
20.	White cross marking the landing of J. B. Gribble	97

21.	"The First Aborigines at Yarrabah, 1892"	101
22.	St. Alban's Church interior, 1901	104
23.	Senior girls, Yarrabah	105
24.	The Yarrabah band with man in Native Police–like uniform, 1907	108
25.	The Yarrabah band girls and boys	109
26.	Married quarters at Yarrabah village, ca. 1905	111
27.	Authority figures and lawmakers at Yarrabah	114
28.	Government men visit the mission	115
29.	Murragun Outstation	123
30.	Karpa Creek Outstation	124
31.	Ethel Gribble's wedding, 1906	132
32.	Junior girls outside Yarrabah schoolhouse, ca. 1900	135
33.	Front page of the *Cherokee Phoenix*, April 10, 1828	151
34.	*Cherokee Phoenix* masthead	152
35.	George Washington medal	159
36.	Vann House	165
37.	David Vann	166
38.	Rose Cottage, home of John Ross	175
39.	Sequoyah	189
40.	Letter from John Ross to Mary Stapler, 1844	198
41.	Watercolor portrait of John Ross, 1841	207
42.	*John Ross*: A Cherokee Chief	208
43.	Silhouette of John Ross, 1841	210
44.	Dolley Madison in turban	224
45.	John Mix Stanley, *International Indian Council*	239
46.	Samuel Bell Waugh, *Mary Stapler Ross*, 1848	242
47.	Photograph of Mary and John Ross	244
48.	Chinese man in front of his hut, ca. 1890	255
49.	Archibald Meston and Walter E. Roth	266
50.	Postcard from Wild Australia Show	268
51.	Aboriginal men with hunting and fighting equipment	269
52.	Chinese prisoners, Croydon, 1894	277
53.	Cartoon of Archibald Meston	280

54. Alexander Meston, ca. 1890	282
55. Archibald Meston, ca. 1895	283
56. Walter Roth, 1918	286
57. A Chinese cook in a bush camp, 1886	310
58. *The Black Predecessor*, from the *Bulletin*, 1894	335
59. Locket images of Elias and Harriett Boudinot, ca. 1826	372
60. Boudinot family portrait gallery	376
61. Caroline and William Penn Boudinot	377
62. Cherokee delegation to Washington DC, 1866	378
63. Daguerreotype of John Ross, ca. 1850	379
64. Ernest Gribble, Nola Clark, Winnie Massey, and Madge Leftwich	380
65. Generations of the Clark family on their property, ca. 1940	382
66. Nola Clark's children, 1930	384
67. Ernest Gribble's farewell address, 1930	385
68. Ernest Gribble at Gribble Point, Yarrabah	386
69. Ernest Gribble's grave	387
70. *Children of John and Mary Ross*, by Samuel B. Waugh, ca. 1847–48	388

Maps

1. The world	xii
2. Australia	xxxiv
3. The U.S. Eastern Seaboard with Indian tribal areas featured	34
4. U.S. intermarriage sites	34
5. Queensland intermarriage sites	86
6. Yarrabah and surrounding region	122
7. The Cherokee Nation ca. 1820, overlaid with modern state boundaries	146
8. Cherokee Nation towns, 1820s–1830s	146
9. Trail of Tears routes to Indian Territory in the West	354

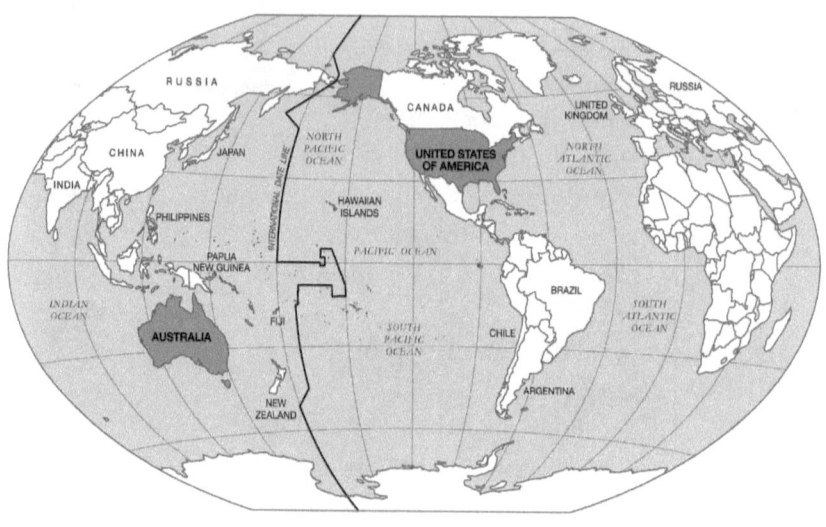

MAP 1. The world: nations across seas and hemispheres.

PREFACE

Flowers for the Bride

We are waiting on a file. Sitting together in the archives of the Gilcrease Museum in Tulsa, Oklahoma, Clara Sue and I are having lively chats while hoping to learn more about the Cherokee chief John Ross. Although he had opposed intermarriages between Cherokees and whites, after his Cherokee wife died, he ended up marrying a white woman. The opening cast of this part of the story: Clara Sue Kidwell and the author. From different sides of the hemispheric divide, we are time-line jumpers, historians of frontier, especially of the colonizing interface. Myself, a Queensland-born Australian, and Clara Sue, a senior Native American scholar from Oklahoma in the United States of America. Our research expeditions have crossed the Equator and the date line — those invisible geometries that partition the world. Although we sit on different sides of the settler-colonizer divide, these cross-lines are not so simple. Clara Sue Kidwell's ancestry is Choctaw, Chippewa, French, English, and Scotch-Irish. Despite our Scottish, English, and other ancestors, my grandparents and great-grandparents said we were Irish. My paternal grandfather was indeed the son of a Galway man, but along with Viking genes, his deep-toned skin suggested the Spanish or Roman heritage that people referred to as dark Irish. Then there was his English-born mother, my great-grandmother, Marion Smith. Illegitimate, she never knew who her father was, or her birth name. Brought up by foster parents, she traveled alone to faraway Australia at age sixteen. Soon married, she eventually bore and raised ten children. Her daughter-in-law, my grandmother, confided that her missing father was "something to do with royalty." "Sure," I scoffed to myself when I first heard this: "It's one of those family history myths; everyone is related to a king—or perhaps an Indian princess." That is, unless history is indeed stranger than fiction.

These days, the urge to connect with ancestors seems driven by something deeper than curiosity. With the Internet, digitalization, and DNA testing bringing within closer reach distant and even ancient generations, finding lost ancestors has become a favorite pastime. Yet even in close family history, it can be difficult to go back far, and with missing fathers, displaced families, and missing birth records, even more so.

In histories of colonialism, the stories of marriages across colonizing boundaries have not entered the main plotlines. Further, broad patterns of marital and family histories have gone missing from the histories of nation-states. Yet these marriages delivered new branches of family histories and expansive diasporic connections that present different family trees and connecting forests. We need to explore why these became such an uncomfortable fit in colonizer nations—to the extent that they were razed by a systemic forgetting. Perhaps it is because these marriages blurred the dividing lines between Indigenous and settler-colonizer space.

Although historians turn their attention to a relatively small chunk of written time, it is worth turning our eyes toward the deep history of the global journey—one of rising and falling land bridges and ocean voyages, where a bevy of our ancestors traveled from Africa.[1] On epic migrations, people took northern, southern, western, and eastern routes around the globe, encountering different peoples and intermixing with them as they did so. Following different motivations, and in different epochs, they departed again, journeying back to where they came from and then onward, in other directions. Human history is an expansive story of separation and reunion—of peoples traveling, departing, fighting, severing, cooperating, and again meeting up—in turn amazed, curious, and anxious about their similarities and differences. Connecting, pairing, having families, departing, dividing up, and doing it all over again; this is central to the story of how the world's cultures and peoples came to be.

It has seemed a very long time, but now the Ross file has finally arrived. My research is about to become a lone business again. That is, as alone as one can be in an archive, where the fresh pages of someone else's present day still manage to speak to a distant future. With full hearts, those writers sometimes shared their most intimate emotions. When I untie the white ribbon and open the Ross Collection's manila folder 94, registration no. 5326.290, the sea of words I had anticipated is missing. Instead, protected by old paper inscribed in India ink are the corpses of flowers.

A spray of fine twigs and a bud have been tied up with string. Powder-dry, faint imaginings of color tinge the otherwise sepia remains. Maybe the stems were once a sprig of cedar, lavender, or some other woody bush. As for the bud, it is crushed almost flat, petal and stem fused. I discern the remains of an old-style pink or red rose.

Who has inspected them before me? Who laid them there so carefully? The thick, hand-cut paper containing them is yellow-stained with organic impressions of archival movement. Powdery botanical scraps nestle in the creases. Judging the stains, perhaps only one or two people have opened and shut this file before me. Then I read the paper's notation: "Presented to Mrs Mary B. Ross By Mrs Madison the widow of Ex President Madison." The file is dated September 2, 1844. The occasion was the wedding of the Cherokee chief John Ross and Mary Bryan Stapler of Wilmington, Delaware. In the same file is an ornate marriage certificate, dated 1844.[2]

It is the summer of 1999 and now we are speeding along the highway in a Honda sports car, en route to Clara Sue Kidwell's parental home in Muskogee, Oklahoma, stopping at places that I knew only through the archives. Clara Sue is generously hosting her Australian colleague on her first whistle-stop tour of this region. She is brushing up against childhood and family stories, including her birthplace of Tahlequah, Oklahoma, the Cherokee capital founded in 1838 in the western territory and the location of her old school.

In interludes from university teaching positions, we had both worked at national museums — she at the Smithsonian Museum of the American Indian, then in New York, and I at the then-just-opened National Museum of Australia in Canberra. When we arrived at the Gilcrease, Clara Sue and I soaked up the galleries, including one full of Wild West landscapes, before heading to examine the nineteenth-century painting *The Trapper's Bride*. The work of the American artist Alfred Jacob Miller, it was first sketched in

FIG. 1. The remnants of flowers from the wedding of John Ross and Mary B. Stapler. A note in the museum's file indicates that Dolley Madison presented the flowers to the couple. John Ross Collection, registration no. 5326.290, folder 94, Gilcrease Museum Archives. Courtesy Gilcrease Museum, Tulsa OK.

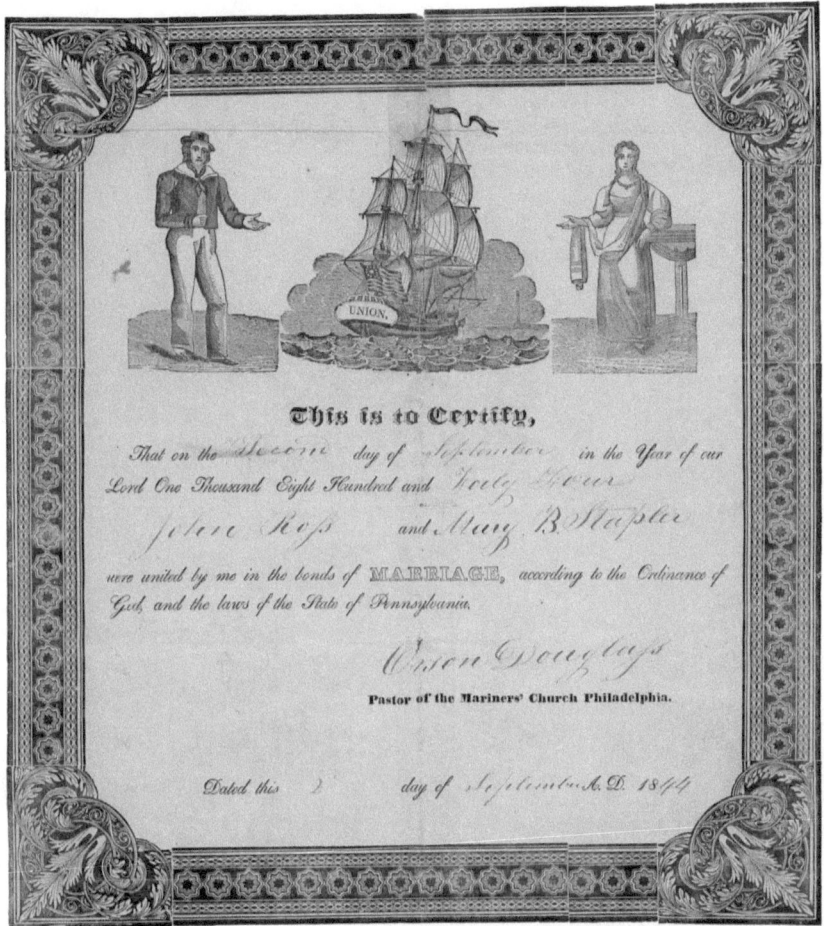

FIG. 2. Marriage certificate for John Ross and Mary B. Stapler. John Ross Collection, registration no. 5126.52, folder 94, Gilcrease Museum Archives. Courtesy Gilcrease Museum, Tulsa OK.

watercolor in 1837, then completed as an oil in 1845. A section from a later commissioned watercolor appears on the cover of this book. In this romanticized "Indian" scene, a gallant European-looking groom and a beautiful Indian maiden are about to be betrothed. Like the artist, who had traveled through the Rocky Mountains but who painted the more formal, oil version of this work in a Scottish castle, we historians live in worlds separated but not entirely severed from that once-seen, once-walked-in past. We try

FIG. 3. This image of Dolley Madison (Mrs. James Madison) soon after her marriage depicts her as an elegant, stylish young woman in a formal gown, carrying a fan as an accessory. Her expression suggests a confident and friendly woman who takes pleasure in her public role. "Mrs. James Madison, (Dolly Payne)/from an original picture by Gilbert Stuart, in possession of Richard Cutts, Esq. M.D. Washington." Courtesy Library of Congress, reproduction no. LC-USZ62-68175.

FIG. 4. This cartoon recognizes the power of the political wife as hostess and as a force for developing powerful networks of loyalty. With the words "The Reign of Dolly Madison," it subjects the president's wife to ridicule, yet against the often-harsh diatribes of the era, this is gentle, suggesting that Dolley had earned acceptance of her role in this regard. Louis M. Glackens, artist, courtesy Library of Congress, reproduction no. LC-USZCN4-179.

hard to find the routes and connections that help us travel alongside those fleeting particles of time.

Two feet by three feet, the painting we are taking in is far from life size but big enough in conception to create an epic drama. The bride and groom enact what appears to be a formal ritual of frontier union. The rich-toned woman with flowing dark hair wears a fringed buckskin dress, its pale hue conjuring the white wedding gowns of a later era. The light-skinned trapper is dressed in hybrid clothing that could place him on either side of the colonizing frontier. Their eyes do not meet, but yes! their hands are about to touch. Although the painting's composition evokes a European-style proposal, the calumet or pipe suggests another cultural world with different marriage rituals. Trade goods for marital exchange signal a negotiated, familial contract, while a mother and baby nearby evoke the promise of offspring to come. The bride is regal, commanding, yet stands with eyes

FIG. 5. Clara Sue Kidwell outside the Cherokee Female Seminary at Tahlequah, Oklahoma. Photo by author.

humbly downcast. In a seated position, the groom looks up entreatingly. He is mesmerized, enthralled — as much trapped as trapper.[3]

Whiffs of fresh leather, tobacco, and the dust of people and horses moving about. If we could pierce time and step into these action scenes, we would confront a complex story of individual personalities, hopes, and power struggles permeated by global mobilities — of wide, unseen networks of connection. Although populated with archetypes, this painting evokes larger histories generally known only to insiders: private sagas of attraction, emotion, and family.

As a historian of gender and colonialism, intermarriage has preoccupied me as a subject of metaphoric and tangible significance. Why was a painting like this so rare? I had many questions. Behind the steering wheel and over many meals, Clara Sue introduced me to the complexity of factors that shaped her people's history, including American Indian women's struggles with a gendered colonialism.

Beyond the vast oceans separating their land masses and the contrasting seasons of their upside-down hemispheres, we tried to work out why

FIG. 6. Alfred Jacob Miller, The Trapper's Bride, ca. 1837. Watercolor, courtesy Walters Art Museum, 37.1940.12, Creative Commons license.

such a chasm divided North American and Australian history. I could not think of any Australian artist who romanticized the marriage of a white man and an Aboriginal woman.[4] Quite the opposite. I could not think of one Australian case in the nineteenth or the early twentieth century where a respectable white woman would be congratulating another white woman on her marriage to an Indigenous man. Let alone a woman with the stature and gravitas of the wife of a former president and founding father of the nation. It would be challenging, but the history of marriage in settler-colonizer nations demanded a larger canvas. In order to spark more conversations between seemingly disparate national histories, I wanted the histories of these distant settler-colonizer nations to be placed side by side.

When I tried to explain my intermarriage project in its early stages, most U.S. historians presumed that I would be looking at marriages between blacks and whites in both nations — that is, those between whites and African Americans and whites and Aboriginal people. This made me realize that I had not envisaged this as a "color" juxtaposition project but rather as one linking people experiencing a common set of power relations — those between colonizers and Indigenous peoples. Indigenous peoples tried to hold on to land that they occupied and knew to be their own; the colonizers attempted to take over lands, to populate them with their own people and create their own nations.[5] In unpredictable and multidimensional ways, color, race, status, gender, and class tinged each and every historical landscape.

The bars to marriage between black and white Americans — segregation laws and practices dubbed Jim Crow — have a high profile in popular consciousness. Having taken place in the lifetimes of the living, their legacies remain. But another segregation history — one engineered to keep "Indians" apart from whites and whites apart from Indians — burbles below the surface. Similarly, the history of Australia's marriage restrictions remains below the radar of national sensibility. In Australia, the term "antimiscegenation" was not even in the lexicon; this was an American thing — something to do with the "Deep South" after slavery. In the cities, schoolchildren who grew up during the twentieth century were taught that British navigators discovered Australia, that the British first colonized it, and that the local Aboriginal people simply "disappeared" or "died out." Australian society imagined itself as white, with some "remnant" Aborigines segregated somewhere else—somewhere far away in remote areas and out of sight. American schoolchildren learned of dramatic wars between Indians and whites, especially on the western plains. Most American Indians were safely relegated to the "West" or "on the reservation" and distanced from the central stories of nation.

History is a discipline devoted to interrogating what people assume to be "common sense." One day, as a child of eleven or twelve, I recall standing next door, in the food-basket backyard of my Australian-born grandfather Joe. A humble man, he never forgot the Great Depression of the 1930s, when his brothers had to travel from one farm to the next to toil for a meal. As miner, then tram driver, he had led a frugal life and his garden now catered to most of his family's food needs. Joe believed in hard work and workers' rights. He respected other people's privacy and he deeply distrusted police and authority figures. That day in the backyard, he switched to a whisper about one of our neighbors, confiding, "He has a touch of the tar brush." I was thrown into confusion, as racism seemed at odds with his nature. So why was the marriage of a white Queenslander to an Aboriginal man or woman something shameful—something to keep hushed and secret?

While Aboriginal and white Australian histories were mixed up in every direction, being readily visible on every Brisbane street, I was mystified as to how, in "settled" suburban zones, such mixed unions had become too illicit to have a name. I did not appreciate how "color" mattered so much, how "whiteness" was entrenched as a category of privilege. To use a hushed tone and a coded language zoned these marital unions inside a perimeter of social exclusion. Only after studying history at university and researching Queensland's Aboriginals Protection Act did I realize there was a law against it—against intermarriage and, for decades, against Aboriginals living in the same areas as whites. The act was first introduced in 1897 but was actively implemented until the 1970s. Better not let the police hear you; better not to let out some secret that could see the couple's children taken away.

Joe did not speak this way about the Sericos. Our house looked directly out to theirs. Their son Nurdon was Dad's best playmate as a boy. Nurdon had helped train me for the school athletics, teaching me how to improve my sprinting. His sister Eve was selected for the Olympic discus team. However, as "Aborigines" were supposed to live on reserves, not in suburbs, and indeed, in *gunyahs*, not houses, the presence of Aboriginal people as neighbors was somehow impossible. On their side of the street, Aboriginal families had compelling reasons for silence about their Gubbi Gubbi identity.

As we headed out on our regular jaunts to our beach shack near Mooloolaba, I was curious about the Aboriginal names. And I was repeatedly awestruck as we passed Mount Tibrogargan, the beast-like extinct volcano that rose suddenly from the edge of the highway. On the gleaming white beaches of Maroochydore and Coolum, where we drenched ourselves with sun and surf, I always wondered where the people who named these places had gone. These places, and the Maroochy River, where my grandparents, Dad, and then the next generation loved to fish for whiting and bream, were all Gubbi Gubbi country. My grandparents refused to holiday or fish anywhere else, building an unwitting connection to their neighbor's country. While encouraging the magic their land worked on others, the Serico family protected the secrecy of their Indigenous lives, holding tight the cultural knowledge of places that most people by then saw as the lands of white Australia. Their full life stories emerged only at their funerals.

By the 1970s many other Queenslanders had become so complicit in burying hidden ancestries that keeping such secrets seemed like common sense. Not only had Aboriginal people supposedly just "gone" from the landscape, with no heroic battles, but it was as if they had never shared the same spaces, let alone fallen in love or gotten married, or lived in our streets, on their land, and among us all.

When, during the early 1980s, I was undertaking my doctoral research project with Aboriginal people who worked in the Northern Territory cattle industry, I had expected to hear accounts of brutal sexual exploitation. And I did. However, I was surprised that several older Aboriginal women spoke candidly, and some even joyfully, of their longer-term liaisons with white men. In what appeared a form of serial monogamy, they recalled stories of agency—of entering and leaving lengthy relationships at will. The Gurindji woman Amy Laurie spoke of how she didn't mind having friends of "different colours.... Some people don't like colour, but better to be mixed like the birds and the flowers mixed."[6] Not all of Amy's family agreed with her optimistic inclusiveness. Rape and incest left cross-generational legacies of intense bitterness and anger. Most of the Aboriginal men fiercely resented white men's "stealing" their women.

Memorialized for its impact on equal wages and land rights, the now-famous Gurindji stockman's "walk-off" strike on Wave Hill Station during the 1960s was driven by the men's desire to curb white men taking Aboriginal wives.[7] Why could white men take their wives, and they not have white wives? For Aboriginal men, rebalancing and redressing colonialism's impact was a continuing dynamic that could be played out in intimate relationships. Recently, certain Aboriginal men of power accumulated a number of white wives, who followed the local protocols for polygamous marriage. Nowhere can be color or gender neutral. The researcher walks into worlds where the ripples of the past disturb the surfaces of the present.

When it came to my own marriage to a New Zealand man, there was no law against it, and despite its transnational aspect, it did not affect anyone's citizenship, rights, or entitlements. My mother was troubled by our being born into different brands of Christianity and no prospect of a Catholic wedding. My father was thrilled with our marriage in Alice Springs and outback honeymoon in Uluru. Dad sent me a huge bunch of banksias and kangaroo paw flowers. My mother was desperately upset. At last, after the birth of our first child, her first grandchild, all was forgiven. The proud grandmother remembers our wedding anniversary more often than we do.

Some years after this big life event, and now with two young children, my American research journey was launched. Under the neo-Gothic spires of Sterling Library at Yale University, New Haven, I found an astonishing archive of the courtship of a Cherokee man and a white woman from Cornwall, Connecticut. Although this was not the West, and by the early nineteenth century neither a new nor an archetypal frontier zone, a New England case of intermarriage had made deep tensions resurface. I needed to work out why.

Inside the marble walls of the Beinecke Library, with their strange red glow of filtered sun, exciting moments of discovery followed, helped greatly by fellow travelers in history. From places with gleaming tropical fronds to pillows of bright snow and singing streams, I would search for some of the clues that long-gone people had left behind. Letters, images, photos, voices, and the flowers for a bride — all promising portals into a cast of living, breathing, loving characters. These people were the ones who held the potential to glue new worlds together — or to smash them into smithereens.

ACKNOWLEDGMENTS

In researching worlds wedded and unwedded, I was humbled by the weight of this subject, and I was buoyed by the new work being published. I had the good fortune to be supported by a patient bunch of colleagues, friends, and family. Nicholas Thomas, now of Cambridge, provided a great boost by awarding me a two-year senior fellowship at his newly opened Centre for Cross-Cultural Research at the Australian National University (ANU). For stimulating conversations about my work, I thank everyone I met in this wonderfully collegial interdisciplinary environment, especially Dipesh Chakrabarty, Roger Benjamin, Iain McCalman, Margo Neale, Donna Merwick, Joan Kerr, and Greg Dening. Starting out at the University of New South Wales, colleague Ian Tyrrell showed that anything was possible, while Allison Holland was a wonderful researcher. Since taking up my post at the Australian Centre for Indigenous History at the ANU, I have learned much from foundational research fellows Gordon Briscoe and Frances Peters-Little, and then from Shino Konishi, Maria Nugent, and Jeanine Leane.

Being welcomed by the great Howard R. Lamar as a visiting fellow at Yale University during the 1990s was one of the highlights of my career. A gentlemanly exemplar of American hospitality, Howard honored me by taking the trouble to read all my publications before my arrival. He then offered his vast knowledge and expert scholarly networks to assist in the development stages of this research project. Dining at the Faculty Club as Howard Lamar's guest was a way to meet leading historians and, equally, to be sustained by tastes of Yale history. Ever thoughtful, Howard chose an Australian necktie to make me feel welcome in that new scholarly home. John Demos and Robin Winks were helpful hosts, as was my sponsor the courageous Ben Kiernan. Carrying on not only the deep-rooted tradition of Dolley Madison's hospitality but also that of her Cherokee grandmother, Glenda Gilmore shared her storytelling. The gregarious Jay Gitlin engaged with my scholarship at conferences in Australia, North America, and various other parts of the globe. George Miles supported my research, encouraging me to apply for the Archibald Hannah Junior Fellowship in American History at the Beinecke, which provided excellent opportunities. I was honored to present a keynote lecture at the newly opened Lamar Center, with my work critiqued by experts of the caliber of Theda Perdue and Nancy Shoemaker.

The exceptionally talented Nancy Cott of Harvard University convinced me of the significance of the marriage theme to national history as we dined together on various occasions in New Haven and at her Cambridge home; the scope and vision of Nancy's work continues to inspire. Johnny Faragher and Alan Trachtenberg impressed with their intellectual energy, while Cherokee historian Jace Weaver asked me probing research questions. Donna Akers of the University of Nebraska shared her family history and gender insights. During the early stages of this project, Lynne Harlan of Cherokee, North Carolina, explained aspects of Cherokee women's attitudes toward intermarriage, opening more doors to Cherokee history. At the Menmuny Museum, Darryl Murgha, Bradley Higgins, and Elverina Johnson were extremely helpful; they and the Yarrabah Council encouraged me to take in the sights of their ancestral homeland. The Brumbys, the Hollingsworths, Kay Schaffer, and Sidonie Smith provided insights into tackling North Queensland research. I am particularly grateful to Charmaine Hollingsworth for sharing her family's Yarrabah history. My research on this topic could continue for a lifetime, but I owe it to my many historical helpers to get my work out during their lifetime, not to mention my own. I owe it to the historical actors too. As I want this book to reach the widest reading public, I acknowledge many more valiant scholarly guides in the references rather than throughout the text.

My many rendezvous with colleagues like Margaret Jacobs, Gunlög Fur, Pamela Scully, Myra Rutherdale, Susan Armitage, Phillipa Levine, Sonya

ACKNOWLEDGMENTS

Michel, Antoinette Burton, Sonya Rose, Nancy Shoemaker, John Maynard, Jacquie Huggins, Marilyn Lake, Patricia Grimshaw, Sylvia van Kirk, Kat Ellinghaus, Victoria Haskens, Lynette Russell, Sioban Nelson, Dan Cobb, Dan and Judy Walkowitz, Clara Sue Kidwell, and Daniel Smail have taken place in various historical hemispheres — at conferences in the United States, Australia, and Europe, at swimming pools, resort lakes, and Swedish farmhouses, and in the warm comfort of their homes. True, with friends and locales like these, being a historian is not a bad career move. More fleeting encounters with Annette Gordon-Reed and Ann Laura Stoler have been memorable and enriching. My dear friends Gunlög Fur, Mickey Dewar, Rebecca Smith, Sue Chamberlain, and many more go way back in autobiographical time. All these people have readjusted my historical and personal compass. Having enjoyed their company, enthusiasm, and ideas over the years, I thank them fondly; I am honored to know them. All of you are my extended kin-networks across the planet and, as several are also Facebook friends, I can enjoy a twenty-four-hour illustrated news cycle.

My doctoral students have been inspiring fellow travelers, but I especially thank Tiffany Shellam, Karen Fox, Christine Hanson, Ingereth Macfarlane, and Val Cooms for their insights. The Dean of my college, Toni Makkai, and Head of School Douglas Craig have been very supportive, while the company of long-term colleagues Allison Cadzow, Mick Dodson, and Peter Read is much appreciated, as are the sanity and wisdom of Mary-Anne Jebb and Malcolm Allbrook. ANU history office staff provided much assistance over the years, while colleagues Tom Griffiths and Pat Jalland have always offered helpful advice. Historians Bain Attwood and Damon Salesa set strong examples. Ann Curthoys and Desley Deacon provided reliable founts of calm wisdom, while Pat Grimshaw never fails to take useful action. I enjoy the company of a gaggle of ANU professors, including Hilary Charlesworth, Kim Rubenstein, Mandy Thomas, Alison Booth, Kaarin Anstey, and Margaret Jolly. I am also fortunate to have more wonderful colleagues than I can thank by name, including all those who helped and stood by me during the early stages of my academic training. And not to forget all those who listened to me whinge and whine about the latest academic dramas. On the subject of spiritual and emotional sustenance, I thank the soothing magic of beaches, the power and unpredictable moods of the Pacific and the Atlantic

Oceans, the beauty of birds and mountainous vistas, my yoga teachers, my calm dog Sebastian, and the baristas at many lively coffee shops.

For sheer effort, I offer warm appreciation to my office neighbor and mentor Barry Higman, whose conscientious reading and troubleshooting meetings enabled me to reach the final stages of this book. He read the manuscript twice. I thank Paul Spickard for his support when I most needed it, and the anonymous assessors for sharing their constructive critiques. Margaret Jacobs, Kat Ellinghaus, and Russell McGregor kindly read chapters. In the final stages of this project, Naomi Parkinson and Laura Rademaker provided timely assistance. Matthew Bokovoy of the University of Nebraska Press has been an intelligent, responsive, patient, conscientious, and supportive publisher. What more could one ask?

The Australian Research Council provided the grant that started up this project, while the University of New South Wales, the Australian National University, and Yale have provided financial support. I have benefited from various visiting lectureships and specialist library and archival visits to the University of Canterbury, the University of Sydney, the University of Queensland, Johns Hopkins University, the University of Baltimore, Harvard University, the University of North Carolina, and the Newberry Library. The Institute for Advanced Study, Princeton, was the magical locale where the book was completed. Special thanks to Didier Fassin, Joan Scott, Danielle Allen, and Robert Dijkgraaf for the perfect scholarly environment that they create there and for their warm support when I needed it. At the Rockefeller Center, Bellagio, I met a team of amazing people. I learned about the importance of supportive networks from our group, including Jacqueline Novagratz—and from Pat Mitchell, who told me about that missing piece of the national history jigsaw—her Cherokee grandmother.

I am grateful to the many librarians and archivists and to several Indigenous and tribal liaison officers who supported my research. These include staff of the Library of Congress, the National Australian Archives, the Queensland State Archives, the Queensland Department of Aboriginal and Torres Strait Islander Policy, the National Library of Australia, the Houghton Library at Harvard, the Sterling and Beinecke Libraries at Yale, the Library of Congress, the U.S. National Archives, the Smithsonian Libraries, libraries at the University of Maryland, the Gilcrease Museum Library, the Western

Collection at the University of Oklahoma, the Museum of the Cherokee Indian, the New Echota Historical Site, the Oklahoma State Library, the Oklahoma Historical Society, the Pennsylvania Historical Society, and the Delaware Historical Society, and those who assisted with email and other queries. Many organizations also assisted with photographic permissions, and these are acknowledged with each image. Cultural permission was sought and received from a recognized representative of the Yarrabah community before reproducing any photographs of the community. Paul Sjoberg and Kay Dancey of the Australian National University expertly prepared the maps.

While many people helped put a roof over my head during my historical travels, it is family who have launched and steadied my world. My parents, Betty and Brian McGrath, have made me what I am and have encouraged me for decades. While my mum still says that she is "not interested in the past, only the future," this is the kind of maternal statement that makes a rebellious daughter ever keener to do the history that matters. She always listens to my gripes. My dad became crazy about history and reads what I write. My brother Paul and sister-in-law Atsuko have been relaxing hosts. My brother John and sister Mary have been supportive as only siblings can be.

I add the caveat that the mistakes of this book are no one else's fault but my own, which I mean sincerely. Some things, however, are the *book's* fault. My husband, Milton Cameron, and daughters, Venetia and Naomi, did not necessarily consent to family weekends ruined by the mantra "Sorry but I have to finish the book." These days, my daughters' demanding university projects are stimulating me toward refreshing perspectives from other disciplines. My husband's interests are unbounded, reminding me of some of the potential fun things I might do after finishing a book. As I witnessed Milton morphing from architect and artist into historical researcher and writer himself, I am grateful for his willingness to accept my ban on discussing endnotes after 10:00 p.m. Strange, when I think of the serendipity of how we met, with its chance kinship encounters across the northern and southern hemispheres, and how enmeshed our lives, if not our formatting issues, then became. I will spare you our courtship story and, before that, the story about the time we first met, momentarily finding ourselves on the same piece of ground, each heading in opposite directions, and supposedly toward different destinations.

ILLICIT

LOVE

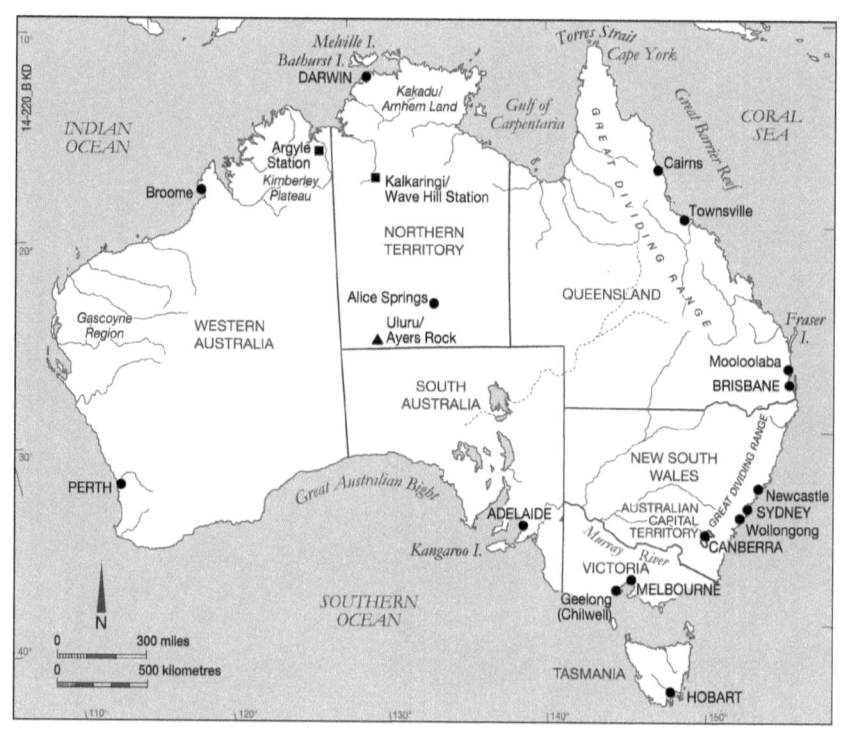

MAP 2. Australia

Introduction

A Perfect Marriage?

Illicit love crossed boundaries. When a man and a woman married across colonizing boundaries, they broke one law or another. Even if their union was not against any official colonizer or Indigenous law, it pitched against family and community wishes. It was inherently transnational. Illicit lovers began to absorb the worlds in which they lived, and to create, and make worlds anew. In so doing, they challenged the vision of what the nation would be. For when people wed, they enacted the future nation in tangible and intangible ways. Yet, whose nation, and what kind of nation? Some couples united in lands of shifting languages, double place-names, and contested, plural understandings of law, marriage, and how to live your life.[1] Illicit love would transform geographic frontiers or separated worlds into landscapes of deep family connection. It would give birth to new worlds and new domains. Love, that eternal intangible, is integral to this history. Subjects moved between cultures, places, and nations and along an emotional trajectory. This book aims to carve some space in the history books for feelings, for tenderness and tender emotions.

We will explore marriages across colonizing frontiers in the early national periods of two modern nations, the United States and Australia. At this particular stage of colonialism, negotiations around intermarriage intersected with founding nationalisms. The main stories take place in the early nineteenth century and in the early twentieth century, respectively. Across each landmass, these boundary-crossing intermarriages created messy, idiosyncratic human dramas. Entangled in state, community, and family politics, they exposed difficult choices and tricky, still unresolved national legacies. They crossed sovereign borders. Metaphorically, "a marriage of nations" stands for a fairy-tale union, living happily ever after. It could also end in divorce. Or be lived unhappily ever after.

Intermarriage became a hidden plotline in settler sovereignty. Casual sexual relations did not attract the same concern, perhaps because it was the longer-term unions that entwined families. During times when nations were trying to define themselves and to imagine their futures, the power nexus of colonizer-Indigenous nations became complex. In their attempts to contain heterosexual unions across colonizing and color lines, settler states used various techniques to assert the authority of their liminal state entities. Negotiations around intimacy, sex, color, family, land, and property left indelible legacies.

This introduction considers marriage as a performance of sovereignty and introduces its significance across sets of laws. It proposes a multilayered approach to transnational history in settler-colonizer contexts and argues that this marital middle ground presented a fundamental challenge to the social, sexual, and colonizing dynamics of settler colonialism. It considers the ideas of some of the founding fathers of nations and refers to the enduring settler mythologies that constrain our current-day thinking.[2]

When I refer to "new worlds," I include the changing worlds of all those who experienced colonialism — the colonized, colonizers, and those who crossed the boundaries.[3] The term "settler-colonizer nations" is used here for colonies where expatriate European populations constituted their own states and aimed to become the majority. This is not meant to imply that colonizer takeover was complete in every realm of life. White settler-colonizer nations referred to themselves as the New World, but of course they were someone else's Old World. Associated with imperial expansion and maritime prowess, the concept of the New World has a long European history. Imperialism, that great land and treasure rush that changed the global map, was a multifaceted human thing — an embodied, embodying encounter. Beyond their known worlds, individuals entered into the worlds of others. These peoples had been geographically separated over deep time, but when they resided on the same ground, they did not stay apart for long.

This work reflects upon the lives and the emotions of people who engaged in heterosexual unions across colonizing frontiers. Here the identities of the people and the groups who held domain remained mobile and unstable. Authority over different aspects of life was constantly disputed. Fundamentally, these were grounds where dual and dueling sovereignties were enacted.

When Indigenous nations intersected with colonizer nations, something specific happened. Relations between colonizer and colonized took place between what were essentially two competing polities. Stuck together, they vied for the same land. Settler colonialism required first the takeover of lands from the people there before the colonists, and second, repopulation through immigration. According to the historian Patrick Wolfe, settler colonialism was premised upon a "logic of elimination" that aimed to rid the land entirely of its Indigenous populations.[4] However, the history of intermarriage demonstrates how colonial projects were fraught with human attraction, contradiction, and competing interests.

This book explores intermarriage across colonizing boundaries as a dynamic of sovereignty and of kinship.[5] In newly emergent nations, orderly marriage was understood not only as key to creating a civilized, modern nation but as essential to the design and weave of its very fabric. The term "nation" is used here in both its older sense, referring to a group of people, and in its modern sense, for a centralized state. During the historical periods under review, the older and modern meanings of nation were used interchangeably. The nation-state is generally defined as a form of political organization under which people who share the same history, traditions, or language live in a particular region, under one government.[6] In any nation, the regulation of gender and family was an important assertion of power. And the ordering of marital relations, eventually through state codification, was arguably the most fundamental of all.

The nation to which an individual belongs helps define a person as a social being, and it requires them to fulfill certain social obligations. In a marriage entered into across colonizing boundaries, each person's relationship to the state and nation was distinctive. It brought new demands on people's loyalties and identities. They were obliged to act as subjects of nation-states and Indigenous societies alike. Would their loyalties remain as a member of the colonizer group and/or of the Indigenous/being-colonized group?

Take the example of white men who joined an Indigenous polity. The derogatory terms "squaw man" or "gone native" were used to imply barbarism or savagery, as if they had stepped backward in history. This narrative configured a world surging toward whiteness and concomitant definitions of race and marital progress. By the same token, white commentators classed Indigenous people who entered colonizer space, or who modernized, as "assimilated" or "civilized," albeit conditionally so. On each side of New World colonialism, people incorporated new knowledge, technologies, concepts, explanatory frameworks, and law. In the eyes of Indigenous landowners, newcomers who entered "Native space" were becoming assimilated and civilized too. Neither culture nor polity was static. Fresh ideas were constantly incorporated and gendered institutions were being remodeled. Everyone's worlds were becoming new. While some rejected their changing worlds, many insiders understood their locales as modern places for modern nations.[7] Like colonialism itself, intermarriage history is intrinsically relational. The realm of neither colonizer nor colonized, it takes place across shared zones of law and history.

In settler-colonizer nations, "perfect sovereignty" was to be achieved through imposing one judicial system to control people and land. From the 1820s, on both the Cherokee lands and in southeastern Australia, sovereignty and territoriality became entwined. According to the historian Lisa Ford, this decade was the turning point at which the concept of the modern nation became increasingly associated with landownership.[8] The threat and enactment of violence asserted control over property. Through military imposition of law, colonizer states were gaining exclusive control over land, resources, and people. At the same time, heterosexual and marital unions were proceeding. In order to achieve what the law referred to as "perfect sovereignty," a judicial system had to assert authority.

The American Constitution declared its aim was to secure "a more perfect Union" and "domestic tranquility." Yet in law, Indians were both domestic and foreign.[9] Across colonizing boundaries, could there ever be such a thing as a "perfect marriage" of state? Both the analogy and the institution of marriage became associated with domain and authority. Backed up by social action at a community level, in attempts to control intimate relations and marriage, Indigenous and colonizing nations alike exerted their law.

In tackling such subject matter, I see value in expanding historical vision beyond a single nation-state; however, the marriage stories do not necessary function as comparative case studies. Instead, in order to apply a strategy of juxtaposition, I put together and tease out a selection of emblematic narratives. When one set of marital history scenarios is placed alongside the other, each looks slightly more peculiar, and fresh perspectives emerge. The aim is to explore and delve into stories that were worlds apart, with the expectation that each will unsettle the other. Rather than attempting a comparative or survey approach, I looked for eye-opening exemplars of what happened between peoples and polities in different times and places. My aim is to engage with the vitality of the micro — the courtship and marital experiences of particular people in discrete times and places. In order to shed a spotlight on the bigger picture, wherever possible, I foreground those vivid details that individual actors have managed to transmit across vectors of time.

In both Australia and the United States, present-day national histories still tend to portray distinctly separate colonizer and colonized pasts. Indigenous history is either relegated to the periphery or finds its way back there. This book tells a story of multiple, intersecting Indigenous and colonizing "nations" — ones that operated interconnected social formations.[10] It focuses upon the Cherokee nation and upon the North Queensland–based Indigenous landowning groups that increasingly call themselves nations.[11]

Indigenous people used marriage strategies to negotiate colonialism and to develop modernizing strategies. It could go either way: marriage could draw their worlds closer together or rip them further apart. However they played out, these unions became the platform for cross-generational cultural transmission and for new formulations around gender, land, and transnational entanglement.

In recent years, a tendency has been to judge Native Americans on appearance, being criticized as too white or too black to be Indian.[12] Within Indigenous nations, questions of blood quantum can be deeply divisive. Meanwhile, Aboriginal Australians are judged as too white, too Indian, or too Asian, sparking bitter controversy and court cases.[13] Somehow people forget the longue durée — that for generations, colonizer and colonized had sex, courted, and married each other. In settler colonies, aspects of the national story have only been partially told; there is a forgetting of entangled histories, and an unwillingness to join the dots. This book will explore how the histories of colonizer and colonized are intimately interwoven.

Perhaps you have mixed ancestry yourself. Or your close friends or family do. In which case you may have heard insider family accounts. It is these historical experiences, your history — and everyone's extended family histories — that constitute the nations in which we dwell. Despite the American penchant for an Indian princess ancestor, many historical border-crossing marriages remain secret. Family secrets. National secrets. Indigenous Australian writers have started to write of the family romances, and the sustaining mixed unions, that were often staged against the law.[14] In Australia, the shame of Aboriginal ancestry has started to tilt the other way, but only very recently. A plethora of stories are still held tightly inside families, confessed on deathbeds, or never.

To return to the question of "nation," this book aims to take the *trans* in "transnational" across a deeper layer of terrain. The flowering of *transnational history* has expanded historical understandings beyond the confines of any one nation. In the United States, it has started to work against a sense of national exceptionalism. Transnational histories have helpfully searched for global linkages, especially across the seas. Yet these have obscured those transactions taking place between nations within the same landmass.[15] This project directs attention to what I call the "colonizing transnational." That is, the intersections, relations, and links *between* colonizer nations and First Nations. By examining the formative early national periods of two colonizer nations as inherently *transnational* ground, we might gain a better vantage point from which to view colonialism. As a contest of intimate power, it was played out across multiple geopolitical borders. Indigenous nations were not considered foreign, so regulations relating to foreign marriage did not apply. However, categories of exclusion proscribed marriage partners classified as Indian, Native American, or Aboriginal.

Historians can be very reluctant to compare similar themes across different nations, let alone different centuries.[16] Nonetheless, the heightened, even frenetic, activity over intermarriage that occurred during the early national periods of the United States and Australia warrants attention. Against a perceived threat to evolving national polities, we will explore how different national entities were trying to deal with regimes of intermarriage. In North

Queensland and in the Cherokee nation, forced to move from east to west, individuals and groups of people revealed that they were self-consciously concerned about marriage, nation, and the transnational.

Specific chapters will discuss intermarriage negotiations between Cherokees and Anglo-Americans, and other chapters will discuss those between Aboriginal people and newcomers in North Queensland. Indigenous groups navigating the pressures of colonialism also had to negotiate different marriage dynamics between different tribal entities.[17] However, the emphasis in this book is upon marriages that took place across colonizing boundaries.

PERFORMING MARRIAGE

When I talk of marriage, I refer to a longer-term, as opposed to a casual, union. This includes informal and formalized unions. These were inscribed in the law of the land by Indigenous peoples and in the printed laws of Indigenous and colonizer nations. Marriage confirmed public recognition and acceptance of a couple's intimacy. It implied wider familial entanglements. In her superb study of marriage and nation in America, historian Nancy Cott explains that the American wedding is the ultimate performative utterance. Whether simple or elaborate, the modern western marriage requires consent, and it seals a potentially lifelong contract. Words of agreement must be spoken aloud, and then agreements signed on paper, before witnesses.[18]

Marriage was not only about individuals and couples. Consent, taking place in given historical cultural contexts, could be a complex and sometimes problematic concept. The nature of marriage, especially regarding same-sex and plural marriage, has been controversial for the U.S. Congress and the Australian parliament alike.[19] In modern western states, marriage law defines the union as monogamous. It has usually been between a man and a woman. Yet the idea of how marriage is constituted is not static; it reflects changing social values and aspirations. Same-sex marriage is increasingly welcomed and legal. In *early national periods*, marriage was seen as the essential building block that constituted new nations. After all, it made them heterosexual or straight; it made them mono, unified, monogamous. Fundamental to liberal logics, marriage potentially shaped a certain kind of heteronormative polity and, in turn, a specific national character.[20] Indigenous nations also had a strong stake in using marriage for nationalistic purposes.

So what's it all about? Marriage is about love. Or so people say. We will follow some such stories. But marriage is equally about law and a legal and social status that comes with specific expectations. Within a liberal framework, a contract between parties is anticipated, alongside other kinds of societal agreement.[21] Between cultures, the rules, rituals, and expectations differ in so many ways.

Marriage can happen due to obsessive human impulses: sexual desire, infatuation, and longing. It commonly produces, adopts, or incorporates children, who in turn provide new targets for love, cultural transmission, property transmission, and dispute. Marriage nearly always creates new networks or strengthens or expands old ones. It sparks cross-generational feeling and loyalty and consolidates or splinters group identity. The sociology, law, philosophy, ethnology, songs, poetry, art, and literature on the topic of love and marriage are endless.

Marriage can be strategic: economically or religiously so. It can create new knowledge exchange. Between families or kingdoms, it is associated with peacemaking and diplomacy. Marriage is at once political—public and state controlled—and intensely private. It is implicated in the orderings of patriarchy and matriarchy. It is both a key symbol of social order and control and suspect because it can be ruled by passion. It increases or decreases status; it confers rights and obligations. It brings in useful skills or attributes and it involves labor exchanges. It is associated with economic exchange, land, accumulated wealth, inheritance. Binding bonds, kinship, extended family, community. Gender roles, submission, compromise, influence.

Sexual unions across colonialism were both tense and tender ties.[22] With this evocative phrase, the cultural theorist Ann Laura Stoler alludes to both colonizer anxieties and bonds. There is more to be done with the word "tense." For, as the legacies of intermarriage crossed past, present, and future tense, they not only endured beyond frontiers, they dissolved them.

Given the atrocities associated with colonialism, including sexual violence and exploitation, the possibility of noncoercive relations between colonizer and colonized seems incongruous. Massacre, poisoning, warfare, neglect, disease, starvation, abduction, rape, and all kinds of horrific cruelties do not appear to lend themselves to courtships between nations. So colonizing invasions were hardly conducive to happy marriages. Nonetheless, imperial mobilities facilitated new sets of intimate connections.[23] Marriage, like gender, constitutes both a category and a connecting sinew of historical analysis.[24] As a crucial social dynamic, it points to gendered and cultured intersections that are imagined, embodied, concrete, enacted, and lived. This book interrogates how marriages across colonizing boundaries disrupted and unsettled settler colonialism. The visibility of people in cross-colonizer marital unions potentially reconfigured ideas of nation, gender, and race. Intermarriage nuanced people's everyday lives, leading to new trends, exchanges, laws, and demographic outcomes. Consequently, marital decisions shaped the public sphere and in turn contributed to the making of nations.

Colonialism offered the marital voyager an option akin to heading east or west. Intermarriage occupies the bamboozling crossroads of gender, race, class, and colonialism — if not of history itself.[25] It is too easy to fall into the teleological trap of seeing colonialism as one way and the colonizers as all-powerful.[26] This is where a focus on courtship and upon the families that jumped the colonizing gap is especially useful.[27] In the quest to secure national, community, and family futures, race and gender continually resurfaced to create a unique politics of intimacy that was at once public and private.

THE RULE OF MARRIAGE

Throughout history, and across cultures, many societies around the world had value-laden ideas about marriage as constituting social order. Marriage made families, but families could not then beget themselves. Marriages within forbidden degrees of kinship and family affinity were commonly banned. In other words, you could not marry a brother or sister, either biologically defined or according to classificatory kinship. You had to marry either outside or inside your local area and group or to marry a person in a particular category. Age, class, and religion mattered. Different states and nations outlawed mixed marriages on the basis of national citizenship, slave status, race or ethnic affiliation, and Indigenous identity.

Alongside warfare, European monarchs, colonizers, and Indigenous people alike deployed marital diplomacy to retain or enlarge their sovereign domains.[28] In eighteenth-century New England, the Algonquins used the courts of the newcomers to codify their marital practices in writing.²⁹ In the hope of sustaining the "common pot" of resources and sustenance that ensured harmony amid periods of intense warfare during the eighteenth century, Mohegan sachems formed strategic, often multiple, marriage alliances with other peoples.³⁰

Intersecting class and nation, the gendered politics of marriage mirrored larger colonial struggles. Britain sustained concern about marriage as a device of empire. For example, despite their often having wives and husbands back in England, convicts in Australia were encouraged to marry each other. In 1865 Britain's Colonial Marriages Act validated all marriages "contracted in Her Majesty's Possessions abroad" provided that both parties were "competent to contract the same."³¹ In this strange imperial twist, the law of marriage effectively preempted the establishment of a state. It also meant that prior marriages that took place far away could be disregarded.

Marriage histories offer special insights into the gendering of colonialism. Imperial and settler-colonizer rule needed the institution of marriage, for they held that it was vital to creating and maintaining social order. It was a way to tame felons and frontiersmen. Although modeled on British law, marriage law diverged across the American colonies, and later between its states. Most states restricted intermarriage between whites and black slaves, rules then extended to free blacks. Several states banned intermarriage between whites and Indians.³² In Queensland, the Aboriginals Act restricted intermarriage on the basis of race, targeting people with the labels of white, Chinese, and Aboriginal. However, as the Marriage Act itself was not changed, this temporarily weakened the act's authority.³³ After federation in 1901, the Australian self-governing colonies became states, each of which exercised power over both Aboriginal affairs and marriage. The Queensland Act became a precursor of policies in Western Australia and the Northern Territory.

In the United States, after Congress met in 1789, the federal Department of War had responsibility for relations with Indian nations. Tribal leaders had a direct line to the leaders of the United States. The Cherokees fought court cases to gain legal recognition of their national status. By the early 1830s they gained a judgment that they were a "domestic dependent nation." Not that this necessarily helped. Although their sovereign status was recognized, Georgian and federal authorities became ever keener to override this ruling in order to pursue their conflicting interests.[34]

SOVEREIGNTIES

Sovereignty is still a vital concern for settler-colonizer states. In 2007 Australia, New Zealand, the United States, and Canada formed a block that refused to sign the United Nations Declaration on the Rights of Indigenous Peoples, arguing that it would conflict with their national laws. Eventually, they relented.[35]

Both nations have trouble coming to terms with their role as colonizers and its associated almanac of violence and injustice.[36] We can observe this in the way they tackle Indigenous rights issues and the way they remember their histories.[37] Despite Australia and the United States being wealthy countries, Indigenous peoples in both nations suffer poverty, serious health and economic disadvantage, and disproportionately high imprisonment rates. Being Indigenous in a settler-colonizer nation remains an economic drawback.[38] This and overall population disparities led to high rates of Indigenous out-marriage in Australia and the United States.[39]

In order to make authority over domain real, in international law, sovereignty required assertions and performances of power. For the early national periods, this book will show how intermarriage became an enactment of transnational sovereignty. Just as the wedding and marriage had to be contracted, lived, and observed, so too did Indigenous and colonizer sovereignty. I apply an understanding of sovereignty as the operation of group power — one enacted through performative practice: orally, on paper, in kinship and clan, and in other social and familial relationships.[40] Popular sovereignty went beyond the monarch to share power and consent with the people. As with other cross-cultural categories, using the term "sovereignty" for Indigenous polities has limitations.[41] We engage in flawed acts of translation.

For settler sovereignty to take effect, human bodies needed to enact and perform it. Ships arrived, people planted crosses with royal arms, hoisted flags, made speeches on behalf of a king, read out official instructions to gathered audiences. Employees of states wrote journals, explored, mapped, and surveyed land. Wars were fought with Indigenous peoples; many were killed. Sometimes treaties were negotiated with the original landowners.

Later, the victorious colonizers wrote constitutions, laws, and histories of what had come to pass—histories suited to new kinds of nations.

To install security over real estate, settler sovereignty required a displacement of longue durée prior sovereignties. Colonizers attempted to impose structures of governance that would clarify authority. In British colonial and later in American law, sovereigns and state agents sealed treaties and new sets of title deeds. In Australia, Britain's refusal to negotiate official treaties created a situation anomalous to those of the United States, New Zealand, and Canada. In both North America and Australia, however, Indian agents, representatives of the Department of War, missionaries, military officers, police, Aboriginal protectors, and others acted as state agents and intermediaries in regard to law and order, trade, and other intersecting interests. Depending on national policy, their intermediary role could also include the encouragement or discouragement of marital unions. Regardless of which way this went, some of these men fell in love and intermarried with Indigenous women.

Indigenous peoples enacted sovereignty in a myriad of ways. They conducted warfare to protect lands and extended their kinship and social practices. They enforced land-based laws and conducted ritual and custodial practices involving travel, art, dance, song, and storytelling. Their sense of group identity derived in part from holding the lands since "time immemorial."[42]

For Indigenous peoples today, sovereignty is an empowering concept, an expression of ongoing landed power and authority with special utility for scholarly analysis. Lenape scholar Joanne Baker explains, "As a category of scholarship, activism, governance, and cultural work, sovereignty matters in consequential ways to understanding the political agendas, strategies, and cultural perspectives of indigenous peoples in the Americas and the Pacific."[43] Furthermore, as Aileen Moreton Robinson, a professor of Indigenous studies and a Geonpul-Quandamooka woman, explains, sovereignty is about ways of being and knowing. Indigenous sovereignty "allows for a different sense of power, materiality and embodied relationship with landscapes in a more holistic sense." Partly due to their rejection of race-based, essentializing arguments, she argues that scholars have not adequately considered embodied ways of knowing and the significance of group traits.[44]

Australian Aboriginal peoples enacted their sovereignties through embodied acts, such as speaking the appropriate language in "country." Today, Aboriginal Australians use that term to signify a visceral, emotional and spiritual connection with land that can be painted on flesh and danced. "Belonging *to* country" is an oft-used phrase. In many ways, this concept is akin to that of nation.[45] Country is whole; it is *you* as well as *it*. Both biography and history, it is cultural, family, and spiritual inheritance that — like "history" — goes back to a storied, deep past that explains the world. Reflecting the nontranslatability of key concepts, it is as if the country owns them rather than their owning the country.[46] People today are called custodians rather than owners; they have specific duties toward country that must be carried out. Whereas there is much cultural diversity among the numerous Aboriginal groups, purposeful travel is a fundamental way of life. Through journeying, Aboriginal Australians create continuity and change, resolve conflicts, hold ceremonies, and memorialize their deep and recent histories. And they arrange marriages. All these acts bind distant peoples.

In both Cherokee and Australian Aboriginal ontologies, a material, ecological domain provides an explanatory framework of living philosophical truths about how to live and behave. The Cherokees hold a profound sense of their connectedness to the storied land of their ancestors, to family, and to a balanced way of being and living, or *osi*, that accords with the processes and pace of nature.[47] Backed by rich linguistic metaphors, their language contains cyclical concepts of history, time, and space that emphasize continuity and the need for moral pathways. The beneficent earth is mother; Selu, the Corn Mother, is creative/creator being. Beloved elders, a special revered status for both men and women, ensure the health of forests, inspirited waterways, and connected landscapes. In the Green Corn festival, the Cherokees celebrate and express gratitude for family, resources, and land, reinforcing matrilineal social order and matrilocal residence, whereby the wife and husband live on the wife's mother's country. Significantly, Cherokee politics consisted of different towns and clans, brought together from time to time for wider group purposes. Colonialism created terrible ruptures, ones that demanded constant cultural renewal, reinvention, and reconfiguration.

INTRODUCTION

Here, thinking about sovereignty and marriage helps to remind us of how sites of power, agency, and action were always located in more than one place and that settler-colonial sovereignty was embodied and, at its core, plural.[48]

TRANSNATIONAL MARRIAGE

A handful of transnational historians have managed to bring the two settler-colonizer nations of Australia and the United States together with convincing results.[49] Due to disparities in population and economies, Australians look to America, while the United States has little reason to return the gaze. In order to allow for Africa, the Atlantic diaspora, and South America, it becomes inconvenient to squeeze the enormous Pacific Ocean and the Australian continent onto a flat map projection. Consequently, on some maps, much of the Pacific and Oceania is missing altogether. When they do include Australia, most American maps locate the respective land masses at the opposite edges of their flattened world, as if signifying little hope of their connecting. In contrast, Australian maps tend to feature Australia in a prominent position and the United States facing it across the sea. Nonetheless, both look out across oceanic vastness.

Certainly, the geographical, demographic, and sociopolitical characters of the two settler-colonizer nations diverge, as do their colonial time lines, their state systems, and key policies. To reach America, European maritime intruders had far less distance to travel than to get to Australia, and they arrived centuries earlier. Many wars between powerful tribal nations followed in their wake. Imperial powers vied for North America, including the Dutch, French, Spanish, and British, then generations of native-born Anglo-Americans. North America had a much larger population much sooner, and great cultural and historical diversity within and between its regions. In the United States, independence was celebrated after the revolutionary war against the English of the 1770s and 1780s, spelling out a divorce from the British sovereign and from other parts of the British Empire.[50] In the shadow of the American wars and the severance to follow, the first British colonies in Australia were established in 1788.

Although occupying different hemispheres and geographically distant, the New World nations of the United States and Australia share histories of white rule, Anglophone dominance, and settler colonialism. A desire to populate lands with their own kind created ambivalent, often contradictory attitudes toward intermarriage with Indigenous peoples.[51] In contrast, Spanish colonizers were less concerned about the issue of intermarriage and racial intermixing; the French openly engaged in *métissage*, accepting offspring as full French citizens.[52] Although British fur traders also paired with and married Indigenous women, English-based colonies had trouble even finding a word for such marital untidiness. They consciously acted against the racial amalgamation outcomes in Latin and French countries and in neighboring Mexico.

Sharing an identity as modern, white man's countries brought the United States and Australia together, and they swapped notes on many issues. With the migrating journey transforming European emigrants into colonizers, severance from one's ancestral home became weighted with historical purpose. Settlers settled. Migrating Europeans brought their mixed cultural, political, and ethnic backgrounds, appearances, and styles. Gradually, settler status became an emergent ethnic identity and homogeneity developed as its precept. By the early nineteenth century, the concept of white Britons evolved. In colonized zones, this became associated with entitlement to land and authority.

Intermarriage across ethnicities, nationalities, and religions reinforced identities of whiteness. As indicated earlier, the state did not discourage intermarriage between different categories of colonizers from different parts of Britain or Europe. Even the convicts serving time could marry the free. Cheap land and the status of being a colonizer transcended many of the old class and ethnic divisions, creating an egalitarianism of whiteness. Disregarding the dead bodies of old European rivalries, marriage brought different lands and peoples together.

Conditioned by its emergence and dispersion through empire, coupledom was a vital element of the Enlightenment project of "contractual constitutional democracy and capitalism." Well, at least that was the ideal. As anthropologist Elizabeth Povinelli advises, "If you want to locate the hegemonic home of liberal logics and aspirations, look to love in the settler colonies."[53] Permeating the fields of family and state, liberalism brought implicit beliefs in equality, freedom, and notions of the self. People from

Indigenous nations also engaged in the Enlightenment project, but from a platform of different precepts and intellectual traditions, including those pertaining to gendered governance and marriage.[54] If the body politic is an embodied political maneuver, its carnal side is especially relevant to nation.

FOUNDING FATHERS

In both Australia and the United States, the founding fathers envisaged new nations that would be underpinned by a regime of monogamous marriage, patrilineal inheritance, and patriarchal governance. Men would be in charge. White men. President Thomas Jefferson, the admired polymath and Constitution drafter, owned Monticello, a plantation where slaves performed the labor inside and outside the home. His property looked out west across to the Blue Ridge Mountains, beyond which stood the Appalachians, still Indian territory in the early nineteenth century.[55] Jefferson envisaged an untroubled land of virtuous yeoman farmers. It was 1808, and just five years after the landmass of the United States had been significantly expanded with the purchase of Louisiana from the French. He wrote of the future native American as a "chosen people laboring quietly in the Earth's fertile soil."[56] Jefferson was deeply influenced by French philosopher Baron von Montesquieu, whose ideas linked ideals of popular sovereignty with the contemporary ideal of a family with a male patriarch as head.[57] In Anglophone colonizer states, to evoke a sense of shared sentiment and national cohesion, terms such as kin, blood, race, family, and the marriage of states came to be used interchangeably. The Declaration of Independence mentioned Britain's encouragement of "domestic insurrections" by "merciless Indian savages" on "*our* frontiers." In an "us and them" binary, the American Constitution included Indians in the same clause as foreigners.[58] Clearly, American Indians had an ambiguous place in the new republic.

Pondering how to unify the new nation, President Jefferson was excited by the intermarriage pathway. He predicted, "The day will soon come when you will unite yourselves with us, join in our great councils, and form a people with us, and we shall all be Americans; you will mix with us by *marriage*; your *blood will run in our veins* and will spread with us over this great continent."[59] Had he made the same comment about African Americans, let alone declared a desire to marry Sally Hemings — his house slave and lover and the mother of six of his children — his political career would have been over.⁶⁰ This family secret showed the lengths that even a highly intelligent, philosophical, and genuinely questioning humanist would go in order to avoid a politically dangerous crossing.

Slaves were prohibited from having the right to marry. In American law, they were property, denied a status as people in their own right. They could not enter into a contract; they did not have the legal right to observe duties and obligations other than their master's. State laws dictated citizenship status or lack of, chances of liberty, and rights to marry and to rear children. Race attitudes toward slaves were imbricated by perceived threats to their financial and labor value for white people.

Unlike British convicts, American Indians were free men and women. Unlike black American slaves, they were free to enter into a contract, to consent, and to marry. Several of the early Scottish traders who married American Indian women from nations such as the Choctaw and Cherokee established successful businesses. In 1816 President Madison's secretary of war (which included Indian wars) and treasury, William H. Crawford, followed Jefferson's lead, publicly advocating intermarriage between Indians and whites, which he saw as enabling of their equal citizenship. He considered that it would "preserve the race with the modifications necessary to the enjoyment of civil liberty and social happiness." The "true interests of the nation" and the "national honor" would be well served by such "a humane and benevolent policy."⁶¹ Thinking of the citizen as a heterosexual white male, Jefferson and Crawford imagined such marital unions would proceed between white men and "Indian maidens."

Eight years later, however, with growing panic over freed slaves and African American mobility, Crawford's political rivals attacked and ridiculed his intermarriage advocacy. His stance hit a sensitive nerve for the white male voters who held the suffrage. They protested that they did not want their sisters or any of their female relatives to marry an "Indian." Political opponents urged fathers to protect their white daughters from being forced to marry Indian "savages" — and by extension to marry black men and slaves.⁶² These American leaders had advocated intermarriage as a utopian gesture of national unity. At the same time, this was gender delimited, for they implicitly backed marriages only where ascendant white man married an Indigenous woman — in a world where all women were understood to be subordinate. The prospect of Indigenous men marrying white women was an atrocity.

In 1901, the year of Australian federation, Alfred Deakin, one of the nation's most influential leaders and intellectuals, envisaged a liberal, egalitarian, and homogenous new state. Aboriginal people were left out, but it would be a nation where race and marriage mattered: "A *united race* means not only that its members can *intermarry* and associate without *degradation* on either side, but implies one inspired by the same ideas, and an aspiration towards the same ideals, of a people possessing the same general cast of character, tone of thought — the same constitutional training and traditions — a people qualified to live under this constitution, the broadest and most *liberal* perhaps the world has yet seen reduced to writing: a people qualified to use without abusing it, and to develop themselves under it to the full height and extent of their capacity."[63] Marriage "without degradation" was race-coded rhetoric. The nation was to be turned into a body politic, with stature, color, and gender. When federationist Henry Parkes referred to the "crimson thread of *kinship*" (emphasis added), he meant to remind people of the metaphoric blood that united white Australians of disparate British roots. Framing marriage as a civil right associated it with the inspiring principles of freedom, liberty, and democracy, Deakin looked to America, whose "manhood" he greatly admired, for its race lessons — especially on how to avoid the "dangers to whiteness" posed by black slavery.[64] With slavery outlawed in the British Empire and convict labor — another manifestation of unfree servitude — now phased out, employers searched for new options. Indentured laborers from the Pacific Islands and various countries in Asia were imported to work on pastoral stations and railways and, in greater numbers, as cheap labor on plantations. In inland areas, cameleers from present-day Pakistan, Afghanistan, and neighboring states provided key transport services. Larger groups of workers arrived from China, India, from Ceylon, Java, China, Japan, from Fiji, the Cook Islands, and many other Pacific islands.

Although relative newcomers themselves, white workers opposed these newcomers. Violence took place in both the Australian and American goldfields against the Chinese, and maritime and wharf workers also opposed their arrival.[65] Transnational ideas about whiteness soon morphed into the nationalist race platform known as White Australia. Being dark-skinned, Australia's Indigenous people did not fit this color palette. But, unlike imported laborers, they could not be exported back to their homelands. At the time when populous Asian neighbors were dubbed "the Yellow Peril," Aborigines were depicted as a doomed race.[66] The men once remarked upon for their manly physiques and courage came to be seen as sickly and weak.

In a readily observable colonizing pattern, Aboriginal people of full descent had been rapidly wiped out of the earlier settled convict colony of Tasmania, while by 1901, only about 850 such people survived in Victoria.[67] Forcible child and family removals and a system of reserves weakened the health and hopes of these families. However, Aboriginal Australians still lived on their own territories in North Queensland, Western Australia, and the Northern Territory. Nonetheless, political leaders imagined a declining Aboriginal and mixed-descent population that would not last long enough to constitute part of the national family. The commonwealth government of Australia had jurisdiction over marriage and welfare, but the states held the power to exclude Aboriginal people from entitlements.[68]

As in the United States, Australian intermarriage policies were inconsistent. With eugenics science riding high in the 1920s, the tropical medicine expert and Aboriginal protector Dr. Cecil Cook introduced incentives for white men to marry Aboriginal women of mixed descent in the commonwealth's Northern Territory. Buttressed by new research that proved that Aboriginal ancestry did not produce "throwbacks," he saw this as a solution to the "problem" of Aboriginal people of mixed descent swamping White Australia.[69] However, as recent scholarship of New Zealand/Aotearoa and the trans-Pacific has shown, amalgamation policies were not necessarily destructive; as Indigenous people took marital initiatives in their own directions, they did not mean the end of culture or political claims.[70]

Against rapacious colonialism, hunger, and disease, certain Indigenous people in Australia and North America used marriage with the newcomers as a group survival strategy. By the same token, in order to prevent intermarriage and other destructive forces, various Indigenous factions—if not united nations—proposed marriage bans in order to ensure permanent separation from whites.[71]

INTRODUCTION

TWO COLONIALISMS

Colonizing wars go to the heart of sovereignty questions. With treaties being whittled away and plenty of reason to be unsure of their position after the Declaration of Independence, American Indians quickly mobilized to undertake diplomacy with the leaders of the new republic. Having fought a succession of wars, including on the English Loyalists' side during the Revolutionary War, the Cherokee population was depleted.[72] Mobilizing in new ways, by the early nineteenth century the Cherokee Nation developed formal governing bodies with a written regulatory framework and a national constitution.

The British government based its entitlement to Australia not upon conquest or war but upon acts of "discovery" and "settlement," which meant not only populating the country with immigrants but rendering previous discovery and settlement illegitimate. Such colonizing takeovers could also be equated with conquest, and with taking over absolute rights to the land and its occupation. As American legal scholars David E. Wilkins and K. Tsianina Lomawaima argue, the doctrine of discovery became a legal principle that exerted property rights over tribal lands. This expansive idea of sovereignty could lead to Indigenous peoples being viewed as mere tenants, incapable of managing the land, and consequently being stripped of property rights altogether.[73]

Although the territory was declared as British on the basis of discovery in 1770, it was quite some time after the British convicts arrived at Botany Bay, and later at Sydney Cove in 1788, that the whole continent became assumed as British Crown land.[74] Convict labor was the vanguard of Australia's British settlement.[75] Rapid industrialization, land enclosures, and alienations had displaced numerous people in Britain and led to a crime wave. Britons once facing the gallows back home were transported to lands unimaginably far away. It was no longer possible for Britain to send them to the United States. Most convicts sent to Australia were freed in a short time and rewarded with land grants — that is, of Aboriginal land. Ignoring and dismissing Indigenous occupation, the doctrine of *terra nullius* — that it was "empty" or wasteland — became the legal justification for a continental takeover.[76]

The lack of a readily recognizable warrior tradition, and governance based upon boards of elders rather than chiefs, befuddled the British imperial agents. Aboriginal Australians acquired authority over the law of the land through merit, knowledge, totemic and landed affiliations, and consensus building. Speaking five hundred distinctive languages in discrete sovereign zones across the continent, linguistic groups were linked by travel, trade and expansive marital routes over hundreds of miles.[77]

Queensland, the main focus region of this study, saw the establishment of a British penal colony at Moreton Bay in 1824. It separated from New South Wales to become a self-governing British colony in 1859 and was named in honor of the sovereign, the long-reigning Queen Victoria. She lived to sign and seal the establishment documents of the Australian nation in 1901. To avoid losing another chunk of its empire, Britain delivered self-government early to the Australian colonies. For various reasons, Australia's colonial Republican movement lost ground during the 1890s. As a minimally populated white nation in "Asian seas," Australians harbored an exaggerated desire for "mother country" support.

In North America, warfare and conquest had been endemic. A history of imperial wars with Spain, France, England, and Mexico, and with contingents from different Native American tribes, deflects attention from the enormity of Indigenous dispossession. In a self-protective gesture, the only civil wars that took place in Australia, the colonizing wars with Indigenous peoples, are not officially recognized as wars at all.[78]

Between 1684 and 1820, the Cherokees signed over thirty treaties. They lost so much land that their hunting economy became unsustainable, leading to competition with other tribes facing the same decreasing range. Entering complex alliances, they fought and suffered losses in intertribal and British wars. From the early nineteenth century, the Cherokees modernized their economic and social structures. They united their town and clan and governance networks to form a more centralized state.[79] The republic recognized the Cherokee Nation as such, and the Cherokees hoped to gain greater parity with the other American states.

Historians refer to the end of the American Revolutionary War in 1789 as the end of the colonial period. Referring to the end of British imperial authority, this terminology obscures the fact that the beginning of the republic did not mark the end of colonizing contests.[80] By the Revolution's end, it has been asserted, most European Americans distrusted each other less. However, the violent clashes with Indians, including ghoulish imagery of scalped corpses, were constantly revived in popular memory, keeping colonizer anxiety fresh. White Americans came to see two all but unbridgeable worlds—one was white, one was Indian.[81]

COLONIZING MARRIAGE

If the colonizer state had aimed for total elimination of Indigenous peoples, the practice of interracial sexual relations and marriages meant that the colonizers were not following their own logic. Certainly, after or during the land wars, women constituted a second appropriation. Newcomers first abducted but later paired up more peaceably with Indigenous people for casual or short-term sexual liaisons and for longer, committed relationships. Frontiersmen and Indigenous women entered informal and formal marriages on the basis of Indigenous or colonizer state law, or both. So did some white women and some Indigenous men.

Colonialism entailed a whole array of individual, competing and confounding desires, interests, and approaches. Colonizers were not a uniform or unified group and they were not carrying out an undeviating project. Many feared unfamiliar others; some hated them, or found excuses to do so, and some came to love them.

Although I avoid deterministic binaries, the categories "colonizer" and "colonized" are useful for indicating the overarching power dynamics in operation. Neither group was a homogenous entity. Many contests ensued between and among Indigenous peoples and among different groups of colonizers. Some of the most heated disputes took place inside family circles. There were times when each group's hold of the power over life or death, survival or starvation, was not entirely certain.

In the rearview mirror, colonialism looks like a well-engineered highway to Indigenous destruction. For those traveling along the road, the outcome was less knowable. Newcomers arrived in native space, in *their* country—often a long-entrenched domain.[82] Indigenous people tried to force the colonizers to obey *their* laws of the land, which they saw as superior and sustainable.

Nonetheless, in the United States' early national period, the early republic gained narrative momentum, representing American Indians as history's shadow.[83] During the early nineteenth century, a New England literature extolling the "firsts" of Anglo-American ancestors served to memorialize the end of Indigenous time.[84] As a premise of colonialism, First Nations peoples could have no history. Nonetheless, people needed a history to be modern and to move forward to a national future. Primitivist tropes are endemic, whereas modernization theories for Indigenous history are lacking.

Nineteenth- and twentieth-century legends starring white frontiersmen, the frontier wilderness, the bush, and the outback glorified national beginnings but obscured interactions across gendered frontiers. Manly sagas remain etched into the psyche of the citizens.[85] The American West is popularly known as the locale of frontier histories and conflicts, with prior Indigenous histories tending to go missing.[86] Somehow the "open land" had made the man, which in turn made the national character. Historian Frederick Jackson Turner's treatise on the lone American frontiersman included the famous phrase "The wilderness masters the colonist." His frontiersman undergoes an intimate undressing and redressing. It is the wilderness that "strips off the garments of civilization and arrays him in the hunting shirt and the moccasin." Furthermore, "it puts him in the log cabin of the Cherokee and Iroquois and runs an Indian palisade around him."[87] In this apocryphal narrative, the Indian woman disappears. Similarly, in historian Russell Ward's influential study of the Australian bushman legend, it is the bush or the outback that shapes the man. Aboriginal women appear only as an antidote to sodomy and as a dirty joke.[88] At once absent and present, the Indian and Aboriginal woman hover in the background, expunged from white man's wilderness baptisms. And somehow expunged from history. In these seemingly unoccupied landscapes, certain girlfriends, wives, and families go missing. Such nation makers are white men, either alone or with heterosexual male mates. Yet these frontiersmen commonly paired with Indigenous women. It seems difficult to recover from the hangover belief that the only real nation is a white nation.[89]

In popular histories, Indigenous people first appear at moments of European arrival, via the European gaze. Most people are familiar with the foundational romance of Pocahontas and John Rolfe. In Australia, the best-known intermarriage story is that of Ethel and Jimmie Governor. After racist jibes were directed at Ethel the Governor brothers murdered nine people, including white women and children.[90] Jimmie Governor was hanged in January 1901 — the same month and year that the Australian colonies federated, but just weeks later so as not to spoil the celebrations.

Intermarriage prohibitions started in 1691 in Virginia, where Pocahontas once lived. During the late eighteenth and early nineteenth centuries, many American states introduced prohibitions on intermarriage between blacks and whites and between Indians and whites. In Australia, restrictions on intermarriage came into force around the same time as federation.[91]

MARITAL MIDDLE GROUNDS

When I first discovered the archive revealing the Boudinot-Gold intermarriage controversy explored in chapter 1, I wondered what to make of those hyper reactions to intermarriage. Something big was at stake: could it be possible that it was marital boundaries that demarcated the peopled ground of sovereignty? In decades when ideas about new nations were being consolidated, why else did cross-colonizer marriages lead to tensions that frenzied and imploded whole communities? I started to wonder whether we should speak of the existence of a "marital frontier" and, equally, a "marital middle ground."[92] If so, this emotionally charged space might offer significant clues to the gendered power dynamics of colonialism.[93]

New theoretical developments help historians to see beyond imperial eyes — especially Indigenous standpoint approaches, critical approaches to whiteness, and memory studies.[94] In order to examine colonialism's interactive spaces, historians have used various metaphors to jump between past and present. Frontier, the other aide of the frontier, marchlands, dual economies, middle grounds, contact zones, intercultural zones, borderlands, diasporas and native spaces. Although they hold different nuances for audiences in the United States and Australia, all assist the historical imagination.

The terms "intimate frontier" and "middle ground" are useful too.[95] In Australia, "frontier" has radical implications, as it acknowledges a long-denied war over territory, culture, and politics. Admittedly, the notion of a sharp-edged geographical line or a progressive march forward blurs complexity. However, as a spatial and gender concept, intimate frontiers can denote multiple layers of human interactivity. A problem, however, is that the intimate is usually considered sexual and private. Being state and community endorsed, marriage is public. If it is implicated in social order, and in shaping the composition of nations, it may be misleading to relegate it to the intimate.

American historian Richard White's middle ground conceptualization eschews dividing lines and opens the imagination to multiple actors and voices. In his significant study of the fur trade era, White noted that "intermarriage created bonds of kinship and obligation."[96] French and British men working for major companies united with Cree, Algonquin, and other Native American wives and reared families with them. However, the short-term nature of their employment meant that most returned to their European homes of origin, or moved elsewhere, leaving the local wife behind.[97] Consequently, the intimate cross-cultural exchange of the middle ground has been represented as being transient, like some fast-passing dust storm.[98] The middle ground was portrayed as a moving-on ground.

Yet, however temporary, cross-colonizer sexual and marital unions were not necessarily ephemeral. Rather, they formed a special kind of middle ground that composed the formative, enduring bedrock at the core, if not the heart, of the modern nation. I argue that the marital middle ground was a generative, enduring phenomenon. As a space of dual sovereignty, it was made of different stuff — of complex cultural and national compounds. It was skin and blood, metaphoric and physical. Intermarriage was central to the "colonizing transnational" — or those social and reproductive dynamics that ensued between colonizer and colonized peoples. In contested sovereign space, intermarriage was a site of creative agency across divided fields of influence.

CONTRACTS WRITTEN IN BLOOD

So, we will explore how nations preoccupied with their futures responded to cross-colonizer marriages. The individual's relationship to the modern liberal nation is premised upon a social contract, with implicit ideas around a citizen's willingness to be governed, anticipated rights, and mutual obligations. In the modern nation, the social and legal institution of marriage plays a key role in ordering gender relations.[99] Political scientist Carole

Pateman termed marriage "the sexual contract." Heterosexual marriage thus constitutes a complementary social contract, in which a state-authorized marriage holds special weight. Once a couple's public vows were made, the contractual basis of marriage created rights to property, inheritance, and national citizenship.[100] Power was differentially apportioned between husband and wife. In tandem with gender and race, marriage conferred one's place in society and one's civil status.[101]

Over various periods in both the United States and in Australia, for a white woman, marriage outside one's nation meant defection; she had no choice but to become a citizen of the husband's nation. For example, when a woman entered a western-style marriage, she was *femme covert*, taking on the civil status of her husband under the legal notion of coverture.[102] Henceforth it was the husband rather than the state that held authority over important aspects of his wife's and family's lives, including financial support. He had obligations, having to perform the duties anticipated of a good husband.[103] Women were not passive, however, and if their expectations were not met, they used the courts for recourse. Although marriage laws in Australia and the United States were primarily under state jurisdiction, ideas around marriage were cherished as a wider national value.

In another asymmetrical relation of power, colonizer and colonized became implicated in a reciprocal "*colonizing contract*" — or at least a one-way promise of such. For Indigenous peoples, the issue of consent is problematic. The violence, theft, and coercion of colonialism precluded choice, and settler-colonizer states operated on a liberal logic that Indigenous groups did not necessarily share.[104] Nonetheless, colonized peoples were agents who, among limited options, negotiated rights and benefits. The Cherokees were offered something explicit, so they provide a special case in point. In the words of one Cherokee memorial, they were promised a "solemn compact" that entailed spoken and written promises of "humanity," "kindness," and "protection" for "natives," as "children" of the "Great Father," as "subjects" of the Crown, and as "citizens" of the republic.[105] This was all conditional upon the Cherokees becoming "civilized." They were led to believe that fulfilling this obligation would deliver benefits, including assured treaty annuities and rights, the right to remain on their own lands, and finally, the right to be treated as equal partners in the nation.

Colonizing contracts were not built upon the framings and promises of the colonizers alone. The ubiquitous bodily metaphor of "blood" is implicated in constructing various group and national identities, having become conflated with race, color, and culture. For the Cherokees, "blood politics" evokes women's power and emphasizes the principle that unites a people as one of kinship and genealogy. Origin histories and cultural ontology associate blood with a vital essence and way of being.[106] Clan, conferred maternally, connected Cherokee people with an animal, bird, or vital quality that was elemental to Cherokee identity and social order.[107]

Aboriginal Australians were supposed to be "subjects" of the British Crown, but in reality, they were often treated as enemies. Where Indigenous law retains some authority today, many Aboriginal Australians use not blood but kin or "skin" as an individual's chief identifier. Kinship becomes the tactile principle and guide for creating and conducting relations between people. It makes outsiders part of the human world—making them into "fictive kin" who are obliged to follow Aboriginal law and protocols.[108]

Marriage cemented the social arrangements of Indigenous Australians and Cherokees alike, restricting and connecting families according to class, religious, kin, clan, or tribal networks. Among the Cherokees, women usually married outside their clan, whereas Aboriginal Australian women generally married a man outside their larger common language group. In both societies, exogamy or out-marriage was a well-worn means of incorporating or adopting outsiders into their groups. Models of clan, blood, and nonbiological classificatory kin networks explained the world, your place in it, and your expected roles and behaviors toward every other individual. Marriage agreements epitomized and underwrote Indigenous law, creating an expansive politics that extended human networks, territory, and resources.

In Aboriginal Australia, dangerous consequences, punishments, and death could follow a marital union contrary to kinship-based law.[109] Marriage negotiations entailed travel across other people's country. Marriages connected clans and territories, playing a role in uniting them into loosely organized constellations of broader, nation-like polities. Although patrilineal descent was more common, matrilineal groups required the man to move to his wife's family home and land. For the Cherokees, rights to lands, residence, children, inheritance, and National citizenship were passed through the mother. Due to their enmeshment in the colonial economy and ideas around gendered modernity and patriarchy, changes followed.

In settler states, colonizers self-consciously referred to themselves as belonging to new nations. Their belief in a hierarchical order of human difference was a fundamental dynamic of the early national periods. Race is a category of changing meanings, becoming more hard-wired from the late nineteenth century.[110] It could also be used as subterfuge for justifying the pragmatic continuance of inequalities. It was not either/or. Race mattered. Citizens understood that liberty, equality, and citizenship would be distributed along gender and race-coded lines. However, on both sides of the increasingly uneven frontier equation, colonizing imperatives were given preeminence above race.

So many words in our historical lexicon usefully indicate power relations but simultaneously reinforce binaries. Indigenous and non-Indigenous peoples, colonizer and colonized are not separate camps. To avoid overuse of negatives such as "non-Indigenous" or a power term like "colonizer," I sometimes use the terms Anglo-American, Euro-American, Anglo-Australian, European, or whites. They are not intended to imply homogeneity or to obscure hybridity and multiple identities.

The sidedness of "frontiers" both clarifies and confuses colonizing boundaries. After all, who was on which side of the colonizing frontier during sexual intercourse, let alone during a marriage? When the sides were united in another generation, did this mean that the offspring then became colonized or colonizer? And in any mixed families that followed, who was assimilating whom? Hybridity confounds both the color line and the colonizing line.[111] Indigenous people today share European descent and Europeans share mixed heritage. Who even knows about their families' extended multigenerational branches? Identities rely not only on descent but also upon family, upbringing, education, politics, property, class, culture, and changing incentives and disincentives.[112]

Given that the colonizing gap was often bridged and that "perfect sovereignty" was not necessarily accepted or complete, I use the term "colonized" advisedly. Settler-colonizer nations are not instantly transformed from unsettled to a fully settled endpoint of "perfect sovereignty." Although

"Aboriginal and Torres Strait Islander people" is often preferred to "Indigenous peoples" in Australia, in dealing with this combination of Australian and North American studies, the term "Indigenous" is useful.[113] Furthermore, "Indigenous" has gained empowering meanings in international law and in a growing global scholarship. I use the term "First Nations" occasionally to indicate primacy of occupation and to evoke international diplomacy and recognition. Where appropriate, I also use generic terms in common use today, such as "Native Americans" and "American Indians." As long as peoples assert themselves as First Nations, or Indigenous, colonialism has not been entirely settled.[114] In settler-colonizer nations, the term "postcolonial," like the term "postracial," may be fantasy rather than fact.

Rather than referring to specific Australian language groups (the term "tribe" does not well describe their social organization), I often rely upon the generic term "Aboriginal people." Because intermeshed families lived and married across multiple linguistic boundaries, these implicitly transnational histories cannot always be readily mapped. Maternal and paternal descent and exogamous marriage make for multiple landed identities.[115] In North Queensland, by 1900, a range of tribal groups gathered on the same reserve sites, forced to establish new landed relationships and mutually agreed governance with the local Indigenous landowning group. The archive does not distinguish language groups, and today's native title boundaries are disputed. Additionally, the history of oversurveillance by the Queensland state has heightened demands for privacy and confidentiality. However, as it cuts Aboriginal individuals out of national history, I do not agree with fictionalizing names entirely. In some sensitive cases that were not published and in the public eye in their day, I have avoided the use of full Indigenous names and language identifiers to protect identity.[116]

The dynamics of cross-colonizer secrets deserve attention. Such studies could enable us to reimagine our countries and futures afresh. Stylistically, I sometimes switch between past and present tense in order to remind readers that history happened in somebody's present, in the immanence of a particular moment.[117] I am constantly inspired by the many people whose histories I have encountered, and by the many American and Australian historians, writers, and storytellers whom I deeply admire and upon whose quality work this book is built.[118]

INTRODUCTION

In the chapters that follow, you will be introduced to some citizens of the Cherokee Nation during the period known as the early American republic or early national era—especially between the decades of the 1810s and 1840s. This was also the early national period for the Cherokee Nation. People were self-conscious about being part of new national projects; they were not yet looking back in time to a war that had not yet come or to a slavery era not yet over.[119] In the later-colonized, tropical region of Queensland, I examine events that took place during the decades of the 1900s through the 1930s, the early national or federation era of Australia. At Yarrabah near Cairns, different amalgamations of people, speaking numerous languages, were gathered together on a mission reserve on the territory of Menmuny's Gunggandji group.

Across the colonizing transnational divide, in the selected periods and places in focus, individuals fell for each other. Disparate communities reacted differently. In Australia and the United States, people were living through periods when the very makeup of their nation-states was still being constituted. The North American cases happen earlier in calendar time but during a later phase of colonizing time.

The pastoral and tropical frontiers of Queensland had underdeveloped economies in which significant tracts of land remained under Aboriginal control.[120] Queensland colonizers were aware of the southeastern Australian frontiers that now seemed long gone—their Indigenous populations decimated and their mixed-descent populations hidden on missions and reserves.[121] New Englanders were learning to forget that the local frontiers in which they lived were also native space, and they looked somewhat anxiously south and west to frontiers in process.

Via their sometimes serious, sometimes humorous writing, we will follow several boundary-crossing couples as they share their bubbling sexual attractions. These historical scenes take place amid contrasting geographies and divergent political and colonizing spaces. Shaping the colonial experiences of Australian Aboriginal and American Indian peoples were differing intellectual and ideological landscapes pertaining to race, science, education, the British Empire, and white settler-colonizer democracy. Due to Indigenous literacy and good record keeping, the Cherokee sources portray individual courtships in first-person accounts. Although the voices of many would-be husbands and wives are recorded in the Queensland government archives, Aboriginal women and their partners had much less control over the written record.[122] Family correspondence, as more comes to light, may allow for different kinds of stories than those found in the archives of state.

Rather than being representative, the regional studies explored here are emblematic of significant national themes. No single group of Indigenous or non-Indigenous people can represent *the* American story or *the* Australian story, and the selected studies are not meant to imply this. I often followed archival trails. The richest American stories of this formative national period are about Indigenous men who married white women, whereas the Australian cases feature white men with Indigenous women.

In the first two chapters, I juxtapose narratives of marriages across colonizing boundaries—one from the United States and one from Australia. These allow room to witness the tumult and confusion, the drama and romance, of power brokers in action mode. I aim to share something of the texture of life before the happy and tragic endings. From individual studies, we can prize out the wider dynamics of gender, nation, and colonialism. We can also follow some of those human emotions missing from most national histories—the passion of courting lovers and the love and affection of certain husbands and wives.[123]

In chapter 1, you enter an American family story that becomes a raging controversy in 1820s New England. When an Anglo-American woman is engaged in courtship with a Cherokee man from the South, letters lost and found reveal and preserve their secrets. Chapter 2 takes us to a relatively raw frontier in far North Queensland, and to a visibly Aboriginal, albeit missionized, world. Here even a fanatical same-nation marriage and segregation policy could not stop the growth of transgressive intimacies.

Chapter 3 discusses the Cherokee Nation's legislative efforts to control interracial marriage. In chapter Four, we read of the playful romance and self-conscious treaty talk that takes place when the Cherokee chief is courting a young white woman. Traveling across the land, Cherokee men and women forged close family connections across the urban and governing centers of the early republic. The Cherokee romances and legal interventions that followed take us across the United States of the early republic—between its iconic centers of nation, the settled North and the frontier South, between the northeast metropole and the Indian Territory to the west.

Chapter 5 shows how Queensland frontiersmen undermined the moral authority of the senior government men who were trying to police their intimate relationships. Chapter 6 reveals the way Aboriginal women and men used marriage as a means of renegotiating gender and sovereign rights in country. Across colonizing boundaries, marriage sparked transnational moments in law that in turn reconstructed the relations of gender and state. As demonstrated in chapter 7, marriage across colonizing frontiers was not necessarily monogamous. Colonialism was peculiarly conducive to plural unions and multipronged families across frontiers. Chapter 8 explores the links between illegitimacy and sovereignty across the colonizing transnational. It suggests that colonizer states intentionally ruptured the marital middle ground by introducing Indigenous zoning policies.[124] The epilogue follows up on the poignant stories of particular couples and their families, revealing how Indigenous sovereignties lived on in love.

This book asks how marriages between colonizer and colonized defined, subverted, and entrenched the body politic of liminal nations. Even in the first story, which takes place in the "settled" New England of the 1820s, boundary-crossing marriages unsettled colonialism. In New Worlds, we might wonder: Who was the good wife, the good husband, the good colonizer, the good colonized? What bearing did intermarriage have on colonizing sovereignty? What bearing could it have on domain over land? In the intermarriages and intimate unions of Indigenous peoples and colonizers, one thing was certain: something dangerous was going on.

Part One

Secrets of New Nations

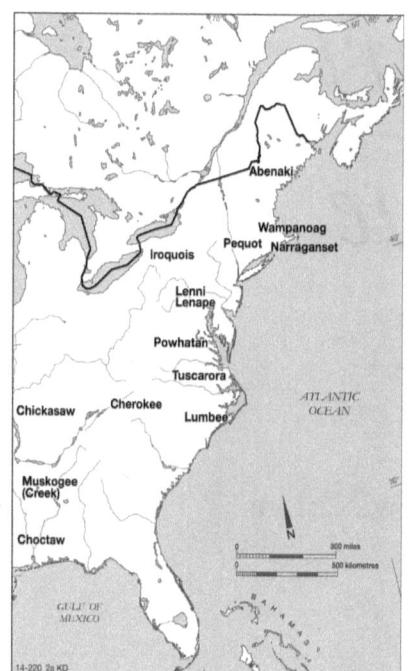 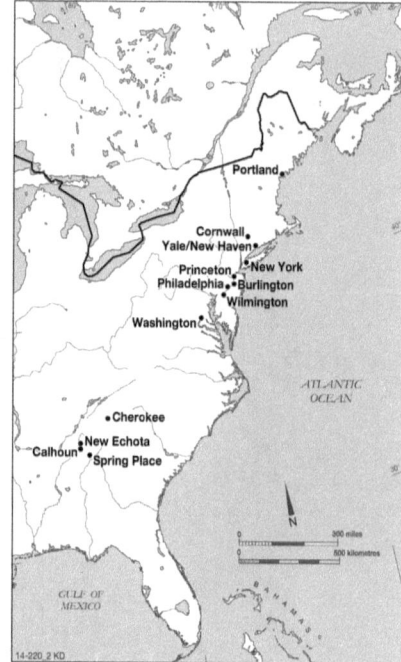

MAP 3. (*left*) The U.S. Eastern Seaboard with Indian tribal areas featured.
MAP 4. (*right*) U.S. intermarriage sites discussed.

CHAPTER ONE

Harriett Gold and Elias Boudinot

Against History?

THE MARITAL FRONTIER

Burnings Enough

It is June 1825 and we are in Cornwall, Connecticut.[1] Led by her older brother Stephen, Harriett Gold's childhood friends are stacking wood to make a funeral pyre. Harriett and Stephen had been close. They had enjoyed singing, walking, and riding together.[2] After Harriett disclosed her romantic interest in Elias Boudinot, a young Cherokee man who had studied in their village, Stephen turned on her. The proposed marriage tipped the whole orderly town upside down. Testing the boundaries of frontier, of social inclusion, and of colonizer virtue, the prospect of this marriage fractured this not-so-new New England.[3]

Generations of white New Englanders had enjoyed a relative sense of settled security, bearing babies who would create ongoing dynasties. A nativist sense of belonging was starting to displace any thoughts of the prior residency of the Indigenous peoples.[4] Occupying a new nation demanded fresh visions of the past. In the early republic, these events suggest how far New Englanders would go to draw lines between the Indigenous past and their imagined national futures.

The main protagonist in this story is the nineteen-year-old Harriett, who usually lived in the Gold family home. She is hiding in the house of a family friend. Looking out the window toward Cornwall's attractive village green, she writes that she witnessed a "full prospect of the solemn transactions in our valley."[5] Although Elias's letters are not reaching her, she finds out from someone else that he is seriously ill. He is back home in New Echota, capital of

FIG. 7. Portrait of Harriett Gold, by an unknown artist. The artist has depicted Harriett as a doleful and serious young woman—perhaps overly earnest, but of strong character. Courtesy of the estate of Henry Meigs Boudinot; despite extensive enquiry by the family, the artist and date are unverified.

FIG. 8. Elias C. Boudinot. From an oil portrait; artist unknown. Courtesy of the estate of Henry Meigs Boudinot.

the Cherokee Nation, near Calhoun, Georgia. Recently, Elias had received a letter containing an ink drawing of a gallows. He was warned off ever returning to New England, let alone to Cornwall. Although he had lived there for four years, his old friends are now preparing to burn an image of Elias too.

The house in which Harriett is writing overlooks the village green, but she is too frightened to go out. In a letter tempered with deep emotion, she speaks of herself in the third person. She had lived in Cornwall all her life. Music and voice meant a lot to her. Harriett loved singing; she enjoyed the harmonies of the church choir. Sunday hymns gave her an exhilarating communion with her peers and a way of communicating with God.[6] However, Harriett was no longer permitted to join her choir group. Indeed, the last time she attended, the choirgirls had worn black crepe around their arms — bands normally used to mourn the dead. In Harriett's words, "the publick," "good people and bad" are against her. Not all, she reassures herself — although her few allies are afraid to offer open support. As she writes this letter, she musters a sense of moral rectitude, stating that she can hardly describe "the scenes we have witnessed the week past. Yes, in this Christian land. The members of the Mission School many of them said it was more than they ever knew among the heathen."[7]

Harriett smells the fresh smoke. She looks down on her fine writing paper and breathes in the aroma of the moist black ink. She hears a chorus of youthful squeals, jeering, and rude shouting. As she writes, the metallic vibrations of the church bell fill the town, continuing to toll and echo.

Accused of "wrecking God's work," Harriett stands strong: "I have seen the time when I could close my eyes upon every earthly object and look up to God as my only supporter, my only hope — when I could say with emotion I never felt before, to my heavenly Father, 'other refuge have I none, so I helpless hang on thee.'" Perhaps she quietly sings the words, for they came from a hymn.[8]

Resonating through the fields and sky, the tolling of the town bell, she explains is "speaking the departure of a soul." This sound marked Christian time, day after day. Recently, it rang for her older sister. Disease had struck Cornwall badly that past year, killing children and young women.

Cornwall's Cherokee and Mohegan residents had different signals to denote death, such as the appearance of a particular bird or animal acting in an unusual way.⁹ As she thought deeply about matters of the spirit, Harriett, too, may have wondered about signs. Was the bell's voice to counter the pure silence of the departing one? Or had this ritual peal *become* the sound of a departing Cornwall soul? It was her death they were marking.

Now, in burning Harriett's effigy, the Cornwall residents were providing a preview of hell. The bonfire on the town common had been prepared alongside the mission schoolhouse — the same building that Harriett, as a young child, had witnessed being officially opened.[10] Now, around it, she reported, her old school friends danced "wildly," angrily, riotously.

Church missionary agents had assessed the local youth as "sober and promising" and well educated, for their family libraries bulged with religious tracts. Harriett recognized the wild dancers as "our respectable young people, Ladies and Gentlemen." Harriett's writings echo her detachment from their revelry, which lasted from early evening until after 10:00 p.m. "The flames were huge" and the smoke ascended to the heavens — so she told her sister Flora and brother-in-law Hermann. Harriett's older brother Stephen brought and lit a barrel of tar.[11]

Harriett knew the exact reasons behind the spectacle. She provides details from firsthand observations. Specially constructed and carefully painted "corpses," as she put it, were to be ritually burned. One, she penned, was "a woman, an instigator of Indian marriages," and the other "an *Indian*"; the third was "a beautiful young woman." "Woman" applied to an Anglo-American female, and she knew the most beautiful painted effigy was meant to be herself. Her beloved fiancé, Elias, was rendered as a comical antique, the generic "Indian."[12]

This public rite resembled the peasant Carnival of the Old World and perhaps recalled the Salem witch trials and New England's earlier practices of lynching unruly women. Meant to punish, to ostracize, to symbolize and threaten violence, it was shocking to see Cornwall's usually temperate males going into a frenzy.[13] Harriett wrote, "My heart truly sung [*sic*] with anguish at the dreadful scene."[14] She knew it was too dangerous to step outdoors.

Earlier that month, in June 1825, leading Congregational Church elders had posted the marriage banns — notices of the intent of Harriett Gold and Elias Boudinot to marry — on the church door.[15] The banns were accompanied by a proclamation condemning the secret engagement. This was signed by the agents of the board of the Foreign Mission School — highly influential church men who were close friends of Harriett's parents. This sheet of paper incited the local community into uproar.

From 1817, the Cornwall congregation had accepted the unusual evangelical mission of educating Indigenous people from other countries in their own town. The Foreign Mission School was designed to redeem "heathens" from the "darkness and corruptions and miseries of paganism to be sent back to their respective nations with the blessings of civilized and christianized society."[16] Perhaps the mission's success might justify colonization and dispossession as part of God's plan. Opukaha'ia, or Oobookiah as it was spelled by the missionaries, was a stranded Sandwich Islander or Hawaiian who shared with divinity scholar Timothy Dwight his desire to gain an education like the young white men at Yale. Opukaha'ia inspired Dwight to action, and he became the first Cornwall student, with other displaced Pacific Islanders soon joining him.[17]

Cornwall's Foreign Mission School was one of the earliest local ventures of the American Board of Commissioners for Foreign Missions, an interdenominational organization established by Congregationalist clergy and laymen in 1810. Notable names associated with its establishment included Reverends Samuel Worcester and Timothy Dwight, a Federalist who promoted the new historical narrative of Plymouth and the Old Colony as "the cradle of New England."[18] Their missions carved the globe into historical timelines: peoples of "ancient civilizations" and "Islamic faith"; Native Americans came under the mantle of "peoples of primitive cultures."[19]

Another founding figure was the Calvinist preacher Lyman Beecher, a modernizer who played a key role in adapting the Congregational Church to fit republican ideals. Beecher hoped to extend both the church's and the republic's ambit beyond the nation. The Congregational Church's effort to spread American religion and culture to "dark" lands hinged upon assumptions about race and gender in which true "womanhood" was conceived of as white. Although Beecher advocated women's rights, he believed that a missionary woman should serve only while under the authority of a white husband.[20]

Calvinists like Beecher believed that God was sovereign and that humanity's natural inclinations were essentially depraved. Despite their understanding that a person's future was predestined, they sought direct guidance from God about correct choices.[21] The recent flowerings of nativist Euro-American evangelicalisms merged with narratives of their ancestral Puritan past, especially with earlier revivalist traditions of the Connecticut Valley.

Cornwall's Foreign Mission School delivered an exotic immigration directly into the Congregationalist heartland. Without entering the privations and dangers of foreign travel, the small Cornwall community could reach out to distant strangers from beyond its boundaries. In an approved context, Harriett and other Cornwall youth could share their educational and advancement opportunities with people from a wider world.

The Anglo-American citizens of Cornwall seemed happy to be educators of "primitive" peoples from the Pacific. For they were confident regarding their moral and cultural superiority—in social progress, religion, and the written arts. Although the instigators did not have American "heathens" in mind, when Cherokee and Choctaw converts sought higher education, it was difficult to refuse. Besides, they were, in another sense, foreign nationals.

Seeking the skills and social empowerment to fight the battles ahead, the agendas of the all-male students diverged from those of their teachers. One Cherokee student, John Ridge, had already courted and married the young Sarah Northrup in 1824. The community uproar spread to Hartford and the influential newspapers. Boudinot's wealthy cousin John was the son of the Cherokee planter and slaveholder known as The Ridge—from the Blue Ridge Mountains. John and Elias were fellow scholars and friends. When Sarah Northrup first announced her intention to marry an Indian, churchgoers threatened to lynch her fiancé. Vitriolic newspaper editors ridiculed the backers of the Foreign Mission School. In January 1824 Isaiah Bunce, the editor of the popular Litchfield-based *American Eagle*, declared that intermarriage was "a new kind of *missionary machinery*" (emphasis in original). This marriage story was well covered in other papers too, including the *Niles Weekly Register* and the *Eastern Argus*.[22] Bunce felt vindicated, for from the outset, he had opposed the establishment of the Foreign Mission School, predicting that bringing "barbarians" onto "their doorsteps" would be detrimental to "civilization." Senior church figures were mortified by the

FIG. 9. "Major Ridge, a Cherokee chief / printed & coloured at I.T. Bowen's Lithographic Establishment No. 94 Walnut St." Courtesy Library of Congress, reproduction no. LC-USZC4-3158.

marriage, which seemed contrary to fundamental assumptions about New World progress. They declared it would never happen again.

The aftershocks of Sarah and John's engagement curbed open friendships or exchanges between the students and the town's young women.[23] Any hints of friendships between town and "foreign" youth were viewed suspiciously. However, there was no curfew, and the pupils at the Foreign Mission School were still invited to visit the houses of Cornwall residents. Elias had enjoyed invitations and meals at the Gold family home.

Courageously, Harriett had decided to write a letter to her brother Stephen declaring the news of her impending marriage. We have access to many of Harriett's letters, but not this one. After he read it, Stephen bellowed,

FIG. 10. "John Ridge, a Cherokee / drawn, printed & coloured at I.T. Bowen's Lithographic Establishment No. 94 Walnut St." Courtesy Library of Congress, reproduction no. LC-USZC4-3157.

These images of Major Ridge, or The Ridge, and his son John were published by F. W. Greenough, Philadelphia. The portrait artist takes great care in capturing the intensity of Major Ridge's persona. His dignity is highlighted, with his distinctive hair, serious expression, and fine attire. The son John Ridge looks even more refined, as he is wearing an elaborate ruffled shirt with a high neckline unimpeded by a bow tie. He holds a quill, emphasizing his literacy and high level of education. Both are depicted as having richly toned, red-tan complexions.

"Harriett! Harriett! Harriett!" and would not stop. Gold relatives locked him inside their house.[24] A few days later, we witness him whipping up wildfire among Cornwall's youth.

Family Drama

When Harriett told her parents that Boudinot had asked for her hand in marriage, they were extremely upset. Her mother, Eleanor Gold, was highly respected. Her father, Col. Benjamin Gold, was a decorated military man and a church deacon. He owned farmland in Cornwall. He was one of several church leaders to assure the public that another wedding like that of John Ridge and Sarah Northrup would never take place in their town. Her parents refused permission for Harriett to marry and wrote to Boudinot expressing their opposition.

A few weeks afterward, in the cold of winter, Harriett fell mortally ill. Benjamin Gold's views changed. He decided that church and community opposition to his daughter's marriage was "pride and prejudice" and was "against Indians": "the least that can be said and done against Christian connections of any colour I believe to be best."[25] The parents did not believe that marriages between Indian men and white women were "sinful," but at the same time, they explained that they did not wish to part with their "beloved daughter." This greater *distance* would be "like breaking their heartstrings — and they brought up every argument . . . to dissuade her and prevent the connection."[26]

Although Benjamin and Eleanor Gold had firmly opposed the marriage, their view changed. Believing in omens, they saw their daughter's illness as a sign that they were standing in God's way. They feared they would "be found fighting against God." Still grieving over the death of their nineteen-year-old daughter, Benjamin and Eleanor could not bear the thought of losing another daughter, their youngest. So they wrote a second letter, informing Boudinot of their consent — or at least that Harriett was "free to do as she pleased."[27] Harriett recovered. Boudinot received the second letter first.

Meanwhile, one of the church leaders lobbied Harriett's brother-in-law, Reverend Hermann Vaill of East Haddam, to intercede. A former assistant teacher at the school, Hermann was in a position to influence her. And, as good clerical postings were competitive, he was eager to ingratiate himself.

The Foreign Mission School and its board were desperate to maintain public credibility.

Beginning a tirade of emotional blackmail, Hermann Vaill wrote to Harriett. Boudinot, he explained, had been taught the wrong lessons at the Foreign Mission School: "To prove himself thus grateful to his friends and faithful to Christ, it is not necessary that he should marry a white woman." He warned Boudinot against being "one of those who return to their former sins" instead urging him to become one "useful to his Nation" and "grateful" to "christian benefactors."[28]

He blamed Harriett for bringing "dishonour" on the Savior, describing her as "the one female enemy who shall quench the Light which the Mission School may yet shed upon the heathen world."[29] He asked her to look back and remember when, as a young girl, she witnessed the school's opening day and heard the poignant redemption narrative of Opukaha'ia, since deceased.[30] Labeling Harriett's actions as religious arson, he warned that the flames will spread: "*thou* and thy father's house shall be destroyed" (emphasis in original). Must Harriett "put forth your hand and pluck [Christ's] Banners down"? He even called her Judas and suggested hellfire. Nothing was off limits; he accused her of causing Christ to shed tears of blood.

Harriett responded that she had "a perfect and lawful right" to marry Elias and had wronged no one.[31] Hermann then blamed her parents for complicity in deceit over the courtship. Her parents saw no need to make the matter public. This was not only to protect Harriett's recovery from illness but also to hedge their bets in case the marriage did not eventuate. For by this time, Boudinot's health had collapsed; he was dangerously ill.

Benjamin and Eleanor Gold were outraged at Hermann's slight on their personal integrity. His actions were especially upsetting as they from "one of their children" — brothers-in-law were regarded as full family members. Now Hermann Vaill was banned from their house.

When a married daughter, Mary Brinsmade, got the news of Harriett's engagement, she was shocked, then furious. She foresaw danger to the family's, and especially her own, reputation. Her husband, Gen. Daniel Brinsmade, a Revolutionary War hero, was even more incensed, writing this sarcastic reply: "no evil results from Indian marriages [?] — all the blame lies on one side ... we don't ... feel how good and how pleasant a thing it is to be kept by an Indian — to have black young ones and a train of evils. I am sick at heart."[32]

A "calamity" must be prevented. The Department of War had federal responsibility for Indians. Brinsmade may have had some baggage about Cherokee alliances with the English during the Revolutionary War, or perhaps about Indians in general. Above all, both Brinsmade and Vaill dreaded damage to their social standing. Reverend Vaill's career would be in tatters, for a congregation would not "face a clergyman" who was "*brother* to an Indian."[33]

Then Mary Brinsmade changed her mind. After visiting Harriett and her parents, she decided that she was not being very "Christian" in her reactions and that she should instead comfort Harriett. She added that it would be a great sorrow to split apart from sisterly and parental ties. As Harriett explained, Mary's visit to the family home for several days brought pure joy in "praying and singing together."[34] Mary asked her parents' forgiveness for attacking Harriett. Soon after, Mary wrote several letters to "brothers and sisters" advocating Harriett's case: "She has for a long time past been seriously weighing the subject, endeavouring to know her duty, and I believe she has earnestly sought divine direction — and she now thinks that we shall at a future time see that she has done right."[35]

Mary thought "some good" might eventually come of the marriage. Mary admires Harriett's resolve, writing that Harriett "never appeared more interesting than would at present . . . meek but firm as the hills."[36] In the depths of this trauma, Harriett found self-realization and inner strength. Not long after receiving Hermann's toxic letter, Harriett wrote to him with mounting confidence in her position.[37]

Hermann's attacks became more vicious and desperate.[38] To frighten Harriett out of marrying "an Indian," he attacked her on moral grounds. According to Hermann, Harriett's determination and saint-like countenance proved how evil she was: "her meekness was feigned, & her *firmness* . . . nothing but *obstinacy*." She had practiced many "devices"; her illness was a stunt. Her "Gospel sincerity" was "deep and subtle artifice." "She may hope in vain to carry with her a heart that feels for the heathen, & for Zion. Her heart is engrossed with other feelings." How could heathen learn to stop using deception when they learn of what she did "to gain a lover"?

She used to have a "reputable character for her common virtues," but if she goes, they may say,

> Poor virtues that she boasted so, this test unable to endure
> Let home, & friends, & missions go, — to *make an Indian husband sure*.[39]

The poem implied that Harriett failed her key "test" — that of womanly virtue. To marry an Indian was to reject one's Anglo-American family for once and forever. As if that was not damning enough, Hermann goes on to suggest that death would be better than satisfying such lust: "If H. must die for an Indian or have him, — I do say she had as well die, as become the cause of so much lasting evil as the marriage will occasion; — better to die on the side of Xtian honour & Gospel sincerity than to pine away with satisfied love, & its consequences, on the bed of Love."[40]

Mary had previously accused Harriett of sacrificing the whole family in order to gratify her "*animal feeling*."[41] Now Reverend Hermann Vaill portrayed his sister-in-law's desire to marry an "Indian" as purely sexual. The "bed of Love" stood for sexual attraction and passion: a debased emotion. Rather than stereotyping Boudinot on racial grounds, Hermann portrays Harriett as the "savage" or animal that cannot control sexual passions. Harriett's opponents viewed her as exhibiting selfish urges of the flesh rather than the evangelistic "leadings of Providence."[42] Harriett's letters are silent on the topic of physical attraction. Perhaps Harriett *was* being more conniving than we might wish to think. Drawing our sympathy, her compelling letters may underscore her cleverness. Passionate yet asexual.

Harriett knew that "civilized" women had to restrain their passions. A virtuous white woman needed to suppress desires of the flesh. At stake was white women's fidelity to their own "race" and, further, to the highest ideals of the republic. The love of "a savage" — heathen or Christian — represented woman's descent. Any such association symbolized a possible move against the republic itself, a defilement, a pollution, and defection. Gendered respectability was raced. As the "prime exemplars and symbols" of nineteenth-century Protestantism, women had been "elevated" from being "slaves" to having the status of intellectual and moral beings. While religious passion was acceptable, Anglo-American women's entitlement to improved standing was conditional upon their "passionlessness," which implied suppression of female sexuality.[43]

Hermann's barbed comments reflected not only his personal anxieties but also the contemporary tumult over ideas around marriage roles and race. Once a patriarchal decision reifying duty, marriage was now a more individual choice based upon satisfactory companionship. In the new republic, white women, in their ambitions toward perfection, were supposed to embody the nation.[44] Surely they could not find an Indian man, or the prospect of living in his nation, more attractive than one of their own?

When he says that it is better that she *die*, of course Hermann goes way too far. Given the unusually fond and intense friendship between family members, the heat of Hermann's diatribe, including his intrusive comments about Harriett's sexual desires, perhaps arose out of his own sense of being duped. For soon after Hermann had married her sister Flora in 1823, Harriett had approached him for marital advice. Confiding in him like she would a sister, she asked Hermann whether she should marry a certain "lonely old bachelor" farmer with little money.

From the age of sixteen onward, Harriett was perceived as someone on the marriage market. Yet the unnamed suitor — a local older man of "little wealth" — sounded like an uninviting prospect. Due to the age difference, it could lead to local derision. Was Harriett weighing up her future — a safe but unromantic choice where she could help a lonely bachelor? Or was this a ploy to fish for Hermann's approval, even encouragement, toward a more exciting choice? Ruminating on this marriage question, Hermann had written Harriett flirtatious letters referring to her as "a solid junk [a chunk] of Gold above ground," and noting that every old bachelor would be looking at her as "a guide board" — a road map — to a "State of second youth."[45]

We do not know exactly what Hermann offered that day by way of advice, but by post, he asked, "Dost thou affection him, verilie and trulie marry him, and let others talk.... You have intrinsic and extrinsic worth and he has Great Charm." Rather than "your brother-in-law" or brother, he signed the letter "your friend." Hermann had been overly keen to impress Harriett. Perhaps he hoped that if she made a dull choice, he would retain her as his confiding friend. Harriett's ulterior motive may have been to gain the imprimatur of a clergyman who could bring the church around *in favor* of her union with Boudinot, which by this time she was already contemplating. From an unwitting Hermann, she had secured — and in writing — the following golden advice: "You see I do not urge you to 'Forbear' — choose who you please, white, or black or *red*."[46]

Hermann having had no inkling of Elias and Harriett's liaison when he wrote that, the Ridge-Northrup controversy explains his preoccupation with race and intermarriage. The family knew John and Sarah well. Additionally, most New Englanders were becoming increasingly anxious due to the improved status of free blacks, which was ruffling the status quo. In her earlier conversation Harriett might have discreetly raised the topical moral issue of different color matches. While Harriett's letters give an impression of "purity" and godliness, there is nothing passive about her. Harriett's conversations may well have been strategic, and she could have taken Hermann's comment about a "red" match as a clerical endorsement.

On another occasion, June 10, 1823, Harriett and Hermann walked in the garden together. It was her eighteenth birthday. In this familiar, civilized space, midsummer, Harriett now shared a premonition of wild, gloomy forces. When "a thick, dubious cloud" appeared across the sky, Harriett said that she felt a menacing presence in her life. Thinking it wiser *not* to confide in him this time, Harriett remained mysterious and did not reveal what it was. Hermann kindly promised sympathy for whatever was impending.[47]

When the news finally splashed itself across church doors, Hermann may have been upset that Harriett had not confided in him about this big news. Furthermore, he may have toyed with a more than friendly interest in his wife's sister. Hermann's verbose letters sometimes used an overly stiff sign-off, such as "with affectionate fraternal regard" — as if to tone down his effusive feelings. In 1824 Hermann and Flora had decided to name their first child after her, Catherine *Harriett* Gold.

Prior to their marriage, Elias Boudinot had long corresponded with Hermann's wife, Flora. However far their friendship went, Flora had felt obliged to formally inform Elias of her plans to marry Reverend Hermann Vaill. Afterward, the erudite Elias continued to correspond with Flora.[48] Perhaps Hermann realized that his own wife could have married an Indian. Whatever his motives, Hermann tried to justify his opposition to Harriett's marriage.

He argued that Harriett's union was *more* sinful than Sarah Northrup's on the grounds that her engagement was based upon "secret correspondence." Harriett's task was to prove that "negociations [were] carried on, in a proper manner, & without the use of inconsistent & unchristian duplicity."⁴⁹ The previous Ridge-Northrup marriage was unlike Harriett's — that is, not secretive, "except it be the Love for an Indian."⁵⁰ In his letter to her sister Mary, he emphasizes the "public" consequences of Harriett's "secret" actions. Although sarcastic, he attempts consistency with his earlier stance on race: "I have no objections that sister H. should marry the man of her choice, be he white, or black, or even *red*, if that is the colour she prefers." But he then goes on to preach, "*provided* she can do it without endangering the interests of the Great Cause which she ought to love; & without a sacrifice of the Xtian consistency of character which, as a professed Xian, she is under obligations to maintain. If it was only 'the bare act of marrying' or a common case, I will cease to object. (*apart* from dissimilarity of complexion, for that I care nothing about)."⁵¹

Elias was darker-skinned than John Ridge. Some contemporaries refer to Elias as "black." Harriett, too, refers to her chosen partner as having "black skin." However, she notes the color/race hypocrisy, commenting that her sister Catharine's husband has a darker complexion than Elias's.⁵²

Some contemporaries described the Oowaties/Waties as "full-blood" Cherokees while others referred to them as mixed-blood. Elias's paternal grandfather was said to be Scottish, and some accounts state that his mother, Susanna Reece, had European ancestry. While recent scholars often refer to Elias as one of the elite mixed-bloods, differing contemporary assessments of his physical appearance and his ancestry, illustrated by contrasting portrait paintings, suggest fluid categories around color.

By the 1820s, many of the Cherokee ruling elite were of mixed descent. John Ridge and other wealthy men of his nation were the grandsons of Scottish and other traders, some of whom established large plantations based upon slave labor. Bilingual and bicultural skills enhanced the ongoing success of intermixed Cherokee families in trade and commerce, as did their links with Anglo-American networks.⁵³ We know that Boudinot's parents spoke Cherokee and were of high status, living in accordance to Cherokee law. But he knew both worlds. Boudinot had learned western etiquette from living in a missionary family's Anglo-American home; in his demeanor, he may not have acted or dressed differently from the local Cornwall men.

Hermann's jealous, sniping attestations that he is not bothered by "*colour*" — when he mentions it repeatedly — reflect one of the key anxieties of contemporary New England. Colonizers were a group with a sense of entitlement and a sense of whiteness. Carving out a role as benefactors to natives was one way to assuage guilt about the long-term impacts of colonizing land takeover. But color-crossing marriages were not part of that equation.[54]

Hermann challenged Harriett to prove that her marriage would not injure the school, the church, or "the cause of American Missions." He harangues, "'It would be a fatal stroke for the '*School for the Heathen, & for Christ*' that would make 'Xians weep, & the foes exult.'" On a pragmatic economic note, it would dampen the "ardour" of financial benefactors. Obsessing about "complexion," Hermann sarcastically implies that Harriett will ruin the marriage prospects of other family members: "Tell Cousin Eleanor she had better wait awhile. *White* is going out of fashion. Some think '*red*' becomes their complexion best, & *red it shall be*, if the milk dont spill."[55] (Perhaps this "milk" allusion referred to the offspring and whether the "red" would predominate, causing the "milk," or whiteness, to be spilled.) While clearly most worried about his status in the church and his social standing, Hermann strategically elevates familial duty and denigrates romantic and sexual love.

Another pertinent issue concerns mixing "blood"; Mary's husband, Daniel Brinsmade, refers to the "black young ones." As if against nature's laws, when mixed, white and red made "black." The cultural ideas behind these counter-color-wheel descriptions drew upon both historical and contemporary anxieties. Of course Harriett was not truly "white" in color, nor was Elias "red."

Keenly aware of their moral turpitude, New Englanders were nervous about their complicity in the slavery system. This case reminded them of their fears about sexual intermixing with former slaves; they were taught that the prospect of a white woman bearing "black" babies was somehow repugnant. Black was the color of slavery. Via gradual prohibition acts of 1784 and 1797, Connecticut had abolished slavery. Yet black laborers were thought unsuitable for the cold-weather agriculture that dominated the state's economy anyway. African Americans freed after the Revolutionary War were increasingly mobile, since slavery was abolished in various northern states, and more of them were starting to appear in towns and cities. They competed with white labor in factories and commerce. Churches and schools moved to segregate the "negroes." Local aversion to giving people of color an equal footing was raising conflicts over ideals of liberty and equality. Their anxiety over "color" consequently led New Englanders to agitate for the introduction of prohibitions against intermarriage with African Americans.[56]

Nonetheless, both Cornwall residents and the Cherokees were well aware that attitudes toward intermarriage with Indians differed. Presidents Thomas Jefferson and James Monroe had advocated intermarriage with Indians. However, for political purposes, different kinds of intermarriage could be fused. New Englanders and Cherokees observed how William Crawford's presidential campaign of 1824 was wrecked when newspapers and pamphlets reminded the public of his support of intermarriage between Indians and whites. This hit a sensitive nerve for white male voters in an era when changing African American demographics were exacerbating fears of competition with black men. Artists excited the public by ridiculing Crawford's vision. They depicted beautiful white women socializing with and marrying "Indians and blacks."[57] White men — the people entitled to vote — did not want their sisters or any of their female relatives marrying such men.

Although claiming *not* to be opposed to color-based intermarriage, both Hermann and Mary repeatedly alluded to color as a factor contributing to their stance. The Gold family was comfortably well off. "Gold" signified a Christian God's light and wealth. It was also malleable. Playing around with the family name "Gold," family members used it to stand for investment in inner and material wealth. Property and prospects were certainly at issue.

To connect with a sacred, revelatory nature, Harriett spoke of "darkness" and "dark clouds." Indeed, clouds became omens of dangerous enemies, of suffocating forces. Preferring the metaphor of Christ's light coming to the "dark lands" of the heathen, she trusted in "Providence" and knew her side of the day.[58] Harriett revealed her anguish, sadness, and affection, her love for her parents, for her sisters, and for her brothers-in-law.

Nonetheless, in a public letter to her friends, Harriett stated that if Elias made a proposal in correspondence, she had decided to agree to it. After the banns were published, Harriett wrote another formal letter to her friends explaining her decision and outlining the length of time they were betrothed and the propriety of her behavior. As long engagements were seen as a "true test" of feelings, she was keen to explain that her sentiments survived Elias Boudinot's three-year absence from Cornwall.[59] Well before the first wedding of a Cornwall woman to a Cherokee scholar in 1824, the dark visions that Harriett confided to Hermann in 1823 suggest that she had been considering the matter. The awful community ferment after the Ridge-Northrup union was traumatic and may have contributed to her illness, and perhaps Elias's too.

People's attitudes started to change. The biting tone of Hermann's letters prompted a change of heart in her family, and others started to revise their moralizing. Indeed, they decided that Harriett had not been secretive and that she had not lied. After her sister Catherine visited Cornwall, she wrote, "We were willfully ignorant. How often ma used to tell Flora & me that she believed that Harriett *loved* Elias — & . . . that she might marry him. . . . We thought that ma was criminal in saying as she did, & used to tell her so, we thought that it would give people occasion to talk — we were always offended when she introduced the subject." Catherine blames herself as part of a conspiracy of disbelief. They had denied the extraordinary, the unwanted, shameful, and embarrassing truth.[60]

Unlike in several neighboring states, intermarriage was legal in Connecticut.[61] Yet the "criminal" reference indicates the crucial role of the church in defining deviance and in keeping this local world "settled." Many other investments — in blood, in warfare, and even in history writing — had secured it. Yet people knew that to the south and the west, frontier conflicts ensued. No matter where you were, the frontier was not entirely dormant.

The powerful intervention of a dying young woman gave special pathos to the adage "Better dead than marry an Indian." With the authority of a prophet, the local woman stated that she "used to think that she had rather a friend would die, than to marry an Indian; but she did not feel so now, she found that it was a great thing to die she said, we have condemned Harriett for doing as she has — but perhaps our Saviour *loved her, better* than he does *any of us*."[62]

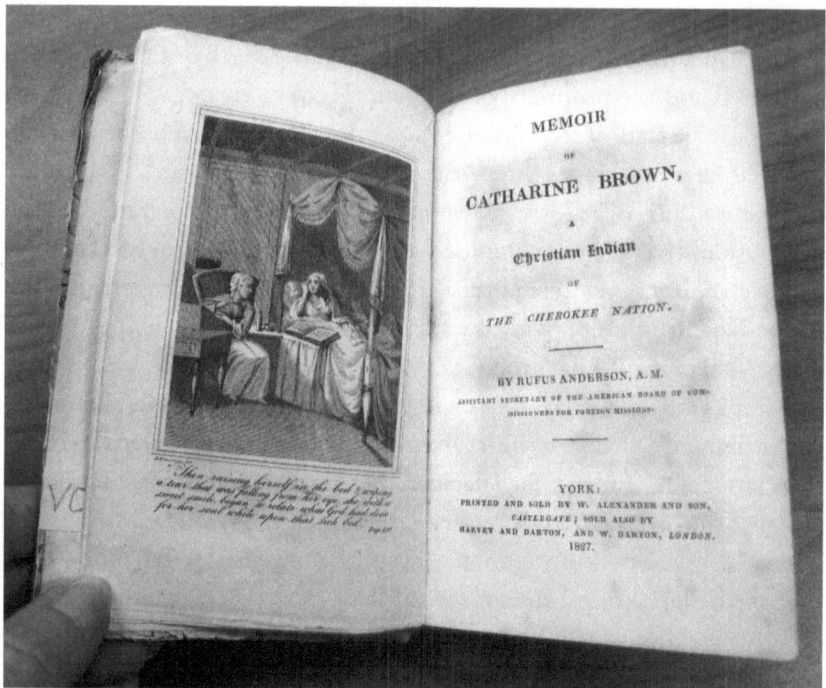

FIG. 11. Catharine Brown, memorialized as the first female Cherokee convert to Christianity, died in 1823, in her early twenties. Rufus Anderson's influential missionary tract *Memoir of Catharine Brown* narrated her transformation from a girl with Cherokee beliefs and "ornamentation" to a life of literacy, Christian simplicity, and perfection. The wording below the frontispiece etching reads, "Then raising herself in the bed & wiping a tear that was falling from her eye, she with a sweet smile began to relate what God had done for her soul while upon that sick bed." Photo by author.

Regardless, hurtful rumors to discredit Harriett continued to spread among the community. For example, that Harriett had been reportedly seen "walking" with a certain Deacon Loomis, perhaps to receive counseling on her decision, was labeled conspiratorial.[63] Having already dispatched missionaries farther afield to Hawaii, the Loomis family knew something of Indigenous matters.[64] Yet anyone associating with her was implicated and imperiled.

Harriett's brother Stephen Gold refused to attend congregation meetings for several Sabbaths. Harriett tried to empathize: "I do not wonder that he feels bad, but he has no right to threaten. I hope he does not mean all that he says."[65]

Meanwhile, Hermann's arguments became increasingly reliant upon emotional blackmail rather than logic. Harriett's parents were shocked not only by his melodramatic vitriol but also by his lack of respect for their authority. Overeager to please church leaders, he had broken protocol by failing to consult his father-in-law, Benjamin Gold. Hermann's letter backfired so badly that he had to beg his way back into their household.

Her brothers and brothers-in-law offered the most vicious personal attacks against Harriett. Hermann Vaill probably knew even before her brother Stephen found out. He could have been the person who informed General Brinsmade.[66] In June 1825 Brinsmade in turn informed his churchmen colleagues of Harriett's wedding plans. Brinsmade referred to "Harriett's craftiness by making them believe that she would die if she did not have her Indian."[67]

Even though he had personally threatened to lynch all parties, as a full brother, Stephen stood on firmer ground. Yet in the famous expression echoing Julius Caesar crossing the Rubicon, there was no turning back: "The dye is cast," he wrote to his brother and sister in June 1825. However, probably after discussions with Harriett and his parents, he changed his position. Family bonds took over from public embarrassment. Stephen agreed to ride, walk, pray, and sing with his sister. However, when he took his place in the congregation's choir, the rest of the company left their seats. Stephen sang a beautiful solo. It was a performance in honor of his pariah sister. Their sister Flora remarked triumphantly, "I have not heard better singing in a year."[68]

Church Wedding Banns

Let us leave the family for now and go back to the church's reaction when the news broke. As marriage demanded a public proclamation and community approval, "banns" were posted for all to see. But they also proclaimed that the church was wiping its hands clean of all responsibility. The prominent church elder Lyman Beecher stated, "A negociation for a marriage has been carried on secretly between Elias Boudinot a young Cherokee, who left the school with a good character . . . and Harriett R. Gold of this village; and that this negociation which has been carried on by secret and covered correspondence, has now become a settled engagement between the parties." With a sense of their authority, the banns proclaimed, "We regard those who have engaged in or accessory to this transaction, as criminal; as offering insult to the known feelings of the christian community: and as sporting with the sacred interests of this charitable institution." "This evil" was an "outrage upon public feeling."[69]

At an earlier stage, when one of the church agents had visited the Gold home in Cornwall to ask if it was true that their daughter was to marry an Indian, her parents answered that the question of her marriage was entirely in Harriett's hands. Col. Benjamin Gold and Eleanor Gold announced that they would not stand in their daughter's — or God's — way.

With an impending second intermarriage announced, missionary board members anticipated even worse publicity and the complete alienation of the school's philanthropists. Indeed, the influential newspaper editor Bunce now argued sarcastically that this intermarriage with an Indian man would allow the board to judge its enterprise as a success.[70] What could they say? The leading churchmen found his sharp logic excruciating. A church color scandal could ruin their missionary and political aspirations.

Like Harriett's white brothers-in-law, Elias Boudinot had adjudged marrying into the cultivated, esteemed Gold family as a good prospect. On a metaphysical level, it symbolized the unity of Christian-kind that he had been taught to cherish. What is more, the masculine prestige of successfully courting a white wife constituted a highly public performance of parity with white men. It might signal closer ties with the republic of the United States. Boudinot, the confident orator and political aspirant, knew the importance of widening his networks.[71]

While Elias understood how to work with the early republic through political and religious friendships, he might well have assumed that matrimony would unlock deeper bonds of intimacy, kinship, and family. Such a marriage might be a way of bringing nations and statesmen together.

The proposed marriage, however, was not going according to plan. Through the window, as the bonfire was being prepared, Harriett Gold was straining to identify the faces and gaits of familiar people. Harriett described many more "trying scenes," and her sister Mary confirmed, "Cornwall is in great turmoil and if the disturbances of the peace would be disposed of and had in safe keeping—it would rejoice the christian publick."[72] As for her brother Stephen's involvement in setting the effigies alight, Harriett wrote, "Even the most unprincipled say, they never heard of anything so bad . . . as that of burning a sister in effigy." Again, indicating a world divided across moral and color boundaries, even the "heathen" would not stoop so low.[73]

Harriett's mother, Eleanor Gold, was shocked and hurt that her own children were ganging up against her esteemed husband, herself, and their daughter. Harriett's letters depict a tight-knit local community promoting specific virtues. Belonging to her family's fifth generation of New Englanders, she had grown up with views of green hills and ploughed fields. She was accustomed to seeing the red barns, useful animal enclosures, and haystacks. The lines of neoclassic churches and the elegant houses marked home.[74] Facing onto a commons, with farm lots dotted outside the town, Cornwall was becoming the typical "white village."[75] Despite their modern commercial genesis, such towns were an emblem of New England's "venerable communal and republican past." As the historian Joseph Conforti explains, "The 'white' village and the Pilgrim story came to promote New England's identity as the American homeland."[76] Civic buildings and churches were constructed along classical lines and painted white, evoking simplicity and orderly, rational belief. However, they also denoted wealth, as only elites could afford this most expensive paint.

By 1820, with the bicentenary of the *Mayflower* landing, local historians invented a pioneer history that fitted contemporary politics and aspirations.[77] Ordaining the local with narratives of settler-colonizer antiquity and progress, they developed tales of Anglo-American "firsts."[78] By Harriett's time, New Englanders could readily imagine their ancestral past as a layered, place-based history. History had transformed their towns into sacred spaces with imposing memorials to an innocent nation with virtuous ideals. Such a history celebrated the founding of a free, white republican nation of high moral standing.[79] These values were also demonstrated in women's dress and style.

In a formal, painted portrait that survived the last two hundred years, Harriett's simply tailored dress and unpretentious hairstyle match a preordained aesthetic.[80] The artist made her face look plain to today's tastes, but she has a long, fine nose, perhaps considered distinguished. Harriett's letters suggest that she cherished values such as parental respect and obedience, truthfulness, humility, and thoughtful restraint. Some of her friends considered her "unremarkable," which was apparently a good thing. Now heading toward adulthood, she was weighing her own life choices.

Harriett's sisters Flora and Mary had married churchgoing professional men of learning and accomplishment. One was an ambitious clergyman; one an accomplished general. After marrying, the couples moved to other towns in the New England region. Through letters and occasional trips by horse and carriage, they kept in contact. After the announcement of her intention to marry, Harriett received a barrage of correspondence from family members. Almost an outcast, she struggled to retain membership of her familiar and family-centered world.

Mohegan World

Long before the Separatist Puritans boarded boats in England to sail to the New World, this place was the family- and clan-centered world of the Mohegans, the people of the wolf. Beneath Cornwall's soil were many signs of earlier occupation: arrowheads, stone tools, and worn pieces of ancient bowls and pots. Each place in that landscape held significance for the Mohegans. Native Americans from Bantam, Schaticoke, and Weatogue passed through Cornwall on a common trail; they hunted, fished, and conducted sacred rituals. The Puritan arrivals entered a conflict situation over land. They built a protective fort and farmers carried loaded weapons on standby.[81]

By 1738 Cornwall land had been officially divided and sold and an earlier generation of the Gold family was farming at Cream Hill.[82] Cornwall's period of dramatic frontier violence between Mohegans, Pequots, and Anglo-Americans, including changing alliances between the different Indian nations and Anglo-Americans, left legacies of fear, anxiety, and loss on all sides.

The Pequot War (1634–38) and King Philip's War (1675–78) scarred New England, with white men from various regions serving as soldiers against the Indian uprisings. The Pequot War was sparked over tensions in the fur and wampum trade and over justice, in response to retaliatory and punitive murders. The Mohegans saw it not as an English-Indian war but as "the warres with the Generall Nations of Indians."[83]

Wampum was part of an embodied, ritual process of exchange that served to rebalance power between peoples and to bring harmony to the land itself.⁸⁴ King Philip's War, named for Metacom, the Wampanoag sachem or leader who had taken on that English name, was "a multi-faceted coalition against English expansion."⁸⁵ In order to fight for control of the lands that are now part of southeastern Connecticut, the Mohegans, who had broken away from the Pequots, allied themselves with the English. Leaders disagreed on strategies for resource sharing. Uncas, in alliance with the English, wanted to draw more families into the Mohegan dish. Miantonomo wanted to create and deepen kinship within the wider Indian union, "to sustain the pot from which their ancestors had eaten together." Mohegan leader Samson Occam stated that "to join in marriage was to eat from the same dish."⁸⁶

The Mohegans pressed a land case to protest relentless colonial encroachment. Their leaders petitioned the British monarchs in 1700 and 1736 and participated in the 1735 meeting at Deerfield that included Abenakis, Mohawks, Mohicans, and English.⁸⁷ They could see that the Connecticut Assembly wanted "to root us out of our land, root & branch," to make them "cyphers in their own land."⁸⁸ Drawing upon oral traditions and English law, leaders such as the Mohegan clergyman Samson Occom embraced literacy to further their title claims.⁸⁹

Although the Mohegans lost the land case, in 1778 they confirmed a more inclusive national identity, that as a people they were "one Family." In 1789 they sent a memorial to the Connecticut Assembly. While their forefathers had lived in "peace, love and great harmony" they now had "hearts full of sorrow and grief." They yearned to return to a time when the dish was "equally divided amongst us" so that they could eat quietly and so that everyone could "have his own fire."⁹⁰ In the 1800s the Mohegans retained a few small parcels of land but were regularly forced to sell them off to pay debts incurred after being cared for in white people's homes while ill and for funerals.⁹¹

During Harriett's time, some Mohegans remained in this now-interpenetrated region of Connecticut, including people of mixed descent identifying as Mohegan or white. A local historian recorded that the Cornwall townspeople saw the occasional "Indian," recalling them fondly as a novelty of the past, as a "last remnant" of their tribe.⁹² Harriett lived at a time when Indians no longer threatened their farmlands and towns. As well as having fought earlier Indian wars, many New Englanders had fought during the Revolutionary War against the British, Indians, and other allies.

Now that that war was over, Cornwall Christians might anticipate enjoyment of the Connecticut lands without interference. Winning the noble war against the British enemy brought a sense of finality, triumph, and new beginnings, but only one kind of colonial era had ended. On a heady mix of Christian ideals that blended concepts of human perfectibility and individualism, the new, "rightful Americans" were building a modern republic. This was an economic and cultural transition period. Major forces were changing the Connecticut that New Englanders had created. The old agricultural perspective of the world, hinging on the drama of the seasons, was being replaced by a more linear concept of the world as a place of advancing technological progress.⁹³ Changes in the landscape, such as the construction of canals and turnpikes, heralded the market revolution. New England farming families were scattering more widely because there was not enough land to distribute among families.

During the 1820s a widespread religious revival was enlivening the complex cultural world of New England. Individual congregation members were encouraged to transform themselves; they argued against predestined fates, creating an optimistic religion looking more heavenward than hell-ward. Through self-cultivation, discipline, and restraint, they believed they could become personally closer to God. New England churches were increasingly evangelical and outward-looking, proclaiming in public prayer that they had been "born again."

Slavery and "color" threw up difficult questions about who had souls and whether inferior earthly social status was part of God's plan. Different religious groups in the northern and southern states of the United States interpreted the Bible to fit specific racial and labor agendas. The proslavery lobby asserted that the Bible referred to man's "sovereignty" over slaves — and over women.⁹⁴ Relationships were changing, however. Nonetheless, convinced of their moral superiority and exceptional role as a people in Providence or God's plan, New Englanders hoped to re-create and extend their ideas of godliness in the wider world.⁹⁵

In Cornwall, the students from many nations learned in English, but their lessons were certainly not all about religion. They read geography, rhetoric, surveying, ecclesiastical and common history, three books of the *Aeneid*, two orations of Cicero, and natural philosophy. When student John Ridge wrote a letter to President Monroe in 1821, he exclaimed that he was pleased to be educated "like the whites!"[96] Unlike some of the Pacific and other Native American youth, the Cherokee youth had the company of a few compatriots. During their leisure hours, the Cherokee youth walked around singing together.[97]

Entangled by Literacy

In order to conduct an effective campaign for sovereignty, the Cherokee Nation, situated almost a thousand miles south of Cornwall, needed to educate its young men. So that their lands could be freed up for miners and settler colonizers, state governments and colonizing entrepreneurs were agitating for all Indians to go west. Oratory, ethics, philosophy, and law would be useful in their battles, as would fluency in English and in the religious rhetoric of philanthropists. From 1823, New Echota, in current-day Georgia, was being established as their new capital. Their nation had implemented modern forms of representative and constitutional government that simultaneously respected their clan-based systems of governance and cultural practices. While the Cherokees asserted a position of strength, their lands were under serious threat, decreasing in size via new treaties and being grabbed by land-hungry white frontiersmen. The Cherokee Nation was facing very serious challenges. Although hunting large game was now difficult, many Cherokee citizens led subsistence lives, growing and grinding their corn and weaving cloth.[98] A wealthy elite held extensive plantations and hundreds of African American slaves. A missionary education, now on offer, might empower the next generation.

Elias Boudinot's father, Oowatie, an influential political leader, and his mother, Susanna Reece, decided that their son should gain this training. In an 1817 record, missionaries transcribed his Cherokee name as Tekuh nah ste sky, translated as "pick him up and throw him down"; they also recorded him as Buck Watie. In 1820 the Foreign Mission School at Cornwall recorded his name as Kuh-le-g-nngah. Later missionaries listed him as Galagina, Oowatie, Buck Watie, and The Buck, an English interpretation of Tekuh nah ste sky.[99] From childhood, he struggled to learn English and literacy from the missionaries. After a shaky start at Spring Creek, the Christian mission in Cherokee country, he was recognized as a promising student. Cherokee parents agitated for their children to be able to attend senior schools and the local missionaries backed them. Along with some other Cherokee youth, the fifteen-year-old Buck Watie was invited to attend the Cornwall Foreign Mission School for advanced schooling. Buck Watie was to live there during his impressionable years.

On their seven-week journey from the Cherokee Nation to Cornwall, the students were taken to visit iconic national locations and to meet leaders of the republic. Although they were part of a church-led youth leaders delegation, such direct network building continued the nation-to-nation diplomacy between the Cherokee Nation and the United States. These visits were also designed to advocate state and philanthropic support for Cherokee education.

They visited Monticello to see the former president Thomas Jefferson, finding him very interested in the Foreign Mission School and in higher education generally. Next the students traveled to nearby Montpelier to visit the Constitution writer and former president James Madison and his wife, Dolley Madison, who defined what it meant to be a First Lady. They all dined together, waited on by Madison's African American slaves.[100]

What did the young Cherokees think of the people in these households? What did they think of Jefferson's library, the paintings all over his walls, his ingenious inventions, his theories about government, and the global plant displays in his garden? What did they think of his many accomplishments? Had they read in newspaper stories that he had a mixed family and children with his house slave?[101]

After Monticello, the students visited the tomb of George Washington, the first president of the republic, to pay their respects. The Cherokees remembered him fondly for making firm and equitable promises and for addressing them as "Beloved," a category of the highest esteem in their culture. Approaching the end of his term as president, in 1796, Washington had promised them that if they embraced "the experiment" of modern farming and such practices, they would gain a place in the new republic.

Furthermore, he considered that their example "may determine the lot of many nations."[102] They were being treated like an older brother to other Indian nations.[103] The Cherokees believed that he had set out the terms of a compact — a colonizing compact.

Testifying to the impressive networks of the Foreign Mission School and the significance of the venture, Buck and his fellow students gained an audience with the reigning president, James Monroe. They also met the secretary of war, John C. Calhoun, who administered Indian policy. Impressed by this native education project, the government promised to pay a hundred dollars each toward the Cherokees' expenses.

Boudinot Meets Boudinot

The student group then ventured on to the bustling town of Burlington, New Jersey, to meet a private philanthropist. Elias Boudinot IV was a New Jersey politician and statesman whose parents were descended from French Huguenot emigrants from La Rochelle. This persecuted Protestant group had sought refuge from their homeland in other parts of Europe and the New World.[104] Elias had been a Republican statesman, a state politician who served as president of the republic's formative body, the United States in Congress Assembled — better known as the Continental Congress. In 1783 he revived Thanksgiving Day as an annual event for the new republic.[105] We do not know exactly what transpired when Buck Watie met the statesman Boudinot in 1818.[106]

Boudinot IV mixed in elite governing and church circles.[107] An education enthusiast, he had established a teaching seminary and was a trustee of the College of New Jersey, later Princeton University.[108] Here one of his earliest tasks was to address riotous student behavior, which was especially bad during the sleighing season.[109] By the 1810s the plump, aging Boudinot still cut the dignified figure of an "old patriarch."[110]

As for so many early American men of influence, a good marriage had helped Elias Boudinot IV consolidate his material and cultural capital. In 1762 Boudinot married his sister-in-law, Hannah Stockton. She was the sister of the wealthy attorney Richard Stockton, Boudinot's legal mentor and teacher and a signer of the Declaration of Independence.[111] Stockton's grandfather had bought land off William Penn. Boudinot's sister Annis

FIG. 12. Elias Boudinot IV, New Jersey statesman. Courtesy Library of Congress, reproduction no. LC-USZ62-54694.

was a prominent poet and fan of Mary Wollstonecraft's *A Vindication of the Rights of Women*. Elias Boudinot IV exemplified how marriage could bring social and cultural cachet, material advancement, personal security, and — in his case — happiness.

In Elias Boudinot's and Hannah Stockton's courtship letters, which flirted around ideas of Perfection and Virtue (in capital letters) Elias used the pseudonym Narcissus, and to Hannah he gave the name Eugenia.[112] Their marriage appears to have been a loving one. They had two daughters. As he grew older, Elias wrote increasingly heartfelt letters and poems to his

FIG. 13. This is the stately home of Elias Boudinot IV, where the young scholars visited, in Burlington, New Jersey. Courtesy Burlington Historical Society.

wife, declaring his "unbounded affection" for his "Dearest Love" and stating his pleasure at his choice of bride.[113] As she had died in 1808, in 1818 his visitor Buck had to imagine Hannah with the aid of her framed portrait. Holding a small book, she appears as a regal woman exuding strength, wealth, and learning.[114]

Elias Boudinot IV published tracts on the history and future of Indians. His 1816 pamphlet *A Star in the West* linked the American Indian people with the same biblical tribes as the Europeans and, more particularly, their New England émigrés. He disparaged assertions that American Indians were merely "savages and barbarians" as coming from "the old world" of Europe. Seeking a common American heritage, his split-tribes theory offered a sacred solution to one of the quandaries of American colonialism. Drawing upon similarities between Mohegan and Hebrew words and customs, he embraced Indians as relatives.[115] In a coup for church and state, in 1816 Boudinot had brought a large interdenominational Christian group together in New York to form the American Bible Society; its secretaries included the Reverend Dr. Lyman Beecher of Litchfield and James Fenimore Cooper.[116]

Boudinot IV's house featured a library of books on theology and history, an impressive writing desk, and various high-quality items of furniture, art, and sculpture. With bas-relief figures of Apollo and the Muses and medallion portraits of Julius and Augustus Caesar, allusions to classical Greek and Roman civilizations abounded. Allegorical figures depicted the known world in white marble. Australia's existence did not yet rank in the European imaginary.

The Stockton-Boudinots owned a huge ornate mirror framed in embellished mahogany and gilt. Dated circa 1776, at the top of its eighty-inch-high frame protruded a standalone carving of the phoenix of Greek and Egyptian legend. Its wings were spread upward, as if to take flight. With its phoenix signifying regeneration after destruction and associated with the sun, the mirror is said to have been a gift from George Washington, with whom Elias Boudinot had been close friends. The gold-leaf finish of the bird and frame gave the appearance of solid gold.

We cannot know for certain that the mirror was in the room when Buck Watie visited, but it is highly likely that it was. Imagine the fifteen-year-old Elias stealing a glimpse of his reflection inside that lavish golden frame. With its trail of bodies and burned-out towns, an America ravaged by Revolutionary War found powerful resonance in the legendary phoenix. Even as recently as in 1814, British troops had burned down the White House. In the ancient legend, the phoenix rose anew from the ashes of destruction, invigorated and reborn. Buck Watie was aware of his own people's history of warfare and national destruction. He also knew the Cherokee narratives of birds, serpents, and other animals, in which the golden eagle was a powerful symbol associated with warfare and peace making.[117]

Approaching the columned portico of this stately home and its manicured gardens must have filled the young Buck Watie with a sense of excited anticipation.[118] A staunch and humane abolitionist, Boudinot saw the increasing numbers of "negroes" as an insurrection risk.[119] Indians were different.

Elias Boudinot IV was so impressed with Buck Watie that he invited the young Cherokee to adopt his distinguished family name.[120] The elder was approaching eighty and in declining health. Although he had no son of his own upon whom to confer the patrilineal title, a nephew already carried the name. The Cherokee scholar accepted the same honor.[121]

While a name change happened routinely when a woman changed her status from single to married, this was not the case for American men.[122] Three years later, in mid-1821, the young Elias Boudinot visited his namesake.[123] Not long afterward, on October 16, 1821, the New Jersey statesman died.[124] Boudinot IV's generous bequest helped fund both the German Moravian school at Bethlehem and Cornwall's Foreign Mission School.

On the day that Buck Watie first visited Elias Boudinot IV on his way to Cornwall in 1818, the two became kin. In his mentor, Buck Watie observed how a learned, thoughtful life of political advocacy had been supported by a well-connected wife. Like an adopted son, the Cherokee Boudinot took the name giving very seriously, keeping and using the title through his adulthood. But what did it feel like to live inside someone else's name? Or, for that matter, inside someone else's republic?

Inside the Homes of the Whites

Before he arrived at Cornwall, the new Elias Boudinot was already better traveled, better networked, and held more career options than Harriett Gold, who was a lifelong resident of the small town of Cornwall and a girl. Harriett assisted in the school, which created some opportunities for the two to get to know each other. As an exceptional student, and with his fancy name, Elias got noticed.[125] Regularly entertained in the white churchgoers' homes, including the Golds', he socialized with their families.[126] As ethnographers of local northern life, the Cherokee students observed what happened inside Cornwall homes. They read the newspapers and other contemporary literature that ruminated on Euro-American and European notions of beauty, true womanhood, and courting etiquette. The local Congregational church had facilitated Harriett's and Elias's friendship, if not their romance. Cornwall teacher Reverend Hermann Daggett attested to the good characters of the would-be couple, for he "loved Boudinot and had been much loved by him" and "the young lady was a most sincere friend of the pastor."[127]

Harriett was well aware that her actions were deeply subversive. Elias was in the process of crossing even more dangerous boundaries. He had been warned that the church had promised the local community that an intermarriage scandal would never happen again. If it did, the Foreign Mission School would certainly close down. But his plans did not coincide with the church's plans.

How could church founders have overlooked the possibility of marriages between the exclusively male Indigenous students and local white women? Had they ignored Connecticut's tribal memory, ever revived in popular accounts, of white women held captive to Indian men? Not to mention the former Revolutionary War soldiers and other freed African Americans whose presence was igniting local anxieties over color?

By 1788 the Cherokees were still fighting unofficial wars with white, predominantly male, usurpers. In frontier and trading zones, Europeans saw the advantages of marriage to Indian women — indeed, such marriages were essential to diplomatic and trading access. In the Cherokee territories since 1803, hundreds of white men had married Cherokee women and many had moved into the Cherokee Nation permanently. The first state-funded Indian agent, Return J. Meigs, was proassimilationist, encouraging intermarriage between white men and Cherokee women. He believed it was for the Cherokees' own good, "because your women are industrious and because I conceive that by this measure civilization is faster advanced than in any other way." Meigs assumed "white blood" would "raise" the Indians from "backwardness." (He put his own "blood" into the mix, living with a Cherokee wife and raising a family.) Cherokee men did not necessarily agree.[128]

With those lands so compromised as native space, Boudinot must have seen contemporary Connecticut as a foreboding, awful vision of an endgame. Here colonialism's battles looked "settled," and the Mohegan world had become part of the Anglosphere. As sovereign space, Cherokee territory remained very different from the established north. The Cherokees were considered a "civilized tribe." They wore lively variations on western-style clothing, milled grain, and wove cloth, and the wealthy elite owned plantations and worked slaves. The Cherokee Nation built townships and engaged in modern commerce and transport businesses. Adopting Sequoyah's remarkable syllabary, the Cherokees began to use "talking leaves" in their language. At the same time, they moved toward codifying their government.

The Cherokee hemisphere had become a transnational and cross-cultural zone. Gender roles and matrilineal property distribution were being realigned toward a more European-style patriarchal practice.[129] For emigrant scholars, however, wearing western-style clothing did not mean they became Euro-American, and residence outside their native space did not mean that they had they given up their sovereignty over land.

Perhaps the people of Cornwall feared that they had been fooled. Were they helping distant strangers or were they helping the foe? Worrying to Christians were the "ghost dances" or the spiritual revelation and revival movements that gave no primacy to the Christian God. Cherokee leaders tried various strategies for dealing with colonialism and notions of modernity. By the 1820s the Cherokees were disputing treaties with other groups, including the Choctaws. They had started to battle the intruders by using literacy, religion, education, and a representative system of governance with a written constitution and laws, and they mounted legal battles in the courts. And now they used letters, too, including love letters.

THE MISSING WORDS: A SECRET AND
COVERED CORRESPONDENCE

When Harriett Ruggles Gold of Cornwall, Connecticut, agreed to marry the Cherokee scholar Elias Boudinot, she knew she would be making the move south to the capital of the Cherokee Nation, New Echota. It would be a forty-nine-day wagon trip south. However, in July 1825, when Harriett had not heard anything from Elias for some time, she suspected that letters were being intercepted in "some office."[130] We will now explore responses to the missing letters through which the courtship proceeded.

The inflammatory proclamation posted on the church doors in July 1825 declared that a "negociation for a marriage" had been "carried on secretly" by "secret and covered correspondence." Being "a settled engagement," it was contractual, and some kind of posting in a public place had to follow.[131] The lead signatory to this extraordinary proclamation was the well-known Yale Divinity School graduate and Calvinist preacher, Lyman Beecher.[132] In it, the church leaders expressed total disapproval; they stated that "the christian public universally" expressed "unequivocal disapprobation of such connexions." With Elias now in the Cherokee Nation and outside their ability to influence or govern, Harriett was their target. In a jointly signed statement, the churchmen labeled Harriett's actions as *criminal*, as evil and an "outrage upon public feeling."[133]

Imagine the effect of such words on a young churchgoing woman.[134] Church authorities proclaimed, "*This negociation . . . has been carried on by secret and covered correspondence*" (emphasis added). When the church posted details of Harriett and Elias's intention to marry, their engagement had civil status. It had gone too far for this "crime" of literacy to be stopped. Correspondence was not permitted to be private; people expected it to be circulated for wider consumption.

Harriett and Elias's union elevated the tensions across a complex political spectrum. Arguing for intimate segregation would make the church leaders sound hypocritical. After all, they propounded the equality of natives and African American slaves alike and had set up the Foreign Mission School to educate and "civilize" Indians. To prevent its detractors having a field day, the church had to prove that such a marriage was not "missionary machinery" designed to undermine the values of settled, pastoral New England, a world with prescribed same-race family amalgamations that had made its own "little Commonwealth."[135]

Love Letters

In a letter to her brother and sisters on June 25, 1825, Harriett Gold announced, "Your Sister Harriett is already *published* to *an Indian*."[136] Printed words had contractual implications. Not to a man, to an Indian. Not a connection sealed by hands but rather, like a land deal, one of pen and print. She knew the intent of the official wording was to publicly disgrace and humiliate both herself and her family, but this terminology made explicit the underpinnings of the public insult to Elias. Although once a friend of the congregation, he was instead given a label that evoked a violent historical stereotype. To be "Indian" represented a masculine warrior threat — a savage enemy at war.

After Elias returned to the Cherokee Nation, the courtship negotiations between he and Harriett were conducted almost entirely through letters. Regular, though expensive, mail services operated between the North and South during the 1820s. Harriett's letters from Cornwall, Connecticut, took five or more weeks to reach New Echota.[137] Over two years, ink-inscribed pages — occasionally in diagonally crisscrossed, paper-saving line arrangements — traveled to and fro.

Providing cover, the Northrup family kept the letters at their place. They were already receiving mail deliveries from their married daughter Sarah Ridge, who now lived in the Cherokee Nation.[138] As Harriett wrote, Elias's letters had indeed been "stolen." Sometime in May, the church agents confiscated the lovers' correspondence from the Northrup home. Despite the preservation of extensive mission and family records, these precious letters are still missing.[139]

While New Englanders had come to accept that marriages were now self-determined, with sons and daughters able to make their own choices, this union was in another league. The nervous community denigrated Mrs. Northrup as having "an unnatural interest" in Indian marriages. After Harriett's announcement, a lynch mob threatened to kidnap both Mr. and Mrs. Northrup, and they were forced to flee.[140] Prejudiced anyway about white women's special role in marriage arrangements, community members accused Mrs. Northrup of being a "Jezebel," making her daughter a "squaw," and "connecting her ancestors to a race of Indians."[141] Marriage's ripples spread far and wide — potentially extending to a different, undesirable future.

So what kind of courtship letters were they? If other letters provide a guide, the adventure and anxieties for would-be lovers coexisted with a desire for restraint.[142] Each would want to demonstrate his or her honesty and belief in self-inspection and improvement.

The early republican era has been dubbed a "republic of letters."[143] Mail services broke down distances, creating and maintaining bonds of sympathy across and between the United States and the Cherokee Nation. Epistolary writing and communication expanded. Correspondence was a place where "an enduring relationship grounded in feeling might be cultivated."[144] Love letters in the suitor's hand were considered of great worth, and it was thought that such manuscripts could be read as signs of "true" versus "false" politeness; they could assess virtue.[145] Handwritten letters mediated personal connection and trust.

Letters acted on individual emotions, sparking feelings, imaginings, and desires. They shaped embodied, private moments of the heart and mind and they expressed one's sexuality. Always relational, whether the bodies in question had previously been together or not, they facilitated the forming of connections. And now, with literacy, Native Americans could enter that same circle.

Concocting their letters on fine paper with ink-dipped quills, the correspondents secreted them in envelopes and sealed them with stamped wax. For a time, these intimate expressions of self *were* the relationship.[146] They were also its tangible proof.

In the early 1800s Cherokee life was not dependent on books, reading, or writing, although Sequoyah's Cherokee alphabet, adopted by the nation in 1821, demonstrated commitment to language-specific literacy. Literacy assisted in diplomatic and legal dealings.[147] The Cherokees, an oral culture, witnessed the literate succeeding at business, wealth accumulation, diplomacy, political affairs, and the gaining of wives. Elias's parents had not learned to read and write, but clearly they saw the value of encouraging their son doing so. The missionary teachers at Brainerd and Spring Place, including Anna Gambold, had taught Buck Watie how to speak English and how to write in a good hand. They taught him the protocol and etiquette of the letter considered appropriate in the American republic.[148]

Upon his initial return to New Echota, Elias first corresponded with Harriett's brother Stephen and then with her sister Flora. The romance between Harriett and Elias appears to have commenced and developed exclusively via correspondence. In any case, letters provided opportunities for intimacy not available in these chaperoned times.

During the two years of their correspondence, from 1823 to 1825, the friendship between Harriett and Elias grew strong enough for them both to make a risky decision. Elias's student letters to various highly ranked Republican statesmen were competent but obsequious. He knew how to craft flattering, if not fawning, letters to Anglo-American and international benefactors.[149] Although sometimes following a stilted, formal style, he expressed himself with sincerity and could draw emotion in the reader. Boudinot pitched his letter-writing abilities to various contexts and occasions. Widely read, he devoured a range of American newspapers, which included news of Europe, the Pacific, and the rest of world. He understood the correct New England protocols and knew that letters were public documents to be passed around and read like newspapers.

Harriett's and Elias's letters tested their emotional engagement, shared meditations of the heart, and eventually became the venue for contracting the serious matter of marriage.[150] Knowing the antagonistic community feeling, Harriett and Elias had privately agreed to keep their letters secret. And now, their confiscation meant they would remain that way.[151] Sadly, they are our missing artifacts.

The flowing prose of Harriett's letters provides glimmers of a thoughtful person who values directness and sincerity. She spreads out her lines on the page but succumbs to the thrifty habit of writing additional, sometimes less guarded, comments in the margins. Her introspection reveals a sense of assuredness. Harriett does not seem overly interested in material things. In an era when individuals strove for godly perfection, one of her friends commended Harriett as "one of the fairest, most cultured young ladies of the pale, a very pious, amiable girl, the nearest to perfection of any person I ever knew."[152] Harriett does not see herself in such a flattering light, revealing her religious doubts and weaknesses in the self-critical Calvinist tradition of the day.

We have no record of her discussing a wedding dress, although this could have been in the missing letters. A distant relative, Eunice Wadsworth Taylor, stated that she had attended the wedding and that she had hand-made Harriett's wedding outfit.[153] Elias had arranged to have a miniature version of Harriett's portrait made to wear in a locket, which he probably pinned to his waistcoat.

By all accounts loving and dutiful, Harriett cherished family, church, and Christian ideals. Perhaps she attempted to impress Elias Boudinot with the Christian insights of her simple everyday life. Within the framework of New England culture and ideals, Elias felt assured of Harriett's sincerity and integrity. Her parents epitomized a world of Christian sophistication and a fusion of Republican and church statesmanship.

On the other hand, the illicit nature of the match on both sides added a frisson of danger. Both were lonely in their own ways. Harriett lacked excitement, had always lived in the same place and known the same close circle of visitors and locals. We hear of only one other suitor. From Elias's perspective, very few of the Cherokee girls from his community had a New England—style cultural education. However, Elias had other reasons for apprehension. In his matrilineal society, only children of Cherokee mothers had clan-based land entitlements and full Cherokee status in their law. Unlike in Cornwall society, the husband was expected to move to the land of his wife, and his children would inherit their mother's property. Although he would not be moving north, the children of a well-educated Cherokee man being lost to the nation in this way was troubling. Elias had every reason to anticipate disapproval and resentment of his choice, especially from Cherokee women, who guarded their powers within their evolving nation. Had he thought that Harriett would be more compliant than a Cherokee wife, she was not showing much sign of it.

The emotional richness of this story relies upon the correspondence hoarded by Hermann Vaill. The immediacy and candor of these letters makes it all the more frustrating that we do not have the correspondence of the courtship transactions and negotiations. Did these missives discuss where Harriett would live? Did Boudinot say what he expected of her? How did she feel about leaving all that she knew? Did they quote song verses to each other? We might expect that the two would have been formal at first, observing protocol. It would be intriguing to read those vital clues to their evolving emotional entanglement. While we know that church people confiscated them, we do not know what became of them. Possibly the letters, like the effigies, went up in smoke.

AGAINST HISTORY? THE TEST

With her own direct family now on her side, Harriett still had to contend with collective notions of colonizing history. Indians could be uplifted toward a progressive future, but a white woman should not be pulled backward. In this conception of history's predetermined path, Harriett was swimming downstream, against the tide of history. A marriage between a white woman and an Indian man was against the assumed order of things; it was against historical logic.

Captives to Colonialism

As in other parts of New England, the people of Cornwall, Connecticut, and the wider New England region knew the captive women stories well.[154] A white woman's union with an Indian was understood as forced — as brutality and rape. Somehow a white woman's consent was impossible. Many local people thought it a good thing to have rid the country of "savages" all those years ago. Wasn't blood spilled and danger felt by families in respect of their sons and daughters? They ruminated not on their ancestors' actions toward Indians but on *Indian* atrocities. Generic stereotypes of American Indians portrayed white women like Jane McCrea as raped and debased. During the 1820s, Anglo-American captivity narratives, with their central trope of white women's encounters with Indian men as sexual slavery — a "fate worse than death" — were reaching a peak of popularity in New England. The 1824 publication of the story of Mary Jemison's capture and transformation into a Seneca "squaw" was a best seller. In contrast, another nonfiction book published that year, by Lydia Maria Child, a Unitarian, took the reader into more unsettling territory. In *Hobomok*, Child described the world of an upper-class white woman who voluntarily marries a Native American chief, has his child, then deserts both of them. To Child, interracial marriage symbolized an alliance that might provide "a natural resolution of America's racial and sexual contradictions." In defiance of white patriarchal order, Child thus provided an alternative vision of race and gender relations.[155] We cannot be sure if Harriett or Hermann had heard about or read *Hobomok*; evangelicals of the time tended to consider novel reading somewhat trivial and unladylike, instead encouraging their youth to read pious religious tracts.[156]

The prevailing captivity narratives expose white male anxiety, providing parables about how white women require white male protection from ravaging Indians. Simultaneously, they reveal white women's desire to imagine the horror of such a "primitive" fate, ostensibly so much worse than their own.

Moreover, New Englanders did not wish to imagine themselves as connected with a history in which it was Indigenous women who were commonly raped, abducted, or exploited and in which it was peoples other than themselves who were forced into exile. "Civilized" societies needed to maintain the status quo and to feel good about themselves as colonizers.

When a white woman "connected her race" to an "Indian," it was portrayed very differently than when a white man married an Indian woman. The latter had long been condoned for traders and Indian agents in Indian territories, but now something had changed. At play were the politics of the white wife, who was expected to forge the new "egalitarian" white republic.[157]

Elias Boudinot's Cherokee translation of the popular missionary tract *Poor Sarah; or, Religion Exemplified in the Life and Death of an Indian Woman, a Sentimental Tragedy about an Indian Wife*, would further reinforce the image of a downtrodden wife with a violent Indian husband.[158] "Squaw," an oft-used trope for a native woman, now stood for oppression of Indian women by their men. To be a "squaw," an "Indian's wife" was to be degraded. This conveniently deflected attention from white men's ongoing exploitation of Indian women.

Soon after the Cornwall events, a popular poem mythologized the "Indian marriages" story, reinforcing stereotypical racial discourses:

She thinks great splendor there is seen,
And she be crowned for a queen.

She would be disappointed of her home,
To find a little, small wigwam.
And nothing allowed her for a bed,
But a dirty blanket, it is said.

And this be hard for Sarah fair,
Who long did live in splendor here,
To lay aside her laces and fine gowns,
Her Indian blanket to put on.[159]

"Sarah" of the poem conflated Sarah Northrup, Harriett Gold, and the "Poor Sarah" of the religious tract. Despite the Cherokees' prosperity and "civilized" accouterments, the white wives of Cornwall had to be imagined as "reduced," as forsaking a comfortable world for blanket and wigwam. In reality, Sarah Northrup had moved from a humbler home to a stately plantation home with many black slaves. Yet in the early nineteenth century, republican New Englanders' perceptions of historical progress hinged awkwardly upon a vision of local Indigenous worlds as places left behind by time, while they, the "New World Pilgrims," took on the future. Even the brilliant Yale scholar Ralph Gabriel subscribed to the "two temporalities" view: "American Protestantism confront[ed] not only a race problem but that of adjustment between two cultures separated by a thousand years."[160] As if she encountered a historical full stop, "the squaw," like "the Indian," was frozen outside modernity.

Since Anglo-American women's bodies became emblematic of the American republic, sexual or marital association with "an Indian" symbolized an act of theft in a subterranean war. Although reformers believed in an equality of man and perfectibility via instruction, they too could readily fall into the pervasive thinking that a "savage" remained "savage," no matter how civilized he appeared. Ruled by passion, these indelible associations meant (white) women's defilement and pollution, jeopardizing not only their purity but that of American Protestantism itself. In this sense, perhaps white women served as the territorial boundary markers of empire.[161] No amount of Christianity or successful gentlemanly performances, oratory, or literary ability could make an "Indian" deserving of a white woman.[162]

Race and color categories were less stable than categories like "heathen" and "savage." "Indians" were sometimes described as red, vermillion, tawny, or black. Use of the slave-associated category "black" for Elias may have been an intentional fusing of nonwhite status.[163] Defiantly, Harriett praised Boudinot's "black skin," saying she would not exchange his "complection."[164] Denoting another moiety to "pales" or whites, the Cherokees called themselves "the red man." They also used the term to assert original occupant or First Nation status.[165]

By attempting to create their own mirror images in converts, missionaries affirmed their colonizing selves. They did not do so by living with missionary subjects as man or wife. Indeed, the thought of one of their own women migrating to another nation, protected by, subordinate to, an Indian or "foreign" man as head of the family, seemed to defy a deeply held logic.[166] The American Board of Commissioners for Foreign Missions endorsed the idea of women traveling to foreign shores only as wives of (white) Anglo-American missionaries.[167] Outside of the United States, white women's clear mission was to "advance the natives" by exemplifying good family practices and by reproducing their own kind.

Influential members of the Cornwall community and the American Board of Commissioners for Foreign Missions condemned marriages between American Indians and white women, but others also thought that they were "correct, and scriptural" and even "that such connexions should be formed."[168] Churchmen and community members often proved to be independent thinkers. Local ministers Smith, Starr, and Talcott were all willing to conduct the wedding of Elias and Harriett. Certain churchmen told Harriett's parents that the impending marriage was "a good plan." As their engagement had been news throughout New England, opinion started to form that if it must go ahead, it should be done in "as honorable way as possible."[169] Now some of the most vehement earlier opponents convinced Harriett that she should be married in Cornwall like other folks.

The wedding took place in the Gold family home on that classic spring day, the first of May, in 1826.[170] Whether guilty about his actions or plain confused, Harriett's brother Stephen found it beyond him to attend. He kept on working at the timber factory.[171]

Unity?

Christian thinkers of Connecticut had long used metaphors concerning the "unity" of peoples. They had a nice ring: inspiring, optimistic, and suited to a forward-looking, inclusively democratic republic.

Cherokee scholars styled themselves as thoroughly "modern" or Anglo-American. In Boudinot's portrait, he wore fine clothes in the fashion of the day — a ruffle-collared white shirt, dress jacket, well-styled short hair. It was an outfit that evoked modern white masculine power and authority, with visual lines that led the eye to focus on the wearer's head rather than the rest of his body.

High achievers like Boudinot and Ridge were so immaculate and polished in every detail of grooming and dress that their public performances rivaled New England youths'. Living a life against the historical clichés, Elias drew upon his knowledge of biblical and European history to argue that the Cherokees had made faster progress in civilization than many European peoples and that they would only improve further.[172] Isaiah Bunce's *American Eagle* considered that the "poor white boys of Cornwall valley" would object to this competition for eligible young women. Presenting a great blow to their pride, it was no joke to the youth of Cornwall: "We spurn the intimation that we have been cast into the shade, by our rivals, white or tawny."[173] Perhaps the Cornwall youths who had never left home did harbor resentment, for those handpicked Cherokee geniuses had met current and former presidents and were already outdoing them — and not only in the classics and church oratory.

Young Cherokee males were angry too. They felt betrayed by what had happened in Cornwall. After all, they had been urged to believe that the Christian people were "one" and all equal in God's eyes. Realizing that they were still classed as "a grade of inferior being," the young Cherokee men had their pride injured by the Cornwall marriage controversies, which made them question the integrity of white Christians.[174] Subsequently, they questioned the "civilizing project" and whether it would fulfill its contractual promises of protecting their nation's rights. White men had long been marrying Cherokee women and the practice was all around these young men. In Cherokee country, Reverend Jeremiah Evarts feared the extent of the damage to his Cherokee mission. He stood out on a limb, opposing the church agents' reaction to the Cornwall intermarriages: "I can see no evil in it." Reverend Daniel S. Buttrick, also stationed in the Cherokee Nation, wrote a letter to the Northrups that was so supportive that it moved Mr. Northrup to tears.[175]

Having no doubt about the Cherokees' equal, if not superior, standing to the whites, in 1821 John Ridge called upon Congress to give his people "the hand of strong fellowship — that they will encircle them in the arms of love, and adopt them into the fond embraces of the *Union*."[176] When Ridge married Sarah Northrup a few years later, his "fond embraces" became more than rhetorical flourish. At the same time, his words gestured toward inclusion in the United States. Cherokee scholars had admired the unifying exhortations of political figures such as Thomas Jefferson, James Monroe, and William Crawford, who advocated intermarriage with Indians. There was no parity if this meant only marriages between white men and Indian women.

In contemporary New England, a suitable white groom was assessed by his prospects, including family, property, and wealth.[177] Reverend Evarts of Brainerd, Cherokee territory, attested, "Mr Ridge is a young man of good talents . . . good manners . . . worthy of respect in any community." He added, "What crime then to marry a young lady worthy of his station?" His "prospects" were good; his family owned a number of slaves and a grand house. What is more, he had "the appearance of a gentleman." Elias Boudinot, too, was polished in the ways of the New England gentility, well groomed, industrious, enterprising, ambitious, with the makings of a good writer. Darker skinned than his cousin John, Elias was thought to "look" more "Indian."[178] Although Boudinot was not as wealthy, his family was influential. Harriett had no personal estate to be jeopardized by her marriage, nor were Anglo-American married women entitled to own property.[179]

Nonetheless, property losses endemic to settler colonialism, and confirmed by the long, painful history of Indigenous dispossession, must have tinged parental concerns. For a father, the thought of New England's white daughters sharing the future with men whose nation was being dispossessed, like the Mohegans before them, was a difficult one to bear. A woman needed economic security and safety. With the Cherokees' holdings near Georgia already known to be under threat from state-backed white frontiersmen, any Indian-owned property had uncertain tenure.

Rather than breathless admiration or an ecstatic meeting of minds, Harriett was compelled to offer a more spiritual rationale for her marriage. After all, "love" and "romance" were base reasons to marry.[180] While Harriett inferred that God had been consulted on the matter, her zeal seemed directed more toward marriage than missionary work.[181] Elias was a rising star and a snappy dresser. Highly intelligent, a brilliant orator and author, he was already becoming active in Cherokee politics. His intelligently crafted, inspired prose engaged with, critiqued, and subverted mainstream colonizing ideas.

Having finally apologized, Hermann Vaill wrote a farewell letter to Harriett that was peppered with personal regrets about her impending marriage and departure. Marking the death-knell of her singledom and citizenship, Hermann lamented that "Harriett Gold" would "soon be no more" and how Harriett's "Gold" would soon "dim."[182] If marriage signified social death for a white woman, emigration to the "being colonized" side of the frontier forecast a double social death.

In settled white American society, this "Indian marriage" controversy exposed latent colonizing discourses. Intertwined notions of property, gender, race, color, church, and community cast a long shadow over evangelical ideals espousing civilization through education and example. Inside Harriett's family, their community, and their church, this "Indian marriage" crisis exposed her people for the colonizers that they were. The Cornwall events unraveled national and religious identity, if not everything individuals thought they stood for. While reaching out to "the heathen" was supposed to unite New Englanders in an expansive mission, the journey was now rerouting.

Before she left Cornwall, Harriett's wedding departed from the imagined historical trajectories of her sex and her own nation. Not only that, she was immigrating to a nation that the early republic was beginning to dismantle, if not demolish. She was exchanging her citizenship in New England, and that of the noble, modern early American republic, for a world seen as old — rooted in the past: a fate, for a white woman, that signified sexual defilement and captivity, and according to the cliché, a fate worse than death. In effect, the marriage thus brought a competition of sentiment, a fraught contest of emotion and belief.

Despite their religious precepts, New England society wanted to maintain certain colonial hierarchies — in particular those of white men's patriarchal sovereignty over white women.[183] Their mantras reinforced the incongruity of any marital-style relationship between Indian = savage and white woman = civilization. In a kind of national separatism, narratives of mismatch guarded the crucial borders of gender and frontier. Populist thinking in New England favored keeping the two groups apart. Had not the "Indian problem" been "solved" by their ancestors? Why hand over white women as booty? "Connecting *her* race" was literally "unsettling" because it reversed the ways in which history — here specifically the settling and gendering of new lands — should proceed. Harriett was stepping on the wrong side of the colonizing line.

A Test of the Republic

Amid the crisis of the Cherokees' struggle against Georgian dispossession, Elias Boudinot wrote that his nation's struggle was a *"test of the virtue of the republic."*[184] Indeed. But now, in that republic's heartland, he was implicated in an intimate test of its virtue. While his soul might be equal to a white man's, it hit him hard to experience how being an Indian husband or brother was unacceptable to white families. With implications far beyond the individual, it was intermarriage that became a litmus test of a nation. So what, if anything, was proven by this marital "test of the republic"?

Reflecting back, every part of Harriett and Elias's story seems redolent of a story of broader national significance. Harriett and Elias's Christian marriage between nations stands as a metaphor for wider processes taking place at the intersection of cultural, spatial, and gendered frontiers. Even to these thoughtful, inclusive people, this conventional, heterosexual, clerically conducted marriage, undertaken "in as honorable a way as possible," remained subversive, shocking.[185] It went too far.

Harriett would be leaving behind the protection of her nation and whatever truncated and tightly controlled citizenship it permitted for its female members. Her marriage meant she would switch her national allegiance and citizenship and would come under Cherokee law.[186] This kind of marital union would not comfortably fit into the Union of the United States. An emigration against prescribed routes, it unsettled notions of race, modernity, and nation. As her community had articulated it, her actions went against the flow of history itself. For Harriett's marriage involved a category of reverse emigration — heading south into an Indigenous nation. There the process of Indigenous dispossession was far from over, and in the face of increasing federal and state pressure to move west, the Cherokees were losing ground.

In the early 1820s, Boudinot plotted a nationalist narrative of progress for the Cherokee Nation. Connecting respectability with national success, he wanted the Cherokee Nation to be "respectable among nations" and no longer "despised."[187] Marrying the lovely Harriett might indeed be one strategy, his own kind of modern machinery, toward manufacturing such an outcome.

Just as New England residents thought that frontier binaries of the region had been replaced by a virtuous history all their own, colonialism's tensions had resurfaced with great intensity. Cornwall's solid foundations had been rocked and colonialism's hidden fault line had opened up. Belief in the equality of man and in Christian benevolence had collided with color-tinted barriers. Opposition to the marriage clearly reflected the conflicting ethics of an ongoing colonialism in the heart of the early republic.

Writing her farewells to her brother and sister, Harriett grabbed the moral high ground to depict her emigration as a religious transformation — even an apotheosis. As she put it, in her new role as wife, she would be God's instrument and do his civilizing work among a demonstrably "despised people."[188] If Harriett envisaged gaining a heightened status among the Cherokees, she suppressed this impulse by positioning herself within a narrative of destiny and God's will. In her understanding, Harriett was not, therefore, becoming a citizen without nation. Like Elias Boudinot IV and his "lost tribe of Israel," she belonged to the body politic of the Christian nation — to "light," not "dark." As she wrote, "All the things of life are uncertain. . . . May we . . . live as strangers & pilgrims," for this is not "our Continuing City."[189] Such passages are redolent of John Bunyan's *Pilgrim's Progress*, the still-influential Protestant text that tracked a spiritual journey of "pilgrims and strangers" to a "celestial city."[190] A few years later, Harriett and Elias's antagonist Lyman Beecher published a text called *The Spirit of the Pilgrims*.[191]

The Christian journey and the colonizer journey depicted life as a noble pilgrimage, so as a "moving subject" in her own right, Harriett subverted this "wrong-way" migration into a noble evangelical move. Building herself up for a painful rupture from home, family, friends, and cultural milieu, in 1825 she stepped into a deepening historical narrative. Both the Separatist "pilgrims" and others, the "Strangers" who colonized New England, conceived of life as a geospiritual pilgrimage from the Old World to the New.[192] The Landing of the Forefathers, as it came to be known, conflated the Pilgrim-Puritan historical narrative to expand New England's values into a usable history for the evolving nation.[193] As if belonging to the one patriarchal family, members of the new republic became kin to the forefathers.[194] Harriett was aware of the *Mayflower* ancestor on her father's side. Harriett's renderings fused her embodied, living migration and out-marriage journey with awareness of an ancestral journey story.[195]

The prospect of her marriage symbolically uniting disparate nations into the one Christian nation was hardly the only thing on her mind. Harriett's passion for her "marriage project" was propelled by a sense of audacity and adventure and understandable excitement over this dashing, well-educated man of great talent, great potential, and big ideas.

It was handy, however, to reason that any direction could lead to death and that only the eternal hereafter mattered. To Christians, death symbolized transformation and the hereafter. The step of marriage, like death, symbolized the move from one state to the next. Her emotional entanglement across colonizing hemispheres offered Harriett an alternative New World of relationships, and of historical trajectories.

On a practical level, Harriett had needed to find a husband. Elias may have recognized something special in Harriett, too — not only in her deep religious conviction but in the courage it took to rock the pious establishment off its pedestal. She proved her talent, convincing those closest to her that her decisions were right, good, and godly. It is difficult not to admire the mettle that it took to marry Elias.

Neither Harriett nor Elias would forget that their hurried departure soon after the wedding was to avoid being lynched. Ominous dark clouds or not, as the horses kicked up dust, Harriett was heading on a long and rough journey south toward her chosen land, her new nation.

In the new Cherokee Republic of Harriett and Elias's domestic future, the Europe/America binary of Old World and New World became redundant, for they were bringing once-separated worlds and histories together through marriage. Once starry-eyed, the Cherokee prodigies had learnt that the optimistic early republic to the north had failed its test of virtue. Its true colors and its gender-specific restrictions on marital intermixing had been shown up by what Elias sarcastically described as the "gross crime of matrimony."[196] From now on, Elias would be propelled by the Cherokee Nation's politics, and so too would Harriett.

The power of family love, of affinity and sentiment, eventually transcended politics and notions of godliness to create a bridge between still-warring sides of colonialism's history. It was Harriett's own "blood," her direct family, that ended up getting behind her and against the larger community. Perhaps this was precisely why intermarriage was so dangerous.

Soon after their wedding, Elias gave his *Address to the Whites* in Philadelphia: "What is an Indian?" he asked quietly. "Is he not formed of the same materials with yourself?"[197] Of "one blood" God created "all the nations that dwell on this earth"? Speaking to his white audience, Elias switched to a modernizer's argument, explaining that the Cherokee Nation had long been a civil, admirable society that embraced "civilization" — a value that he equated with modernity. Elias railed against the saying "Do what you will, an Indian will still be an Indian."[198] That suggested stasis, as if his people were living outside history. While he insisted that his nation could no longer be described as "barbarians," he made it clear that they did not want to be white. Drawing upon the best of biblical prose style, his electrifying oratory argued for the Cherokees' readiness to be integrated as equals in the national polity of the early republic.[199]

In 1826 Boudinot was arguing for a seat inside the halls of the Great Republic. This is the same year that northerner James Fennimore Cooper published *The Last of the Mohicans*, the eulogy for Indians that placed them outside modernity, and outside of America's future. In his eloquent address, Elias Boudinot explained that the Cherokee marriage system was modernizing. And it was ousting polygamy. However eloquent and convincing were Boudinot's words, in these settled parts of white America, being confronted by the sight of a Cherokee man marrying a white woman was like seeing an apparition of the fires of hell. Despite threatened violence, however, the newlyweds set out safely for their new home in the Cherokee Nation.

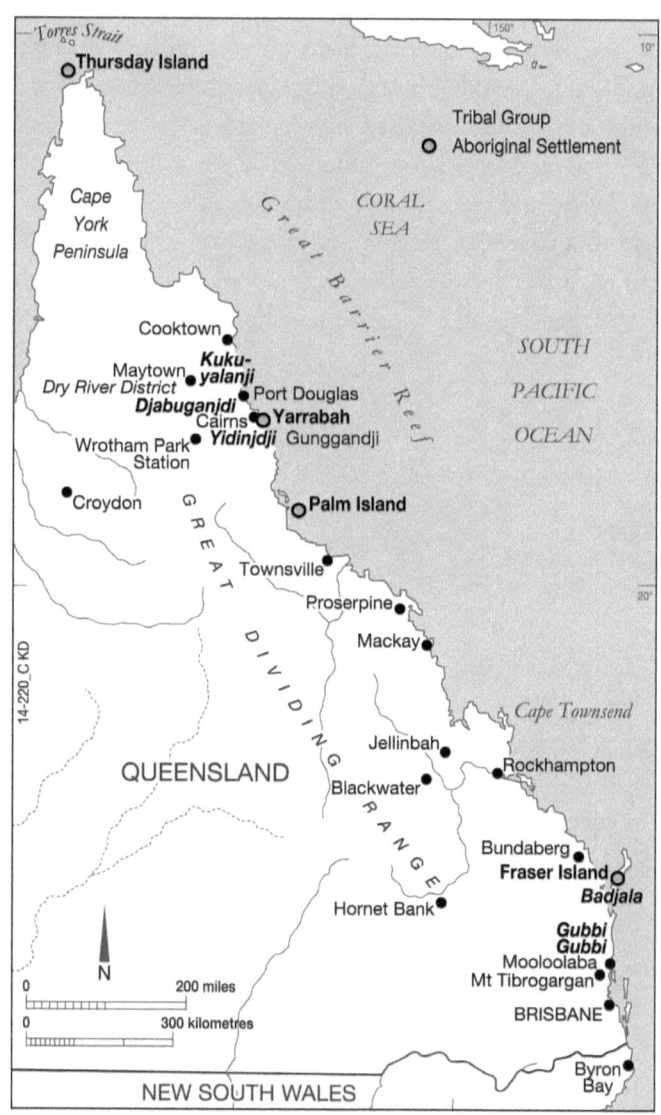

MAP 5. Queensland intermarriage sites discussed.

CHAPTER TWO

Ernest Gribble and Jeannie

BRIGHT WEDDINGS

When I visited the Aboriginal community–run Menmuny Museum at Yarrabah near Cairns, Queensland, a batch of historical wedding photographs was displayed on its walls. Wearing lovely white dresses that gleam in the bright sunlight of decades past, Aboriginal brides beam gorgeous smiles. Alongside them, their young Aboriginal husbands stand close, wearing printed cottons from Pacific islands. The brides hold huge bunches of native ferns and wildflowers. In reprints on glossy photo paper, these suspended moments serve to memorialize the significance of a public ritual that anticipated a future.

The Gribble family, the missionaries who had taken up residence in Aboriginal "country," made weddings a big community event — something to look forward to and celebrate. By 1892, when Ernest Gribble arrived at Yarrabah to assist his father, J.B. Gribble, the Anglo-Australian political leaders of each self-governing colony met regularly to discuss how they might unite into a federated nation.[1] Ernest aimed to establish a different polity, a mini commonwealth based upon Christian-style marriages between Aboriginal men and Aboriginal women of similar ages. Today the Yarrabah community has extended and reinvented this ritual, making church weddings cherished cultural events.

Even in the black-and-white photographs at the Menmuny Museum, the intense, pale aura of Ernest Gribble's eyes stands out. In this land of brown eyes and dark skin, they contrast with his reddened, sunburned

FIG. 14. The wedding of Mathilda and Cuthbert Simpson, 1926. Courtesy Hollingsworth family and AIATSIS.

FIG. 15. Yarrabah beach. Photo by author.

face. Among those who knew him, nobody forgets the intensity of Ernest Gribble's electric blue eyes.[2] Many of the older people at Yarrabah, now an independent Aboriginal community of about three thousand, still hold Ernest Gribble in high regard. Other Yarrabah residents attest that some of what Gribble wrote was lies. The exhibition at the Menmuny Museum is not critical of the museum's founder, Gribble. Nor was the exhibition that was prepared for the State Library of New South Wales in consultation with Indigenous curators with Yarrabah connections. However, Yarrabah residents and descendants hold a variety of views.[3]

At the museum, both the Gunggandji elder Menmuny, the senior figure in the local landowning group, and the mission's key founder, Reverend Ernest Gribble, are honored like kings.[4] Despite Gribble's interference in Aboriginal family life and culture, his legacy is commemorated everywhere. With Yarrabah no longer a mission and now an independent, Aboriginal-run town, the church that Gribble built remains an imposing presence. On Gribble Street, it looks out to the turquoise of the Coral Sea. To the east is the Pacific Ocean, to the north are Timor and South East Asia. Taking place at Yarrabah, this Gribble family story is emblematic of how an attempted

FIG. 16. Yarrabah shipwreck. Photo by author.

reordering of gender and marital relations shaped the very bones of the "white" Australian nation.

From the early nineteenth century, thousands of British convicts were being sent to Moreton Bay in southeastern Queensland. It was a long ocean passage from home and too expensive to return. As long as they helped clear "the blacks" out, the convicts had plenty of chances to gain work, business opportunities, and freehold land to call their own. European free immigrants followed, seeking more and more land for large-scale cattle stations. Timber getters, farmers, pearlers, and others arrived from Europe, from America, and from southeastern Australia, on Indigenous land. By the 1870s Chinese miners, looking distinctive with their braided queues and light clothing, arrived in large groups in Queensland's tropical north. Indentured as farm laborers or gold workers, they were caught up in a system that required them to work off the debts of family in their home provinces. Southeast Asian laborers arrived bewildered, not knowing what to expect so far away from home. It was worse for the Pacific Islanders (dubbed Kanakas). Initially, many were blackbirded (kidnapped) from their small villages and islands for intensive sugar plantation work in the tropical heat, under contractual arrangements that they did not necessarily understand. Later arrivals had a taste for modern goods — choosing to come in order to bring back bicycles for traveling fast on their home islands and rifles for fighting-out conflicts. The food, conditions, and local diseases shocked their systems. A high proportion died. It was called seasoning sickness.[5] Slavery was banned in the British Empire, but coerced labor was not. Convict, Kanaka, Chinese, and other forms of indentured nonwhite labor were far cheaper to import and employ than the less pliable, free white laborer.

Local Aboriginal people worked as stockmen, drovers, and domestics in the pastoral industry, especially if this enabled them to stay on their own land. But they had no interest in plantation labor and their expert bush knowledge meant that could readily escape servitude. They were the only ones not far from home.

Aboriginal people were still living on their own lands, conducting either their bush economy of hunting, fishing, and gathering or a dual economy in which they used their skills and learned new ones working with horses, in the cattle industry, and as domestic laborers. Repeated colonizer intrusions forced many into finding other means of sustenance. Growing interest in horses, new foods, goods, opium, and alcohol were pull factors. Just decades after it received self-government in the late 1860s, Queensland's treatment of Pacific Island laborers had earned it a bad reputation. Horrific frontier warfare against Aboriginal people also filtered into the British press, partly thanks to Ernest's father.

The emigrants knew that these faraway Englishmen would never understand. Aboriginal people were spearing their cattle, ruining their enterprises. Queensland frontiersmen thought it manly and perhaps good business to retaliate; they shot whole family groups. They called it a "surprise." Police called it "dispersal." The massacres were many, and horrific. Aboriginal women were also abducted, raped, and held captive. This sparked retaliatory murders. White men were found with spears sticking out of their bodies. Two thousand white people died in the conflicts. Between ten and thirty thousand Aboriginal Queenslanders are estimated to have died by violence. Evidence for the higher figure is mounting.[6] The Martini Henry Carbine and the Winchester revolver, imported from New Haven, Connecticut, spoke loud and fast. Queensland was marked as the most violent of Australia's colonial frontiers.

FIG. 17. A multigenerational family group in traditional housing. Courtesy Cairns Historical Society. Note: Cultural permission was sought and received from a recognized representative of the Yarrabah community before reproducing any photographs of the community.

FIG. 18. Men carrying *woomeras*, spears, and decorated shields. Courtesy Cairns Historical Society.

Frontiersmen and frontierswomen had been terrified of Aboriginal spears and tomahawks, keeping guns at hand. Colonizers wanted more access to land for pastoralism. The Queensland government set up a Native Police force to tame the violent conflicts over land, resources, and Indigenous governance that were taking place between Aboriginal residents and the British newcomers. Under the military-style command of police inspectors, an armed Indigenous militia known as the Native Police killed competing Indigenous groups with frightening efficiency. Aboriginal recruits had deep knowledge of the environs and were well-armed. This force was used to curb the activities of other Aboriginal groups and to mete out revenge attacks. Recruits were often prisoners who had been charged with cattle theft and were sometimes serving out their time for acts of violence against white men. One lot of killings led to another. Indigenous law had to be enforced. Bitterness, malice, more violence, and more retribution. Bloodshed became virulent. Warriors were not discouraged from carrying out their law. But they acted outside and beyond their law. Aboriginal populations were devastated.

Between the white colonizers and Aboriginal people, and between competing Aboriginal clans, there was bad blood. Repressed stories of torture, murders, cruelties. Awful visions. Some white men bragged about their conquests, though generally only to the in-crowd of like minds — other white men. Much they kept inside. Having blood on one's hands could change a man.

For Aboriginal people throughout Queensland, the impact of extreme violence was matched by resource depletion due to agriculture, mining, and tree felling encroaching on their lands. This led to stress, conflict between groups, malnutrition, abuse, and exploitation. All combined to make traveling in their own country, a vital act in the clan and community's connective tissue, and their different "bush economies" increasingly difficult for Aboriginal people to sustain. Using antislavery rhetoric, British humanitarians publicized kidnappings and horrible abuses. Labor and sexual exploitation drew their attention. Interracial sex was very much on their minds.

Meanwhile, in addition to a humanitarian problem and an "Aboriginal problem," the colonial state thought it had a race problem. Scientists predicted that the white race could not survive in the tropics. Yet Queensland's "colored north," with its blend of so many different peoples, was an image that its leaders wanted to dispel. "Perfect white sovereignty" in the far north looked impossible. Thus, in 1897, the self-governing British colony of Queensland introduced a new law called the Aboriginals Protection and Restriction of the Sale of Opium Act, which attempted to bring race control of Asians and Aboriginal people under the same umbrella. The act introduced race surveillance partly to prevent the intermixing of Aboriginal people with the increasing numbers of whites and Asians in their midst. They could also be forcibly removed from their residences onto a state-controlled or approved reserve. On the ground, however, between living people, intimate relationships would play out very differently from how the planners had hoped. The act's authors and its implementation will be discussed in more detail in chapter 5.

In reaction to intimacies that had crossed colonizing boundaries and hence transgressed the desired order, a shared politics of secrecy arose. Mixed up with the endless stories of murders, of bad blood, the secrets of love became equally painful. Illicit although not explicitly against the law, they took on the import and gravity of secrets of nation, secrets of state.

Indigenous people's later testimony played a crucial role in the sexual revelations that were eventually to surface about Ernest Gribble. The official records of the Australian Board of Missions (ABM) also provide convincing clues and pointers. Gribble's assiduously kept diaries are now in the ABM records in the Mitchell Library, Sydney.[7] As with the Gold-Boudinot story, documentary sources abound. However, crucial months and years are missing from the record. These blank spaces in the jigsaw reveal colonizers' quiet collusions.

The Australian Board of Missions, like the American Board of Commissioners for Foreign Missions, elevated its Christian initiatives to national projects. Within mission borders, it hoped to ameliorate the impacts of colonialism in each settler-colonizer nation. During this crucial time, Aboriginal Australians were thought to be a dying race.[8] By 1901, the year of national federation, the constitution did not include them in the count of citizens. A "primitive" or black-skinned people would not fit a modern white Australian future.

Nonetheless, Gribble wanted to save the "Aboriginal race" from total obliteration. This was believed to have occurred in Tasmania, where the "last of her tribe," Trucaninni, was sentimentally lamented. However, such beliefs overlooked the sons and daughters of Aboriginal women sealers who had been abducted by white men and who bore and raised children with them. Some other women had paired with the newcomers, too.[9] Gribble looked toward another hemisphere for an American "solution": "Force them all onto reserves as they did the Indians in America and then let teachers go amongst them."[10]

Yarrabah, on and around the lands of the Gunggandji people, was located in lush rainforest. A shiny, viridian, evergreen landscape, it contrasts with the changing foliage, the colorful autumns and cold winters, of Cornwall, Connecticut. There white Americans had effected that ultimate "segregation" of Indians, a stage where they were no longer a visible community on their own lands. However, after they invited other "Indians" back inside the boundaries of their white town, that "settled stage" of colonialism was rocked. The Yidinjdji, Kongkandji, and Djabuganjdi people had been exposed to regular visitations by white intruders for only about ten years. Around Yarrabah, maritime workers and frontiersmen negotiated and exchanged food and goods with Aborigines in exchange for casual sexual services. The Indigenous landholders were still attempting to live a bush lifestyle,

FIG. 19. Ernest Gribble in a Yarrabah classroom, ca. 1900. Gribble stands to the left, holding a young girl tightly. The emphasis is on reading, writing, and solemnity. A map of Queensland features on the wall (upper left), demonstrating the colonizing role of geography in redrawing the boundaries of ownership. Courtesy State Library of New South Wales, SLNSW/nca128744h.

surviving off their country, while incorporating newcomers into their system of kin relations in order to acquire new resources.[11] In North Queensland, many Aboriginal people suffered disease and malnutrition. As can be seen from photographs taken of local Aboriginal men in the 1890s, they were well muscled and healthy. Cicatrices on their upper bodies revealed that they had gone through the full initiation ceremonies that tied them as adults to secret stories associated with landscapes and kin. Other photographs of people still attempting to practice bush lifestyles show adults and children with pleading faces and swollen, distended bellies — evidence of how decreased access to land resources and fears of violence were causing physiological harm.

FIG. 20. The white cross that marks the landing of J. B. Gribble. Photo by author.

On this violent frontier, missionaries could easily see themselves as the good guys, the native rescuers.

Soon after Ernest's father, John Brown Gribble (J. B.), started up the mission in far North Queensland, he took seriously ill. He was assisted by South Sea Islander Willie Ambrym, an Aboriginal man called Pompo Katchewan, and a white man, James Tyson; it was only Tyson who proved a disappointment. Suffering a cocktail of diseases — tuberculosis and mosquito-borne malaria and dengue fever — J.B. had to be evacuated. He called on his son for help.[12]

John Brown Gribble had been born in the Cornwall of "old" England in 1847; he had come to Australia not as a pilgrim but as a miner. In 1876 he became a minister of the United Free Methodist Church and then joined the Congregational Union, to work at missions along the Murray River, in New South Wales and Victoria, before moving to Western Australia. J. B. and his wife, Mary Ann Elizabeth Bulmer, established several missions with varying success, having nine children along the way, who eventually assisted them. Ernest was born in Chilwell, Victoria, in 1868. His father courageously reported on how white frontiersmen bought and sold Aboriginal women and men, bashed Aboriginal men, and cruelly ill-treated the women.[13] Exposing ill treatment and colonizer violence against Aboriginal people in the Gascoyne region of Western Australia, Gribble's reports embarrassed influential settlers and gave that colony a bad name in England.[14]

Taunted by white Australian "towns-folk" about having "blacks on the brain," J. B. nonetheless raised funds for Aboriginal welfare in England during the 1880s and published a book about Australian Aborigines entitled *Black but Comely*.[15] Another book, *Dark Deeds in a Sunny Land*, exposed the sexual exploitation of Aboriginal women by white men in the Western Australian cattle industry. This made him deeply unpopular with influential pastoralists and police and eventually with his own church, which relied upon their philanthropy and political clout. Considered traitorous by their white compatriots, the family was abused and ostracized. While the father campaigned against Aboriginal exploitation, the family lived in dire poverty, with hardly enough food to eat.

The Yarrabah mission represented another attempt to convert and baptize Aboriginal people as Christians and to protect them from labor and sexual exploitation by white frontiersmen.[16] Churches were loath to support the venture, with newspapers already attacking them for destroying the fishing industry and for preventing access to cheap Aboriginal labor. Eventually the church provided some meager support; however, it demanded that J. B. not publicly criticize the behavior of local white men.[17]

At the age of twenty-three, Ernest steeled himself to fulfill his dying father's dream, reluctantly taking over the isolated and poorly funded mission of Yarrabah, or Yarraburra.[18] Also called Gimuy, after the slippery blue fig tree (*Ficus albipila*), the mission site is near Point Grafton, close to the current-day tourist destinations of the Great Barrier Reef and Cairns.[19] Situated on a Pacific Ocean beach, it was sheltered by the Murray-Prior Range and Yarrabah or Wambilari Range. The traditional owners of the region are the Gunggandji, Djabuganjdi, Yidinjdji, and Mandingalbay. Their histories are deep; Yidinjdji people have stories of events experienced by their ancestors at least thirteen thousand years ago, including the volcanic activity that formed what is now known as Lake Eachem. They talk of how the open lands changed into rainforest; they explain the rising of the seas that formed Kobahra or Fitzroy Island and how the Barrier Reef marks the old coastline of the Pleistocene age.[20]

Unlike in Cornwall, Connecticut, Europeans were only an intermittent presence around Yarrabah. Its reputation for cannibalism and murders of whites deterred visitors.[21] In a location accessible only by boat, Ernest set about carving up a mission township comprising local Indigenous people with sovereign authority over the land, as well as Aboriginal people pushed off homelands with nowhere else to go and those whom the state forcibly relocated there.

Queensland's interventionist Aboriginals Protection and Restriction of the Sale of Opium Act of 1897 authorized northern police and government officers to remove Aboriginal people from their places of residence. Some had already been forced off lands due to colonizing activities, including the establishment of sugar and tobacco plantations. Many were suffering or starving, while others were a mere inconvenience to new agricultural and mining enterprises that preferred imported Asian labor or indentured immigrants. After earlier colonizing warfare, some Aboriginal groups achieved a détente with pastoralists, proving an indispensable labor force in that industry. However, the act also provided a way for pastoralists to control workers who demanded better remuneration and conditions — they could get police to send them away to a distant reserve.

The act also enabled police to separate Aboriginal children — from toddlers to teenagers — from their families, thus severing them from country, camps, and other residences. This was a form of colonizing social control generally clothed in humanitarian rhetoric — such as "rescuing" children from neglect or "moral danger." Yet they were classed as "neglected" purely on the basis of being Aboriginal or "half-caste" or of mixed descent.[22] There were also other reasons for their removal; sometimes the children were the unacknowledged offspring of the local pastoralist or policeman.

Agreeing to take such children into the mission secured much-needed government funding for Yarrabah. While Ernest Gribble committed to "Save the Remnant," Aboriginal people were already attempting to save themselves. As we will see in chapter 6, strategies included intermixing with the Asian and white newcomers, participating in introduced industries, and trading knowledge and resources to obtain goods and resources from newcomers.

Local Aboriginal people, forced and unforced Aboriginal immigrants, Ernest, his mother, his sisters, and Pacific Islander missionaries — all toiled to create the new Aboriginal world of the Yarrabah mission. By late 1899 Yarrabah had a printing press, a newspaper, plantations, numerous substantial wooden dwellings, and an extensive book of rules. Outbreaks of endemic tropical diseases and oppressive heat and humidity provided scientists with more proof that the climate was unsuitable for white people and even created race degeneration. Of course, the tropics also had their pleasures: sea views, fresh air, exotic birds, waterfalls, and the protective, glossy canopies of native fig trees, numerous varieties of elegant palms, and astonishing flowers — including stunning water lilies and bright red flowers that Gribble described as the size of a dinner plate.

The elite classes of Yarrabah were not color exclusive. They included Gunggandji; Djabuganjdi; white Australians; other Aboriginal people from mainland Queensland; Aboriginal people born of white fathers; Badu, Darnley, and other Torres Strait Islanders; and Melanesians. While a variety of clans had migrated into the Yarrabah settlement or had been removed there by the Queensland government, the original Gunggandji-Djabuganjdi-Yirritja groups predominated and the other residents had to defer to them in certain matters.[23] However, the gradual arrival of forty different tribal and language groups over a decade or so was increasingly disruptive to the authority of Indigenous elders. Very young, displaced children had limited or no knowledge of kin identities or the Indigenous law.

Trackways, rivers, and sea routes, songs and corroborees linked Gunggandji, Djabuganjdi, and Yidinjdji people's dances and stories with those of Torres Strait Islanders and Pacific Islanders.[24] Biblical and Christian stories and notions of sin were merged into stories of sacred places in this ancestrally familiar landscape. These soon came to include recent historical stories about the coming of Ernest Gribble, the founding father.

Today the Indigenous past remains, evidenced in the landscape itself. For example, a significant rock overhang at King Beach holds some of the historical epics underpinning Menmuny's custodianship over country. Still-discernable rock paintings map the story of Bindam, the wife who ran away from her husband, Gamburrguman. Dots represent her path to the beach and its nearby sacred waters, while other markings follow her

FIG. 21. "The First Aborigines at Yarrabah, 1892." Names are inscribed around the photograph, which appears to be from an official government census. Menmuny is standing on the right. Albert Maywe is squatting on the right. Courtesy Cairns Historical Society.

travelogue, where she encountered and named the geographical features of Yarrabah's dramatic surrounds.[25] The stories of the spirit or ancestral creation journeys tell of where every plant, tree, and animal was encountered and named and explain a landscape of human, plant, and animal connection. Their spirits exist in the "everywhen" or dreaming, the term commonly used for the Aboriginal way of seeing the world. Outside of linear time, complex journey stories are laden with moral messages about Aboriginal law. It is a living, instructive history constantly refreshed and reinvented through oral traditions, songs, dances, craft, and rock art.[26]

Many Yidinjdji stories deal with men's troubles finding brides. Ancestral characters become impatient waiting for a bride to be bestowed; men become resentful of others with multiple wives. In several stories, men forcibly abduct brides from people with different languages. As Indigenous marriage arrangements forged and reinforced connections with outside groups and distant lands, this connects with living practice. One story tells of two brothers who stole one bride each from an unfamiliar tribe. A brother, Damarri, kept both but on one of his journeys, a crocodile bit off one shin and he had to crawl back to die at Yarrabah. Another tells of Bibiyuwuy, a man who killed his brother because he thought he was having an affair with one of his two wives. A bride could also escape. In the story of the water sprite bride, a man stole *burrawungal*, or water creature. Grabbing the slippery teenager, he tied her up with vines in order to take her back to his people. After dissolving her fishy slime by the fire, he took her as a wife; they sat together, talking happily "as a married couple should." One day she said she was going to soak vegetables in the water and never returned.[27] In this personal landscape, configured out of human relationships over millennia, morality tales remind people of the drastic results of infringing marriage laws.

Despite an autobiographical history in which individuals held deep connection with storied landscape sites, under the new regime, Aboriginal people had no state-recognized land title and no treaty rights. Indeed, Aboriginal land rights had not been officially acknowledged by the colony of Queensland, or by any other Australian colony. With no official recognition of Indigenous sovereignty, the colonizing state portrayed Australia as a blank slate. Consequently, few white power brokers boasted much insight into the ordered system of kinship, gender, and land-based regulatory systems that inscribed ownership rights to these lands, and which could potentially incorporate newcomers, too.

Living alongside Aboriginal people since childhood, Ernest knew them as people and had witnessed the pain they were going through. He also witnessed how his father was excluded by elite society, including his own church. Although not keen on the missionary life, Ernest hoped to assist the Aborigines and, as he put it, to emulate Jesus, who — as he wrote conspicuously — "took manhood into God." With a difficult paternal model, Ernest pondered what it meant to be a good man. His solution was to mix muscular Christianity, with its ideals of sexual restraint, with a form of High Church Anglicanism.

Agreeing to walk in his father's shadow, Ernest Gribble justified the Yarrabah mission as a way to prevent white men from pairing up with Aboriginal women. Interracial sex he declared as illicit on every count. While they were common practice in each and every Australian frontier zone, he viewed these unions as despicable, exploitative, and degrading. As he did not think that men could control themselves, he distrusted any white man placed in the path of an Aboriginal woman.

Gribble classed the lifestyle of white frontiersmen as one of "vice" and predations that led the Aboriginal "pagans" astray. He used this to justify his mission rescue enterprise and to bring bush dwellers into the sedentary life of a township. Gribble complained that they were "trading their women and receiving [in] exchange flour tobacco etc." Some had "taken up their abode in the vicinity of these men. One of our mission girls complained that her step-father had been lending her mother for immoral purposes." It was true that such negotiated exchanges had been going on for some time.[28] Yet local Aboriginal people did not see this as a purely commercial trade, for it operated in a more complex values nexus, including a system of kin reciprocity that enabled them to incorporate strangers into their law and polity. Normally, a kinship designation would be given to an outsider male to ensure the sexual union conformed to the correct "skin-group." Depending on varying tribal rules, this would require a cross-cousin kinship classification and/or moiety affiliation. We will explore how this operated in chapter 6.

As ameliorator of the doomed race, the mission's motto was, "Lift thy prayer for the *remnant* that is left" (emphasis added). By segregating Aborigines from sexually depraved outsiders, Gribble aimed to create a mission world to "civilize" Aborigines and, he believed, thus save them from extermination. While condemning temporary partnerships between white men and Aboriginal women, Gribble ruled out respectable marriages too. Aiming for strict segregation from the rest of the colonizing world, he intended to create an orderly system of monogamous, race-segregated marriage. Gribble would control the choice of partners for the Aboriginal couples. He would organize Christian unions and act as official celebrant at their marriages. By this means, he would "seal" the Yarrabah community to his God.

FIG. 22. St. Alban's Church interior, 1901. Note the hand-hewn logs and timbers used for pews, the earthen floor, and the pebbles used to create an aisle. The banner proclaims Gribble's motto, "Lift up thy prayer for the remnant that is left," which reflected the doomed race theory justifying Aboriginal rescue. State Library of Queensland, no. 76955.

Gribble, who ordered "his" mission girls to dress in plain, shapeless tunics, wanted them to know that they were NOT as good as white girls and would not marry as well. In other words, they should not aim to marry good white men in the hope of achieving economic prosperity. "No self-respecting white man will as a rule marry Aboriginal or 'half-caste girls,'" he reasoned, so they were better off marrying "decent" "full bloods." He characterized the men who wanted to live in stable relationships with Aboriginal women as "Chinese and other aliens" and "the dregs of our own civilisation." Ernest detested the rough and "disgusting" behavior of lower-class Australian men.[29] At the same time, Aboriginal people found their generous supply of goods, alcohol, and opium more appealing than his scant mission offerings.

Requiring Queensland government backing to expel all other white men from the Yarrabah environs, Gribble lobbied the Aboriginal protector to

FIG. 23. Senior girls, Yarrabah. Only one girl has been permitted to keep her child with her. Courtesy Cairns Historical Society.

assist in his scheme of creating a new generation of Aboriginal-only space. He persuaded Dr. Walter Roth, protector of Aborigines, to use Yarrabah as an appropriate place to send the young Aboriginal girls singled out for separation from their territory and their families. Whether for moral or race reasons or both, such separation was purportedly to avert the risk of sexual liaisons with non-Aboriginal men. Gribble promoted Yarrabah as a haven where Aboriginal girls could escape sexual exploitation and molestation.

However, his own diary reveals his personal struggles trying to talk himself out of "falling" for their glamor. When they dressed and acted as "perfect ladies," he labeled it a conceit. Preaching against vanity, but perhaps also against upward class mobility, he argued that it was what the girl looked like inside that counted.[30] "Black girls" brought up by white people often had "exaggerated notions about their looks and thought that because they had fine clothes on they were good as white girls though all the time they were as black as saucepans."[31]

Tides

> The white waves
> are the wings of the sea
> they jump and
> break away to nothing.
>
> Gunggandji song[32]

On his first voyage to Yarrabah at age twenty-three, his father is still alive and Ernest is cheerful and excited.[33] As his boat approaches, he appreciates the beauty of the region, enjoying the vistas of rocky islands along the Great Barrier Reef. Short of his destination, however, he has to wait for four hours in the becalmed cutter. With him are a male missionary, Mr. Pearson, and Willy, a "Kanaka boy" — probably Willie Ambrym of Vanuatu. The three eventually attempt to use the dingy, but low tide requires them to haul it for half an hour and then walk ashore through knee-deep mud and razor-sharp seashells. While not a portentous arrival, after a day of drama and excitement, Ernest's energy amazes: "After cooking bread a few cakes and clearing up the house I retired to bed really done up."[34] The stoic young Ernest made light of physical hardships, but his isolation often sits sadly on his diary pages. With his father remaining very ill in Sydney, on February 19, 1893, he writes, "Alone with the natives today the only white person among 100 natives."[35]

Earlier Ernest had laughed about how, upon his first arrival, he found Pompo, "a native boy," with a fishhook in his foot — apparently from playing some kind of high-kicking game.[36] Two days afterward, a depressed and deadpan Ernest writes that he nearly cut off his own hand with an ax.[37] After giving up smoking, he craves his pipe, castigating himself when he repeatedly takes it up again. Quipping that "any extreme churchman" (not himself) would appreciate the lack of temptations to break his Holy Week fast, he complains of his boiled fish diet and craves "a cold mutton chop on a greasy plate."[38] Having run out of fat, he spoils his coral trout and other delicious local reef fish by boiling them. Ernest had not discovered Indigenous culinary techniques such as wrapping his fish in flavorsome leaves and roasting them in the coals of a fire. He does not seem to know how to catch crabs or collect shellfish.

As well as a place for self-reform, Ernest Gribble saw Yarrabah through the eyes of an optimistic community builder: "The mission is very prettily situated near to Cape Grafton with very high mountains the Bellenden Kerr . . . at the back. A lot of work has been done. A nice two-roomed weatherboard cottage built also Kitchen and Blacksmith shops and a farm house built by the kanakas, also the blocks laid ready for the school house. . . . The forest scenery is really magnificent. Just near the house is a fine large tree with stag-horn ferns and two other varieties and ferns adhering to its trunk right up."[39] He performs church services throughout the day and reports on "alligators" (crocodiles) on the beach near their boats.[40] "In the afternoon took bible and Hymnbook and had a pleasant time by myself in a very pleasant and picturesque spot. I saw a beautiful waterfall while strolling along the hills homewards."[41] At the evening service, he speaks of the importance of prayer. Gribble luxuriates in the beauty of the giant fan-palm rainforests around him. What he does not realize is that he is traveling in the Gunggandji dreaming lands, a place where each waterfall, creek, plant, and animal is imbued with storied and spiritual significance.

When Ernest arrived at Yarrabah in 1893, he was also shadowed by past secrets. While the nature of his sins is open to speculation, his diaries are full of lamentations in which he begs for God's forgiveness. We wonder at the godly standards set by his brave and demanding father.[42] Ernest suffers a kind of self-loathing: "My thoughts have been evil from my Youth up."[43] On October 29, 1892, soon after his arrival at Yarrabah, he writes, "I live the curse sinful do I find myself. Help me oh God to battle against sin." He confides falling out of God's grace. When members of his flock — young girls whom he considered promising converts — become fatally ill, he believes that God is punishing him personally. Gribble believes that he is the "most unworthy" of his family. "My God My God forgive all my Sins and unworthiness."[44]

As a missionary, Ernest Gribble's position was oppositional — against traditional Aboriginal culture and religion and against the sexual and labor demands of white frontiersmen and pastoralists. Although he took a passing interest in local languages, he banned body scarification and numerous ritual practices.[45] Not learning Djabuganjdi songs, dances, or body art, he instead encouraged what he generically termed "corroborees" — the Sydney Eora–derived Aboriginal term for dancing and musical performances. But he

FIG. 24. The Yarrabah band with a man in a Native Police–like uniform and the bandleader holding a riding crop, 1907. State Library of Queensland, no. 64082.

repopulated them with popular English songs, piano accordion, euphonium, piano, brass bands, and dances in the hall. Gribble taught the Bible, English literacy, and a range of physical, military marches and musical activities. In his own person, he exemplified new body techniques, including the postures of Christian devotion, and new clothing forms. His enthusiasm impresses: he taught athletics, gymnastics, and cricket as manly forms of Anglican "muscular" Christianity.[46] Despite the crocodiles, he sometimes enjoyed a swim with the Aboriginal boys.

Child Brides

When the unmarried Ernest first arrived at Yarrabah, he had a particular kind of marriage in mind. He was appalled by Aboriginal marriage practices. In one of his earliest diary entries — for January 21, 1893 — he writes that polygamy and "child betrothal" were two practices he felt he must wipe out. Gribble describes one man with six wives: "all of them young women and

FIG. 25. The girls and boys in the Yarrabah band. Cairns Historical Society, P16524.

one is a girl of about 13 years of age. The man being about fifty years of age. Another has two one a mother and the other a little girl of about nine."[47] Menmuny has three young wives. In one of these early diary ruminations, Ernest writes, "We will as Missionaries have exceeding difficult work with the Children especially the girls on account of these early marriages. All the girls attending the school have been given to certain men of the tribe all of whom already have one or two wives." These girls were not expected to take up their position as wife until they came of age. However, when a promised husband visits Lizzie, a twelve-year-old, at the school, Gribble despairs: "The work ahead looms up like a great strong wall but with God's help we will break through the wall of senseless customs and traditions and save souls for Christ."[48] In the tropical glare, Gribble uses the same "light" and "dark" allusions earlier applied by Harriett Gold and other Christian missionary writers among the Cherokee; he offers a prayer to assist an "unworthy servant" — to convert the "poor dark skinned and *dark-minded* brothers and sisters" to Jesus.[49]

Three years after his arrival in the north, at the age of twenty-six, Ernest himself had married. His wife was Emilie Julie Wriede, who, because "Emilie" sounded too common, preferred to be called Amelia. Ernest called her Millie. Married by the bishop at St Johns' Anglican Church in Cairns, they had three bridesmaids, a choir sang, and then they journeyed off to honeymoon at Port Douglas. Daughter of the Cairns Harbor pilot, Amelia was brought up in comfortable circumstances and her comportment gave her a somewhat aristocratic air, accompanied by a certain humorlessness. her family's social standing enhanced the appeal of this marriage to Ernest, who was strategizing the creation of networks with influential sectors of Cairns society. Their marriage followed a measured courtship. It did not arise out of any great romance, and Ernest later mused about another girl he had once known in Victoria.[50]

Gribble's obsession with the civilizing and sexual orderings of marriage dominated his mission plans. He organized a dormitory system that separated boys from girls and other residential zones that separated married couples from other adults. He introduced curfews, restricted fraternizing, and enforced monogamy, age parity, and other western-style marriage notions. Significantly, Gribble created a system of strict sexual policing designed to ensure monogamous, heterosexual unions between Aboriginal people. Aboriginal women and men were accustomed to conducting certain rituals and ceremonies separately, and the boys and girls were also involved in different initiation rituals. However, people lived in extended family groups, which combined into clusters of families or clans.

At Yarrabah, married couples would now live in nuclear families; they were supposed to mix only with other married couples and to sever links with people living in towns. Extended family members were prohibited from sleeping in the "married" houses. Gribble prevented visiting boat crews of white timber-getters and maritime workers from having access to and engaging in casual sex with Aboriginal women. He restricted any mixing with white and other frontiersmen. Gift giving and exchanges between them were banned. Mission couples had to follow strict curfews. When their husbands were away, Aboriginal women were barred from having visitors or walking in the dark. Indeed, to prevent sexual activities, they were ordered to sleep overnight in the children's dormitories.[51]

Even white tourists and fellow missionaries were instructed to acknowledge and honor the married couples. In Gribble's 1890s *Rules and Regulations*, he

FIG. 26. The married quarters at Yarrabah village, ca. 1905. State Library of Queensland, no. 69602.

prohibited newcomers from using the derogatory, often American-derived terms like "nigger," "mary," and "benjamin" and the Sydney Eora term "gin." They were to instead use terms like "woman" and "black" or "wife" and "husband."[52] Recognizing Aboriginal couples' Christian marriages would perhaps curb white male visitors' propensity to see Aboriginal girls as sexually available and would enforce monogamy. Aboriginal people had to choose which newcomer system of kin and marital alliances to follow — that of the white male frontiersmen or the strange white missionary family.

Gribble introduced some disincentives: the names of those on the "Black List," as Gribble labeled it, were written in his annual diaries and read out at church. In the familiar trope common to European nations, black was bad, white good. This "Black List" included girls going with white men.[53] Achieving a pattern of monogamous Christian marriage between Aboriginal couples — and *only* Aboriginal couples — was Gribble's fundamental strategy for preventing the "vices" of intermixing and those "pagan" practices that tolerated evil sexual relations with white men. With the aid of his assistants, Gribble punished Aboriginal offenders and absconders with imprisonment in a cell built on the mission grounds; here they could be deprived of food, publicly shamed, and corporally punished. During his church services, he singled out anyone who broke his rules, refusing to provide Holy Communion to offenders.

Polygamy and child betrothal were not only "unchristian"; in the Euro-Christian historical narrative they symbolized the "primitive" as opposed to the "civilized," as will be discussed further in chapter 8. Somewhat peculiarly, Gribble took cases of violence against wives into his own hands, using a whip to personally "thrash" any husband for wife beating.[54]

To ensure colonizers optimal benefit from their status, marriage had to reinforce colonial power and authority. In Gribble's eyes, this meant white should marry white and black should marry "black" — although he was not particular about intermarriages between people of different degrees of "black" or from different clan or language groups.

For Gribble, monogamous Christian marriage was indeed a new "mission method."[55] Instilling the western marital institution was as important as instilling notions of God and of "manhood"; they went together. Christian marriage was the path to civilization, the way to tame Aborigines' savage passions. Marriage was civilization's building block. With western marriage, Gribble, mission builder, could construct his own "great strong wall" against evil. By constraining girls and boys in separate dormitories and preventing their parents from taking them back to camps, Gribble introduced a particular kind of heterosexual, Christian, and companionate marriage for twosomes of similar ages. Rather than worrying about color, Aborigines were more concerned that they be "right-skin." That is, their marital regulation system dictated that only cross-cousin kinship marriage according to kinship classification was acceptable. And often a girl's first marriage was to a much older man. Gribble discouraged Aboriginal people from marrying according to their traditional customs. In Australian Aboriginal society, control over religious knowledge framed a political economy premised upon land, kin exchange, and social obligation principles. Marriage law and the alignments based upon marriage negotiations created and cemented peaceful relations among landowning groups.[56] One of the central facets of their social organization, marriage cemented family and clan relations and ensured crucial diplomatic ties with other clans. The key social laws were negotiated within the marriage laws. The earliest Christian weddings created great fear and anxiety among Aboriginal couples. Broken arrangements caused anxiety for the families of promised brides, who had to ensure they compensated their kin and contractual partners in various ways with goods, services, or future wife exchanges. In Indigenous law throughout most of Australia, marrying "wrong way" — to a person of the forbidden kinship classification — was punishable by death.[57] This could apply to a white man, too, and to someone intent only on a casual sexual relationship. In severing the Aboriginal women's and men's control over marriage, the new system created unimaginable tensions and stresses.

Aboriginal Marriage and Political Authority

By the 1900s Yarrabah had a mission government of "twelve church elders," including "chiefs" of neighboring settlements or camps, which represented clans and landholding groups presumably identified by their people. They met monthly. As a representative model, this was unusual for Australian missions; most colonies required Aboriginal people to live under more authoritarian institutions. What is more, in 1910 the franchise for the Yarrabah Court, a kind of mini parliament, was open to men and women. The court was separated into different electorates for single and married people.[58]

This was a commonwealth of landowning groups that mirrored elements of the regional electorates in the emergent Australian federal system. One photo depicts the court all dressed in British-style attire, with several of these Aboriginal leaders wearing the white shirts and jackets that commonly signified white colonizer authority, particularly in the tropics. Use of terms like "Nation" and "Commonwealth" and a representative system may have panicked the central Sydney-based mission. Sovereignty issues contrasted with those of the Cherokees, for the Queensland government did not openly acknowledge that Indigenous people held any sovereignty. Despite promising beginnings, however, the Yarrabah people were a mixed group that lacked the diplomatic status, authority, and degree of independence of the Cherokees.[59]

Yarrabah had already become a refuge for different Aboriginal groups under pressure from white colonizers in nearby areas. By occupying their own land, albeit with a mission base and lifestyle, some Aboriginal groups continued their hold over "country" or their traditional landowning estates.

FIG. 27. The different authority figures and lawmakers with their family members at Yarrabah. Gribble stands tall in the doorway. The senior Aboriginal men are distinguishing themselves through a variety of headwear. Courtesy AIATSIS.

Still dictating terms for other groups to also reside there, they retained a degree of authority and power. At first the mission recognized Indigenous law authority over the people who resided there. In his *Rules and Regulations*, Gribble recognized the leadership of "chiefs" or elders in ensuring law and order, especially encouraging them to enforce law and order in outer camps.[60]

In 1909 readers of *Missionary News* were taken on a promotional "Trip Round the Reserve," on which the moral geography was clear: "Passing on again we cross the cricket ground, a large square, with the married people's cottages built on three sides, conspicuous amongst which is the palace of the King recently erected, with a neat paling fence enclosing a garden in the front, close by the King's flag-staff, upon which every Sunday a flag is hoisted by King John."[61] Marriage, the flag of empire, a complicit local king, and an authoritarian mission king: they all went together at this Church of England mission. Under the Gribble regime, marital and gendered geographies were highly visible, with inbuilt incentives. Space and

FIG. 28. Government men visit to inspect the mission and, in this case, its girls. Courtesy Queensland State Library.

residence were gender segregated for the unmarried, while married people lived in individual houses rather than dormitories. In a reversal of their usual gendered practice, before the wedding the would-be husband had to build a house in his spare time — that is, after mission work hours. Before being allowed to marry, he also had to be a Christian convert and to demonstrate an exemplary work ethic. Once married, life was controlled by sets of rules and regulations regarding residence, movement, and association. Married couples were expected to mix only with other married couples.[62] Tables had to be regularly cleaned and flowers displayed at all times. Married women who took little interest in garden competitions would be ridiculed in the *Aboriginal News*. Married couples had discrete communal eating places, their small homes mainly for sleeping.[63] The married men played against the single men at cricket. Athletics, picnics, and church services all emphasized the division between married and singles.

Town planning was designed around Christian marriage and a sedentary notion of domesticity in which the modern nuclear family spent set periods of time within the marital home. Ernest's architecture for a good marriage included indoor living and decor — a domestic scene with flowers on the table grown from the couple's own garden, a neat, nuclear family–styled house with restricted inhabitants, and friendships exclusively with other married people within its walls.

It is difficult to ascertain how much gendered and political authority this commonwealth could exercise. Gribble successfully pressured the Gunggandji, Djabuganjdi, and Yirritja landowners to leave their children in dormitories. In return, they gained a food supply, childcare, and education for their children in literacy, English, and the newly introduced Christian cosmology and lifestyle. Although often demanding their children back, mothers came to use the dormitory system to fulfill their own agendas. Some did so to circumvent their young daughters having to join a promised husband or their sons having to endure a frightening, painful initiation ceremony. Lightening parental fear of retribution, the mission now had to share the blame for failure to fulfill early betrothal promises.

They were up against other difficulties. Under the government protection policy, more and more Aboriginal people were regularly arriving from different "country." Sometimes mothers used the new system to give their daughters more freedom in marriage choices. For example, they might negotiate marriages with local residents rather than have their daughters move to a distant camp, as in previous exogamous marriages. Uninitiated boys did not go over to the male hierarchy but stayed under the mother's and women's authority, including in the boy's dormitory, which, for a time before 1909, was run by a woman. From the Aboriginal men's perspective, the mission provided an advantage in that the young women were not all drawn into white men's camps. Some elders foresaw that this trend would deplete Djabuganjdi Yidinjdji society and make it unsustainable. But they also saw that the mission rules were preventing Aboriginal men from joining their promised brides.

However, the chiefs were to be enlisted in Gribble's new governance system. Through the lens of hindsight, historians can too hastily presume that the presence of colonizers and intruders immediately eroded Indigenous landed authority. Given the tenuous hold of newcomers in the landscape and the longevity of Indigenous traditions, this was simply not possible.

Whether Gribble viewed this as a true chiefly alliance or a superficial ploy, although it was an unusual recognition in Australia, local Indigenous people would have expected this as a protocol in recognition of their long-held landed authority and law.

"King" Menmuny agreed to participate in a grand coronation ceremony in 1899. Gribble orchestrated this to exert his own authority via Menmuny's status.[64] As one of the most senior Gunggandji elders of the Yarrabah area, Menmuny had gone through the law, evidenced by the cicatrices across his abdomen that marked his transition. Although Menmuny had authority in the lands of the vicinity, his mother, who was less amenable to Gribble's overtures, had superior authority. Gribble recognized Menmuny as the law-maker or "law man" in the male domain. By negotiating man-to-man with this leading elder, Gribble hoped to encourage the settlement of Aboriginal people from the Gunggandji, Djabuganjdi, and Yidinjdji into the Yarrabah mission township. Menmuny's mother opposed the move. She had a dream, a vision, of all the cultural changes that were to come and asked Menmuny not to accept the missionaries. Other elders also held back, asserting that they wanted to come and go, not settle there for good. Apparently Menmuny later regretted not listening to his mother, but given the ceaseless land take-overs in their region, he had very little choice.[65] His agreement to relocate suggests he or his kin came to see some benefit — perhaps an opportunity to enhance their own power and the clan's standing in relation to other land custodians in the region.[66] Yarrabah was certainly to become a "super waterhole," a center for new food supplies and numerous other resources, including, in the eyes of Aboriginal men, the potential procurement of wives.

Menmuny was an elegant, dignified-looking man with a lean, muscular physique. He practiced hunting and fishing and exercised his rights and responsibilities over nearby land.[67] When Gribble conferred upon him the title of king or, in the American style, chief, Aboriginal people may have appreciated this as a valid acknowledgement of his seniority in Indigenous law over this particular location.[68] Like the British Crown, he held authority over land. Aboriginal governance was complex, contingent upon constellations of sites in the landscape and a range of land and kin rights and duties; there was no single authority figure, line of royal inheritance, or singular decision-making body.

Gribble persisted in trying to talk Menmuny into giving up at least two of his three wives, listed as Maggy 1, Maggy 2, and Nora.[69] But Menmuny pointed out that deserting one would be bad behavior for a husband, and he asked what would become of her. On what was classed as "Crown land," or state-owned, "unalienated land" that was technically under the control of the British sovereign, the public spectacle of a Christian wedding ceremony had a double meaning. It implied a new form of governance that was premised upon imperial and colonizing hierarchies. It was embodied in, and underwritten by, new forms of gender and marital relations.

In mission literature, joking asides about the "royal" nature of Menmuny's son Albert's wedding in 1908 alluded to the authority of British royal weddings as defining spectacles of authority.[70] His bride had eight bridesmaids, including "one of his tribal girls," and they were all dressed in white. Lorna Schrieber, daughter of Albert, the "king of the Gungganyi tribe," described his "coronation." Her father wore a lap-lap and a white, long-sleeved singlet and her mother wore a crown. The bridesmaids' crowns were made of native ferns with colorful flowers stuck into them. Lorna explained, "And we carried that crown for some time and then it faded away."[71] Albert wanted to ease tensions between incoming language groups and the Yidinjdji. He is said to have proclaimed that anyone born at Yarrabah belonged equally to their territory.[72]

While giving up on Menmuny's less compliant mother, the King Menmuny-Gribble alliance recognized male authority and at least represented limited power-sharing arrangements with traditional landowners. Other Indigenous people were making key decisions behind the scenes, and nearby Indigenous groups were exerting and consolidating a new generation of landed connections. The visions and revelatory dreams of Menmuny's mother were valued as explaining lawful belief and action. Despite the fact that Queen Victoria currently reigned over the British colonies, Gribble could not think of this Aboriginal woman elder, an important law woman, as any kind of authority figure. Or perhaps her power *was* the problem, for she opposed his ideas of modern progress and even rejected the "light" of biblical narratives. Recording his relief at her death, Gribble hoped that he could now exert more suasion over Menmuny.[73]

Gribble's role as marriage organizer and broker propelled a dramatic reconfiguring of Indigenous land and geopolitical and social organization. Gribble's interventions into betrothal, initiation, and polygamy eroded and, along with other factors, would eventually wreck the promised marriage arrangements that were fundamental to kin and clan landowning networks. Gribble-ordained unions undermined Indigenous promised marriage law. Gribble's usurpation of the role of marriage broker and his taking, in fixed, written regulations, of the role of new "law man," conferred an increasing share of personal authority upon himself. Gribble had introduced a new cosmological frame of reference, with specialist knowledge based on literacy and a liturgy. Local Aboriginal people were sometimes intensely interested in these new stories from the European diaspora. While some used the new schema to advantage, community resistance could be strong.

Indigenous residents probably tried to incorporate and adjust to mission marriages as something to do with love matches and Jesus. But they could not avoid their responsibilities in matters of crucial kinship and marital law. Kinship obligations, which determined appropriate social behavior towards classificatory kin and which conferred and explained each individual's niche in their social world, started to become vexed. In 1909 the mission newspaper acknowledged that "great care has to be taken not to upset the native ideas of justice with regard to their tribal marriage laws."[74] As the mission marriage was more likely be "wrong skin" way and subject to serious punishment in Indigenous law, it created tensions between clans. Although unmarried people were cloistered in dormitories, older mission residents found ways to advise them surreptitiously. To avoid the danger of marriage among inappropriate kin-groups, wherever they had some knowledge, many young people would have discretely selected appropriate partners according to kin classification. To please Gribble's regime, they had to select ones much closer in age than previously. However, a few years of missionary authoritarianism could not evaporate deep cultural knowledge, nor Aboriginal people's shared commitment to a world ordered by kinship, land, and spirit affiliations.

It is difficult to know how much or how little Gribble understood of Indigenous cultural precepts. When, in his later years, Gribble called himself "Judja" — his skin or classificatory kin name from Forrest River — this may have been transposed from a status that he had already received at Yarrabah.[75] After all, Menmuny would have been unlikely to go along with any of Gribble's wishes without some kin relationship having been established. Whether the Gribbles acknowledged it or not, the whole family would have been given skin names, with their associated obligations and rights. Gribble himself may have had at least one "right-skin" female partner picked out for him.

Under the missionary regime, any girl and boy seen talking to each other unchaperoned would be told they must get married.[76] Yarrabah residents recall that Gribble forced some marriages on unwilling couples. Sometimes they were very unhappy and broke up.[77] In some cases they may have been in a strictly forbidden classificatory category like brother and sister, where they were strictly required to avoid close physical contact and eye contact. There was even a special "avoidance language" to be used in Yidinjdji.

On the other hand, Aboriginal girls and boys wanted to get out of the dormitories. The promise of marriage motivated other young people to Christianize. Indigenous men were perhaps likely to become complicit — at least to embrace Christianity overtly.[78] White frontiersmen's interest in Aboriginal women, whom they sometimes forcibly abducted, led to dwindling numbers of Aboriginal women in the camps outside the mission. This made it difficult for men to find a "correct" spouse along "straight" kinship lines.[79]

The idea of "premarital sex" as a problem held no sway with Aboriginal people, who had their own strict guidelines about illicit unions. In consequence of removal from lands and families, Aboriginal people continually feared that they would unwittingly marry their brother or sister. Whether classificatory kin or biological siblings, this made little difference to their law. In several cases, people came dangerously close to infringements before other residents gathered more details of their family ties.[80] By placing priority on garnering information on paternal identity, Yarrabah residents continued to follow their own law, while outwardly complying with precepts of monogamy and Aboriginal-only marriage.

Gribble punished those involved in early betrothal and polygamy by caning, locking people in chains, and denying them food. Recalcitrants had to endure a day's exposure on the bakery roof. Punishment for illicit sex was particularly harsh; women's heads were shaved, followed by banishment.

Punishment places like Palm Island and the neighboring Fitzroy Island/Kobahra recall the use of islands for incarceration during Australia's earlier convict regime. White authority figures were empowered to banish, remove, and relocate, making exiles of Aborigines, who feared leaving family and friends. Male offenders had to go to lonely Fitzroy Island for a month and burn lime for paint and mortar — a hot, dangerous process that could lead to serious burns.[81] When the private sexual misdeed was proclaimed to all, the secret became public. Banishment removed people and bodies from sight, allowing for new layers of cover and secrecy.

Moral Geographies

We cannot fully know the extent to which Yarrabah evolved into a "moral community" with shared values about the constitution of good and evil. Writing recorded only missionary perspectives. Queensland government agents had sent many children and adults there against their will; several escaped. As outlined in the *Rules and Regulations* booklet printed on-site, certain offenses led directly to banishment and ostracism from the inner circle of "good" Christians. Gribble was keen to teach the moral implications of illegitimacy and adultery. In the role of father to all, he introduced the personal shaming devices standard in the contemporary white Australian community, but in exaggerated form.

Gribble codified good and bad in terms of spatial parameters. For men and women whose premarital sex led to pregnancy, Rocky and Fitzroy Islands became spaces of moral quarantine. As traditional land and geography played such an important role in explaining and organizing the Aboriginal world, forced exile may have appeared a familiar, logical enough punishment. Yet as the coming birth of a child was never classified as an offense, banishment for pregnancy and giving birth was therefore inexplicable and cruel. Aboriginal mothers traditionally gave birth in special places with long and meaningful traditions and within easy hearing, in case assistance was required. The *njumbubu*'s, or newborn baby's, birthplace conferred a special relationship with a site in the landscape. When some women gave birth in inappropriate places under mission

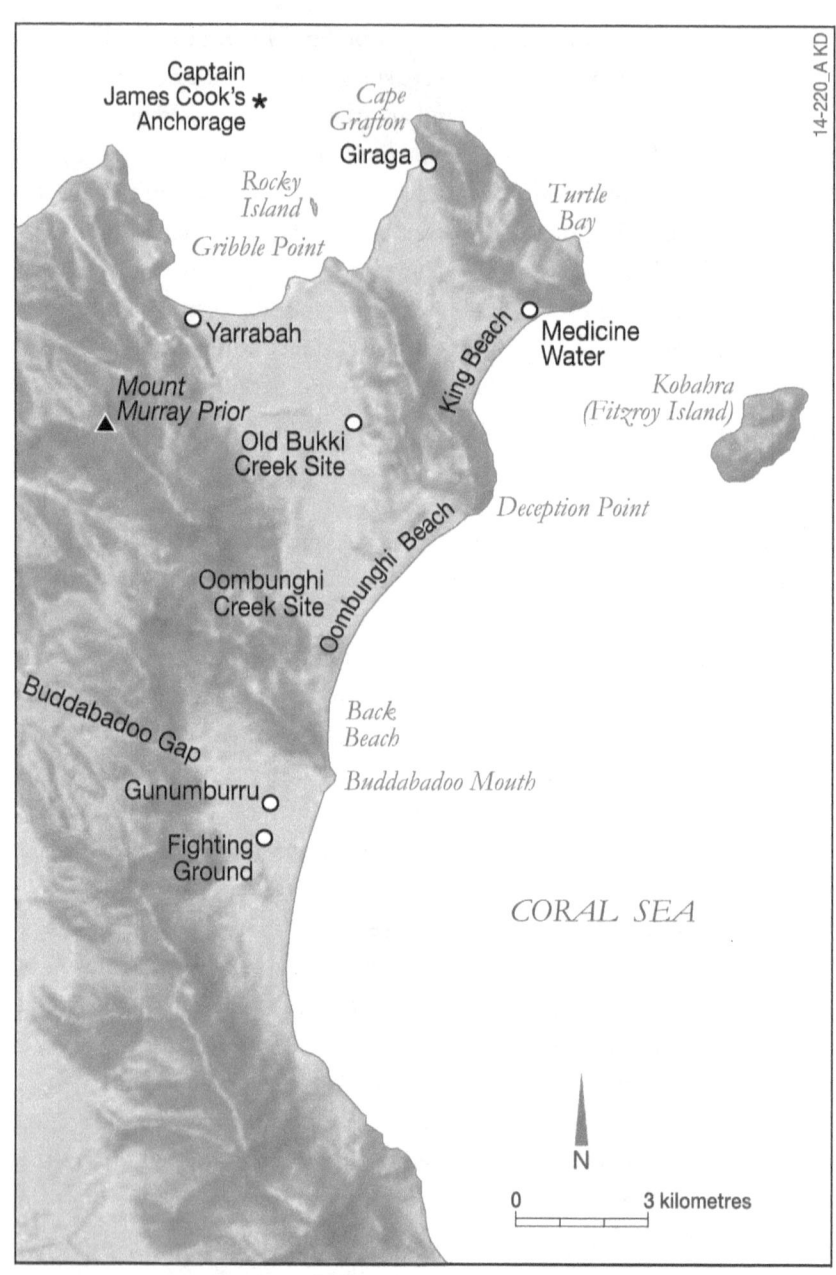

MAP 6. Yarrabah and surrounding region.

FIG. 29. Murragun Outstation. After clearing local forests, the residents are growing exotic fruits such as bananas and pawpaw. They are modestly dressed for the photograph, and the men wear military-style uniforms, generally supplied to those who served in the Queensland Native Police. Cairns Historical Society, P00183.

intervention, it caused anxiety and had future ramifications for the child's land connections and duties.

The Gunggandji people taught Gribble the names for sites, many of which they ran themselves as outstation settlements with new enterprises. Murragun was the place where two married couples lived, growing the newly introduced crops of mangoes, bananas, pineapples, cassava, cotton, and sweet potatoes. Bukki was where the beach joined a range of hills. Judu had an angora goat farm. Other outstations were Bolbahroo, Buddabahdoo, and Karpa Creek, while a creek of clear running water was known as Moorbundie.[82] The wider Yarrabah region thus became a convergent moral and cultural landscape imbued with clan hierarchies and land associations, including secret, sacred places and dreaming stories. Songline, body painting, dancing, and performative traditions still connected vast tracks of country via stories, trade, exchange, and marriage routes.

FIG. 30. Another outstation of the Yarrabah, Karpa Creek, is a cleared village with coconut palms planted and poultry being reared. The woman wears a Victorian-style dress and the men wear Fijian-influenced attire. Cairns Historical Society, P00182.

Musical Performances

Away from Yarrabah, Gribble used public performances to convey his marriage and modernization strategy in an upbeat way. In 1903 he brought a large contingent of Yarrabah children to Cairns to perform a public concert.[83] Dressed in white and red to evoke the British flag, young Aboriginal children sang English nursery rhymes, punctuated with rousing renditions of "God Save the King" and "Rule Britannia." Their endorsement of the second imperial anthem "fairly lifted the roof" with laughter and applause. The newspaper commentary referred to the cute "pics" or "picaninnies" — a comical term contemporaneously used for African Americans, especially via Harriet Beecher Stowe's *Uncle Tom's Cabin*. Ernest's father had loved this novel, which was now further popularized in musical theater and contemporary piano music.[84]

That night in 1903, the white audience both relished the British imperial tunes and readily connected the status of Australian Aboriginals and blacks of the British Empire with slavery in the United States. Following pole exercises, gymnastic performances, and Indian club drills, they listened to a talented Yarrabah youth narrate the poem "The Last of His Tribe" by the leading Australian poet, Henry Kendall. Following this somber moment, the audience delighted in the children's rendition of "Ten Little Niggers," a song that had become popular throughout the Anglo-speaking world.[85] Also rendered as "Ten Little Injuns" or later "Ten Little Indians," this nursery rhyme was first put to music in the 1860s. More common versions had the last "nigger" and/or the last "indian" hanging himself. In Gribble's version, one by one, each boy departed the stage after scripted "catastrophes," with only one remaining to sing verses solo. The white audience roared with laughter, refusing to quiet down for at least five minutes. Offering a happier ending to the settler colonial audience, the newspaper described the finale: "a small 'pic' black as the ace of spades, came onto the stage attired as a bride and taking up his place by the side of the singer, took up the theme of how there were soon 'ten little niggers more.'"[86] Here was Gribble's social contract — the promise that if mission residents intermarried with other Aboriginal people in Christian "white" weddings, they would be saved from extinction. The cute, racialized performances of the "pics" or "picaninnies" were designed to appeal to the benevolence of the white Cairns audience. Not only was the nursery rhyme well known and enjoyed, its allusion to the popular "black and white" minstrel shows from the United States and to the wedding and race "remnant" survival theme resonated with the local white audience.[87]

Gribble's didactic version of the song centered monogamous western-style marriage, epitomized by a bridal outfit and ceremony, as ensuring a reproductive future. Helped by his mission, his survival formula would save the race, or at least its "remnant," from disappearing. A boy in a white bridal outfit was funny enough, but a black-skinned boy was sure to create a roar of hilarity and, at the same time, at the finale, relief. They would not all die out. With audience donations, mission segregation of Aborigines from whites might prevent their total demise.

WHICH SIDE OF THE WALL? STAGING THE WHITE WEDDING

After they arrived at the mission, Gribble and his sisters Illa and Ethel introduced the ritual of the white wedding, which soon became the top Yarrabah social event. Ernest sent wedding photographs to mission newspapers to advertise his success. In the western lexicon, this color-coded ritual signified sexual purity or virginity in the bride. White was also a special color, symbolizing status, luxury, and religious ceremonial; it was also worn at Yarrabah's first communions, confirmations, and Sunday mass. The groom sometimes also wore a white cotton *sulu*, or sarong.

Prior to mission days, a woman joining her betrothed or *dunggarr*, especially in patrilineal societies, could involve moving to his country, sometimes with fear of unknown people and places, decreased freedom, and increased work duties. No specific ceremony was required; the fact of the betrothal was already well known in the community. While Aboriginal men also had clear obligations to perform for wives, having a wife or an additional wife usually made the man's life easier. Although Aboriginal women had previously played a key role in organizing marriages, mission segregation of married and nonmarried residents could get in the way. However, behind the scenes and unknown to the Gribbles, Aboriginal women still negotiated matches within the amended system.[88] Local groups tried to make them right. Gribble frowned upon initiations, which involved sex rituals and male genital mutilations.[89] He also banned the cicatrices, *muyngga*, or raised scars for body decorations that indicated full manhood and womanhood status and access to the deepest secrets of Indigenous dreaming law.

Under the mission regime, Christian marriage became one of the few ways to move from the boys or girls dormitory to adulthood status, and away to the wider settlement. Under the reverend's authority, the church became the new site of ritual observance and the marriage ceremony increasingly became the key coming-of-age ritual that signaled personal maturity and greater social independence.[90]

To Yarrabah girls, marriage came to symbolize an opportunity for greater freedom. In some ways this inverted aspects of the traditional age cycles of Indigenous life, in which childhood was a time of freedom and early adulthood one of increasing responsibilities and tasks. The later generations of Yarrabah girls said they could not wait to find a boy to marry.[91] Mission residents came to view a wedding as an escape from a repressive childhood of single-sex dormitory living, supervision, curfews, and other restrictions.

Rather than the usual mission baptisms that marked conversion, under Gribble, it was weddings that were the key highlight of the Christian calendar. Mission weddings were accompanied by large corroborees, including Gunggandji, Djabuganjdi, Yidinjdji, and Samoan and Fijian songs, dances, and feasts adapted for the occasion.[92] A glamorous picture of a Yarrabah bride and bridegroom under a mango tree appeared in the 1910 *Western Australian Church News*.[93] The bride wore a white, high-collared, full-length gown, broken only by a flower on her breast and a long veil decorated with a floral wreath and carried an enormous vertical bouquet. The groom had slicked hair, a white shirt bedecked with flower, a formal tie, and a white wrap-around *sulu* secured with a sash. So the latest Australian and English fashions for the bride were matched with Pacific Island and tropical fashions for the groom. Possibly Gribble entertained an idea of Yarrabah's residents fitting into a gradual uplift to "civilization" channeled through a Pacific missionary diaspora.

Ernest set himself up as the key marriage broker, but others played roles, including the matrons of the Girls' Home and the Boys' Home, other teachers, and his mother, Mary Ann, who cared for the "senior girls." As if a wedding represented a personal trophy, Ernest liked to count and publicize each and every one. As marriage celebrant, he dressed in special robes to perform a ceremony that reinforced his command over sexuality and marriage. The more Gribble's authority grew in this sphere, the more he took over Indigenous law from the elders. The underlying principles of marriage law ordered their society — shaping internal clan relations, relations with distant clans and lands, assurance of safe passage, and congenial relationships with outside groups.

Queensland government officers feared that meddling in Indigenous promised marriage arrangements would lead to retaliatory murders, but Gribble assured them he was not interfering. Smoking their pipes together and exchanging knowledge of Aboriginal practices, he and ethnologist W. E. H. Roth, the northern chief protector of Aborigines, who was concerned about Ernest's actions, had long conversations.[94] Gribble knew the potential violence and disorder that could arise from tampering with this system. However, with marriage his platform for Indigenous Christianization and civilization, Gribble was willing to take big risks.[95]

Yarrabah's white weddings involved painstaking preparations and heavily symbolic performances. The Gribble family slaved over preparations. As clothing was at a premium and had to be repaired constantly, Aboriginal girls were excited at the chance to wear beautiful new garments for their special day. Calico or cotton for the bridal gown was purchased with the mission's scant cash. Ernest cut out the patterns, and his mother, Mary Ann, and sisters Ethel or Illa sewed them. Who took the measurements is uncertain. Floral wreaths and huge wedding bouquets were prepared on a Friday evening, as weddings were often held on Saturdays. Depending on the season, Aboriginal residents picked different varieties of ferns, orchids, and blue water lilies from the surrounding hills. Flowers grown by other married couples were added, with elements of white and additional greenery. A feast, including cake, provided an exciting change for hungry Yarrabah inmates and staff.[96]

The allure of a white wedding was used as a tool to attract conversion. Under Ernest's system, conversion became a prerequisite for obtaining a condoned wife. Lorna Schrieber, granddaughter of Menmuny, described her father's wedding from a photo as a "bright wedding, a church wedding." Mission newspaper writers of the day commented favorably on how married couples proudly displayed framed photographs of their wedding party in their homes.[97] The intending bride and groom must have felt very special indeed, embraced by the extended Gribble family and their special efforts for the day. The sewing and festive activities confirmed for the affection-starved girls that they were indeed part of a family. It cemented their sense of reciprocal kinship relations with the Gribbles and other white missionaries. It was a time of reaping rewards from the boss, of receiving the nurturing and attention that the institutionalized children craved. That is, if they had an approved, "clear" or "bright" wedding.

Ragtime Wedding

On the other side of the coin, Gribble's errant daughters had to act out a private performance of "disgrace" involving disapproval from the patriarch. The *Rules and Regulations* contained a punitive clause regarding "forced marriage": "Any girl falling into disgrace necessitating marriage hurriedly, no bridesmaids, best man, wedding dress, decorations or cake allowed at the wedding. The ceremony to be performed privately in the church in the presence of the Mission Staff only."[98]

Yarrabah marriage was thus divided into sinful and nonsinful, with the mission introducing a serious social stigma for the unwed mother. In such cases, marriage was enforced to curtail "illegitimate" offspring—to cover up a sin. Both the man and woman had their heads shaved and were forced to wear hessian sacks or old rag clothing. As one Yarrabah resident recalled in the 1970s, "I got married *clear*, ya know. Another couple my mates, they got ragtime wedding. No tea."[99] The "rags" contrasted with the beautiful clothing of the sanctioned bride. In white weddings, the dormitory also had a big feast. "They go back there and have a good old feed, ya know. Invite people.... Not ragtime wedding.... They cut your hair you know.... We used to get bawlie [bald] head too... in the boys' dormitory... as punishment."[100] They enjoyed no celebrations. Only Ernest, as official marriage celebrant, and the obligatory witnesses attended, in punitive mode.

Discriminating against women who had premarital pregnancy and likely illegitimate births, this regime was obviously set up to attempt to enforce western notions of sexual and marital regularity. In Gunggandji society there was no equivalent concept of an "out-of-wedlock" pregnancy. The child would be classified as the child of the male spouse or promised spouse, and although biological paternity was usually common knowledge, it was not considered so consequential. In the mission, the pregnant bride participating in the "shotgun wedding" was barred from inviting family or guests. To indigenous people, such "shaming" (*girrany* in Yirridny) had parallels in the temporary ostracism and enforced banishments experienced by those who married "wrong way"—according to a "love match" as opposed to conventionally promised or arranged correct kinship classificatory unions. No such shame, however, would be involved in any pregnancy—premarital or not. Under Gribble's regime, visible proof of premarital sexuality was to become a subject of humiliation for the pregnant woman. While her "disgraced status" would become commonly known, even the spectacle of the wedding itself was hidden from the public eye. Her growing, pregnant body would be secreted away via banishment.

Via the Queensland government, such moral policing had prompted individual girls' removal to the mission.[101] Because they were pregnant "out of wedlock," several of the girls had been forcibly removed from their work situations and residences and relocated to Yarrabah. Queensland police also took them away from Chinese camps or those of men whom white government authorities regarded as "undesirables." Said to be in sexual "danger," the girls often came from live-in domestic positions with white middle-class families who made complaints. Sometimes it was the employers or authority figures — the white husbands or wives, the sons, or the local policemen — who wanted them banished to avoid being exposed as race transgressors or to avoid the obligation to support their offspring.

The midnight timing of the "bad wedding" evokes the Cinderella fairy tale gone wrong. However, we cannot assume that the girls fully internalized the guilt and shame message of "rag-time" weddings, for, removed from kin and country, they had worse punishments and more hurtful social rejection to fear from unknowingly breaking "skin laws" and accidentally marrying a classificatory brother.

The older Aboriginal women certainly had their own agendas, and their status and authority demanded that the missionaries give them latitude. Nora, an elder and one of Menmuny's wives, liked to smoke her pipe under a tree rather than attend church. While Gribble convinced her to marry the king in a Christian-style wedding, she agreed only on the basis that she could wear her red coat.[102] She would not convert to Christianity or wear white.

Crossing the Line

Gribble had mixed success in staging the performances of his own family or the other missionaries. Soon after taking up his position in 1893, Gribble's first white missionary assistant, Pearson, became sexually involved with an Aboriginal woman. Gribble expelled him from the mission.[103] Then Gribble's own brother Bert was accused of raping a fifteen-year-old Aboriginal girl, Jinnie, who was the promised wife of Pompo.[104] She gave birth to Bert's daughter, Susie. Ernest and his church colluded to find Bert another job, despite jobs being in scarce supply during the 1890s depression. Bert was dispatched from the mission without charges being pressed. Poor Jinnie was later sent to the Goodna mental asylum in the Brisbane hinterland, and from Gribble's diaries it does not appear that Susie was adopted into the Gribble family.[105]

Then, in a committed relationship more difficult to keep under cover, Ernest's sister Ethel fell in love with Fred Wondunna, a talented trainee Indigenous preacher. A Badjala man of Fraser Island, he was eight years younger than her. Concerned that his people would "wander about in the world like lost sheep having no shepherd," he had found his solution. Later he wrote of how the sounds of the church brought happiness: "Ever heard bells ring merrily from church tower steeple? What do they mean? Joy? Yes But they are calling people."[106] In his case, they were calling him to sing along with Ernest's musical sister.

Gribble panicked. Harnessing his forceful personality, somehow he pushed Ethel instead into marrying his shy, malleable white missionary William Reeves. Although she delayed the wedding for sixteen months, Ethel eventually acquiesced, probably under pressure to put her family's reputation ahead of her own desires.[107] An exceptional teacher, Ethel led the Yarrabah choir, loved playing the piano, and was a zestful, resilient young woman who enjoyed horse riding and bush picnics. Yet Ethel's wedding photo shows her smiling insipidly, her weak eyes as impassive as that of a stunned rabbit. Reeves, too, looks captured — maybe frightened — in an unsure moment. Given all the effort Ethel put into the Aboriginal weddings, the joylessness of this photo is poignant. It is likely that the eye behind the camera apparatus was that of Ernest Gribble. We cannot know whether the marriage was happy, but they called their lovely, curly-headed girl Faith.[108]

In January 1906 Gribble must have feared God's wrath again, as Ethel's husband, Reeves, contracted a severe illness. His final hours coincided with a cyclone rampaging through Yarrabah, destroying their years of backbreaking building and gardening work. Desperately trying to keep Reeves alive and to prevent the family's abode from flying and smashing through the air, Gribble clung onto ropes all through the night. When Reeves died the next morning, the grief-stricken Gribble resolutely went about constructing a coffin with building materials from the cyclone wreckage of mission buildings.[109] Gribble's diaries poignantly reveal his love for and deep gratitude to this self-sacrificing and loyal man. Ernest's sense of deep indebtedness to Reeves continued.[110] Indeed, Reeves had been his strongest ally, willing even to assist in curbing Ethel's dangerous aspirations.[111]

FIG. 31. Ethel Gribble's wedding, 1906. Mitchell Library, State Library of New South Wales, MLMSS 4503, add-on 1822.

To Gribble, this white missionary marriage stood as his last hope that his own family, the "good white colonizer" exemplars, would remain white. If they crossed the color line in an official way, it would throw into question the mission's rationale in segregating Aborigines from white colonizer men. Furthermore, his own mission could be accused of undermining the national race aspirations of the new commonwealth.

After Reeves's death, Ethel became even more convinced of her feelings for Fred. In 1908 she was pregnant by Fred, and, probably because her brother refused to marry them, they decided to marry in New South Wales. This was kept a family secret. Ethel had not wanted it so and informed the ABM about it. Except in the restricted files of its executive committee, in the church's eyes it is as though Mrs. Wondunna never existed. In Ernest's several memoirs, Ethel appears only in the guise of the dutiful wife of saintly Mr. Reeves. Ernest's diary omits his sister, reporting only his own faithful care for Reeves. However, Ernest's published autobiography invents a reassuring tale of his sister's loyal, wifely nursing of the dying Reeves to his last breath.[112]

Already, in his personal diary entries Gribble had started to obscure the facts. In regard to Ethel's pregnancy, he mentions only her hurried departure by boat before Christmas, an event coinciding with his own ill health and increasing irrationality.[113] With the 1908 diary missing, Ernest's autobiographies say nothing of Ethel's later elopement and marriage to Fred Wondunna in a Congregational church in Sydney. Nor do they indicate that he knew the bride was pregnant. Later, with inadequate means and lack of either family or church support, she had to deliver her first child somewhat shamefully in the Salvation Army home for the poor in Brisbane.[114]

Ethel's decision to marry Fred Wondunna sent the mission establishment reeling. The shocked executive board of the ABM called for the marriage certificate. Having seen it, in cold bureaucratic words, their minutes noted that she was legally married, the place of marriage, the church, and the names of celebrant and witnesses.[115] Although the event was considered significant enough to warrant an agenda item, the ABM minutes stuck to the marital legalities. With a telling silence, no congratulations were sent, nor was there any sign of regret that two of their missionaries were unable to wed in their own Anglican church. She was referred to as "Mrs Wondunna née Reeves."[116] They, too, preferred to see her in relation to the compliant Reeves, omitting to note that she was actually née Ethel Gribble.

Star-Crossed Lovers

The other important woman in Ernest Gribble's life was a young Indigenous woman, Janie Brown (also referred to as Jeannie, Jane, and Janey and by the surname Forbes). A long-serving Gribble family nanny promoted to matron of the Boys' Home, her omission from Ernest's 1930 autobiography suggests a strained silence.[117] As one of the few Yarrabah residents who wrote for the mission newspaper, her first-person testimony alone would have been a useful addition.

Jeannie Forbes's removal from Mareeba by state police officers at the end of 1900 under the Reformatory Act clause relating to "neglect" had aroused public controversy in Cairns.[118] Often such actions were prompted because of sexual fears pertaining to the male members of white households. However, the girl's removal was sparked by government intervention in a dispute between female employers and their husbands. Jeannie had been well cared for and a police bench ordered the child be returned to the wife of the subcollector of customs — an important job in this port town.[119] This was overruled and she was instead sent to remote Yarrabah. White male writers ridiculed Yarrabah as an Aboriginal "cannibal camp" where she would eat half-raw human flesh. Of course, Gribble needed the state subsidies that came with the support of such wards. Jeannie's arrival there caused a stir. Described as "Mrs Forbes' black gin," Jeannie was used to every luxury. Wearing silk frocks, stylish boots, and expensive jewelry, she was beautifully dressed and, upon arrival, became the envy of local Yarrabah girls.[120]

Her removal to Yarrabah had sparked strong opposition, even leading to comments being made in Queensland's parliament in December 1900 and in Cairns's *Morning Post* on national federation day, January 1, 1901.[121] Alluding to the Bible story in which a dispute over a child's rightful parent led to a ruling that the baby be divided in half, the article was subtitled "Solomonic Fooling." Thomas Givens, the Tipperary-born Labor member of the Queensland Legislative Assembly for Cairns, who had been a miner and bush worker himself, opposed tearing Aboriginal people from the "native habitat of their tribe." They had "an inordinate love for their native hunting-grounds, and would return when they could." He commented to the home secretary, "Though white people were excluded from the mission station, half-caste children were still born there. Of course Mr Gribble could not be blamed for *all* that went on there, because he was often away."[122] The innuendo and local white men's skepticism about the mission project as a national project were plain.

Employed by the Gribble family as a housemaid, Jeannie also became their friend. In the June 1908 edition of *Aboriginal News*, she reminisced about accompanying Emilie and the Gribble children as a nanny during a visit to Sydney a few years earlier, recording her excitement at seeing the magnificent Blue Mountains, with their spectacular sandstone rift valley. As Ernest had been estranged from his wife the year beforehand, he may have encouraged Jeannie to write this article to gain some good publicity about his family life.[123] Although we do not know her exact age, Gribble was then in his thirties, so about nineteen years older than Jeannie. Like other Aboriginal domestic servants, she was vulnerable to the sexual desires of white males in the employer household.[124]

FIG. 32. Junior girls outside Yarrabah schoolhouse, ca. 1900. Cairns Historical Society, P02262.

Gribble promoted the trustworthy Jeannie to be matron of the Boys' Home. Jeannie also supervised the work of married women in the dormitory. In the *Aboriginal News*, she complained that these women put in only a cursory hour or two and that the boys broke too many mugs and did not take enough care of their clothes.[125] Poor resources and the reluctance of many mission residents to work as hard as she did stretched her patience. In her position of authority and commitment to high standards, she identified closely with mission goals and shared some of the same anxieties as Ernest. By early 1908 Ernest was estranged from his wife, though still married. He had moved in under the same roof as Jeannie — in the Boys' Home.[126]

In terms of mission politics, Jeannie occupied an elite position. Her status was tenuous in terms of Indigenous landowning politics, as she was not a member of the Gunggandji or adjoining landowners and so lacked family support there. Her mixed descent and upbringing in white homes may have aligned her culturally with the missionaries. As a live-in domestic servant who was removed from her family so young, her chance to learn Indigenous cultural knowledge was impeded. We do know, however, that by the mid-1900s she was literate and had a strong work ethic. In her twenties she was tall and elegant. With wavy, shoulder-length hair, she was a smart dresser and people thought her "startlingly attractive."[127]

In a race-conscious political climate, Ernest Gribble's heightening love affair with this young Aboriginal woman had to be a well-kept secret. In 1907, six years after the formation of the new nation, the Commonwealth of Australia, Jeannie had grown more mature and self-assured. Their union was heading toward its crescendo. Nonetheless, it remained under cover. Eventually Gribble was forced by the ABM to leave Yarrabah, and the church barred him from ever returning.[128]

Ernest had excused his white wife's initial absences from Yarrabah as being for health reasons.[129] Emilie Wriede, whom he had married three years after arriving at Yarrabah, had regularly departed for Cairns, then later Sydney, giving birth to her children away from Yarrabah. Emilie and Ernest had three boys, two of whom became dangerously ill. Rampant life-threatening tropical diseases, food shortages, and a life of mission poverty worried this white mother with young children. Emilie must have felt great relief to return to her well-off family's home in Cairns or to retreat to Sydney.[130]

At Yarrabah, Ernest had surrounded himself with his own zealous missionary family and the privations and exhaustion of his colonizing mission project. The intensity of his dedication, even with his own bouts of rheumatism and malarial debility, would have been irritating to anyone not raised a Gribble. Ernest channeled every ounce of his energy into his Yarrabah project, with its rapidly growing population. In the shadow of Ernest's deceased father, his mother's life of privation and unswerving loyalty to the mission cause intensified the pressure placed on Ernest. His mother, Mary Ann Bulmer, had vowed to his father that if God was calling him to the work, "Go and I will be with you. I will do all I can to help you in your work."[131] Perhaps Emilie saw that with the Gribbles, Aboriginal people came first, ahead of herself and possibly even her boys. Perhaps she noticed the spark in Ernest's eyes that revealed another kind of interest.

To assure the mission's credibility and continued church and government funding, Ernest's respectability was essential. Ernest was unwilling to share his romantic secrets with anyone. His mother's sacrifices and his need for maternal approval only exacerbated matters. He could hardly speak about his personal feelings with a sister whom he had banished for her boundary-crossing romantic passion. While family members surely knew, they were becoming expert at cover-ups.

With his own marriage, Ernest fudged the issue of his separation, officially reporting that Emilie was on "leave."[132] It was as if her marriage was a mission duty. Ernest never applied for divorce, and in church records, her status as missionary wife thus continued. Like his family, he incorporated his wife into the church project; it was if the church's permission was required to sanction their failure to cohabit. The tensions between the pair can only be imagined. Among Yarrabah descendants, Ernest and Emilie's marital altercations have become legendary. They particularly relish the story of a fight when Ernest hit Emilie over the head with a plate and beat her with a duck.[133] The poultry incident perhaps convinced Emilie to stay away. Clearly the Yarrabah residents loved to laugh when their drill-sergeant-like authority figure displayed antics that were clearly out of control.

But how do we explain this unlikely, yet so likely, romance? Jeannie was a senior employee, a newspaper correspondent in the paper Ernest edited, and closer to him in status than most others on the mission. She was a child who had grown to womanhood there, someone who had lived with his family and who knew him well. Emilie relied on her as a nanny for the children. Jeannie's father was reputedly a white man who "gave her" to a white family.[134] For Jeannie, the "race/colonizer" sexual and color boundaries had already been crossed, just as they had been all over Queensland and in every frontier region of Australia.

Jeannie's youth, her having been treated as both servant and family member, and the fact that she was, despite her responsible role, under Ernest's guardianship and authority, would make it easy for her to become emotionally dependent. Yet Gribble had not only drawn but also blurred many lines in the Yarrabah sand. He had concocted cover-ups over his brother's sexual violence, then over his sister's romance; he had devised an arranged marriage and tried to cover up his sister's out-of-wedlock pregnancy and her clandestine wedding. Now the fact that he had crossed the "race boundaries" of his own construction, and with a young woman under his guardianship, was too much for him to rationalize. Gribble's affair with Jeannie, who was in her early twenties at best, while he was in his late thirties, not only transgressed the age and race boundaries of his monogamous missionary design, it also transgressed the amorphous sex and race boundaries of the wider colonial regime. His cohabitation with an Aboriginal woman was illegal in state law. In Christian law, he was an adulterer. That the authoritarian ideologue Ernest yearned for intimate and sexual companionship across colonizing boundaries revealed a great crack in the many edifices that, brick by brick, he had painstakingly constructed.

In other ways, perhaps we should not presume to judge their emotions too readily. Jeannie had sympathy for Ernest. Perhaps she also yearned for her missing father. As they shared first the space of the family home and later mission goals and mission management roles, the boundaries between Jeannie and Ernest had eroded. Uprooted and dislocated from her parents as a child, then seized from her willing guardians, Jeannie's emotional battles must have been fraught. Gribble was the man Yarrabah people called "Dadda" and whom Jeannie took the liberty of calling "Daddy."[135] Was this also "Djaja," a kin classification, or Jaja, for Rocky Point, also known as Gribble Point, the place where he had preached the word of God?

In the Aboriginal community, Ernest's attraction to an Aboriginal woman was seen in a very different light. While the hypocrisy was obvious, this was not necessarily a "fall." For them, it was an endearing sign of his humanity, perhaps even an indicator of his good taste and a hopeful clue that he did not really find Aboriginal women or "blackness" inferior. Rather, it confirmed their attractiveness as good sexual and life partners. Perhaps this was tangible proof that they could all be truly one family. Yarrabah Aboriginal descendants still fondly recall this story as one in which Ernest and Janie "fell in love." They were so obviously smitten with each other that everyone could see what was going on.[136]

With their child now on the way, Gribble acted quickly. True to form, he used a "regular" Aboriginal marriage strategy as a solution. Not a shotgun wedding between Jeannie and himself. Gribble was still married, but even outside that bond, he could not possibly recognize Jeannie's child. He therefore came up with an alternative: ordering Jeannie to marry another Yarrabah resident, the hard-working young Willie Clark.[137] As Willie was already in a serious relationship with another Yarrabah woman, the order was destined to ruffle the Aboriginal community and to create grudges.

Jeannie Brown kept the paternity of her first child secret. While Yarrabah's strict and puritanical Christian morality was dissuasion enough, this was at Gribble's request. Plus, if exposed, she would fear banishment to Rocky Island, where unmarried mothers had to give birth, or to Fitzroy Island, farther away and a punishment place.[138] Or, with the assistance of the Queensland protector of Aborigines, she could be banished to the dreaded Palm Island. She now held a role of political and moral authority and belonged somewhere. To let out the truth would offer no good example for the boys' dormitory. A revelation like this would reverberate to destroy everything she and the Gribble family had worked for.

What appeared as Ernest Gribble's tightly run ship had now smashed into a coral reef, with every prospect of sinking rapidly to the bottom of the Coral Sea. Becoming increasingly deranged and unable to manage the mission or its precarious finances, Ernest ignored the ABM's increasingly strident instructions for him to leave. In desperation, to force him out, the board obtained doctor's orders for a "health cure." Out of loyalty, Ernest's mother, Mary Ann, and his sister Illa resigned. This left them in dire financial straits, relying upon the charity of others.[139] This was not the only Gribble family, however. There were now at least two other mixed Aboriginal branches of this family whose existences were officially ignored by church and family; this new one, too, would be a shared secret.

Blue Eyes

It is 1908. Upon the baby's birth, Gribble makes a somewhat unusual public announcement in his church newspaper. At Sunday church service, he reads out its announcement that the Reverent Ernest Gribble congratulated Jeannie and Willie Clark on the "birth of their first born, a splendid little girl." Then, for the benefit of *Missionary News* subscribers, the announcement adds, "Jeanie will be known to many of our readers as the girl who was with Mrs Ernest Gribble in Sydney. Since her marriage she has been Matron of the Boys Home." In the Yarrabah baptism register, kept by Gribble of course, Willie Clark is listed as the child's father.[140]

Before Jeannie gives birth, public fighting incidents nearly blow the lid off Jeannie and Ernest's denials. Ada Pickles, Jeannie's cousin, is having a relationship with Willie Clark, now Jeannie's legal husband.[141] Jeannie accuses

Ada of wrongdoing, of stealing her husband, and of being pregnant with his child. Ada retaliates by threatening to expose the secret, fairly well known anyway in the small community, that Jeannie is carrying Ernest Gribble's child. This rapidly escalates from argument to physical fight. Their second fight occurs after their babies are born. Physical resemblances confirm suspicions. After this fight, Gribble reports in his diary that he has banished Ada "forever" to Fitzroy Island.[142] Perhaps realizing he is losing credibility in the eyes of the Yarrabah community, he relents from this self-serving punishment. Before long, Ada is permitted to return.

What else was common knowledge among the Yarrabah Aboriginal people? Did they snigger in church? Earlier, the community knew that Ernest had banished his first assistant, Pearson, and then his brother Bert Gribble for sexual transgressions. Yarrabah people knew that Gribble had been separated from his wife, Emilie, for years. As much as Ernest Gribble might protest that he was married, they judged him to be the lonely single man he was — without wife, without his own children nearby. Perhaps they whispered and laughed about his sinfulness, or his hypocrisy, but Aboriginal women and men would not necessarily consider a white man's love of one of their people as an affront.

At Sea

In 1910, as fallen man, Gribble did not see it this way, and he had no place to go except into himself. As the banisher, there was no higher authority over Gribble in his Yarrabah kingdom. He had argued with and fallen out with Menmuny. Gribble had devised books of rules, regulations, and a world of order, routine, and conformity in appearance and behavior for "inmates." Nowhere in his rules was there anyone to hold himself — the "head of mission" — accountable. So who was it to be? His wayward sister was gone — to the family's and church's embarrassment. His mother had handed authority to her son Ernest so many years ago. Who could he turn to but God? The Board of Missions in faraway Sydney had handed Yarrabah's management to him years ago. He was king and king maker. But the church used its financial strings to override Ernest the only way it could. For Gribble, anywhere *away* from Yarrabah was his place of banishment, of loneliness. Gribble was now so enmeshed with Yarrabah that severing him from this place would be like taking him out of the world. By 1909 Ernest is drowning in his own confusion. It turns into despair. He is talking about how he would like to die with "his people" — the Yarrabah community. In an ominous tone, he writes that he is thinking about taking "a holiday" at sea.[143]

As much as Ernest had created a mission order and community, it too had created him. As much as he forcibly installed the nuclear family, Gribble himself had become part of a large extended Aboriginal and mission family, albeit one in which he placed himself at the top of the hierarchy. He left many records concerning the implementation of his "Christian regime," but the extent of such records can too easily warp the viewer's perspective.

Gribble had become acculturated into Yarrabah Aboriginality and its community structures, and Yarrabah had thus become his only place of belonging. Yarrabah's exterior shapes — its architecture, road, and clothing — displayed a transnational modernizing sensibility. However, the human landscape and the embodied experience of being human in this landscape remained, to a significant extent, Gunggandji. For Gribble, this in-country mode of being on the earth had become both familiar and normal. Despite his efforts to dismantle the functions of the complex kinship system of obligation and exchange, it was the extended structure of community, mutual obligation, and place that connected him with Aboriginal community and family. Aboriginal cultural tunes permeated Yarrabah. Despite his guilt, Ernest was unable to separate himself from this dislocated mission family or their shared landscape.

We do not know what would have happened if the ABM had not forcibly plucked him from Yarrabah. North Queensland and the mission itself were awash in "filthy" rumors about Gribble. Ordering him off the settlement, the ABM isolated him in a hospital a thousand kilometers away — in metropolitan Brisbane. His "cure" for "incessant anxiety and no rest" consisted of rest and milk, the Weir-Mitchell remedy for nervous exhaustion and breakdown.[144] He was "not enjoying" his furlough. What happened next only made him more distraught. Bishop George Frodsham pressured him to resign and Primate Charles John Wright banned him from ever returning — a lifetime ban indicating the gravity of his transgression.[145]

In all his writings, Gribble consistently portrayed sexual relations between Aborigines and whites as exploitation, as vice, as evil colonialism exemplified.

Such debauchery would lead to doom — to death for the whole "race." Ernest now found himself cast, in his own eyes, as the evil one. Worse, his evil reeked of duplicity. It had been discussed at ABM meetings; any contemporary church figures knew the shameful story. Ernest was now to suffer the banishment that he normally meted out as a punishment to others.

In this crisis, he was made to remember that, rather than being white king of Yarrabah, he was just a church employee, subject to its final authority. Relying upon income from the Church of England and its aspiring national body, the ABM, Gribble now had no private means of support. In order to sustain his extended family, himself, and the Yarrabah enterprise with which he was so personally identified, he could not lose favor altogether. He knew the church's reliance on the congregation's contributions. Any suggestion that the mission was not going well, let alone an officially confirmed scandal, would be the end of that.[146]

Colonial Hide-and-Seek

Unsurprisingly, Yarrabah residents took an intense interest in evolving sexual liaisons in their community. New relationships could mean a realignment of their kin duties. As discussed, it was crucial to know their classificatory brothers and sisters in order to practice avoidance relations and to prevent marriages between them. As a resident in their world, Ernest Gribble was already incorporated with a kinship classification that integrated him into networks of obligations. This added layers of kin loyalty toward Gribble; perhaps the Yidinjdji saw it as their success — that they had included a powerful man and his legacy in associated kin networks and that he had stayed among them to provide certain things, including security for their land. This did not protect it from intrusions and colonizations by other Aboriginal groups, which could involve ongoing tense power plays. But at least their land did not become freehold, in the hands of colonizer entrepreneurs, and taken from them forever. This would have had worse ramifications for their own secret information networks.

In Yidinjdji, one language spoken at Yarrabah, the word for quiet, clandestine is *munim*, and the word for sneaking and hiding is *wurrgay*.[147] Aboriginal people may have been inventing their own colonizer legends about intimate secrets; they knew well that stories of sexual dalliance could realign power and the paths of history.[148] This narrative runs close to so many revelations of paternity and illegitimacy that have been kept secret from children but were known or easily spotted by those around them.

Although the Earnest-Jeannie story had long circulated among Yarrabah residents, it was supposed to be the tightest of secrets. It is said that only Jeannie's best friend, Myra, seen in a photograph with her and family members years later, was told the story. Only Ada Pickles, who had been having an affair with Willie, mentioned it to her daughter. Gribble's daughter by Jeannie did not know, for her mother had not told her. Nor had her father. At Holloways Beach, near Cairns, in 2000, Charmaine Hollingsworth, the granddaughter of Willie Clark Senior and Jeannie Brown, told me her version of the story. In one sense, the lid was kept on the secret, but secrets gain momentum because they rely on being privileged information. The Yarrabah people already knew about it. "Yes, it was hushed up. She had real blue eyes though and was really light-skinned, as light as me. The Yarrabah people said that she was his [Ernest's] daughter.... And the Yarrabah people know the father of *every single child*" (her emphasis). In 1984 Elva Sands had stated, "Nola was clearly a Gribble. She had these bright blue eyes. Father Gribble had bright blue eyes."[149] Charmaine Hollingsworth, a devout Christian, was keen to note that she did not know for sure but commented that Nola was very light-skinned. While Nola's mother was also light-skinned, her husband, Willie, was dark. Nola had "these blue eyes." Sadly, Charmaine told me that Nola and her two children had by then "passed on."[150]

As a social building block and building block of new nations, Gribble wanted monogamous marriages to build a dividing wall between Christian and pagan customs. Ernest had taken on the power of marital arrangements; unions as important as life and death, these were what would constitute Yarrabah's mini commonwealth. In binding Christian ceremonies, Ernest acted as celebrant, including some designed to obscure his family's crossings.

Today such submerged memory might potentially redefine colonialism, revealing the intimate permeability of its dividing walls. It is often only via the revelations of Indigenous people that colonial secrets surface. They, too, colluded in the game of hide-and-seek, even initiating it. Their ongoing cooperation may have come out of affection, loyalty, and a desire to cherish special knowledge and its potential advantages.

Against his nature, Gribble, in his late thirties, had made his face and body into illegible spaces. The Word of God may have been heard among great Yarrabah boulders. One of Ernest's favorite quotes, about "taking manhood" into God, suggested his sense of human frailty and a quest to understand his own masculinity — in the face of the downfall of his father.

While assisting with Ernest's family in Sydney, it was Jeannie who wrote to Ernest in place of "poor Mamma," his fatigued, depressed wife. In 1906, about two years before she gave birth to Nola, Jeannie signed off, "I remain your true little girl."[151] Any consent she exercised was much compromised. Yet the Aboriginal residents of Yarrabah cast it with the spice of forbidden love. In unexpected ways, Gribble's missionary "word" was made flesh.

The people of Yarrabah still honor Gribble's memory. Despite his drastic change agendas, Gribble's mission helped the Yarrabah people hold onto some country, to survive as an amalgamated community identified by expanded, multilayered land and marital connections between language groups. Without being entirely destroyed as a sovereign people, they were able to modernize and expand. Via the pull of shared landscapes and of emotional family connections, their Ernest Gribble story was not told in his biographies or other mission texts. Instead, it has been inscribed in rocky, inspirited seaside landscapes sometimes known by his name. One, in large painted English letters inscribed on the rock face, is called Gribble Point.

Gribble used his photographs of white weddings as visual evidence to substantiate his assertions that heterosexual marriage was creating a group of Aboriginal Christians. In fact, these marriages signified a multilayered negotiation of authority, often involving only a thin layer of observance. When the Anglican bishop visited the early mission, Gribble organized the marriage of seven couples for him to witness. The brides wore fine dresses donated by the women of Croydon and carried startlingly blue lilies from the rainforest. Gribble later admitted that these people were already couples — having been united according to Aboriginal marriage protocols. Serving to impress the bishop, the group wedding would simply confirm "native marriage laws by the Prayers and Blessings of the Church."[152] So that ceremony was mainly for show. But it was not only Gribble's show. Weddings are, after all, public performances serving multiple agendas.

Part 2

Marriage and
Modernity among
the Cherokees

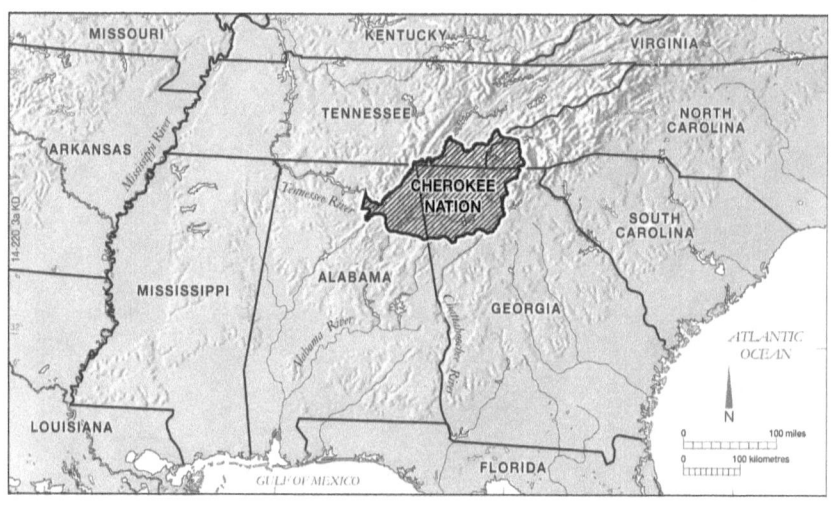

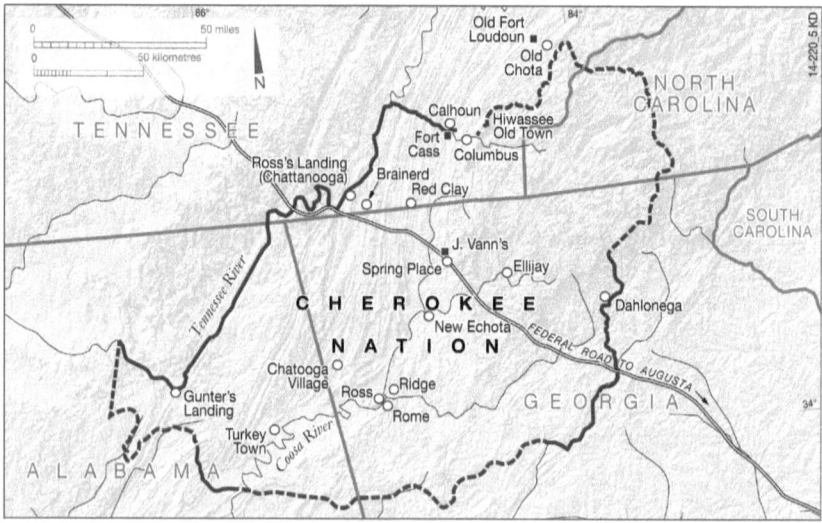

MAP 7. (*top*) The Cherokee Nation ca. 1820, overlaid with modern state boundaries.

MAP 8. (*bottom*) Cherokee Nation towns 1820s–30s.

CHAPTER THREE

Socrates, Cherokee Sovereignty, and the Regulation of White Men

In March 1828 an article in the *Cherokee Phoenix* appeared under the pen name Socrates. It intermeshed concerns over intermarriage with the Cherokee Nation's tenuous grasp on sovereignty. Socrates explained, "This nation owes to its character and safety, the establishment of a systematic policy, to preserve both." Implying the need to maintain both cultural integrity ("character") and national security, the author continued, "The exercise of sovereignty must necessarily embrace, and touch many, and various objects and interests, but the interests of individuals must sometimes be surrendered an[d] give way to the interest and existence of a nation."[1]

In its early national period, the Cherokee Nation became an innovator in restrictive intermarriage legislation. Fusing the issue of marital controls with the exercise of their sovereignty, Cherokee leaders devised and introduced a series of special laws between 1816 and the 1830s. While neighboring American states enforced restrictions upon intermarriage with people labeled as slaves, "negroes," and "Indians," it was a novel development for an Indigenous nation to enact them by written law.[2] We will consider how the Cherokee Nation's intermarriage restrictions directed attention at the monitoring of *white* men.[3] We will also consider how a racial approach to national inclusion and exclusion became an assertion of their Indigenous sovereignty.

Under unrelenting assault from the large numbers of intruders on their lands, the Cherokees used diverse strategies to hold on to the land of their ancestors and their autonomy as a nation. The crush of numbers of white men trespassing, stealing, raping, and committing other acts of violence on Cherokee land increased each year. By the 1820s, ten thousand white men were invading Cherokee land in Dahlonega, threatening to swamp the Indigenous population and, in some localities, already outnumbering them.[4] The gender imbalance of a male-dominated frontier was socially catastrophic. The relatively few white women living in frontier zones were in demand and far less likely to be looking for partners than was the case for white men. Eager to find minerals or to take up land, white intruders took little notice of Cherokee national rules and cultural expectations. To the state of Georgia, the existence of the Cherokee population was a practical and a legal impediment to its citizens' right to settle the land.

With backing from President Andrew Jackson, Georgia ignored the frontiersmen who were stealing whatever Cherokee land and assets they desired. Many white frontiersmen shared a presumption that they were entitled to exploit Cherokee women sexually. Others assumed that they could take a Cherokee wife without any ongoing commitment. Against the quickening stream of encroaching intruders, the Cherokee Nation was facing huge challenges for its survival. Neither the Georgian state nor the federal government assisted the Cherokees when they appealed to prevent illegal encroachment.

These pressures were highly stressful, with repeated criminal and murderous acts being committed against the Cherokees. They were reeling from many losses suffered during the Revolutionary War, when many of their men fought with the English. Tensions and fighting with the Creeks had also eased off. Now they sought a period of peace. As the Cherokees had agreed to numerous land cessions to ensure security, their territories were increasingly limited.

The Cherokees had plenty of reason for anxiety about the future viability of their nation. With so much pressure from outsiders, would they be able to exercise sovereignty and autonomy at all?

During the early nineteenth century, when both the early American republic and the early Cherokee republic were still developing their identities, Cherokee leaders used many strategies to hold on to their communal lands and to ensure authority over them. Their sovereign rights were collective, dependent on consent and consensus. Their domain comprised territory that was at once embodied, political, ecological, historical, and spiritual. Village centers were locations for decision making over resource usage and distribution, trade networks, and village governance.[5] They were centers for law and politics, including diplomatic dealings and legal challenges to the neighboring states and the federal government.

The early Cherokee national period was a time when they reworked their traditional narratives to fashion fresh approaches to contemporary political and social problems. A smaller group integrated insights from the teachings of western education, including the philosophers of ancient Greece and Rome. Such ideas permeated the thinking of the new republic, especially the development of its intellectuals and orators and the designers of its founding documents. At the same time as the classical thinkers of old Europe were enjoying a revival, they inspired the cutting-edge transatlantic writers and poets known as the romantics, who ruminated on love, marriage, history, and much else — including the politics of nation.

Although contributing only a handful of articles, the Cherokee Socrates was well read and versed in both political theory and law. His identity is mysterious. His? I assume by the tone of the writing and by the landscape of Cherokee journalism and educational opportunity that it is a male author. Socrates's application of liberal theory prized freedom of choice, echoing the thinking of the Constitution author James Madison. Nonetheless, Socrates conceded that elected representatives must put the health of the nation ahead of personal liberty.[6] By arguing that individual interests should be surrendered to the "interest and existence of the nation," he warned of the need to consider the wider polity.[7] For a nation to hold on to its sovereignty, Socrates backed intervention. His intermarriage plan touched the sensitive nerves of diplomacy between the Cherokee Nation, the neighboring states, and the federal polity. He identified the necessity for their nation to become proactive in controlling gender relations — thus proposing a microdiplomacy at the level of marriage and family.

Young Cherokee men were rocked by the rabid, race-based opposition to the Cornwall intermarriages that resulted in the closure of the Foreign Mission School. Hurt, they had trusted the northerners' belief in their humanity and equality. In particular, they hoped their allies would assist them in fighting Georgian intrusions. Socrates acknowledged that his anti-intermarriage recommendations would "touch feelings," engender "severe remarks," and even risk "*a settled animosity*." Perhaps Socrates feared putting white newspaper subscribers and supporters offside. In a carefully worded rumination, he stated that he would nonetheless "disregard" this concern, knowing that "no respectable white man, will consider it personal to himself." He also thought that "respectable parents" would not "disapprove . . . for the better security to his offspring's matrimonial connection."[8]

Socrates wanted action because outsiders were neglecting their Cherokee families and gaining way too much Cherokee land. But so as not to offend their white allies, he had to exercise tact. Although his recommendations were aimed at all white men, he explained that only those of bad character would be excluded: "the thief, the robber, the vagabond and the tippler, and adulterer."[9] Yet with the exception of resident missionaries, whom they respected as allies, the Cherokees classified most of the white American colonizers in this way.[10] And indeed, Socrates went further, arguing that all intruders into their nation should be denied "the privilege of intermarrying with Cherokee women." For as these white men rendered Cherokee women's existence "wretched," an intervention was imperative. Furthermore, white men were to be excluded not only because of their color but because they were lowbrow types, of inferior class and education. They inflicted "a deep rooted and corrupted ignorance among our people."[11] As Cherokee women freely chose their marital unions and clans were not policing these unsuitable unions, Socrates therefore proposed that the national representative government should enact new laws to prevent his people's degradation.

In his playful engagement with neoclassicism, when Socrates chose his pen name in March 1828 he instantly created something of an enigma. It was only the second month of publication of the *Cherokee Phoenix*, the first Indigenous-run newspaper in the world. It was bilingual — in English and Cherokee. What is known of the Greek historical character Socrates is limited, but he has come to stand for the wise man, the father of modern philosophy, an acute scholar of politics and a trickster.[12] A popular figure, the Greek Socrates managed to reach the newspapers. For example, in the 1820s and 1830s secular and mission newspapers alike commonly featured the latest translations of Greek philosophers. In particular, Socrates's wisecracks and humorous anecdotes appealed to readers of the time.

FIG. 33. The front page of the Cherokee Phoenix, April 10, 1828.

FIG. 34. The *Cherokee Phoenix* masthead.

Some of the Cherokee Socrates's comments could almost be channeling one of his transatlantic contemporaries, Jane Austen. Socrates wryly notes that perhaps intermarriage is "the most important object in the esteem of all classes of society, however defective their prudence and judgement might be in their selections." He is both earnest and wry: "Far be it from me to cut asunder the ties of Love, or to part those who are now happily or unhappily united in destiny by marriage."[13]

Socrates's articles enable novel perspectives on Cherokee intellectual and political life. His one on intermarriage drew attention to the deep divisions of opinion and the personal conflicts of interest aroused by the topic. It provides insights into the sociology of intermarriage and why, in regard to the Cherokees' interface with colonialism, it became a crucial aspect of contemporary Cherokee thinking. Keen analysts of the latest governance ideas and practices, Cherokee leaders were constantly asserting their sovereignty in intellectual, political, cultural, and gendered performances. Politicians of the early Cherokee Nation documented and archived developments in their new capital, New Echota. As the first Indigenous newspaper in the world, the *Cherokee Phoenix* received international attention, with some of its articles widely syndicated.

By 1825 the Cherokee Nation was a sizeable entity, with 13,583 citizens. Their traditional territories covered 130,000 square miles of southeastern

North America, taking in the Appalachians and many states of the "New South."[14] We know this because their Cherokee clerks registered, counted, documented, and monitored the population. Yet collecting census and life data is more commonly noticed as an effective tool of imperial governance, bureaucracy, and biopower. While Indian Agent Return J. Meigs hired George Barber Davis to make the first statistical table, Cherokee clerks were trained to collect data themselves, organizing a national census that made specific note of social practices such as intermarriages.[15]

The Cherokee census recorded that 17 percent of Cherokees had at least one white ancestor, and among the wealthier slave-owning classes, almost 80 percent had a white relative. According to the 1825 census, 147 white men were married to Cherokee women and 73 white women were married to Cherokee men.[16] By 1835 the proportion of "mixed-bloods" had increased to 23 percent of the population.[17] This shows that intermarriage was not rare; however, in total, such couples represented only 1.6 percent of the Cherokee population. Nonetheless, intermarried families, and especially their male heads, held disproportionate wealth and influence.[18]

During the early decades of the nineteenth century, the Cherokee Nation was practicing its right to exert jurisdiction over those within its borders. The Cherokees elected to do so upon the grounds of "race" difference.[19] Unlike Queensland's Yarrabah example, it was not the missionaries or the colonizing states who were restricting intermarriage for "the good of others." Between the 1810s and 1830s, the Cherokee Committee and Council introduced and continued to tighten intermarriage and citizenship restrictions. In 1819 it introduced the first intermarriage laws targeting white men. Later, from 1824, marriages with "negro slaves" were officially restricted.[20] The Cherokees had long brought war captives into their societies as slaves. Most of the slave owners ran plantations and other enterprises and were of mixed Cherokee and European descent.

After 1821, when John Ridge's proposal to Sarah Northrup became public in the North, the Cherokee Nation was shocked at the New England furor over the Cornwall students. After all, white American reactions seemed counter to the "Great Book of the whites," the Bible. The Cherokees had been taught that it said that all men came from a single set of parents and that God "hath made of one blood all nations."[21] This concept obviously appealed to them far more than the eighteenth-century Christian notions of a Great Chain of Being, where "Indians" were placed below "whites" on the basis of skin color.

"Blood" came with many additional layers of meaning, as the concept had central significance to the Cherokees, being the important identity factor gained from one's mother's clan. Blood was the essence of personal, clan, and wider collective belonging. It was fundamentally associated with national belonging.[22] It was Selu who united the Cherokees as a people, and it was her harvest cycle that was celebrated in their calendar. Blood held an ontological connection with the sustenance that came of the shed blood of the great mother Selu, the corn goddess. Selu had a formative role in verifying Cherokee women's authority over land, religious power, agriculture, and the staple food, corn.[23] Endorsed by Selu and the blood that was her essence, matrilineal clan bodies held substantial power, including the very wealth and resources of the land itself.

Privately held property and private wealth-building in transport, trade, and plantations were rapidly starting to change all that. Curiously, mission educators were shocked that Christian teachings to Native American men would encourage "affairs of this world" and its lusts.[24] As John Ridge's Cherokee mother was very upset at the idea of his marriage to a white woman, she asked local missionary Daniel Buttrick of the American Board of Commissioners for Foreign Missions for advice. He tried to dissuade the couple, arguing that white women would "feel above the common Cherokees." Perhaps under pressure from the northern church leaders, Buttrick advised that Ridge would "promise more usefulness to his people were he connected with them in marriage." Ridge eventually convinced his parents to support him.[25]

With seventy-five white women already living in marital unions with Cherokee men in the nation, such a marriage would not have seemed particularly unusual. The Cherokees had invested hope in the thought that the northerners were more enlightened than the apparently non-God-fearing frontier intruders currently destroying their lives. Now, having seen that even many refined northerners really viewed the most high-achieving Cherokee scholars as inferior savages, they had to reassess their approach to a multiplicity of colonizers. The northern church leaders, the southern, locally based missionaries, and the Georgian and Tennessee frontiersmen from different European places of origin had contrasting beliefs, motivations, and agendas. However, in the business of constructing whiteness themselves, the Cherokees lumped those with different European ethnicities and conflicting colonizing interests into the racial or "color" class of "white." In their regulations, this then took on the status of a legal category.

In 1826 John Ridge saw an appeal to the United States as one of the Cherokees' only hopes for honoring their treaty agreements. Yet he recognized that the Cherokees faced a crisis that might be irretrievable: "We are in the paw of a Lion—convenience may induce him [to] crush and with a faint Struggle we may cease to be!"[26] While the lion is a clear symbol of exotic power and dominance, Ridge also saw his people's mutability as part of what we might now call the deep time history of nations, and that of all creatures. Change within and without—modernization—seemed to offer the only hope of staying in the power game. As Ridge stated, "Mutability is stamped on every thing that walks the Earth." Assessing the long-term impacts of intimate mixing, Ridge appreciated how intermarriage could serve as one biological and cultural lifeline to the future. Here is the climax of his 1826 address: "Even now we are forced by natural causes to a Channel that will mingle the blood of our race with the white.... In the lapse of half a Century if Cherokee blood is not destroyed it will run its courses in the veins of fair complexions who will read that their Ancestors under the Stars of adversity, and curses of their enemies became a civilized Nation."[27] Not only their valiant efforts to become "civilized" but the biological essence of Cherokee people—their "blood," as they put it—might survive to carry on their ancestral legacy and their story. Marital mingling might serve as a contingency against their nation's final destruction.[28]

By the time of Ridge's speech, the Cherokee Constitution had both restricted intermarriage and granted citizenship to the children of intermarried white women. Perhaps they had inheritance and material wealth in mind. According to historian Theda Perdue, the controversial move that "divorced citizenship from matrilineal kinship" had actually been sparked by the marriage of John Ridge.[29] Scholar Circe Sturm argues that Cherokee blood no longer belonged to the distinct matrilineal clan bodies, but thereafter "Cherokee blood itself... became the possession of a single national body."³⁰ Their constitution now stated that "the descendants of Cherokee men by all free women, except the African race . . . shall be entitled to all the rights and privileges of this Nation." Based upon patrilineal descent, their new laws spelled out this radical shift to entitlements. If born to an African or "unfree" parent, you were excluded. All other male descendants of Cherokee *men* were entitled to stand for elected positions — as were descendants of women married to free men. Cherokee men and women could vote, and they were all entitled to citizenship. Without the requirement of official documents or specific rituals, the children of any recognized Cherokee-style marriage were included. Children qualified "whose parents may be or have been living together as man and wife, *according to the customs and laws of this Nation.*"³¹

In 1825 the Cherokee Council first met in its newly designated capital, New Town, later called New Echota. The Cherokee Constitution was written in 1827 and adopted after the elections of 1828. Power to negotiate with the United States was now placed in the hands of the council.³² After Socrates expressed concern that outsider intermarriage was destroying the fabric of Cherokee society, in 1829 the nation increased restrictions. These included a system of registration, monitoring, and surveillance of intermarried husbands. During the 1830s the Cherokee Council and Committee tightened restrictions, fees, and penalties affecting intermarriage and citizenship rights. While the Cherokee clans had usually sorted out intimate family and local matters, in order to deal with non-Cherokees, their national representatives ordained to use written laws to provide a marital governance tool, with fixed punishments as part of that design.

Although the Cherokee Nation had already introduced restrictive intermarriage laws before Socrates's article, these appeared to be ineffectual. In 1828 Socrates felt it necessary to call upon the Cherokee powers to get serious about implementing their policy. Socrates recommended much tighter controls on marriages with "outsiders" — a nonspecific race category. He also recommended the appointment of two senior officers who would undertake background checks to ensure that the prospective groom could pay a bond and security of up to $500 and had "good and sufficient recommendation for good character." A citizen of the Cherokee Nation would be required to countersign. If the man's behavior toward his wife and family turned out different from what the character reference promised, Socrates recommended that he be "expelled from the nation as a Base intruder." To monitor the situation, an officer would provide an annual report of licenses issued, a "faithful account of his superintendency," and a list of "the names of the Cherokee women so married, according to the law."[33] To emphasize that only whites who were officially married to a Cherokee citizen could presume any chance of permanency or citizenship, Socrates persistently used the terms "outsiders" and "intruders." White men had to understand that they stood outside the category of belonging; their residence was limited, temporary, and conditional.

The enactment of Cherokee authority over Indigenous lands included the right to enforce their laws over all residents. Commenting on the *Joint Committee Report on the Republic of the United States* in another, lengthier article on colonizer sovereignty, Socrates notes that Georgia was claiming a "good, legal, and perfect title to the lands in question." In fact, it claimed an entitlement to possession by any means. Socrates is outraged by Georgia's justifications of "discovery" when it is "country that never yet belonged to any other."[34] Subverting it for his own use, Socrates quotes what he refers to as the "textbook" of the "whites," Emer de Vattel's international treatise *Law of Nations*, on rights to land and national status. In a clever ploy owing something to Plato, the Cherokee Socrates poses questions, then answers them with direct excerpts from Vattel.[35] Defining the terms "domain," "empire," and "sovereignty" via this device, Socrates argues for Cherokees' claims on the basis of their having occupied the lands "since time immemorial." The proof was in their ancestor's bones that lay beneath their soil. Socrates goes on to quote a published local history (by a white American author) that confirmed the Cherokees' long connection with their lands.

Via multiple assertions of "nationhood," the Cherokees performed and enacted their sovereignty over lands and people. As political historian Hideaki Shinoda concludes, "The American Constitution [1787] was a historical achievement of the constitutional theory of sovereignty."[36] Here, power resided in the will of the people. Although colonialism undermined Cherokee sovereignty at every turn, the Cherokee Nation worked to meld its own notions of governance with the governance concepts embodied in the American Constitution. As discussed in this book's introduction, sovereignty goes to the core of political relations. Modern sovereignty, or a people's assertion of authority over land, embraces "popular sovereignty," in which power is invested in the constituency rather than in a king or queen. The people have a say over electing leaders. While theories of sovereignty are complex, in the Cherokee territories both Indigenous and colonizer competed for exclusive authority or "perfect sovereignty."

With their new laws, the Cherokees were trying to harness what the theorist Michel Foucault called state biopower, in which a government introduced external, centralized controls of life, including controls over reproduction, birthrates, and in this case, over marriage and race.[37] The Cherokees based their new national government upon a representative model with a clan-based and consensus decision-making system, with every citizen entitled to attend gatherings, to speak, and be respectfully heard. Cherokee sovereignty was polymorphous across and between regions. While their courts had previously decided punishments on a case-by-case basis, a system of stipulated penalties reflected new ideas of progress and modernity to be enacted through exercises of law. Since President Washington made his promises to them in 1796, the Cherokees had had a contractual understanding with the United States. If they complied with the colonizing contract and its expectation that they would attain "civilization," then full entitlement to treaty rights and benefits would follow; they would retain rights to their lands and would share the same benefits as other modern states in the United States.[38] And they believed that their example would be followed in other Indian nations too.[39]

In order to ensure that they could attain these goals, the Cherokee Nation needed to exercise its own "perfect sovereignty" via the civil and criminal law. As earlier discussed, from the 1820s onward in North America and Australia, the introduction of their law in settler polities created what in European law was considered to be "perfect settler sovereignty." Furthermore, as colonizers needed to shore up the legitimacy of settlement, from the 1820s the Georgia-Cherokee story actually represented the moment of this global transformation of sovereignty. As historian Lisa Ford explains so well, "Empire changed sovereignty because it altered the relationship of people with space. In the process, it created the conditions for the redefinition of sovereignty through the legal subordination of people in defined

SOCRATES, CHEROKEE SOVEREIGNTY, AND REGULATION OF WHITE MEN

FIG. 35. This silver medal was presented by President George Washington to Chief Red Jacket. On the right, the seal of the United States, as much phoenix as eagle, is featured. Note the arrows held in the bird's feet and its upstretched wings. On the face of the coin, note Red Jacket's distinctive dress compared with Washington's suited attire. Symbols of agriculture, the plough and domestic animals, and a hut are featured in the background. "The original silver medal presented by George Washington to Red Jacket." Courtesy Library of Congress, reproduction no. LC-USZ62-125642.

territorial units."[40] Through public performances and writings by Cherokee intellectuals like Socrates, the Cherokees, too, became adept players in the sovereignty game.

CHEROKEE WEDDINGS

In weddings that involved public ceremonials, ideas of modern Cherokee sovereignty could be performed. Although varied and not obligatory, these rituals reveal shifting, convergent meanings. Weddings usually honored the corn mother and matriarchal creation figure Selu. In 1819 the Anglo-American missionary Cephas Washburn attended a Cherokee marriage ceremony in New Echota. First discarding their clothing and dipping themselves several times in a fast-flowing stream in the freshness of the morning, the Cherokee bride and groom performed a "going to water" ceremony that signified purification and renewal. Enhancing the symbolism was the new capital's location at the union of rivers; the Coosawatteea and Conasuaga merge to become the Oostanaula River.[41]

Clothed in fresh garments, the couple then moved to the New Echota Council house, a venue signifying the civil authority of the Cherokee Nation, with its now-centralized polity and modern constitutional government. The bride and groom stepped toward each other to meet in the center of the main room. The groom brought venison for the woman and, in choreographed fashion, she presented him with corn.[42] They exchanged the food, then the blankets. The groom's mother presented her son to the bride's mother and mother's mother, signifying that he now belonged to the bride's clan, with whom he would reside. Then the bride and groom tied together blankets or shawls of blue or white, confirming their deep belonging to Cherokee land and waterways, a respect for the foods they provided, and the gendered narratives informing them. The blankets marked the couple's agreement to share a bed, warmth, and comfort. After gifts were presented to the woman's family, the bride and groom hosted a huge feast. Each year, all Cherokee marriages were reaffirmed as part of the proceedings of the annual Green Corn festival. Several villages gathered to reenact the story of Selu, the first woman. Domestic and community purification and renewal rituals, including their famous running dances and musical performances were conducted.[43] Selu performances were compelling, dynamic narratives that connected living people to a landscape-based life force. Like many foundational stories, the Selu story had been carefully reworked by the Cherokees to address contemporary life, thus serving as a platform for both origin stories and critiques of contemporary colonialism. Incorporating themes of imperialism, technology, age, gender, race, and blood, contemporary versions also considered the politics of intermarriage.

There were many different tellings of the Selu narrative, for it was a living story serving a changing world. Some provided rationales for a segregationist message, premised upon a hierarchy in which black people had been ordained to occupy the lowest rungs.[44] A version circulating between the 1810s and 1830s went like this: Selu's sons feared that her power over the creation of food made her a sorcerer. They attempted her murder, but Selu escaped and "flew up into the heights." When their father discovered their plot, he gave his sons a book instructing them how to act and live, but one brother stole the book and kept it to himself. On his deathbed, the father drew a line that became the great Atlantic Ocean. On one side, the people made small boats; on the other, they made large boats. Eventually those on the eastern side of the ocean sailed their large boats to the North American side, bearing gifts from their leader King George. Because young people seized the goods intended for the elders, their greed disrupted the world. The different skin colors on each side of the ocean could be explained. Although both brothers had originally been white, those people who had not taken the same trouble as the others to avoid the sun became red. Whites and reds were thus the same people, but those descended from the thieving son were morally bankrupt. The others, the Real People, continued to respect the authority of elders and to exercise self-control.[45]

In order to explain colonialism's immorality, Cherokee leaders drew upon divine visions. At times, such movements gathered revolutionary and segregationist momentum.[46] The historian William McLoughlin has described the Ghost Dance movement of 1811–12 as "a spiritual struggle to reconcile the old myths and the new ways."[47] On a journey via Rocky Mountain in northwestern Georgia in 1811, a Cherokee man and two women saw a remarkable vision ride out of the sky while the earth quaked. A large group of Indians thundered toward them on black horses, beating a drum. Their leaders announced that the Cherokees were made of red clay and the white men of white sand; the two peoples were distinct and should remain so. They warned that the Cherokee women should grind with mortars and dispense with the white man's corn mills. When a beautiful light and a vision of white horses appeared, they proclaimed that all whites (with a few exceptions) should live *outside* the boundaries of their nation and must give back the land in their sacred towns. The three witnesses returned to urgently report their ghost-riders vision to all the Cherokee chiefs and to the Cherokee agent, Colonel Meigs. When John Ridge's father, the wealthy plantation owner chief called The Ridge or Major Ridge, scoffed at such lessons from the spiritual world, Cherokee law enforcers wanted to kill him, and they almost did so.[48] A Cherokee speaker and nationalist, The Ridge nonetheless rejected the revelation medium and its anti-integration message.

From 1815, Chief Elk used Selu as a cultural platform to explain British and American imperialism and to develop historical counternarratives. Messianic insights gesture toward new solutions outside western thinking.[49] As historian Claudio Saunt notes, the Cherokees described America as "the Old World, the site of creation, and Europe as the new." Not only did this reverse the direction of migration from Europe to America, it made the Cherokees senior to Europeans and enhanced the primacy of their land claims.[50] Elk and his followers believed that the Great Spirit had established different lifeways for whites and Indians and that the peoples of different colors were meant to remain culturally distinct. The story mirrored another shift in power relations: between mothers, and between older men and younger men with book knowledge. While the old chiefs may have struggled with foreign powers to negotiate the Cherokee future, they foresaw that the young, bicultural Cherokees would not necessarily hold dear the same values.[51] These Cherokee histories attempt to mediate social change on their own terms. King George sending his boats represents the basis of British claims to sovereignty, while Selu explains the foundations of the landed, ongoing basis of Cherokee sovereignty.

Dramatic visions noting colonizer immorality and offering solutions to the colonizer onslaught provoked revolutionary momentum.[52] The Booger dance was performed in winter; with a mock erotic theme, dancers acted out the role of awkward men from a distant land dancing ludicrously. The dance is believed to have preceded the coming of whites, having represented monsters with stony skin. However, the dance had warned of the imminent arrival of strange Indians, "negroes," and Caucasians from the east. This historically themed dance was a cure for the sick. For an ailing society, it had a healing intensity.[53]

Interpreting history through their own prisms, the Cherokees reasserted narrative authority and made sense of their changed world. They also drew upon the authority of certain biblical explanations. In this largely prescientific age, Euro-Americans routinely deployed the Bible for insights into what they saw as their prior history. They also used the Bible to map their futures. Such ideas converged into new Cherokee narratives, creating critical syncretic discourses that reconfigured gendered concepts of color, family, and nation. The Cherokees thus used various strategies to map their relationships with other Indian nations and with the new republic.[54] Although these narratives mapped alternative modernizing futures, they were premised upon anti-African, antiwhite, and antimodernity discourses.[55]

Dramatic social change required drastic solutions. Without wider rangelands, the Cherokees had to convert their social order to rely upon agriculture over hunting. Their wealthiest members were now running plantations and trading enterprises with the labor of African American slaves. While some Cherokees harnessed a strategy of cultural revival to accommodate change inside their own cultural ethos, others sought to be respected within modern models of progress, which in the South still included plantation slavery. The Cherokees valued their own gender practices. Married women owned property and had communal rights in land. During marriage, the woman continued to own her own property, and if the marriage broke up, she retained it. The children were under the mother's guardianship and the husband was not entitled to custody. By the same token, he retained his property, including wealth accumulated during his marriage. However, in the face of the powerful forces of Euro-American colonialism, even the Cherokee traditionalists' strategies required innovation and reorderings.

As we have seen, specific stories depicted how an external imperialism had distributed goods inappropriately and had valorized the written over the spoken word, thus disturbing the power of Cherokee elders. A proposed solution was a politics of cultural separation between "white" and "red" that valued "red" values over "white." In some versions, certain "good whites," such as missionaries or Indian agents who advocated and supported Cherokee sovereignty, were exempted from exclusion. Overall, an explicit prosegregation message opposed all associations and intermarriage with white men. And it aimed to exclude "negroes" or African Americans from Cherokee citizenship.

LESSONS FROM PLATO

Although committed to the strict regulation of intermarriage, the Cherokee Socrates referenced neither the revelations of chiefs nor the texts of white missionaries. Fitting his nom de plume, the Cherokee Socrates turned to the secular philosophy and logic of his western education. Just as the title of their newspaper references the Greek myth of the phoenix rising from the fires of destruction, Socrates's nom de plume conveys the virtue of a questioning, interrogatory approach to national struggles. It provides insights into the transnational intellectual character of the early Cherokee Nation. At a sophisticated level, the Cherokees were engaging in the same conversations over statehood that were ensuing in the early republic of the United States and across the Atlantic in Europe.[56]

So who was this enigma, the Cherokee Socrates? His article about intermarriage has attracted plenty of scholarly attention, yet his identity has not been cracked. As no women wrote for the *Phoenix*, we have presumed it was most likely a male author. We can assume that the potential reactions of influential individuals may have necessitated secrecy. In a society with a relatively small well-educated elite, exposing the author's identity risked retaliation by white men in the nation or other intermarried people. Or perhaps it would alienate the backers of a person who could have been an aspiring politician. Intermarriage was an emotive issue with a strong personal aspect, and intermarried friends and relatives could take offense. Perhaps the author himself was married to an outsider.

It may be that the Cherokee Socrates was one of the Vann brothers, delegates to the National Council. In 1829 David Vann moved the council to tighten intermarriage restrictions. His brother Joseph Vann opposed the motion, putting up another option.[57] Like other wealthy, slaveholding families, they had white grandfathers—and some had great-grandfathers.

There are so many possibilities. Perhaps Socrates held political office or had a conflict of interest; perhaps he was using this opinion piece as a political device to garner public support in the buildup to the council discussion. The newspaper editor Boudinot, who published the piece, surely knew his identity. As a young student, John Ridge took an early liking to Socrates, quoting him in his "Indian Address" of 1822.[58] Having famously married the white woman Sarah Northrup from Cornwall, Ridge, if he were the author, would understandably be trying to avoid accusations of hypocrisy. Whatever the true identity of the Cherokee Socrates, his arguments to curb intermarriage were compelling enough to see the intermarriage law change the following year.

ANTI-INTERMARRIAGE LAWS

So what were the laws that were already in place but ineffectual? In the Cherokee Nation, "Black Africans" or "negroes," as they were then called,

FIG. 36. The Vann House exemplified the wealth and influence of certain Cherokee elites who prospered with the plantation system and the use of slave labor. Courtesy Library of Congress, reproduction no. HABS GA,107-SPLA,1-7.

were not permitted to marry Cherokees at all. Restrictions against whites were qualified. The initial law was passed in 1819 and required "that any white man who shall hereafter take a Cherokee woman to wife be required to marry her legally by a minister of the gospel or other authorized person, after procuring license from the national Clerk for that purpose."[59] Only in these circumstances would a white man "be entitled and admitted to the privileges of citizenship." The regulation's intention was "in order to avoid imposition on the part of any white man."[60] Definitions of "imposition" include burden, nuisance, annoyance, and obligation. If white men resided in their territory, the Cherokees would be obliged to share entitlements with them. Oblivious to or intentionally ignoring Cherokee protocols and expectations, and outside the governance of the clan structure, such men posed a social risk. The male-run Cherokee Committee aimed to stop unscrupulous white men from using marital partnerships to gain land and other benefits. They also wanted to punish them for wife desertion, marriages of convenience, and not meeting approved standards of the good husband.

FIG. 37. "David Vann. A Cherokee chief / drawn, printed and coloured at the Lithographic & Print Colouring Establishment, No. 94 Walnut St., Phila." Courtesy Library of Congress, reproduction no. LC-USZC4-12424.

After the law was passed, a white man wishing to marry a Cherokee woman therefore had to obtain permission for a western-style marriage. If approved, Cherokee clerks could scrutinize whether they fulfilled family obligations.[61] No such requirements applied to Cherokee couples.

After 1819, in the Cherokee Nation "any white man who shall hereafter take a Cherokee woman to wife" had to obtain a license from the national clerk and "to marry her legally by a minister of the gospel or other authorized person."[62] In another gesture to control intermarried whites, the Cherokee Committee and Council resolved that the wife's property was not subject to the husband's disposal and that if a white man parted from his wife "without just provication [sic]," he had to pay a suitable sum to her and be "deprived of citizenship." Furthermore, a white man was no longer permitted to have more than one Cherokee wife. For Cherokee citizens, for whom polygamy had long been an accepted practice, having only one wife was thereafter "recommended" but not compulsory.[63]

The Cherokee Constitution self-consciously referred to the "Sovereignty and Jurisdiction" of their nation, emphasizing its distinctive and separate legislative, executive and judicial functions and its eight district electorates.[64] Ideas about sovereignty shaped both the high politics of national and international structures and the orderings of "domestic property." This included intimate gendered and familial unions. Slaves, another form of property, had no "sovereignty" at all — not even over their own persons.[65] Cherokee women had earlier intermarried with white men as a way to trade with and to integrate intruders under their own regulatory systems pertaining to family and nation. In the context of early nineteenth-century political and economic developments, increasing rates of intermarriage had begun to dramatically realign the gender and power order. For the Cherokees, it is no accident that the anti-intermarriage regulations appeared at a time when Cherokee women were starting to lose out to Cherokee men in status and power. Women's ability to endow matrilineal inheritance and to have formal representation in the governing body of the Cherokee Nation was being eroded. At the same time, sovereignty contests between the United States and Cherokee citizens were intensifying. This nexus would flavor the Cherokee Nation's approaches to women's entitlements.

Cherokee political organization was intensely local, with landed roots underpinning knowledge systems. Political allegiances also emphasized the village and the town. The nation's four main regions were divided by the geography of the southern Appalachians, rivers, and bogs. Individuals shared multilayered identities of kinship and clan. Clans were categories of people who believed themselves to be of "one blood."[66] However, the village was the organizational focus, and speeches, meetings, dances, and ceremonies took place at the town center.[67] With decreasing acreages of lands, the loss of numerous towns and regions, and moves to the capital of Echota and then in the 1810s to New Echota, the nation was becoming increasingly centralized. Regardless, the local power of village leaders and the political power of towns continued. Beyond this, there was a wider sense of place, of life amid mountains, and of communal ownership of land. Constellations of associated groups identified with a wider landscape of spiritual association. Such groupings shaped their interface with the fur trade and other trading systems.[68]

As previously mentioned, in the eyes of the United States, Indians fell between the categories of domestic and foreign citizens, and in the Declaration of Independence they are mentioned alongside foreign nations in regard to commerce. In this light, the fact that Indians attended a Foreign Mission School in the middle of New England was not so odd. Indicating no assurance of a cessation of conflict and conquest, Indian relations came under the Department of War.[69] Furthermore, when the Cherokees took the matter of their sovereignty to the courts in the early 1830s, the outcome evoked the entwined, multilayered orderings of sovereign power in the United States.

These cases included *Cherokee Nation v. Georgia* (1831) and *Worcester v. Georgia* (1832), both decided by Chief Justice Marshall of the Supreme Court. In 1831 the court ruled that the Cherokee Nation was a "domestic dependent nation," secondary to the United States. The state of Georgia was arguing for greater authority to rule over Cherokee lands, including the rights of people to live there. Although the judgment recognized a subordinate sovereignty, this was a breakthrough decision for the Cherokees and for Indigenous people globally, as it acknowledged an entitlement based upon historical and prior occupation. It also ruled on federal authority over that of nearby states. However, for the Cherokees it declared that they were not autonomous; their fate was intertwined with and subordinate to that of the republic of the United States. And, although they had a special status as an Indigenous nation, it was not counted as one of the states.[70] Whether a president and Congress would follow through and honor the court ruling was another matter. Once a sovereign, independent Indigenous people, the Cherokees were now both "domestic" and "dependent." At once, they were precariously subject to the will of Georgia, the state in which their nation was located, and that of Congress.

The Cherokee Nation faced a conundrum. Amid the outsiders' disruptiveness, lawlessness, and acquisitiveness toward Cherokee women and lands, how could they retain sovereignty? They campaigned in the North; they published a newspaper; they established a modern government; they critiqued and analyzed their past and future. With astonishing acuity, strategic action, and modernizing acumen, they tried to assert and shore up their entitlements on multiple fronts.

As previously discussed, the Cherokees understood that they had entered into a colonizing compact with President George Washington, then with Jefferson and his successors. If they fulfilled their part of the deal and became "civilized" and progressive, they understood that they would be entitled to recognition as a modern people entitled to autonomy and sovereignty under the Great Republic of the United States. In this, they were assured, they would be judged upon their degree of civilization, to be measured by a range of social indicators. Their gender practices would be expected to follow the modern division of labor between men and women.[71] Women would weave and make clothing, prepare food, care for small animals, and practice other domestic arts, while men engaged in government, the law, and heavier work, including farming, building, infrastructure construction, and outdoor labor. Promoting their own tribe and nation at the expense of others, the Cherokees also hoped to jump ahead of neighboring "civilized tribes" like the Choctaws and Creeks, with whom they had long competed to establish the strongest nation. The Cherokees identified as the big brother in a politically extended family of "little brothers," though their aspirations did not extend to empire in the same sense as the later Comanche exemplar.[72]

Cherokee delegates made formal representations and petitions to the city of Washington, undertook diplomatic negotiations, renegotiated treaties, appealed in courts of law, and persisted in pursuing treaty breaches. Although many Cherokees refused to embrace all aspects of modernity or civilization, even against the externally set criteria, their nation had proven its civilized status time after time through economic independence, the incorporation of modern political institutions and laws, establishment of a newspaper, educational achievement, and even modes of historical narration and critique. In the light of past presidential and other assurances, and in the light of fairness, many Cherokee leaders held on to the hope that such advancements would guarantee cultural and territorial sovereignty.[73]

To Georgians, Cherokee advancement created an obstacle to their own.[74] They considered that their whiteness and colonizer status entitled them to carry out land thefts. In order to do so, they conducted brutal acts, which went unpunished. After the discovery of gold in the mid-1820s, Georgia became more strident in its plans for the takeover of Cherokee lands.

Although the universalizing language of colonialism that permeates colonial legal documents can obscure gender and culture, contests of sovereignty were both gendered and cross-cultural. When the Cherokees tried to assert the authority of their own state and its laws, they chose to use restrictive intermarriage regulations targeting white men. Perhaps they had greater hope of exercising marriage power over white men than of exerting any authority over criminal law.

The first Cherokee Nation intermarriage law represents a significant turning point in the nation's assertions of modern sovereignty. After all, Cherokee women's intermarriage with white men was not a new phenomenon. Leading men such as Oo-wat-ie, the father of Buck Watie (later Elias Boudinot) and Stand Watie, traced their non-Cherokee lineage back to the Spanish conquistador Saladin. Others, such as the Ross family, were descendants of Scottish fur traders who were themselves often vanquished sons of clan chieftains.[75] Indeed, during the 1780s, most of the British and Euro-American traders operating in Cherokee country were white men with Cherokee wives. Being in such marriages proved economically and politically advantageous. Besides acting as female companions and sexual partners, Cherokee women played essential business roles, serving as translators, diplomats, and cultural and business intermediaries. The Cherokee women's farming skills provided agricultural products for sustenance and sale; they cooked, performed domestic and shop duties, and in the trader's absence, ran the stores.[76] Active partners, their contributions were crucial to wealth creation.

Some intermarried white men became "countrymen" by definition. Leonard Shaw, the first federal agent sent to the Cherokees and a graduate of Princeton, arrived in the Cherokee lands in 1792 and soon afterward married a Cherokee woman.[77] As with earlier traders, the Cherokees integrated Shaw into their clan-based society and culture, community networks, and belief systems. Accused of insubordination and "inebriety," Shaw's advocacy of Cherokee rights against the federal government's interests may have been the real cause of his dismissal.[78] We can instantly see an example of how marrying and establishing a family across colonizing boundaries led to a shift in allegiance. Was he fired because he was putting his new family and their nation first? Or, as a paid agent of colonization, had he been so absorbed into Cherokee society that he was neglecting his duties? These Indian agents, sent by the War Department to Cherokee lands to conciliate and control frontier relations, frequently married Cherokee women. The federal "Indian" agent Col. Return J. Meigs, a veteran of the Revolutionary War who was born in Middletown, Connecticut, married a Cherokee woman. The couple had children together, and Meigs, who was sixty-one years old upon his arrival in 1801, remained in the post until his death in 1823.[79]

Nonetheless, when Meigs advocated intermarriage of white men and Indian women, the Cherokee chiefs wholeheartedly protested. In 1808, this is how Meigs responded: "You said I encouraged marriages between white men & Cherokee women. I always have and shall do it because your women are industrious & because I conceive that by this measure civilization is farther advanced than in any other way having always considered the whole human race as brothers."[80] In other words, Meigs viewed Cherokee women as good wives and as "civilizers" who would civilize not only their offspring, but the wider frontier society. The Cherokee chiefs thought his assimilative thinking unjust. Cherokee women were not simply a resource put there to keep white frontiersmen from being lonely and lacking domestic comfort. Or a third-column strategy for assimilation. There was no parity for Cherokee men, and less discussion of marrying a white woman in a reciprocal "civilizing" exchange.

Several Methodist missionary men and their sons had married Cherokee women, who were highly praised as wonderful women and wives. Despite opposition from her uncle John Ross, the president of the Cherokee Committee, Mary Coody married a white man.[81] Meigs's grandchildren also married into the Ross family. During the earlier phase of trading relationships, when only a handful of white men were present, Cherokee men were in a much better position to control the marriages and to use them to their advantage.

AFRICANS AND SLAVES

There was nothing very godly about the behavior of white frontiersmen. The Cherokees feared losing control over their women, families, and nation. Separatist narratives in regard to the "red man" — and their objective that the Cherokees should not be fused culturally or biologically with the "whites" — had popular appeal in their communities. Ideas of blood and Cherokee identity and rights were at stake. Increasingly, the Cherokee Nation expressed its determination to exclude slaves and ex-slaves or "blacks" from Cherokee citizenship.

Their leaders were concerned about including people who lacked sovereignty and/or equal status in the prevailing American republic. Since the 1810s, several American states had been weakening the citizenship rights of "free negroes," as they were then called. The Cherokee already had their own entrenched system of keeping and working slaves, who had originally been captives of war adopted into clans. They could be from other tribes or be white children, men, or women. However, by the early nineteenth century the slaves held by the Cherokees were mostly of African origin. Slavery became associated with blackness. In 1809 the Cherokees held 583 slaves; in 1827, 1,038; and by 1835 there were 1,592 African American slaves living in Cherokee territory.[82] Although the most common form of union was between male Cherokee masters and female slaves, the Cherokee Nation prohibited intermarriages with blacks of either sex. Cherokee women also held slaves. For example, the Beloved Woman Nan-ye-hi (1738–1824), a warrior also known as Wild Rose and Nancy Ward, was one such slave owner. She remains a heroine today due to her outstanding leadership in fighting for Cherokee independence. In later years she married a white man, Bryan Ward.[83]

The Cherokee Committee feared that social intermixing with "blacks" could damage their status in the eyes of neighboring states. The acknowledgment of sexual intimacy between slave and master — especially its public performance through marriage — was prohibited by many American states, including their neighbors. They appreciated how southern prosperity and private wealth were premised upon the world of slave and master — a hierarchical and publicly segregated racialized space. Nonetheless, the Cherokees were not simply following Euro-American race policies. They were making choices and setting policies for their nation. Responding to both external influences and internal factors such as Cherokee race concepts and their goal to protect Cherokee "blood," the Cherokee Nation adopted self-serving notions of inferiority around the category of blackness. Selu narratives were also used to justify black servitude and inferiority.[84]

With a few exceptions, from the 1810s the Cherokee Nation increasingly excluded "negroes" from citizenship.[85] After passage of the new marriage laws in 1819, intermarrying with slaves was prohibited altogether. From 1824, punishment for any male marrying a "negro slave" would be fifty-nine "stripes on the bare back," while an Indian or white woman would receive twenty-five stripes.[86]

The Cherokee Nation was participating in a wider global system of slavery that had been adapted in particular ways in the United States and was most entrenched in its southern plantation states. Originally torn from their African homelands or halfway stops, slaves were at the disposal of and subject to relocation by their sellers, and then their American and Cherokee owners. American property laws meant slaves had no legal rights, including rights to own property and even to enjoy a family. Indeed, their children were for sale. As property, slaves were very valuable — often an owner's most saleable asset. In spite of laws that denied their humanity, slaves maintained whatever integrity and autonomy they could. Between legal owner and slave, bonds of mutual dependence and patronage sometimes became complex emotional ones. Although property interests repeatedly and tragically outweighed slaveholder bonds of affection, of course they were human relationships too, and as Annette Gordon-Reed's study of Jefferson makes loud and clear, they became far more entwined and intrafamilial than any legal contract might suggest.[87]

For wealthy Cherokees, relationships between master and slave drew upon contemporary western notions of capital and former Cherokee practices of slavery associated with warfare. Wealthier Cherokee men such as John Ross, James Vann, and their families became major clients of the African American slave trade and kept numerous slaves, whose labor built their plantation, transport, and domestic enterprises. As household arrangements between slave and nonslave had tended to be comparatively fluid, the Cherokee situation differed from that of their Anglo-American southern neighbors. Significantly, the open acknowledgment of some marital-style unions between Cherokee men and slaves disturbed the hierarchies of the South, where slavery was understood as an irrevocable category of servitude. Slaves might belong to the white family, but they were not the family as such. At times, to their northern advocates, Cherokee ideas about color, slavery, and justice appeared incongruous. Cherokee leaders and white northerners alike admired outstanding statesmen like Washington, Jefferson, and Madison, and it was no secret that they had built their comfortable, cultured lifestyles and even their notions of a good republic upon the backs of slaves. Indeed, their slaves served political delegations of the Cherokees at table.

When in Cherokee country, white missionaries from northern abolitionist churches also succumbed to the temptation of requesting—and receiving—slaves to ease their household burdens. Despite their abolitionist beliefs, Cornwall residents, including Harriett Gold's Christian community, were impressed by the arrival in their town of the Cherokee Major Ridge in his luxurious coach. This rocked the race stereotypes about Indians held by so many New Englanders in the early nineteenth century. Ridge's wealth, contingent upon owning at least fifty slaves, was considered tangible proof of Cherokee advancement and "civilization."[88]

In most states of the United States, race-based intermarriage bans were associated with fears of losing rights to property in the slaves and in their offspring, which, under U.S. law, came under the master's legal entitlements. For example, if a free white woman paired with an African American slave, would the children remain slaves? However lowly their class or living standards, in the early republic white women were ideologically differentiated

FIG. 38. Rose Cottage, the Park Hill home of Chief John Ross at Rose Hill, Oklahoma, shows the chief's large household, which included numerous slaves, including children, responsible for different household and outside activities. The grand portico of the classically designed two-story home displays its domestic staff and the slave families required for its maintenance. A group of people standing between the columns appear to be attired in the uniforms of domestic staff, whereas the people in the front may be outside staff or people who attend to the coaches and horses. Their long sticks suggest they may work with horses. The formality of the image makes me wonder if it could have been taken on the occasion of a funeral. Many of the workers appear to be African American and were probably owned by John Ross. Sadly, the young children are already primed for service and endowed with a property status as slaves. The home was destroyed during the Civil War. Courtesy Oklahoma Historical Society.

from slaves. The possibility that white mothers would bear dark-skinned children — and, shamefully, children with slave status — created fissures in a color-based system — ones too confronting for the settler classes to tolerate.[89]

For southern whites, the subordination of African Americans became a contingency of civilization — a system understood by those around them as advanced, and facilitating further advancement. In turn, under the "colonizing compact" with the founders of the Great Republic, the Cherokees understood outward conformity to its protocols to be a condition of continuing Cherokee autonomy.

The Cherokees knew that intermixing with blacks still went on among their people. This explains John Ridge's apologetic tone in his 1826 account of the "state of Cherokee civilisation." He wrote, "There are a few instances of African Mixture with Cherokee blood & wherever it is seen is considered in the light of misfortune & disgrace." Paradoxically, racism against "negroes" could be used as proof of the Cherokees' superior standards of civilization; it could thus secure a promise that their own "blood" or race "superiority" would be upheld. In order to prove the Cherokees' cultural conformity with white Americans, Ridge explained their modern slaveholding customs: "The African Slaves are mostly held by half breeds & fullblooded Indians of distinguished talents.... Servants attend to their meals & the same rules and etiquette is observed at table as in the first families of the whites."[90] Indeed, he had been inside the homes of some of "the first families." Despite such declarations of conformance with southern hierarchies, de facto partnerships and marriages between Cherokees and slaves continued. Although intermarriage was banned from 1824, the Cherokee Council occasionally awarded full citizenship to children of Cherokee men who married slaves.[91] This was the ruling in the case of Tahseekeyarkey or Shoeboots, although it was conditional: he was no longer to live with his African American slave or have any more children with her. Nonetheless, Cherokee legal definitions and regulations were more flexible than those of their white neighbors. Slaves continued to be adopted into clans, entitling them to citizenship status and rights to land.

The public orations of Ridge and Boudinot during the 1820s already underplayed the extent of black-Indian intermarriage, and over the ensuing decades the Cherokee Nation rigidified its laws regarding blacks and slaves. The *Cherokee Phoenix* advertised sightings of escaped slaves within their nation; this gained not only revenue but also a modicum of goodwill from neighboring states. In particular, the Cherokees hoped their conformity would nullify accusations that their nation destabilized the southern institution of slavery. After all, this was one of the powerful arguments promulgated by proponents of the Cherokees' removal west.

The Cherokee Nation was searching for some common ground with their neighbors. In competing performances of race-based sovereignty with the United States, Georgia, and nearby states, race demarcation from others was a strategy for defining the Cherokee polity. Lessons in the classics even supported their position, for the ancient Greeks of Socrates's time had founded democracy from a slave society.

Preventing intermixture would enable the Cherokee Nation to argue for a distinctive polity based upon common Cherokee "blood," or race. Whereas intermixture with whites might lead to a wider union of common "blood," they had to be vigilant about prioritizing the common good or "common wealth" of the Cherokee Nation. In the contemporary economic and political milieu, intermixture with blacks offered no political or economic advantage. But what of segregating whites?

SEGREGATING WHITES

After the Cherokee Socrates's intervention, we have seen that a broader set of regulations was enacted around intermarriage and access to Cherokee citizenship.[92] One of the Cherokees' main goals was to keep *whites* out of their nation. In October 1829 the Cherokee Committee and Council tightened access to citizenship by suspending the right of Cherokee citizens to give permits to noncitizens. Without permits, even white men with crucial skills, such as mechanics, blacksmiths, ferrymen, or turnpike keepers, could not be readily employed. With the exception of schoolmasters, all families of white workers were prohibited from actually residing in Cherokee territory. A series of additional laws curbed the rights of intermarried whites further. For example, noncitizens who had married Cherokees and were widowed lost all rights of citizenship, unless the couple had children. Such widows or widowers would remain citizens of the Cherokee Nation only as long "as they shall remain single or shall marry any other citizen of the nation again." If they married a white person, they "shall be considered intruders upon the soil of the Nation, and be liable to expulsion and removal from the nation."[93] The new restrictions inadvertently created a marriage incentive, as formal marriage to a Cherokee citizen was a pathway that entitled outsiders to residency and citizenship.

Although directed at white men, the intermarriage laws significantly affected Cherokee women. Socrates had criticized Cherokee women's poor marital choices. During the 1820s and 1830s, Cherokee women held rights unthinkable for contemporary white women, playing key roles in political affairs. Before marriage, a young woman could enter into various sexual relationships without being obliged to marry. The woman's relatives had to approve and help with marriage arrangements, after which the new wife continued to live with her relatives. The groom moved to the wife's farm or her village, into one of the family group houses, amid an arrangement of seasonal dwellings, corncribs, menstrual huts, and storage sheds.[94] Usually a woman had various male partners over the course of her life, with marriage not anticipated as lifelong. Indeed, the *Phoenix* found the constraints of Euro-American marriage amusing. It featured a humorous story from a Philadelphia editor who had invented a contraption, with the attached message "marriage is like a mouse-trap, easy to get in, but hard to escape."[95] It was much harder for American wives. The Cherokee wife could choose to leave her husband or divorce him without recriminations.

Despite the nation's stated aim to protect Cherokee women's rights, by the 1820s its marital policy and practices were changing rapidly in the men's favor. From 1808, some of the wealthier Cherokee families adopted patrilineal inheritance, a European system that eroded not only Cherokee women's economic power and status but also the matrilineal clan system itself.[96] It drew them into a system closer to the Euro-American gender system of private landownership and male hegemony.

For Cherokee women, European-style progress and civilization may not have looked so attractive. Modeled on the U.S. example, the new Cherokee Constitution excluded women from the vote and from being on the key Council and Committee, which meant they could not be politicians. Senior Cherokee women had traveled to Washington during the 1790s and early 1800s in order to represent their people to the male political leaders of the United States. However, the American government leaders and representatives addressed only the Indian men, with the women present being included only as "wives and daughters."[97] Cherokee delegations subsequently became exclusively male. From the 1820s, Cherokee women's traditional power bases, including farming, politics, and warfare, were being relinquished for roles confined to the domestic or the home. White American missionary wives encouraged Cherokee women like Catharine Brown, who was from an elite family, to follow a celibate, self-denying, and humble "path of duty" — not to seek high rank, material wealth, or adornment.[98] Aside from the respective female and male virtues promoted by missionaries, on the male-led Cherokee Council only men could vote and hold official position. While women could exercise clout behind the scenes and through male representatives, the new constitution was a very public statement of their loss of formal economic and political clout.

Intermarriage laws played out in intrinsically gendered ways.[99] Cherokee women ensured that even under a Christian-style marital contract, the Cherokee wife should not be subjected to the same disadvantages as her Anglo-American counterpart. Unlike American women in the United States, if they married a noncitizen, intermarried Cherokee women did not lose their citizenship rights. If they lived outside the nation, however, they came under U.S. law and would be subsumed under the laws of coverture, and thus under their husband's citizenship and rights to own property.[100]

Senior women's influence on the Cherokee Council and Committee ensured that women's property rights were protected. While women in the United States lost substantive property rights upon marriage, in 1819 the Cherokee Council ruled, "That any white man who shall marry a Cherokee woman, the property of the woman *so marry*, shall not be subject to the disposal of her husband, contrary to her consent."[101] Recognizing this as a matter of national interest, the council sought to protect Cherokee women's traditional power base in property ownership. The Cherokee Committee thus introduced the Tenth Law of the nation to "protect the Orphan and Widow to the father's or husband's property after death."[102] In 1826 Ridge boasted of this as a fair, equitable, and superior system: "The laws of our Nation from time immemorial recognizes [sic] a separate property in the wife and husband, and this principle is universally cherished among the less informed Class and in fact in every grade of intelligence. If they are so disposed, the law secures to the Ladies, the control of their own property."[103] The introduction of Christian marriage and European expectations of patrilineal inheritance had already destabilized women's rights. In 1829 another law was thus passed to further codify the matter of tradition for all Cherokee women, not just those who intermarried. "*Whereas*, It has long been an established custom in this Nation and admitted by the courts of law, yet never committed to writing, that the property of Cherokee women after their marriage cannot be disposed of by their husbands." Any disposal was a matter of "her will and consent."[104] Strategic Cherokee use of Vattel's concept of "time immemorial" allied women's property rights to a key platform of Indigenous sovereignty — rights based upon long historical occupation, ancestral connections, and the assertion of their own legal system.

The Cherokees were selective — contesting, rejecting, and adopting elements of dissonant legal and belief systems. Themes of exile, migration, and reunions with lost tribes echoed with colonizers and dispossessed alike. Aware of the new Christian calendar that marked and measured time, the Cherokees understood their present-day world via a selection of Christian ontologies and other historical narratives that drew upon multiple sacred histories.[105] Certain Cherokees drew upon notions of the history of human and the earth as a relatively recent, short span of time. Some Cherokees looked to the belief promoted by Elias Boudinot IV and the American Bible Society that they originated as one of the lost tribes of Israel.[106] Some reinterpreted the stories of Noah and other Old Testament figures, repositioning them into a familiar Cherokee landscape and moral world intricately connected with their own sacred explanatory frameworks.

With modern sovereignty based upon a written constitution and in the hands of the people, the relative powers of the United States and of individual states were undergoing a major test. The federal ruling of domestic dependent national status for the Cherokee Nation did little to clarify its relations with the new republic of the United States. Slavery, a formative institution in the polity of the United States and also integral to the Cherokee Nation, was legally a *domestic* relationship. Although the slave was primarily under the authority of the owner rather than the governing state, states regulated slavery and could delimit the power of the owner. Capital accumulation via plantation economies facilitated, allowed, and created a strong impetus for the Cherokees to protect property along the patrilineal lines of the American republic. In *A Vindication of the Rights of Woman*, Mary Wollstonecraft analyzed how prescribed roles for women as subordinate to men, along with their lack of access to education, made them "abject slaves."[107] As Nancy Cott has pointed out, the two "domestic relations" shared "structural and legal similarities."[108] Marriage was the ultimate domestic institution, crucial to the reproduction of the nation-building state and its gendered, family, and race-tinged socioeconomic order.[109]

Both the United States and the Cherokee Nation agreed that the domestic institution of marriage was a precondition for an orderly state under the new regimes. Both agreed with the goal of civilization. However, where exactly this left women was unclear. In America, Europe, and the Cherokee Nation alike, women writers and activists were constantly challenging the form and practice of marriage and the state.[110] Regulated forms of marriage had complex legal and religious histories. The English term "sovereignty" is used in the King James Bible, where Genesis explicitly refers to man's sovereignty over woman as wife, and over slaves.[111]

In Britain, America, and transnationally, female and male intellectuals were contesting the implicit gender roles of marriage. Around 1815, the English romantic poet Percy Bysshe Shelley drew upon the Greek classics to reflect on the meaning of love and the institution of marriage.[112] Absorbed at the time by his English translation of Plato on Socrates, Shelley became preoccupied with thinking through issues of sexuality, beauty, and the meaning of love. His romance with Mary Godwin, daughter of the protofeminist author Mary Wollstonecraft, made him well aware of these gender politics. In one of Shelley's essays, he argued that marriage corrupted love because it arose out of a desire "in rude ages and in rude countries" to make women the "property of men" who wished to "retain undisturbed possession" of them in the same manner as "beasts." He concluded that fears about the insecurity of ownership of other kinds of property were thus behind the "spirit of marriage."[113] That the Cherokees were imposing western property models that led to a loss of female entitlements was outside the gamut of his thinking. However, the world of the European romantics was closer than we might think.

In 1828, the same year Socrates's "Intermarriages" appeared, the *Cherokee Phoenix* published views on the American Indians by the author and historian Washington Irving. He had been a member of the continental circle of romantics that included Shelley and Byron.[114] So too was the famous actor, writer, and lyricist John Howard Payne. Around 1824, the year of Cornwall's Ridge-Northrup wedding, Payne fell madly in love with Mary Wollstonecraft Godwin, the author of *Frankenstein* and widow of the poet

Percy Bysshe Shelley. Mary only had eyes for Washington Irving, and John Payne took it hard. Percy and Mary Shelley and Byron became inspired by the legend of Prometheus, who suffered a torturous fate after he stole fire.

Elias Boudinot adopted not only the name of the New Jersey federationist but also the creature adorning his grand mirror. On the Great Seal committees, Elias IV had campaigned to have the phoenix as the main feature on the U.S. national crest. Although the new republic decided upon the bald eagle, Congress's Third Seal Committee, of which Boudinot IV was a member, retained the upward wings used to depict the phoenix rising again. With its choice of a native bird, the new republic of the United States was attempting to nativize or Indigenize its iconography. The Cherokees had no need to prove their Indigeneity, opting instead for an archetypal myth from Greece.[115] With the flames of its destruction clearly depicted, that wondrous creature — the sign of hope and renewal rising above the flames of a burnt earth — now bedecked the masthead of the *Cherokee Phoenix*.[116]

Once John Howard Payne returned to America, he wanted to learn not Greek mythologies but the traditional stories of the Cherokees and other Native Americans. Perhaps he wanted to deploy them to create nationalist narratives. From 1835, Payne worked with John Ross and Cherokee elders to assist with their political advocacy and to collect their histories and legends.[117] He wrote and published on the Cherokees' matrilineal marriage traditions. In order to underline the matrilineal dynamics upon which Cherokee marriages were premised, Payne described the significance of the Cherokee groom being stripped and then dressed in fresh clothing by the bride's kin.[118]

The Cherokees excelled at establishing high-profile literary networks and engaging in transnational conversations. In March 1828 the *Cherokee Phoenix* published a three-part article by none other than Washington Irving about how the "unfortunate aborigines of this country" had been "doubly wronged by the white man." After being driven away by the invaders' sword, they were "darkly slandered by the pen of the historian."[119] With Cherokee self-generated performances of story and history going strong, their leaders enticed talented writers like John Howard Payne to agree to document and write a balanced account of their history. Similarly, women leaders such as Nancy Ward and Peggy Vann Cruthchield attracted talented white feminist authors like Catharine Beecher and Lydia Howard Huntley Sigourney to their sides in support of antiremoval campaigns.[120] With great effect, the Cherokees cultivated their relations with iconic transnational figures of contemporary intellectual and literary movements.

MARRIAGE NOTICES: THE *CHEROKEE PHOENIX*

When Albert Gallatin, formerly of Thomas Jefferson's cabinet, asked the young John Ridge to report on the state of Cherokee civilization, Ridge used the opportunity to promote their progress.[121] As a key measure of Cherokee advancement and of women's elevation, he singled out the institution of marriage. Aiming to impress a skeptical audience, he stressed Cherokee modernity and that the women were not slaves or beasts of burden. As proof of their "advancement" and of the triumph of civilization over savagery, Ridge explained that "the better class of females prefer to be united in Marriage attended by the solemnities of the Christian mode."[122] Despite Gallatin's invitation coming during the height of the Boudinot controversy, Ridge's report offers the controlled voice of the participant-observer who bridged cultures. Ruminating over the supposed contrasts of primitive and civilized, he drew on his Calvinist training at the Foreign Mission School, which had taught him that historical "progress" was a one-way street. Or at least that is the way he articulated Cherokee modernity.[123] In the same speech, Ridge valued distinctive aspects of Cherokee society, emphasizing their reliance upon the spirit of natural law or common sense. Outlining the Cherokee legal system, in order of priority, he listed the intercourse laws designed to secure peace on the frontier, then, secondly, those prohibiting whites from introducing "ardent spirits," and thirdly those "regulating intermarriages with the whites, which makes it necessary for a white man to obtain a license and be married by the Gospel minister, or some authorized person." Next came murder and theft, followed by penalties for Cherokees who did not obtain permission to introduce whites to the nation and to rent them land.[124]

The Cherokees banked on demonstrating their progress to the outside world. Bilingual and parading the Cherokees' own written language, the *Cherokee Phoenix* valorized modernity as a means of propelling their vision of a unified, civilized Cherokee people. Stories that made the Cherokees appear "backward" or nonprogressive were unlikely to appear in this paper. The traditional, Selu- oriented wedding had been similarly modernized, being officiated with reference to the centralized powers of their new national constitution. Yet, although Cherokee-style marriage ceremonies remained far more popular than Christian ceremonies between the 1810s and 1830s, the *Cherokee Phoenix* was more inclined to report Christian-style weddings than traditional ones. Although probably less than 10 percent of the population was Christian, western-style nuptials associated approved pairings with authorized, formal ceremonies.

In 1828 the *Phoenix* described a Methodist wedding near New Echota. The Cherokee bride wore a gown of "white cambric," a plainly woven fabric with a glossy finish, and the Cherokee groom a "clean northern domestic suit." While we lack an image, this was probably a high-collared white shirt, shiny cravat, and buttoned vest, framed by a long, dark coat and trousers.[125] The couple's well-costumed performance in the latest European fashion intersected with ideas of orderly, patriarchal governance. Indeed, the *Cherokee Phoenix* portrayed western-style marriage as elevating—as part of "the march of civilisation."[126] To citizens of the new republic of the United States, such weddings constituted tangible proof of advancement and enlightenment. They represented embodied performances of individual modernity and, more generally, of a social transformation from savagery. For the matrilineal Cherokees, however, the Christian ceremony embodied a reordering of gendered and epistemological power.

Yet neither a civil nor a Christian ceremony transformed the learned cultural behavior of bride or groom. Historian Kat Ellinghaus has analyzed how some white women of the late nineteenth century took up marriage to Indigenous men as an assimilative strategy. However, these earlier marriages of white men and Cherokee women might also be seen as an assimilation strategy in the other direction.[127] Could it be, therefore, that Cherokee women assimilated white men into conforming to the expectations of Cherokee husbands and fathers? Cherokee mothers inculcated Cherokee values into the minds and hearts of their mixed-descent children, who were considered full Cherokees in clan and spirit. Mothers instilled knowledge of and pride in women's clan and tribal authority and forms of childrearing that did not necessarily complement the colonizing project. Indeed, when given a choice, many mixed-descent children identified culturally as Cherokee and wanted to stay on Cherokee lands.

Despite endorsing the virtues of Cherokee civilization, John Ridge's report did not praise colonialism. Rather, to encapsulate its impact on his people, he drew upon the Judeo-Christian idea of the serpent or Satan. The Cherokee Nation was thus experiencing a state of national emergency caused by a "tide of white population . . . advancing on all sides."[128] Their nation was becoming a theater of hideous crimes of a sexual nature, included the rape and kidnapping of young Cherokee girls and women.[129] Furthermore, since the Cherokees were acquiring destructive vices such as alcoholism, they too would be "crushed in the folds of the encroaching Serpent!"[130]

John Ridge characterized colonizer greed as akin to that of a satanic figure. The rattlesnake was a potent symbol in Cherokee ontology, having quite different meanings. Indeed, the Cherokees' original name, Aniugatena, identifies them as the people of the winged serpent: a powerful fire people or dragon clan whose culture hero had "the head of a snake and wings of a bird."[131] By the early nineteenth century, Cherokee lands, imagined as once a Garden of Eden–like creation place, had been invaded and compromised; like Satan, unruly frontiersmen brought the twin evils of sexual assault and alcohol into the bodies and lands of the Cherokees. The leading historian of the Cherokees, Theda Perdue, came up with the adage "Selu meets Eve." Unfortunately, it does not appear that either managed to formulate an antidote to the serpent of a masculinist, patriarchal colonialism.[132]

With Cherokee leaders arguing over the best strategies to grapple with colonialism, and thereby to maintain their sovereignty, the initiative to introduce marriage restrictions for outsiders found some common ground. Across the Cherokees' cultural, ideological, and factional chasms, here was a degree of consensus. Deep political rifts were growing between those who wished to retain traditional lifestyles and those who favored western education, printing presses, and centralized corn mills. The modernizers armed themselves with knowledge of the U.S. legal system, bilingual literacy, and influential Anglo-American friends. Additionally, social differences based upon wealth, education, clan status, gender, age, lifestyle, and belief had created divisions.

Responding to revelation histories, some Cherokees called for the total expulsion of whites from their land — and even from established family units.[133] Although not banning whites outright as new marital partners, the compromise proposition would weed out the many "evil whites" who refused to conform to either Cherokee or Christian standards of the good husband. The process gathered momentum: in 1839 the Cherokees made stronger laws against amalgamation with blacks and slaves; in 1840 a prosegregation group tried to ban all marriages with whites, only narrowly failing to get this through the Cherokee Council.

SOCRATES AND THE WHITE HUSBANDS

In a blatant contest of authority with the settler colonizers, the Cherokee Nation had decided to exert control over marriage. From the outset of the establishment of their new capital, New Town/New Echota, the Cherokees identified intermarriage as a high-priority national issue. Indeed, after they established a new centralized structure of governance, the regulation on intermarriage was one of the earliest laws introduced. Such a national system would be more comprehensible to the whites.[134]

Socrates offered practical solutions to the Cherokees' white problem. His March 1828 "Intermarriages" explicitly connected control of intermarriage with citizenship rights and with the national security of the Cherokee Nation.[135] He deployed contemporary political theory to justify what were radical recommendations from an Indigenous nation. And he recognized the need to exercise sovereignty through enacting written, printed laws. As authorized by its constitution, he argued that the Cherokee Nation should use the same imperial technique of jurisprudence that the colonizers exerted globally over Indigenous peoples. Negotiating and redefining Cherokee gender roles and marriage formats was a way of negotiating both colonialism and the gendered social and political aspects of modernity. Despite ongoing female influence, the male leaders now placed their signatures — or, if not literate, their marks — on the new national laws.[136]

A brazen means of legislating white *men's* sexuality, Cherokee intermarriage laws were a noticeable intervention in the processes of Euro-American colonialism.[137] At the same time, the Cherokee lawmakers did not see the need to restrict white women from marrying Cherokee men. As only Cherokee women owned land and held it in their families, this did not jeopardize land ownership. Rather than being presented as antiwhite race exclusionism that might offend, the new law was cleverly dressed up as a form of internal civil order. In reality, empowering themselves to decide upon a white man's moral, husbandly, and economic worthiness, Cherokee officers grabbed the moral high ground and turned the tables. The law allowed them the power to judge the good husbands. Yet laws that curbed the sexual and marital freedoms of colonizer men provided the Georgia legislature with an infuriating reminder of the Cherokee Nation's power to govern themselves and others.[138]

The laws targeted intermarriage as one of the forms of mixing with whites with the greatest impact. Although relatively moderate, these laws were therefore a step toward placating the extreme Cherokee segregationists in an intense internal political scene. Consequently, antiwhite intermarriage laws assisted greater national unity among the Cherokees envisaging the national future.

Unlike the marriage restrictions of other states, Cherokee intermarriage and property-control laws were designed to protect their people and their territories against colonialism's cataclysmic impact. Through jurisprudence in the gendered realm of marriage, the Cherokees designed and implemented laws that asserted their sovereignty over lands and people. Hence they reasserted a degree of control not only over land and property but also over domestic sovereignty, family constitution, and reproduction.

Socrates, the Intellectual, and the State

Some Cherokees believed in a higher, godlike sovereignty or authority expressed via Selu, land, and their ancestors, while others rejected this because of its associations with primitive people following the law of nature rather than the precepts of a republican-style constitution.[139] Combining new and old forms of gendered sovereignty and cultural power, the Cherokee Nation thus guarded its social norms, governance, philosophy, religion, and marital practices. Under the old gender regime, Cherokee matriarchs held the power. Intermarried white women gained very few entitlements, being outside that system. Indeed, if widowed, a situation that confronted Sarah

Northrup Ridge in later years, they and their children faced dire straits and had to plead for charity.

With their own alphabet or syllabary and newspaper, the Cherokees easily worked across literate and oral traditions in two languages. In written laws, the nation attempted to single out one of the most socially constitutive and potentially destructive forms of encroachment. Not only were they threatening to beat the colonizers at their own legal games, their modernizing successes made it harder to destroy their nation without leaving a telltale paper trail.

Opposition to intermarriage was based upon shoring up property and sovereignty and building a homogenous national identity. Cherokee sovereignty was contingent not only upon symbolic acts but upon residence or occupation. As the Cherokees could not risk being outnumbered in their own territories, the 1828 marriage-permit system provided a means of preventing white men from occupying or using Cherokee land.[140] As well as promising to create social order, restricting marriage further excluded white men from entering and freely living on Cherokee territory. Potentially, the permit initiative closed the borders. Calling the shots over residency, citizenship, and other benefits therefore became a key strategy through which to protect their nation.

The new law represented a race-based *immigration restriction act* specifically aimed at preventing the permanent occupation of white male colonizers and potential husbands in the Cherokee Nation. In 1829 the principal chief was also looking into various ways to remove "citizens of the United States out of the nation."[141] A form of territorial border control based upon intimate unions, Cherokee intermarriage laws thus amounted to a kind of nonmilitary, morally based "border control" through which the Cherokees battled transnational immigrations. By introducing a covert, race-based immigration restriction act through marriage law, the Cherokees hoped to protect sovereignty from colonizing impositions.

Cherokee restrictions on intermarriages with African Americans drew the black-red color line even more rigidly. Anti-intermarriage laws restricted blacks purely on the basis of color lines, whereas for white men, assessments of their capital, character, and behavior by appointed clerks were also factored in. In a novel move against colonizers, the Cherokees were now policing the "global color line" along an Indigenous values meridian.[142]

FIG. 39. Sequoyah, the inventor of the Cherokee alphabet. "Se-Quo-Yah / R.T.; drawn, printed & coloured at I.T. Bowen's Lithographic Establishment, No. 94 Walnut St." Courtesy Library of Congress, reproduction no. LC-USZC4-4815.

Border control became a self-protective strategy that policed not just geographical boundaries but marital, civil, and status boundaries as well.[143] In various ways, intermarriage restrictions addressed multiple ideological and political agendas. With the power to approve the moral underpinnings of formal marriage, female subordination, and good husbandly behavior, the Cherokees imagined that a kind of civilization barometer might police the borders of their state. On paper, that is. Unfortunately, the Cherokee Nation did not have any adequate form of policing or guards to enable them to ensure policy implementation. Additional strategies had to be found.

The Cherokee Elias Boudinot and other men who had intermarried insisted that they shared the same patriotic goals and dilemmas as other Americans. They started to argue for a more portable form of sovereignty. Boudinot chose intellectual and political arguments that gave primacy to feelings and emotion. Defining patriotism as "love of country" and "love of people," he worried that being "attached *to*" their country could lead to their coming under "the dominion of the oppressor," in which case they would face "a *moral death*." If his decision to be removed west was wrong, he argued that it was "an error of *judgment*, not of the *heart*."[144]

Transatlantic intellectual influences and transnational webs of friendship shaped the Cherokees' sovereignty campaigns. New cultural narratives were required to justify and explain the new laws, forming a bridge between the Cherokee and white nations. The transatlantic revival of the classical pedagogy of Greek philosophy, with its debates about the relationship between individual and state, preempted and converged with the contemporary culture of sensibility and the more individualistic, sentient, and sentimental musings of the romantic age.[145]

Like the original Socrates, the Cherokee people adopted a questioning and creative approach to tackling colonialism, Christianity, law, and governance. In Socrates's evocation of Diotama contained in the Shelley-translated *Symposium*, the sovereign people themselves became *the composer*.[146] Socrates was interested in conversation, dialogue, and finding satisfying explanations for the world in which he lived. He reflected on the relationship between knowing, memory, and writing.[147] Selu also provided explanatory frameworks of a different kind, embedding in the Cherokee landscapes her stories of how the present came to be. We hear that Socrates, who was interested in myth and the power of myth, lay down by a river to think and perhaps to talk. Between the 1810s and 1830s, many Cherokee people also lived beside the fast-flowing streams. In an even faster-moving history, Selu, Satan, and Socrates engaged in unpredictable conversations. Our encounter with the Cherokee Socrates finds a clever man who had become deeply disillusioned with colonizer promises. As he wrote, "After being tantalized with the hypocritical language of friendship and offers of Civilization and Religion," the Cherokees had "their rights and liberties crushed in the cold embrace of Iron power."[148]

Given the Cherokees' powerful educational, literacy, and other achievements, it seems apt that a Cherokee man invented not only an Indigenous phonetic system but a new Socrates who would enter the present days between 1828 and 1830. Drawing upon the intellectual fashion of neoclassicism, the Cherokee Socrates engaged with the subject of marriage, ruminating over intermarriage's problematic relationship with the state. When Socrates became Cherokee, he thus became a clever player in a crucial moment of modern sovereignty. As a political strategist and as a cultural deep-time expert, this Socrates reflected upon a longer history of human mutability. He delved into philosophy and ideas around the body politic and, like his namesake, into the meaning of love.

In turn, Cherokee thinkers recognized the gendered political dynamics around the control of intermarriage, citizenship, blood, and the sovereignty of their nation. During the early national period of the Cherokee Nation, their male leaders and thinkers would increasingly assert jurisdiction, in written law, over the supposedly *domestic*, intimate realm of marriage. In their eyes, intermixture with white men and black men would dilute their sovereignty over land and women. Through unsupervised, uncontrolled intermarriage, outsiders could take away Cherokee women, children, and land. Understanding this as a key factor that would shape their nation in the present and future, they adopted a more rigid race hierarchy. Later they would measure blood in a different way. In the meantime, rules on who should marry whom applied only to Cherokee women, not men, who were free to marry whomever they liked, as long as she was not "negro."

By 1831 the Cherokee had taken their wider sovereignty complaints to the courts, first litigating against the state of Georgia. When Elias Boudinot heard of Judge Marshall's decision that the Cherokee Nation held the judicial status of a nation, he had exclaimed, "Glorious News!"[149] It had little impact on Georgia. The state made no pretensions of cross-border diplomacy, continuing to create sufficient disorder to push as many Cherokee people off their land as it possibly could. Much would depend on the political judgment of the president of the United States and whether he would honor this court ruling. In the context of an acquisitive, expansive colonizer state, outcomes would depend upon the relative military strength and political determination of neighboring states.[150] Backing a removal policy, under Andrew Jackson's presidency the federal government refused to assist the Cherokees. Jackson had no interest in being classed with the derogatory title of "Indian lover." With an eye to gaining land through casual sex and informal or unscrupulous intermarriages, white men's swamping of the Cherokee Nation numerically and reproductively worked in Georgia's favor.[151] State authorities were relentless; the lion — or the serpent — did not sleep.

Despite being confronted by anti-Indian prejudice, it was crucial for Cherokee leaders to muster support from and conduct diplomatic relations with their New England allies. To what extent the Cherokee Nation could use control of intermarriage to "have and hold" on to sovereignty was uncertain. Whether Cherokee individuals would decide to remain separate from or integrate into the kin and blood networks of white Americans was another matter. The Cherokee Nation may have ruled that Cherokee *women* would be restricted from marrying into the kin networks of whites, but this did not apply to the Cherokee men now taking over the reins.

CHAPTER FOUR

John Ross and Mary Bryan Stapler

COURTSHIP

In his words, Chief John Ross, the Cherokee Nation's principal chief from 1828, had "warmly opposed" intermarriage between Cherokee citizens and outsiders. Before 1820, he prevented two sets of marriages in his family. In particular, Ross had objected to intermarriages of "adult white women without clan ties to Cherokee men."[1] Many Cherokee women publicly voiced their objections to marriages between Cherokee men and white women. Nonetheless, as one Cherokee memorial phrased it, there had been a "long and intimate connexion" between the Cherokees and their "American neighbours" — one evident in John Ross's own ancestry.[2] According to the missionary Ann Paine, John finally consented to a request from a third family member to intermarry only "because he believed opposition would do no good."[3]

Since both Elias Boudinot and John Ridge, the men instrumental in the breakaway Treaty of New Echota of 1835–36, had married white wives, John Ross and the majority of Cherokees had additional reasons to be skeptical. Many thought these women led their husbands to place too much trust in whites, leading to political treachery. Already, given his light skin color, education, family businesses, and wealth, John Ross risked being seen as too "white." So why, after his Cherokee wife's death, did he go looking for and choose a white woman for a wife? In an already unstable polity, why would he change his stance in ways that could risk his chiefly position? His fellow Cherokee citizens were likely to see such an intimate union as counter to the national principles that he stood for. Here we follow what he made privately of such a decision. And we consider the repartee between himself and his fiancée, which made much play of community attitudes toward the prospect of her leaving the colonizer side of the frontier.

When John Ross fell in love with Mary Bryan Stapler of Wilmington, New Castle, Delaware, he felt no compulsion to explain his change of heart to his people.[4] She was a young white schoolgirl when they first met in 1841. Historians of the Cherokees have noted Mary and John's relationship, but they have tended to pass over it as a curious, slightly amusing occurrence.[5] In a life spent campaigning to hold on to Cherokee political and cultural autonomy, it does seem an odd contradiction.

Mary and John's first meeting was apparently during his visit to her boarding school at Bethlehem, Pennsylvania.[6] Established in the 1740s, by the 1840s this girls' academy was known for holding high academic standards, having a fine library, and providing an excellent music education. Perhaps Mary and John attended a school social gathering or an associated event organized by a mutual friend. John Ross was about fifty-one years old when they first met. Mary was sixteen.[7] Youthful marriages were not uncommon, but the degree of age difference was. As was marrying the chief of the Cherokees.

Their courtship exchanges provide an invaluable archive that enables close tracking of a story of affect and of romantic love across different boundaries — not so much those of their age difference as the borders of an active and ongoing colonialism. John and Mary's intimate correspondence reveals the mystery of their personal futures entangling. Across national divides, John and Mary's letters reconfigure one corner of the colonizing archives.

From the beginning of their courtship, John Ross was acutely aware of the parallels between negotiating the politics of marriage and negotiating his nation's future. As it follows their correspondence, this chapter sets a slower pace in order for us to experience the connections the couple make between the public negotiations of statecraft and the intimate diplomacy of love.

In the banter of their exchanges, the peculiarly *transnational* character of their interaction and growing relationship keeps bubbling to the surface. In the 1840s the United States was an amalgam not only of states but also of nations — including Indian nations that were desperately struggling with the federal and state governments to retain sovereignty, political integrity, and treaty rights. The Cherokees had "treated" with the founders of the American republic as a foreign nation, their students attended a "foreign mission," and the government department handling their affairs was the Department of War. Although the "domestic dependent nation" status decided in the 1831 Marshall judgment in *Cherokee Nation v. Georgia* partly subsumed the Cherokee Nation under the rules and balances of the federal system, this was not as a state or territory of the United States. In some ways, they were more akin to a sovereign nation than to a state. Through John and Mary's courtship and marriage, we will see how both marital and state contracts could be carefully constructed, proclaimed, and enforced through symbolic acts.

Choosing a name revealed much about identity, about one's life story. As a child, the man best known by the Scottish-English name John Ross used the dual names Tsan Usdi and Little John.[8] He spoke fluent English and had served as a Cherokee interpreter since childhood. We can presume that he was at ease working across languages and cultures, and although he did not write in Cherokee, it is difficult to believe he could have maintained his chiefly status without reasonable Cherokee fluency. He signed off "John" or "Jno Ross" in most of his letters. His Cherokee name, Kooweskoowe, which stood for a rare white bird, was more precious to him.[9] He tended to use this appellation in correspondence with close friends. Mary knew this one from the beginning.[10] Although it would be easy to refer to either, in order to remind us that John's world was constantly on the move, in this chapter I will use both his adult names — John Ross and Kooweskoowe — each empowering in different ways and milieus. Chief John Ross traveled regularly across the United States — across cultures and states and across himself — the diplomatic within and without.

The courtship letters of John Ross and Mary Bryan Stapler enable us to read the gradual, and sometimes rapid, progress of their romance. Revealing a courtship story of increasing emotional intensity, these intimate letters reveal their attempts to speak from the heart. The letters are witness to a growing relationship. Intended only for the other's eyes, they create impressions of sincerity and gauge sentiment. Although the correspondence is extensive, we are missing some of their first letters. In 1842 perhaps there was a standoff between the two, as one letter has a stilted tone, discussing a possible meeting in formal prose. By 1844 things warm up again. Letters of teasing and titillation follow, then ones that start to express more tender emotions. Nervous entreaties test the other's feelings. When rapid reassurances follow, the letters suddenly release their full voices of mutual infatuation. When John writes to Mary, you sense him relaxing, switching off from his other cares and matters of state — liberated to joke, cajole, and make playful comments. His nerves rise only after certain pivotal letters are dispatched. In the waiting lapse, he panics about what Mary will think of that small package of words in her hands.

Mary Bryan Stapler and John Ross's meeting came only a year or two after the federal government had forcibly removed the Cherokees from their land. Elias Boudinot and John Ridge, the two Cherokee graduates of the Foreign Mission School, were the leading signatories to the December 1835 Treaty of New Echota. The implications for the nation could not have been more momentous or more likely to lead to permanent rupture from their land or between their people. Although Boudinot and Ridge had once vigorously fought against the federal government's plan to move them west to the Indian Territory, their hopes were fading. Georgia was stepping up its aggressive destabilization campaigns, without any prospect of being reined back by the federal government under President Andrew Jackson, who held power between 1829 and 1837. What is more, Jackson pushed for the Indian Removal Act, which only narrowly passed Congress in 1830, becoming law the following year. Jackson was determined to force the remaining Indians in the southeast to move west.

Boudinot and Ridge now decided that negotiating a treaty was the only way the Cherokees could gain some compensation and survive as a nation. They garnered support from wealthy plantation owners and some chiefs, but they lacked full national authorization. By the mid-1830s, the state of Georgia was sending out guardsmen to confiscate Cherokee properties and belongings. Homes still occupied by their Cherokee owners were given away in lotteries. Principal Chief John Ross opposed signing any treaty endorsing removal west. On November 7, 1835, the Georgia Guard consequently arrested Ross and the Anglo-American writer John Howard Payne and confiscated the nation's papers, including the substantial collections from the historical and cultural project that the two men were working on together. While they were in jail, federal commissioners negotiated with the Treaty Party.[11] The majority of Cherokee people remained adamant about staying on what remained of their lands.

Because they saw that the key to national strength was in following their own ways, Ross's supporters have been classed as conservatives or traditionalists. Yet they could equally be labeled radicals, for they acted against colonizer domination; they did not trust whites, wanting their people to have much less to do with them and their ways. They backed segregationist policies that excluded whites. The signatories to the Treaty of New Echota, known as the Emigration or Removal Party and later as the Ridge-Boudinot or Treaty Party, have often been labeled progressives. They now considered it impossible to stop Jackson's plans for Indian removal. The Marshall judgment seemed most unlikely to be honored by the current U.S. government. The *Worcester v. Georgia* judgment (1832) had recognized the Cherokee Nation's right to exert a limited form of national sovereignty and autonomy, including the right to make and enforce its own laws. Georgia continued to enforce its laws at the expense of the Cherokees, and its officers had also imprisoned the missionary advocates Samuel Worcester and Elizur Butler.[12] Even some of the Cherokees' key allies were backing away from supporting them.

With no chance of federal intervention curbing Georgia's actions in Cherokee territories, the politics looked increasingly hopeless. Economically, the Cherokees were suffering too, with the federal government not paying their usual annuities. Again, this made their continuance in the East seem a losing cause. Boudinot and Ridge took legal and strategic advice. Under the current presidency and political regime, they were told, the Cherokee situation indeed looked hopeless. Facing the prospect of ongoing warfare and possibly even complete destruction as a people, they opted to sit at the negotiating table to try to strike a reasonable deal before being removed west.[13] But the majority of Cherokees continued to oppose capitulation.[14] Understandably, the Cherokee negotiators had not wanted to be wrenched from their cherished sovereign lands. They were being courageous about it. With migration, they would have to desert their homes and their landscapes

5836

Washington City
June 16th 1844.

My Dear Mary—

If you had not long since found out how timid and irregular a correspondent, I have always been, on soft and bewitching Subjects, I should almost despair of ever receiving forgiveness from you, for so long omitting to return you my acknowledgments, for your very kind favor of the 22d Ult°.— but, relying upon the goodness of your heart, and subscribing to the prevailing sentiment, that "it is better late than never", I have this morning, after returning from Church, concluded, to write and send you these desultory lines—. I have been much interested in the particularity of the information given in your letter, respecting an old friend and acquaintance,— but, as regards my Brother the Col: I must confess, I was not a little astonished to find that you have seen and known so little of him since I last saw you! You seem to think however that he is like a bird of passage, and not to be one of dame Fortune's favorites—. Is it not possible, that, in one of his cheerful flights, he might have lit upon a green spot — where there is an object of attraction, and that his eyes have become so transfixed, by gazing upon the Charming beauty, that, he cannot extricate himself from the lovely sight before him? O! that Cape Cottage—I have had a hint of the place before — Can't you tell me something about it, and of the captivating folks there? yes, I think you can — Will then, do tell me!

You believe there has been no hands given away since my absence — But, as to the hearts that have been disposed of, away you seem unwilling to account for—!

FIG. 40. Letter from John Ross to Mary Stapler, June 16, 1844, pages 1 and 4. Courtesy Oklahoma Historical Society, no. 5836, and Gilcrease Museum, Tulsa OK.

I await your answer —! I am fond of the "friends," and am well pleased to see, that, you have turned to be quite a quaker girl —!!!

I should like to have seen the gravity of your countenance when you were writing your remarks, respecting that, fair Lady, of whom you say, that, "as far as my knowledge extends she is no nearer tying the hym'n' Knot" than when thee saw her"—. and that "there is still a chance for thee," as "I have always thought, that little Cupid had sent forth his darts from her bright eyes into thy heart"—. A chance for me? Prithee, What sort of a chance can you mean? Surely no other than that, of being puzzled into an inextricable dilemma! for, it would really be a funny joke to dream of the heart of one so fair being won by a Sachem of the Western Wilds.— How serious a matter then would it be, to insure that the delicate hand can ever be given to such a personage —! But to cap the climax, how peculiarly romantic would the scenery be were t'a Lady, in all her graceful charms, seated in a circular wigwam, canopyed and carpetted with the soft flexible skins of the buffaloe, and there as might other be, receiving the salutations of the painted and plumed Chieftains and their dark eyed Brunettes, as they come to offer their congratulations to her & the partner of her bosom —. I will not dilate upon the picture, lest you might be horror stricken by its aspect, and be deterred from responding kindly to the question submitted for your decision —.

Very sincerely
Yours with much Esteem,—
Koowes Koowe

of deep cultural and historical significance — places where their elders performed and told ancient stories, on which their ancestors' remains were buried, and which they had a deeply felt duty to protect.[15]

In the meantime, without the support of the Cherokee Council or all the chiefs, the Boudinot-Ridge group of influential Cherokees met with President Jackson's treaty commissioner, Rev. John F. Schermerhorn, and twenty-two men eventually signed the treaty. Principal Chief John Ross certainly did not sign it, however, and it was without the required authority of the nation, including other major chiefs.[16] Like most of the nation, Chief John Ross viewed the Treaty of New Echota as fraudulent, invalid, and arguably not a treaty at all. The politics were complex, worsened by the fact that previously cooperative relations between the Cherokee leaders had broken down.

In signing the treaty, Boudinot, Ridge, and the others acted against Cherokee law, selling their land without full authorization from all the Chiefs and thus selling their people out. Both would have known that in Cherokee law the penalty for such an action could be death. John Ross's large number of supporters held out for as long as possible, refusing to migrate to the Indian Territory.

Seven thousand army troops rounded them up in spring 1838. Eighteen thousand Cherokees were herded into holding camps without adequate food or water. People soon started to sicken and die of dysentery and endemic disease. As an eyewitness testified, families were marched off from their evening meal at the point of bayonets: women taken from spinning wheels, men from working in the fields.[17] As they were marched along, some turned to see their homes burning behind them. They called this forced exodus the Trail Where Everyone Cried. Now it is the Trail of Tears. Children, women, and men weakened, took ill, and died along the way. With four thousand people dying on the trail or soon after reaching the Indian Territory, nearly every Cherokee family was affected by a loss. Suddenly, they had lost their homeland, villages, and livelihoods. Holding out until the bitter winter increased the human toll. Yet resisting any longer would have led to greater violence at the hands of whites and an even higher death toll.[18] Some people did manage to hold out in the Blue Hills and surrounds, forming what is now the Eastern Band of the Cherokee Nation, and their descendants still live in the East and South today.

By 1840, however, the majority of Cherokees had moved to the Indian Territory many miles to the west, to land considered inhospitable for whites but good enough — and far away enough from the white towns — for Indians. Separated from the pressures of the colonizing populations, removal from their eastern lands threw the Cherokee emigrants into a more concentrated Cherokee society, without the same political structures of the old village centers. Furthermore, they had migrated into a new Native American diaspora — a world of other "civilized tribes" of Native Americans already removed from their country.

Quatie, John Ross's first wife and the mother of his children, died on the trail on February 1, 1839. Short of her family's destination, Quatie, who may have already been ill for some time, died just before their steamer reached Little Rock, Arkansas. Quatie had also been known as Elizabeth Brown Henley, for she had been married previously to a man by the name of Henley. She had one child from that marriage, Susan Henley, born in 1808. Quatie was about the same age as John. They married in 1813, when they were around twenty-two years old. She is thought to have been a traditional Cherokee woman with strong ancestral lines and was generally referred to as a "full blood." The union between Quatie and John was long and appeared successful; they reared five children together. Sadly, one died at birth and Susan died in 1838, the same year as the commencement of the forced Cherokee removal.

Unfortunately we know relatively little about Quatie. The Ross papers contain no correspondence from her — or to her, from John. Whereas it is assumed she was not literate, if this was the case, you would think John could still write her letters that others could read out to her. But perhaps that was not expected. Ross's biographer, Gary Moulton, commented that "Quatie likely had little impact on Ross' life"; however, this opinion is difficult to sustain. She and her family connections may have enhanced and consolidated Kooweskoowe's power base. Moulton's conclusions are probably based on the lack of written record, especially in the context of Ross's many other letters written to family members over his long absences on diplomatic and trade trips. Moulton speculates that Quatie may have been an invalid, but evidence to support this is also lacking.[19]

Admittedly, it is odd that Ross did not mention Quatie in his correspondence. Marrying young, John Ross may have taken Quatie for granted. However, a lack of written evidence of exchanges between them certainly cannot be taken as proof that they lacked a deeply loving relationship. Quatie did not accompany John on his Washington visits, but she had charge of his substantial home and plantation during John's long journeys away. By 1833 their large house at the Head of Coosa was taken over by Georgian land lottery winners. Humiliatingly, Quatie and the children were confined in two rooms, no doubt creating shock and stress. Like everyone else, in 1839 she then had to travel on the long, enforced journey from the East to Oklahoma. With greater means, the ailing Quatie was traveling along the water route and in more comfort than most. But like so many others on the trail, she became ill with pneumonia and died.[20]

In the early 1840s, John Ross needed to journey between the Indian Territory and the diplomatic and business metropole of Philadelphia and New England. Ross was attempting to claim back withheld federal tribal annuities and to renegotiate the treaty between the Cherokees and the United States.[21] John's travels among elite circles of influence in northern cities have a lighter side, as they enabled him to visit the homes and attractive holiday locations of the wealthy and to gain opportunities to mingle in polite society.

Now, two years after Quatie's death, Ross planned to use such openings to find a wife from New England. Why not from among his people? Perhaps he wanted a European-educated wife. Or, as principal chief, he may have worried that choosing a Cherokee wife would appear to ally him too closely with a particular clan or political faction. The Cherokee Nation in the Indian Territory faced its own schism — between the Old Settlers — those now more established Cherokees who had arrived during the 1820s and 1830s — and the New Settlers, or the newer, unwilling arrivals who were part of the forced exile. These rifts could weaken Ross's tenuous support base and foster fresh tensions. In one sense, choosing a white wife could offer a more neutral option. In another, it could create deeper resentment and be interpreted as a shift toward biological assimilation or cultural assimilationist politics. This would raise special problems among those Cherokees who had grown to distrust and detest the whites. Governed by class, race, religion, and gender, all marriage choices have a certain political element. But for an astute leader and statesman like Ross, his marital choice was more likely to be governed by political instinct.

Whatever his motives, in the same year as he met Mary, 1841, John Ross brazenly courted at least two other white women, including Elizabeth Milligan. She and her mother had run a boardinghouse in Washington, which is perhaps how she and John became acquainted. Elizabeth was a sophisticated and educated woman, and they discussed such topics as developments in sculpture and interior furnishings. It is unclear how well John knew her, for there are few signs of warmth or familiarity in their letters. However, John thought he had a chance and was serious enough about her to draft a formal letter containing a marriage proposal. In contrast to his usually flowing prose, however, it reads as an odd, awkward correspondence.

His letter commences with an outline of his recent sufferings, then details his onerous tribal responsibilities and duties. It falls rather short in eloquence and charm. Even his marriage proposal, which awaits the letter's conclusion, prioritizes Ross's treaty preoccupations. Like an afterthought, his expression of affection and regard for the addressee comes late. Nonetheless, John rallies sufficient passion to propose "a petition craving your reply on the subject of my fervent desire for negotiating a treaty with you for the purpose of uniting our hearts in the bonds of matrimony!"[22] The exclamation mark adds excitement; however, as oratory, or as an endearing proposal, the letter falls as flat as cardboard.

At the beginning of this letter, his complements to Elizabeth and his declaration of feelings seem contrived. John Ross was at least being candid when he stated that he was more practiced in political than in intimate treaty negotiations. Worried that Elizabeth might think him too old for her to marry, he voluntarily testified to his "healthful tone of mind and body."[23] Yet perhaps this information was really directed toward her guardians. Surely if they knew each other at all, this is something she would have already noticed. His letter was unconvincing. Perhaps Elizabeth also thought it irksome and declined. Or perhaps Ross himself was unconvinced and reconsidered. Due to too much missing correspondence, we can do no more than speculate.

Perhaps John Ross was not yet able to separate himself from his political and national worries. A high level of Cherokee statesmanship was required locally and in Washington, and much diplomatic responsibility fell on John Ross's shoulders. Many Cherokees admired Ross as a heroic leader, but he faced recriminations for the excruciating death toll of their winter journey, not to mention the financial impact of lost assets and income and the poor compensation for their expenses.[24] Several people accused Ross of mishandling the westward journey and its federal finances. Others had sympathy for Ross, as he had shared the pain of losing family members as well as his home and assets. His wife's death on the journey had elevated her to heroic status. It also served to enhance public sympathy for the high-profile grieving widower.

Cherokee internal politics posed enormous challenges for Chief John Ross. Deep conflicts over modernization, traditionalism, and how to deal with the ever-growing momentum of Euro-American colonialism threatened unity. Although the state of Georgia and the federal government were the true instigators of the forced removal, the traumatic events caused the Cherokee Nation itself to further fracture. Ross had to be ever vigilant, guarding against old and emergent enemies. In the western territories, political strife took fresh forms; the eastern Cherokee arrivals became intruders themselves. The Old Settlers resented the arrival of the poverty-stricken, distressed Cherokee newcomers, unsettling their established community. It was difficult for them to cope with the arrival of a large, traumatized group of unwilling immigrants who held different political values. And the New Settlers demanded much in the way of entitlements. Deep divisions threatened to escalate into a Cherokee civil war. The conflicts between the Old Settlers and the New Settlers had some uneasy parallels with the eastern Cherokees' efforts to keep out Georgian intruders. On the Indian Territory in the West, no group could claim sovereignty on the grounds of deep historical rootedness. By the same token, even if associated with storied traditions from a now-distant land to the east, Cherokee narratives, clan membership, and other aspects of Cherokee political identity were portable.

Representatives of both the Ridges/Treaty Party and the Old Settlers were simultaneously lobbying senior government figures in Washington. So it was problematic for Ross to pretend to Cherokee national unity.[25] When Elias Boudinot, John Ridge, and John's father, The Ridge, were assassinated in 1839, the prime suspects were members of John Ross's party, who had by far the majority of Cherokee support. Although there is no evidence that Ross himself approved the assassinations of his former allies, he did not remain entirely neutral. He argued that the unknown executioners had acted within Cherokee law and, following discussion at an 1839 National Council meeting, authorized an amnesty for the assassins.[26] Perhaps his stance was true to Cherokee law, but in consequence, other Treaty Party chiefs and their families harbored simmering anger. In one incident, they threatened to carry out revenge, against which John Ross had to station guards around his house. Delight Sargeant, a white woman who was the widow and second wife of Elias Boudinot, was the person who tipped him off.[27] This confidence possibly suggests that she trusted Ross, believing he was not responsible for her husband's murder. Like John Ridge's widow, Sarah, who fought to retain assets and a livelihood, Delight's security and ability to make a future in Cherokee territory would have been tenuous.

With such unrest and threats of violence, no one could blame Ross for being deeply preoccupied with the affairs of state during the early 1840s. However, at least in the case of Elizabeth Milligan, it was no recipe for romance. In a later letter, just before Ross departed for the Indian Territory, he switched to addressing Elizabeth in a cooler, businesslike tone. Already she was guarding important documents of the Cherokee Nation. Perhaps she cared about the plight of the Cherokees and valued their archives. John certainly trusted her. Referring to them as national documents concerning events not yet "consummated," John asked if she would look after them for a longer period. While readable as a joke about their failed private "treaty," or even a lovers' correspondence, the tone suggests that he was serious. His other purpose was to seek a secure place for additional documents of the Cherokee Nation. He may have feared their safety on his journey west through the badlands or their security in the unstable Indian Territory. It is possible that he had simply run out of time to retrieve them.

To mark the end of their intimate negotiations, Ross arranged a very expensive gift for Elizabeth. It was a bust of Red Jacket, the Seneca Indian chief. Fancying himself a man of taste, Ross observed that he thought it "an improvement in sculpture" with a "true likeness."[28] No doubt this impressive piece was to serve as a perpetual reminder of the association between

Elizabeth and himself, the Indian chief that she knew. His talk of marriage as a treaty suggests a level of purposefulness about his planned union with a white woman. Perhaps this marriage strategy would consolidate his commitment to diplomacy between nations — into the private and intimate world of marriage.

With his next love — or perhaps his concurrent one — Ross enjoyed a more frivolous and longer-lasting correspondence. We now meet Mary Bryan Stapler of Wilmington, Delaware. Mary was born in 1826, and when they met she was a schoolgirl of sixteen. Her parents were committed Quakers. John was equivocal about Christian churches. For years, John resisted adopting an allegiance to any particular denomination. Although interested in Cherokee belief, Ross's parents did not appear to have instilled the teachings of Cherokee religion and philosophy in any strict sense.

Mary was ill-informed about John's political efforts and about the plight of Indians more generally.[29] Nonetheless, their common social networks helped bridge the divides. John's appearance was much like that of the other people with whom Mary and her family associated. Kooweskoowe stood about five foot six and lacked an imposing appearance.[30] Anglo-Americans sometimes thought John looked Scottish. As one contemporary Anglo-American observer stated, he was of "calm and quiet deportment." He was "plain and unassuming in his appearance."[31] Known for his charm, he left memorable impressions upon people, some being reported in New England newspapers. Cultivated and cultured in both Euro-American and Cherokee style, he enjoyed the good life, holidaying at fashionable locations such as Saratoga Springs and on the Maine coast at Cape Cottage, not far from Portland.

Mocked for looking like a white boy as a child, John became assiduous in wearing the right garb for the occasion. Ross's biographer, Gary Moulton, states that he "favored the ancient dress and customs of his people." When the young Tsan Usdi attended the Green Corn festival, he insisted upon wearing Cherokee dress rather than Euro-American styling.[32] In New England and diplomatic circles, he donned the fashionable gentlemen's apparel available in city stores: a city suit with a starched white shirt and long jacket. Often portrayed as thoroughly acculturated in white ways, he was relaxed in his comportment in Euro-American society.

FIG. 41. This watercolor portrait of John Ross was painted in Washington in June 1841. Cherokee writing is included, as well as an ornate signature that may have been done by Ross himself. National Portrait Gallery, Smithsonian Institution/Art Resource NY.

It is unclear how much Cherokee cultural knowledge John received as a child, but he certainly received a good European-style education. He became a wealthy entrepreneur and slave owner, owning at least twenty slaves during the 1830s.[33] From childhood, he had been a cultural intermediary, moving easily between different Cherokee and Anglo-American ways of speaking, thinking, and seeing the world but deeply committed to the Cherokee Nation.

FIG. 42. *John Ross: A Cherokee Chief.* Courtesy Library of Congress. This portrait of Ross appears in *History of the Indian Tribes of North America*, a compilation by Thomas L. McKenney and James Hall. Many images of American Indian leaders were published in Philadelphia, where they visited the president and conducted diplomatic visits. Exhibitions were held of their portraits. The artist depicts Ross as dressed in exquisite clothing, with good taste. He is seated on rich, velvet-lined furniture. Ross has luxuriant hair and eyes that appear bright with intelligence. His forehead is creased in a frown, but there is a warmth, seriousness, and sincerity in his persona. His right ear is exaggerated as if to accentuate that he listened attentively. His hands are fine and unaffected by manual labor. He holds a legal document that appears to be some kind of formal treaty manuscript. The artist makes no attempt to depict Ross as "other," as exotic. Rather, the image attempts to capture the man's character, his wealth, and the genteel masculine style of dress that he adopted for his Washington visits.

In 1841 John Ross was still relatively new to being a widower. Perhaps he was becoming lonely. Although most of his five children were now adults, his sons Silas and James were only eleven and twelve.[34] Having backed the establishment of schools in the eastern Cherokee Nation from the 1810s, Ross passionately believed in a European-style education for Cherokee girls and boys. He funded the school fees of extended family members in prestigious northeastern schools, corresponding with and cajoling them about their studies. En route to Washington and other cities and resorts where he undertook diplomacy and business, he made a point of visiting them. Although they resided at good boarding schools and private residences, being so far from home, John feared that the Cherokee children would become lonely.[35] Furthermore, he worried that the girls might start to behave too much like white women. Observing the way young American women were being socialized, he feared that the Cherokee female students could be swept up in the "senseless flippancy" of "fashionable society."[36] He was about to become more flippant himself.

Ross's regular visits to the Northeast were bringing him into plenty of respectable Anglo-American female company. However, it was the young and feisty Mary Bryan Stapler whom he found captivating. She was boarding at the Moravian Female Academy in Bethlehem, Pennsylvania, also known as Linden Hall. It appears they first met in 1841, the same year as Ross's proposal to Milligan; however, we do not know the exact sequence of the events or exactly when his first meeting with Mary took place.

Although she lived a privileged life, with her mother's death in 1837 the ten-year-old Mary Stapler had experienced personal tragedy.[37] In the wake of her mother's illness young Mary became dangerously ill too, but her older sister Sarah nursed her through it. Mary became inseparable from Sarah, her primary guardian and confidante, to whom she was fiercely loyal. In 1841 Sarah was twenty-eight years old, while Mary, born in 1826, was twelve years younger. Mary recognized how her family duties had impeded her older sister's marriage prospects. After all, their two brothers John and James were well set up, being in the process of entering the professions of lawyer and minister.[38] Like John Ross, Mary's father, John Stapler, was a successful merchant or trader, owning real estate and businesses in the mill town of Wilmington and the port city of Philadelphia. John Stapler Sr. was little

FIG. 43. Artist Auguste Edouart created an image of John Ross during one of his visits to Washington in 1841. It is a lithograph of chalk and cut paper on paper. The wording reads, "John Ross Principal Chief of the Cherokee Nation Park Hill, Cherokee Outlet. Washington City April 22 1841." The landscape appears to be suggesting his mountainous homeland. There is additional script on the lower edge of the portrait that is partly cut off in this photograph. It may be part of a portrait series of visiting dignitaries. The long coat, high collar, and top hat are distinctive. National Portrait Gallery, Smithsonian Institution/Art Resource NY.

mentioned by his kin — even for his absences — and is thus obscured as a historical character. Often traveling for business, Stapler had apparently not remarried and may have become aloof from family life.

After John Ross sent a letter to her at the Bethlehem school, Mary Stapler was reprimanded, as this was against regulations. Somewhat melodramatically, she responds that her school is a prison. Ever the strategist, in 1842 Ross writes apologetically to her sister Sarah, indirectly cajoling Mary at her complaints and pointing out a contrary view, of the need for restrictions and regulations: "I hope she will not think me cruel, for believing, the discipline to be very proper." Indeed, Ross was keen to obtain enrollment there for his Cherokee relatives, and he continued lightheartedly, "Tell her that I have along with me a niece of sixteen years and in compliance with her own desire I may imprison in female Cage at Bethlehem, if I can get her in."[39] He was referring to Eliza Jane Ross. Possibly in anticipation of the union, John's letter addresses Sarah as "My dear Sister."

From 1841, Ross penned his letters to Mary from Washington DC, Philadelphia, Delaware, New York, Boston, and New Haven, Connecticut. In September 1841 he handed a letter to Thomas L. McKenney, the former superintendent of Indian trade, who was his long-term friend. McKenney passed it on to Mary at the school.[40] We are missing Kooweskoowe's first letter to Mary, but she had insisted that *he* should write first. The insinuations of Mary's earliest available reply suggest that he had already hinted at a marriage proposal. She may be trying to be sure about exactly what he is proposing, but more likely she is playing a flirtatious game. As if feigning ignorance, she addresses him with the biblical and Quaker usage of "thee," impishly skirting his offer. Mary alludes to making promises and refers to being *counsel* on a *fair* court (a female court). Using a pun on courts to obfuscate references to courting, she asks "what court it is I am to appear in" and who will be the "presiding judge." Mary then writes about "addressing a case to a court which has no record" and mischievously asks, "Has thee a *record*?"

Although conscious of her inexperience in love, she is astute enough to suspect that Kooweskoowe is "courting" other women simultaneously. If Elizabeth Milligan was still in the picture, she was right. "Tell me, I accept thee as my client but then thee must make thy case openly and clearly before

I can speak to it, I will wait thy answer and then maybe I may talk of the regions of mountains and pure air."[41]

The pointed reference to mountains evokes transcendent, private spaces. John's former home is surrounded by the Appalachians, while his new abode in the Indian Territory to which his nation was forced to move, in present-day Oklahoma, near Tahlequah, is Plains country. Although Mary invites him to visit her in Wilmington, in placing value on pure air she reminds us of the gritty, suffocating atmosphere of contemporary industrializing cities. John responds that such places must be a "very delightful retreat for ambulation and meditation," allowing the "mind" to "soften" from the "hum and bustle of life" and to reflect on the "Great Creator of the Universe." Flatteringly, Mary refers to John's letter as so lyrical that he must be quoting a notable poet. Showing off her education, she suggests that he is quoting the exotic "Assan," possibly the Kerala-based poet laureate who was a writer of Christian hymns of praise.[42]

Ross's concoction of a legal allegory with a "court/courting" case and a pending "judgment" flows from his daily preoccupation with appeals for treaty justice with the United States. Pretending naïveté, Mary deflects Ross's wordplays, asking about what "case thou intended to initiate." Their flirtatious early letters are full of lighthearted allusions that skirt around the notion of a potential intimate contract.[43] Displacing the seriousness of Ross's premature proposal, Mary avoids expressing her own feelings. She is interested enough to write — but is it just an exciting game? Ross's veiled private language attempts to compensate for his fear of directness and possible rejection.

Ross's friend Col. Thomas Lorraine McKenney was implicated in their first meeting and in passing on their early correspondence. A close mutual friend of both the Stapler family and John Ross, McKenney had business dealings with John Stapler. Despite his prominent — and pacifist — Quaker parents, he rose to the rank of major in the War of 1812.[44] Whether he was actually a colonel is somewhat uncertain, but his dignified, military-like bearing and white hair made people think he suited the part.

McKenney had earned his reputation as a negotiator at the interface of the American Indian and Euro-American nations. After serving as superintendent of Indian trade from 1816 to 1822, he was appointed commissioner of Indian affairs between 1824 and 1830.⁴⁵ He later attempted to muster philanthropic efforts toward Indian "civilization," especially via education projects. An energetic "advocate of the Indians," he conducted lecture tours where his self-styled persona and stories of noble chiefs appealed to white female audiences. In Portland, Maine, one of the numerous states that had declared all marriages between whites and Indians null and void, it was reported in the local newspaper that he attracted a swooning female crowd.⁴⁶

Keen to work under President Jackson, McKenney had backflipped on his original antiremovalist position, backing forced removal of Indians to the west. Despite this, John Ross did not cut him off, later calling Thomas "my cheerful *Brother* the Gallant Colo. [Colonel]."⁴⁷ By 1844 the two had met and been corresponding — albeit intermittently — for at least twenty years.⁴⁸ McKenney needed this alliance with a high-ranking chief more than Ross needed him.⁴⁹ Although McKenney's political influence and personal finances were declining, Ross appeared to appreciate not only his political and trading networks but also a genuine sense of friendship.

McKenney and Ross enjoyed a jocular man-to-man confidence that included exchanging views about attractive women and potential lovers. Introducing John to a potential bride was the kind of thing such a friend should do. It would also incur a debt of gratitude. Having brought Ross and the Staplers together, McKenney then convinced the Stapler family to take an interest in Indian affairs. In a letter to John, Mary acknowledges McKenney's history lessons, for she explains to John that she has now learned that "your people" have "endured much." Colonel McKenney's sympathy has enabled her family to learn "to sympathise too" — and perhaps to offer philanthropic funds.⁵⁰ Mary wishes John "a speedy close of thy mission." While her subsequent courting letters express little or no curiosity about Cherokee national affairs, she displays plenty of interest in John. Mary points to alternative ways by which John could send letters privately. Naïvely, she suggests he send them to the school principal, Reverend John G. Kummer.⁵¹

Despite causing trouble at Mary's school, Ross was invited into the Stapler family circle. He traveled with members of her family from Mary's school at Bethlehem, Pennsylvania, to the Delaware Water Gap — a place where the Delaware River dramatically cuts through a mountain range. By stage, steamer, and the new railroad, he journeyed toward Mary's home. Here Mary and John had opportunities to spend time together, possibly unchaperoned. The river continues two hundred miles on to Wilmington and Delaware Bay. Because of its role in establishing their rapport, Ross was later nostalgic about his journey, reminiscing that he recalled "the charming circle" and the "kind hearted relatives" as "pleasures of the past" that were "refreshing to my mind and can never be forgotten." Fondly, he recalled his views of the "green lawns and the yellow harvest" and the beauty of "the rising hills and the towering blue mountains, that formed so beautiful a landscape."[52]

Anglo-Americans understood landscape grandeur as God-given, as gifted according to their manifest destiny as colonizers. Landscapes could be appreciated, nurtured, and owned.[53] As Ross moved between trade and agriculture, his own business interests embraced that American vision. As a trader and planter, Ross was excited about the national future — variously referring to rural America as "harvest" and New York as "emporium" — a place of boundless possibilities for trade, commerce, and business exchanges. In other public addresses he referred to the Great Spirit, whose force permeated Cherokee landscapes and histories.[54]

Again, Ross's lineage, education, and political and social experience enabled him to move with grace between different landscapes and their aesthetic and religious visions. John and Mary's love letters also connected different worlds. Their letters conjure an immediate, intimate world of feeling. Although intensely romantic, they are vivid, witty, and often sardonic. Seemingly flowing and spontaneous, two sharp intellects are contriving to excite each other. Perhaps John learned from his dealings with Elizabeth Milligan, for notably absent from both his and Mary's letters are the politics of state. Although Ross is engaged in detailed treaty work, strategic meetings, and negotiations at the highest levels of the U.S. government, when addressing Mary, he speaks of his political networking and advice-seeking activities in personal terms — as friendships, discussions, and social exchanges.[55]

Transnational and Transatlantic Identity Games

As perceptively analyzed by the historians Rayna Green and Philip Deloria, the cartoonish race caricatures of the "white man's Indian," such as the noble chief in an elaborately feathered headdress or the Pocahontas princess, laid out scripts for cross-cultural performances that American Indians soon embraced for their own purposes.[56] By the 1840s the stereotypical Indian was already appearing as "factual" in U.S. history texts.[57] Kooweskoowe grabbed the subversive potential of "playing Indian," appropriately casting himself as "chief" in a mixed-marriage drama.

From the earliest, John's letters hammed up the perceived differences of his national identity. In an 1842 letter to Sarah he refers to himself as "your *Cherokee Brother* in the region of the great Prairies of the West."[58] As if the recipients did not already know about his Cherokee status or where he lived! Drawing attention to his Cherokee identity could increase his exotic allure and perhaps also activate their philanthropic urges. Although this "brother" and "sister" language was common between Christians, humanitarians, and Indians, this device also had Indigenous overtones, with the capacity to bond nonfamily into kinship, with its associated sentiments and obligations.

When Ross visited Mary one year — it was late 1842 or 1843 — he made a personal proposal of a more serious order. Presumably Mary had insinuated that she would think about it but wanted plenty of time. Referencing Cherokee kinship, Mary uses its well-known cultural protocols of adoption to scamper over their age difference. Playing Indian maiden, she invents the title of "adopted niece," addressing her letter to "uncle." Creating a culturally condoned kinship relationship jokily hints at her willingness to be included in a Cherokee cultural world — and, more particularly, in Ross's intimate family circle.

The witty and intelligent Mary lived in a domestic world of women, with her sister as confidante and parent figure/guardian and in the company of a few other female friends.[59] In stark contrast to her relatively sedentary life, Ross's job required a lot of dangerous travel between the East and Tahlequah in the Indian Territory, which is west of Fort Gibson and Muskogee.[60] Horse-drawn "stages" or stagecoaches covered many routes, while steamboats carried passengers along rivers and lakes and the brand new rail lines and locomotives operating in the East. However, outlaw bands and general lawlessness still made travel between the West and the East quite dangerous. Mary hoped that Ross would step back from his public role as leader. By then madly infatuated and totally preoccupied with her own happiness, Mary placed too much faith in Ross's assurances. For John had led her to believe that, once married, he would cease journeying away from her side.⁶¹ In the meantime, it was Ross's diplomatic travels that were making their courtship possible.

Spring 1844 had an effect on the young Mary. In a coquettish tone, she writes to her "uncle," inviting him and his cousin to pay a visit to what she calls their "Humble Home." Belonging to a wealthy business elite, it was never too humble. However, because of Ross's known wealth and his habit of mixing with presidents, rich philanthropists, writers, and other celebrated Americans, Mary's concerns may have been sincere. The humble home allusion evoked the popular song "Home Sweet Home" and its lyrics: "be it ever so humble there's no place like home." Ross knew the song very well indeed, being a good friend of its lyricist, John Howard Payne, with whom he had been arrested by the Georgia Guard and imprisoned, while their papers were confiscated. In at least one of his letters to Payne, Ross pointedly underlined the chorus word "home," gently reminding him of the many layers of emotional and political meaning the concept held for supporters of Cherokee rights and rights to their homeland.⁶²

Mary continued,: "We flatter ourselves that you could pass a few weeks very pleasantly in our Native City Wilmington." Her choice of words could be a knowing reference to John's recent uprootedness from his own "native city" in the East. Mary writes invitingly, "Some of our walks are truly romantic." Addressing her letter to "Kooweskoowe," and perhaps reflecting upon his Cherokee name, she describes the birds that take her fancy along the Brandywine River: "The little songsters of the grove that took their departure during the cold and chilly blasts of winter, are once more heard singing their Hymns of praise. . . . The beautiful flowers hid themselves from our view while the Snow, and Frost, covered the ground. . . . Is this not a fitting season for Friends to meet that have been separated."⁶³

Artificially subscribing John into the community of Quaker Friends that she has now formally joined, in her land of long winters, Mary overtly co-opts the romance of nature in spring. In buoyant mood, she evokes the excitements of seasonal renewal, change, joy, and fertility. Significantly, Mary's allusion to natural feelings neutralizes the unnaturalness colonizers placed upon mixed marriages between Indian men and white women. Alongside images of sexual excitement and fertility, she purifies any accusations of lustful intent by cunningly throwing in the pious hymns-of-praise exhortation. With John named for a bird himself, it is as if their union is endorsed by nature, including even the birds of the woods. John is now fully integrated into the musings of Mary's youthful imagination.

The 1840s were a high point of American romanticism. The rationalist priorities of business, state, and religion had already been challenged by the unemployment and poverty of the economic depression of 1837.[64] Rather than dry rules, nature itself was to spark intuitive insight and metaphysical solutions to the industrial world. Spontaneity, feeling, and passion were elevated above rationalism as indicators of truth. This was the era of the meltingly romantic Lord Byron and the nature-loving American writers Henry David Thoreau and Ralph Waldo Emerson. In 1836 Emerson, whose book *Nature* was considered revolutionary and influenced the rise of transcendentalism, indeed wrote to President Martin Van Buren to protest against the forced Cherokee removal.[65]

Romanticism appealed equally to Mary, the passionate young woman who read poetry in a girls' academy, and to the fatigued political wrangler John Ross, who reminisced about the beauties of his lost Appalachians. With their appealing attention to natural wisdom, American romanticists were also drawn to Native American themes and imagined sensibilities.[66] Memorials to the "lost" and "last of the" Indians became embedded into the romanticism of the age — for example, in the noble portraits by Charles Bird King and in the God-in-nature landscapes of artists like Thomas Cole. The Cherokees had different love stories and songs, but Ross's classical European education, first with a private tutor and then at a boarding school, meant John and Mary shared the same classical Greek and Roman and European romanticist reference points.

Although their exchanges cleverly engaged with the intellectual milieu of the era, the young Mary remained somewhat insecure about their bond. In her letter of May 22, 1844, she needles her "esteemed Uncle" over his purported romantic interest in the family friend Grace Levy, who, she pointedly reports, is "no nearer tyeing the Hymenial knot." (Hymen was the Greek God of marriage; in English parlance of this time, it commonly applied to wedlock as well as to the female membrane associated with virginity.) Perhaps Grace also flirted with John Ross. Of this, Mary teases and sweet-talks: "Does thee know I always thought that little Cupid had sent forth his darts from her bright eyes into thy heart."⁶⁷ They knew well the Greek myth in which Venus's son Cupid was associated with the rapture of passionate love and desire.

Aware that Ross was interested in herself and not necessarily in Gráce, the mischievous Mary offers to play matchmaking intermediary between Grace and John. In her youthful identity quest, she swings wildly between rebellious boarding school student and virtuous member of the Quakers, the Society of Friends. Her invitation toward intimate commitment also comes with an implied threat: "Do not let it be long for delay is dangerous. Farewell. I have turned [*sic*] to be quite a little Quaker girl. I remain thy adopted Niece."⁶⁸ Perhaps Mary Stapler had heard that Mary Connelly, also of Bethlehem, a friend of both John's niece Eliza Jane Ross and McKenney, was making overtures to Ross. Indeed, Connelly considered John "the first and only that I could ever love."⁶⁹ Although Ross had written her a flirtatious letter citing the words of a song a few years back, he claimed he had not noticed her attentions and that the feelings were not mutual. Connelly was heartbroken, more so by feeling snubbed when he did not even bid farewell to her.⁷⁰

In a letter to his niece, the student Eliza Jane, in 1844, Kooweskoowe denied his love interest in the much younger Mary Stapler. Ross reassured Eliza Jane, "Were I to seek a heart that is congenial with my own, in view of uniting both into One — I think, I should be inclined to search for it amongst the teachers."⁷¹ Eliza Jane viewed Mary as a peer, and she was probably embarrassed by their age difference. At the same time, Ross's next reply to Mary sees the flirting meter rise. This letter is more seriously entreating of marriage.

Aware of her nickname, John asks what has become of "Molly's hand." McKenney had used "Molly" when introducing Mary; it was also what Ross called his mother. In his reply, Ross falls for Mary's trap, spelling out that it is not her friend Grace Levy but only *she* who interests him. Intriguingly, he refers to "soft and bewitching subjects" — "bewitching" being a lovely word to describe the alchemy of a growing infatuation.⁷²

Perhaps dreaming of a time that they might spend together there, both mention the charms enjoyed during separate stays at McKenney's Cape Cottage, Maine, and time they spent as guests of their mutual, high-living friend McKenney, whose exotic Indian tales rendered him so popular with white women. Each presumably dallied over the uneven tables of angular rock slabs that require navigation to get to the beach. They thoroughly enjoyed the fun-loving crowd at the fashionable holiday retreat, where people ate delicious meals of crayfish and lobsters.

The visit of the "distinguished Chief" John Ross to Cape Cottage had been excitedly reported in the Portland newspapers.[73] Ross enjoyed "fishing, rambling along the rock bound shore, and through the adjacent groves and then peeping out from the deep foliage upon the many vessels floating upon the widespread Ocean." But, despite all the attention and charming female company, he stated that he pined for Mary.[74] Whether they ever stayed there at the same time, we cannot be sure.

Only her sister Sarah knew about Ross and Mary's secret correspondence — and Ross wanted to keep it this way. By June 1844 he remains insecure about their future. While obviously titillated by the images conveyed in Mary's hand, he is haunted by fears of white women's frivolity. He writes that she may be flirting with his affections "for the sake of mirth." He is anxious that "the fairer Sex" might tend to use "a cunning coquettish negotiation" to "*cheat and rob* the poor unsophisticated and confiding man *of his only heart*." He worries he would be left "to pine away and die upon the green fields of love."[75] Ross may be unnerved and vulnerable, but it seems absurd for this leading statesman to call himself "poor unsophisticated and confiding." His words may be facetiously evoking the savage stereotypes of Indian men. Knowing, however, of other "learned Indian men" who were humiliated in a love for a white woman, he may have harbored anxiety that even a wealthy and erudite man such as himself might be too "unsophisticated" for the wiles of a fashionable white woman.[76]

Mary's next letter to John does not pull back; she fishes for even more precise written words that express his feelings and intentions toward her. And she succeeds in drawing him out. Finally, John replies unguardedly. Before waiting to receive his latest missive, Mary writes back. The orderly to and fro of correspondence is thrown out of sequence. Ross panics. A delay in the mail leaves his heartfelt expressions of romantic love in limbo. Mary's ploy of insinuating that he was interested in her friend's hand, not hers, had worked with startling success. Responding to her demands for an exact statement of his feelings, he writes,

First — *I* and *you* ... makes ... two
Second — *you* and *me* ... makes ... both
... So, if, you love me — I love you!
And *as* — I *do love you* — Do *you love me?*⁷⁷

If he feared he could be tricked or let down before, the risk is escalating. Now he fears that his poetry and mock courtroom tactics will land awkwardly, be misinterpreted — or perhaps even land in the wrong hands. Although described as having a calm, unflappable personality, Ross is now wracked by emotion. His life course, he writes, is stuck "betwixt two fires," "consumed by the flame" or "by its extinguishment, I might be obliterated from your remembrance!"⁷⁸ Despite his expertise at operating between the polarities of states, nations, and factions, Ross has found himself caught on unfamiliar territory — between widowhood, infatuated love, jilted lover, and the prospect of being a husband again.

No longer hiding behind sardonic humor, he seems to lay bare his raw emotions. Suddenly, John has second thoughts about revealing his feelings so unguardedly — or perhaps he is simply ashamed of his sickly-sweet couplets. Ross the public man fears that his love-struck persona will bring him embarrassment or humiliation. He writes to request of Mary that the "crazy lines" of his reply remain confidential.⁷⁹

Romanticizing Mixed Marriage

John Ross's letters contain plenty of sophisticated wordplay and satire. He lampoons contemporary stereotypes of mixed marriage, remarking that it would be a "funny joke to dream of the heart of one so fair being won by a Sachem [chief] of the Western Wilds." The identity of the "one so fair" could apply to both Grace Levy and the fair-skinned, albeit dark-haired, Mary. He provides this vignette: "How peculiarly romantic would the scenery be were lady, in all her graceful charms, seated [*sic*] a circular wigwam, conopyed [*sic*] and carpeted with the soft dressed buffalo skins — and there as mistress of the lodge receiving the salutations of the appointed and plumed chieftains and their dark eyed Brunettes as they come to offer their congratulations to her and the partner of his bosom."⁸⁰ Such intellectual and political games displaced his awkwardness. This was a heightening emotional relationship that transgressed colonizer expectation — and in some ways, his own. When portrayed by a modern Indian man who dressed in fashionable suits, the primitive Indian caricature was amusing. Furthermore, as an elected chief, Ross led a constitutionally governed Cherokee Nation. Cherokee men did not wear plumed head regalia, nor had the Cherokees lived in wigwams.[81] Unlike the Indigenous ceremonial dress favored by many Indian chiefs, Cherokee leaders of the day tended to conform to European dress. When engaging in diplomacy with U.S. politicians, Ridge, Boudinot, and Ross all wore high collars and three-piece suits.[82]

Ross's word picture of a white "mistress" married to a chieftain was taken straight from the popular "captive white woman" literature. He unwittingly revealed his own prejudices, for some white women — as it happened, those with darker hair — would be more suited than blondes in adapting to the fantasy wigwam life. Ross thus flattered Mary at the expense of Grace Levy, whom he adjudged to be the haughty "blond." (As it happened, Grace ended up marrying one of Mary's brothers and then moving to live in the Indian Territory, so it seems she was not too haughty after all.)

Educated Cherokees were embracing these ideas about the Indian at the same time as they were refashioning democratic ideals for their own nation. John's nephew William P. Ross, during his school studies, wrote an essay entitled "The Romance of Indian History." Although pleased with how it was developing, the student regretted not having access to George Caitlin's recent publication, which John Ross had apparently recommended.[83] John Ross and the Stapler family alike socialized in romanticist circles. As discussed in the previous chapter, one of John's dearest friends, John Howard Payne, had associated with its leading lights in Great Britain and Paris. Rejected by Mary Shelley, he never married.[84]

We can imagine conversations between Ross and Payne about these famous circles. Mary Bryan Stapler loved the poetry of the Shelleys' friend Lord Byron. She quoted these lines at the end of a letter to John: "Farewell, if ever fondest prayer for others weal availed on high, mine will not all be lost in air, but waft thy name, beyond the Sky. Thy Friend, Mary."[85] Perhaps she liked another of Byron's poems — one of repressed emotion, lust, and struggles with the spirit that was entitled "To a Beautiful Quaker" and addressed to a "sweet girl."[86] Everything was becoming clearer. The romance between John

Ross and Mary Stapler had now become a real prospect. Whimsically, they connected places of happiness with their romantic interludes — consequently *Prospect* Hill received some purposeful underlining.[87]

Negotiating a Treaty

Acutely aware of the power of symbolic acts, Kooweskoowe observes all the rituals associated with a contemporary American marriage. In June 1844 he buys a large gem for Mary, using a postscript to explain the gem's personal symbolism: "As I have no Secrets to Conceal from you my Dear girl I will tell you that, I have this day negotiated for a *gem* that is to be a bosom Companion for me all the days of my life!"[88] The wordplay on "gem" beautifully conveys his elation, while the reference to concealing secrets conveys Kooweskoowe's sense of the delicacy of the negotiations in hand.

By July 1844 Mary knows that this is a time for other things to be sorted out too. She is not willing to sever herself from her primary family tie with her sister. When she lays this out in a letter, Ross is shocked and disappointed. He assumes that Mary is unwilling to leave her family home at Wilmington — even after marrying him. However, his fears are misplaced, for Mary only wants his consent for Sarah to accompany them to the Indian Territory. Stating the importance of Mary's happiness to him, Ross agrees, though slightly reluctantly. Unenthused at the idea of sharing Mary, he nonetheless understands the art of negotiation and compromise.

In late July 1844, in the buildup to the final agreement between them, when their letters cross over, Ross becomes paranoid that his avowals have gone too far. He does not know that Mary's letter, written two days previously, would at last address him as "My Dearest Friend."[89] Their chosen forms of address provide a barometer of their seesawing emotions and evolving affection for each other. In May 1844 Mary's letter to John had opened with "Most esteemed Uncle," which revivified their coy game of 1841.

The temperature is rising. Both John and Mary start to mention the "true pleasure" of receiving each other's letters, as well as their anxiety and the suspense and pain of not being able to spend time together. In response to a letter of early July, John says that he "felt the heat of its contents as they came hot from your pen."[90]

Although keen to embrace speed in communications and transport, John is forced instead to rely upon the "tedious conveyance of the mail."[91] Yearning for a more immediate form of modern communication, he complains that Samuel Morse's telegraph does not yet link Wilmington.[92] At its launch in Washington that same month in the northern spring of 1844, Dolley Madison sends the first-ever personal telegram — to her cousin in Baltimore.[93]

By early July 1844, Mary becomes less evasive. From May onward, John directs his letters to "My Dear Mary!" — the joyful exclamation mark declaring the possessive. Until June 1844, John signs off "Jno Ross." The intimate letter with the "*as — I do love you — Do you love me?*" banter is signed off, for the first time, as "Kooweskoowe."[94] Was this used simply as a more exotic name, possibly more alluring to a white woman enamored with "Indians"? Or was it a name for more intimate occasions, a "truer name" in some way? When Mary switches to "Esteemed Friend" in her letter of July 30, John takes this as expressing heightened feelings, replying with the endearment "My Beloved Mary!" Her next letters contain various expressions of intensified feeling, repeating words such as "joy," "joyful," "pleasure," and "delighted to see you," with Mary signing off as "your Devoted . . . Mary."[95]

Some of their correspondence is torturous to read, making palpable the suspense and wrenching emotions they endured between replies. To describe his tumultuous feelings during May 1844, Ross draws upon nature clichés like "the ebb & flow of Tide" and says his heart palpitates "like the wounded fluttering bird."[96] Mary portrays the "romantic scenery" of the Brandywine River and Quaker Hills as pristine nature parks. Here she leaves the "noisy world" to focus upon the actions of birds, though she takes care to connect these moments of joyful transcendence to "nature's God."[97]

When her latest correspondence is at last received, Ross confides how its endearing tone, "incites the tender feelings of my heart which can not [sic] be described! Confiding love, innocence & timidity seem to unite in thought as regards the step you are about to take from the present, to a future relation in life." He sees this as "important *movement*."[98] This step may be part of any life journey that will travel its course, but Ross knows this is no ordinary event. Rather, it is life in a new note: a rupture between present and future that will dramatically redefine Mary's role from single to married woman.

FIG. 44. An older Dolley Madison wearing her trademark turban. Engraving by Joseph Ward. Courtesy Library of Congress, reproduction no. LC-DIG-hec-00962.

Furthermore, at a time when women who married foreign nationals took on the nationality of their husbands, this marriage would qualify and redefine her relationship to her birth nation and to her future nation. The citizenship status of white wives remained controversial in the Cherokee Nation.[99]

Ross knew that the details of intimate pacts had to be as carefully negotiated as other alliances. This one required the support first of Mary, then her sister, her friends, and most significantly, her father. Mary had advised John that "a second person interested in the welfare of both parties can often work wonders."[100] Sarah was the most suitable emissary, and she was the only one who knew about their continuing secret correspondence. Furthermore, John considered that Mary would have "a fair chance of preparing the way for him without any thing being known about it." Ross also sought the consent of "friends," referring to the Quaker meetinghouse to which Mary had subscribed.

John went about sealing this deal with great seriousness. In order to "be certain of your own consent first before I made it known to her," he writes to Mary before Sarah, signing off, "Yours very affly" — that is, affectionately. By the end of July, Ross tells Mary that he gives her his "whole heart." He refers to a "sacred union" being formed. And he asks her not to show his letters to anyone. Although pleased and relieved that Mary thinks him sincere, this stilted prose suggests he still fears he might be dreaming: "Perchance the monitor within should tell you that your heart remains unalterably fixed upon me as you have more than once already intimated."[101]

Whereas they write romantically of "hearts" and "hands," anxious-sounding phrases reveal Ross's fears about the cruelty of unreciprocated love — when one gives the "entire heart." "Remember the happenings in this world and the one to come depends upon it" — a crossed-out line, Ross wants to tell Mary that if she has regrets, she should let him know immediately, not later.[102] Perhaps he was thinking of the case of the talented lawyer and Choctaw man James Lawrence McDonald, who fell in love with a white woman. When his proposal was rudely rejected, he plunged off a cliff to his death.[103] At least this is the version of events poignantly told by the same Thomas Lorraine McKenney who, in an assimilation experiment, took the studious McDonald into his Georgetown Heights home. He supervised McDonald's education and reared him alongside his own, less talented son. McDonald suffered deep psychological pain. His sense of despair for his people, especially the rest of his family, and his sense of not having any real home to go to, were intensified by the racism he encountered in Washington.[104]

Nineteen-year-old Mary Bryan Stapler was now at the stage of being able to offer both "your hand and heart . . . in the bonds of matrimony."[105] The time had come to seal the contract. From early days, Sarah had played intermediary, encouraging the liaison. Ross knows it is Sarah's opinion that really matters, so he requests information on her "private feelings." John goes through a prescribed process to gain the consent of both Sarah and Mary's father, passing the letters on to Mary to deliver.[106] On August 17 Sarah writes, "My dear sister is young and the thought of so soon resigning her to another as well as the great distance she will be removed from us is most painful." However, John has won her allegiance: "Having such entire trust and confidence in you, and her happiness having always been the desire of my heart I yield trusting Heaven may smile upon your union."[107] Despite family reservations, he gains Sarah's assurance to go ahead.

John Ross then wrote a formal request to John Stapler Sr., Mary's father, for Mary's hand in marriage. Although both were traders and businessmen, the letter does not suggest an ebullient relationship. A master of treaty and contractual negotiation, Ross writes in a formal style, adding the stilted, legalistic assurance that he can provide Stapler's daughter with "the ordinary comforts and happiness of this life." Then, becoming rather convoluted, he advises, "I should certainly never wantonly be instrumental in bringing about any change in her situation, calculated to render her condition less happy than it is at present."[108] Perhaps a standard phrase, in this context it anticipated Anglo-American anxieties based upon Indian race stereotypes, particularly on the captive white woman transformed as wife into a "squaw." Ross could not laugh off the degrading stereotypes entirely. With the prospect of civil unrest and warfare breaking out in his nation, the danger of ruin was all too real.

We receive few clues to John Stapler's personal reaction. His letter is missing from the extensive John Ross collection. Sarah told John that her father was absent but that she would forward the letter to him "as early as possible." She could predict his response: "The desire of my parents heart is to see his children happy and I feel at liberty to say he will not object when he finds Mary's *affections* are so entirely *yours*."[109]

We might speculate a lack of emotional connection, and perhaps even authority, on the part of her father. Or perhaps it was because Sarah had taken on the role of guardian and that marriage arrangements were essentially women's business. Mary provides more insight into the process. John Stapler arrives the day after Sarah dispatches John Ross's letter. There is a backup plan. Ross has thought to prepare other copies of his formal letter requesting the patriarch's consent, so Mary is able to provide the copy that is in her "possession." After reading it, John Stapler tells Mary that he respects John Ross "highly as a Gentleman" but that "separation" from Mary would "weigh heavily upon him." Her father was concerned about the distance and her youth. Despite this, as Mary explains to John, "after I had convinced him that my happiness was so much connected with you, he gave his Consent." John Stapler wrote a letter confirming this, which he sent to John Ross in Philadelphia. When Mary wrote to John on August 26, 1844, she advised him of the letter awaiting him and of its contents.[110]

In August 1844 John Ross writes to Mary, asking if she approves his planned wedding outfit.[111] She replies that she is happy with everything but would prefer if he wore a black satin vest rather than silk. Somewhat taken aback by his thoughtfulness in consulting her on such matters, because she has not sought John's opinion before selecting her own wedding outfit, Mary becomes remorseful.[112] Could Ross be more alert to the expectations of the new companionship style of marriage than Mary? Certainly Ross publicized his willing compliance: "It is the wish of Mary & I that our marriage should take place in as private a manner as possible, yet, Mary has notwithstanding assured me that, any of my friends or relatives, I wished to have present, will be agreeable to her!"[113] A couple of weeks before the wedding, Ross writes a letter to McKenney from New York reveling in boyish excitement:

> When we separated, I intimated to you that, it would give me pleasure to see you in P [Philadelphia], on a special occasion — and that, I would write and let you know what that occasion is to be. I will now tell you my friend, it is nothing more nor less than that I am engaged to be married to a young Lassie in the city of P on Tuesday morning the 3rd day of

Sept 1844! Are you surprised to hear of it? If not, pray then, who do you believe that lassie is?? I think you may guess & guess, over & over again, and not hit upon the right one! Now, if you are not yet astonished; I am sure you have at least become curious to know who she is. And when her name is revealed to you, I believe that you will wonder! Well then, without further exciting your curiosity, or keeping you in suspense, I will deliberately and softly whisper into your ears, that, it is the same identical little school girl, whom you once called Molly! And at this time known as Miss Mary Stapler of Wilmington Delaware!! Yes, my friend, strange and unexpected as this news may be to you, yet, it is nevertheless true.[114]

At last, with John and Mary's flirtation and courtship games about to reach a settlement, John had the chance to brag to his male confidante.[115] The extent of his excitement, if not pure glee, is revealed in his mischievous "P.S" to his "Dear Friend." Playfully, he boasts that he expects "to take from the banner State, Delaware, a captive quaker lassie, to preside over his wigwam."[116] This goes beyond the earlier wigwam whimsy, for although using the third person, Ross places himself explicitly in the role of captor. We know that, like Mary, he enjoys satire, but here his revelry and sheer acquisitive delight suggest more than a grain of emotional truth. Was he celebrating a historical moment when a Cherokee man could at last demonstrate equal masculine entitlement to a charming white woman from polite society?

Going further, he proclaims to his male friend that he has a "trophy" of "civilisation" to take to Indian country.[117] The reference to the Tuskaroras, a Native American group that had taken up residence in western New York and Maine, in the context of his "trophy from Maine," obliquely connects his boast with earlier histories of Tuskaroran captures of white women. And it links them all with McKenney's Cape Cottage resort. Ross had observed how white audiences voraciously consumed stories of wild savages capturing white damsels. Toying with the popular history of gendered conquest, he slotted himself as protagonist in their plotlines.

Kooweskoowe's success in securing a consensual union with a white girl not only subverted the dominant captivity narratives, it placed him — at least as an individual — on the winning side of history. Ross's unique position as educated Cherokee chief and his strong grasp of European history narratives meant he could—however ephemerally—occupy the same victorious league of successful conquerors as the colonizers.[118] As well as gaining a sense of masculine triumph, he found the gender and race politics exhilarating.

Although Mary had initiated the coquettish correspondence games, she would now agree that she was "captured," albeit by infatuation. When she fails to hear from John, Mary suffers her own "feelings of excitement": "Countless doubts and fears possess my bosom." Plaintively, she writes how "time passes heavily during your absence" and refers to the days ticking away until she sees "him my Soul holds most dear." She starts to refer to her faults and to adopt a meek tone: "I feel each day how unworthy I am of the affection of one so talented honorable, noble, and kind as I consider you [sic] all I have to offer in return is a heart which is all your own."[119] Ross's enjoyment of games that unsettled contemporary colonizing narratives was contingent upon Mary's cooperation. New chapters in their life stories and new histories of wider worlds were in the making. Yet none of these plotlines quite fit into any preexisting prototype.

From the beginning of their courtship, Kooweskoowe had been acutely aware of the parallels between the gendered politics of marriage and the transnational politics of negotiating his nation's future. Indeed, from mid-1844, he anticipated an important National Council meeting in October that could determine his nation's future. The planned wedding in September coincided with the three-year anniversary of Kooweskoowe's first letter to Mary. Beforehand, he was invited to visit various important men; as he puts it, "the first men of the New England States."[120] In stitching up key political support for Cherokee restitution, he follows a social networking process with staged protocols. Harking back to the "fair court/courtship" analogy of Kooweskoowe's first letter, in a practiced line, he assures Mary that after his business dealings, he will return "as soon as I can to Wilmington to consummate the treaty negotiation with you."[121] Around the exact time of his letter, his July business travel included a visit to Saratoga Springs with one of his beautiful young "nieces," where both drew attention. Intriguingly, she was also called Mary. This highly educated young woman of about seventeen years of age was there to "take the waters" and to learn more about fashionable society. Although she was slightly "tawny," a newspaper writer reported, this brunette "belle" was extremely beautiful and so alluring that white men repeatedly asked about her marital intentions. In reply, and possibly under Ross's instruction, she stated that she would only marry a man of her own nation.[122]

WEDDING HISTORIES

Symbolic Acts

John and Mary are to be married in Philadelphia. You can read about it in the major newspapers, for John and Mary placed official notices of the Ross-Stapler marriage on September 2, 1844. Using a standard format, they specified Mary's city of birth and residence and noted that John belonged to the Cherokee Nation. No mention was made of his birthplace or current residential town. Perhaps, after the Cherokee exodus west, the nation was no longer place-bound. The Cherokees, too, had become an emigrant people.

Preserved in the same file as Dolley Madison's flowers, John and Mary's wedding certificate (fig. 2) is flamboyant.[123] Like an elaborate tarot card signifying global journeys, its decorative border is an engraving of leaves and flowers that frames a ship tossing on choppy seas, against a cloudy background. On either side of this maritime image are portraits of a man and woman facing toward each other with outstretched hands. These figures are too wooden to evoke a suspenseful drama, but they do articulate a leveling respectability. A humble working-class man, the depicted groom wears antique seaman's trousers and waistcoat, and the woman wears a simple gown in an antiquated style for its day. Leaning on a baptismal font to suggest future offspring, her pose and stylized drapery allude to Greek and Roman statuary. (Following the Christian protocols of the day, however, the only bare flesh exposed is hands and faces.) John and Mary may not have glimpsed this certificate before their wedding day. Combined with their names in a fine calligrapher's hand, and the grand flourish of Pastor Orson Douglas's signature, this sheet of printed paper provides us with official proof of their marriage. And the wonder of it — over one and a half centuries later.

The union between two people in matrimony has often been signified by the distinctly human action of "taking one's hand." Holding European and Cherokee meanings, hands physically connect one human being with another, and the act of holding hands publicly communicates a connection between them. In their dealings with presidents, earlier Cherokee chiefs had stressed the need to bind men to their word via a physical connection of hands. In 1816 the young John Ross and his diplomatic party had been instructed to take "our Father the President" (Madison) "by the hand" in order to express the nation's satisfaction at being able to participate in the war "with our white brothers."[124] Western-style marriage relied upon another kind of intimate and political contract — one sealed by the meeting of hands and on paper. Words of love had been written in the lover's hand; the ring adorned the bride's hand with a significant gem or two. For John and Mary, the taking of hands was now publicly documented — before witnesses, in the newspapers, and on the certificate.

Although containing no reference to Native Americans, the wedding certificate features a display of nation and vital aspects of its colonizing history. The ship flies a version of what is now the U.S. flag. Travelers from distant places across the seas come together under a flag; marriage unites them, with the certificate's iconography indicating sovereign, legal, and church authority. With allegorical flourish, the ship is named *Union* — in large, noticeable letters. Like the colonizing settler states now governing marriage law, on landfall, a man and woman from afar seem destined to become settled. Its iconography connects immigration, commerce, wage labor, distances traveled and the vast oceans that can divide the sexes, and the Old and New Worlds. The hands outstretched across threatening seas connote a migrant nation based upon marriages. And perhaps also across the distances created by nation, culture, and histories.[125]

The many-layered certificate falls short of explaining why this particular couple chose to be married by Orson Douglas, a pastor of the Mariner's Church. Neither John nor Mary was a maritime worker, church member, or affiliate. The Quaker meeting hall of Wilmington had appealed to Mary's parents and quite recently, around the age of sixteen, she herself had joined. Whereas the Quakers stressed tolerance, civility, antislavery, and pacifism, they were religious exclusivists, vehemently opposing out-marriage and ostracizing anyone who married a non-Quaker. Dolley Payne suffered the same fate when she flouted the society's regulations to marry the non-Quaker James Madison in 1794.

It would have been impossible for John Ross to obtain the sanction of marriage within the Quaker meeting. He was ambivalent about Christianity and we do not have any evidence that he attempted to do so. According to the historian William McLoughlin, the Cherokees saw John Ross as a prophet and spiritual leader, although there is little evidence that he saw himself that way. He often referred to the syncretic notion of the Great Spirit who created all red, white, and black and who favored the red man. His views sometimes drew upon Christian rhetoric. Although incorporating elements of biblical frameworks, "Great Spirit" had a rather different meaning than "God."[126] It had become an acceptable transcultural translation. When making his official address to the Cherokees in 1896, George Washington had adopted the term "Great Spirit."[127]

When Mary attempted to encourage John toward godliness, he had responded tactically, with a pointed reference to buying a Bible and later to having heard a sermon.[128] Initially Ross had hoped to gain support for the marriage from Mary's "Friends" in the Quaker society. Aside from his not being part of the society, the Quakers opposed slavery, and the businessman John Ross was not planning to relinquish his valuable slaves. If Mary had to choose a substitute religion and Ross to select a marriage celebrant, a pastor from the Mariner's Church was indeed an inspired choice. One of its most charismatic and celebrated preachers was the Boston-based John Taylor, an orphan who had gone to sea and then been converted. He articulated an inclusive, democratic doctrine:

> For we being many are one bread, and one body,
> We have no artificial national meridians,
> Truth is our Meridian and Equator
> We have no sectarian lines of latitude[129]

Although affiliated with Presbyterianism, the Mariner's Church preached an antidiscriminatory religion that eschewed all kinds of bigotry. The elaborate graphics of its churches may have catered to a congregation who were not all literate. The church's catechism was designed like a mariner's compass, depicting an expansive moral worldview.

Although their ceremony did not take place in a church, for these lovers, their union transcended a civil treaty. Despite the couple's romantic interchanges reified nature's allurements more than God's, Mary referred to their "sacred union" and John to having their union "sacredly fulfilled."[130]

Philadelphia

The mariner imagery of John and Mary's wedding certificate aptly resonates with Philadelphia's history as a meeting place of colonizing frontiers and with a history fusing Old World and New. The couple chose to be married in this bustling port town that linked the key maritime routes of trade and commerce. Philadelphia was a center for industry, trade, and commerce. The Stapler family stayed here often, with business and friends there. Ross also had business and numerous relatives nearby.

In Philadelphia the memories of the settler-colonizer nation were celebrated and reconfigured, as they still are today. The city was forever associated with William Penn, after whom the state of Pennsylvania was named. Informed by the Quaker principles of compassion and tolerance, Penn presided over an idealistic regime where the English and the Delawares were to "live in love" for as "long as the sun and moon give light."[131]

Penn's "holy experiment" commenced when the English king Charles II granted him twenty-nine million acres of land in 1681. With Penn recognizing their sovereignty, the Lenapes, the Delawares, and leaders of other American Indian groups negotiated substantive treaties; Penn respected them deeply and exercised decency toward them. The Conestogas called him "Onas," referring to his quill pen used in signing treaties; the Delawares called him "miquon," meaning "feather."[132] Despite relations turning sour when his sons and later settlers took over, William Penn's example became a beacon of benign colonialism, if not of respect for Indigenous sovereignty. White philanthropists memorialized Penn's memory as a nonviolent reconciliation story. Native Americans saw it as exemplifying what might yet be possible from the colonizers.

Educated Cherokees were particularly enamored with keeping Penn's memory alive. In 1826 Elias Boudinot chose Philadelphia in which to deliver his eloquent *Address to the Whites*. When, four years later, he and Harriett named their first-born son William Penn Boudinot, they were honoring the conciliatory story of Penn and the Delaware chiefs. And they put this ahead of memorializing their own names. In a letter of 1836, John Ross explicitly used Penn as exemplar: "Most sincerely and ardently do we pray that the noble example of William Penn may be more generally followed, and that the rich rewards which attended his exertions may be showered upon the heads of those, who like him, never outraged the rights, or despoiled the property of the Indian." For them, "the blessing and prayer" of "the friendless native."[133] The missionary Jeremiah Evarts, who had written numerous newspaper articles and essays under the nom de plume William Penn, including tracts pleading against Cherokee removal, regularly corresponded with John Ross.[134] Years later, in one of Mary Stapler's letters, she evokes Penn's memory as a model for future American statesmen — one that she hopes will benefit her children.[135]

To John and Mary alike, the Philadelphia setting evoked a shared history of significance. Philadelphia's heritage included hosting key events of the American republic. It was here that the founding fathers of the United States met and where men of the caliber of Thomas Jefferson, James Madison, and George Washington had thought about how to constitute the republic.[136] The idealistic founding fathers of American democracy had offered to continue elements of Penn's legacy. Here were the hotels where presidents stayed; here were the homes of Washington and Madison and the streets that they walked. Here, too, were the homes of leading women such as Martha Washington and Dolley Madison.

Philadelphia was now a stage upon which national histories were being enacted anew. Its wharves witnessed ongoing arrivals of new immigrants and the loading and unloading of raw materials and new types of manufactured goods. Facing the sea where European visitors had made earlier landings, Philadelphia's port connected the American continent to Europe, Africa, and the rest of the globe. It was a place where nations met — not only the Delawares and the English but the rest of the industrializing world.[137] New waves of strangers continuously arrived on its Atlantic shores, along with the rise of modern forms of governance, global mercantilism, and new factories and industries.

In the first half of the nineteenth century the city remained boisterously democratic and a site of popular, often violent, protest. In the 1830s riots against African American slavery took place. In May and July 1844 troops quelled an anti-Irish uprising by Protestant Philadelphians.[138] Calling themselves the "Native American movement," the protesters paired colonizer nationalism with an assumption that white Protestants had already replaced Native Americans as "natives." (Similarly, in Australia the Australian Natives Association became powerful later in the nineteenth century, playing a populist role in the moves toward federation of the colonies and sardonically adopting Indigenous motifs such as decorative boomerangs and *gunyahs* for event shelters.)

Washington House

The Mariner's Church had outgrown itself and a new one was under construction. Consequently, although presided over by Orson Douglas, John and Mary's wedding was held in a hotel. They chose Hartwell's Washington House Hotel at 223 Chestnut Street in the city center. (Under the current numbering system, the hotel would have been located at approximately 709–13 Chestnut.) It was a home away from home for John. If you walk down the street's length, you end up at the legendary Penn's Landing site — memorialized as the supposed place where Penn later signed the treaty under the famous elm tree.[139] How many years John had been staying at this hotel we do not know, but he was certainly there in 1842 and in July 1844. Washington House catered well to business people and travelers, with its own stationery stamp for the mail service.[140] John's friends, his nephew William Ross, his cousins, and his relatives the Coodeys had also frequently stayed there, while McKenney, too, regularly stayed somewhere on Chestnut Street.[141]

Washington House's plain, symmetrical exterior contrasted with the Gothic windows and castellated parapet of the Masonic Temple next door.[142] On one side of the hotel was a piano and melodeon shop and various "fancy goods" stores. On the other side was Warne's Rifle and Pistol Gallery, with enticing painted images on its façade. During the day, women in hats or bonnets and dressed in tight-waisted, voluminous, floor-length dresses walked along the sidewalks chaperoned by finely dressed men in smart hats, well-fitting patterned trousers, vests, and jackets. It was a place to be seen. Groomed horses pulled along small and large coaches with seated passengers. At night, jaded businessmen walked along Chestnut Street to enjoy "places of amusement" with a "choice of every variety."[143]

Its name, Washington House, might suggest that George Washington, the first president of the republic, stayed there at some stage, but more likely it had simply been named in his honor. As the architectural historian Jeff Cohen points out, people of the 1840s would expect a far more palatial interior than would have been common during the lifetime of Washington, who died in 1799.[144] Possibly after the capital was moved to Washington City, at least one president had undertaken business at the hotel in Philadelphia. If John Ross was looking for historical continuity, this hotel obliquely associated him with historical legacies of great statesmen.

Ross did not need to try hard. He had personally corresponded with and negotiated with numerous presidents. Ross was only nine years old when Washington died, but the first president's name was revered in the republic's capital as the "father of his country" and for having chaired the Constitutional Convention of 1787.[145] (Elias Boudinot IV had chaired the Congress in 1782–83.) Washington House nicely reflected the trajectory of John Ross's intensely political life. And it also resonated with the memory of the idealistic founding fathers and the "Republic of virtue."[146] Monogamous marriage was implicated in national virtue, and holding on to their diplomatic history was crucial to having treaties ratified.

The settlement of Kooweskoowe's and Mary's marital contract took place in the same city where George Washington gave his contractual and heartfelt promise to the Cherokees in 1796. As a founding father of the Great Republic and a man of high ideals who recognized Cherokee sovereignty and who called them brothers and friends, Washington was beloved by the Cherokees. Indeed, John Ross and his first wife, Quatie, had called one of their sons, born in 1830, George Washington Ross. (He was born the same year as William Penn Boudinot.) Honoring Madison's fair-minded drafting of the Constitution and dealings with the "beloved" Cherokees, another Cherokee couple named their boy James Madison. Such naming paid homage, bestowing a role model and rejuvenating a legacy. Naming honored someone; it also forged a kind of kinship, with a reciprocal family tie. As with Elias Boudinot's assumption of a Republican statesman's name, it created obligations by association. In the case of figures like Washington or Penn, it engineered a remembrance of contractual promises, thus rejuvenating a legacy of living personal connections and ongoing agreements and expectations.

Washington had hoped to introduce policies "to advance the happiness of the Indians and to attach them firmly to the United States." He lamented that existing laws could not preserve peace with "our Indian neighbours" and that nothing "scarce of a Chinese wall, or a line of troops" could "restrain colonizing encroachments upon their lands."[147] That time, the bonds were between men — between brothers, fathers, and sons — and the rhetoric was warm and affectionate. In their letters of formal negotiation with current presidents and leaders, Cherokee leaders repeatedly reminded them of Washington's and Jefferson's earlier promises. Consequently, in his September 1841 letter to the Cherokees, President John Tyler had acknowledged these historical compacts: "I have read with interest and emotion the solemn address of our first President, the venerated Washington, to the delegation of your Nation, recorded in the silver bound book which he presented to you at Philadelphia, as the record of the mutual obligations then existing between the Government and the Cherokee Nation; and I have also read the eloquent talk made to you by the illustrious Jefferson, inscribed upon a parchment surrounded with an endless chain of gold. Let us still keep that chain bright and unbroken. In its preservation consists our mutual happiness."[148] The parchment and gold chain were cherished as artifacts of the United States — inspiring archival texts of even greater significance to the Cherokees. Written texts, and written contracts, now had embedded, hopeful meanings in Cherokee society, even more so among the literate and English-speaking Cherokees.

The Wedding

It was a significant event. Major newspapers announced the wedding. The day afterward, the *Pennsylvania Inquirer and National Gazette* proclaimed,

MARRIED

Last evening, at Hartwell's Washington House, by the Rev Orson Douglas, JOHN ROSS, Chief of the Cherokee Nation, to Miss MARY B STAPLER of Wilmington, Delaware.[149]

Similar notices about the transnational union also appeared in the *Public Ledger* of Tuesday, September 3, 1844, and in the *Pennsylvanian*. On

September 5 the leading paper of the time, the *Public Ledger*, published a feature article in the editorial section, on page two:

"MARRIAGE EXTRAORDINARY."

> John Ross, the celebrated Cherokee Chief, was married in the President's parlor of Hartwell's Hotel, in the city, on Monday night, to Miss Mary B. Stapler of Wilmington, Del. He is about 55, and she is only 18 years of age; she is said to be a very beautiful girl and highly accomplished, and belongs to the Society of Friends, or did. Her father was formerly a highly respectable merchant of the city. She was given away by her brother and attended by her sister and a niece of John Ross as bridesmaids. He had collected several of his daughters and nephews from the boarding school &c., in N. Jersey, to be present at the wedding and after the ceremony a family party of twenty of the Rosses (all half breed Indians) sat down to a most sumptuous banquet. Ross is considered to be worth half a million dollars.[150]

Their marriage was newsworthy for a number of reasons. For one thing, Indians were not expected to be wealthy or to host lavish feasts in the most prestigious venues of the early republic. The parenthetical "half breed Indians" indicated an effort to explain the anomaly. No "Indian," however, was expected to marry a desirable, respectable white girl or to have a community of relations residing nearby in elite schools. Rather, they were supposed to be segregated and to live far to the west in "Indian Territory." The bride's sister and John's niece—perhaps Eliza Jane, who attended school in Bethlehem—were attendants and bridesmaids. The matchmaker McKenney was unable to make it, so he did not act as a witness.[151] One of Mary's brothers gave her away, not her father. As we have no record of her father's formally objecting and Sarah assured Ross that he would follow Mary's feelings, we can only speculate as to why he did not perform the task. This was the first wedding of a daughter. Was it illness, business, or something else that kept him away?

Marriage, Home, Sovereignty

Following their September 1844 wedding, before heading west, the newlyweds traveled to New York. Philadelphia, Washington, and other major

FIG. 45. *International Indian Council* (Held at Tallequah, Indian Territory, in 1843), by John Mix Stanley. John Ross presides. Note the variety of dress styles indicative of different tribal groups. One man is smoking a peace pipe; others appear to be wearing medallions and chest ornaments, some of which may signify a tribal recognition, while others may have been awarded in diplomatic negotiations with a president. Smithsonian American Art Museum, Gift of the Misses Henry.

cities were places where Kooweskoowe had many friends, but he had to reach the Indian Territory in time for the October National Committee meeting. Cherokee politics were tense; civil war could break out; the nation could split.

Good political news arrived in the same month as the wedding. In September 1844 Ross received a letter from the president of the United States. After the hard line on Indian suppression of Andrew Jackson's presidency during the 1830s, President Tyler's words offered hope: "So far as it may be in my power to prevent it, you may be assured that it shall not again be said that a Cherokee has petitioned for justice in vain. I have looked over the several treaties that have been made between the Cherokee nation and the United States, and I find there promises of friendship on the one part, and of protection and guardian care on the other; and I now again promise you, and through you, your whole people, that the protection and care, so promised, shall be given."[152] This presidential assurance to abide by earlier contracts was the culmination of an eight-month-long delegation to Washington led by John Ross. An expert in using networks, Ross possibly had encouraged McKenney or Dolley Madison to play a mediating role. Ross was entitled to a sense of personal accomplishment, as well as measured hopes for the Cherokee Nation's — and his own — political future.

Yet was Ross really going *home*? In the 1840s he dramatized his ambivalence by calling the Indian Territory the "great Prairies of the West," the "expansive West," and the place of the "Sitting sun" and "setting sun."[153] Kooweskoowe had seen going west as not only leaving the Cherokees' sovereign lands but as going backward as a nation. Their forced exodus associated the Cherokees with the undeveloped lands of the West rather than the civilized, agricultural, and more culturally cultivated East, especially in New England. Yet, as if there were no routes leading toward modernizing futures, contemporary colonizing narratives situated Indians in static, dead or dying pasts. The highly mobile Ross had modernized and his sense of nationhood was now a migratory one.

So where was John going? For both Mary and John, shared confidences had turned into a public ceremony and formal announcements. In this marriage, John was stepping inside Mary's nation and Mary was stepping outside hers. If she married a foreign national born overseas, as a married woman, Mary would lose her citizenship status. In this case of "dependent sovereignty," however, the matter was somewhat opaque. Living in the Indian Territory would subject her to Cherokee law. Reference to John's national status in the newspaper wedding notice underlined the wedding's significance in transforming the wife's citizenship. However, being married to the Cherokee chief would put Mary in an elite position. Additionally, whereas her status became unstable in both nations, there was no bar to Mary returning to her Wilmington birthplace.[154]

In colonial imperialism, nations in contest had to assert sovereignty repeatedly — not only through historical texts and public enactments but through informal means such as repeated asides and humor. Although not unknown by the 1840s, for residents of New England a voluntary union between an "Indian" and a white woman was still an oddity. Ross was aware that the idea of a consensual mixed union would remain, in his words, a "funny joke." One nervously repeated at the expense of Indian masculinity.

In his case, however, a white bride had consented to "marry an Indian." She would leave the colonizer stronghold of New England to head west to the Indian Territory, lands to which the Cherokees had been recently expelled. The only way a white wife could fit into existing historical narratives was as his "captive quaker lassie." In Kooweskoowe's hands, his "playing Indian" satire at once exposed the limitations of colonizer thinking and defused colonizer ridicule.

As the imagined "chief in a wigwam" had long ago moved into a different architecture, Ross had particular reason to enjoy that joke. Rose Cottage, his impressive new residence, was located four miles outside present-day Tahlequah. The state of Georgia had sold his Coowasee home to lottery winners, forced Ross and his family out of the home, and taken over all his assets. By 1844 his splendid home in the Indian Territory was ready for his new bride.

As chief—whether in letters, in statesmanship or in council—Ross's public persona inevitably represented his nation. In dress, hairstyle, occupation, and gravitas, Ross's cultivated performances in the United States, including his wedding, were also about "playing modern American." At the same time, he unequivocally identified as Cherokee, using his totemic name in his own language for personal correspondence.[155] Adept at crossing worlds, his achievements, his lifestyle, and his life choices mediated the Cherokee present and future.

To Ross, something more needed to be done to record a nation's progress: the collection of national archives and the writing of national histories. Initiating various history projects, John recognized that written records and histories played an integral role in modern nationalism.[156] Valuing all kinds of written documents, and these especially, in early 1844 Kooweskoowe wrote to Mary emphasizing that he did not want their courtship letters destroyed, as she had wished. He requested that they remain "under cover" and confidential. "Do not be surprised at me for requesting you not to show that strange correspondence which passed between us whilst I was in Washington—but, let us keep those papers as a relick of curiosity, [by]

FIG. 46. *Mary Stapler Ross*, by Samuel Bell Waugh, 1848. Oil on canvas. Museum purchase, 1942.12.2. ©2015 Philbrook Museum of Art, Inc., Tulsa OK.

which wonders have been produced."[157] By "strange," he is alluding to his discomfort and joy at the strange ways of the heart, and of love.

We do not know why the young Mary was so ashamed of her letters, stating, "The sooner they are destroyed the better."[158] Both engaged in their romance via the transnational romanticism of their age. In urban America, ideas first developed in England and France were reverberating, including in the mind and heart of the chief of the Cherokee Nation.

Perhaps, after she received his very first letter, Mary allowed an obsequious foray into romanticism to go too far, flying too high on the scent of love. After all, she had written that it was "no less than a letter from Kooweskoowe the Chief of a generous and noble race for whom flambeaus were lighted and music was made to resound among the mountains even of Bethlehem."[159] But Ross had equal cause for embarrassment, echoing and building upon Mary's titillating "nature" descriptions of the Brandywine River in Wilmington. Ross's 1844 letter from Washington City included a reference not only to the "little songsters of the forest" — the birds Mary had repeatedly referenced to Kooweskoowe — but to the "gay and pretty May flowers of the valley" and "the sweet odour of the shrub . . . wafted upon the breese [sic] over the romantic scenery along the sylvan Brooks, gently gliding into the majestic Delaware."[160]

Mary relented. She never destroyed their letters, thus ensuring that the pen work of their hands — folded, inserted in envelopes, and stamped — remained safe. Successive generations of the Ross family kept the archive intact. A descendent finally sold them, along with the wedding certificate and the flowers, to the safekeeping of the Gilcrease Museum in the 1940s.[161]

So what clues do we gain about why John Ross changed his mind on intermarriage? In one sense, the letters strongly suggest that John and Mary simply fell in love, in the romantic sense that we might understand it today. We glimpse sustained infatuation, obsession, both of them feeling high on love. John's life was busy and serious, his energies caught up by the affairs and perplexing worries of state. In Mary, he discovered that the "frivolity" he once despised in young white women enabled him to relax, to enjoy himself, and to exchange intelligent, even politically incisive, humor. At the same time, transnational diplomacy had filled his life from boyhood. Making it tangible via a sexual and marital relationship may have enabled

FIG. 47. This glass-plate image shows John Ross in the pose of a dignified, affectionate husband, with a gleam in his eye and a look of pride, happy to place his arm around his wife's shoulder. Mary's eyes reveal a sparky sense of the mischievous, while her warm smile exudes contentment and happiness to be with him. Courtesy Oklahoma Historical Society, no. 19615-45-b.

him to find another dimension of himself, of Kooweskoowe. There was more to it, too. As principal chief, his choice of a white wife might have been a necessary political strategy. For John as a man, it provided a gratifying sense of victory in a game his people were losing — the masculine game of colonialism, with its landownership and its female trophies.

Kooweskoowe and Mary were both keenly aware of the place of their marriage as a juncture in a complex story of colonizing diplomacy. They seemed to sense that their actions potentially redefined the meanings of union, home, and nation; they stood inside the transnational, the mobile and transformative. Contractual moments of nation and of marriage were sharp turning points that had led them down new roads — in John's words, to a "*future relation* in life" (emphasis added) Together, they expanded the range of acceptable kin and familial relations that Ross had used in his lifetime of letters with national leaders, philanthropists, and missionaries — those limited to brother, sister, and father. From the outset, Mary and he had stretched bonds of relation by adopting the purported family relationships of uncle and niece. An uncle owed much to a niece. Now the familial categories were properly — and legally — extended across two nations, to that of husband and wife.

Via a written, mailed correspondence, they had negotiated the terms of their intimate relationship. To empower his people, Ross relied upon the pen and the mail service. Literacy and the letter-writing traditions of the new republic were fundamental to their courtship. Their printed and signed wedding certificate was proof of a legal contract. The iconography of their chosen venue — the city of Philadelphia, the Mariner's Church, and the Washington House hotel — summed up their purposeful deliberations. Each had sharp eyes for telling motifs that might be inscribed into useable histories; they harnessed the memories living in the popular imagination and in places, scenes, and symbols of deep national significance.

Mary and John's correspondence consciously reflected upon the contrasting histories into which they were born. These transnational histories had shaped their consciousness, their worlds, and in turn, what was to become of any relationship between them. They explicitly drew parallels between the negotiation of intimate and state contracts. In surprising ways, their letters have provided us glimpses into vital national discourses and their self-conscious subversion of their tropes. Indeed, their correspondence enables us to readily see that they recognized the strange nexus between the history-making potential of intercolonial marriages in a settler-colonizer nation. Although Ross's courtship letters offered escape from higher duties, their gentle mockery of the colonizer's version of history was also part of a serious transnational game with high stakes.

John and Mary's seemingly flippant exchanges cleared the way beyond historicized stereotypes, suggesting alternative narratives of gendered intimacy. In so doing, they carved out a space between nations that two people could journey between, and where some Indigenous power might survive and assert itself.

Ross knew that the theater of national sovereignty and the softer performances of marriage involved symbolic and public acts. Sometimes unintentionally, sometimes by careful choices, John and Mary defied the limits of a single nation to inscribe their wedding rituals with a transnational iconography. On the most intimate scale, through webs of connection and kinship, their courtship and marriage became a means of enacting, extending, and consenting to the reach of nation in which a two-way inclusiveness seemed possible.

Archival Afterword: Dolley Madison's Flowers

The file containing John and Mary's marriage certificate also held the flowers. This formed a direct link with the president's widow. Playing a key role in thinking through the principles of the Constitution, and in putting it into words, President James Madison worked closely with Thomas Jefferson. Dolley herself has been mythologized not only for being the ultimate hostess who set the standard for future presidential wives or "first ladies" of state but also, according to a widely held legend, for preserving Washington's portrait, an important state relic, just before enemy attacks destroyed the White House in 1812.[162] So she had honored the first man of state, the first president, and the greats like Jefferson and her husband, James Madison. In sending Mary flowers, she was honoring the woman married to the chief of the Cherokee Nation. In the Anglo-American republic, it was marriage that conferred First Lady status. In the Cherokee Nation, it would not be so simple. But John Ross was the chief, the leader of that nation.

Marriage and nation featured powerfully in Dolley Payne's life. As mentioned earlier, when she married the non-Quaker James Madison, Dolley was forced out of the Quaker church and rejected by the Friends. Additionally, as the official consort of the widowed President Jefferson, Dolley played an intimate role in obscuring his sentiment for his slave Sally Hemings. Their children, their secret family, could not be classed as family at all.

The trail linking Dolley Madison's flowers with John Ross and Mary Bryan Stapler had grown over. However, its remains lead back to John and Mary's matchmaker, William McKenney. The heyday of his career had been under President Madison, and so he knew Dolley as an old acquaintance.

Corresponding with her from time to time, he put her on a pedestal, awestruck by her persona as a legendary American and her continuing influence. In extravagant words of praise, McKenney dedicated his published memoirs to Dolley Madison.

When I sought evidence of direct contact with John Ross in her mellifluous records, the research trail ran cold. It is highly likely, however, that they met during delegations to Washington. An archetypal story was included in the biography written by her niece, of how Dolley was one day entertaining a delegation of chiefs. When she slipped into her boudoir, she was surprised by one of the "Indians" supposedly in "full war paint." The image of this elaborately painted and attired "savage" in this private female space of her home appealed to an early and mid-nineteenth-century audience, being retold many times.[163]

That the elderly First Lady of the nation sent a wedding gift of flowers to Mary Bryan Stapler was surely significant. The widowed female elder of the early republic thereby conducted an exchange with the First Lady of another nation. As an icon of the republic, Dolley Madison stood at the heart of national protocol on marriage. She had a fine understanding of the pact between presidents and chiefs. The Great Father, the president, had become kin to Indians, with the fiduciary responsibilities that entailed. In Washington's terms, Dolley understood a compact of mutual obligation. The Cherokee Nation would cultivate the soil and become civilized, in return for the full benefits of the republic. A gift respecting John and Mary's wedding stood as one remembrance of that trust-based agreement. Perhaps she was also endorsing the words of her close friend Jefferson: "You will mix with us by *marriage*; your *blood will run in our veins* and will spread with us over this great continent." The United States would be complete: "we shall all be Americans"[164] Dolley Madison's role was one of gender diplomacy, acknowledging the symbolism of a deeper kind of transnational marriage: a marriage of state.

One marriage, even one of the chief or king, cannot settle everything between nations. It was certainly not an ultimate solution to the vulnerable Cherokee Nation's suffering of the pain of multiple dispossessions and loss. But its symbolism was there. And, if his later letters are any indication, John had found the great love of his life.

Part 3

Queensland's Marital Middle Ground

CHAPTER FIVE

Husbands under Surveillance

It is 1901. If you are a man who is not an Australian Aboriginal person and you are living with an Aboriginal woman, you have just become a criminal. Take the case of Goon Goo, a Chinese resident in North Queensland. He was prosecuted for "harbouring" Kitty, an Aboriginal woman who had been his partner for seven years. A local policeman advised Goon Goo that if they wanted to stay together, he now required permission from the chief protector of Aborigines, from whom he had to obtain an official marriage license. Otherwise, he would risk being sent to jail. Three days after his prosecution, Goon Goo applied to the local protector of Aborigines for a marriage permit. However, police charged him for supplying opium and alcohol to an Aboriginal person and he was fined three pounds sterling. Following his conviction, Kitty was forcibly "removed" from their home and transported to the Yarrabah mission, then under the auspices of Reverend Ernest Gribble. Kitty lost her right to live with her de facto husband and to live on her own land. She also lost her liberty. Torn apart, both Kitty and Goon Goo were deeply shocked and confused.[1]

Jauntily confident about Queensland's white future, the administrators of the Queensland Aboriginals Protection Act aspired to create an idealized social order befitting of a "modern nation." At first, however, they did not articulate a clear concept for implementing the new framework. Contests would be fought between colonial and Indigenous knowledge systems, over colonizer and class entitlements and definitions of respectability. The morality and sexual propriety of the act's enforcers would be seriously challenged.

By the late nineteenth century, Aboriginal Queenslanders were still applying their law of the land. While Aboriginal people all knew where their particular "country" and linguistic regions began and ended, to newcomers these were borderless lands — ones in which they hoped to find new lives. These were also places where nations met. In some areas it was only twenty years, or even a few years, earlier that Chinese, whites, and had others started entering Aboriginal territories. Aboriginal laws were not published; although message sticks and other forms of written communication were used, Aboriginal people did not apply the symbolic systems known as literacy. Unlike in eighteenth-century Algonquin history, their marital law had not been tested and codified in the courts. And unlike the Cherokees, these Aboriginal groups had not formed a centralized national unit with written marriage laws. Explained in diagrams and paintings, Aboriginal law was embodied in the landscape, reenergized by rituals, storytelling, painting, weaving, and traveling. On light wooden shields and smooth rock surfaces, rich ochers left striking circles and stripes that delineated personal and land-based identities. Correct moral behaviors and right-way marriage rules were associated with continuously peopled pasts. These were present and immanent in the living landscapes that they could feel and touch around them — places that noticed who was there and cared.

The spine of all their law was marriage law. It *made* kinship, which was the premise of human identity and behavior, and it was what linked individuals to constellations of other language groups and to great sweeps of country and their neighboring custodians. Before discussing this further in the next chapter, this one focuses upon state perspectives. Unlike the self-generated Cherokee private and public archives, in Queensland it was acts of government surveillance that created an extensive marriage correspondence of the intimate transnational. The archive was created by state officers involved in a social project. For often-contradictory reasons, this enterprise attempted to impede the free-form development of these liminal and transactional societies. Through speaking with state officers, recording testimony, and writing or having pleading letters written, some Aboriginal and intermarried people actively constructed the record too. Many also refused to provide witness statements, so actively avoided inclusion in the archive. The octopus of intrusive state surveillance has left its legacies among Aboriginal Queenslanders, so for privacy reasons I restrict this discussion to cases already in the public record.

In lives both public and private, North Queensland's emergent new societies had become places of intricate intergroup and family connections. Following a period of violent warfare, various common grounds of cross-cultural negotiation emerged — a New World landscape that saw the interface between people from Asia, Europe, and Aboriginal Australia. Queensland's Yarrabah region was one of many regions where Indigenous people were living on or near their traditional lands. Although they formed the majority of residents, they were also living alongside communities comprising predominantly male groups of newcomers from the continent's south and from across the seas — from Europe and America.[2]

Morals campaigners accused European frontiersmen of abductions, kidnappings, and rapes of Aboriginal women. They portrayed Aboriginal men as pimps and the Aboriginal women as prostitutes. Queensland frontiersmen could be brutal and lawless. Only some cases of violent coercion and horrors found their way into the archive. By the same token, much of today's thinking about Aboriginal sexuality is flavored by presumptions of female victimhood. It reflects a contemporary European cultural and Christian sensibility around sexuality and gender. It overlooks the fact that Indigenous people saw their sexual and marital protocols and local law as sovereign in their land.

Indigenous husbands frequently enforced their marriage law, punishing infringements against their strict kin-based marriage laws violently — sometimes executing the transgressor. If the husband or partner did not meet reciprocal obligations toward kin, his life was in danger. This could equally apply if the union was approved under Aboriginal law or legally endorsed by the colonizer state. Aboriginal women had not asked for "protection" from white men or for a new layer of marital restrictions.

As the police magistrate reported in 1891, "Every murder that occurred on the coast was due to the carrying off of gins in the boats. There was not the slightest doubt of this being the case."[3] "Gin" was a word used for

Aboriginal women at the time; thought to derive from the Eora people of Sydney Cove far to the south, it took on derogatory connotations.

So what kind of society did Kitty and Goon Goo inhabit? Some of this has already been discussed in chapter 2. While the Australian colonies federated on January 1, 1901, most of Queensland remained "unsettled" — a frontier zone, with the ever-present specter of violence. The "great land rush" that had divided Queensland into privately owned urban, pastoral, and agricultural properties under British rule had exacerbated extreme frontier conflict.[4] Indeed, as outlined earlier, from the 1870s, state-backed imposition of law and order imposed British sovereignty over Indigenous lands, making Queensland Australia's most violent frontier. Free white settlers carried out violent incursions, including numerous massacres, leading to one of the heaviest death tolls in Australia.[5] Aboriginal girls and women suffered rape, abuse, torture, capture, enslavement, and murder at the hands of brutal white men. Introduced sexual and other diseases and malnutrition due to land encroachments wreaked further devastation. By 1910 Queensland's Aboriginal population — estimated at between one hundred thousand and two hundred thousand in the precontact period — stood at twenty thousand.

Against this horrific tale, the frontier also brought mutual interdependence and cross-cultural cooperation. Intimate associations brought links with introduced economies, new ideas, and new peoples. In the archive of colonial paperwork, the imagined social landscape changed far more suddenly than it did on Indigenous lands. Nonetheless, the sudden implementation of the new marriage laws came as a surprise to many mixed couples.

Local white men and women in Kitty and Goon Goo's community supported them strongly. A white businessman, a bank manager, and a sergeant of police pleaded for Goon Goo's right to live with Kitty. They all argued that he was a "good husband." Kitty's white female employer objected to her removal to Yarrabah because she was a quality worker. Other people from the Dry River district vouched for her work as a cook and laundress and stated that she was well regarded and admired. Defending her husband's reputation and his domestic arrangements, his lawyer commented that "if all the blacks were as well treated as Kitty there would be no necessity for interference by the authorities."[6]

FIG. 48. A Chinese man in front of his hut, ca. 1890. Queensland State Library, no. 70254.

MARITAL ACTS

The Queensland government sought to regulate and phase out intermarriage and intermixing between all newcomers and Aboriginal women. However, the self-governing colony did not introduce race-based marriage prohibitions like those in the United States of America. Modeled upon English law, Queensland's marital laws did not proscribe any racial categories of people from marrying.[7] Queensland's Marriage Act, "An Act to amend and consolidate the laws affecting the Solemnization of Marriage" (1864, effective 1865) was one of the early acts assented to by Queen Victoria, and it correlated with Britain's Colonial Marriages Act, effective the same year and passed in order to validate marriages in its colonies abroad.[8] The Queensland act was assented to only five years after the colony gained its self-government and separated from New South Wales. Close relatives were prohibited from marrying, a bride under twenty-one years of age required the consent of the parent or guardian, and "lunatics" were considered unable to provide consent. Marriage was disallowed if the applicant was already married. Various issues later arose regarding the marriage of foreign nationals, and also marriage to foreign nationals.

The Queensland act required witnesses to the ceremony and a registered clergyman or district registrar to officiate. The couple had to swear oaths or a "solemn affirmation" and, whether literate or not, they had to sign forms. The oath — a Christian-ordained ritual that required swearing "on the Bible" — was to include that "there is no impediment or lawful objection by reason of any kindred relationship or alliance or any former marriage or the want of consent of parents or guardians or any other lawful cause."[9] Family permission was required only for minors. The key prohibitions were incest and bigamy.

Marriage could not be secret; it had to be done in open view. Clause 11 required that marriages performed by the registrar be held in the public space: "The doors of such office must be open at the time of the celebration of such marriage, so that any person wishing to be present may be enabled to enter."[10] This also allowed objections to be heard. Marriages had a timetable; they had to take place between eight in the morning and eight at night. While the Queensland act made special allowances for the distinctive traditions of Quakers and Jews, Aboriginal customary law and ritual was not considered relevant. It was not the Marriage Act but the Aboriginals Protection Act of 1897 (amended 1901) that became Queensland's key mechanism to curb intermarriage between Aboriginal and non-Aboriginal people.

During the early Australian national or federation era, the Queensland government's radical social interventions needed to be acceptable in a global imperial context. The "White Australia" policy was designed to stop nonwhite immigration and to deport Asians and Pacific Islanders. State legislators had to do something to assuage Queensland's bad reputation both for exploiting Pacific Islanders, who suffered a high death toll, and for watching over the demise of Aboriginal people on violent frontiers.

In this context, and following a reign of anti-Aboriginal terror, the 1897 Aboriginals Protection and Restriction of the Sale of Opium Act's rhetoric of protection was a disingenuous ploy to appease British humanitarians. As colonialism brought employer exploitation, disease, and drug dependence, it was difficult to argue against the act's good intentions. After all, its stated aim was to protect Aboriginal women from harmful sexual and labor exploitation.[11] Equally, however, its "protective" arsenal could be harnessed as a new colonizing tool to serve pragmatic, local ends.

Scientific racism was an aspect of the cultural and political landscape of this era in a way that had not been the case for the Cherokees in the early nineteenth century. The popular post-Darwinian doctrine of the "survival of the fittest" positioned the decimation of Indigenous peoples as an evolutionary fact, like a large wave in the advancing tide of history. Humanitarians argued for ameliorative strategies—one method was to try to create survival opportunities by segregating Indigenous peoples from the perpetrators of their demise, the colonizers. This had the advantage of getting rid of potentially violent competitors to the colonizers for land, resources, and women.

If this didn't work, at least it might "smooth the dying pillow" for the "remnants."[12] Those of mixed descent were not counted in the equations. They did not belong to a "race"—either whites or Aborigines. Perhaps to suggest a "species" difference, armchair scientists of the early nineteenth century thought that Aboriginal women could not reproduce with whites at all. However, nobody in early twentieth-century Queensland thought this for a moment.

Initially, the 1897 act targeted Aboriginal-Asian couples. On the rationale that they supplied opium, all Chinese men were banned from employing female Aboriginal labor and from associating with Aboriginal females altogether. As white male workers resented Chinese competition for Aboriginal employees, they approved such color-coded restrictions, which were designed to appease the labor movement.[13] The fact that white men also supplied opium and alcohol was underplayed.

Despite the race coding of the Queensland act, its 1901 amendments extended restrictions on employment and cohabitation to apply to *all non-Aboriginal* men. As the act contained regulations to prevent social fraternizing between Aboriginal women and outsiders, any non-Aboriginal man living in an informal marriage with an Aboriginal woman became a potential police target.[14]

Heterosexual relations, cohabitation, and intermarriage now came under concentrated state surveillance. Any man who wanted to live with an Aboriginal woman and was not Aboriginal himself now had to seek permission from the protector, via a police officer. The protector was entitled to refuse all requests.

From 1901, local police were instructed to observe any white or Asian men living with Aboriginal women, to compile evidence, and to report offenders to the senior protectors. One was based in a government office in Brisbane and another in Cooktown, North Queensland. If a man was apprehended for cohabiting with an Aboriginal woman, the local magistrate's court heard the case. If proven guilty, he was fined or jailed. As Kitty discovered, state authorities had the authority to send the Aboriginal woman and her children away to an Aboriginal reserve in strange country, with strangers.

This was no clear-cut antimarriage policy. The state held powers not to ban but to *restrict* heterosexual mixing between Aboriginal women and all non-Aboriginal *men*. Cohabitation was criminalized, not marriage. To obtain a legal marriage, an applicant could officially apply for a marriage permit via the local police officer, who would then refer the request to the regional protectors of Aborigines. The chief protector then assessed the "suitability" of the potential non-Aboriginal husband for the Aboriginal woman. The Aboriginals Protection Act was introduced at the highpoint of pre-federation nationalism. It relied upon a system of race classifications based upon hybridity, or percentage of non-Aboriginal parentage. Yet, despite a polemic emphasizing race and aliens, in actual practice, administrators frequently made moral judgments that overlooked color. Their decisions were often based upon contemporary notions of fairness and European values around marriage and family. As the rules applied to all men who were not Aboriginal, this included the white men who were making the rules. The reasoning behind the decisions of the act's administrators provides a window into contemporary ideas around not only race and nation but also the precepts of masculinity and marriage. In particular, it reveals what was expected of the good husband.

In Queensland there was no ban upon *white women* marrying Aboriginal men. This was in stark contrast to the United States, where the possibility of a white woman marrying a slave and black children being born to a white mother was considered repugnant. Consequently, numerous states had banned all mixed marriages with African Americans.[15] With more freed slaves mixing in North American society from the 1820s, several states introduced new or stricter bans against marriages between whites and "negroes," "blacks," or Africans.[16] As well as "color" difference, issues of slavery and property, and of class and labor hierarchies, prevailed. By the early twentieth century, the one-drop rule was creating the Jim Crow segregation policies that targeted African Americans.[17]

In various Australian states during the late nineteenth century, colonizing contact had been taking place since the late eighteenth century. Some white women had married Aboriginal men — for example, Ernest's sister Edith Gribble — but most of these women's stories are yet to be told.[18] Queensland's extremely high masculinity ratio, plus increasing Indigenous impoverishment, made white women's intermarriage with Aboriginal men relatively uncommon.

Additional considerations account for the anomaly between state laws in the United States and Australia. It was not only the shift toward scientific racism and eugenics. On the Queensland frontier, when an Aboriginal woman married a white man, it was regarded as "uncivilizing" for the man. White women later lobbied to be protectors themselves, arguing that when white men mixed with Aboriginal women, it reinforced white male "savagery."[19] Although the American term "miscegenation" — which after the 1860s came to infer a crime against race or genus — was not in use in Australia, the term "combo" became its derogatory equivalent. Signifying the combining of "types" specifically across the colonizing line with Indigenous peoples, "combo" became a slander implying a social offense against race. It also implied the production of children with the derogatory label of "half-castes."

White men were appalled by the thought of police and protectors impeding their rights or adjudicating their intimate behavior. Across all classes, they were angry about state interventions in their intimate lives. After all, the state's marital acts set a precedent that potentially affected the rights of any man to choose a wife and to assert male "sovereignty" in marriage.[20]

Threatening male authority in the realm of marriage was a risk-laden policy. By rupturing the common ground of cross-cultural marriages, the gendered authority of men was potentially jeopardized. The act authorized the chief protectors to assess whether any man living with an Aboriginal woman was a worthy husband. Consequently, a man could be put under surveillance and charged and his wife moved away and placed under the authority of a strange man, a "reserve" manager or superintendent. White male colonizers were in a mood to assert their democratic rights. They had high hopes for an egalitarian, classless society that would benefit them in any way they liked — sexually, in semisecret unions or in public. Living in frontier regions only enhanced their sense of entitlement.

Because their heterosexual choices were under threat from the state, in order to fight back, white working-class frontiersmen deployed both their democratic powers and "race powers." They conducted antiprotection and antisegregation campaigns. This even included campaigns in support of the Chinese and Pacific Islanders whom they had previously opposed due to cheap labor competition. In this transnational zone, white men effectively resisted efforts to inscribe state boundaries between men and women. They refused to relinquish their rights to live with or marry an Aboriginal woman. Instead, they made a morality-based case, pleading that the state recognize that, as consenting adults, they had every right to take on the role of husband across colonizer boundaries. If they were to lose these rights to partner choices — to being good husbands, to keeping their family together — it would defy all gendered and emotional logic.

BREAKING UP THE COMMON GROUND

In many regions of northern Australia by the 1900s, Aboriginal people were still the majority. True, diverse outsider peoples had arrived and were now living upon the lands of the rainforest and cape dwellers, the Kuku-Yalanji, the Yidinjdji, the Djirbalngan, the Wargaymaygan, the Kaantju, and many other landowning groups. With their ancestors having sustained a civilization on the continent for fifty thousand years, they had certainty over their land entitlements. They cherished a deep-time sense of belonging and knowledge of their sovereign lands and their respective languages and cultural traditions. The imprints of journey routes, creation stories, and kin, marriage, and moiety networks linked histories of connection over a longue durée. While the colonizer state did not recognize Indigenous land title or laws, individual newcomers were becoming enmeshed in their society and some were agreeing to follow key aspects of their land-based systems of law.

Along with workers in the maritime industries and cattle enterprises, large groups of Chinese and other men started arriving as gold-seekers in the 1870s. Intensifying resource exploitation was making the hunter-gatherer economy untenable. Queensland Aboriginal people had to migrate across other Aboriginal groups' increasingly limited lands and to constantly negotiate new kin, shelter, and economic alliances with them. They had to do the same with the colonizing newcomers. To avoid violence, to replace livelihoods, and to acquire new goods, Aboriginal people adopted proactive strategies that would entwine them in the introduced economies of gold, pastoralism, agriculture, and port towns. Excellent horse riders, stockmen, and drovers, and in demand as domestic workers and cooks, by the late nineteenth century Aboriginal people of the north became a sought-after labor force on the vast Queensland pastoral stations. Often this work allowed them the mobility to travel large range areas.

Aboriginal people refused to work on plantations and to be tied to sedentary labor. Consequently, from the 1860s to 1900, Queensland sugar and tobacco planters imported tens of thousands of Pacific Islander workers from New Caledonia, Malaita, the New Hebrides, the Solomons, and Fiji. In a substitute for the slave trade, unscrupulous "blackbirders" recruited and transported labor to meet demand, a trade that was more tightly regulated after the 1880s. When Pacific Islander recruitments suffered decline due to depopulation, British Australian employers imported labor from Asia—including Java, Ceylon, Japan, and China. In order to maintain international competitiveness with former imported labor and slavery economies such as the Caribbean and Fiji, employers argued that imported colored labor was essential for tropical industries.[21]

Additionally, numerous scientists believed that white men working in Queensland's tropical climate would suffer race degeneration. A proliferation of sunburned drunks seemed to prove the case. However, the unionized white labor movement had long campaigned against cheap imported labor, and by 1908 all "colored labor" was to be deported and repatriated. In joining the federation, Queensland was dragged into a wider population and immigration project. Australia's race fears were exaggerated due to its geographical location—far distant from larger "white nations" and close to populous Asian nations. From 1901, to avoid giving offense to Britain's ally Japan, Australia's immigration policies drew upon American policies and developments and the Natal model from South Africa. Rather than explicitly restricting entry on the basis of race, the new law duplicitously made entry contingent on a dictation test in a "foreign language."[22]

Arrivals to Queensland's shores were predominantly male, creating the highest non-Indigenous sex imbalance of all the Australian colonies. In rural areas in 1861, there were 200 white men to every 100 white women; by 1900 there were 171 white men to every 100 white women. Many white men were looking for wives.[23] Only half of the white men then residing there ever formally married; even lower rates applied to Asian and Pacific Islander men.[24]

As a basis for developing new economies, the Queensland state was highly motivated to create and sustain segregated zones between black and white. Intermarriage had already been a catalyst for waves of frontier violence, undermining the colonizer's grip on law and order. Frontier violence was too recent to be forgotten. When Aboriginal men killed eleven residents of the Fraser family's pastoral station at Hornet Bank, Central Queensland, in 1857, it was commonly accepted that these acts were provoked by poisonings of Aborigines and acts of rape and sexual cruelty by the Fraser sons. This did not stop local settlers from retaliating in amplified vengeance, with hundreds of Aboriginal people randomly killed throughout the region.[25] During the 1890s the notorious case of the intermarried Aboriginal bushranger Jimmie Governor from neighboring New South Wales reinforced colonizer fears. On the farm that had employed his white wife, Governor murdered several white women and young children. This young man had been complemented for being literate, intelligent, and a hard worker. Racist comments made to his pregnant white wife are believed to have provoked him into creating an outlaw gang and carrying out these murders.[26]

Despite the risks of inciting Aboriginal men's ire, for white men, unions with Aboriginal women remained highly attractive. First, they did not arrive with wives, and the gender imbalance among the immigrants on the frontier created high demand for women. White men across the class spectrum — pastoralists, employers, and skilled and unskilled workers in other frontier industries — were attracted to the beauty of Aboriginal women. Indigenous knowledge of water, food resources, trails, and terrain provided strong incentives for newcomer men — whether white, Asian, or Pacific Islander — to engage cross-culturally. Aboriginal women were skilled in identifying and gathering bush foods and general survival. They were less threatening than the men — that is, assessed as less likely to kill you. Many white men took advantage of this and were cruel and exploitative.

Frontiersmen regularly and eagerly entered into casual liaisons with Aboriginal women. Some negotiated marital partnerships with women and Indigenous kin or husbands. Many settled into longer-lasting unions. Some fell in love. Many became practically and emotionally dependent upon their partners. Out of economic, sexual, companionate, and familial arrangements, close cultural knowledge exchanges took place.

With such intermingling in progress, making Queensland "white" and a matching part of white Australia would be no easy business. For example, in 1901 there were 2,017 Chinese men and only 61 Chinese women residing in the Cairns district. In that year, the Chinese (many of whom arrived during the Palmer River gold rushes of the 1870s) made up 48 percent of the population in the Cairns hinterland and 18 percent of the town population. On the Barron River, up to twenty sampans ferried Chinese corn, bananas, and other produce to the northern port of Cairns, which had a bustling Chinatown with two temples.[27] While marriage laws in the Australian states did not generally prevent Chinese intermarriage with whites, from 1901 a forced repatriation policy was in place. For two more years, the spouses and families of the few Chinese men allowed to remain were permitted to immigrate to Australia.[28] The policy used loneliness to freeze out Chinese men.

Another way of looking at peoples uniting across colonizing boundaries is that they were in the process of creating a "*borderless* land." That is, in the western sense of state borders. In regions where Chinese, Pacific Islanders, and others predominated, a league of nations prevailed, without clear-cut boundaries. Despite their differences, North Queenslanders lived in a network of mutual cross-cultural interdependence across many national and cultural origins. These worlds were inherently transnational—simultaneously opening and erasing borders. With endemic demand for local Aboriginal women as lovers, sexual partners, and domestic and pastoral workers, every man and woman of the colonizer classes had cause to enter into some cultural diplomacy. Consequently, to various degrees, First Nations people became interconnected with a range of colonizing peoples; they became families across frontiers.

As we will explore further in the next chapter, Aboriginal people had a clear sense of landed boundaries, as defined by clan affiliation, language spoken on certain tracts of land, and place-names. Although more organic, complex, and interconnected than marked lines on a western map or grid, intermarriage was used by clans and wider constellations of nations to extend a group's domain. Marital law was powerful for bringing lands, networks, and peoples together cooperatively.[29]

Indigenous notions of borders remained, but the toll of murder and disease meant that Indigenous laws could no longer be policed. Varying locally and regionally, it would be difficult to date the beginnings and ends of the incipient borderless grounds of the colonizing frontier. However, such societies certainly endured in the north between the 1880s and 1930s, way beyond the official declaration of nation. The colonizing lines that delineated private and state property on maps were abstract, remote. Perhaps it is more useful to call these lands transnational spaces, for these were sites upon which sovereignties, laws, and politics were being negotiated. People's embodied selves exaggerated this blurring of the boundaries. By 1900, at least two thousand people of mixed Aboriginal and other descent had been born in Queensland. This is the official count, and the real figure would be much higher. After all, there was only unmitigated disadvantage in claiming Aboriginal descent. It meant you lost many liberties and the state could exert more control over your residence and actions.

Where they had the choice, the children of mixed unions usually lived within Indigenous communities, as did many born to second-generation families. Queensland had not developed the Métis societies that evolved over centuries in Canada and around the Great Lakes via the fur trade and for different reasons on the Spanish frontiers.[30] On its borderless ground, these boundary-blurring offspring, living on transcultural, colonizing ground, were visible. They jarred against the racialized timbre of the colonizer project, yet their existence could not be denied. This created conflict between Queensland authorities and its white male colonizers and between the metropole and the transnational periphery.

With no signs of residents wishing to disengage from this common ground, colonial governments had cause for anxiety over the intimate spaces of transnational diplomacy. They wanted permanent solutions by which to break up the intricate familial networks and to bring Queensland more in line with the "settled" southeastern states and with an ideal picture of a hegemonic white settler society.

Due to frontier violence, many white men bore hatred against Aboriginal people. Blood was fresh; passions ran high. Some suffered guilt for the blood on their own hands. The same men, or others like them, were perplexed by nagging anxieties about the children they had fathered. Not all fathers wanted to see their children taken into the arms of the state and separated from them forever. Nor did the ruling white men ever wish to admit their love for an Aboriginal woman. They and their laws worked to tarnish such sentiments with social stigma — partly about race, but mainly about colonizer status. Indeed, lovers would come under the surveillance of the new colonizing system of law, with its punitive measures of fines and jail sentences.

FATHERS OF THE BRIDES

In European conceptions of state and family, the newborn paternalistic state was taking on the role of the white male parent, whether the biological father was absent or not. The first chief protectors of Aborigines became the state fathers in question. As such, they also became the architects and authors of the new state. Archibald Meston was appointed for the southern region and Walter E. Roth for the north. Talented men, they believed they had much to offer in implementing a new colonial policy. In different ways, both admired Aboriginal people, but they were inextricably caught up in the nationalistic and racial aspirations of their day, a time when British imperialism and whiteness were in their ascendency. The social planners were anxious about the collateral damage of colonialism, especially in the eyes of the humanitarians of London and the metropole. At the same time, they worried about white men's racial suitability for the tropics.[31] The sight of tanned, sun-ravaged men confirmed race anxiety that pure "British" whiteness might be imperiled in tropical zones.[32]

Chief protector of the northern region from 1898, W. E. Roth worked from Brisbane until 1906. Roth was born in London to a Hungarian refugee family in 1861; he was educated in France and Germany and at Magdalen College, Oxford. His gifted scientific family immigrated to Australia. Roth's

FIG. 49. The two protectors: Archibald Meston (left) and Walter E. Roth. Courtesy Queensland State Library.

credentials were in ethnological practice, based upon scientific observational techniques. He was a fine draftsman and clear writer. His published articles reveal his appreciation of Aboriginal skills, their rules, gender, sexual practices, initiation into adulthood, childbirth rituals, art, and material culture. Yet he thought nothing of walking off with Aboriginal weapons and crafted artifacts from campsites, then selling them to museums.[33]

The chief protector of Queensland's southern region from 1898 to 1903, Archibald Meston was born in 1851 at Donside, Aberdeen, in Scotland. His parents then emigrated, setting up a farm at Ulmarra on the Clarence River in New South Wales, Bundjalung country. Meston's reputation rested upon a close practical knowledge of Aboriginal people — qualities better prized by white frontiersmen than book learning. Yet chillingly, Meston had boasted of killing Aboriginal people. Among the Queensland frontiersmen, where exploits in frontier violence were not only a conversation topic but a badge of white masculinity, he found like minds.

Meston employed Aboriginal people in various pastoral, exploring, and other enterprises. Their camps and communities shared his property. As an entrepreneurial self-promoter, a journalist, editor, and publicist, Meston ensured that his manly imperial accomplishments became well known. Using at least one Aboriginal tracker as an assistant, he had climbed the highest mountains of both New South Wales and Queensland. On lands near present-day Yarrabah, he had "discovered" a mangosteen plant that was subsequently named after him.[34]

Meston gained a seat in the Queensland parliament, where he served as party whip. Although he had once had a plantation enterprise, in his role as whip he vociferously opposed the importation of colored labor.[35] During the 1890s Meston famously managed Wild Australia, a traveling show in the style of Buffalo Bill's Wild West circus in the United States. Here he performed muscular feats, including practicing boomerang throwing and engaging in fighting contests with Aboriginal men.[36] Aboriginal dance troupes performed in body paint and grass skirts, demonstrating their skills with spears and painted shields.

In such public performances, Meston valorized Aboriginal people in their "pure" or "full-blood state," implying not only a physical state but a style of living. On both counts, he worried about the impact of colonial intermixing. But he did not talk about an Indigenous "state" or governance entity or the existence of their own law. However, he admired Aboriginal men's physiques, leaving titillating, homoerotic descriptions in which he relished comparisons with the ancient Greeks. When Meston drafted Queensland's first Aboriginals protection legislation in 1897, his written ruminations focused mainly upon the "breeding effects" of the white men. "The question of *mating* must be faced at some time or other. . . . The problem of half-castes, quadroons and octoroons" was one that the Australian colonies should solve.[37] To avoid "the breeding of half-castes," he recommended "*the absolute isolation*" of Aboriginal women from contacts with whites; otherwise contact would produce "attendant quadroons and octoroons among whom *the law of atavism* will assert itself in [the] after years with unpleasant results."[38]

Australians were well aware of the law of atavism concept—the idea of a distant ancestor's features reappearing—when phenotypically "white" parents had a black child, which so troubled citizens of the United States at this time.[39] Yet the livestock-like categories applied to mixed European and Aboriginal offspring do not fully explain why these children constituted such a "problem." This was the colonizers' secret. Such children made visible the hidden socio-sexual relations, hitting the most sensitive nerve

FIG. 50. A postcard marked "Wild Queensland Show," although it was also known as the Wild Australia Show; most of the Aboriginal people were from various Queensland locations. This theatrical image depicts Aboriginal men, wearing body paint, creeping up on two white men relaxing "innocently" in their camp. The image was sold as a Christmas and New Year's greeting card. Macleay Museum, University of Sydney, H P83.3.13.

of colonizer anxiety. After anticohabitation laws were introduced, darker children being born to white-skinned families contravened the clear-cut color lines the protectors hoped to police.

In the imperial world, ideas around whiteness became entwined with those of modernity. "Blood" classifications turned mixed Aboriginal-European parentage into a problematized category subject to state scrutiny and commentary.[40] Racial terms such as "full-blood" and "half-caste," already used in the earlier-settled New South Wales, merged the race metaphor "blood" with that of class or "caste." From the 1890s, allied with evolutionary science, racial classification became an obsession across the British Empire. In Burma, India, and Australia, government demographers like T. A. Coghlan collected statistics to measure racial sturdiness and survival capacity. They compared death- and birthrates to assess which groups were declining and which were multiplying. Those not reproducing at a particular rate were confirmed as "dying" or doomed races.

FIG. 51. This postcard depicts Aboriginal men with hunting and fighting equipment, adorned with body paint. The cicatrices across the men's chests indicate that they are fully initiated men who have been through Indigenous ceremonies, so they are authorized "law men." The man with a moustache on the left appears to be Meston. Macleay Museum, University of Sydney, HP83.3.14.

Government agendas derived from global ideas about eugenics, social planning, and public health. Ideas of a superior white colonizer race became central to the Australian self-image and the new nation's future hopes.[41] Basing their ideas upon a construct that all humans could go backward in evolutionary time, the newly appointed protectors superimposed a hierarchy of virtue upon white men that stood separate from race.[42]

In such discussions, the role of a recent history of dispossession in creating living conditions was frequently ignored. Malnutrition, venereal diseases, alcohol and opium, grieving, loss, and repeated deep shocks to the psyche were among the causes of population decline in frontier zones. Race "degradation," as the powerful rhetoric went, was explained away, not due to the colonial project in general, but as due to mixing with white men of inferior class. In 1900 Queensland's aboriginal protector Archibald Meston's concerns resemble some of the Cherokee Nation's: "I hold in utter abhorrence these marriages between Chinese and Aborigines, or whites and Aborigines.... They are unfair to the woman and degrading to the man, though in nearly all cases the man is of very low type.... An alliance with a white man who cannot get a woman of his own race is a degradation to any decent aboriginal woman."[43] We can note that Meston did not see the "Aboriginal woman" as inherently degraded but rather believed that outside men of "inferior" rank and wealth would destroy her decency. Segregation thus featured in a project to enhance Aboriginal health and well-being and a more pristine Aboriginality.

Imagining themselves as imperial heroes acting to "save the race," the ambitious, Darwinian-inspired social engineers Meston and Roth argued for drastic state intervention. They propelled a national project to breed "superior races." Whether their "protector" role aimed to protect the white race or the Aboriginal race was confusing. How they should treat people who did not neatly fit either group was even more puzzling. They focused upon the policing of intermarriage.

In 1899 Roth, the northern protector of Aborigines, expressed his frustration because marriages with Aboriginal women were "at present taking place with Europeans and colored aliens."[44] Some white men supported Aboriginal women having Pacific Islander husbands. Roth wanted to prevent the marriage ceremony becoming "the Harbour of Refuge for those men who (under the Aboriginals Protection Act 1897) were deemed unfit to employ or to harbour natives." Chinese, he reasoned, might merely use marriage to Aboriginal women as a means of gaining cheap or free labor.[45] As the new policies now prohibited Chinese from employing Aboriginal women, and it was illegal for any non-Aboriginal man to cohabit with an Aboriginal woman, this encouraged Chinese men to gain state permission to marry. Indeed, Roth suspected that interracial couples would try to marry merely "to defeat provisions of Aboriginals Protection Act." In other words, the act might create incentives rather than disincentives. This was the same gauntlet being run by Cherokee legislators; whereas white men wanted to marry to gain land and labor, marriage was one of the powerful ways by which the Cherokee state could control them through the rule of written law.

THE COLOR OF A GOOD HUSBAND

In a sense, the Aboriginal protectors became fathers of the bride to all Indigenous women. They exercised authority over marital regulation and approved or disapproved choices. State controls impeded the rights of association of white frontiersmen with Aborigines, curbing the freedom and life choices of potential husbands and scrutinizing their suitability as grooms. Even after marriage, the intermarrying husband was more likely to be penalized for his behavior to his wife, whom the act placed under special state protection.

Certain ideas of "civilization," or modern habits and a western notion of marriage, were linked in the minds of the ruling elite. The new protectionist rhetoric promised rescue by paternalist intervention. However, its implementation had to pander to the realities of colonial power, awarding priority to *white* community needs—the colonizers' labor, sexual, and marital needs that were causing trouble in the first place. Demands could be contradictory: most local townspeople wanted Aboriginal camps and dwellings to be *away* and not in sight of urban centers. This would make them look modern and settled and would improve their sense of security and real estate values. But at the same time, they wanted their cheap Aboriginal labor close by. State authorities therefore placed Aboriginal people on reserves outside towns. After their work was completed, they were no longer welcome in the town and were subjected to evening curfews. Regulations involving fixed distances prohibited whites and others from entering or getting too close to Aboriginal reserves and Aboriginal women. These forced people into more surreptitious rendezvous.

According to their correspondence, in order to assess a man as permitted to marry, Roth and Meston applied eugenicist thinking and contemporary values around the constitution of the good husband. By the same token, both chief protectors were openly prejudiced against white men who lived with Aboriginal women. Labeling them "combos," they thought of them as the "lowest order" of white man. Nonetheless, as captives to their own protectionist rhetoric, the protectors had to apply a fair test as to whether a man applying for a marriage permit matched up to their criteria for a "suitable" husband. Their aim to protect Aboriginal women was also balanced by the need to keep the peace in unstable, only tangentially settled communities. In many cases, they were dealing with tender emotions, when the male applicants strongly depended on the woman and the relationship.

The adjudication of intercultural marriages in frontier zones was far more difficult than devising the policies. In this context, defining the anticipated duties and behaviors of a good husband was especially challenging. Ideal husbandly attributes of the time included home ownership and settling down to a sedentary lifestyle, yet transient frontier zones had little substantial housing and highly mobile work patterns. Drunkenness, violence, transience, and vagrancy might define the "unrespectable," unsuitable husband elsewhere, but on frontiers these traits were too commonplace to be considered deviant. Furthermore, the rough-living frontiersmen were willing to engage lawyers and religious men to vouch for their morals.

For example, one white man asked an Ingham pastor to impress on Chief Protector Roth the integrity of his feeling for his Aboriginal de facto wife. The pastor complied, stating that the man was "fond of her and I believe is honest in his intentions to make her his wife and care for her." In cases like these, protectors often approved the marriages, referring to the good character of both parties and to the stable employment of the man or woman.[46] Having a child together was another favored argument. J. Nicol, a farmer from Seymour River, wrote that he had hoped to marry the woman he lived with for the "last 7 years . . . and I will marry her with your permission; She has one child and I do not want to desert eather [sic] her or the child. This is all I have got to say in the matter."[47] A minister of religion, Reverend B. Bryant, backed him, writing that this man had applied to marry an Aboriginal woman "with whom he has been living and to whom he has one child. The man seems to be fond of the woman and I believe is honest in his intentions to make her his wife, & care for her." The minister got the man's name wrong, however.[48]

The protectors' determination to measure the respectability of the potential husband contained a stark paradox. After all, in the protectors' thinking, any white man's open interest in marrying an Aboriginal woman already rendered him "unrespectable." When Joe Simpson, a white resident of St. George, went before the court in 1898 seeking permission to marry his Aboriginal companion, it was simply refused as a "ridiculous request." Before fines and jail, social ostracism was a powerful deterrent, although some men were willing to buck white social mores and fight back. In an 1885 incident, when Bill Smith of St. George abused Bill Freeman as "no white man" because he lived with "a black gin," Freeman retaliated by "combing" "Smith's hair back with a garden rake."[49]

Despite Roth and Meston's stated desires to prohibit marriages between Aboriginal women and Chinese and Pacific Islanders, marriage records show that "colored" men had equal, if not higher, chances of gaining permission to marry Aboriginal women as white men. Between 1901 and 1934, 62 couples were refused permission to marry and 302 couples were permitted to marry.[50] During January 1901, the month of "White Australia's" federation celebrations, five marriages of "colored" men with Aboriginal and "half-caste Aboriginal" women were officially permitted in Queensland. Of the forty marriages of Aboriginal women approved in that year, only 7 percent of them were to white men. Divided into birthplace and colony, three applicants were described as "Queenslander (white)," "New South Wales (white)," and "English/British (born at sea)."[51] All the other permits were for men of South Sea Islander, Javanese, and Malay birth, while the other twelve were to Pacific Islanders, Filipinos, West Indian, Indian, Cingalese (Ceylon) and one Chinese.

However, with Asian and Pacific Islander men soon to be repatriated under the Immigration Restriction Act, a de facto Aboriginal wife would have to either migrate to the islands or eke out a precarious living in hiding. Although Aboriginal women did not have citizenship in the new nation, having a legal marriage to a local Aboriginal wife enabled some Asians and Pacific Islanders to avoid forced repatriation. Over sixteen hundred men were permitted to stay, and another five hundred escaped into the bush. Local police revealed surprising sympathy for Asian and Pacific Islander frontiersmen requesting marriage permits. Forgetting the "White Australia" principles behind the Aboriginals Protection Act, Protectors Meston and Roth noted these men's community contributions, lifeways, and survival struggles with considerable empathy. They became involved in their human stories and struggles, extricating the individual man from eugenic framings. This reveals yet another layer of the complex links between gender, marriage, and colonial and national policy.

Being in competition over Aboriginal women, white men sometimes deployed Asian-vice discourses to convince police to break up the relationships of Chinese husbands and highly desirable Aboriginal women. They accused Pacific Islanders of running prostitution, underage, and group marriage rackets. This exacerbated police harassment, including inspections of the sleeping arrangements of certain couples in stable unions.[52]

Enthusiastic police could run up against other competing interests, including white female employers. In 1898 Constable Buckley accused Ah Chin of locking up his Aboriginal partner, Topsey. She denied any ill-treatment, stating, "That fellow Constable never ask me, that fellow tell em lie, me like Ah Chin, no leave him, me long time sit down long him." Indeed, the couple had been living together for six years and Topsey worked for Mrs. Flynn, the local schoolteacher's wife. Sergeant Bradley was angry about the intrusions: "What right had the constable to absent himself from town duty, to spy about Ah Chin's house" on several occasions? "She is a good-looking gin and much attached to the Chinaman Ah Chin. There is a rumour that some white men have offered her money for immoral purposes. In fact it has been suggested to the Sergeant that Constable Buckley's zeal might be at the suggestion of some other party, so as to get the gin away from Ah Chin."[53]

Marriage applicants of mixed Aboriginal and other descent flummoxed administrators. When a man called Tony Bing, thought to be of Chinese and Aboriginal descent, requested to marry a "half-caste Chinese girl" in 1909, police did not know if he required permission or not.[54] When East Woodlands grazier W. H. Jackson decided to legally marry Emily Clark, he tried to take her to a place where they could marry, but she refused to travel for fear of being "taken away by Mr Meston" to a reserve. When police traveled to the station in 1903 to question Jackson about his de facto "half-caste Aboriginal," he explained that they had been living together for eighteen months and had a one-year-old child. Eventually Meston authorized the union, but it was on the grounds that Jackson himself probably had some Aboriginal ancestry, with an Aboriginal mother: "but to all appearance he shows no trace of it." Furthermore, he was the "acknowledged father" of the child.[55] Other reports described the child as "perfectly white."[56] In his assessments, Meston frequently commented on color, and in another case he referred to a girl's "very light" coloring, "even for a quadroon, and any children she might have would likely be pure white."[57]

They were policing color lines that were already blurred. Their preoccupation with whiteness created concerns. Protectors started to categorize blood proportions, using the ugly terms "half-caste," "quadroon," and "octoroon." Authorities did not enforce segregation with second and third generations of mixed parentage, reasoning that they were not necessarily "Aboriginal" and not necessarily "white." Confirming a mishmash of eugenics and welfare concerns, when a marriage permit was granted to a light-skinned woman, protectors sometimes explained that that this was on the basis that she had already produced or was likely to produce "pure white" offspring.[58] In this liminal, intermeshed society, eugenic talk was explicit. Across absent boundaries, the protectors were trying to draw clear lines on paper.

Police and protectors sometimes extended their marital approval role into the realm of matchmaking. Men wrote to the protectors, police, and superintendents of government and mission reserves, stating the sort of "lighter-skinned" Aboriginal woman they liked and assuring them of their respectable intentions.[59] Understanding outback loneliness, local protectors were keen to help, but sometimes they were more interested in retaining their good female staff. When William Buchanun, a white man, applied to marry Ada, an Aboriginal woman of mixed descent, in 1903 the police disapproved on the grounds that Buchanun was an alcoholic living in a makeshift tent. However, they also admitted that they wanted to hold on to Ada because she was a reliable worker.

After her husband's death, the inspector of police came up with the suggestion that Ada marry a "half-caste" tracker called Jumbo, who was one of their police staff. The police inspector knew of the high demand among white men to marry her. Protector Meston quickly approved, advising "that the woman be sent to Jumbo to marry."[60] Under the Aboriginals Protection Act, marriages between Aboriginal people did not actually come under the protectors' authority. However, this did not stop them from pleasing a reliable Aboriginal tracker, who they may have feared would leave his employment in search of a wife.

COLLUDING HUSBANDS

On other occasions, to evade restrictions on their association with Aboriginal women, Chinese men actively colluded with the women and with other Chinese men. Those in longstanding de facto relationships enlisted lawyers to challenge police authority. Many had already won the respect of local residents, including some police officers. For example, in 1906 Ah Kow, a storekeeper who had lived in the region for thirty years, was charged with harboring an Aboriginal woman and attempted bribery of a police officer. A newcomer, Constable Creedy, and the Aboriginal tracker Tiger had visited Ah Kow's store and residence in remote Byerstown, in the Palmer River region, inland between Cooktown and Port Douglas. Tiger allegedly saw two female Aborigines, one chopping yams in the kitchen and one with a "piccaninny." When they saw the police, the women ran away.

Ah Kow reportedly said, "That is my gin and you are not going to take her away as I got a letter through my solicitor from big boss telling me I could have the aboriginal gin Nelly."[61] Ah Kow was no longer entitled to a permit to employ Aborigines, as this was now prohibited under section 5, subsection 2 of the Aboriginals Protection Act. Creedy alleged that Ah Kow had offered to bribe him with gold valued at one pound, four shillings. Ah Kow stated that Nelly was "his gin, he liked her" and that he had spent a lot of money on her. "Aboriginal Nelly sometime carries water, sometimes washes shirts . . . looks for job and looks for horses."

When Nelly ran away, Constable Creedy caught her down the river and whipped her. As if the cruelty charge was not bad enough, Ah Kow counteraccused Creedy of demanding gold as a bribe. Creedy had actually taken the gold from Ah Kow's house and had it valued, which weakened his credibility. Creedy was subsequently transferred from the district and the charges against Ah Kow were dismissed.

In a well-documented 1912 case, another gold miner, Lee Chew, accused Constable Casey of bribery. Casey had alleged that Dolly was "cohabiting" with Lee Chew at a mine between Maytown and the evocatively named Cannibal Creek, in north Queensland. When Casey handcuffed Lee Chew for harboring an Aboriginal woman, the vital witness, Dolly, fled into the bush. Lee Chew then charged Constable Casey with assault, accusing him of getting drunk on his premises and wanting gold as a bribe. Casey's arguments that the gold he took was for "evidence" were unconvincing, and he was subsequently transferred to another district.[62]

While some police sought to gain monetary advantage from the laws against cohabitation with Aboriginal women, others were ambivalent about applying the law at all. When Chong Choy of Byerstown was charged with

FIG. 52. Chinese prisoners, Croydon, 1894. This photograph shows an Aboriginal Native Police officer looking down on the Chinese prisoners with bemusement. Queensland State Library, no. 44909.

harboring an Aboriginal woman named Maria, she claimed she was there only to exchange fish for potatoes. Once again, Aboriginal friends and intimate partners knew the drill, and the case was dismissed. Subinspector Bowen complained about "two Justices who have been a long time in the locality and who apparently consider the chinamen benefactors to the aboriginals for years past." Indeed, the bench "considered that were it not for the Chinese support the aboriginals would be often wanting provisions on the Palmer."[63] As Chinese men were prohibited from employing Aboriginal labor, it was easier to charge them for harboring an Aboriginal woman than it would be to charge a white man.[64]

Attempts to define what constituted "the good husband" conflicted with nationalistic race ideas. This created a quandary for those implementing policy. Taking Aboriginal protection and welfare literally, various local police, clergy, and others frequently supported interracial marital pairings — even in opposition to the chief protectors. Against the grain of the race-based law, state authorities and police frequently made allowances for the respectable, good husband and father. The interests of frontier social order and often a genuine respect for the good husband transcended color boundaries.

It would appear that white policemen's regard for Chinese men as human beings, as intelligent, and as potentially good colonizers was never in question. Despite the Aboriginals Protection Act's officially singling them out as unsuitable husbands, when Chinese men actually requested permission to marry, protectors and white police often treated these applicants favorably. This was especially so if there was proof of a long-standing relationship and the care of children.

Relatively few marriage applications were refused, and police correspondence of around 1901 contained surprisingly few derogatory race-based comments against Asians. Apparently the Chinese worked hard, had valued skills, were good employers, and whether married under state law or not, acted as good husbands. Few were drunks. Chinese men's cohabitation with, intermarriage with, and general support of poverty-stricken Aborigines was creating a system of community-based protection that Queensland's segregation-oriented protection acts could not hope to achieve.[65] "Dutiful husbands" were allowed to take on the role of "protectors" of Aboriginal women, saving the state from having to pay rationing, blanket, and welfare money.

The Aboriginals Protection Act's experiment exposed internal contests over the values and meanings of marriage. There were many unknowns in this state intervention into human liberty. What administrators saw as satisfactory justification for separating a couple was then applied to couples who were mutually reliant upon each other. Or — let me use the word — who *loved* each other. Consequently, the chief protectors responsible for enforcing the new interventions themselves became the prime targets for opposition.

In this budding democracy, frontiersmen fought back against the protectors' upper- and middle-class pretentions. As well as competing for Aboriginal women, white and "colored" men even supported one another in order to retain their rights as husbands. White men deeply resented Meston's interference into the authority of the husband — albeit in colonizer law. In reaction to one couple's forced separation, the local newspaper characterized Meston as a "cruel monster." It called him "an arrogant sultan," insinuating that his removal of Aboriginal women was done in order to collect a personal harem. It likened Meston to "the long-legged brolga," a gray and white bird with a long beak — a "sticky-beak," perhaps.[66] This bird, *Grus rubicunda*, became known as the "native companion" because Aboriginal people often reared and semitamed them. Curiously, this brolga is known for elaborate mating dances; it jumps, bows, dances, throws and catches grass, and even lines up in choreographed dancing ensembles.[67] A mating game indeed. White men resented Meston's powers over them, so they tried different means of attack.

His jurisdiction over the colonizing classes — that is, over any white man or woman who associated with or employed Aboriginal people — led to his vilification. Newspaper cartoonists delighted in portraying him in the seminaked postures of his Wild Australia shows. On other counts, he was attacked as having hidden "the heart of a frog . . . under the plumage of a peacock."[68] As Aboriginal people excelled at animal-inspired caricatures and hilarious mimicry of individuals, we can only wonder about their impersonations of Meston, the man authorized to circumvent their family lives.

White women were deeply distrustful of a system in which the "protectors" of Aboriginal women were all male. They had special cause for colonizer anxiety, as they often had to compete with Aboriginal women for their husband's affections. Archibald Meston's wife, Frances Prowse Shaw, was one of these. Helped by her husband's authority, she had been appointed an aboriginal protector in Brisbane city, and she had ambitions to stop Aboriginal women's exploitation. However, when she invaded the home of another white woman, Mary St. Ledger, and confronted her about the wage conditions of her employee — an Aboriginal girl called Nina — it started a train of dramatic events. Opposing Aboriginal labor competition and accusing the "respectable" urban middle class of exploitation, white male unionists backed Mrs. Meston's efforts to enforce decent wages. They published various newspaper articles and editorials supporting her. St. Ledger retaliated, however, with an insinuation that Frances Meston's husband had engaged in scandalous behavior with this very domestic servant. Perhaps this had something to do with Frances's invasion of the St. Ledger home in the first place.

Chief Protector Meston's stance against intermarriage had won him many opponents. Now the man whose legislation threatened to rupture private lives and marriages had himself been sexually exposed. We do not know the veracity of allegations of his inappropriate behavior with the young Nina. Despite his wife, Frances's spirited defense of her own actions,

FIG. 53. A cartoon of Archibald Meston entitled Native Protector Meston's Black-Guard and featuring Aboriginal performers in the background. Wearing Scottish apparel and a headband reading "All Scotch," Meston carries a boomerang and shield and appears to be in the business of selling them for profit. The parenthetical comment reads, "infants in arms will not be treated with." Implying he is a charlatan, this possibly also alludes to the key undercurrent of the act regarding Aboriginal offspring with white men. Queensland State Archives, no. 1461074.

she had little choice but to let the matter drop and to resign her post. She must have adjudged this humiliating retreat and retirement from the public domain as less damaging than ruining her husband's reputation. The loss of his government income and a possible family breakup would ruin her. Her dream of exercising leadership in the service of vulnerable young Aboriginal women had blown up in her face and in the family domain.

This was a "domestic" dispute on several fronts: a marital contest over a domestic servant that potentially destabilized Archibald Meston's authority in the public sphere. Both Archibald and Frances had stepped out into the gendered minefield of Aboriginal protection. The normally hidden crossfire of colonizing anxieties taking place inside the respectable marital home was thrown open to public scrutiny. Under their breaths, other women may well have asked whether Mrs. Meston had sexually "civilized" her own husband. This was no ordinary gender contest between a prominent husband and his wife. Meston's interference with the authority of the intercultural husband in white law had made him many enemies.

Although white women had the vote from 1901, the parliament remained a male enclave. Pressured by peers and vocal male constituencies, white politicians tended to oppose white women's involvement in Aboriginal protection. They mocked the very idea; they said it was too shocking for them to see. There was too much to hide.[69]

The other chief protector, Walter E. Roth, was subjected to an even more sustained and damaging newspaper and parliamentary campaign than Meston. Although presiding over a scheme to decide suitable marriages, Walter Roth's marital life was shaky and his paternal efforts rather uneven. In 1887 he married Ada Toulmin in London, but he soon deserted her to travel to Australia, where he married Eva Grant. They had a son, Vincent, but Eva died when the boy was only ten months old. Afterward Roth departed for England to study medicine, leaving Vincent in an orphanage run by the nuns of Parramatta Convent. Later, Vincent was cared for in England by Eva's English relatives.

When, due to a chance visit by some Australian women, the young Vincent discovered that his father had a new "mother," he asked to join them. Roth was living with Edith Humpherson. He is said to have fathered various children by different mothers, some out of wedlock. Details of Roth's marriages are sketchy; as his biographer summed it up, "Walter had a number of children from different marriages and other relationships."[70] There is no evidence that these offspring haunted his conscience, although his relationship with Vincent, who had proactively sought out a father, saw them working together for years in another imperial and scientific enterprise — a study of the ethnology and government of British Guiana (now Guyana).

While his private life went unremarked on in the local papers, Roth's public role intruding into other people's unions did not. In the early days of

FIG. 54. Alexander Meston, ca. 1890. Archibald and Frances's son displaying the family pride in Scottish heritage and lost titles. Queensland State Library, no. 16522.

FIG. 55. A dashing Archibald Meston, ca. 1895. State Library of Queensland, no. 53084.

the new intermarriage policy, we have seen how the Goon Goo and Kitty case created public outcry and sympathy for both husband and wife. For Kitty, her forced removal meant separation not only from her partner but from her employment, severing her from her traditional homelands, kin, and community. Roth dismissed Goon Goo's admission of "supplying opium and drink to aboriginals" as commonplace, remarking, "Beyond being a chinaman, I can find nothing against Goon Goo's character."[71] Although the Aborigines Protection Act was ostensibly designed to segregate Aboriginal women from Chinese men and from opium, Roth provided permission for a state-registered marriage in order to "rectify as far as possible the wrong already committed." Roth's defensive reaction at the removal of a "good husband" only added to popular confusion about the act's intentions.

Furthermore, Roth's ethnological work, which he continued to practice as chief protector, opened him to ridicule, especially from those white men who considered themselves the true "white bushmen." White frontiersmen and parliamentarians thought that his report, as informed by Aboriginal people, that crocodiles would not swim upstream was hilarious. Much more powerful ammunition was to come. His white male opponents outed him for arranging to take naked photographs of an Aboriginal man and woman — a husband and wife — allegedly "in coitus." In his 1897 *Ethnological Studies* text published by the Queensland government, Roth described this subject as an "interesting position" or a "wheelbarrow," where the man pulls the woman toward him. Roth referred to it as "the peculiar method of copulation in vogue throughout all these tribes."[72] In the proto-anthropological style of the day, the photographs were impersonal representations, with no clan, location, or individual names specified. The couple's white employer had assisted Roth in the negotiations.[73] Roth implied that this intermediary action demonstrated an ethically obtained consent. Although the pastoralist spoke the Aboriginal couple's language fluently, as landholder and resource supplier he had significant sway over these people.

In 1902 the nude photos created a sensation in parliament. Hamilton, a politician representing a North Queensland electorate, posed questions about the chief protector. Reasonably enough, contemporary critics asked, if Aboriginals are treated as animals, how can this be "protection"? Anonymous ethnologists described the photographs as "terrible," "disgusting." One expert stated, "Those pictures haunt me." In parliament, the photographs were described as "disgusting, immoral" and the sexual position as "unnatural," "filthy," obscene, and "grossly indecent." For offending morality and the standards of "decent society," Roth, the state-appointed guardian of other men's sexual behaviors, was now rendered the transgressor: the immoral one. As one anonymous ethnologist commented, "What manner of man took these? He ought to be in gaol." Hamilton agreed: "Any Queensland Judge would reward such an offence with imprisonment in St. Helena."[74] The very men threatened with prison for living with Aboriginal women delighted in catching out the protector.

Roth's moral demise would be their moral victory. The frontiersmen could claim the high moral ground. Ironically, one of the few public expressions of support for Roth over the "pornographic photos" came from Bishop White of Carpentaria. Like Ernest Gribble, churches had the common goal of segregating Aborigines from white frontiersmen, whom they saw as uniformly "immoral." Possibly the educated Bishop White also had an appreciation of "science" and its modern scientific observational and recording practices.[75]

Conceding no wrongdoing, Roth drew upon the Crown and its supreme sovereignty. He argued that a copy of his work had been presented to parliament and another had "been graciously accepted by the son of my Sovereign, HRH the Prince of Wales."[76] Such a remote figure held little traction among the white frontiersmen, who, as local "settlers," considered themselves more authorized arbiters of moral authority than any distant royal figure.

After being attacked in parliament, Roth could no longer continue his reign as chief protector. Although afterwards he led an important enquiry in Western Australia, Roth eventually left Australia to take up a government job in British Guiana. That blurry coital photograph, his "ethnopornography," as he put it, probably impressed the esteemed scientists of the Berlin Anthropological Society for whom it was intended. But it was later published in an unsavory subscriber-only book "for gentlemen" entitled *Venus Oceanica* — its titillating context giving it an even more malodorous effect to a viewer.[77]

Via their local politicians, white frontiersmen had started a contest of morals, raising important questions about Roth's relationships with the Aboriginal men and women under his care. As we have witnessed, white

FIG. 56. An older Walter Roth, who spent his later career in British Guyana, in 1918. Queensland State Library, no. 162059.

men deeply resented not only the surveillance of their sex and marital lives with Indigenous women but also attacks on their codes of ethics and sexual and familial morality. Motivated by the threat of losing what they viewed as their sexual and partnership rights to Aboriginal women, they formed alliances and campaigned energetically. They wrote petitions, arranged well-attended public meetings, and, via their local politicians, put embarrassing questions to parliament.

Turning the glare of the public spotlight away from their own frontier and urban intimacies, white men and women effectively exposed both Roth's and Meston's sexual and marital inconsistencies and improprieties. Intense public scrutiny followed. At stake was an intensifying conflict of authority over government interventions in intimate relations and privacy. In contrast to Roth's behavior, frontiersmen could portray their own dealings with Indigenous people as relatively decent and honorable.

Albeit self-serving, this contest of morals had a genuine aspect that went to the very core of frontier life. Where should the loyalties of intermarrying white men lie? Who, after all, was truly one's "own kind"? In law, intermarriage with white men had no place on land now zoned as "Aboriginal." Men in established unions and families with Indigenous Australians now risked jail. So what were they to do? Commit a crime against one's natal family by recognizing the marriage, against one's wife and progeny by deserting them, or against one's "nation" by having already sinned against a policy only just proclaimed?

TRANSNATIONAL CITIZENSHIP

In Australia's early national period, the photographic scandal exposed some of the deeper tensions in colonial democracy to the harsh light of day. Men from different ethnicities and classes competed for Aboriginal women. Local white men, including senior white police, defended ongoing "decent" relationships. In 1901 Roth backtracked from policy wording, explaining that if the local police were satisfied with an Aboriginal woman's well-being, they should not interfere.[78] Not only did the restrictive intermarriage policy expose all the ethical and cultural dilemmas of the frontier, it also exposed the inexperience of the policy makers. For many reasons, the protectors knew that they were treading a fine line and that their actions should not renew outbreaks of frontier violence and instability. Transnational marriage disputes and the supposed protection of Aboriginal women via state marriage law could interfere with carefully negotiated arrangements within Aboriginal marriage rules.

The British-derived marriage law had evolved over some centuries. Unsettling laws as fundamental as this would be no easy business. Crown lawyers and church authorities were well aware of the difficulties, which is probably why the restrictive marriage regulations were placed under the Aborigines Protection Act rather than the Marriage Act. Churches, also involved in enacting marriage rites, challenged the authority of the chief protector over the churches.[79] The Crown solicitors had serious doubts about the Aboriginal protector's authority to stop a marriage celebrant performing a mixed Aboriginal–non-Aboriginal marriage. The government solicitor was asked to seek clarification. He advised Roth that, under Queensland law, the protector indeed lacked the authority in law to prevent intermarriages. Civil and religious celebrants could still go ahead and marry people; the chief protector only had the power to "dissuade" them, not to stop them.

Although churches were initially upset about caveats on their power as celebrants, after receiving the solicitor's advice, Roth admitted to having powers of persuasion alone. The churches kept quiet about the confusion. Missionary churches relied upon government funding and agreed with the state's aims to segregate Aboriginal women from white and other newcomer men.

Despite so much energy being put into its enforcement, to the protector's astonishment, the colonial and state marriage law was clear. Race-based marriage restrictions were an expensively administered folly. After all, the Queensland Marriage Act, which followed the New South Wales Marriage Act, mentioned nothing about race-specific rules. And the marriage acts overrode the Aborigines Protection Act.[80] It appeared that the actions of protectors in forcibly separating, breaking up, and even jailing people in mixed marriages was in fact beyond their powers. Needless to say, the protectors never made this embarrassing finding public. They persevered, ignoring the shaky basis of their powers of jurisdiction.

Roth soon attempted to firm up his powers by adding amendments. An instruction from Justin Foxton stated that the minister had authorized Roth "to give permission, in writing, for the celebration of the marriage of female aboriginals with persons other than aboriginals" (section 9). What the authorization did not do was to prohibit intermarriages. This appears to be an assertion of a potential power but not a firm prohibition. Intermarriage was still not prohibited under the Queensland Marriage Act.[81]

Legally speaking, it was no easy business for the colony of Queensland to start interfering in British-derived marriage codes that had evolved over some centuries.[82] Authority over the celebration of marriage revived rifts between church and state over marriage. Unlike in the United States, where each state introduced its own marriage regulations, Queensland was not authorized to interfere with the sacrosanct Colonial Marriages Act signed with the pen of Queen Victoria, after whom the state was named. The act referred not only to the woman's consent but to the "Consent of the Lords Spiritual and Temporal."[83] Consequently, Roth tried another route that he called "moral suasion." He requested rather than ruled that ministers of religion and "marrying justices" refuse to marry mixed Aboriginal–non-Aboriginal couples.[84] While some were happy to comply with this very official looking "request," others were not.

The shaky standing of restrictive laws exposed problems regarding the status of all Aboriginal couples married under the Queensland state system, including those not in mixed unions. Like Ernest Gribble, many of the mission managers running the communities where they lived were keen to encourage Christian-style weddings, yet they now discovered that they were not properly state-authorized celebrants. When investigations revealed that marriages of Aboriginal couples conducted at certain northern missions were invalid in the eyes of the law, government officers wondered whether they should inform the affected couples or not. In 1901 Roth requested a gazettal of his authorization "to give permission in writing for the marriage of female aboriginals provided for in and by the 9th section of the said Act."[85] Roth was happy with at least gaining some extra muscle in the Aboriginals Protection Act that he implemented, and the Marriage Act was not amended.

HISTORY'S HUSBANDRY

This is the story of how, with mixed results, the Queensland government messily attempted to grab control of the entangled world of cross-cultural marital coexistence. It tried to regulate marriage within a vision of orderly national progress. While theorists have applied the term "colonial project" to colonizing initiatives, this suggests a unified logic and streamlined implementation. In the case of intermarriage, white male colonizers were split, colluding with others of their gender across race and cultural boundaries to challenge the precarious logic behind the Aboriginals Protection Act's marital regulations. Police in remote regions were likely to turn a blind eye to wealthy landowners with Aboriginal mistresses or wives. This created class resentment among working-class men. And unlike Aboriginal people, who were not counted as citizens and generally lacked voting rights, white men had democracy on their side. They mobilized the press and politicians to back what they saw as a basic colonizer right — the right of white men to partner with their choice of Aboriginal women. And significantly, if they infringed Indigenous law doing so, they expected to be protected from retribution by the state police force.

On a local level, white men from the colonial lower classes thus formed themselves into a protonationalist group, joining with professional men, including lawyers and politicians, to fight against prurient attacks on their characters. They confidently asserted the superiority of their own values, which incorporated open or surreptitious boundary-crossing lifestyles and systems of adaptive cross-cultural protocols for marital morality. In an evolving democracy that espoused egalitarianism, their campaigns undermined the credibility of the government protectors and questioned their suitability as marital arbiters.

The state authorized and regulated marriage, yet frontiersmen argued that personal control over the sphere of sexual partnerships and family was a fundamental liberty. A marital union was the site where men and women's secrets were supposed to be protected from state interference. The government occasionally opined on the Aboriginal wife's worthiness, but under Queensland's Aboriginals Protection Act, it was usually the white man, the potential husband and "guardian," who was placed under state scrutiny and surveillance.

This frontier society, composed of displaced peoples, was in need of some stable family relationships. White men were often lonely rovers who drank too much alcohol. In such a context, police and senior administrators attracted outrage for breaking up successful heterosexual unions. Surely, as people on all sides reasoned, the state had no right to break up the good husband and the good wife.

The official archive reveals disquiet about the legitimate targets of policing and confusion about the actual purpose and power of restrictive legislation. When administrators tried to make sense of it in relation to real partnerships and families, they offered only empty ideology, contradictory arguments, and inconsistent decisions. Protectionist ideas concerning the good husband disrupted any strict eugenicist approach. In the novel context of frontier colonialism, administrators tried to balance tangled expectations around gender, family, race, and the presence and color of offspring. In attempting to distinguish the savage husband from the civilized husband, administrators applied their own moral values, energized by the racial and class bigotry that passed as social planning. Protectors and local police knew that they were playing with other men's lives. More often than we might expect, along with muddled and racist logic, this created an archive containing some surprisingly heartfelt moments of empathy and sincerity.

Under the White Australia policy, the threat of state expulsion of Asians and Pacific Islanders from Queensland, provided an incentive for them to seek more formal marital unions with Aboriginal women. Marriage sometimes enabled them to stay in Australia. However, by the same token, if they married, Aboriginal women were sometimes expected to live in Asia or the Pacific. An inherent problem with the system was that chief protectors became flummoxed about whom they were protecting from whom. Scientific intrusions into other people's sex lives seemed respectable in centers of European scholarship, but not so in a liminal nation. The protectors' authority came completely unstuck when their private sexual ethics entered the full glare of public scrutiny.

Intimate cross-cultural relationships were sites of colonialism that blurred racial and national boundaries physically and reproductively — and in other unexpected ways. As state administrators did not make any effort to reconcile imperial and colonial law with Aboriginal marriage law and protocols, they created a recipe for yet more poor logic. And try as they might, the white male protectors were no experts at either assessing or playing the good husband. They had trouble weighing the many competing gendered, class, race, and clan interests that crisscrossed the transnational borders of settler colonialism. Although hardly unusual, because they were ostensibly protectors of the colonized and engineers of a new nation, their masculine sexual dalliances shook their moral authority to the core.

CHAPTER SIX

Consent and Aboriginal Wives

"I do." The words, or words to this effect, are uttered separately. By the man, then the woman. The third party has a state-ordained power to hear these utterances and to ask the question "Do you take this man to be your lawful wedded husband?" And the husband is asked the same regarding the wife. Each needs to find breath and voice. Alone in voicing their individual consent, but people are there, listening, looking. Separately, they must see each mouth move and their ears must hear them speak. Those with cause to object have their chance. This double act of "free will" is an embodied practice that must be witnessed as such. In a legal, or state-authorized, marriage, the consent between the two separate individuals cannot be secret. The public proclamation of their agreement makes them two, and one.

Switching the angle from husbands to wives, this chapter explores how people directed and managed complex cross-cultural negotiations and, in doing so, how they redefined what it meant to be a husband or a wife. The intercultural meaning of consent, which was an essential requirement of Queensland's marriage law and its marriage contracts, will be considered. As the non-Aboriginal husband was the one who had to apply to the protector, his consent was presumed. However, if one of the two protectors approved a particular marriage between a non-Aboriginal man and an Aboriginal woman, he reminded the white police officers that the union could only proceed *"provided she is willing."*[1] This was the precept fundamental to British marriage law.

When an Indigenous woman entered into a formal marital contract under Queensland's colonizing regime in the early 1900s, her understanding of *what* she was consenting to differed dramatically from that of the colonizer. The increasing arrivals of a predominantly male population into their country called for new strategies. To fit changing times, Aboriginal women and men reconfigured their usual kin and land relationships to allow the women to engage in marriages with men of other nations. We will explore how, as a logical way of negotiating the modern world and bringing the lawless insiders under their system of law, they developed a transnational form of marital diplomacy.[2]

In Queensland during the late nineteenth and early twentieth centuries, Aboriginal men and women held a strong sense of belonging and commitment to sustaining their people and their land. Wherever possible, they devised strategies for harnessing marriage law as a means of asserting and extending their land-based sovereignty. Indigenous peoples saw their traditional marriage laws as proper, orderly, and far more sophisticated than those of the newcomers. Based upon complicated classificatory kinship rules, their highly regulated marriage laws prevented any possibility of marrying a close or classificatory relative. They also allowed for the incorporation of distant peoples, potentially facilitating orderly relations and influence over wider areas of lands and resources. Their precepts were the markers for a truly *civil* society.

Furthermore, their land-associated dreaming stories, including epic creation stories with strong moral undertones, were inscribed not on paper but in verifiable features — in the storied mountains, rocks, plants, rivers, seas, and secret places that made up their country, their nations. Landscapes not only contained and provided proof of but they actually embodied their ancient narratives; "country" witnessed and policed the law underpinning them. Lands were understood to contain the narrative essence of individual and collective biographies of particular individuals, above and beneath the layerings of the present. Inspirited landscapes were the palimpsests that operated in metaphoric and material ways to contain their law. Senior elders conveyed their secret knowledge only to the worthy. The visceral pull of place, people, and nation entangled each individual into kin networks and into an inclusive system of marriage law. In turn, this grounded people in a land-based system of kinship-based law, and family connectedness, in which individual identity became intricately bound up with specific sites and the geospatial, familial politics that connected them.[3]

Queensland's state marriage approvals process created another kind of archive, in the marriage files of the Queensland State Archives that were generated by authorities dealing with the intermarriage regulations of the Aboriginal acts of 1897 and 1901. Once located across from the Brisbane River, the archives are now located in the newish outer Brisbane suburb of Runcorn.[4] As well as its extensive paper archive of correspondence in the masculine voice, this man-to-man conversation contains vital clues into Aboriginal women's views and actions. How were they navigating intimate gender relations across societies in a contest for land, resources, and Aboriginal women? These intercultural marriage stories involved political and social ideas of civilization, freedom, and consent, all of which had multiple, shared, and conflicting meanings across cultural and colonizing boundaries.

At the colonizing interface, the gendered constitution of marriage was integral to negotiations over sovereignty and the state. Imported laws reflected distinctive European histories of religion and industrial and social change, as well as the lessons and laws of empire. Far from Europe, they pertained to the many places the British now called Her Majesty's possessions.[5] European newcomers saw their laws reflecting an advanced society primarily based upon English Protestant values. Others preferred Irish Catholic values, although few of these people were senior administrators. Asian and Pacific Islander immigrants had different legal ontologies and held on to their own ideas of the civil and of civilization.

Marriage law was a vital principle — arguably *the* most vital principle — of Indigenous law. So marital negotiations between Aboriginal and European systems involved a contest of laws fundamental to each nation or group. A male newcomer in an intimate relationship with an Aboriginal woman fell under an Indigenous system of authority and law. The outsider became insider. "Constituting marriage" is a helpful way to think about marriage at the colonizing interface of nation building.[6] The word "constitution" refers to the makeup of something — from the physical constitution of the body of an individual person to the larger collective, the nation. Among modern nations, including the United States and Australia, the constitution is understood as a written, public document that lays out the basis of governance and laws and marks the beginning of nationhood itself. The *Macquarie Dictionary* defines "constitution" as "the system of fundamental principles according to which a nation, state or body politic is governed."[7] *Merriam-Webster* offers a definition that includes principles that "determine the powers and duties of the government and guarantee certain rights to the people in it." Other useful definitions include "a written instrument," the "mode in which a state or society is organized," and "the manner in which sovereign power is distributed."[8]

Many Aboriginal women who lived with men from Europe, China, or other parts of Asia were not in unions authorized by the written marriage legislation of the colonizer state, the Marriage Act. Rather, they were in relationships authorized by Indigenous marriage protocols. When a man entered into a European-style marriage, this might imply proper respect for the Aboriginal woman as a "real wife." At the same time, it is doubtful that this foreign system meant much at all to many of the Aboriginal woman involved in these unions. This is not to say that views did not vary between individuals and change over time. Perhaps some women reasoned that, if the outsider husband did not comply with the Aboriginal system of social obligations, he would at least respect those of his society of origin. Some women came to understand that, by entering contractual obligations that were underwritten by colonizer family expectations, they could obtain certain civil protections under the new regime.

As we have seen in the previous chapter, in Queensland's marriage approval process, any non-Indigenous man who wanted to marry an Aboriginal woman had to obtain permission to marry from the regional chief protector of Aborigines. The local policeman making enquiries often had trouble working out how to ascertain whether the Aboriginal woman had given her consent. Some Aboriginal women clearly exercised choice. Even after a prospective husband had received permission from the protector to marry, a chosen Aboriginal wife had the right to refuse, and they did. According to the archival files, rebuffs were not uncommon.[9] This suggests that they did understand the matter of consent under Queensland law, that they had a clear sense of their autonomy and of having a choice.

In fundamental ways, the oppressive and violent nature of colonizing power relations obviously worked against free choice and consent. In many instances, it was a uniformed police officer who enquired as to whether a woman agreed to marry. Many Aboriginal women may have logically presumed that they were therefore obliged to marry the man concerned, and possibly that they would be forced to do so. They carried the psychological scars of recent frontier atrocities, including murder and rape — often at the hands of police, including Native Police. The innumerable coercive legacies of colonialism, including the horrors of child removal and family breakup, left emotional pain beyond measure.

While Queensland's efforts to impose an orderly marriage regime in these regions were confusing for everyone, from the perspective of Indigenous kinship laws, they made no sense at all. Intimate relations across the colonizing frontier continued apace. Aboriginal women saw intermarriage from inside the world of their own complex system of laws and values — one in which the strict laws applied to marital pairings did not preclude the question of consent. Usually marriages were exogamous, meaning that a woman married a man from another language group rather than someone within her own extended family, clan, or tribal unit. Endogamous marriages, or ones within a larger group entity, still required unions with men of more distant clans. White men living with Aboriginal women learned, accepted, and became acculturated to these kinship and marital value systems. If they wanted to find a wife, they usually had to.

Contemporary European studies of "primitive peoples" were preoccupied with the notion that primitive peoples used force to obtain brides. Europeans seemed to measure their manhood against these stereotypes, having a stake in pretending that such peoples never allowed for female consent. Pioneering sociologists argued that humanity had developed from primitive into more sophisticated social forms. Their evolutionary thinking posited monogamous European-style marriage as the yardstick. E. Westermarck's 1891 study *History of Human Marriage* explored the "origins and development of marriage," while Ernest Crawley's 1902 work *The Mystic Rose: A Study of Primitive Marriage and of Primitive Thought in Its Bearing on Marriage* portrayed marriage ceremonies as deriving from a "primitive religious mental habit."[10]

Laws requiring consent to marry consequently became privileged as an essential marker distinguishing sophisticated from primitive manhood. In the highly descriptive scientific method of his day, Roth looked for ancient remnants of "marriage by capture" in Australian marriage traditions. While some Indigenous courtship and prenuptial rituals were played out as dramas of abduction and coercion, Roth sometimes read too much into these performances. However, he did admit that, even when agreeing to the marriage, girls could enact the ritual of being unwilling captives.[11]

Although Roth's ethnographies used what he considered the language of the scientifically dispassionate, his chosen English terminology was laden with historical and religious values. For example, Roth wrote of wife "exchange and barter," "marital and first-night's Orgie," and "wife capture." He noted that incest was unheard of, suggesting that Aboriginal people's exogamous system and complex system of marriage classes prevented it. Revealing his social evolutionary thinking, he reported this as indicating "a gradual development of the moral sense."[12] In various localities, he observed various betrothal ceremonies. These included painting and putting feathers in the hair of the young girl who was the promised bride. He explained the gradual, controlled stages and ceremony that preceded her going to her husband at a later age. He also explained that, before being granted his promised wife, and in order for a marriage to be "publicly recognized," the husband had to be at the highest level of initiation.

Increasingly, colonizer-state registrars and bureaucratic systems of permission started to endorse Aboriginal marriages. Rapid demographic and economic impacts, combined with the system of Queensland reserves that concentrated Aboriginal people from many distant language groups or nations, extended the range of peoples who could marry each other. Those groups who practiced endogamy, or marriage within their country, often later switched over to marrying people from more distant regions. This may have been due to increasing mobility.[13] Potential marriage partners now included non-Aboriginal people, who did not pose the same challenge in terms of close affinity and the need to match with "right-way" kinship classification. In the changed circumstances, Aboriginal societies modified their internal marriage arrangements. Although it is unlikely that Aboriginal women saw themselves as goods, Roth speculated that the colonizer economy had "contaminated" them by creating a "selling" and "trading" system for brides.[14]

INDIGENOUS MARRIAGE AND KINSHIP LAW

Indigenous Australian marriage relied upon a masterfully ordered mechanics. Lengthy, patient negotiations achieved an eventual consensus across ordained groups of kinspeople, often involving long-distance travel that cemented wider alliances. Among North Queensland's Aboriginal people, appropriate kin negotiated the bestowals according to the rules of correct marriage affiliations. However, there was always room for variations and realignments.

From birth, everyone was allocated a skin name or kinship classification that mapped out who could and could not marry each other. Ideally, marriages functioned as a means of ensuring cooperation between different clans, cementing ties between them, and providing expanded access to lands and journey routes. Transgression of marital-related kin obligations and appropriate behaviors could lead to bitter disputes, ritual violence and death. A valid way of looking at the kinship system is that it was structured less by biological descent than categories of marriageability. The critical question was not "Who am I descended from?" but "Whom may I marry?"[15]

While Aboriginal children readily grasp kin and marriage rules, to the untaught western observer, the complexity of kinship relations has been likened to advanced algebra. Anthropologists comprehend it with the aid of extensive diagrams and specialist study. Many groups had two moiety systems, which also determined marital partners. Kinship classifications derived from mother and/or father. "Correct" marital partners usually jumped two generations, according to putative kinship relations — and not necessarily biological descent. The North Queensland marital system was based on what anthropologists dubbed the Aranda framework. For example, the Lardil, Yangkaal, and adjacent mainlanders had an eight-class subsection system. In principle, it was based upon "the exchange of women between two patrilineal land-owning groups or clans every second generation and the maintenance of 'brotherhood' groups at two different levels — the moiety and the clan complex."[16] Marriageable kin would therefore be the children of female or male cross-cousins. Only certain men were allowed as marriage partners for women of a specific kinship group, as they had to be the "right-way" kin classification. "Wrong-way" marriages — to use the colloquial — were one of the most serious and antisocial offenses, punishable by physical ordeal or death. Such unions were thought to be dangerous and destructive. On loved ones, they would wreak social and spiritual havoc, causing natural disaster, illness, or death. In turn, these outcomes would require avenging. "Wrong-way" marriages caused intense and lasting conflict, Indigenous law killings, and terrifying sorcery.

Although marital systems differed regionally from one language group to the next, they precluded unions between classificatory brother, sister, mother, father, uncle, and other classificatory kin, even when these involved no blood tie. Some anthropologists call this "fictive kin," but for Aboriginal insiders, there is nothing fictive about it. Kinship is real; it need not rely on blood alone. The same could be seen with the Cherokees — when adopting people into their system and forming alliances.

Regardless of rules and feared punishments, the Australian Indigenous marriage system offered safety valves to allow for irregular marriages to come under the law. Transgressive "love matches" were common enough throughout Aboriginal Australia. Such couples usually eloped. After they observed an extended period of absence, and sometimes a ritualized physical chastisement upon return, their match was frequently accepted.[17] But time and negotiations were prerequisite. Kinship classifications were realigned to correct the irregularities.[18] While "love" was emphasized in marriages by elopement, these were not necessarily associated with "free will." "Love magic" and/or sorcery meant that the will of one was used to influence the will of another, the would-be partner.[19]

The bride could be promised at a young age, or even prior to her birth. Such arrangements were crucial to ensuring good relations between neighboring linguistic and landowning groups. Aunts, uncles, and other relatives usually participated in protracted marital negotiations between neighboring clans and tribes that involved meetings and long journeys.[20] Pieces of story were shared across the land, making for a larger, more intricate memory canvas. The marital contract was negotiated to arrange sexual, labor, and familial relations into a system of social cohesion. Relatives policed the appropriate behavior of spouses and protected women against excessive violence. Marriage according to the kinship law was an essential thread weaving storied ontologies into the social order. Not only did it make the world, and individual humans within it, but marriage law functioned for their mutual well-being.

Polygamous unions were common, especially for older men, with multiple wives signifying prestige and high status. Aboriginal women rarely had multiple husbands, but communities permitted discreet sexual relations with another partner.[21] By 1900, Indigenous betrothal practices were still in place, with only girls raised by non-Aboriginal families potentially excluded. Marital arrangements were matters of public knowledge, the news circulating during the time when long family and community discussions were aiming to reach consensus. However, population displacements, colonizer incursions, and other frontier economic, social, and spiritual impacts created rapid changes in the system.[22]

The presence of Europeans, Asians, and Pacific Islanders had a dramatic impact, widening the range of available husbands and facilitating exogamous or out-group marriage. Outsiders would be given "suitable" kinship classifications. This was obligatory, for otherwise they would lack any status as a social entity. In this sense, they would be without a place in a known world, without social codes to govern anyone's interaction with them. They would not be truly human, with no name and no one linked to them. However, as blank slates, they could have kinship bestowed upon them strategically, according to the logic of existing associations, especially with prospective partners. Because he had no preestablished or born-into kinship classification, relatives could allocate a kinship status to a non-Aboriginal man that was congruent with being a right-way marriage partner in the proper kin alignment to his sweetheart.[23] Due to the ease with which tactical kin classifications could be created for outsiders, a right-way marriage of an outsider to a particular woman could be far more readily organized than a marriage that required realignment of the kin status into which an Aboriginal man was born.

In conjunction with kinship, marriage regulations underwrote a gendered system of law and order. In early child raising and later interfamily and intergroup negotiations, parents, aunties, and other elders taught the principles of marriage. And they organized the appropriate pairing of couples. Husbands who ill-treated their wives or failed to meet the required obligations to their spouse's kin could be punished with illness or death. Social and ceremonial exclusion played their role too. Marriage law was understood as pivotal to a functional, healthy community. Disobeying it brought disharmony, sickness, and catastrophe. Even today, elders in remote communities (who tend to follow modified forms of customary law) often explain a dysfunctional community as a result of people marrying wrong-way.

While Aboriginal Australians often held low estimates of white men's morality, they judged white people's random mating behavior as proof of a moral status that was animal rather than human. Just like dogs, they would "mate with anyone."[24] By arranging an Aboriginal female partner for an outsider, however, Indigenous power brokers could attempt to train them in their community obligations, thus bringing the outsider into humanity and under the control of customary law. Marrying "straight" reflected a cherished value and, through songlines and stories, it embedded people in landed histories comprising epic journey stories and protocols.[25] This metaphoric journey in the "right" direction defined personal identity and obligations to specific areas of land, in turn reinforcing a correctly oriented moral universe.

THE RIGHTS OF THE INDIGENOUS HUSBAND?

The state bureaucracy was wresting control of Indigenous marriage out of the Indigenous community's kin-based authority system. The so-called protection policies detracted from Indigenous people's powers to independently and freely negotiate marriages. Under the Aborigines Protection Act of 1897 and its amended version of 1901, the police had powers to remove people and to break up family groups. For Aboriginal people, these intrusions could be virtually impossible to avoid. Given passage of the act, it appeared that the freedom of choice and consent fundamental to democratic national thinking simply did not apply to them.

At the same time, however, if a man applied to marry an Aboriginal woman, protectors were obliged to pay attention to the consent issue required in the Queensland Marriage Act and in British and colonial marriage acts. To respect the monogamy requirement, the applicant could not already be married. Consequently, protectors had to take elements of Indigenous marriage law into account. This also meant taking the rights of Indigenous husbands into account. The local policeman was required to comment on whether the woman consented to the marriage and had to ascertain whether she had "a tribal husband," which was the term Europeans used for an Indigenous or customary law spouse. Women's existing marriages with Indigenous men created a quandary for the chief protectors and police who administered the act. After all, a woman was usually promised to the man who would be her future husband from childhood. Few mature women who had grown up in their own communities would not be already promised or married. Yet polygamy and bigamy were illegal under British law.

In several cases, Chief Protectors Roth and Meston refused permission for Aboriginal intermarriages because of conflicts with Aboriginal marriage law. Roth feared that as Aboriginal women might already be married by "native law," authorizing such a marriage would create a *"grave moral wrong* inflicted on the tribally recognized husband."[26] Chief Protectors Meston and Roth had insights into Aboriginal ways of being and understood the strength of Indigenous conceptions of marriage law. While not always getting the details correct, Roth's ethnological writings reveal a close interest in and a certain knowledge of Aboriginal marriage arrangements and betrothal practices. Often the protectors' interventions reflected a desire for fairness.

They were also driven by a desire to avert more murders of white men. The need for protective laws may suggest that Aboriginal people had lost the battle, but this was not necessarily so. Protectors were enforcers of colonizer order with a duty to ensure peace across colonizing boundaries. In Indigenous law, the Aboriginal husband was entitled to avenge himself against a man who stole his wife with violent punishment—even death. Colonizer anxiety about the Aboriginal *husband's* consent during this period demonstrates that this law was still in operation; threats of violence had not been eradicated. The police enforcing the new laws of the colonizer state therefore needed to be acutely aware of Aboriginal marriage law, its sway over their people, and its significance for law and order. On Queensland's transnational ground, Aboriginal cultural knowledge thus became an essential colonizer commodity. As police regularly sought advice from Aboriginal trackers and police staff to assist with cultural translation, those they consulted were provided with direct opportunities to advance their own clan politics. Rather than expecting a written document, protectors had to rely upon oral testimony for proof. The requirement to look into the marital status of an intermarrying woman meant that, in this sense, the state acknowledged Indigenous marriage as valid. Perhaps it even took precedence over a written license under the Queensland Marriage Act.[27] This recognition of the Indigenous husband represented an unusual acknowledgment of Indigenous protocol and law.

Nonetheless, when an Aboriginal woman entered a marriage under the Queensland state-endorsed registry system, the protectors did not necessarily appreciate her understanding of the situation. For example, the Aboriginal wife may not have shared an expectation that a woman's coresidence with a white man was permanent or until "death do us part." Cessation of the relationship was at the woman's discretion, and perhaps her prior Aboriginal husband's, or both. In one such case in 1902, Chief Protector Meston instructed police to remove an Aboriginal woman, Minnie, from her home with a Pacific Islander husband and send her to a government reserve where her tribal husband resided. She had previously been living with a "Mr T," having married him in a registry office in Rockhampton. Given their powers under the act to arrest any non-Aboriginal man who "cohabited" with and openly acknowledged an Aboriginal female partner, Queensland police detained her. Perhaps the police were not aware of the legal marriage into which she had entered.

Purportedly outraged about the attack on the non-Aboriginal "legal" husband, who held a written marriage contract, local white working men launched an energetic campaign. Claiming they were interested in protecting the rights of the married man, they conveniently ignored the rights of the Indigenous husband and possibly the wife as well.[28] This controversy was fought over which husband was the most entitled, authorized, or valid husband and over the competing authority of two sets of marriage laws.

Whereas protectors had to honor the limited amount they knew of Aboriginal law, colonizing priorities came first. What, indeed, did the woman want? And the Indigenous husband, who was the original husband and from whom she was not "divorced"? Aboriginal society had no formal divorce process, with men and women separating by mutual consent and often the approval of parents or elders. If one party did not agree, however, he or she could seek to fight or punish the former partner or the new lover or could seek compensation.[29] From the perspective of the protectors, it came down to the matter of consent ensconced in Queensland's British-derived marriage law. Culturally different notions of gendered sovereignty arose when marriage took place across colonizing and legal boundaries, confounding the law enforcers. They came up against two sets of marital laws.

As they usually saw them as cheap labor, and as competition for Aboriginal women, it was unusual for white men to agitate for the rights of *nonwhite* males. Yet, as with Kitty and Goon Goo's case discussed in the previous chapter, Minnie's banishment by Aboriginal Protector Meston to an Aboriginal reserve gave vent to white men's bitter resentment of interference into the rights of the colonizer husband. Given white men's opposition to cheap "colored" labor, by publicly supporting an Asian or Pacific Islander husband, they reasserted the authority of all non-Aboriginal husbands.[30] Without having to out white men like themselves as exemplars, they advocated for the primacy of the "legal" husband.

Minnie's understanding of the marriage contrasted with both her husband's and Meston's. Minnie had reportedly agreed to move to the reserve "cheerfully enough," telling Mr. T at the last minute, "You clear out of this I don't want to see you no more." Meston stated that Minnie told him she wanted to return to *"her husband"* — in this case her customary-law husband — because her own people had left the district and she did not want to be "alone with" the "Kanakas." Fearing offshore deportation to their husbands' homelands, Aboriginal women with Pacific Islander husbands faced particular problems. Minnie did not want to risk being deported on the grounds of being the legal wife of an alien.[31]

It is surprising that Protector Archibald Meston recognized the rights of the Indigenous husband. Perhaps he was prompted by his fascination for ethnography and respect for Aboriginal rules, or his desire to maintain a "pure race" unspoiled by mixing with Asians and Kanakas. In wishing to recognize the Aboriginal customary-law husband, however, Meston isolated himself. Sternly rebuked by his superiors, his actions were overturned.

Predictably enough (as had been the pattern with land law and sales), state law ruled in favor of the primacy of its own law. The Crown solicitor advised the government that even in the case of a prior customary marriage,

British law overrode Aboriginal law.³² Northern Protector Walter Roth remained concerned, stating, "Although our laws do not recognize aboriginal marriages, there is no doubt that a woman may often be already married according to native laws, and trouble hence arise."³³ "Trouble" was a popular euphemism repeatedly used to mask Queensland's ongoing frontier violence. The contest over which husband's rights won out was about security for white men and women. This indicated that Indigenous law was still being implemented; outsider transgressors were still being published. Although the frontiersmen's rhetoric emphasized the rights of the "legal" husband and of the "Christian" marriage, their primary concern was to discount the standing of the Indigenous husband.

Yet white men could not actually plead ignorance of the Indigenous husband's existence, for those seeking partners often had to negotiate with him directly. In entering a relationship, they were then obliged to fulfill reciprocal obligations, such as supplying new foods such as flour, tea, and sugar and new technologies such as tomahawks, pots, knives, clothing, blankets, and other desired commodities.

Nevertheless, by diminishing the legal significance and entitlement of Indigenous husbands, white and nonwhite men ensured and morally justified their own access to Aboriginal women. Supporting the rights of a Pacific Islander enabled colonizer men to assert supremacy over the Indigenous "colonized." But more to the point, it enabled them to assert their primacy as negotiators of marriage over the authority of metropolitan protectors. They alone should be the organizers of colonizer-colonized relations.

The chief protector was attempting to work a "two-law" system that reflected the current state of play and power and cultural relations on the contemporary frontier; however, when disputes arose, Queensland's legal marriage law overrode not only the protectors' conciliatory intentions, but also the Aboriginals Protection Act.³⁴ Nonetheless, as another government department had ruled on the legality of Minnie's marriage, it is surprising that committing a "grave moral wrong" against *Aboriginal* marriage systems apparently still rated as a serious concern.

Indeed, the chief protectors continued to take account of the woman's freedom to choose. This was especially so when further public controversies erupted in the Queensland newspapers. Given the removals that the

Aboriginals Protection Act made common, it seems paradoxical for Roth to argue that it was "a very serious matter thus to take away an aboriginal's *liberty*." So he then specified what Queensland's policy really meant. Intervention, he wrote, was designed for preventing sexual danger, removing "young girls where every hour may add to the risk." Roth sought to claim the high moral ground, stating that, by contrast, removing a mature woman from a long-term partnership was not only illegal "*morally* speaking, it was *forcible*."[35]

Trying to juggle and adjudicate ideas of free will, two marriage systems, and the cross-cultural nature of knowledge systems was quite a challenge; they were often irreconcilable. Where were their tools? Rather than exploring Minnie's understandings of the matter or reflecting upon the status of the tribal husband in a colonizing society, Meston considered civilized gender roles as a modernizing paradigm. Pondering whether Aboriginal women fully comprehended their duties as wives, he wrote in 1903, "Much depends on the degree of civilization to which the woman has attained to [*sic*] as also is the character of the man. If she is above the ordinary type of 'Gin' and if both he and she would recognize the responsibilities it might be well to insist on legal marriage."[36] Here this kind of marriage was understood as a civil privilege to which only an educated Aboriginal woman was entitled. In this context, "civilization" implied conformity with the cultural and legal protocols of British marital contracts. Only in this way could a woman understand and agree to the bounded obligations and the loss of freedoms expected to follow her consent.

In such thinking, the matter of whether the Aboriginal woman consented to the norms and delimitations of this cultural and sexual contract fell out of the picture. Around this time, in Australia and in Great Britain, women's rights and married women's rights were a subject of contention. Married women's property rights were granted in Queensland in 1890. However, Aboriginal protectors could remove an Aboriginal widow to a reserve, thus denying her the right to remain in a privately owned house. In 1902 Australian women gained the vote nationally, which was well ahead of their British and American counterparts. Although eligibility varied across states, Aboriginal men and women either were not included or were being gradually excluded.[37] As the same time that Meston was presuming that only British-style marriage was nonbarbaric and "civilized," contemporary feminists were depicting this same form of marriage as akin to slavery.[38] In various ways, the British-Australian institution of marriage rendered the wife the property of her husband, who in law could assume rights to all material possessions and offspring and could force sex.

Aboriginal women saw their subjectivity and their responsibilities differently. In a changing colonizing context that required drastic adaptations, Minnie's views accorded with her personal and cultural priorities. Faced with isolation from her own community, her legal marriage under Queensland law had decreased in importance to her. According to Meston, Minnie's Aboriginal husband, Linnay, complained bitterly that she was his wife and had lived with him for over four years. Meston tried to obtain the Indigenous husband's consent to permit Minnie to leave him. Linnay refused, seeing himself as the rightful husband in Indigenous law — a system he clearly recognized as having continuing jurisdiction. Although not necessarily for love, Minnie herself was making strategic decisions in regard to her marriage options, residence, and community affiliations.[39]

The case sheds light on one woman's ideas about what she was consenting to in legal marriage. While her husband under British-Queensland law stayed in or near her people's country, and while she stayed near her Indigenous husband and community, she had no objections to the marriage to Mr. T. However, she did not wish to be too far away from her people. She was willing to stay with her newcomer husband only when her Aboriginal community was living nearby. Meanwhile, her relatives and husband Linnay had supported her concurrent marriage to a non-Aboriginal outsider.

Certainly it appears that Minnie agreed to live with Mr. T and to participate in a sexual and domestic relationship. But the contract had limits; Minnie thought she could leave Mr. T whenever she liked to return to her other husband.[40] Put simply, she was agreeable about having two husbands, for this enabled her to fulfill her responsibilities to land and kin across two economic and social systems. However, she agreed to continue the arrangement only on the condition that she did not have to be separated permanently from her Aboriginal kin and community, and from her Aboriginal husband.

PROTECTORS OF PLURAL MARRIAGE?

In the previous chapter we discussed the case of Police Constable Casey arriving at the premises of Lee Chew in 1906 and sighting his Aboriginal companion Dolly as "proof" of a cohabitation offense.[41] Yet when it came time to test Dolly by presenting evidence in court, she was nowhere to be found. A police expedition was sent out in pursuit but was unsuccessful. Casey explained that Dolly went "away in the ranges at Stoney Creek to hide." Not alone, though, for she was with her *Aboriginal husband*, Jacky. "I did my best to secure her, as also did acting Sergeant Magee, but it was impossible to find her in time for the hearing."[42]

Many of the Aboriginal women "cohabiting" with non-Aboriginal men similarly had Aboriginal husbands living in the district or its surrounds.[43] Dolly's arrangement with the Chinese man enabled her to stay around her own people and in her own country. Knowledge of country and support from her tribal husband gave the "cohabiting" woman an alternative and sustaining world to which she could go at any time — either to leave the other husband or to evade Queensland's marriage restriction law. Similarly, the relationship with a newcomer man — some of whom had market gardens or farms — enabled access to new food resources for her wider family group.

As well as ending the perils of police harassment, for an Aboriginal woman, legal marriage to a non-Indigenous man sometimes had other advantages. In the 1900s out-marriage was one of the few ways that she could be exempted from the powers and restrictions of the Aboriginals Protection Act, which enforced residence on a reserve, broke up families, and controlled employment and wages. Despite their interest in marital consent, the chief protectors did not seek a woman's consent to remove her from her own land or from her normal residence.

For example, when Lizzie L. was married to a white man, under Section 10, she could not be forcibly removed from her residence. After her husband died, police tried to remove her from Croydon. This was despite the fact that he left his cattle and horses to her. Lizzie objected, stating to a protector that she "had never been in a black's camp in her life, having been born on a Station and brought up by white people. She does not associate with the blacks nor does she speak or know anything of their

FIG. 57. A Chinese cook in a bush camp, 1886. Queensland State Library, no. 414267.

language." Chief Protector Richard Howard believed she was exempted from the act due to her marriage. The Crown solicitor disagreed. Her marital status was annulled upon being widowed. Her exemption from the Aboriginals Protection Act applied only "so long as she resides with such husband."[44]

Marriage under the colonizer system was thus Lizzie's best method of ensuring her children stayed with her too. Although a woman might be subject to "governance" or the demands and authority of a husband, being married under the colonizer regime released her from the Aboriginals Protection Act's residential control and surveillance. In effect, only being married to a non-Aboriginal man and then staying married gave her citizenship status and exemption from the act. It was a conditional status, and if widowed, she would again come under the provisions of the Aboriginals Protection Act. The temporary, marriage-tied nature of her citizenship impeded her access to property.

In another case, Jackson, a man of mixed Aboriginal and white parentage, had to go through the process of proving his suitability as a husband. Protectors had removed his de facto wife from Blackwater in Central Queensland to the Barambah (later Cherbourg) reserve, making him desperate to get her back. Presumably the couple had been satisfied with their relationship and had no need of formal endorsement, but after her removal, he had to file an application to marry her or lose her. She was pregnant by him and, according to Jackson, was "willing to become my wife." Not only was the relationship well established, but the man was a horse breaker on Jellinbah Station — a prestigious occupation with a reliable income.

Her unmarried status and her pregnancy may have been the reason behind her removal in the first place. The chief protector granted permission for them to wed, upon condition that the husband pay her train fare back from the reserve. The positive outcome was based on the grounds that Jackson had some Aboriginal descent anyway. On April 20, 1909, only a few days after she arrived back at the station, they were married in the Methodist chapel at Emerald.[45] Their child would therefore be legitimate under state law, and as long as the father was alive, the child could remain free from the forcible removals of the Aboriginals Protection Act.

Indigenous women married to Indigenous men under the tribal system did not share the same freedoms from state intervention as those married to other men. Within the Indigenous marriage system itself, they might access greater choices, depending on age, circumstance, the individual husband, and their place as a wife in a traditionally polygamous marriage system.

Freedom is a difficult quality to measure, and the Aboriginal world itself brought gender, clan, and family-based restrictions, scrutiny, and expectation. In Aboriginal-style marriage, however, an Aboriginal woman had far greater freedom of movement, choices in sexual activity, and overall autonomy than a white Australian wife of the early twentieth century. Aboriginal women also had custodianship over sacred places, resource sites, ceremony, and special knowledge that gave them power and status. Moveable property was not a major component of the Aboriginal economy, although rare commodities — like ocher, stones with special properties, or pearl shell from a distant coast — often became shared property of sacred significance. A marriage ceremony might also incorporate some special trade objects from afar. In some North Queensland groups, the ceremonial components of marriage included the girl or her mother building a hut and lighting a fire and the husband's seizing the girl's wrist.[46] Any ritual would confirm certain sets of sexual, labor, and resource relations and obligations.

CROSS-CULTURAL CONSENT

In western thinking, consent refers to voluntary agreement, concurrence, and permission.[47] Consent to marriage did not imply the presence of affective bonds, or love. Although regulated by the state and wider society, the contract required an agreement between two individuals. Adults were free agents, not requiring parental or kin permission. Marriage involved a public declaration and signatures on paper. It also required an authorized celebrant. In current Australian legal parlance, it implies "affirmative acceptance, not merely a standing by and absence of objection," "freely given by a rational and sober person."[48] In marriage, consent refers to acquiescence to a proposal.

In European cultures, marital consent had a long and changing philosophical, political, religious, and legal tradition. Dissent had often centered on the marital partners' maturity, differences of ages, and affinity or close blood relations. For example, in 1589 church minister John Stockwood objected to children marrying without *parental* consent, especially the father's.[49] In Samuel Bufford's 1696 *Discourse against Unequal Marriages*, he objected to old persons marrying young persons and to persons marrying without the consent of at least one parent or friend.[50] There were some caveats about categories of people considered unable to provide consent. For example, a lunatic was not considered capable of providing consent. In following British precedent, the Queensland Marriage Act barred marriages based upon close affinity — that is, incestuous unions.

Marriages between the families of feuding British lords, and between European royalty, were a widely used peacemaking strategy. In the United Kingdom during the late nineteenth and early twentieth centuries, members of key political families intermarried, thus consolidating their power bases and property.[51] Such marriages continue to play a political role in royal, governing, and elite circles.

From the early nineteenth century, "companionate marriage" was based increasingly upon individual choice and love matches. Although the principles of European marriage had been contested over the prior century, the institution retained certain historically evolved values and rituals.

Conceptualizations of individual consent need to be culturally contextualized. For example, in Australian Aboriginal law, the matter of marital consent tended to rely partly upon the decisions of those with bestowal rights over the wife. I wondered whether there was an equivalent for the bride's consent in Indigenous languages. By considering related concepts that are laid down in language, hopefully we might gain significant clues to the cultural complexities of betrothal in Aboriginal Australia. A widespread Central Australian language, Warlpiri, has a metaphoric term used to describe a young woman's agreement to go to a promised husband. It is *jarralyku*, or "floodout." Here the water frees itself of its banks; it is freed up or unbounded.[52]

Australia's climate of drought and flood gives flooding special significance. In flood, the land changes; river channels join up, divert, and get isolated into billabongs, creating an intricate network of potential linkages and bypaths. Indeed, due to the multiple veins of intermittent streams, one region of Queensland is known as channel country. Confluences and new connections enabled travel across vast areas of land and across the current-day boundaries of large states. This kind of thinking turns western ideas on their head; for one thing, flooding is seen as bad: it washes away houses, agriculture, and stock and endangers life. Western newspapers do not talk about rivers being freed, liberated in a positive way. Nor do many western cultures tend to think of promised brides that way.

In current-day American and Australian sensibilities, to be a promised bride is often taken to mean a loss of choice and freedom, while in contrast, *jarralyku* conveys a notion of liberation and freedom from containment and the earth's restraint. Like the river itself, the girl could range beyond her confines, from the smaller area of her own clan to lands farther afield, extending her land associations and networks.

Perhaps the water metaphor also has sexual meanings associated with pubescent awakenings. Again, the concept reflects how marriage opened up new spaces and new dreaming and journey routes and, like a flooding river, linked areas of previously dry land once out of bounds. In flood, some Queensland rivers connect up to travel south to New South Wales, then Victoria and into the Great Australian Bight to the south of the continent. With the aid of canoes, floods expanded the possibilities for journeying and for the establishment of new relationships and enhanced areas of influence.[53]

Marriage routes — where people historically journeyed to negotiate for wives and to hold ceremonies — traverse hundreds of miles and more. They provide important points of connection, uniting different tribes up and down the east coast of Australia, extending networks, range areas, and connections into something more akin to large "nations."[54] Around Australia, Indigenous people tell marriage narratives in their songlines and "dreaming stories." Around Byron Bay in New South Wales, a waterfall stands for a powerful love and marriage story, "Eelemarni," which brought about the unification of two nations of people and wedded two vast land areas as one.[55]

The linguist Robert Dixon depicts the tribe as the key political unit in North East Queensland. He explains that each inhabitant has three group affiliations — to tribe, local group, and section or moiety. The "national unity" in this region, which comprises geographically distinctive terrains, is maintained "through predominantly endogamous marriage" and through tribal gatherings for "food procurement and recreation." Marriage may take place within the wider group but not within the small group or clan, which is further divided into moieties.[56] As the ethnographer and protector Roth stated in 1910, "Marriages are still largely arranged according to the section system," with old people being consulted about procedure.[57] A diagram of such interconnecting networks contrasts with the discrete branches depicted in the western-style family tree.

The appropriate bestowing kin member was more influential in the matter of marital consent than the prospective wife or husband. Usually a girl's uncle on her mother's side or another person in the girl's parents' generation conducted contractual arrangements, but her or she also sought her mother's consent. In practice, such arrangements could not always be enforced and, depending on her age, the girl or woman had a degree of choice and autonomy. Whereas a young girl was not in a very strong bargaining position, a grown woman could be, and a mature woman usually was. Although her mother would also exercise a certain say, she could assert her own wishes as she grew.[58] At the same time, relationships were carefully monitored to try to avoid wrong-way sexual partners.[59]

In the two-laws zone, the legacies of European and Indigenous marital histories merged and shaped the colonizing experience. An Aboriginal woman's agreement to intermarry on a colonizing frontier — and that of her kin, community, and husband — became part of a crucial social and trading negotiation among all parties. In Queensland, Aboriginal people could strategically negotiate with likely husbands who sought legal marriage. Although relationships with landowners and managers might be long-lasting and committed, such men were more likely to be or have the prospect of being legally married to a white woman. Consequently, white men of high status and wealth usually sought more discreet unions with their Aboriginal lovers. Dwelling in remote areas created a sense of being away from prying eyes.

At various points, Aboriginal men grew fed up with the number of their women in unions with white men, especially when the white men did not perform anticipated kinship obligations under Aboriginal law. For example, this led to the leading Aboriginal stockmen at Wrotham Park station (inland from Port Douglas) taking allegations of sexual exploitation, harassment, and other matters to the police in the 1920s.[60] In the Northern Territory of Australia, white men's monopolizing of Aboriginal men's wives contributed to the Gurindji walk-off of the 1960s, and possibly to numerous earlier protests.[61]

Nonetheless, Indigenous-colonizer marriage had the potential to deliver, at least for a time, a kind of dual sovereignty. In these zones of negotiation, a two-law system operated, with sinews of connection between them. Human, embodied engagements across colonizing frontiers, they delivered land access and substantive rights, potentially enhancing Indigenous authority over land and law. And like Eelemarni's waterfall, it could unite peoples, forming a confluence — a new kind of intimately connected and interconnected nation.

BRIDE RIGHTS

During the period of the late nineteenth and early twentieth centuries, the Queensland landscape was a place of ongoing Indigenous power over bodies and space. And, as with the Cherokees in the 1820s and 1830s, Aboriginal people's sovereignty was constantly under threat from colonizers. Aboriginal Australians were not entitled to the standing and treaty rights that had enabled their North American counterparts to exert a system of law under a centralized system of governance with a set of written regulations and a constitution. Few Aboriginal people were educated to the level of certain Cherokee politicians.

Under Queensland's Aboriginals Protection Act, the state effectively took on the role of father, and Indigenous families lost more and more power over their own families and their children. Such protective guardianship effectively saw Aboriginal Australians categorized as people who required the state to make decisions in regard to their life choices, in a kind of in loco parentis and father of the bride role. In effect, the protector was entitled to make decisions in the same fashion as would occur in the case of a minor or a lunatic.

Under this regime, an Aboriginal woman's authority and status in Aboriginal marriage was confusing. If she was married under British or Australian law, certain common-law protections for women and rights applied. If married to a white man or an Aboriginal man of mixed descent, the Indigenous woman was covered by the legal principle of coverture. As mentioned in the introduction, as wife, she became *femme covert*, taking on the legal status of her Australian- or overseas-born husband. As H. R. Durham, a missionary in Geraldton, wrote to the protector of Aborigines, "Our marriage laws make man and wife one."[62] Upon entering this contract, she could no longer sign other legal contracts in her own name. She also took on the citizenship of her husband.

Aboriginal people had initially been "subjects" of the British Crown; however, under colonial self-government and federation, they became an exceptional category, without clear-cut status as citizens. This changed only in the 1960s.[63] With no treaties or state recognition of Indigenous title rights, their groupings were not recognized as having any standing as nations in themselves. Under Australian colonialism, Aboriginal nations were not recognized as entities with their own systems of recognized citizenship. Before 1992, the legal idea of *terra nullius*, or the idea of Australia as having been unoccupied, would ensure no recognition of native title. This did not grant any entitlement to sovereignty — even in a limited "dependent nation" form.

Unlike the Cherokees, Aboriginal people were not seeking to ban intermarriage. With different motivations, they were seeking to maintain control over it. Nor did they want the protectors to prevent or restrict it. For an

Aboriginal woman, the ability to formally marry a non-Indigenous man under the state system was a pathway to certain freedoms. Potentially, it enabled her and their children to stay in her own country — benefits that informal and secret unions could not always guarantee. Marriage to a non-Indigenous man also enabled her access to goods for herself and her family. When making their decisions, Indigenous women had wider community and resource pressures in mind; out-marriage might bring in new foods and trade goods, enabling her to fulfill her own reciprocal kin responsibilities in her community. Other Aboriginal women took up an outsider pairing to escape unwelcome or violent marriages.

Some Aboriginal women married to white Australians could gain the entitlements of Australian citizenship, which included civil status and civic freedoms, including rights to their children's education. Of direct practical impact, such a union could free a woman from the many other powers of the Aboriginals Protection Act — powers that would affect her freedom of movement, employment, and wages. She would have more rights to keep her property, including a home and earnings, and to enjoy greater freedom of movement.[64] Although Indigenous people were not a discrete nationality, under the act their rights were severely impeded.[65] Marriage to a white, Asian, or other non-Indigenous man could protect an Aboriginal woman from forcible removal to a state-run reserve and would enable her to keep her own wages.[66]

On an individual level, legal colonizer marriages would often seem a viable, logical choice. Entering such a marriage could prevent an Aboriginal woman's non-Indigenous partner from being harassed by police, fined, or imprisoned. Only through this means could she live with him and prevent herself being exiled onto a distant, government-run Aboriginal reserve or institution. In other words, formal marriage to a member of the colonizer class allowed Indigenous women a quick route to improved civil status and the freedoms of the new state's citizenship rights. The so-called bondage of marriage thus enabled them to escape the bondage of state institutions and allowed their non-Aboriginal husbands to escape repeated arrests and prison sentences. There was also another significant consideration. Marriage allowed them to protect their children from removal by state authorities.

MARITAL ACTS

Many Aboriginal women on Queensland frontiers agreed to long-term sexual partnerships with colonizer men. Under Queensland state law, some legally married them. Despite the introduction of state restrictions on intermarriage and cohabitation, when populations mingled on common lands, sexual unions, whether de facto or authorized by marriage, created families that traversed cultural and colonizing boundaries.

In the context of colonial dispossession and frontier violence, asymmetrical power relations and violent coercion flavored and delimited choice, and they qualified the idea of consent, too. Aboriginal women conducted ongoing sexual liaisons with outsider men — white, Asian, Pacific Islander, or others — in marriages regulated by the colonizer state and in marriages authorized under Aboriginal kin and kinship laws.

In other states, some of these stories have been told. Writer Stephen Kinnane narrated the courtship and patient love story of his English grandfather Edward, from Westminister, London, and his Aboriginal sweetheart Jessie Argyle, a Miriwung woman from Argyle cattle station. As Kinnane writes, "There are different versions of how Edward and Jessie came together.... What I do know is that when he fell, he fell hard. What I do know is that they used every spare moment to spend time with each other."[67] Pam Rajkowski relates the determination of Jack Akbar, an Afghan cameleer who traveled the breadth of Australia in order to avoid state obstruction so that he could marry his Aboriginal love, Lallie Matbar. Gillian Cowlishaw tells a story of Nelly Camfoo and her battles to conquer love against the race law.[68] Many more such stories are contained within Aboriginal people's autobiographies.

Such modern unions pitted individuals against colonizer law. Other marriages fitted less into the individual consent model and more into an Indigenous model built upon a more complicated kin-based nexus of consent. To many Indigenous people, the entry of a western legal marriage arrangement, or even a marital union with a white man, did not nullify their existing arrangements. Aboriginal societies viewed white and Asian husbands as part of system of extended kin, land, and trading relationships. Irrespective of color, Aboriginal kin reciprocity obligated her allocated husband to fulfill a range of economic and social responsibilities. The Aboriginal wife did not envisage an exclusive contract, nor did her Indigenous husband. As we have seen in the case of Minnie, her understandings of the marital agreement contrasted with Mr. T's. While Dolly may have been living as wife to the Chinese man Lee Chew, with her Aboriginal husband she could readily evade police. Jackey was not merely a decoy but a concurrent and alternative husband with whom she was in a longer relationship, and one more tightly bound into her familial and cultural world. Perhaps she spoke the truth when she explained she was at Lee Chew's only for *ki-ki*, or food.[69]

More often than not, Aboriginal women ignored the new marital boundaries being superimposed, supposedly for their protection, on their own land. Zones restricted to Aboriginal people were intended to make it easier for authorities to police white-black sexual liaisons. Yet paying too much attention to written policy tends to give elements of the Aboriginals Protection Act more credence and clout than it could exert, especially during this relatively early implementation period. The lived experience was very different from laws on paper. Where people lived in camps, life was self-governed in day-to-day interactions and in localities that Aboriginal people knew intricately. The cartographies of government acts were neither seen nor applied.

What is more, in such zones, state efforts to control marital intermixing threw up continual contradictions between intent, implementation, and law. Despite its lack of formal recognition of any kind of Aboriginal law, it is a matter of note that in the new state of Queensland senior government officials sought to respect both the Aboriginal woman's consent and the contractual rights of her Indigenous husband. In intermarriage applications, the two senior protectors instructed police to consult the Aboriginal husband in order to ascertain whether he had agreed to let go of his wife so that she could live with the non-Aboriginal man. The Aboriginal husband and his relatives may not have seen any particular arrangement as permanent; also, they wanted to know if the prospective husband had correct right-way kinship status according to their marriage law.

It is frequently assumed that Australian Indigenous law was unilaterally quashed by British declarations of law and sovereignty, yet the attention that the protectors paid to Indigenous customary laws of marriage prompts further thought. While colonial authorities believed that Indigenous men's rights could not be ignored in case this sparked violence, the state had additional considerations. Unlike missionaries, state officers did not refer to biblical commandments such as the one against stealing another man's wife or adultery. Neither Roth nor Meston explicitly brought Christian ethics into his race and gender thinking. However, it appears that they wanted to implement manly fair play toward Indigenous husbands. In a kind of husband-to-husband interplay, the protectors respected the rights of the Aboriginal husband. They did so in a way that transcended their dismissive attitudes toward Aboriginal rights to property in land.

Contradictions in the colonial project abounded. While deference was paid to Indigenous men's bride rights, western marriage law was given primacy, overriding the rights of the Indigenous husband. For example, even if an Asian or Pacific Islander husband was using marriage as a last-ditch strategy to stay in Australia, and the woman already had an Aboriginal husband, the Crown lawyer advised that, under Queensland marriage law, the rights of the "legal," or non-Aboriginal, husband had to be given primacy. The interests of white colonizer men living in frontier zones prevented husbandly collusion with Pacific Islander and Asian men from going too far.

Given the colonizing context of high male demand for Indigenous women, attempts to favor the interests of the Aboriginal male spouse would be fraught. White frontiersmen's orchestrated campaigns for free rein over Aboriginal women for sweethearts and wives received plenty of attention from the newspapers and parliament.

Meanwhile, Aboriginal women were conducting marriages with newcomer men in a range of ways. These included ongoing sexual liaisons, de facto or living-together relationships, marriages regulated by the state, and marriages authorized by Aboriginal kin and kinship laws. And perhaps most commonly, marriages regulated by both. Aboriginal women had to negotiate their sexual and marital contracts across two societies — each patriarchal, but with very different marital and sexual norms and economies. Cross-cultural gender and familial interactions created dramatic flux for a nation in the process of formation. But more important than cultural differences were the politics of colonialism, with its purposeful power plays over land and people.

In reality, Indigenous people in colonizing zones were subject to two "governing bodies" — Indigenous community and kin governance and that of the increasingly powerful colonizer state. As an arm of colonizer and Indigenous law, at the intersections of zones without visible boundaries, marriage law might prove more significant than previously allowed. After all, if perfect settler sovereignty through juridical processes was to be achieved, the two marriage laws posed a constant destabilizing threat that also had the potential to reproduce itself down the generations.

On the Indigenous side of colonizing frontiers, modernizing and hybridizing forces were at work.[70] Gender contestations from women, between clans, and across age groups were part and parcel of Indigenous as well as colonizer society. Within acceptable frameworks, men and women had always nudged the boundaries. Colonialism shifted the range of options and variables available to both groups. Values and expectations might be deeply internalized, but they could also be adjusted according to perceived advantages and disadvantages and according to who might be watching.

In the long run, the growing settler-colonizer populations, their policing, the ever-replenished resources base, and their rapacious industries made the colonizing power relations way too uneven. However, what I have attempted to capture here are the locales and moments of frontier possibility and a moment and place where things could have turned out differently. Was this a time when Aboriginal women had marriage power? White frontiersmen needed to sustain themselves with food and water. Not complying with Indigenous law endangered white men's lives. In ignoring Indigenous law, white men may have delivered an advantage to Asians and Pacific Islanders.

Out of intimate assertions of sovereignty, Aboriginal women's consent to formal marital arrangements with colonizer men thus represented one of many social and legal innovations. In this new era, by using kinship and land law to reinforce their sovereignty over "country" and by adapting customary marriage law, women attempted to empower themselves and their wider communities. An intimate transnational diplomacy, their engagement with newcomers was conducted as much as possible on their own terms and, quite often, by balancing husbands and marriage systems on both sides of the colonizing frontier. After all, these frontiers were places where "countries" converged, where nations met, and where marriages were made. This story was not about white women marrying Indigenous men nor a quest to take assimilation to heart.[71] Assimilation cut both ways. Through individual relationships, Indigenous governance was widened; acculturation became two-way. Marriages sped things up. People exchanged ideas across cultures; they met and became something else again. These women were "taming men" to their law of the land, a rule of law that entangled land and kin to constitute "country."

An Aboriginal woman's participation in a state-endorsed marriage under Queensland law did not imply her consent to monogamy. A woman with an Indigenous husband may have considered relations with non-Indigenous men as secondary. She understood these marriages as bringing the colonizers/outsiders into an Indigenous kinship system. At a time of forced dislocation from land, marriage to an outsider could enable a woman to stay near her own land and to perform her custodial duties toward special landscape sites. So marriage did not indicate compliance with any drive toward cultural assimilation or marital conformity. These diverse frontier marriages instead reflected a proactive strategic engagement with new peoples and new economies. Necessary negotiations between colonizers and various Indigenous networks created a fluid two-way marital frontier with a cross-cultural, often plural marriage system. Marriage destabilized just who was the colonizer and who was the colonized. Who was coming under whose law? And when they fell in love, on which side of the frontier were the lovers falling? Was this marriage between only two sides or several?

Indigenous modernizing agendas did not imply that wives had consented to monogamy or to permanency, let alone to dislocating themselves or their children from their Indigenous community. As we have seen, neither had they rejected the principles of the Indigenous marriage system or their obligations toward their Indigenous husbands. They were hoping to integrate outsiders into their own systems of family and ways of living in country. They wanted to extend the reach of their cosmology, its landed moral authority and law, and at the same time to ensure a new means of sustenance and access to new goods. Aboriginal women had different agendas from their husbands, both Indigenous and non-Indigenous. Nonetheless, through the incorporation of outsiders as kin, they exerted their landed sovereignty and, to an extent, incorporated the newcomer men into their own governance networks. Under colonialism, marital routes provided pathways for expanding the gendered grounds of influence.

Part 4

Embodying
New Worlds

CHAPTER SEVEN

Polygamy's New Worlds

If monogamy was the building block of modern nations, polygamy was the crack in its walls. At discrete moments, the intimate bonds between Indigenous people and newcomers stretched across the colonizing transnational — its lands and laws. The founding fathers of America and Australia dreamt of a homogenous, national family — albeit with different ways of achieving it. Indigenous peoples viewed their futures differently.

Inside these bounded visions were histories of at least two, often multiple, competing gendered sovereignties operating across frontiers and within families. Two wives, two husbands, two nations, two sovereignties? No national domain was discrete or united, for each was made up of many tribes, clans, and competing groups. Each staged transnational contests over gender, family, and community.

During their early national periods, the *practice* of polygamy was an aspect of the colonizing frontier in Australia and the United States that was at once controversial and hidden.[1] Settler-colonizer nations were not built out of the neat twosomes implied by the code of heterosexual, same-race monogamy. In the early national zones under scrutiny, alliances were happening at multiple levels. The verb "to ally" can refer to the connection of individuals or families through marriage — a practice with deep foundations in the history of European elites and royalty. The forging of alliances was also important for the Algonquins, the Cherokees, and various constellations of Australian Aboriginal groups.

This chapter discusses how Australian and North American colonizers prioritized the eradication of polygamy. We will revisit the Cherokee Nation during its early republic era and will again travel to White Australia's north. Although colonizers and Indigenous peoples had contrasting, deeply conflicting quests, when their intimate paths crossed, points of convergence emerged. Ideas about heterosexual monogamy and polygamy, and expanded or decreased opportunities for enacting them, shaped a conflicted, gendered colonialism.

I use the general term "polygamy" to refer to any plural marriage, that is, where one partner concurrently had two or more wives or husbands. More gender-specifically, polyandry is the practice of a woman having more than one husband and polygyny is the practice of a man having more than one wife. The marriage could be condoned by a colonizer or an Indigenous nation or practiced as a heterosexual union between two people. This does not necessarily mean that the relationship was freely admitted to the wider public, let alone spoken about as part of national narratives. Nor am I implying that participants were admitting to the practice of polygamy or polyandry. Status disincentives and the ease of collective denial worked against identification. Colonialism had its many secrets, which were later perpetuated by conventions, including a matrix of secrecy and braggadocio around sexual exploits.[2] The practice of polygamy provides a revealing lens into the multiple marital practices of early settler-colonizer nations.[3]

THE MONO AND THE POLY

The marriage laws of the new nation-states of the United States and Australia recognized a specific kind of monogamous contract between a man and a woman "till death us do part." Divorce was possible, but very difficult to obtain. By contrast, in Cherokee society and Aboriginal Australian societies, marriage was not necessarily anticipated to be lifelong, so a succession of marital partnerships was socially acceptable.[4]

Under colonialism, in both Australia and the United States, in unions both secretive and open, families were being created across frontiers. In substantial numbers, white, Asian, Melanesian, and other newcomer men were uniting with Indigenous women. Newcomer women also paired with Indigenous men, but since the white frontier population was predominantly masculine, this was less frequent. This, however, is only the colonizer side of the equation.

The interconnection of families disturbed the sexual and marital boundaries of individuals' hemispheres of origin. Significantly, when Europeans interacted with Indigenous custodians, they entered into another cultural zone, a world with divergent definitions of common law and of what should constitute normal family life. As settler-colonizer states hosted at least two cultural conceptualizations of marital and family laws in specific localities, their cultural collusions led to shifts in marital practices.

The distinguished historian Patricia Grimshaw has argued that the Australian family was "born modern." This was because of the dislocation of British convict and other immigrant woman that detracted from older extended-family formations.[5] Distance from England meant that earlier marriages were overlooked and that people could marry someone closer to hand. But these early immigrants, predominantly convicted felons, had entered land where regulated Indigenous systems of marriage had prevailed for millennia. The same can be said for the early republic of the United States. Yet monocultural frames have beleaguered historical approaches to colonizing marriages. The newly "modern" or nuclear family met societies premised upon webs of kinship stretching over sovereign landscapes. For First Nations peoples, family and clan dynamics conferred landownership. Embodied connectivities linked property and social roles. Written or unwritten marital agreements prescribed mutual obligations and community expectations. Kinship, clan, and marriage delivered title rights to storied — or more aptly, *historied* — landscapes.[6]

When First Nations peoples and colonizers lived in proximity, it changed the dynamics of kin, family, and sexual relations. North America's mountain men and fur traders settled into a mutually accepted arrangement known as "country marriage" or "mariage à la façon du pays." In every frontier zone, different sets of marital laws and practices were applied and redeveloped.

Indigenous and colonizer groups did not necessarily agree on monogamy and permanency as essential elements of marriage. For the Cherokees, the equivalency of the term "husband" meant "the man I am living with." Although the union was often honored for long periods or for life, neither party expected or vowed permanency.[7] During the early nineteenth century, loss of the men's skilled roles as hunters and warriors created a potential gender crisis. Men did not necessarily wish to switch to the agriculturalist role expected of them — for one thing, this was understood as women's work. In these societies during the early nineteenth century, alcohol abuse and domestic violence created additional strains on marital relations.[8] Under British and American colonialism, expectations of women's roles were increasingly associated with greater subordination of women and fewer rights. Adaptive or strategic alignments with western models of national and gendered governance tended to be detrimental to women's status.[9]

As discussed previously, an Australian Aboriginal woman was permitted to go with a white man for an agreed time, dependent upon her husband's and her own consent. Aboriginal parties understood these sexual pairings as an incorporative gesture toward a newcomer man in their country. To Indigenous participants, it was a way of acknowledging the humanity and ensuring the safety of outsiders. Significantly, these unions marked the beginning of diplomatic relations between sets of nations, drawing outsider participants into obligations toward kin, inspired landscapes, and law.[10] White men and humanitarians understood these arrangements as promiscuity or commerce, as prostitution. According to their gendered terms of reference, they could not understand them as otherwise, or as marital, especially when the woman already had a husband.

In Australia, a transgression against Aboriginal marriage law was one of the most serious offenses, warned against in numerous dreaming stories. Outsiders knew that going against this law could be fatal, although without any set date. In entering sexual relations, an outsider man or woman became enmeshed in a system of corporal law and punishment. A judicial spearing in the leg could follow minor offenses. For a transgression as serious as stealing someone's wife, the punishment was death. The offense might include taking a wife without permission from the right people, confining her or refusing to allow her to return, or failing to fulfill reciprocal obligations, such as supplying specified resources.

In remote areas, white men's failure to either understand or comply with the strict betrothal and temporary wife-stay system provoked violent punishments and executions.[11] Were their actions fueled by ignorance of Indigenous marriage law, foolhardiness, or a sense of entitlement? Sexual transgressions certainly led to numerous executions of white men. Although what they witnessed was an authorized killing as punishment for a crime, journalists and other writers memorialized such actions as proof of Aboriginal savagery.

Such acts were also exercises in sovereign law. In Australia's Northern Territory during the 1920s, a Japanese fishermen and a white police constable were killed in Arnhem Land. Police interviewed Aboriginal men and attributed both executions to offenses against Aboriginal women. In Central Australia, the most notorious example was the killing of the white man Fred Brooks, who was accused of stealing an Aboriginal man's wife.[12] This set off a spate of revenge killings of Aboriginal people by whites that were known as the Coniston Massacre. Similarly, Indigenous men enforced their laws on the Queensland frontier. In the Hornet Bank Massacre of 1857, they killed eleven white colonizers in retaliation for the rapes of Aboriginal women. When a colonizer man failed to await the promised marriage system or to return a wife or took too many wives, his actions could create punitive havoc on frontiers.

Many white men unscrupulously, and brutally, stole Indigenous women, whom they perceived as part of their colonizer entitlement. Viewing the women like sex slaves, they acted regardless of the violent consequences. Frontiersmen demanded that colonial police protect them. Consequently, they united with police to conduct terror campaigns against the Aboriginal people still trying to live freely on their own lands.[13] Even before restrictive colonial marriage legislation was introduced, frontier negotiations entwined state and Indigenous policing and marriage law. On frontiers characterized by violence or its threat, people knew that transnational marital interactions could serve as detonators.[14]

Marriages across colonialism's borders introduced new complexities. In all societies, people lived in the spaces between culturally prescribed marriage models, balanced against their preferred choices of partner or partners. On Australian and North American frontiers, many marriages involved consent and, concurrently, an expectation of plurality. After all, frontiersmen were usually aware that they were pairing with the wife of an Indigenous man. On Australian frontiers, they often had to ask the Indigenous husband's permission to live with his wife. As the previous chapter showed, when he granted permission, this did not necessarily mean that he ceased being the husband.

As Indigenous women came to exploit the outsiders, they expanded the number of husbands available to them and could do so in accordance with clan and kin rules. In addition to any possible attractions and emotional bonds, these polyandrous unions provided economic benefits — a practical means for a woman and a community to ensure ongoing access to new foods and resources and, in a threatening environment, greater personal and family security. Without relinquishing their wives, Indigenous husbands exploited newcomer opportunities too. In order to conduct new relationships and to engage in new economies and polities, they reconfigured the expectations and parameters of plural marriages.

The Enlightenment, Missionaries, and Polygamy

As if someone had drawn a clear line between good and evil, missionary rhetoric placed polygamy on the dark side. Polygamy presented a particular challenge to British-style notions of marriage practice and law. As the historian Nancy Cott has argued, the writings of the French political theorist Montesquieu contributed to the Enlightenment's association of polygamy with despotism: "The harem stood for tyrannical rule, political corruption, coercion, elevation of the passions over reason, selfishness, hypocrisy." Monogamy, in contrast, stood for a government of consent, moderation, and political liberty. By 1785, writers were singing the praises of monogamy, whereas polygamy led to "voluptuousness, abasement of women, and neglect of children." Cott concludes, "A commitment to monogamous marriage on a Christian model lodged deep in American political theory, as vivid as belief in popular sovereignty or in voluntary consent of the governed or in the necessity of a government of laws."[15] Monogamous marriage was thus enforced as a significant element of colonizer sovereignty and property law.

Christian missionaries to the Australian Aborigines and to the Cherokees sought to eradicate polygamy, defining it as contrary to Christianity, to civilization and progress. Any woman who entered into multiple sexual relationships was classed as licentious and/or as a prostitute. The historian Theda Perdue explains that Europeans understood polygamy as "rendering women contemptible in men's eyes" and as reputedly degrading for all women.[16] Feminist scholars of First Nations history have celebrated the power that Indigenous women gained in sororal marriages — where a man's wives were sisters.[17] Indeed, the women often enjoyed sharing household tasks with other wives, especially with cousins or sisters. As Perdue argues, "Multiple marriage as practiced by many polygamous Cherokees tended to strengthen matrilineality and the bonds among women."[18] However, Yarbrough complicates this by explaining that in Cherokee society, the usual benefits of polygyny for men — such as increasing wealth, creating new leadership ties, and providing access to more sexual partners — did not necessarily apply. Rather than the man accumulating wealth through multiple wives, the Cherokee wives retained their property rights, and their clan affiliations did not change. Although men in polygamous unions might expand or solidify relationships with other clans and gain prestige, their offspring remained part of their mother's clan, and Cherokee women in polygamous unions still retained custody of children.[19]

To the colonizer states, however, polygamy proved problematic and potentially divisive. Slavery and marriage, each a *domestic* institution in Anglo-American law, became caught up in political rhetoric. Polygamy was considered inimical to the values of Protestant Christianity, which in the United States was aligned with modernity, progress, and civilization. In the Bible, alongside Genesis's explicit rulings on gendered sovereignty are stories of incest, the keeping of mistresses, and plural marriage. In order to civilize Indigenous people, missionaries and state authorities alike considered that such practices as polygamy, attitudes toward premarital chastity, and certain gendered divisions of labor, property, and inheritance had to be reformed.

In the 1820s Reverend Jedidiah Morse, whose geographies helped Americans reimagine the landmass in terms of colonization, was called upon to conduct an investigation into Native American groups. In his view, the "marriage institution, in its purity" would serve as the vehicle for civilization. By this he meant heterosexual monogamy. In order to produce "new generations who would merge with the American people" and thus enter "civilized life," Morse advocated intermarriage between educated Indian women and white men.[20]

Infamous contests over Mormon polygamy were fought out in the federal arena by the mid-nineteenth century, further entrenching the significance of monogamy to the polity of United States.[21] Joseph Smith, who founded the Mormon Church as a religion based upon American-based revelations, took a positive interest in Native American polygamy. Unsubstantiated stories allege that Smith had "two squaws." (This term for Native American women became associated with a derogatory category of racial and marital difference.)

According to church historians, in 1831 missionaries in Missouri were instructed via a revelation: "For it is my will, that in time, ye should take unto you wives of the Lamanites and Nephites that their posterity may become white, delightsome and just, for even now their females are more virtuous than the gentiles."[22] Mormon men were to "marry with wives of Every Tribe of Indians."[23] Smith started his "private practice" of polygyny in the 1830s and by 1843 was making public declarations about "celestial plural marriage," a practice further promoted during the 1850s.[24] As Mormon leaders had earlier urged an alliance with converted Indians to overthrow the "gentiles," polygamy became freshly associated with a subversive threat to the nation-state.[25]

An American-originated religion, Mormonism drew upon and appropriated understandings of Indigenous beliefs. This was partly to assert a local spiritual belonging or landed connectedness for the new "natives" — the white citizenry. By the mid-nineteenth century, Mormon polygamy raised controversies around future visions for the American family and the nation. For example, in 1860 Justin Morrill of Vermont used this form of marriage as a way to condemn slavery, stating, "By the license of Polygamy, one man may have many wives, all bound to him by the marriage tie, and in other respects protected by law. By the license of Slavery, a whole race is delivered over to prostitution and concubinage, without the protection of any law."[26] In the social hierarchy, plural marriage became entwined with gender and race issues of national significance.

By the twentieth century, early social scientists studied marriage in "primitive societies" as if they provided frozen exemplars a primeval human time. Edward Westermarck's *The History of Human Marriage* (1901) and later Ernest Crawley's *The Mystic Rose: A Study of Primitive Marriage and of Primitive Thought in Its Bearing on Marriage* used Australian Aboriginal people as exemplars of the origin phase of marriage.[27] They argued that communal marriage had gradually evolved into polygamy, asserting that Indigenous people such as Aboriginal Australians provided evidentiary proof. Although they did not consider them to be nearly as "primitive," they also drew upon American Indian examples. Aboriginal courtship rituals were depicted as brutal, involving marriage by capture of the bride rather than by consent. Predictably placing Europeans at the evolutionary pinnacle, these proto–social scientists narrated a Eurocentric human history that evolved from barbarism to a vision of modern, gentle courtship and monogamy.[28] Only monogamous marriage laid the necessary preconditions for modernity, civilization, freedom, and democracy.

God's Police

Anglo-American and Anglo-Australian preoccupations with Indigenous polygamy mirrored anxieties arising from gender contests among European peoples. In both nations, Mary Wollstonecraft and other early feminist authors left their mark on marital politics. In the new republic of the United States, companionate marriage, a break from the patriarchal notion of heterosexual marriage, promised a more equitable wifely role as a mutual companion. No longer was the husband master, the wife servant. To a degree, this assuaged women's concerns about their status in marriage and seemed to fit better with a nation premised upon popular sovereignty and equality.[29]

Companionate marriage was uncontested monogamy, however, and not exactly equal. It was the wife who bore the children and ended up with most of the domestic and child-rearing work and little chance of professional education, public power, and acclaim. At a time when white American women were trying out modern marriage styles, they were also curious about the virtues of Indian marriage and social organization. During the 1840s, in Portland, Maine, white women enthusiastically attended Colonel McKenney's lectures on Indian culture.[30] Some female authors skewed the captivity narratives. Published in 1824, Lydia Maria Child's novel *Hobomok* reflects an interest in imagining alternative and cross-colonizing unions. Its protagonist is a white woman who falls in love with an Indian man.

In Australia, the early granting of women's suffrage in South Australia in 1895, and nationally in 1902, brought political power for white women. Like other women around the world, at this time the search for "new woman" icons led Australian women to embrace Annie Oakley, a transnational icon of modernity and the New World. She displayed the gun-toting, hybrid American Indian styling of the Wild West frontier, along with the outdoor dexterity of the modern white frontierswoman.[31]

Furthermore, looking for meaningful roles in the new colonizer nation, white Australian women became keen to take an active role in Aboriginal protection.[32] In particular, they hoped to police white frontiersmen's behavior toward Aboriginal women.[33] First they campaigned vociferously against polygamy within Aboriginal society. Australian human rights campaigners like Mary Montgomery Bennett were influenced by feminist antislavery discourses.[34] Bennett portrayed polygamy and infant betrothal as exploitative of women — to the point of turning them into chattels. Furthermore, Bennett argued that sexual exploitation by white frontiersmen had caused a revival of Indigenous polygamy.[35] She and other white feminist campaigners believed that frontier life transformed white men into savages and Aboriginal women into slaves. Deep tensions between Indigenous and newcomer men, and between women too, arose from sexual competition. White women and white men fought battles for control over frontier sexual relations.[36]

In the 1890s through to the 1920s, cartoonists played upon the concerns of white women in rural areas about their husbands' illicit offspring. Ignoring the veil of secrecy, in these images Aboriginal female protagonists make the revelations. One cartoon depicts a white mistress talking to an Aboriginal domestic who is about to marry. The mistress expresses her hope that her servant's man will make a good husband — to which the Aboriginal woman replies, "By cripes, missus, if him bin no better'n yours, I be back plurry quick!" In another cartoon, *The Black Predecessor*, a barefooted Aboriginal woman reveals to a shocked, well-dressed and newly married white woman that she is the previous wife of the husband. In another, an Aboriginal woman comments on the likeness of her baby to a white woman's husband, the joke making a play on the anxious white wife's relief when the Aboriginal woman reveals that the similarity is in their baldness.[37]

Aboriginal people themselves delighted in sexual joking and teasing. Between people in certain kin relationships, such jokes were not just condoned but expected. Aboriginal people enjoyed gossip about sexual relationships, which featured anecdotes at the expense of white men. The

FIG. 58. *The Black Predecessor*, from the *Bulletin*, 1894. Courtesy National Library of Australia, BibID 1085805. The caption reads, "Mary the Gin (*to squatter's bride, just arrived at homestead*): 'You Missus Jackson now?' Bashful Bride: 'Yes.' Mary: 'Oh, me Missus Jackson once!' — (*Conversation ends here.*)" "Gin" was an Eora term commonly used among Sydney people to refer to an Aboriginal woman; colonizers later used it as a derogative. "Squatter" was the term for wealthy landowners who had displaced smaller landholders in nineteenth-century Australia.

various polygamous structures of cross-colonizer family relations dispersed power across many sites; humor defused this.

Because of the high demand for Aboriginal women, Indigenous husbands could exert some authority over colonizer men. So too could Indigenous women. As Michel Foucault famously argued, desire and the sexual relationship constitute one of the many levels at which power operates.[38] The family is also a locus of power. In Indigenous societies, cultural and land knowledge were bases of authority. The multiple marriage configurations in frontier landscapes engendered both oppression and potential power. Take the cases of Minnie and Dolly discussed in the chapter 6. Indigenous people could experiment with arrangements that enabled on-country economic survival. Not uncommonly, Aboriginal people's transgressions against strict Indigenous marriage laws led them to seek refuge among the colonizers to evade punishment.

Changing Indigenous Marriage Models

In both Australian and North American Indigenous societies, the men tended to view customary polygamous arrangements as a form of opulence and social well-being that offered deep satisfaction. Ann Marie Plane's *Colonial Intimacies: Indian Marriage in Early New England* provides important insights into the way the colonizer's antipolygamy agenda troubled the Narragansett people during an early contact period. One man made the poignant statement that "My heart did love the having of two wives." He conveyed his deep enjoyment of these marital arrangements, for polygamy was not only normal to him but, in a deeply felt way, true and proper. He lamented that the newcomers "have made a law against it."[39] In the longer term, the Narragansetts' disputes over the constitution of marriage in seventeenth-century New England enabled them to "plant potentially useful ideas of custom and culture alongside colonial constructions of Indian identity."[40]

Frequently in colonial spaces, public contestations centered around the plural nature of marriage. Indeed, Plane explains that it was in the early English written accounts of New England that "Indian marriage" was articulated as a concept. This "helped to express, and to contain the frightening divergences between European men and women and their North American 'others'; a concept that helped to shape the very meanings of being Indian or being English; a concept that would later have force in special legal categories." In such a schema, Indian marriages were "sinful, reminiscent of [a] pre-Christian past," Old Testament Judaism, and polygamy. Flexible marital unions became sinful lust, with troublesome labels like adultery and fornication.[41] During this time, the Narragansett ontology started to shift; some came to worry, and had been schooled to worry, that their own way of life and family practices were degenerate. For example, in 1652 a "praying indian" knew that he "must have but one Wife, and at first [God] did make but one man and one woman; but I followed many women."[42] According to his European teachers, God the Creator founded the human race along the lines of Genesis, with Adam and Eve modeling monogamy.

On the other hand, Algonquin prophets believed that any unions with whites, monogamous or plural, could potentially destroy their nation and any hope for their people's future. They rejected cultural syncretism in favor of invented tradition, sometimes in order to put forward masculinist gender claims over their women. The Shawnees called for bans on Indigenous women's cohabitation with whites. They also banned drinking and trading. In the early 1800s Tenskwatawa, Tecumsah, and other nativists rejected "an American vision of the future which promised them only alternative routes to obliteration."[43] With this in mind, Tenskwatawa denounced intermarriage: "All Indian women who were living with White Men was [*sic*] to be brought home to their friends and relatives, and their children to be left with their Fathers, so that nations *might become genuine Indian*."[44] Algonquin women were in demand by outsiders. Whether for individual, family, or collective reasons, the women appeared to actively seek out this option.

By the early nineteenth century, male Cherokee leaders, along with some other groups of Native Americans, similarly called for a return to exclusive marriage within their matrilineal nation. Cherokee men and their prophets wanted to keep the women in the Cherokee Nation. Women constituted a powerful land-controlling force. Among the Cherokees, the chiefs and other leading figures — who were often custodians of knowledge and materially well-off — also took on multiple Cherokee wives.[45]

In the relatively egalitarian society of the Australian Aborigines, having multiple wives conferred special prestige and power for men.[46] Aboriginal males earned entitlement to more than one wife by proving their worth — through display of knowledge, talent, skill, and discipline and by means of their connections with important sites and rituals.

Polygamy was part of the fine-tuned workings that bound Indigenous societies together, which enabled them to govern themselves and to incorporate outsiders within their own system of law. In Australian Indigenous societies, which differed regionally between matrilineal and patrilineal systems, exogamous marriage patterns brought the spouse into the country of the female or male spouse, respectively. A system of negotiated promised marriage ensured active trade routes and enforced the kin and clan alliances that made one human. It also played a role in nurturing country, extending one's domain and enabling the resolution of differences. When the distant clans united for marriage business, their journeys followed marriage routes that connected sites via song cycles and ceremonies. Incorporating larger networks of diverse newcomers, marriages melded groups across wider landscapes.[47]

In native spaces that were also colonizing frontiers, Indigenous women embraced the enhanced opportunities to take on multiple husbands or to practice polyandry. In both Australia and North America, Indigenous women and men used their engagement with colonizer law to reformulate their own marriage rules, creating new gender-differentiated discourses around polygamy and monogamy.

Against Modernity?

The more that an idealized western marriage stood as an index for modernity and civilization, the more that polygamy came to stand for ignorance and savagery. In the United States, this appeared to be the case for Cherokee modernizers and Anglo-Americans alike. The Cherokee Nation of the early nineteenth century emulated the written regulations and the centralized organizational structure of the early American republic. To a degree, and partly to fit changing economies of wealth creation for a minority, it also emulated a citizenship model based upon an idealized European family fitting the modern nation-state. Again, this was ostensibly premised upon monogamy.[48] The wealthy elite's plantation, slave, and other holdings led to changes in Cherokee legislation in favor western-style patrilineal inheritance.[49]

When a white man entered unions with more than one Cherokee woman, conflicting value systems caused problems in the application of Cherokee matrilineal inheritance and property law. With the aid of cross-frontier trading, with slavery and plantation systems, and with Cherokee women as cultural intermediaries and providers, some of these intermarried white men in Cherokee territory had become very wealthy. Others used marital partnerships to gain Cherokee land and treaty annuities.[50] Reasoning that observance of monogamy would curb white male peddlers of prostitution, alcohol, and other vices, Anglo-American missionaries among the Cherokees and other neighboring groups attempted to eradicate polygamy.[51]

Not long after they set up their national government in 1819, the Cherokee Council legislated to counter white men's adoption of polygamous practices. By taking several wives, some white men in marriages to Cherokee women exploited customary acceptance of polygyny. Cherokee men were understandably irked by white men's monopolization of their women. The Council ruled that white men "should also have but one wife thereafter."[52] Furthermore, to keep tabs on them, they were obliged to marry in the more formal Christian fashion.

After 1825 the Cherokee Nation decided to further restrict polygamy. Wishing to respect the old chiefs who were married under "older customs," the Cherokee Council was very cautious about imposing the antipolygamy rule on Cherokee men.[53] In order to avoid upsetting existing polygamous families, they did not outlaw polygamy, but instead the Cherokee Committee only "recommended" the end of polygamy as practiced by Cherokee men.[54] This law proved useful against white men who exploited Cherokee women.[55] In 1829 a white man, James Pettit, was charged with bigamy and mistreatment of his Cherokee wife. He was fined $500 and had to forfeit his plantation to his wife, who retained custody of their child.[56] Basically, this Cherokee legislation empowered the nation to enforce an orderly monogamy upon white intruders.

As we have seen, by the 1810s and 1820s, colonizer pressures on the Cherokee Nation intensified. Occupying, mining, and farming their land, white frontiersmen and frontierswomen were creating unmanageable pressures. White men's persistent appropriation of Cherokee women was a cause for anxiety and social disruption.[57] Family neglect, cruelty, violence, and murder were not uncommon, and the nation had little authority over American citizens. Strife and alcohol abuse occurred inside Cherokee society too, and Cherokee men found it increasingly difficult to obtain wives. By regularizing cross-colonizer marriage in their nation, the male leaders aimed to at least prevent any white man taking more than one Cherokee wife.[58]

In high-level transnational diplomacy and communications, enactments of monogamy and condemnations of polygamy featured prominently. In the colonizer's republic of virtue, statesmanship and evangelical values went hand in hand. It is hardly surprising that the Cherokee Nation was keen to demonstrate parallel values. The educated Cherokee elite appeared to accept that monogamy had now become a signifier of masculine honor and modernity. In 1825, in an address to John Quincy Adams, the president of the United States, the former Cornwall student John Ridge made pointed comments about polygamy. He stated, "This last vestige of our ignorance is not respected by our people, & increased intelligence and morality [& respect for their characters & matrimonial happiness] is fast consuming it."[59] By this time Ridge was married to the Cornwall steward's daughter, Sarah Northrup.

In 1826, soon after his marriage to Harriett Gold, the other intermarried graduate of Cornwall, Elias Boudinot, delivered *An Address to the Whites*. Of Cherokee progress, he proclaimed, "Polygamy is abolished. Female chastity and honor are protected by law."[60] Elias concurred that polygamy was sexually degrading to women — perhaps even a product of lust and vice, and associated with rape. Cherokee women probably had different views on the matter.[61] Although vocal in influencing the Cherokee Nation's directions, women lacked the right to join the council and were seldom speakers in front of white audiences.

As students, Cherokee girls and boys who lived in the homes of Anglo-American missionaries were taught Christian family models that contrasted with their own gendered divisions of labor. Familial modeling was a key aim of such residencies. With their white wives, John Ridge and Elias Boudinot followed monogamous marriage models, favoring Christian wives and observing Christian weddings. Other literate and record-leaving Cherokees outwardly followed some of the same scripts, advertising this in contexts where they might garner political and humanitarian support.

Why were men like Ridge and Boudinot, Indigenous progressives among the Cherokees, motivated to speak out against polygamy? For one thing, they wanted to assert their compliance with the call of Washington, Jefferson, and others toward modernity, maturity, and civilization. Although neighboring white frontiersmen could do as they pleased, they figured that for Cherokees to declare support for polygamy would detract from their nation's label as one of the five progressive or civilized tribes. After all, polygamy had been compellingly associated with the past and the primitive. On another tack, in Christian historical thinking, polygamy signified social chaos, backward peoples: the noncivil. Despite the Cherokee spokesmen's modernizing rhetoric, standard Christian formulas did not necessarily subsume the cherished Indigenous values that glued loving families together.

Anglo-American missionaries among the Cherokees, the Choctaw, and other Native American societies made efforts to ban polygamy, often stating this was designed to curb white male peddlers of prostitution, alcohol, and other vices. Similarly, Ernest Gribble labeled white men's sexual relationships with Aboriginal women as "prostitution," which he considered a "vice" that was a direct product of polygamy, being due to a man having (what he saw as) "spare wives." After arriving from a perilous schooner voyage on the cyclonic Coral Sea, Ernest Gribble had walked into a world where Aboriginal women were engaging in a new economy of sexual exchange and kin networking with the white timber-getters who were felling their rainforest and with white fishermen.

Gribble's moral universe was particularly challenged when he realized that Menmuny, the most conciliatory power broker of the Gunggandji people and son of the leading female elder, had several wives. This influential man, with whom Gribble had formed an early alliance and upon whom community support relied, was practicing exactly what Gribble preached against. In long conversations, Gribble tried to convince Menmuny to relinquish at least one wife. Menmuny explained that he could not do the wrong thing and desert any of his wives; this would be to fail in his duties. As we saw earlier, in order to cement his transnational alliance with Menmuny, Gribble held a coronation ceremony.[62] And Gribble's effort to orchestrate a white wedding with Nora, one of Menmuny's wives, led to her disinterested response. She did not like going inside the church and insisted on wearing red. According to Gribble, Menmuny eventually "gave up two of his wives," and they married other men.[63] But possibly the women had given up on Menmuny. Although he was a handsome, fully initiated man and a good hunter, his decision to cooperate with Gribble, and more so, to share Kongkandji/Yidinjdji lands with displaced Aboriginal peoples, met disapproval within his group.

Gribble progressed his "same-race" marriage agenda by soft-selling it to the general churchgoing colonizer public. Unlike his father, he was determined to retain the support of the white community and so avoided publicizing white men's rampant sexual exploitation of Aboriginal women.[64]

At Yarrabah, we saw how Ernest Gribble aimed to develop a new system of Christian monogamous marriage. He knew that white husbands and sons in Queensland towns and on rural properties were having sexual affairs with their Aboriginal domestic servants. Reflecting racial attitudes that he shared, Gribble accepted that white men would not consider marrying the servants. After all, in a liminal white colonizer nation, this would defy a white man's aspirations to middle-class respectability.[65]

Gribble's obsessive agenda to create an intra-Aboriginal marital system ignored kin protocols and tribal imperatives. To showcase his plans for respectable "same-race" monogamous marriage, we have observed how the churchman arranged photography, news articles, a traveling band, concerts, stage shows, and other popular entertainments. Although the marriages were between Aboriginal couples, they were not necessarily "same-nation," as, due to Queensland state policies, many different Aboriginal language groups and "nations" now resided at Yarrabah.

When Gribble surreptitiously took up with an Aboriginal woman, he had not publicly acknowledged that his strained marriage to his white wife, Emilie, was over. Nor did he apply for a divorce. Although their stories were kept private, a number of other missionaries also engaged in relationships with Aboriginal women on their missions.[66] In the case of Bishop F. X. Gsell, who set up Bathurst Island mission in the Northern Territory in the 1930s, he became known as the "bishop with 150 wives." He claimed he had "bought" the wives in order to eradicate Tiwi polygamy and to start the mission. Aboriginal men saw this transacted accumulation of women rather differently. Because Gsell, as a Catholic priest, had taken a vow of celibacy, he found his reputation humorous. He claimed that the initiative to "buy" wives was to *eradicate* polygamy. Nonetheless, Tiwi men saw him as a "big man," a polygamy practitioner extraordinaire. Paradoxically, by appearing to practice what he preached against, he enhanced his local status.[67]

Polygamous Frontiers

On New World frontiers, a new form of polygamy was being practiced — one endemic to frontiers but that crisscrossed these zones in multiple directions.[68] Colonizing exigencies and asymmetries, especially economic factors, meant that white men gained opportunities to freely obtain a sexual partner among Indigenous women. For one thing, there were few white women on frontiers. For another, the single white man had less compulsion to act with propriety or to be monogamous than in his previous milieu, where people such as his mother or sisters might disapprove. Without the regimes of familial sexual and social surveillance, missionaries and state planners grew uneasy.

By having more than one Indigenous wife, or by "sharing" a wife with an Indigenous man in a polygamous marriage, many colonizer men effectively became cross-cultural practitioners of polyandry, polygyny, or both. They could have a wife residing elsewhere, or they could "keep" a white wife and an Indigenous wife simultaneously. They might not live in the same house, but in the vicinity or in the same compound at a cattle station or other enterprise. The kin and family networks allowed for in polygamous marriage protocols potentially enabled the outsider man to enhance his strategic and economic position and to gain expanded networks of influence. Each wife might perform specified roles. White men sometimes took advantage of First Nations polygamous marriage, distorting it into arrangements not in keeping with custom. Different kinds of sexual, casual, and longer-term relationships ensued.

White Australian men were well aware of Indigenous polygamous marriage practices and contrasting attitudes toward women's sexual options. Indeed, Australian Aboriginal forms of marriage became a counterpoint to white society's gender contests. By 1920 the popular magazine *Smiths Weekly* featured cartoons commenting on Aboriginal marriage practices and interrelationships between white and black, men and women. In a curious transnational borrowing, they drew upon the popular literature of black American English to evoke Aboriginal English. Providing a masculine critique of European-style marriage, their humor engages with their observations of Indigenous marriage. One cartoon depicts a white man asking an Aboriginal man whether his wife ran off with another "darkie." Replying that the white man is now his "step-husband," the Aboriginal man's response suggests that both remained husbands.[69] In another, an Aboriginal worker philosophizes that having only one wife is "no good"; having two wives, on the other hand, is preferable, for the women could leave him to relax while they fought each other.[70]

In Australia, many wealthy landowners covertly pursued lifelong relationships with Aboriginal wives and children. Often such men were concurrently married — or later married — to a white woman, and the two sets of children and families often lived near each other. However, they were in separate camps, and only the white side of the family was publicly acknowledged. The white wife was in the homestead and the Aboriginal wife was in the makeshift camp. In rural areas with larger Aboriginal populations and workforces, this was extremely common for many decades of the twentieth century.[71]

Colonizers tended to perceive the longer-term relationships between a white man and an Indigenous woman as that described by the European term "mistress" or "concubine," not as polygamy. The mistress was a longer-term, out-of-law relationship. But was this label justified? Such a relationship might or might not preempt a legal marriage with a white woman. If it continued after such a marriage, would not this make the Indigenous woman a first wife? In a frontier zone, there was a qualitative difference. A frontiersman who viewed an Indigenous woman as a mistress ignored the full situation. After all, "the law of the land," the local Indigenous system of law, likely considered her as a legal wife. One or two systems of marital law were in operation. Under two laws, two sovereignties, an Indigenous woman had a wifely status. Only in the constructions of the colonizers was she a nonwife.

In Australia, a middle- or upper-class man in a close relationship with an Indigenous woman could not hope for a state- or community-endorsed marriage across colonizing frontiers. White society as a whole, and especially people physically distanced from frontier zones, never condoned them. However long they endured, these transcolonizing unions were considered transgressive and not truly substantive. Observers tended to view the white man, as a colonizer man, to be in the superior, controlling position. He might feel the same, but this was not always so. He might be smitten. He might also be ensuring the sustenance of a large extended Aboriginal family or community.

Just as colonizers rarely recognized Indigenous political sovereignty, few recognized relationships across the colonizing transnational. So, in their eyes, if a white man was already married to a white woman and he had an ongoing relationship with an Aboriginal woman, there were *not* two marriages. In fact, it was not so simple. One was legal and socially endorsed under one national system, the other under Indigenous law. Although knowing that, by simultaneously having an Aboriginal husband, a long-term Aboriginal female partner was practicing polyandry, the white man did not see himself as implicated in a multiple marriage system. Along with other forms of colonizer denial, white men were rarely challenged about having a white female partner and an Indigenous female partner, and two sets of children. They did not take time to think about what constituted polygyny.

Was this knowledge, and the pretense of ignorance, the beginning of a self-induced form of national blindness? Whether it was possible for the white wife to "not know" about these relationships in such close-knit societies is doubtful. It appears that colonizers were well aware of these partnerships across frontiers — which were publicly acknowledged among Indigenous people — but held them as either denials or shared secrets. Authority, status, and economic factors were at stake.

Plural Sovereignties

Colonizers were enmeshed in a system of transcolonizing relationality. In Queensland, white, Asian, and Pacific Islander frontiersmen participated in a system of plural marriage, or polygamy. Colonialism at once presented a binary — of colonizer and colonized. Yet this binary was readily broken down by the power sharing required by intimacy. Colonialism enabled Australian Aboriginal men to agree to a woman going with newcomers in a temporary exchange and at the same time to retain their multiple wives. Aboriginal women took up opportunities to practice polyandry, which offered the benefits of food and community security on a violent frontier.

Many Indigenous groups certainly used their polygamous practices as a means of integrating newcomers into their clan and family alliances, their kinship system, and its associated law.[72] As we saw in the previous chapter, women could actively negotiate and gain access to new resources and opportunities for clan and families.

The colonial interface created new marriage routes — new directions toward polygamy on the Queensland frontier. Class mattered. In Queensland, a wealthier white man with an Aboriginal wife could use the existence of a white wife to legally protect himself from police interference.[73] Queensland pastoralists presided over the state system of justice and government, so they were well positioned to avoid punishment. Publicly acknowledging love for an Aboriginal woman or making her his "legal" wife would destroy the authority and social status of any aspiring colonizer man. Falling in love with or marrying an Aboriginal woman was considered an illicit act that dealt a blow to an unspoken principle of settler colonialism. Yet, among one's peers, bragging about such relationships was quite acceptable.

In all, we should not forget that out of these unions, people had children together. Aboriginal women had children with both white and Aboriginal husbands. Sadly, many white fathers did not acknowledge their children. But however they might deny it, and however the national history might omit the facts, they were theirs, all the same.

As discussed in chapter 3, for the Cherokees, customary marriage enforced matrilineal codes of property ownership, under which the husband lived in the wife's country. By the 1820s and 1830s, with numerous Georgian intruders in Cherokee land, increasing numbers of white men in the Cherokee Nation were living with more than one Cherokee wife. It was sufficiently common for the nation to introduce a law to prohibit the practice.[74] A white husband might also be married to a white woman elsewhere, as before the law changed, he was not required to formally marry the Cherokee wife. While not ruling out that white men's intentions may have been genuine, many took advantage of marriage, using it as a means of gaining access to Cherokee lands and property.[75]

In a way, the above arrangements constituted a dual system of marriage across an unstable frontier, producing a special kind of boundary-crossing polygamy that could break down or reinforce the line between colonizer and colonized. Unhappy with its results, the Cherokee Nation introduced regulations to police polygamy, at first targeting only white men. Although it goes against the grain of what historians might expect, both Queensland state law and Cherokee national law were designed to police and to segregate white and other outsider men.

On the Georgian and many other American frontiers, white frontiersmen engaged in relations short- and long-term, monogamous and polygamous. The Cherokee male leadership tried to rein in Cherokee women and to take control over intermarriages. In order to prove that the Cherokee Nation had achieved their promise to become civilized, their leaders and legislators declared marital monogamy as the future. Certain men publicized their compliance with this "civilized" norm, making speeches and writing articles about Christian-style weddings in their internationally syndicated newspaper. Public addresses and new regulations demonstrated their rejection of polygamy, yet the Cherokees respectfully condoned it among their own. Despite the antipolygamy and adultery rhetoric, many Cherokee men lived with more than one wife — and loved it.[76] The literate Cherokees did not publicize or write about its practice — especially in letters to their benefactors in New England. Nor did the missionaries and powerful white men of colonizer society choose to write about their intimate plural relationships across the colonizing line. Knowing the power of written words, they chose not to record this part of their lives. They probably destroyed evidence that contradicted their religious convictions and their place in a race-based settler nation.

Cherokee, biblical, and Mormon revelations addressed issues around marriage, intermarriage, and polygamy. All purported to provide moral pathways by which to navigate changing new worlds. The monogamous imaginings of early settler-colonizer nations were challenged. Between the 1820s and 1850s, several Native American nations legislated against polygamy. In the first half of the twentieth century, white pastoralists used various techniques to prevent their secondary marriages to Aboriginal women from entering official family trees. Whole branches went missing. When more accurately constituted, however, the full family tree takes on a distinctly polygamous appearance. We have seen how various kinds of husbands operated across colonizer boundaries: tribal husbands, Indigenous lovers, legal colonizer husbands, and those outsiders married on the side of Indigenous law. The same can be said for wives. Based upon monogamy and homogeneity, the familial model of modern settler nation-states needs to be reconfigured. On transnational colonizing frontiers, families were not neat, and they were not born "modern," in the sense of the nuclear family. But they were modern in their need to innovate and create something new. Gendered sovereignties shaped marital and kin connections that spread out concurrently in multiple directions. Across colonizing frontiers in Australia and the United States, the largely unacknowledged practice of plural marriage created fluid and multiple threads of kinship that became a vital means of circulating the politics of Indigeneity and of creating connectivity.

CHAPTER EIGHT

Entwined Sovereignties and the Great Unwedding

Intermarriages installed an Indigenous mandate into the future of colonization. Juxtaposed sovereignties became entwined, as did their intrinsic cultures of belief and entitlement. In the longer term, sexual unions and intermarriages created new generations that were neither exclusively European nor Indigenous. Intermarriage across colonizing boundaries formed a bridge for two-way traffic between entities, but not everyone wanted that bridge to stay open. Mobile middle grounds hosted dueling sovereignties. The power plays of family and nation could be overtly violent and confronting, subtle and secretive, or cold and legalistic. Then followed the great unwedding of entangled sovereignties.

This final chapter will explain how colonizer nations intervened in order to put an end to Indigenous sovereignty and its mutual entanglements. To close the permeable boundaries of colonizing frontiers, tough policies combined geographic distance with regulatory frameworks. Segregation policies relocated Indigenous people onto Indian and Aboriginal reservations and reserves. The legal principles of legitimacy and illegitimacy placed Indigenous families beyond the visible boundaries of the larger nation. Various strategies reinforced the outsider status of intermarrying husbands, wives, and children. Across that marital middle ground, the multiple threads of connection were frayed, often beyond repair.

Shaped by human idiosyncrasy and contradiction, colonialism's meetings had created sets of private, emotional dilemmas that seared the human heart. On both sides of the colonizer divide, individual desires jumped the blockades of collective political reasoning. People paired up. According to different laws, or no law at all, many of them married and raised families together.[1] Whether compelled by political or economic strategies, sexual attraction, or crazed infatuation, these marriages stood as acts of defiance.

Out of intimate relationships could come the deepest kind of love that stuck through thick and thin, and even beyond the grave. At the same time, the most hateful diatribes and bitter denials could come from people hurt by love across colonizing boundaries — love of a sister, a son, a sweetheart, a husband or wife. With the news that Harriett Gold planned to marry Elias Boudinot, it was her dearest brother Stephen and her closest brother-in-law who evoked the fires of hell.

When the usual gender pairing of colonizing intermarriage — the white frontiersman with the Indigenous woman — switched key, community anxiety became extreme. In ways embodied, matrimonial, and reproductive, what colonizers now saw as their domain had been invaded. Symbolic and corporeal competition over the white woman cannot be dismissed. When Cornwall's church elders closed their school doors, this was in accord with the perfectionist ideals of the new republic, in which the white woman's virtue was a key investment.

To ensure their high-minded republican project went ahead unimpeded, reverting "their town" into an exclusive "white zone" seemed to make sense. Although some Mohegans still lived in and around Connecticut, freshly minted history tellings enabled the Cornwall churchgoers to lose sight of complicity in the Indians' demise. The Mohegans' diminished sovereign power and numerical decline meant that they posed no immediate threat to local whites. Whether seen or unseen, the descendants of the intermarried Indigenous and European couples used expanded networks to move between the South, the North, and the West.[2]

In colonizing contexts, marital diplomacy had been carried out on multiple scales. Intermarital zones signified and enacted transnational contestation. Those individuals courageous enough to intermarry had to walk a tightrope between competing nations, if not between enemy states. Cultural exchanges paved the way for the subtle, ambiguous power plays of intimate diplomacy, in which shared spaces held transformative, unifying potential.

In this book we have observed how marital acts complicated the many contests of colonialism. What is more, in the most intimate and the most public of ways, human communions became crucial acts of sovereignty. When colonizer and colonized peoples negotiated their systems of law across fluid frontiers, the marital middle ground endured. Such spaces are indicative of imperfect colonizer sovereignty. As long as intermarriages continued, no single rule of law, no final elimination of the Indigenous presence, no absolute, "perfect sovereignty" would be possible.

The love game propelled and defied colonialism's endgame. In Australia and North America, in order to populate the land with their own, settler colonizers aimed to displace the previous occupants. As the preceding chapters show, colonizers saw that marriages across the boundaries of colonialism had the capacity to subvert, contradict, and qualify ongoing colonizing projects. Colonizers surveyed and divided up land and thereby made it their own.[3] Meanwhile, intermarriages dissolved the mapped boundaries that colonizers hoped would become solid walls.

It was not that easy for a state to keep individuals apart. Colonizing contracts of the marital kind facilitated multidirectional cultural and economic exchanges. Intermarriage prompted wrangles over land, property, and children. It demanded reformulations of Indigenous gender dynamics. Where Indigenous authority over domain still operated, the generative potential to grow new cross-cultural worlds offered hope to Indigenous nations.

Gender-nuanced performances of sovereignty had complex meanings across transnational boundaries. At multiple national levels, wars were fought and deals over land and women were repeatedly negotiated. The engagement, the wedding, the signing of the marriage papers, and the journey to the new home — these marital performances contractually entangled multiple sovereignties. Marital unions across frontiers became familial unions. These were one of many strategies Indigenous people sought to survive against the odds. Where Indigenous people had power to exert their law on their sovereign territory, a marital middle ground blossomed.

In spaces of plural sovereignty, gendered power relations were multilayered. Colonizers are not privileged as the only agents, power brokers, or generators of discourse. Residence on sovereign lands had enabled Indigenous people to exert authority over laws of marriage, kinship, clan, and social order. This was more feasible when the worst frontier warfare had eased off, where they composed the majority population, and where they still controlled resources. In situations where Indigenous people held on to landed sovereignty, a marital middle ground could prevail for longer. Colonizers and Indigenous people potentially shared not only the same space but also the same families and communities.

Colonizer sovereignty was premised upon intensive white settlement and economic development. In order to avoid being outnumbered in frontier zones, the most straightforward plan was to encourage more European immigrants to reproduce their own kind. Nonetheless, the importation of forced labor — African slaves, indentured Asians and Pacific Islanders, and other unfree laborers — created populations that countered homogeneity. By the early nineteenth century, Anglophone settler-colonizer nations started to consolidate their vision to populate the land with their own kind. Liberal ideals of freedom, democracy, and the modern nation were seen as contingent upon white exclusivity and homogeneity. In the new republic of the United States and later in federated White Australia, leaders self-consciously constructed nations premised upon rule by a white male hegemony. These ideals, however, did not stop white men or some white women from intermixing with Indigenous people who were still in-country. Hence legal prohibitions had to be introduced.

Europe watched as the new republics grappled with the "race" issue. By the respective early national periods in Australia and the United States, white colonizers were convinced that they were the only rightful residents. This was the case even for very recent arrivals. This sense of entitlement was reinforced through their religious revivals, anniversaries, national days, cultural activities, and history writing.[4] In early nineteenth-century America, the antislavery lobby was protecting national virtue but also, perhaps foremost, the whiteness of the nation — the whiteness of their families. From 1817 some abolitionists favored an emigration project out of the United States, most notably to Liberia. In 1901, under the White Australia policy, the new commonwealth government enforced an exit window for Chinese and Asian residents and Melanesian or "Kanaka" laborers.[5] Somehow, these people threatened the newcomers' imagined futures. These nonwhite workers were repatriated to their homelands.

Indigenous peoples remained patriated. After all, they happened to have originated in the countries of these early nations. In being at home, they posed a distinctive problem. Evangelical Christians and other humanitarians in settler-colonizer nations and in Europe were highly critical of the ways other colonizers treated slaves, kidnapped and forced laborers, and Indigenous peoples. Consequently, if they could not export the Indigenous overseas, colonizer states needed to develop ostensibly nonviolent, even benign, responses to their presence.

With gold rushes sparking demand for Cherokee territory in Georgia, the United States engineered a solution to transform contact zones into no-contact zones. An internal repatriation strategy would enable colonizing nation-states to encircle and enclose the frontiers of viable settlement for the exclusive benefit of the white population. Many people from the Cherokee, Choctaw, and other tribes responded to the pressures and incentives to move west, but this did not complete the job. President Jackson's Indian Removal Act of 1830 authorized the forced Cherokee migration to the Indian Territory in the West — now Oklahoma.[6] Jackson argued that to achieve extinguishment of Indian title would be "a happy consummation." Chief Justice John Marshall had referred to the requirement that land be "consummated by possession."[7] Jackson's compact was akin to a divorce of nations. These territories, and the larger West beyond them, are what has most commonly been seen as the American frontier. This western notion of the frontier came to displace the idea that the lands of Tennessee, North Carolina, Georgia, New England, or the Atlantic states were colonizing frontiers.

When Chief John Ross used the term "consummation" in sealing the marriage treaty with his white sweetheart Mary Stapler a decade later, this Jacksonian verbiage was stuck in his mind. Both treating parties were aware of the how contests of marriage and land might play out between dueling nations. In the face of Cherokee removal from their lands, Ross had told his white male friend Thomas McKenney that marrying a white woman was akin to stealing a "trophy." This signals the claiming of a certain dignity — grasping a masculine standing equivalent to that which colonialism had robbed the Cherokee men.[8] Recall that McKenney had supported removal, but he did not oppose intermarriage, he encouraged it.[9]

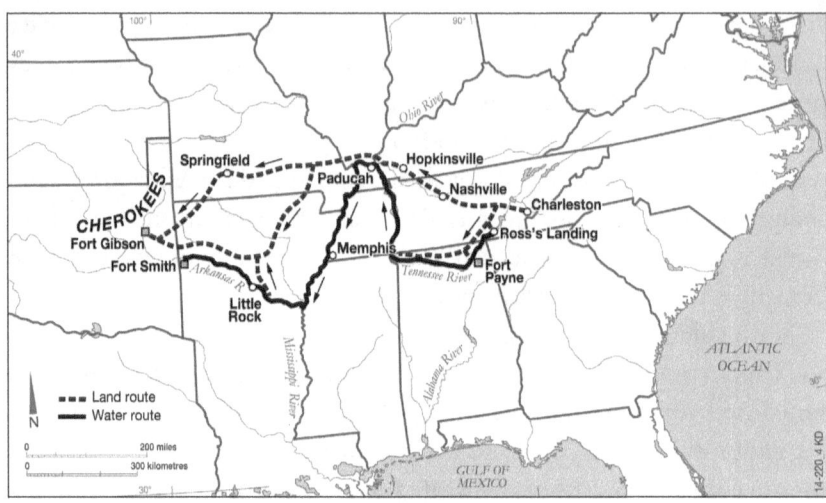

MAP 9. Trail of Tears routes to Indian Territory in the West.

For pragmatic reasons, Jackson and his supporters aimed to ensure the republic that Indian men and women would be taken off their sovereign lands and out of the way. This was the neatest method for the states and federal government to distribute lands for colonizer benefit and to conduct economic pursuits unimpeded. Jackson referred to Indian removal policies and actions as a "compact" located "at the heart of the Confederacy." He shifted the discourse away from President Washington's "compact," in which the Indian nations were required to civilize their societies in exchange for parity with other American states. Regardless of their success at performing "civilization," Indian nations would now be pushed away. With a beguiling rhetorical flourish, Jackson argued that, like other Americans, by becoming *emigrants*, Indians would actually benefit by disassociation from their "old worlds." Mobility and emigration would lump them into the same national narrative. However, while exodus and exile applied, the God-given entitlement to lands and freedoms under the rubric known as American exceptionalism did not.[10]

As a fellow colonizing nation, Australia actively looked to America to identify risks and to propose race solutions.[11] The earliest Australian penal colonies drew upon the model of an Indian territory that relocated tribes from many places. From the mid-1820s to 1830, the newspaper of Van Diemen's Land (now Tasmania) reported favorably on the Cherokee removal policy. In order to eradicate Aboriginal people on the large island of Van Dieman's Land, British colonizers proposed what they termed the "Georgian solution."[12] Without an expansive frontier, they chose exile to small islands — places of no escape. The death toll in these reserves was severe. The "last Tasmanian," Trucaninni, was lamented in poignant narratives. Although she had pleaded for her remains to be spared from grave robbers, in the late nineteenth century they were exhibited as solid proof to memorialize Aboriginal demise. In fact, Tasmania became the international exemplar of the doomed-race theory. The flaw was that this contention was based upon a count of "full-bloods," the Aboriginal Tasmanians of full descent. Descendants of intermarried Aboriginal women who worked in the sealing industry and elsewhere had survived. And to this day, their descendants carry vital Aboriginal traditions and identities.[13]

During the 1900s Australian statesmen still referred to the "successful" American reservation policy. In the lead-up to Australian federation, the Queensland government introduced a comprehensive reserves policy that became a model for other states. Almost in tandem with the earliest legislation — the introduction of the Immigration Restriction Act — this other race-based act was further tightened. The Queensland government published notices in the newspapers declaring various zones with curfews prescribed exclusively for Indigenous people. White men and other non-Aboriginal people were prohibited from entering within so many yards of these designated reserves.

The state now had full authority to forcibly remove and relocate Aboriginal people to these closed institutions. If a woman was formally married to a white man and thus under his guardianship, this sometimes helped prevent removal, but sometimes not. Yarrabah and other church-run missions assisted the state in putting segregation policy into effect. In 1907 the zealous Ernest Gribble upheld the settler-colonizer exemplar, publishing this call: "Force them all onto reserves as they did the Indians in America."[14] (See map 5, indicating lands of the Aboriginal groups discussed and the distant reserves to which they were moved.)

Both Australia and the United States devised novel schemes to forcibly move Indigenous peoples from their sovereign lands to unwanted, usually poor-quality land, distant from key population centers. These spaces were located outside the gendered and raced boundaries that encircled the white national family. In most parts of Australia, the reserves remained Crown land, owned by the state, with Aboriginal residents placed under the jurisdiction of superintendents or missionaries. Even when they were granted land ostensibly for their exclusive use, if it proved good agricultural land and if they proved successful agriculturalists, as in parts of New South Wales, it was rezoned and they were again dispossessed. Reserves were like internment camps for enemy aliens, with residents stripped of autonomy and of the citizenship rights and entitlements enjoyed by other Australians.[15]

Although they lost their valuable eastern lands, the Cherokees retained a national sovereign government in the Indian Territory in the West. The interests of the republic continued to intrude, however, and their government became increasingly concerned about keeping the non-Cherokee people out. They had an eye to their already diminishing wealth and their status in the eyes of the nation-state. In the ensuing decades after removal, the Cherokee Nation hardened its intermarriage and race policies, especially toward African Americans and Cherokees of mixed African American descent.[16]

PERFECT SOVEREIGNTY?

Although an imperial power might declare sovereignty, perfect sovereignty did not apply until colonizer law was fully implemented. Settler-colonizer sovereignty relied upon the imposition of its juridical system on the newly acquired territory. Criminal and property law offered assurances of colonizer landownership and personal security. In Australia, Aboriginal people suffered violent punishment and massacres for killing sheep and cattle. While land and property law penalized trespass, for our purposes, laws against gender trespass are especially relevant.

At certain times, the leaders of white men's nations envisaged Indigenous out-marriage as a way to get rid of the "Native" or the "Aboriginal problem." As discussed in the introduction, in the early nineteenth century President Jefferson and Secretary of War and the Treasury Crawford proposed that intermarriage would civilize Indians, ensuring that multiple sovereignties were united in one blood. In the 1920s Australia's Northern Territory Aboriginal protector envisaged that marriages of "half-caste" women to white men would "breed out the colour" and thereby solve the "Aboriginal problem."[17]

In addition to race-based arguments, on fluid frontiers, more pragmatic motivations often prevailed. The historian Peggy Pascoe argues convincingly, "As long as Indians retained effective control of land Whites wanted, and as long as Whites considered them formidable rivals, intermarriage offered a powerful symbol of the creation of a uniquely 'American' body politic and a seemingly peaceful alternative to outright conquest."[18] And as long as the prospect of Indigenous women as sexual and marital partners made frontiers more attractive and safe for white men, these unions made perfect sense. Colonizing regimes wanted to expand frontiers and rapidly transform them into settled zones. At certain moments, members of the governing classes welcomed unions comprising white frontiersmen and Indigenous or mixed-descent Indigenous women. Perhaps, as Jefferson proposed, the peoples should simply blend together. In addition to the appeal to white frontiersmen, perhaps they reasoned that intermarriage would reduce violent conflicts and eventually alleviate transnational divisions. But something changed. It was not so simple, for intermarriage simultaneously settled and unsettled frontiers.

During their respective early national periods, an entwined world of kin and family did not match national visions for the future in the United States and Australia.[19] Modern liberal nations were white. Australian government men and missionaries condoned a vision of *same-nation* marriage — between whites and whites. And, in faraway locales, between Aboriginal peoples. Their populations were declining and ravaged by illness, so Queensland missionary Ernest Gribble and Aboriginal Protectors Alfred Meston and Walter Roth encouraged Aboriginal people of different tribal groups to marry each other — whether from different language groups or otherwise.[20] Aboriginal Australians were Indigenous, like Indians in the United Sates, but they were considered "black" like "negroes" and slaves. With their color and lack of treaty and land rights, their status in relation to the colonizer state was not equivalent to that of American Indians. Nor was it the same as "negroes." Gribble's "ten little Niggers/Indians" rendition crudely alluded to American popularizations of race themes. Blackness was relevant but not an equivalency like the "native mind" of the Indigine. It was not blackness but Indigenous status that was the factor prompting the reserves policy across the hemispheres and seas.

Mixing Indigeneity may have been confounding for race and nation planners. However, it did not stop white frontiersmen from finding Aboriginal and American Indian women attractive.[21] They got away with rape, cruelty, and acts of abduction. State attempts to curb such behavior and to *prevent* white men from cohabiting with and marrying Indigenous women were perilous. With land at stake, the Cherokees had battled to enforce intermarriage laws, while white frontiersmen battled to challenge them. In Queensland they used the democratic machine, including parliamentary representatives and newspapers, to undermine the anti-intermixing agendas of the early Aboriginal protectors, Walter Roth and Archibald Meston. Yet states did not give up. In order to exert control, colonizer nations required authority not only over land but also over the orderings of race and gender. The colonizer goal of "perfect" or same-nation marriage sat side by side with the goal of "perfect sovereignty." Yet when the British colonizers and Georgians arrived, Cherokee sovereignties of long duration, with preemptive earlier entitlements, along with their developed structures of gendered law, did not disappear.

COMPETING SOVEREIGNTIES

Frontiers were supposed to be fast passing — fought, won, and then melded into a colonizer-led nation.[22] At least that is how the historical narrative has tended to be told. Frontiers tested the colonizers' ability to assert and sustain power. At the same time, benign colonialism became a test of colonizer virtue. In effect, intermarriages made contact zones unstable, multidirectional grounds. Gendered virtue was rocked. Intermarriage worked against the set historical destination of Indigenous disappearance. At the point of union, the middle ground became a freeze-frame. For intermarriage created a familial connectivity that constituted a space of longevity. This marital middle ground contained the political and corporeal essence, the body politic, of an enduring plural sovereignty.

Marital boundary-crossers were more than local intermediaries on a frontier or middle ground; they were engaged in reproducing a different kind of world than previously imagined. As we saw in chapter 6, on the Queensland frontier intermarriages became innovation sites for modernizing and reconfiguring clan, land, and culture. Love matches and marriages became part of an arsenal of Indigenous nation-making. At various times, Indigenous people deployed marriage to create political and economic alliances and to expand kinship and adoption networks. When Indigenous people held a strong negotiating position, and held the "marriage power," they gained greater leverage over colonizer infiltration. When they did not, they sometimes tried to prevent intermarriage altogether. Colonizers had the weight of ever-replenished immigrant numbers. Local Indigenous men such as the Cherokees witnessed the repeated pattern of their nations being swamped.[23]

At the same time, colonialism's competing gendered sovereignties potentially reshaped the constitution of marriage. At least this was the case on the marital middle ground, when Indigenous people still held some economic and cultural power and authority. Here the marriage contract was subject to negotiations inside and between nations. In transnational marriage scenarios, gendered values and ideals, and the dynamics of class, equality, freedom, and citizenship, were performed and experimented with.[24]

Frontier violence and its legacies left behind many ghosts in the landscape. Consequently, marriage across the colonizing transnational could be a harrowing, unpredictable affair. Take, for example, Ernest Gribble, Harriett Gold, and Cherokee chief John Ross. Not everyone agreed to conform to the modern ideal of same-nation marriage, including those propounding these very ideals. Participants became embroiled in volatile contests of state, with bullets fired inside and outside the home. Sovereignty led to tournaments both martial and marital, which could destabilize the homogeneity of national citizenship and individual identity. Meanwhile, across the United States and Australia, marriages were binding individuals, families, towns, clans, and wider socio-geographical zones of town and country.

LEGITIMACY — NATION, WIVES, CHILDREN

In a world of at least two laws, and the sovereignties that underwrote them, one of the great successes of colonialism was to introduce a hegemonic notion of legitimacy. Legitimacy means acceptability, legality, lawfulness, and validity. As a key concept in national and international law, modern sovereignty determines the legitimacy or illegitimacy of rule over people and territory. In these settler-colonizer states, this also operated at the most intimate and micro level of individual and family.

Legitimacy pertains to governments, children, and the citizens of a nation-state. To be legitimate under the patriarchal system of the settler-colonizer state, you needed a father who was the officially registered husband of your mother. Until European-derived laws phased out in the 1970s, a child born "out of wedlock" was classed as illegitimate. The state legitimized and delegitimized the family. Categories of legitimacy and illegitimacy applied to those who were classed as citizens and who were not, those who were classed as legitimate wives and husbands, and those who were classed as legitimate and illegitimate children.

A perceived fault line of colonialism, certain types of heterosexual intermixing were demarcated as illicit.[25] Colonizer laws over residence, marriage, and children could declare one familial group illegal and the others legitimate. "Illegals" stood outside national citizenship, with its articulated system of law and order. In a fight-back quest, the Cherokee Nation exerted its legislative authority over marriage, in support of male authority. Queensland Aboriginal people living on country attempted the same.

At the same time, with at least two systems of law operating between Indigenous people and colonizers, there could be no complete agreement over the licit and illicit, the legitimate and illegitimate. Grounded in the land and its associated repertoire of story, proof, and meaning, the precedents of Indigenous law were deep. Europeans were also confident in their law, having come to define legal authority as written and as requiring certain procedures of enactment. A modernizing Cherokee Nation combined both; it debated laws and amendments and codified, printed, and enforced them in the nation. Despite the decision by the U.S. Supreme Court to recognize the Cherokee Nation as a legitimate nation in the early 1830s, federal and state politicians still forced their removal soon afterward.[26] As with the imperial governments before it, and even within its own judicial system, the colonizer state might make a decision to ratify Indigenous sovereignty but this was not necessarily binding.

This sense of innate illegitimacy reached inside the home. During the early national periods in Australia and the United States, when colonizer-state restrictions were placed upon certain kinds of intermarriages, this led to loss of status for certain families and offspring. A child born "out of wedlock" was not legitimate under colonizer-state law, facilitating child removal practices in Australia.[27] That there was more than one marital law operating at any one time was not reconciled. The variable and multiple status of partners in legal, nonlegal, and illegal marriages nuanced the dynamics of intimate sovereignties.

In Indigenous societies, the concept of a child being illegitimate was peculiar. In Cherokee society, the children belonged to the mother. In Australian Aboriginal society, all the mother's sisters were also the child's putative mothers, and irrespective of whether he was the conception father, the mother's male partner had paternal responsibilities. Biological descent was of some interest but was irrelevant to parenting roles and family acceptance. After patrilineal inheritance and property laws started to apply, as in the Cherokee Nation, increasing capital and land accumulation meant that illegitimacy had material, wealth-related, ramifications.

The Cherokee Nation's relatively fluid system of marriage and adoption did not require official ceremony or paperwork. Matrilineal descent meant that the mother determined the legitimacy of clan membership. However, after the Cherokee Nation adjusted its governance structures into a patriarchal-style legal and political order, Cherokee women's hold over the transmission of land and property was undermined.[28] Clan legitimacy based upon race and gender started to change. When the Cherokee governing body asserted authority over Cherokee women, they engaged in a game similar to the one played by white patriarchal society in regard to Indian men.[29] By insisting upon the formal marriage of white men in their nation, the Cherokee government applied status penalties against intermarried women and men and against the offspring of a white parent. Black parents were to be denied citizenship rights altogether. Reliance upon treaty annuities meant that Cherokee citizenship was increasingly guarded and subjected to restrictions on the basis of color. Later U.S. government policies, including an 1880s allotment scheme dividing the land into private lots, led to more exclusive criteria for Cherokee citizenship.[30]

CHILDREN

Like the Cherokees, many Australian Aboriginal clans and language groups (or nations) were matrilineal, which determined the husband's residence on his wife's land and in her community. Even where clans were patrilineal, the

Aboriginal husband and his brothers were expected to carry out paternal duties. If biological paternity arose outside of marriage, this did not imply shame or loss of status for mother or child.[31]

A woman in an ongoing relationship with a white male resident was very likely to be in a right-way kin match, agreed under Indigenous law. She was indeed married; she was indeed a wife. As discussed in the previous chapter, the transnational wives and families of many men living and working in rural areas, on pastoral properties, and in other remote industries caused colonizer anxieties that morphed into secrets and denials.[32] As their white children approached puberty, white fathers harbored increased fears that they might develop romantic interests in the Aboriginal side of the family. What is more, the possibility of incest occurring between their unacknowledged secret children troubled them, as did a decline in social status. Some fathers consequently sent their white and mixed-descent children to boarding schools — albeit different ones from each other. For the white wife, fear of having to carve up her children's inheritance with the husband's unofficial offspring was a cause for angst, about which she was too ashamed to speak publicly. Best to go with the fiction that the other wife and family did not exist. The men also tried the same trick, causing festering inner conflicts and creating lingering hurt.

Australia's legitimate children were white. The illegality of intermarriage, alongside the exclusivist patriarchal/paternal concept of legitimacy, gave the state greater powers over the parents and children of mixed marriages. Lack of citizenship status for Aboriginal people, combined with the fact that the children were not legitimate in the usual way of the nation-state, proved a legal impediment to their parents' ability to protect them. Under Aboriginal protection legislation, the Queensland state and its authorized staff took on the powers of *father* or guardian over all the mixed-descent children of white men. Accordingly, neither the Aboriginal nor the white parents were treated as full adults in charge of their own offspring. Mixed-descent children could be taken away from either parent by white "protectors," often police.

Western law was designed so that property inheritance along male lines was protected. This took effect via the formal structures of marriage and parenthood, which were tuned into the *mono-* of monogamy and an assuredness of paternity. Additionally, by not publicly acknowledging polygamy, colonizer men could justify refusal to acknowledge their transnational second family. Informal polygamy meant that colonizers did not necessarily have to confer their name or share their earnings with the second (usually Indigenous) family.

Any couple that stepped outside a white same-nation marriage could be ostracized, fined, or jailed. Public denials of paternity, and state complicity, had devastating impacts upon Aboriginal and transnational family life and upon Aboriginal access to property in the long term. Because they were married in Indigenous law, Aboriginal mothers and their children generally missed out on inheritances. They had already missed out on profits being made from their lands.[33] For many offspring of cross-colonizing unions, the patriarchal nature of European marriage and family law erased their future prospects for capital accumulation and social mobility.

Occasionally, state representatives and some white fathers made displays of concern over paternity and inheritance across colonizing boundaries. In the colonial economic regime, having a legal father was imperative to property transmission and wealth accumulation across generations. Only marriage endorsed by the colonizer state, not Aboriginal customary marriage, could create the legitimacy that made the child a rightful heir. Marriage and reservation or reserve law could entrench cross-generational legacies of poverty — and landlessness.

It was one of colonialism's awful inequalities that a white man in a relationship with an Indigenous woman could easily get away with failing to support his children. A married white woman with knowledge of another family across the frontier had a strong stake in protecting a patrilineal inheritance system — both for herself and for the "legitimate" children. Not all Aboriginal people knew their entitlements, being unfamiliar with the market economy and the patriarchal rules of property inheritance linked to western monogamy. They saw the land as theirs in perpetuity and not necessarily as property saleable in the marketplace. Later generations felt differently, observing the differential economic prospects of a white man's dark children compared with his white offspring. Descendants of the men of Australia's most famous major pastoral, retailing, and mining dynasties are increasingly speaking out.[34]

Confusion and intentional ignorance justified state interventions into the private realm of family. In North America, many Indigenous parents had little say over whether their children attended boarding schools. Given that children were living on native lands, Indigenous people had significant autonomy over governance. Nonetheless, the history of family severance has strong parallels with the experience of white Australia's "stolen children."[35] For, as the historian Margaret Jacobs and others have shown, by the late nineteenth century, the Australian states started to take over guardianship of Indigenous and mixed-descent children. White women proactively intervened in Indigenous family life, supporting the removal of children from their parents.[36] In the battle over intimate sovereignty, the status of the wife, the husband, and the child put mixed families on awfully shaky ground.

TOGETHER THEN APART

Disconnecting Indigenous peoples from tribal or traditional lands, forced emigration to reservations and reserves ruptured many of the personal and national connections forming the basis of First Nations sovereignty. Additionally, the spatial boundary zoning of reserves and reservations demarcated who was and who was not part of the national family. Indigenous and mixed-descent people were removed from the national eye and from inclusion as a legitimate part of a body politic.

Indian territories and reserves marked new sets of transnational boundaries. Effectively dividing Indigenous space from colonizer space, this novel land-zoning scheme arbitrarily introduced spatial segregations that were a kind of precursor to the later nineteenth-century Jim Crow policies applying to African Americans. Restrictions were placed on all movement from and to Australian Aboriginal reserves. White men could not travel onto reserves or even go within so many yards of these places. Except for their administrators, they were effectively turned into "no-go zones" for whites. Aboriginal people were not able to travel outside them without special permission.

Eve Fesl (née Serico), the Gubbi Gubbi woman who grew up across the road from me, recalled that one of her direct ancestors was known by the English name Jim Crow: a probable allusion to the U.S. practice. Eve related the love story of her grandmother Evelyn and her grandfather John Olsen. One day John arrived home from work to find that his wife and their children had disappeared. Eventually he found out that police had taken them all away to a reserve. As a white man, John was not permitted to reside on the reserve. Soon after their arrival at that distant reserve, a disease epidemic ensued, and Evelyn died. Without parents, the young children were grieving for their mother in a strange place. Their father grieved long. Unable to take the shock of losing his family for good and prohibited from being a father to his children, John Olsen suffered a breakdown. He was placed in a mental institution, where he died six years later. In the words of his daughter, "I think his heart was broken."[37]

On marital middle grounds, peoples once worlds apart came together on the same ground. For those already entangled, forced removals tore apart established families. In Queensland, it would no longer be necessary for protectors to assess whether a non-Aboriginal man would fit the category of the good husband. Segregation zones severed Aboriginal people from the privileges of landownership, national citizenship, and freedom of movement, employment, and association. Thrown together, the zones brought them into conflict with other language groups and nations. In the United States, except among the elite Cherokees, distance impeded Indians' associations and, in the East and West, state-forced removal brought them into conflict with their own.

When the United States and Australia introduced forced removals, Indigenous marital power in the contact zones was ruptured. This constituted the great settler-colonizer estrangement. It was not mutual, and even if treaties were involved, it was not a matter of equal decision making. In the case of the Cherokees, a high-performing and well-organized nation — and one that had more than met the "civilizing" side of their contract with the American nation-state — was removed from the centers of American expansion. In Queensland, most Aboriginal peoples now resided in places distant from their own country, which eroded their base of authority and law. Forced emigration had a far more profound effect on their powers of marital negotiation than restrictive marriage legislation could ever hope to have.

With reserves, Queensland's colonizing project moved on from asserting white sovereignty and economic domination over Indigenous lands to ending Indigenous people's ability to be sustained by, maintain connection with, and return to their land. What the Cherokees had suffered in the

1830s, the Queensland Aboriginal people suffered from the 1900s onward. The reserve system blocked travel without permission, curbing meaningful travel over wide areas of culturally significant country to conduct essential ceremonial economic and political negotiations, including journeys required for the arrangement of promised marriages. During the early national era, Queensland and other northern states began to lump Aboriginal people together on someone else's Indigenous land. State zoning actions severed Aboriginal people from their sense of self — that is, from their deeply held, embodied links with storied sites. Like the Cherokees' love of their mountains, Aboriginal links with land were intricately associated with a deeply personal sense of identity and well-being. Unlike the situation with the Cherokees and their lands, however, in Australia these zoning actions were government and mission-run institutions that confined Aboriginal people under restrictive and punitive rule.

Mixed-race couples and their children were subjected to excessive surveillance in their own country.[38] Local Aboriginal women, and the white, Pacific Islander, or Asian men who wanted to join them, suffered imprisonment. The men were not welcome to join their wives on reserves. Under the guise of "protection," the Queensland Aborigines Protection Act criminalized friendly associations across the frontier.[39] To pursue such a relationship, hiding certain facts of a sexual, familial, and national nature became necessary. Race whispering built related communities cemented by secrets. Meanwhile, colonizer demand for Aboriginal labor and female sexual partners and companionship paved the way for more casual, furtive, and sexually exploitative crossings, with less prospect of openly acknowledged families.

The Cherokee Nation did not promote the splitting up of families. However, on the basis of blood quantum, the children of successive cross-generational intermarriages with whites or African Americans lost citizenship status. By the mid-nineteenth century, Cherokees of African American ancestry were usually excluded from tribal status altogether. In order to hold on to their nation, the Cherokees wanted to curb intermarriages with whites too and to keep them out of the nation.

Whether under strict state surveillance or the jurisdiction of an Indigenous national government, geographical segregation did not necessarily succeed in ending the intimate circulation of Indigenous sovereignty. Although colonizer states did not recognize them as legal, intermarriages did not cease entirely. And although intermixing was curbed, some marriages still ensued, with the children of these unions in turn marrying outsiders. On reserves in Australia and the United States, higher rates of intermarriage also took place *between* different tribal groups than had ever happened previously.[40] This created an identity and fostered a politics of pan-Indigeneity — of being "Aboriginal" or "Indian" across the wider nation. From the mid-twentieth century, this took place in an increasingly interconnected and assertive fashion. First Nations, first there. A certain dignity in a world that had placed them always second in the race.

No matter how far colonizers removed Indigenous peoples from their lands, and despite these multiple displacements, Indigenous peoples gripped on to threads of connection with their sovereign homelands. In settler-colonizer spaces, ideas of home were constantly reinvented and disturbed. Indigenous sovereignty breathed meaning into identity, place, and a sense of family. In protesting the removal of his servant to Yarrabah, one inconvenienced white employer argued, "I have frequently spent nights in reading to my sons and Lizzie Johnstone's school lessons, and listening to the sweet music from half-a-dozen young voices singing 'Home Sweet Home' supported by the notes of the violin and concertina."[41] (See fig. 31; Lizzie Johnstone is on far right of wedding photo.) This was the same homesick anthem devised by the Cherokee sympathizer and historian John Howard Payne, who was arrested by the Georgia Guard with Chief John Ross. Those same words appeared underlined in his lovers' letters. Against stories of exile and forcible expulsion, in settler-colonizer nations, the idea of home evoked landscapes of repeated displacement.[42]

Families had good reason to submerge their identities and to submerge those stories from national histories. So many of us who have lived on Indigenous land in settler societies do not really know the family shape of our colonial ancestors. The lineage of my colonial ancestors — the Morrises, the Greatrexes, the McGraths, the Egans, the Clancys, and the in-laws the Scottish Camerons — left families with only partially documented entanglements. Among my fellow historians in the United States, the Yale historian Glenda Gilmore speaks lovingly of her Cherokee grandmother, a great storyteller, to whom she attributes her passion for history writing and teaching. Feminist public broadcasting pioneer Pat Mitchell speaks of how hidden ancestries provide some of the missing pieces of the American history jigsaw, including her own Cherokee ancestry. In both Australia and North America, so many more individuals are starting to find out about the lovers who transgressed the increasingly policed borders between colonizer and colonized.

Amid this reclaiming of lineages, we need to better appreciate how settler states used geographical segregation to wrench the peoples apart. In order to control land and love, and thereby to gain perfect sovereignty, wherever Indigenous marriages persisted, the modern nation-states used their power to rule that the associated wives, husbands, children, land, and property — and even the nations themselves — were illegitimate, outside what they defined as the "law." The same pattern emerged in two hemispheres eighty years apart. In their new nation, the Cherokees attempted to police intermarriage in a concerted way — before and after removal. But, despite fighting through warfare, then through the courts of the colonizing nation-state, they could not relegate the colonizers into a restricted, encircled zone. Unwedding them from their domain over land and women would prove impossible.

Nevertheless, whether against colonizer law or Indigenous law, transnational marriages forged platforms of enduring transnational connection. Such histories make us; nations emerge from and are constituted by them. People carry these histories in their bodies. Intersecting sovereignties continue to be transmitted down the generations. Out of sentiments strained and constrained, embodied entanglements constituted nations. In the longue durée of human history, illicit love generated and regenerated new worlds.

Epilogue

Transnational Families

During their marriages, couples like Harriett Gold and Elias Boudinot and John Ross and Mary Stapler show us how, out of deep emotions, transnational couples renegotiated and reimagined settler-colonizer nations. That being said, marital relationships are not between races but between unique individuals, with all their imprinted biographical and collective histories. All marriages are, to an extent, cross-cultural. Not only do politics differ by gender, but embedded in the psyche of the husband and the wife, people from different families will bring norms and expectations from their different upbringings, practices, and beliefs. While marriage was both public and private, in settler-colonizer societies, marriages across colonizing boundaries became sites of political and legal contests.

Emotions and the connectedness of hearts and hands were the stuff of transnational weddings, and they led to longer-term consequences. The families that followed would create new nations and new worlds. Those involved in that intimate politics were both ordinary and extraordinary.

HARRIETT AND ELIAS

The controversy leading up to the marriage of Elias Boudinot and Harriett Gold left a legacy of personal trauma. This heightened the couple's awareness of race discrimination and created a shared sense of Cherokee national allegiance. When Harriett left Cornwall, Connecticut, she and Boudinot needed security protection. When Harriett arrived in Cherokee country to become a member of a Cherokee Nation, she had no clan status and therefore no official citizenship. The best hope of belonging was by following the patrilineal European approach to marriage and its principle of coverture, which meant being subsumed under her husband's citizenship and clan status.

Upon arrival in the Cherokee Nation, Harriett reported that her new family "joyfully" stated, "You are welcome in this Nation." Pointedly, she proclaimed, "I am now at home. Here I expect to pass the remainder of my days."[1] They treated her like an old friend rather than a stranger. She explained, "Beginning with my Parents. My Cherokee Father often reminds me of my own Father by his cheerfulness. I think [he] is remarkable for his amiable, kind and affectionate disposition. Ma says she used often to speak of me before I came here [and] said I was going to leave all my friends to come and do them good, and they must love me a great deal and both [she] and My Dear Cherokee Mother frequently say that I am like an own child to them."[2] In the estimate of both parties, they quickly became family.

Not long after her arrival there, she told a certain Mrs. Turner that she was aware the "final destiny" of the Cherokees would soon be known. "Whatever may be their doom I shall share and suffer as a Cherokee."[3] She was keen to reassure her mother, however, that it was just like home. "I could wish too dear mother that you could look into the room where I am now writing." Not only was it "nicer than you imagine"; the floor was too fine to cover with carpet, and the furniture was like that of Sister Flora's. They had "a good library of books, a writing Table, Looking Glass, & a small map of the United States."[4]

The year following the wedding, her parents, Benjamin and Eleanor Gold, visited the couple. Deacon Benjamin Gold took a particular interest in the Cherokee system of governance, praising members of the council and court as "gentlemen" with "great natural powers of mind." He became their advocate, expressing strong opposition to the taking of any lands from the nation on the grounds that they possessed it by "acts and treaties of the United States."[5] By now Elias was living a literary life of letters — as editor of the first American Indian newspaper, the high-quality *Cherokee Phoenix*, he was editorial writer, publisher, author and public speaker, leader, and diplomat.[6]

In Harriett's family, it was too late to speak of dichotomies and separate destinies. She performed her wifely duties well, including nurturing new bonds between distant families. When Elias is traveling to New England to promote the Cherokee cause, Harriett warns her family that they must not treat her husband with "coolness and neglect." "My heart is warm and I cannot express half what I feel — you will excuse me for the freedom I have already used"; she hopes "you and Mr Boudinott will have a long pleasant chat." In a gesture of humility to her parents, she ends this letter stating she is "ashamed," for she has "written so much about myself and family."[7]

Harriett's parents were proud of their grandchildren. Previously, Harriett's sister Mary Brinsmade had accused her of creating damaging racial consequences — "to have black young ones and a train of evils."[8] For their grandfather, any thoughts of seeing the children in such a racist fashion were impossible. Benjamin Gold wrote, "The oldest little girl is as smart and pretty and healthy as can be found" and the next is a "bright well looking child. All who see her say, 'she is the hansomest child I ever saw.' You must not think that I brag."[9] Harriett is similarly delighted with their beauty, describing them as her "little Indians" and more "fair," more beautiful than any child in Connecticut.[10]

On her wedding anniversary in 1832, Harriett writes to her brother-in-law and sister who once opposed the marriage: "I think it is this day 6 years since I received the hand of Mr Boudinott and gave my own in the covenant of marriage — I now look back to that day with pleasure, & with gratitude — yes I am thankful — I remember the trials I had to encounter — the thorny path I had to tread, the bitter cup I had to drink — but a consciousness of *doing right — a kind affectionate devoted* Husband, together with *many* other blessings have made amends for all."[11] With a one-month-old baby and other young ones, Harriett remains scarred by her ordeal. Using Christian allusions, she refers to the "thorny path" and "the bitter cup."[12] Although tired from her daily work, she is lighthearted and proud.

Harriett and Elias's "connection of hands" had made Indian connections family connections: material, cultural, legal, and political, with implications for nation and citizenship. Harriett's story is the antithesis of the captivity narrative of alienation and subordination. Upon marriage, Harriett's

EPILOGUE

FIG. 59. Locket images of Elias and Harriett Boudinot, ca. 1826, annotated in 1910 by one of their grandchildren. The initials "F.J.B" may be those of Frank Josiah Boudinot, born in 1866 and one of the children of William Penn Boudinot and Matilda Rogers Fields. He married Annie Stapler Meigs in 1897; she was the daughter of Henry C. Meigs and the great-granddaughter of John Ross. Courtesy of the estate of Henry Meigs Boudinot.

citizenship became a Cherokee one, yet she did not lose her U.S. citizenship. She does not seek to conquer and domesticate the native world. Rather, she is domesticated within it. She is not so much an assimilator as one assimilated within another nation, one standing against some of the fundamental aims of the colonizing state. While identifying as a mother aiming to set a Christian example, Harriett supports the production of the Cherokee newspaper and the intense political struggles against removal, recognition of treaty entitlements, and full sovereignty. Harriett's life narrative moved rapidly from "Puritan-Pilgrim," through an anticolonial journey that headed away from the settled world of settler colonialism to a nation where Indigenous people ruled. At the same time that Georgia and the federal government were moving to dispossess the Cherokees of their remaining land and to forcibly remove them, Harriett became a border crosser, and soon a Cherokee activist and nationalist.

Harriett and Elias's story reveals how intimacy shaped and redefined individuals and nations with a glue that neither colonizer nor colonized state could dissolve: "Indeed I wish you could see us in our family, in our neighbourhood, and our Nation," Harriett wrote to her Connecticut family. "You need not say that I profess that disposition of bragging so peculiar to the Gold family — perhaps I do — but I now only mean I wish you to see how Indians can live — how families and how a nation of Indians can live.... I am much attached to this neighborhood. Almost all the people here are our relations."[13]

Harriett relishes writing about her children and their integrated upbringing: "William Penn has gone to his Grand Pa's [Oowatie]. I wish much to see him — he has been gone 12 days — His Uncles learn him to walk like an old man to jump like a boy, to make bows like a gentleman. This is sometimes very amusing to us." Without an image to offer, she draws a word picture: "Permit me to tell you just how he looks — He is very strait — has a high projecting forehead, dark brown hair — large face, rosy cheeks and perfectly black eyes — and what is more than all, I think he has common sense — a mind capable of cultivation — should his life be spared I hope he will be disposed to improve his natural talents." The lives of children were not assured.[14]

Elias and Harriett's one-month-old baby was christened Sarah — perhaps after Harriett's dear friend Sarah Northrup (now Ridge), who lived in New Echota and shared the notoriety of being a Cornwall expatriate. Or perhaps it was for Boudinot's sister, or even the New Jersey Elias Boudinot's fictional Christian heroine "Poor Sarah." Naming denoted multiple identities. Before the christening, the girl's first name was the Cherokee ᏍᎦᏏ, or Gah-sa-gah. Elias was traveling. Harriett writes, "I shall not say much about her — She is probably like other children of her age — I love her — I cannot say we — for her Pa has not yet seen her — but it is possible for a person to love an object he has not seen."[15]

In all, Elias and Harriett had six children. Eleanor Susan Boudinot, named for Harriett's mother, was born in 1827. Mary Harriett Boudinot came along in 1828. In 1829 or 1830 a boy was born, whom they called William Penn Boudinot. Harriett gave birth to Sarah Parkhill Boudinot in 1832, followed by Elias Cornelius Boudinot in August 1835. In May the following year she gave birth to their sixth child, Frank Brinsmade Boudinot. Elias named his firstborn son for William Penn, and the second took on the name of Elias's benefactor and his own name. As the New Jersey Boudinots passed on the name Elias to more sons over several generations, two strands of Elias Boudinots, descending from the two different kinds of statesmen, were living concurrently on different national grounds.[16]

In 1836 Harriett suffered a severe illness and intense pain, and in August she died at age thirty-one.[17] She was buried in New Echota and her tombstone and grave may be seen there today. Boudinot wrote a heartfelt letter to Harriett's parents, explaining how he had lost both a wife and a friend. Sending this correspondence fulfilled the expectations of a good husband. Of Harriett, he wrote, "Perhaps no one in this country has ever commanded such universal respect as she did. No one has ever entered into our humble dwelling... without going away impressed." Indeed, people commented on her piety and religiosity. Boudinot remarked that even the prejudiced Georgians who opposed intermarriage had agreed that she had an "unsullied character."[18]

Elias had not forgotten the personal pain of their marriage controversy or its impact upon his wife. Harriett feared she had not done enough in her life to warrant a place in God's "glorious kingdom," and toward her last days, she told her children to be kind to each other and to become Christians.[19] Perhaps she had not pushed such beliefs on them until then. One of her final requests was for someone to sing her favorite hymn to her, and her friends obliged.

After Harriett's death, Elias not only grieved but plummeted into depression, finding it almost impossible to leave his bed. Eight months later, on April 22, 1837, he remarried. His new wife, Delight Sargent, was another white woman. The children's schoolteacher, she had assisted in their care after Harriett's death. Elias reported that Delight had been a friend and mother to the children beyond his expectations.[20] A month after their wedding, Elias finally wrote a letter informing Benjamin and Eleanor Gold about his second marriage. It was addressed to his "Dear Father and Mother."[21]

A little over two years later, on June 22, 1839, Elias Boudinot was assassinated. As well as suffering various ax blows, his right hand was cut off. This was in retaliation for his signing the highly controversial Treaty of New

Echota, which consented, without the approval of several chiefs, for the Cherokee Nation to move west. His cosignatories, the other intermarried man from Cornwall, John Ridge, and Ridge's father, Major Ridge, were murdered at the same time. Presumably the supporters of the politician John Ross had found their victims, with the exception of Elias's brother, Stand Watie, who survived the attack. Upon recovery, Stand threatened to kill John Ross. Although Delight Sergeant warned John Ross to depart the nation, he stayed, his house protected by guards.[22]

Assisted by their New England aunts and uncles, Harriett and Elias's children received a good Anglo-American-style education.[23] The boys, William Penn Boudinot and the younger Elias Cornelius Boudinot, were high achievers, becoming well-respected lawyers, businessmen, writers, and orators. They dedicated much of their energy and skills to fighting for the rights of Cherokee people. Elias Cornelius became a Confederate colonel. William Penn prepared a compilation of Cherokee laws that I have drawn upon for this book.[24] The brothers also married white women. Some of their descendants still carry the name Boudinot. It has been my great pleasure to hear their family stories and to see their family photographs and other treasures.

ERNEST GRIBBLE AND NOLA

In a photograph of Nola and Ernest together, Nola looks like the cat that found the cream. Ernest faces the camera cautiously, while Nola beams with proprietorial pride and excitement. Nola is coquettish, flirtatious, the blooming teenager all dressed up, wide hat and all. Perhaps Nola sensed something. Or possibly the elevated status of clergy and protective robes stopped her from entertaining any suspicions. Other local Aboriginal people had plenty of skepticism. They so enjoyed retelling that story of Ernest beating his wife, Emilie, with a duck, and how afterward she left for good.[25] We do not know if Nola understood why Ernest chose to be photographed with her outside the church, but this appears a rare and special moment in her life that was to remain treasured; the photo was kept in the family.[26] We do know that after being expelled from Yarrabah, the exiled Ernest Gribble kept in touch with Jeannie and with their daughter, Nola. Eventually based in Forrest River, a remote part of Western Australia, Ernest returned to

EPILOGUE

FIG. 60. Boudinot family portrait gallery, from images in possession of the Boudinot family, as identified by the family. *Top row, left to right*: Elias Cornelius Boudinot, 1857; William Penn Boudinot; and Frank Brinsmade Boudinot. (The middle image may be Frank at a later age than he appears on the right.) William Penn Boudinot was only about seven when his mother died. At age ten his father was murdered. William is said to have lived for a time with Harriett's mother, Eleanor Gold, in Cornwall, Connecticut. He worked as an engraver in Philadelphia before returning to the Cherokee Nation. Frank Brinsmade Boudinot was an actor and the child of Elias and Harriett. *Bottom row*: the two girls are sisters, Mary and Harriett, daughters of Elias and Harriett. The middle image may be an early photo of John Rollin Ridge. Courtesy of the estate of Henry Meigs Boudinot.

officiate at Nola's confirmation ceremony. The look on Nola's face says it all. Perhaps the private Gribble found ways to address his public denials. Deciding that personal relationships were more important than what other people thought, he sought her out (see fig. 64).[27]

In one sense, there is nothing particularly exceptional about a man finding a lover and someone to live with in his community and place of residence. But in this settler-colonizer nation, these histories had to be hidden. In the

FIG. 61. According to the family, this is an image of William Penn Boudinot and Caroline Matilda Rogers Fields Boudinot when they were first married. Courtesy of the estate of Henry Meigs Boudinot.

preferred national narratives, they represented severe cracks in the colonizing wall. Gribble had hoped to break down the "wall" of evils like polygamy. Between white men and Aboriginal women, he wanted to create the highest walls of all. True to convictions, if not to form, he continued to argue against intermixing, campaigning for laws to prevent the birth of "illegitimate half breeds." Using Canada as an exemplar, he approved its policy that all white men must be forced to support their offspring.[28] Gribble's story reveals only the tip of the iceberg when it comes to colonizer anxiety about "half-castes."[29] Indigenous people knew that missionary men had the same vulnerabilities and desires as any man. It gave them cause to be skeptical of white sexual and Christian moralising.[30]

Whereas Gribble's manic marriage policies were exercised upon Aboriginal couples, he could not even entertain the prospect of his own marriage to an Aboriginal woman. At the same time, he had become part of the Yarrabah family and could not bear to leave this world. There was more to it than that. Gribble had become acclimatized, even acculturated, into a familiar, familial, modern Aboriginal world.

Something in his eyes guarded secrets. As the years of tropical living in North West Australia passed, Gribble's face became ever more taut and his intense eyes sunk deep into his skull, but their piercing pale blue burned into other people's space, making them want to get away. While colonial actors privately disguised the facts of procreation, of bodies dissolving into each other, of people merging, momentarily and permanently, secrecy's complex emotional undercurrents and mutual collusions created subversive

EPILOGUE

FIG. 62. This Cherokee delegation to Washington DC in 1866 aimed to negotiate a new treaty with the United States in the wake of the Civil War. Elias Cornelius Boudinot, the son of Elias and Harriett, is seated on the far right. He was a politician and editor. The others are (*left to right*) John Rollin Ridge (son of John Ridge, who became a well-known poet and author; also known as Yellow Bird or Cheesquatalawyny); Saladin Watie (son of Stand Watie, Elias's brother); Richard Fields; and William Penn Adair. Registration no 4326.3693, courtesy Gilcrease Museum, Tulsa OK.

entanglements. Another missionary said that the older Gribble looked like "a bushranger" or outlaw.[31] And indeed, he had lived outside the colonizer law.

But it was not only Gribble who kept their love secret. It was Jeannie too. Her maintenance of secrecy was likely proof that she cared for Gribble. She confided her affair only to her best friend, Myra Pitt. Not even Nola Clark or any of Jeannie's subsequent children by Willie Clark were told the truth about Nola's parentage. Yarrabah resident Mae Smith said she had overheard the dispute between cousins Ada Pickles and Janey (Janie) Clark about Nola's paternity. Maisie Reading, Myra's daughter, attested that her mother had also confided the secret to her.[32]

FIG. 63. Daguerreotype of John Ross, ca. 1850. In ornate gilt, possibly this twin frame also featured a portrait of Mary Stapler Ross. Courtesy Library of Congress, reproduction no. LC-USZC4-11120.

FIG. 64. Ernest Gribble in his clerical robes and collar stands alongside Nola Clark (*right*) outside St John's Anglican Church in Cairns. Winnie Massey is on the left, and Gribble is holding Madge Leftwich. Courtesy Charmaine Hollingsworth and AIATSIS.

Jeannie's effort to keep the facts undercover for most of her life was not only for the sake of Gribble's reputation but to ensure her own place in the Yarrabah community — the only one she had. Perhaps the reason Jeannie kept her secret so long was to protect her own, or Willie's, reputation, rather than Gribble's. Willie and Jeannie reunited and stayed together to have several other children. In 1916, six years after Gribble's departure, the Clarks quit the mission, moving to Meerawa, in sugarcane country about six miles south of Gordonvale. Escaping mission restrictions, Willie Clark worked hard, managing not only to keep his family fed but also out of the hands of the Aborigines Department — a difficult struggle in these decades of state surveillance and control.[33]

Jeannie's actions were also for her daughter Nola. In her childhood, paternal disinheritance and race thinking had created suffering for Jeannie. She was one of many children born out of wedlock and classed as "bastards" or illegitimate. On top of this, Aboriginal people lacked citizenship rights, so the cards were stacked against her. For Gribble, cohabitation with an Aboriginal woman was a punishable offense. Despite his reification of the monogamous married couple, at Yarrabah, dislocated families were the norm. When Gribble forced marriage on Nola's mother, at least he had created a legitimate status for her child and made it a little harder for the state to take her away.

Years later, Gribble saw the apocalyptic impact of colonizing secrets on a nearby colonial landscape. In 1930 he visited Palm Island, where Superintendent Robert Curry had long run the island Aboriginal community at the behest of the Queensland government. After his wife's death in childbirth, Curry was grief stricken, and he allegedly had an affair with his Aboriginal domestic servant. He was then reprimanded for flogging an Aboriginal woman. Hearing that he was earmarked for a transfer away from the world of Palm Island, Curry cracked. He killed his children, shot down various white mission employees, and burned down the mission buildings that he had helped build. He also torched the settlement's launch, the boat that provided the island's only link to the outside world. Following police orders, an Aboriginal resident, Peter Pryor, shot him dead.[34] Superintendent Curry had destroyed so much more than secrets.

We wonder what rushed through Ernest Gribble's mind as he smelled the scorched earth and thought about the dead children. Gribble pasted

FIG. 65. Generations of the Clark family on their property, ca. 1940. Jeannie and Willie Clark are standing, with Janey Clark and Myra Pitt seated and Rebecca Clark's children Steve and Jean on the grass. Courtesy Charmaine Hollingsworth and AIATSIS.

the photos of devastation and burned-out mission dwellings in his personal album. As if revisiting a scene from his own biography, he added the deadpan caption "Views of Missionary Life."[35] Perhaps in that lifeless landscape he saw the causes and effects of his anxieties writ large; it could have been him. After playing an unpopular role in a royal commission concerning massacres of Aboriginal people, Gribble had returned from Western Australia. Reconstructing the mission wreckage and his own exhausting colonizing interventions, Gribble moved onto Palm Island. At this time of devastation, he took over its rebuilding project.

Ernest Gribble revisited Jeannie and Nola again in 1930. Photographs from the visit feature in Gribble's private album. Like any proud grandfather, he includes a photo of Nola's kids, a boy and girl under five, playing happily in front of his camera. A 1940s photograph depicts Willie Clark with Jeannie, a daughter-in-law, and grandchildren at Harvey's Creek, the place they made their own. The blue-eyed Nola was the eldest of three girls and two boys. Her best friend, Myra Pitt, also appears in that photograph. Jeannie, who appeared to outside observers to have a happy and stable life, always knew that something had been left unsaid. She waited until she was on her deathbed before telling her daughter Nola of her true paternity.[36]

Ernest was awarded an Order of the British Empire and made a canon of the church. Despite his age, he refused to give up his work. In 1957 he moved back to Yarrabah. He died there in October of the same year. As if to say farewell to a king, Aboriginal residents lined up to visit his bedside. Ernest Gribble's bones, like those of the Yidinjdji Djabuganjdi ancestors, were laid to rest at Yarrabah in ground that he had consecrated as suitable for a Christian burial. Unlike Ernest, Jeannie and Nola led private rather than public lives. Nola has passed on now.

Gribble left numerous published memoirs in books and newspaper articles; however, they all ignore the story of the marriage between his sister Ethel Gribble and the Butchulla man Fred Wondunna. Ethel's husband is at least remembered as a successful Aboriginal missionary and Butchulla elder, whereas Ethel slips out of the historical record. Their lonely wedding ceremony was akin to one of Yarrabah's "rag-time" weddings. Although not banished to Fitzroy Island like her Yarrabah counterparts, Ethel had to give birth to their first child in a home for the destitute — a Salvation

EPILOGUE

FIG. 66. Nola Clark's children, 1930. Courtesy Mitchell Library, State Library of New South Wales, MLMSS 4503, add-on 1822.

Army home near Sydney, in April 1908.[37] She and her husband continued to work as missionaries on Fraser Island, Badjala/Butchulla country, and they went on to have a long marriage and four children.

The island is well known for the story of "Mrs. Fraser," after the *Stirling Castle* was shipwrecked there in 1836. Via her sensationalist lectures and memoirs, she entered the colonizer imagination as Australia's most famous "captive white woman" — supposedly in the hands of Aboriginal "savages."[38] Borrowing heavily from the American genre, such captive tales were relatively rare in Australia. Fascinated by the story, Ethel became particularly interested in gaining Aboriginal perspectives on the actual experience of Mrs. Fraser. She recorded the old Badjala women's stories of the "strange white woman" who claimed to be forcibly betrothed to an Aboriginal man. Ethel's accounts offer refreshing perspectives that challenge Mrs. Fraser's sensationalist accounts. Although Fred and Ethel eventually separated, with Ethel living on the mainland, they reared their children together and remained on good terms. Ethel returned to Fraser Island to nurse Fred during his last illness. Her association with Fraser Island, its people, and

FIG. 67. Ernest Gribble's farewell address, 1930. With the rock as his pulpit, he clearly enjoys his status in the community, which appears to have grown in his absence. Courtesy Mitchell Library, State Library of New South Wales, MLMSS 4503, add-on 1822.

their land, endured far longer than Mrs. Fraser's. She was a captive not of force but of love — of familial ties and deeply held landscape associations.

Born in 1920, one of Fred and Ethel's children, Olga Miller, became an Indigenous historian and environmentalist, as well as a political activist who fought for the Badjala people's rights to Fraser Island. As with certain children of the intermarried Cherokees, some of the children born of some Australian intermarriages became outspoken advocates for the Indigenous branch of their people. Olga Miller wrote, "Everybody's got two grandfathers. I was lucky as I had an Aboriginal one and a non-Aboriginal one. So that is why I know both sides of the story. On the colonizing side of her family, J. B. Gribble, who was my mother's father, was born in Redruth, Cornwall, and her mother, the Honourable Mary Bulmer, was born in Hull, in Yorkshire."[39] Her references to "Uncle Ernest" suggest a reconciliation had taken place between Ernest and her mother.

JOHN ROSS AND MARY BRYAN STAPLER

After their Philadelphia wedding, Mary and John settled into their home in the Cherokee territory, which became known for its sophistication,

FIG. 68. At Gribble Point, Yarrabah. Captioned "Rev. E. R. Gribble"—apparently by the reverend himself—the photo shows Gribble standing with two elders. The significant rock behind them has been adorned with English lettering to spell out "Yarrabah" for a literate world. Courtesy Mitchell Library, State Library of New South Wales, MLMSS 4503, add-on 1822.

FIG. 69. Gribble's grave, Yarrabah, with Milton Cameron on the left and the curator of the Menmuny Museum, Bradley Higgins, on the right. Photo by author.

elegance, and hospitality. As planned, Mary's sister Sarah moved to the Indian Territory. John Ross and Mary had two children, a girl called Annie Bryan, born in 1845, and a boy known as John Junior, born in 1847. Mary's father, John Stapler, visited Rose Cottage to see his infant granddaughter in 1846 and then returned regularly after that. He died during his visit to the family in the Indian Territory in 1858. One of Mary's brothers and her sister-in-law Sandra Levy — the captivating woman Ross had thought could not live in a "wigwam" — also moved to Park Hill near Tahlequah, Indian Territory (after 1866, Oklahoma) and in 1851 Sandra Levy's husband set up a trading business with John Ross.

Despite having family in the Cherokee Nation, Mary pined for her husband and was lonely when he was away. The emotional work of John's love letters contrasts with the seriousness of his weighty political correspondence. He was the love of Mary's life. At times Mary portrayed herself sentimentally, as if a character in a romantic novel. A letter from John "cast sunshine around my heart & dispelled the clouds that had gathered there." Like Harriett, she appreciated her acceptance by the Cherokee Nation: "The land over

FIG. 70. *Children of John and Mary Ross*, by Samuel B. Waugh, ca. 1847–48 (my estimate). The dark-eyed children of Annie Bryan and John Junior are featured wearing fashionable attire in a romantic outdoor setting, a park-like landscape with colorful flowers and picturesque mountains in the background. Landscape panoramas became very popular as entertainment in the 1840s, especially when moving landscapes were produced. Annie holds a basket of flowers, and her glorious plumed hat is strewn on the grass below. With a strong resemblance to her mother, she looks pert, holding the viewer's eye. The dreamy boy may be admiring his sister or perhaps looking off into another destiny. The care taken with the children's grooming reveals their mother's close attention to detail. The choice of clothing is intriguing. In apparent celebration of his Old World Scottish ancestry, John Junior wears a red Ross tartan, reflecting what his father, John Ross, wore as a boy. Courtesy Gilcrease Museum, Tulsa OK.

which my dear Husband ruled & ... the warm welcome I the lonely white stranger received far from my childhood's home."⁴⁰ In her new residence, her whiteness may have been exceptional, but she became deeply homesick when away from it, such as when she stayed in Philadelphia during the 1860s to escape the Civil War. Nostalgic about her first arrival, she tried to imagine another home for John and herself together. She reassured him that any home with him, with the blessings of "true Christian love," would be "Home sweet Home," whether "an elegant Manson or a simple little Cottage." She signed off "with a Heart full of Love I am thy Devoted Wife."⁴¹

John did not retire from his post as chief, and Mary consequently endured many long absences worrying for his safety. There is palpable affection in Mary's later letters. Ross also wrote tenderly to his "little wife."⁴² During the dangers of the Civil War, Ross traveled between Washington, Philadelphia, and Delaware to conduct treaty business. The couple enjoyed the advantage of being able to visit family members in her hometown of Wilmington. Mary and her sister Sarah remained close, John referring to them as like Siamese twins. John still had an eye for the beautiful ladies promenading in the cities but wrote that he yearned only to be in the "Circle of My Dear Ones."⁴³

Using her daughter's birthday as an opportunity to look back, Mary writes a sentimental letter to John: "Does it not seem strange nineteen years since Papa & Mama received from their Heavenly Father Papa's Baby, a precious Gift indeed, a little Squaw was added to thy treasurers, [sic] as good Dr. Gibbons said when he gave thee information of her arrival." Mary recalled the attending doctor's comments to her husband with amusement. As a letter writer, she still enjoyed inserting wry allusions about the stereotypical "historical Indian" and "white man"; for example, "Well my dear Husband how is thee & they Brother of the Forest Land getting along. I hope the Red & Pale faces will act together as friendly & well, as in the times of my good old Quaker ancestor, William Penn."⁴⁴

Self-consciously alluding to the transnational play of their intermarriage, she references the sovereignty negotiations of the treaty-making figure of William Penn. Wanting to write herself into a hopeful history, she identifies herself with the idealized exemplar of the "good colonizer." Despite having been ostracized by the Quakers due to her marriage, by the mid-1860s she is said to have talked Ross into giving up his slaves. Although the phrase

"Brother of the Forest" had long been used in formal diplomatic language to refer to Indian people, it was revived among the reading public by the Pequot William Apess's book *A Son of the Forest*.[45] Referring to Native American people as "sons" and "brothers" of the land might today appear quaint; however, the term embodied an important assertion of customary ownership and kinship based upon cross-generational inheritance of land. It also implied relatedness to other Indigenous tribes, if not to all souls, of whatever color, who were now sharing the country.

In working the binary stereotypes of "Red & Pale faces," Mary knew that neither Ross nor their children could be classified simply by such color terms. When John Ross commented on the "coldness" of a church service that he attended, he added that he enjoyed seeing the children, who were "like a beautiful Boquet [*sic*]."[46] It helped that their networks crossed frontier boundaries, especially during the Civil War. On June 4, 1864, John Ross states that he is grateful for "our wonderful & Providential escape from danger, & that I am permitted to have a home in this peaceful location [Philadelphia]." When Ross receives Mary's letter written on their daughter's birthday, he is in Washington City at Willard's Hotel. On June 6, 1864, he replies, "I will remember the first words uttered by our darling Child [Annie B. Ross] in this place, years ago, that have passed away & never again to return. When looking up with eyes of celestial blue into my face, and sweetly said 'Papa's Baby'! As I cannot be with you kiss our beloved 'Annie Brian Ross' for her Dear Father — and present her with the small token of remembrance for her Birthday gift!"[47]

The couple would celebrate just one more birthday for their daughter, as Mary Bryan Stapler Ross died of "lung congestion" on July 20, 1865, age forty. Ross agreed that she be buried in the Wilmington & Brandywine Cemetery. John Ross died a year afterward, in August 1866. He was buried near his wife's grave in Wilmington. The Cherokee Nation later requested that his remains be moved to the Ross Cemetery at Park Hill, Oklahoma, where they now lay.

John Ross's will bequeathed his wife's treasured keepsakes to their children, nieces, and staff. "Old nurse" Maud Jones got "my Wifes Black Bombazine dress," while niece Anna B. Stapler received money and "my second Wifes Breast pin with her Mothers hair in it" and another niece her bracelet with "a likeness of Annie," their daughter. As well as equal shares in the spoils of the Ross estate, John Ross left his son John Ross Junior "my Wifes large gold pencil," while his daughter Annie B. Ross received jewels, two gold watches, and his wife's "marriage ring." We might recall that Ross had punned that would be the "gem that is to be a bosom Companion for me all the days of my life!"[48] Almost — but she left first.

Not discriminating on the basis of gender, John left both the sons and daughter of his first marriage the significant cash sums of $5,000 each. Some of these inheritances included money still owing from protracted legal settlements with the United States. As well as inheriting substantial real estate in Wilmington, Delaware, "to be Equally held or divided," John and Mary's son John Ross and daughter Annie received all the couple's personal papers. This is another step in the story of how their correspondence, including the flowers from Dolley Madison, managed to survive destruction and to tell their love story today.[49] The artifact of the wedding roses, the flowers, was passed down by the generations of the Ross family, and later its biological matter was allowed to stain the protective papers of an archival file in Tulsa, Oklahoma.

Annie Bryan Ross married Leonidas Dodson; she died at the age of thirty-one and was buried at Ross Cemetery, Park Hill. Her brother John Ross Junior married Caroline C. Lazalear and had three children: Addie Roche, Leonidas Cookman, and Mary Ross. All lived in the Cherokee territory.[50] Members of the Boudinot family and the Ross family also intermarried, helping to smooth the fatal feuding between the two families.

Love songs and hymns travel routes between the eastern Cherokees in the Smoky Mountains and the western Cherokees, from Scotland, England, Ireland, and New England. They link diasporas that make for two-way traffic, albeit on different sides of the road, as well as different hemispheres of the world. Marriage routes connect along Australia's Pacific coast, intersecting with the ships, railways, roads, and flight paths of modernity. Meanwhile, the elongated tentacles of family connections spread all the way up to the far north, to Yarrabah in the tropics.

Hopefully this book has shed a few perpendicular shafts of light across the seas and across the marital middle grounds of colonizer nations. In North America and Australia, mutual attractions between First Nations' and colonizers' aspirations undid ambitions toward pure, "perfect" whiteness. But in the case of some people, not in aspirants' godly aims to perfect themselves or their future nation.

Transnational marriage and transnational families ruptured colonialism's longed-for neatness. Ever-expanding constellations of peoples open into the future of humanity. Never mono, never the "perfect sovereignty" fantasized about by settler states, instead the connections across colonizer borders and across generations spiral outward to reproduce the polygamous sovereignties that are settler colonialism today. Across expanded landscapes and new global hemispheres, Indigenous sovereignty became mobile and portable. Some of the pieces of its jigsaw puzzle reside in the lost memory boxes of families of the colonizer classes, where alliances of privilege, wealth, and that uncategorizable concept — love — became mixed up with wills, property, and shame.[51] Unacknowledged, often hidden and rejected by family and officially removed by the state, many children of transnational unions grew up outside any family and outside the narratives of an inclusive nation. All the while, intimate frontiers were permeable and acted as bridges between nations.

Traveling across the date line between North America and Australia, the transnational hemispheres of intermarriage were not ephemeral, quick-passing grounds. When marriages traversed nations, on the level of families, they changed the constitutions of the nations themselves. And, by keeping family memory alive, they leave within these nations the seeds of future contestations over sovereignty. Under national flags of the same color, and under different stars and different flags, people will comingle. In doing so, they will also continue to contest the sovereignties of nations placed side by side like new neighbors. Here we see them located diagonally, in different hemispheres. On different sides of the globe, these distant neighbors were implicated in historical dramas never entirely distinct from each other.

With this history in mind, there never can be a "last of his tribe" and "last of her tribe." In the larger national family, in ways metaphorical and embodied, nations have been entangled, enmeshed, ruptured, partitioned off, and then entwined again. In these significant crossings, worlds had come together and been wedded. It was individual people who wedded worlds. And different stakeholders who attempted to make them illicit, to wrench the couples apart. Often shaky, and often painful, the cross-colonizing marriage nonetheless endures. Another stop on a long human journey, illicit love meant that these nations had fresh faces, fresh "complexions" and constitutions. The unifying principle of marriage tends to create new beginnings. Fueled by an enduring alchemy of transformative connection, Indigenous sovereignty looks unlikely to ever reach a final full stop.

NOTES

ABBREVIATIONS

ABCFM — American Board of Commissioners for Foreign Missions
ABM — Australian Board of Missions
AIATSIS — Australian Institute of Aboriginal and Torres Strait Islander Studies
QSA — Queensland State Archives

PREFACE

1. Shyrock and Smail, *Deep History*; Smail, *On Deep History and the Brain*.
2. Folder 5326.290, Ross Collection, Gilcrease Museum.
3. For more discussion of this work, see Schoelwer, "Absent Other," 138–39, 157; McGrath, "White Brides."
4. McGrath, "Negotiating Entanglement," 76–108.
5. During the twentieth century, Aboriginal political leaders formed political alliances and networks with African American rights movements. Maynard, *Fight for Liberty and Freedom*.
6. Laurie and McGrath, "I Was a Drover Once Myself", 89. See also McGrath, *Born in the Cattle*.
7. Hokari, *Gurindji Journey*; F. Hardy, *Unlucky Australians*; McGrath, "Modern Stone-Age Slavery."

INTRODUCTION

1. This study draws upon a rich scholarship on the history of intermarriage. See, for example, Van Kirk, *Many Tender Ties*; Brown, *Strangers in Blood*; Pascoe, *What Comes Naturally*; Hurtado, *Intimate Frontiers*; Ellinghaus, *Taking Assimilation to Heart*; Jacobs, *White Mother to a Dark Race*; Moran, *Interracial Intimacy*; Hodes, *Sex, Love, Race*; Salesa, *Racial Crossings*; Bouvier, *Women and the Conquest of California*. On hybridity and

multiraciality, see Kennedy, *Interracial Intimacies*; Ifekwunigwe, *"Mixed Race" Studies*; Johnson, *Mixed Race America and the Law*; J. Davis, *Who Is Black?*; Spickard, *Mixed Blood*. Nash, "Hidden History of Mestizo America," valuably analyzed the obscured story of mixed race in America. Australian materials include Haskins and Maynard, "Sex, Race and Power"; J. Huggins and Blake, "Protection or Persecution?"; Grimshaw and McGregor, *Collisions of Cultures and Identities*; Grimshaw, "Interracial Marriages and Colonial Regimes"; Wanhalla, *Matters of the Heart*; Hyde, *Empires, Nations, and Families*.

2. When I write "our" or "we" I refer to you, the readers, and myself and do not intend to privilege or preclude any groups of people.

3. James Merrell entitled his book *The Indians' New World*, and this perspective is in keeping with Axtell, *Natives and Newcomers*.

4. Wolfe, "Settler Colonialism"; Wolfe, "Land, Labor, and Difference." See also Veracini, *Settler Colonialism*. The words "elimi/nation" and "miscege/nation" both manage to semantically swallow the "nation" inside of them. Wolfe, "Nation and MiscegeNation."

5. Thelen, "Of Audiences, Borderlands, and Comparisons"; Tyrrell, "Reflections on the Transnational Turn"; Limerick, "Turnerians All"; Limerick, "Going West"; Blackhawk, *Violence over the Land*.

6. *Merriam-Webster.com*, s.v. "nation-state," http://www.merriam-webster.com/dictionary/nation-state.

7. Chakrabarty, *Habitations of Modernity*.

8. Ford, *Settler Sovereignty*.

9. T.U.S. Constitution, preamble and article 1, section 2, section 8, at "Charters of Freedom," http://www.archives.gov/exhibits/charters/constitution_transcript.html.

10. Witgen, *Infinity of Nations*, 189.

11. The 1988 Bicentenary may have been a turning point.

12. A debate ensued regarding the Racial Discrimination Act in Australia.

13. See Heiss, *Am I Black Enough for You?*

14. Kinnane, *Shadow Lines*, is an excellent Australian example.

15. Ballantyne and Burton, *Moving Subjects*; Tyrrell, "American Exceptionalism"; Lake and Reynolds, in *Drawing the Global Color Line*, argue for the importance of race in nation-building projects. Adopting a transnational approach, they describe North America and Australia in the early twentieth century as white man's country. They compare the different triangulations of race in Australia and North America and valuably assess the extent to which Australia's national planning was influenced by observations of America's slave legacies. Jacobs, *White Mother to a Dark Race*, and Ellinghaus, *Taking Assimilation to Heart*, emphasize the importance of class and education in the contrasting marital trajectories of white women who married Indigenous men in Australia and the United States. Smithers, *Science, Sexuality and Race*, is a transnational study that explores the science of race and how it affected ideas around gender in both North America and Australia. See also Ford, *Settler Sovereignty*.

16. Historian David Armitage has been a liberating force in this regard, arguing the value of transtemporal approaches to tackle significant phenomena in very different time periods. See Armitage, "What's the Big Idea?" See also Aslanian, Chaplin, McGrath, and Mann, "How Size Matters."
17. These constitute a significant history in themselves that warrant further study. See Hannah, "Constituting Marriage."
18. Cott, *Public Vows*; McGrath, "White Brides."
19. Attitudes are changing rapidly and we may see more change shortly, if other western countries are any indication.
20. Rifkin's analysis in *When Did Indians Become Straight?* provides a useful critique of liberal concepts of marriage in settler colonialism.
21. Rifkin, *When Did Indians Become Straight?*, cautions here about the use of the liberal contract.
22. Stoler, "Tense and Tender Ties." See also McClintock, *Imperial Leather*; Stoler, "Sexual Affronts and Racial Frontiers"; Levine, *Gender and Empire*; Levine, *British Empire*; Van Kirk, *Many Tender Ties*.
23. Ballantyne and Burton, *Bodies in Contact*; Ballantyne and Burton, *Moving Subjects*.
24. For a summary of the significant debate engendered, see Scott, "Unanswered Questions."
25. For example, see Stoler, *Along the Archival Grain*; Stoler, *Haunted by Empire*; Stoler, *Race and the Education of Desire*.
26. This has been a question of emphasis. Lisa Ford's excellent analysis in *Settler Sovereignty* focuses upon colonizing impositions, as do Ann L. Stoler's stimulating and influential works.
27. Note that Hyde, *Empires, Nations, and Families*, makes breakthroughs in following families across frontiers, as does Graybill, *Red and the White*.
28. McCarthy, *Marriage in Medieval England*; Hay, "Use of the Term 'Great Britain,'" 61.
29. Plane, *Colonial Intimacies*, 179. Plane also deals with some seventeenth-century cases. Plane's insights are further discussed in chapter 7.
30. Uncas married at least six women, including Pequots and other powerful Algonquins. L. Brooks, *Common Pot*, 60–61.
31. Colonial Marriages Act (28 & 29 Vic. C64), June 29, 1865, included in Pol/J17, QSA. This was the same year that the Queensland Marriage Act would come into effect. The act declared this as "any authority competent to make laws for any of Her Majesty's possessions abroad."
32. For summaries of legislation, see Pascoe, "Race, Gender and Intercultural Relations"; Pascoe, *What Comes Naturally*; Hartog, *Man and Wife in America*; Moran, *Interracial Intimacy*.
33. Following Queensland's example, after federation in 1901 other, less intensively developed northernmost states also introduced regulations that restricted marriage on the basis of race.

34. It was an extremely slim minority that saw this decision eventuate. There is much debate over the 1831 and 1832 rulings in law. See Sturm, *Blood Politics*, 62–63; Yarbrough, *Race and the Cherokee Nation*, chaps. 1–2.
35. Australia introduced Operation Sovereign Borders in 2013 to prevent refugee arrivals by boat.
36. Pioneering work in comparative and transnational history has been undertaken by scholars such as Goodman, *Gold Seeking*; Tyrrell, *True Gardens of the Gods*; Ellinghaus, *Taking Assimilation to Heart*; Smithers, *Science, Sexuality and Race*; Jacobs, *White Mother to a Dark Race*.
37. Also in the way they think of their nations today. Over the past twenty years, Australia has placed increasing emphasis on Indigenous history in a retelling of its national story. This has contributed to changes in the law. A referendum in 1967 saw Aboriginal people finally recognized as full citizens who would be counted in the census. After centuries of struggle, limited Aboriginal land rights were introduced in the 1970s. In 1992 the *Mabo* judgment of the High Court of Australia recognized native title rights. A national apology to the stolen generations followed in 2008. The national consciousness raising has been tremendous, but it met with a backlash that called for a return to less-discomforting historical narratives. Generally only casino wealth gets Native Americans into the national newspapers. For a summary of legislation and recent developments, see McGrath, *Contested Ground*, chap. 1; Attwood, *Telling the Truth*.
38. Although American Indians secured treaties, annuities, autonomy, and national recognition, they suffered terrible dispossessions, disease, hunger, and much cruelty. And today, along with Aboriginal Australians, they suffer disadvantages politically, economically, socially, and in health and well-being. Sure, there are some exceptions, such as where Indigenous rights can generate casino or mining income. But amid a range of historical legacies, problems of alcohol, domestic violence, and poor educational and employment opportunities engender tough struggles. By the same token, many Indigenous people are high achievers inside and outside their communities. They value the exercise of autonomy over family lives, the closeness of community, and various forms of rich cultural knowledge, attributes, and lifestyles that are the envy of other peoples.
39. Heard, Birrell, and Khoo, "Intermarriage between Indigenous and Non-indigenous Australians"; Schmidt, "American Indian Identity and Blood Quantum." As a demographic trend, this is explained as offering improved economic opportunities and upward mobility for the Indigenous partner.
40. Keller, Lissitzyn, and Mann, *Creation of Rights of Sovereignty*; Pemberton, *Sovereignty*; J. Hoffman, *Gender and Sovereignty*; V. Deloria and Lytle, *Nations Within*; Shinoda, *Re-examining Sovereignty*; Bruyneel, *Third Space of Sovereignty*.
41. Rifkin, *When Did Indians Become Straight?*, 7. He uses analogies that draw upon the "logics and structures of the settler state."
42. Chakrabarty, *Provincializing Europe*; L. Brooks, *Common Pot*, xxxv; Bruyneel, *Third Space of Sovereignty*. In one of the earliest migrations of *Homo sapiens* out of Africa, the

Australians arrived up to 60,000 BP (before the present). Dates for early Indigenous Americans continue to be debated but some date arrivals at 15,000 BP.
43. Barker, *Sovereignty Matters*, 1; Bruyneel, *Third Space of Sovereignty*.
44. Moreton-Robinson, *Sovereign Subjects*, 2. See also Fixico, *Call for Change*.
45. On "country," see Rose, *Dingo Makes Us Human*, 119. This belonging "to" concept has been debated in regard to issues of legal ownership. Individual or collective ownership is complex; land cannot be traded, bought, or sold. Rights to its use can be negotiated. Land rights and Native title debates in Australia still imply a different kind of connection with different degrees of duty and responsibility toward sites in a landscape. The management of a place, or the higher status of being its "boss," denote degrees of ownership. Conception dreamings, birth dreamings, and much more create layers of relationship with land. Landmarks denote the range of country, but there are no linear boundaries or other markers.
46. A. P. Elkin was one of main proponents of this expression; see also various works by C. and R. M. Berndt.
47. Heidi Altman and Thomas Belt, "Moving around in the Room: Cherokee language, Worldview, and Memory," in Huber, *Museums and Memory*, 227–33; also available at http://newfoundpress.utk.edu//pubs/museums/chp11.pdf.
48. For a study of families across the western frontier, see Hyde, *Empires, Nations, and Families*.
49. Such historians include Elizabeth Povinelli, Kat Ellinghaus, Margaret Jacobs, Lisa Ford, and Greg Smithers.
50. D. Allen, *We the People*, 95–98.
51. Wanhalla, *In/Visible Sight*.
52. Belmessous, "Assimilation and Racialism"; Sleeper-Smith, *Indian Women and French Men*; DuVal, "Indian Intermarriage and Métissage"; Murphy, *Gathering of Rivers*.
53. Povinelli, *Empire of Love*, 17.
54. Povinelli, *Empire of Love*, 17, 4, 7.
55. As Cott argues in *Public Vows*, formal marriage meant that private relationships between individuals entered the public purview of state and nation. The complex governance of gender through marriage helped make nations. See also Carter, *Importance of Being Monogamous*; Leneman, "Scottish Case."
56. Jefferson quoted in Fiege, *Republic of Nature*, 99. "Friend of the Indian" was a term used in opposition to the "Indian-haters" who wanted them all dead. Note that, as Rifkin asserts, Jefferson also laid the grounds for later removal policies. Rifkin, *When Did Indians Become Straight?*, esp. 50.
57. See Cott, *Public Vows*; Hartog, *Man and Wife in America*.
58. See the U.S. Declaration of Independence, at "Charters of Freedom," http://www.archives.gov/exhibits/charters/declaration_transcript.html (emphasis added).
59. Jefferson, 1808, quoted in McLoughlin, *Cherokee Renascence*, 33 (emphasis in original). Some colonizer statesmen in North America and New Zealand advocated intermarriage

with Indigenous people as a form of national integration that could build bridges across colonizing ruptures.

60. Gordon-Reed, *Hemingses of Monticello*; Gordon-Reed, *Thomas Jefferson and Sally Hemings*; Gordon-Reed interview.
61. T. Cooper, *Strictures Addressed to James Madison*. Crawford wrote a report on Indian policy recommending intermarriage between Indians and whites. Like Jefferson, he linked private property ownership and marriage as a means to integrate Indians and their lands.
62. T. Cooper, *Strictures Addressed to James Madison*.
63. Alfred Deakin. "Commonwealth Parliamentary Debate: The Case for National Racial Unity," in *Commonwealth Parliamentary Debates*, House of Representatives, September 12, 1901, vol. 4 (excerpts). Making Multicultural Australia, http://www.multicultura laustralia.edu.au/doc/deakin_1.pdf (emphasis in original). See also La Nauze, *Alfred Deakin*, 279–80.
64. Lake, "Brightness of eyes."
65. Controversies over Asian immigration and intermarriage were rife in California, and this and related topics have been admirably dealt with by Hurtado, Bouvier, Castaneda, and others. However, most of these controversies do not coincide with the early nation-defining era that is the focus of this study.
66. McGregor, *Indifferent Inclusion*. Neither groups were free labor, as coercion and a period of enforced contractual obligation were involved. Many Pacific islanders were kidnapped; however, various people later agreed to contracts. Chinese workers were often subject to coercion from moneylenders in their home provinces. Maynard, *True Light and Shade*.
67. For an overview, see Richard Broome, "Victoria," in McGrath, *Contested Ground*, 121–67; Kiernan, *Blood and Soil*, 289.
68. Commonwealth of Australia Constitution Act, Section 51, http://www.austlii.edu.au /cgi-bin/sinodisp/au/legis/cth/consol_act/coaca430/s51.html?stem=0&synonyms =0&query=aboriginal. This clause was amended after a referendum in 1967. Section 25 also precluded members of certain racial groups from voting and being counted in the census.
69. They had to leave their Aboriginality behind, in order for their children to grow up "exempted" from Aboriginal status and all the restrictive state guardianship that this implied.
70. See, for example, Salesa, *Racial Crossings*; Wanhalla, *Matters of the Heart*. New Zealand and Australia could be viewed as twins, but intermarriage history confirms they were not. Indigenous-colonizer intermarriage protocols, the clash of peoples, the cultural protocols, the regulatory laws on each side of colonizing frontiers, the climate, the environment, and the lifeways they allowed could hardly have been more different. Arguably the tackling of intermarriage across the ages significantly contributed to making these nations what they are — siblings whose histories hardly know each other.

As more research is completed, we are starting to see how marital dealings might have differentiated the politics and polity of one nation from another's. See, for example, Salesa, *Racial Crossings*; Wanhalla, *Matters of the Heart*.

71. Shoemaker, *American Indian Population Recovery*, 65–66, 88.
72. Several but not all Cherokee town groups fought on the British side during the Revolutionary War.
73. D. Wilkins and Lomawaima, *Uneven Ground*, 12–19.
74. Department of Natural Resources and Mines, *Guide to Compiling a Connection Report*. See also Mabo and Others v. Queensland (no. 2) (1992), HCA 23 (1992), 175 CLR 1, FC 92/014, High Court of Australia.
75. Captain Cook's 1770 planting of the British flag has taken center stage as an iconic moment of Australian "discovery" and British sovereignty. Others preceded him, with Dutch and other navigators also venturing from Europe to sight parts of the Australian continent. Southeast Asian trepangers from Macassar (now Indonesia) visited the north coast of Australia from at least the 1700s, entering into sexual and labor relationships with Aboriginal women, some of whom relocated to Macassar. From 1788, the British established a settlement at Botany Bay, then Sydney Cove. Although the French arrived only days later, they soon moved on.
76. Fitzmaurice, "Genealogy of Terra Nullius"; Reynolds, *Law of the Land*.
77. Reynolds, *Forgotten War*.
78. Attwood, *Telling the Truth*.
79. Boulware, *Deconstructing the Cherokee Nation*.
80. The dates for what is termed the early American republic, 1776–1861, conform to those used by the *Journal of the Early American Republic* and the Society for Historians of the Early American Republic.
81. Silver, *Our Savage Neighbours*.
82. See L. Brooks, *Common Pot*; DuVal, "Indian Intermarriage and Métissage."
83. Conn, *History's Shadow*.
84. Conforti, *Jonathan Edwards*; Conforti, *Imagining New England*. O'Brien, *Firsting and Lasting*. Recent excavations and scientific testing date Native American occupation to at least 12,500 years BP (before the present). New tests are suggesting much earlier dates.
85. As the perplexing exception, Pocahontas is cast in a conciliatory, heroic foundational narrative. Green, "Pocahontas Perplex"; Faragher, "Custom of the Country."
86. Merrell, *Indians' New World*; Calloway, *New Worlds for All*; Brooks, xxxvii; F. Turner, *Frontier in American History*, 4, xiv.
87. F. Turner, *Frontier in American History*, 4, xiv.
88. In August 2004 the Australian Centre for Indigenous History, Australian National University, held a conference titled "Narrating Frontier Families in Australia and North America" with scholars from Yale University as well as Clara Sue Kidwell from the University of Oklahoma. The documentary film about the journey that followed is Haywood, *Frontier Conversation*.

89. For an excellent summary of issues relating to the history of mestizo and hybrid America, see Nash, "Hidden History of Mestizo America"; Gutiérrez, *When Jesus Came*; Castaneda, "Engendering the History of Alta California."
90. L. Moore and Williams, *True Story of Jimmy Governor*. These murders are well documented and were explained as retaliation for racism. They have become well-known through a novel, nonfiction books, and a film.
91. Pascoe, *What Comes Naturally*, 94. See also Hartog, *Man and Wife in America*.
92. Hyde discusses the problem of naming "the ground" — was it "native ground" or "middle ground"? — in *Empires, Nations, and Families*, 35–39. This represents a quandary in writing histories of settler colonialism.
93. Numerous tribes, with divergent cultural, economic, marital, and family practices, occupied the vast lands of North America. From the seventeenth century, they experienced contrasting colonizing frontiers and intruder demographics.
94. L. Smith, *Decolonizing Methodologies*; Nakata, *Disciplining the Savages*; Fixico, *Call for Change*.
95. Pratt, *Imperial Eyes*.
96. R. White, *Middle Ground*, 15–16. Although the book carves a space for cross-cultural gender histories, by its conclusion, the intricate world of the actual *pays d'en haut* marital relations is replaced by metaphoric musings. The "*marriage* of alliance and trade" had passed, and the British imperialists then found "*maintaining the marriage*" too expensive. The fur trade era produced societies where multiple collaborations and exchanges took place. But unlike the later settler societies, they were extractive communities whose settlers returned to their homelands.
97. Van Kirk, *Many Tender Ties*; J. Peterson and Brown, *New Peoples*.
98. R. White, *Middle Ground*; Milner et al., "Historian Who Has Changed Our Thinking"; Sleeper-Smith et al., "Forum"; Reynolds, *Other Side of the Frontier*; Attwood, *Telling the Truth*; Klein, *Frontiers of the Historical Imagination*.
99. Pateman, *Sexual Contract*. For a more recent critique of contract theory, see Webber and McLeod, *Between Consenting Peoples*. See also Pateman and Mills, *Contract and Domination*.
100. Cott, *Public Vows*.
101. Halley, "Behind the Law of Marriage."
102. Brook, "Conjugal Body Politic."
103. Outside this period, from the mid-nineteenth century and during the gold rushes, states competed to introduce liberal marriage and divorce regimes in order to attract women to their states. Hartog discusses the complexity of state and federal interests in marriage legislation and also the postrevolutionary cliché of families moving together. He points out that people often moved to escape marriages. Hartog, *Man and Wife in America*, 14, 17, 20, 24, 41–43. He also states that in nineteenth-century America law was defined by the husband's authority and the wife's dependence.

104. Rifkin, *When Did Indians Become Straight?*
105. "Memorial of the Cherokee Nation," cited in Filler and Guttmann, *Removal of the Cherokee Nation*, 46–47; Perdue and Green, *Cherokee Nation and the Trail of Tears*; Prucha, *Great Father*; Scott, "Unanswered Questions"; Jacobs, "Western History," 297–304.
106. Sturm, *Blood Politics*, 2, 24–68. For a range of comparable Cherokee stories, see also Teuton, *Cherokee Stories*. As Yarbrough argues, however, Cherokee race attitudes hardened; see Yarbrough, *Race and the Cherokee Nation*, chap. 3.
107. Sturm, *Blood Politics*; Boulware, *Deconstructing the Cherokee Nation*; Goodwin, *Cherokees in Transition*.
108. For an overview of Pintupi kinship, see Myers, *Pintupi Country, Pintupi Self*, 180–218. Anthropologists refer to "fictive kin" and "fictive kinship," but I do not find those terms helpful. They are meant to identify a category different from biological relationships that westerners would refer to as "blood relations."
109. Stanner, *White Man Got No Dreaming*, 23–40; Poirier, *World of Relationships*.
110. Salesa, *Racial Crossings*; Wanhalla, *In/Visible Sight*; Wanhalla, *Matters of the Heart*.
111. There is a large literature on hybridity, but a relevant introduction is J. Brooks, *Confounding the Color Line*.
112. Nakata, *Disciplining the Savages*; L. Smith, *Decolonizing Methodologies*; Moreton-Robinson, *Talkin' Up to the White Woman*.
113. The Torres Strait Islanders are a culturally distinctive group.
114. Val Cooms discussed this concept in various conversations. Strong scholarly links have been developed thanks to NAISA.
115. Although the appropriate term for Aboriginal social units is much debated, "tribe" does not accurately describe Aboriginal social organization. Generally "clans" or "language groups" or "traditional owners" (TOs) are the terms used in scholarship and law. Increasingly, members describe their larger amalgamations as nations. Meggitt, *Desert People*, which uses the term "tribe," also provides explanations of the marriage and marriageability system common to many Aboriginal groups. Dixon, "Tribes, Languages and Other Boundaries."
116. For more information on research protocols, see "Ethical Protocols," Deepening Histories of Place project, http://www.deepeninghistories.anu.edu.au/ethical-protocols/. The symposium from this project is discussed in McGrath and Jebb, *Long History, Deep Time*. See Read, Peters-Little, and Haebich, *Indigenous Biography and Autobiography*; Johansen and Pritzker, *Encyclopedia of American Indian History*. For the reader, I would suggest that the wealth of recent life writing and autobiographies is the best antidote to this problem.
117. Scholars such as Martha Hodes, Tom Griffiths, Patricia Limerick, Greg Dening, and others have encouraged historians to tell memorable stories.
118. Although the references acknowledge key sources, it is not possible to mention every influence at each moment, and key works are also listed in the bibliography.

119. Although some historians refer to this period as the antebellum era, my use of the term "early national period" follows the practice of key journals in the field.
120. McGrath, *Born in the Cattle*, 145–75.
121. As if offering proof of the doomed race theory, the woman labeled as the "Last Tasmanian," the last "full-blood," Trucaninni, passed away in 1876. Queensland's population, with its Asian, Pacific Islander, and Aboriginal people, did not fit into the white Australian image; the colony was derided as polyglot. They had to be seen to be doing something about another "extinction" and about such admixtures.
122. Many autobiographical works are currently being published by Indigenous authors; however, for obvious reasons, they do cover much more recent time periods. Although I sought out many conversations with people I knew and conducted some of these conversations on tape, the periods under scrutiny meant that this project could not readily explore the participants' oral memory. Some recent Aboriginal autobiographies have exposed the secrets of white pastoral families in other Australian states. Morgan, *My Place*, describes a journey of identity discovery and shameful sexual histories. See also Camfoo, *Love against the Law*; Govor, *My Dark Brother*; Tonkin and Landon, *Jackson's Track*; Kinnane, *Shadow Lines*; Ellinghaus, "Absorbing the Aboriginal Problem"; Haag, "From the Margins to the Mainstream."
123. Hodes demonstrates her commitment to balancing the personal narrative with analysis in *Sea Captain's Wife*. See also Hodes, "Reflections"; Hodes, "Four Episodes." We have also discussed this in Curthoys and McGrath, *How to Write History*; Griffiths, "Poetics and Practicalities;" Curthoys and McGrath, *Writing Histories*; R. Hoffman, Sobel, and Teute, *Through a Glass Darkly*. Dening, *Performances*, has been particularly inspiring;
124. See Australian Human Rights Commission, *Bringing Them Home Report*.

1. HARRIETT GOLD AND ELIAS BOUDINOT

1. A preliminary version of parts of this chapter appeared in 1998 in McGrath, "Marriage, Citizenship and Nation," and in 2002 in McGrath, "Negotiating Entanglement." Gabriel, *Elias Boudinot*, remains an extremely valuable biography. Theresa Strouth Gaul has since edited an excellent compendium entitled *To Marry an Indian*. My citations from correspondence are from the original letters in the Hermann Vaill Collection, Sterling Library at Yale, unless otherwise indicated. Sometimes additional references are made to Gaul's volume to facilitate ease of access for future researchers. As John Demos's *The Heathen School: A Story of Hope and Betrayal in the Age of the Early Republic* appeared after my manuscript writing was completed, it was not used here.

The nomenclature I use in references to the letters generally follows the letter or a standard name adopted in correspondence. The name "Boudinot" was also sometimes spelled "Boudinott" — at least this is the spelling transcribed from his signature in various official transcriptions from the 1830s. Perhaps this was to indicate the Cherokee pronunciation or to distinguish him from the Bible Society president Elias Boudinot.

Harriett's name is spelled "Harriet" by close relations and in different sources, but she usually signed her own name with a double "t." I have followed the most common spelling, "Harriett."

2. Gabriel, in *Elias Boudinot*, states the pair were four years apart; others say eighteen months. Gaul, *To Marry an Indian*, 18; Parins, *Elias Cornelius Boudinot*, 7; T. Wilkins, *Cherokee Tragedy*, 151; Gaul, *To Marry an Indian*, 135.
3. In many of his letters, Boudinot signs his name as spelled here. In official documents of the Cherokee Nation, the name is often spelled "Boudinott." Because he was a member of the Watie family, some still referred to him as Buck Watie. His taking of this name is discussed later in this chapter.
4. See Conforti, *Imagining New England*; Conforti, *Jonathan Edwards*, chap. 1–3.
5. Harriett to Rev. Vaill and sisters, June 25, 1825, Box 1, MS 519, Vaill Collection. In citing letters, I have used the most prominent dates. Sometimes notes were added over a few days, and the receipt date is sometimes inserted too.
6. Marini, "Hymnody as History."
7. Harriett to Brother and Sister, June 25, 1825, Box 1, MS 519, Vaill Collection. In the original letter, the letters "M. S." stand for Mission School.
8. Harriett to Brother and Sister, June 25, 1825, Box 1, MS 519, Vaill Collection. Also cited in Gabriel, *Elias Boudinot*, 79. The scene-setting details are contained in the letter itself. See also Gaul, *To Marry an Indian*, 87, who quotes a similar line from Wesley and Wesley, *Hymns and Sacred Poems*.
9. Many Aboriginal Australians share a similar belief.
10. Daggett, *Inauguration Address*.
11. Harriett to Brother and Sister, June 25, 1825, Box 1, MS 519, Vaill Collection.
12. Harriett to Brother and Sister, June 25, 1825, Box 1, MS 519, Vaill Collection (emphasis in original).
13. Theodore Gold referred to "the moral character of the people, and especially of the youth; many of them, more than almost in any other society, were professors of religion. The youth of the society were then unusually sober and promising, and many of them were, more than in most other places, informed in books, and had a respectable library of their own, most of which books were chosen by their pastor." Gold, *Historical Records*, 82. On lynching, Hodes explains how members of southern communities bashed those accused of sexual offenses across the color line; although she refers to cases in the 1820s, lynching was more common after the 1850s. Hodes, *White Women, Black Men*, 58.
14. Harriett to Brother and Sister, June 25, 1825, Box 1, MS 519, Vaill Collection.
15. Gaul, *To Marry an Indian*, 1–2. Gaul argues that brother Stephen's letter was more of an incitement.
16. Quoted in Perdue, *Cherokee Editor*, 7.
17. Dwight, *Memoirs of Henry Obookiah*; Gabriel, *Elias Boudinot*, 36–37.
18. Conforti, *Imagining New England*, 181.

19. "American Board of Commissioners for Foreign Missions — Overview 1910–1985," finding aid, Congregational Library and Archives, http://www.14beacon.org/finding-aids/ABCFMOverview; Andrew, *From Revivals to Removal*.
20. Grimshaw, *Paths of Duty*; Schreiner, *Passionate Beechers*. Later in 1826, the Foreign Mission School was permanently closed. Lyman Beecher's talented daughter Harriet Beecher Stowe later came to epitomize high-achieving New Englanders.
21. The works of the divinity scholar Jonathan Edwards and his disciple David Brainerd were deeply influential, documenting a history of conversions and American revivals. The religious native son of the Connecticut Valley, Edwards was lauded as "god's chief instrument of all born in this land . . . for restoring prosperity to our American Sion." His work could "redeem the nation, the church, the age to which he belonged." The notion of disinterested benevolence in *The Life of Brainerd* and an impulse toward evangelical revivalism prevailed. See Conforti, *Jonathan Edwards*, 27.
22. See coverage in *Niles Weekly Register* (Baltimore), July 9, 1825, 298; *Eastern Argus* (Portland ME), July 14, 1825, 1. According to *Webster's* dictionary (1972), "machinery" can be "the means by which something is kept in action or a desired result is obtained.". In this case, he implies that intermarriage was an intentional "civilizing" or "Christianizing" strategy.
23. Sarah and John had become acquainted when he was taken into the school steward's home, where Sarah, the steward's daughter, assisted in nursing him in his sickbed.
24. Gabriel, *Elias Boudinot*, 91; Gaul, *To Marry an Indian*, 2–3.
25. Quoted in Gabriel, *Elias Boudinot*, 87–88.
26. Mary to Rev. Hermann Vaill, July 19, 1825, Box 1, MS 519, Vaill Collection.
27. Mary to Rev. Hermann Vaill, July 19, 1825, Box 1, MS 519, Vaill Collection; Gaul, *To Marry an Indian*, 105.
28. Vaill to Harriett, June 29, 1825, Box 1, MS 519, Vaill Collection.
29. Vaill to Harriett, June 29, 1825, Box 1, MS 519, Vaill Collection.
30. Dwight, *Memoirs of Henry Obookiah*.
31. Harriett to Dear Brothers and Sisters, June 25, 1825, in Gaul, *To Marry an Indian*, 85.
32. Brinsmade to Dear Sister, June 29, 1825, Box 1, MS 519, Vaill Collection.
33. Brinsmaid [*sic*] to Hermann Vaill, July 14, 1825; and Mary to H. Vaill and Sister, July 14, 1825, Box 1, MS 519, Vaill Collection (emphasis in original).
34. The closeness of sisterly and familial bonds and the amount of time spent among extended family is explored in Smith-Rosenberg, "Female World of Love and Ritual," esp. 12–14. The theme also emerges clearly in Gold family letters, especially Harriett to Brother and Sister, January 2, 1826, Box 1, MS 519, Vaill Collection, in which she recognizes the pain of leaving her four sisters, who live in and around Connecticut.
35. Mary to Vaill, July 17, 1825, Box 1, MS 519, Vaill Collection.
36. Mary to Vaill, July 17, 1825, Box 1, MS 519, Vaill Collection.
37. "The pie crust was pretty short . . . we may keep away from his house. . . . We are neither frightened nor angry." Harriett to Hermann, July 1825; see also Vaill to Mary, August 2, 1825, Box 1, MS 519, Vaill Collection.

38. Gaul, *To Marry an Indian*, 25–26, 40–43.
39. Vaill to Mary Brinsmade, August 2, 1825, Box 1, MS 519, Vaill Collection (emphasis in original). For a comparable religious tract, see *Poor Sarah*.
40. Hermann Vaill to sister Mary, August 2, 1825, Box 1, MS 519, Vaill Collection.
41. Daniel Brinsmade to Herman and Flora Gold Vaill, June 29, 1825, Box 1, MS 519, Vaill Collection.
42. H. L. Vaill to Harriett, June 29, 1825, Box 1, MS 519, Vaill Collection.
43. Cott, "Passionlessness," 227. Certain Cherokee brides embraced western-style marriage and its symbolism, one wearing "white cambric" and her husband "a clean northern domestic suit," as noted in the *Cherokee Phoenix*, May 21, 1828.
44. See Cott, *Bonds of Womanhood*, xiii.
45. Hermann Vaill to Harriett, August 22, 1823, Box 1, MS 519, Vaill Collection. See also Gaul, *To Marry an Indian*, 79.
46. Hermann L. Vaill to Harriett Gold, [ca. April 1823], Box 1, MS 519, Vaill Collection (emphasis in original).
47. Harriett to Hermann, [June–July 1825], Box 1, MS 519, Vaill Collection.
48. Box 1, MS 519, Vaill Collection. Boudinot wrote to Flora and Harriett's brother Stephen too.
49. Vaill to Mary, August 2, 1825, Box 1, MS 519, Vaill Collection.
50. Hermann to Mary, August 2, 1825, Box 1, MS 519, Vaill Collection. Vaill's dire warnings proved correct. The local newspaper, under the editorship of Isaiah Bunce, was vehemently opposed to missionaries. The Foreign Mission School did close soon afterward, though church authorities denied that intermarriage was the cause.
51. Herman Vaill to Mary Gold Brinsmade, August 2, 1825, Box 1, MS 519, Vaill Collection (emphasis in original).
52. Flora to Rev Hermann Vaill, with postscript from Harriett, [September 19, 1825], Box 1, MS 519, Vaill Collection; Gaul, *To Marry an Indian*, 34.
53. For example, see Kenslea, *Sedgwicks in Love*.
54. Ellinghaus, *Taking Assimilation to Heart*, describes how white women married for assimilation purposes in the late nineteenth century.
55. Hermann Vaill to sister Mary, August 2, 1825; and Brinsmaid [*sic*] to Hermann Vaill, September 14, 1825, Box 1, MS 519, Vaill Collection (emphasis in original).
56. Litwack, *North of Slavery*, 3.
57. Public knowledge of this endorsement was widespread. Evarts referred to how the "President or Secretary of War recognized intermarriages with Indians as a means of promoting their improvement"; *Brainerd Journal* (Cherokee territory), 18.3.1, vol. 4, ABCFM Archives, Houghton Library. See also T. Cooper, *Strictures Addressed to James Madison*, v.
58. Harriett to Hermann Vaill, [1825], Box 1, MS 519, Vaill Collection. This usage was popular in church literature of the day, including Dwight, *Memoirs of Henry Obookiah*, and in letters of missionaries; 18.3–18.8, ABCFM Archives, Houghton Library.

59. Catherine Gold to Herman Vaill, Box 1, MS 519, Vaill Collection. Boudinot [Cherokee], *Address to the Whites*.
60. Catherine Gold to Hermann Vaill, [postmarked July 18, 1825], Box 1, MS 519, Vaill Collection (emphasis added).
61. Saks, "Representing Miscegenation Law."
62. Catherine Gold to Hermann Vaill, Sabbath, July, Box 1, MS 519, Vaill Collection (emphasis in original).
63. Flora Gold to Rev. Hermann Vaill, [postmarked September 19, 1825]; and Harriett to Brother and Sister, January 2, 1826, Box 1, MS 519, Vaill Collection.
64. Intermarriage by missionary men was strongly discouraged and those who partook were ostracized. This was probably why they were required to choose a bride to marry before departing the United States. Grimshaw, *Paths of Duty*.
65. Harriett to Brother and Sister, June 25, 1825, Box 1, MS 519, Vaill Collection.
66. Mary Brinsmade to Brothers and Sisters, July 14, 1825, Box 1, MS 519, Vail Collection.
67. Brinsmade to Dear Sister, June 29, 1825, Box 1, MS 519, Vaill Collection; Gaul, *To Marry an Indian*, 89.
68. Flora to Hermann Vaill, September 19, 1825, quoted in Gaul, *To Marry an Indian*, 43, 136.
69. This proclamation was cited in a variety of newspapers and journals, including *Niles Weekly Register*, July 9, 1825, 298; *Eastern Argus*, July 14, 1825, 1. The proclamation is discussed in Harriett to Rev. Vaill and sisters, June 25, 1825, Box 1, MS 519, Vaill Collection.
70. Bunce editorial quoted in Perdue, *Cherokee Editor*, 9; Brinsmade to Brothers and Sisters, July 14, 1825, quoted in Gaul, *To Marry an Indian*, 8–9, 107–8.
71. Harriett to Brother and Sister, January 2, 1826, Box 1, MS 519, Vaill Collection. See also R. Hoffman, Sobel, and Teute, *Through a Glass Darkly*.
72. Mary to Sister, June 29, 1825; and Mary to Hermann Vaill, July 17, 1825, Box 1, MS 519, Vaill Collection.
73. Quoted in Gabriel, *Elias Boudinot*, 79.
74. For example, see Foster, "Connecticut Separate Church."
75. Conforti, *Imagining New England*, 131, 141.
76. Conforti, *Imagining New England*, 197–98, 202.
77. From the last decades of the eighteenth century, organizations such as the Old Colony Club started to glorify the Plymouth arrivals. Lending more authority, Jedidiah Morse's geographies of 1789 and 1793 projected contemporary republican values onto an appealing founding narrative that asserted the "ordered liberty" of "virtual republicans." Mirroring the federal Constitution, by a solemn contract, the pilgrims and "strangers" had developed a "body politic," to form the basis of civil government. Conforti, *Imagining New England*, 178–81. See also Conforti, *Jonathan Edwards*; O'Brien, *Firsting and Lasting*.
78. O'Brien, *Firsting and Lasting*, 1–54.
79. This historical interpretation was helpful in smoothing over their internal conflicts and differences. Conforti, *Imagining New England*, 178–80.

80. For a useful cultural study of women's needlework as a social and industrial activity, see M. Miller, *Needle's Eye*; Cott, *Bonds of Womanhood*.
81. L. Brooks, *Common Pot*, 104–7. See also O'Brien, *Firsting and Lasting*; Conforti, *Imagining New England*; Gold, *Historical Records*, 24–25; H. Russell, *Indian New England*; Oberg, *Dominion and Civility*; Snow, *Archaeology of New England*; Calloway, *New Worlds for All*; Demos, *Unredeemed Captive*; Axtell, *Natives and Newcomers*; Mandell, *Tribe, Race, History*, chap. 2.
82. Gannett, *Distribution of the Common Land*, provides a description of land distribution in Cornwall. See also "History of Cornwall, Connecticut," NY-NJ-CT Botany Online, http://www.nynjctbotany.org/lgtofc/cornwallhistory.html.
83. L. Brooks, *Common Pot*, 64.
84. L. Brooks, *Common Pot*, 58.
85. L. Brooks, *Common Pot*, 64.
86. Quoted in L. Brooks, *Common Pot*, 63.
87. L. Brooks, *Common Pot*, 24.
88. L. Brooks, *Common Pot*, 93.
89. Fisher, *Indian Great Awakening*, 155–57.
90. L. Brooks, *Common Pot*, 52.
91. Mandell, *Tribe, Race, History*; L. Brooks, *Common Pot*, 50–105. Den Ouden, *Beyond Conquest*, also explores Native people's struggles in this region. See also Connecticut State Library, Indians, second series, 1666–1820: Mohegan petitions. A century later, they erected a church to stand in Moshop's footprint, thereby maintaining a foothold on the land and its story; Fisher, *Indian Great Awakening*, 215–17; L. Brooks, *Common Pot*, 104, 106–7.
92. O'Brien, *Firsting and Lasting*; 105–43; Gold, *Historical Records*, 24–25; Keegan and Keegan, *Archaeology of Connecticut*. For valuable overviews of publications in relation to New England Indians and Puritans, see Cave, *Pequot War*; Apess, *Son of the Forest*.
93. Demos, *Circles and Lines*.
94. Cott, *Public Vows*, 11, 59; Boyd, *Elias Boudinot*, 181–82.
95. Cott, *Bonds of Womanhood*; Divine et al., *America, Past and Present*, 313–22; McLoughlin, *Revival, Awakenings, and Reform*; Robert, *American Women in Mission*; Tyrrell, "American Exceptionalism." In the words of Boudinot's biographer Ralph Gabriel, "Their faith ... caused the simple husbandman whose horizon lay only a short distance beyond his acres to vision empires to be conquered by Truth." Gabriel, *Elias Boudinot*, 34.
96. Ridge to Monroe, March 8, 1822, in J. Morse, *A Report to the Secretary of War*, 276.
97. By this time, pathways and a more orderly townscape started to enhance walking as a leisure activity of the middle classes.
98. Much of the Ridge fortune was lost after forced removal, and then John Ridge was assassinated for his role in the Treaty Party. As a widow, Sarah suffered hardship but continued to live beyond her means.

99. "List of Students Attending the Foreign Mission School," January 1, 1820, 1987.042.001, Museum of the Cherokee Indian; 18.3.1, v. 2, ABCFM Archives, Houghton Library. One of the names given him was also spelled "Gallegina." Boudinot was from one of the leading Cherokee families, several of whom were of mixed Anglo-American and Cherokee descent.
100. Foreman, "Foreign Mission School," 243–44.
101. Gordon-Reed, *Hemingses of Monticello*; Gordon-Reed, *Thomas Jefferson and Sally Hemings*.
102. George Washington, "Talk to the Cherokee Nation," August 29, 1796, Miller Center, University of Virginia, http://millercenter.org/president/speeches/detail/3941.
103. Foreman, "Foreign Mission School," 243–44; Walker, *Torchlight to the Cherokees*. See also Meriwether, *Papers of John C. Calhoun*. In 1941, Gabriel said he had no information on the topic. Gabriel, *Elias Boudinot*, 33.
104. Grafton, *Bring Out Your Dead*, 157–58. The French Huguenots were known for their literary circle, the Republic of Letters, in the late seventeenth century.
105. In 1783 Boudinot set aside a day in December as a day of thanksgiving, and he later introduced the idea of an annual public Thanksgiving; Boyd, *Elias Boudinot*, 135, 173. His focus seemed to be on thanking "Almighty God" for their blessings rather than thanking the Indians.
106. Perdue, *Cherokee Editor*, 59. See also the *Missionary Herald*, December 1821.
107. Boyd, *Elias Boudinot*, 29.
108. When Philadelphia became too dangerous, he moved the meetings of the Continental Congress to Princeton. Boyd, *Elias Boudinot*, 256.
109. Boyd, *Elias Boudinot*, 263–71.
110. Boyd, *Elias Boudinot*, 287. In one of his portraits, he wears buckled boots, glossy dark stockings, and rich clothes of velvet and fur. With a square, bald crown framed by thick white hair, he has a kind face that looks capable of strong empathy. Portrait, 1816–18, ascribed to Thomas Sully and Waldo and Jewett, Frick Art Reference Library, in Boyd, *Elias Boudinot*, facing 287. This portrait appears to be one that is currently displayed at Morven House, Princeton. Another portrait, around 1810, by an unidentified artist, presents a sterner, more foreboding face. An 1821 portrait shows him wearing a fetching fur cap; however, he has a more vacant stare and his teeth appear to be missing. This portrait, *Elias Boudinot* by John Vanderlin, is held at the Yale University Art Gallery.
111. Stockton was later captured and retracted his signature, but that is a long story. See Boyd, *Elias Boudinot*; Wigginton, "Late Night Vindication," 227.
112. Boyd, *Elias Boudinot*, 13.
113. Boyd, *Elias Boudinot*, 108; Elias Boudinot to Hannah Stockton Boudinot, May 15, 1789, Special Collections and University Archives, Rutgers University Libraries, available at First Federal Congress Project, George Washington University, http://www.gwu.edu/~ffcp/exhibit/p2/p2_7btext.html. As Boudinot's house is now privately owned, the Stockton house displays various items once in situ in Boudinot's Burlington home.

Boudinot arranged for the freeing of a cruelly treated slave, James Carter, whose family he took in and paid generously. Boyd, *Elias Boudinot*, 276.
114. The painting is entitled *Mrs. Elias Boudinot IV* and is by Charles Willson Peale. It is dated 1784. The curator has simply written that she is holding "a book"; apparently the kind is unknown.
115. Boudinot [IV], *Star in the West*. He and Buck Watie (later Boudinot) were also mutually impressed with each other. See H. James Henderson, "Boudinot, Elias," *American National Biography Online*; Perdue, *Cherokee Editor*, 6.
116. Boyd, *Elias Boudinot*, 259.
117. For example, Teuton, *Cherokee Stories*, 20, 156–57. For information on the decision to use the bald eagle for America's seal, see "Original Design of the Great Seal of the United States," Our Documents, U.S. National Archives and Records Administration, http://www.ourdocuments.gov/doc.php?flash=true&doc=5.
118. If the young Buck Waite had a ride in the family's yellow chariot, he would have been assisted aboard by its footmen in lace and powder. Perhaps Elias had a chance to peer out at the world through its crimson curtains. Servants looked after the affairs of the house and preened the garden. Slavery was banned in New Jersey from 1804, but the phase-out process extended right up until the 1860s.
119. Opposing slavery was a race issue, as Boudinot feared that the United States could become "a second Haytee." As his health increasingly failed during his last years, he urged his nephew Elias Boudinot V to "exert yourself" in the abolitionist cause. "It is the most important question ever before Congress. I consider that our Union depends on it." The Cherokee Elias Boudinot might be permitted to fight for a different cause. Boyd, *Elias Boudinot*, 290, 182–83.
120. Boyd, *Elias Boudinot*, 255, 233, 290, 291, 116. Some authors refer to the young Cherokee requesting permission to use the name; others state that Boudinot conferred it upon him, which appears the stronger, best-supported case. Foreman, "Foreign Mission School," 244; Gabriel, *Elias Boudinot*, 53. It appears that the students had already received Boudinot's patronage prior to this first visit.
121. An orphaned boy whom he raised had also been named after him, Elias Boudinot Caldwell; Boyd, *Elias Boudinot*, 97.
122. Other scholars state that taking up a philanthropist's name was not uncommon among mission Indians, but it does not appear to be a frequent practice. New England children often carried their mother's surname as a middle name, such as Harriett Ruggles Gold, and after marriage they often used their paternal name as part of a series of names. I have seen the New Jersey Boudinot referred to as Elias Stockton Boudinot, but it was not generally the case that men took their wife's name.
123. Although it would appear that Boudinot's visit was to say his farewells, the young Elias complained of ill health himself, manifesting dizziness and headaches. The trip cured him not only of his illness but also of a desire to study theology.
124. Perdue, *Cherokee Editor*, 44–45.

125. Gaul, *To Marry an Indian*, 6, 67, 157. Elias also continued to use and be known by different names. See Perdue, *Cherokee Editor*.
126. Gabriel, *Elias Boudinot*; T. Wilkins, *Cherokee Tragedy*.
127. "A Catalogue of the Cherokee Scholars That Have Belonged to the School at Brainerd," 18.3.1, vol. 2, ABCFM Archives, Houghton Library, 158–61; Gold, *Historical Records*, 85.
128. McLoughlin, *Cherokee Renascence*, 70; Sturm, *Blood Politics*, 55–58.
129. These changes were due more to treaties and earlier government assistance than to missionary intervention, which was small-scale and, in line with Cherokee demands, delimited to literacy and western-style education. "Missions to the North American Indians," 18.3–18.8, ABCFM Archives, Houghton Library; Halliburton, *Red over Black*; Littlefield, *Cherokee Freedmen*, 3; McLoughlin, *Cherokees and Missionaries*; McLoughlin, *Cherokee Renascence*; Perdue, *Slavery*; Perdue, "Women, Men and American Indian Policy," in Shoemaker, *Negotiators of Change*, 91, 93, 96–97; Miles, "Circular Reasoning."
130. Catherine to Brother and Sister (addressed Hermann Vaill), Sabbath, July 1825, Box 1, MS 519, Vaill Collection.
131. *Niles Weekly Register*, July 9, 1825, 298; *Eastern Argus*, July 14, 1825, 1.
132. Harriett to Rev. Vaill and sisters, June 25, 1825, Box 1, MS 519, Vaill Collection.
133. Gabriel, *Elias Boudinot*, 77.
134. Pascoe, "Race, Gender, and the Privileges of Property," in Ware, *New Viewpoints in Women's History*, 99–122; Hodes, *White Women, Black Men*; Pascoe, "Race, Gender and Intercultural Relations"; Saks, "Representing Miscegenation Law."
135. Demos, *Little Commonwealth*; *American Eagle*, March 22, 1824, quoted in Gabriel, *Elias Boudinot*, 61–62; T. Wilkins, *Cherokee Tragedy*, 148.
136. Harriett to Rev. Vaill and sisters, June 25, 1825, Box 1, MS 519, Vaill Collection (emphasis in original).
137. Harriett to Brother and Sister, January 5, 1827, Box 1, MS 519, Vaill Collection; Shields, *Civil Tongues and Polite Letters*; Smith-Rosenberg, "Female World of Love and Ritual."
138. Gabriel, *Elias Boudinot*.
139. Harriett's brother-in-law Hermann Vaill kept most of the rich family correspondence about the marriage controversy, which included some letters from Elias; this collection is now in the Sterling Archives at Yale. Additional letters from Elias are held in other collections, including the Museum of the Cherokee Indian in Cherokee, North Carolina, and the records of the Cherokee Nation at the University of Oklahoma, Western History Collection. Elias's "stolen" letters do not appear in any of the collected church correspondence. The American Board of Commissioners for Foreign Missions holds a strong collection of Congregationalist mission sources and records pertaining to the Foreign Mission School in Cornwall.
140. Harriett to Rev. H. L. Vaill, [June 1825], Box 1, MS 519, Vaill Collection. Targeting Sarah Northrup's mother like this was possibly connected with earlier controversies about women's role in "bundling" practice, which allowed engaged couples to sleep together,

dressed, prior to marriage. Rothman, *Hands and Hearts*, 46–52; D. Smith and Hindus, "Premarital Pregnancy in America," 547–48. Sarah, who had grown close to John as she assisted in nursing him through an illness, was only sixteen when she left Cornwall and was more interested in John than missionary life.

141. Gaul, *To Marry an Indian*, 8, 104.
142. Shields, *Civil Tongues and Polite Letters*, 316.
143. Shields, *Civil Tongues and Polite Letters*, 316; M. Warner, *Letters of the Republic*.
144. Shields, *Civil Tongues and Polite Letters*, 318.
145. Shields, *Civil Tongues and Polite Letters*, 316.
146. Rothman, *Hands and Hearts*, 9.
147. Toorn, *Writing Never Arrives Naked*.
148. Gabriel, *Elias Boudinot*, 33; Rothman, *Hands and Hearts*, 9–10.
149. Starr, *A History of Cornwall, Connecticut*, quoted in Foreman, "Foreign Mission School," 249.
150. Rothman, *Hands and Hearts*, 10–11.
151. *Niles Weekly Register*, July 9, 1825, 298; *Eastern Argus*, July 14, 1825, 1; Harriett to Rev. Vaill and sisters, June 25, 1825, Box 1, MS 519, Vaill Collection.
152. Edward Starr, *A History of Cornwall, Connecticut*, 155.
153. Gaul, *To Marry an Indian*, 45, 70–71.
154. Tilton, *Pocahontas*; Namias, *White Captives*; Demos, *Unredeemed Captive*; Ebersole, *Captured by Texts*; Green, "Pocahontas Perplex."
155. Child, *Hobomok and Other Writings on Indians*, xiii, xx. See also Conforti, *Imagining New England*, 191.
156. Cott interview; Child, *Hobomok: A Tale*; Ebersole, *Captured by Texts*; Child, *Hobomok and Other Writings on Indians*, 153; Kinney, *Amalgamation!*; Namias, "Mary Jamison," in *White Captives*; Smith-Rosenberg, "Captured Subjects/Savage Others."
157. Lewis, "Republican Wife."
158. *Poor Sarah*. The tract is attributed to various authors, including Phoebe Hinsdale and Elias Boudinot IV, who was president of the American Tract Society, which published the book. It is also often attributed to the Cherokee Elias Boudinot, a confusion that probably grew because he translated it into Cherokee and had the same name as its publisher and supporter. A popular children's play and a religious book concerned the successful convert Catharine Brown, who was close friends with the Gold family and exchanged correspondence with them; Catharine Brown to Flora Gold, May 26, 1821, Box 1, MS 519, Vaill Collection. Like that of "Poor Sarah," Catharine's story is narrated as a moral tale, which stresses the "progress" of the Cherokees for a New England audience (which involved going from traditional finery and jewels to simple dress), although in the play she is called back to serve her parents in the "dark wilderness." [A Lady], *Catharine Brown the Converted Cherokee*. Cornwall residents also knew the Cherokee scholars personally and had received a visit from The Ridge, whom they judged a highly "civilized" Cherokee chief.

159. Fox, "The Indian Song, Sarah and John," [1830s], quoted in Gold, *Historical Records*, 32. Gold fuses the story of John Ridge and Sarah Northrup with Harriett and Elias' story, including Harriett's near-fatal illness and a threat that she would die if not allowed to marry the Indian. Gold, *Historical Records*, 32–34.
160. Gabriel, *Elias Boudinot*, ix.
161. McClintock, *Imperial Leather*, 24–25.
162. Sweet, *Bodies Politic*, 109.
163. Elias Boudinot to brothers and sisters, September 14, 1829, Box 1, MS519, Vaill Collection. Elias makes much of their appearance as "little Indians" when writing from Cherokee territory. ABCFM records place his sister Polly as "three quarter Cherokee": 18.3.1, vol. 2, ABCFM Archives, Houghton Library, 207; Berkhofer, *White Man's Indian*.
164. Flora to Rev. Hermann Vaill, with postscript from Harriett, [September 19, 1825], Box 1, MS519, Vaill Collection.
165. Various Vaill letters, Vaill Collection; Boudinot [Cherokee], *Address to the Whites*, 15–16; Shoemaker, "How the Indians Got to Be Red," esp. 638, 640, 642. On color, see Melish, *Disowning Slavery*; Stoler, *Race and the Education of Desire*, 7; Stoler, "Sexual Affronts and Racial Frontiers," 198–238, esp. 199–200. Stoler postulates that the "cultural accoutrements" of bourgeois culture, or clarified notions of whiteness, were in part shaped by contrasts forged "in the politics of the language of race."
166. For an excellent study of race and benevolence, see S. Ryan, *Grammar of Good Intentions*. See also Sweet, *Bodies Politic*.
167. Grimshaw, *Paths of Duty*. Harriett later expressed disappointment and frustration in this regard. Teaching had to come second to bearing and rearing children and keeping house.
168. H. L. Vaill to Harriett, March 5, 1826, Box 1, MS519, Vaill Collection. Hermann referred to Elias as "Brother Boudinot" — including notions of Christian "brothers" and perhaps unconsciously accepting the status of future brother-in-law.
169. Bennet Roberts to Herman L. Vaill, August 1, 1825, Box 1, MS519, Vaill Collection.
170. Most authors have it as March 28; however, Weierman argues a convincing case for the wedding taking place in May. Weierman, *One Nation, One Blood*, 179.
171. "The dye is cast." Stephen to Brother and Sister, June 11, 1825, Box 1, MS519, Vaill Collection; Gabriel, *Elias Boudinot*, 91.
172. Boudinot [Cherokee], *Address to the Whites*.
173. Quoted in Gabriel, *Elias Boudinot*, 64. Bunce was an "independent Yankee."
174. "This is placing the Cherokee youth in a very delicate situation. They must not look at any young woman ... [in case they feel affection and it] might render them miserable through life." *Brainerd Journal*, November 11–12, 1824, 18.3.1, vol. 2, ABCFM Archives, Houghton Library. See also McLoughlin, *Cherokee Renascence*, 369.
175. Evarts, 18.3.1, vol. 4, ABCFM Archives, Houghton Library.
176. Ridge to Monroe, March 8, 1821, quoted in T. Wilkins, *Cherokee Tragedy*, 128–29 (emphasis in original).

177. Cott, *Bonds of Womanhood*; Rothman, *Hands and Hearts*. M. Ryan, *Cradle of the Middle Class*, 60–104, argues that the family was in transition, linking this with revival cycles and female evangelical movements. Her study focuses on Oneida County, New York, where the revival movement as well as the "frontier" nature of society differed from those in Connecticut and where women appear to have played more active organizational roles, for example, in the Oneida Female Missionary Society and Maternal Society.
178. T. Wilkins, *Cherokee Tragedy*, 103. Evarts, 18.3.1, vol. 4, ABCFM Archives, Houghton Library.
179. Perdue, *Slavery*, 51–53; Cott, "DeVane Lecture Series papers."
180. Rothman, *Hands and Hearts*; D. Smith, "Parental Power and Marriage Patterns." See also Bredbenner, *Nationality of Her Own*, 16–18.
181. Ellinghaus, *Taking Assimilation to Heart*.
182. Hermann Vaill to Harriett, March 5, 1826, Box 1, MS 519, Vaill Collection. Although Harriett adopted the name "Boudinot" that her husband had earlier adopted from a benefactor, she retained her other appellations: "Harriett Ruggles Gold Boudinot."
183. See S. Ryan, "Save Us from Our Friends," in *Grammar of Good Intentions*, 163–86; Ellinghaus, *Taking Assimilation to Heart*.
184. E. Boudinot to Dear Brother and Sister, [1830–31], quoted in Gaul, *To Marry an Indian*, 174 (emphasis in original).
185. Bennet Roberts to Herman L. Vaill, August 1, 1825, Box 1, MS 519, Vaill Collection.
186. "I hope that you will be the instrument of accomplishing much in behalf of that People whom I suppose you now consider as *Your* Nation." Hermann to Harriett, March 5, 1826, Box 1, MS 519, Vaill Collection.
187. Elias Boudinot to Franklin Gold, April 1823, Box 1, MS 519, Vaill Collection. In the Supreme Court cases *Worcester v. Georgia*, 1830, and *Cherokee Nation v. Georgia*, 1831, the Cherokees argued for separate sovereignty, and Marshall agreed to rule that they were "a domestic dependent nation." Reactions to this judgment suggest Congress and its constituents favored a more tenuous grip for both political status and Indigenous title. They saw the judgment as taking native autonomy too far. Wirt, *Opinion on the Right*. See also Gitlin, "Private Diplomacy to Private Property"; McLoughlin, *Cherokee Renascence*; Perdue, *Slavery*; Plane, "Legitimacies, Indian Identities, and the Law"; T. Wilkins, *Cherokee Tragedy*, 228–29.
188. Harriett to Brother and Sister, January 2, 1826, Box 1, MS 519, Vaill Collection. She also writes of expecting "many trials, hardships & privations," of aiming for the "greatest usefulness." While she cannot wait "to begin . . . work" among the "despised people," intriguingly, she first wrote something else — indecipherable — before crossing it out and replacing it with "despised people."
189. Harriett to Brother and Sister, January 2, 1826, Box 1, MS 519, Vaill Collection. See also R. Hoffman, Sobel, and Teute, *Through a Glass Darkly*; Sweet, *Bodies Politic*.
190. Conforti, *Imagining New England*, 174.
191. Conforti, *Jonathan Edwards*, 45.

192. Conforti, *Imagining New England*, 174.
193. Conforti, *Imagining New England*, 178–80, 183; S. Morse, *His Letters and Journals*; Conforti.
194. Conforti, *Imagining New England*, 190.
195. In another "roots" story, a family historian, T. Gold, would later become the local historian of Cornwall.
196. Gaul, *To Marry an Indian*, 45–46; Elias and Harriett to Dear Brothers and Sisters, January 5, 1827, Box 1, MS 519, Vaill Collection.
197. Boudinot [Cherokee], *Address to the Whites*, cited in Gabriel, *Elias Boudinot*, 4.
198. Boudinot [Cherokee], *Address to the Whites*, 4.
199. King, *Cherokee Indian Nation*.

2. ERNEST GRIBBLE AND JEANNIE

1. Hirst, *Sentimental Nation*, provides a full discussion of the politics and events around what became an "imperial federation."
2. This chapter owes its inspiration to Halse, "Reverend Ernest Gribble"; and Halse, *Terribly Wild Man*, 3.
3. Ross Andrews, council clerk of the Yarrabah Community Council, expressed the view of elders that Gribble's writings were lies. Flo Watson has also recorded such testimonies. Thomson, *Reaching Back*, also contains evidence of the oppressive side of Gribble's rule.
4. The Gunggandji language group's name is also spelled "Kongandji." Language groups and clans often have multiple names, and there are multiple spellings, as non-Indigenous observers attempt to translate them into English script. The spellings used in this book are drawn from David Horton's Aboriginal Australia map (Canberra: Aboriginal Studies Press 1994), http://aiatsis.gov.au/explore/culture/topic/aboriginal-australia-map, which in turn draws upon Norman Tindale's maps. Horton's map is approved for use by the Australian Institute of Aboriginal and Torres Strait Islander Studies (AIATSIS), although they state that it is not definitive. Not all groups are included on this map. This usage here follows that currently used by the Yarrabah Shire Council.
5. Saunders, *Indentured Labour*; C. Moore, *Kanaka*.
6. These figures create much debate. See Reynolds, *Forgotten War*; see also Roberts, *Frontier Justice*; Bottoms, *Conspiracy of Silence*; Ørsted-Jensen, *Frontier History Revisited*.
7. The Mitchell Library houses most of the Gribble Papers within its Australian Board of Mission Collection: Mitchell Library, MLMSS 4503, add-on 1822, Boxes 1–69 (69). The Australian Institute of Aboriginal and Torres Strait Islander Studies (AIATSIS) also holds Gribble manuscripts. A full guide to relevant records in this collection, the boxes, and other details is available from the AIATSIS: "MS 1515: Gribble, Ernest R., Finding Aid." Excerpts from Gribble's diary are sourced from MLMSS 4503, add-on 1822, Mitchell Library; unless otherwise stated, they are in Box 3(69).

8. McGregor, *Imagined Destinies*; L. Russell, *Colonial Frontiers*; W. Anderson, *Cultivation of Whiteness*.
9. L. Ryan, *Tasmanian Aborigines*.
10. *Aboriginal News*, April 15, 1907.
11. "Bush economy" and "bush lifestyle" refer to the precontact Indigenous economy, in which hunting, fishing, and gathering sustained people. It involved purposeful travel linked with ceremony and wider group dynamics.
12. Halse, *Terribly Wild Man*, 19.
13. J. Gribble, *Dark Deeds in a Sunny Land*.
14. After Gribble publicly exposed the sexual exploitation of and cruelty against Aboriginal women by white men on the Western Australian cattle frontier of the 1880s, he was vilified in the press, ostracized by his white countrymen, and then charged with slander. J. B. suffered deeply, as the church was primarily concerned about alienating the elite pioneer pastoralists.
15. *Aboriginal News*, June 27, 1909.
16. E. Gribble, *Forty Years*; "Mission Methods," *Argus*, May 28, 1910.
17. Halse, *Terribly Wild Man*, 16–18.
18. Halse, *Terribly Wild Man*, 20–21.
19. Dixon, *Words of Our Country*, 1.
20. At the time of writing, the Queensland government refers to six thousand years. See "Fitzroy Island National Park: Nature, Culture, and History," updated February 6, 2013, Department of National Parks, Sport, and Racing, Queensland Government, http://www.nprsr.qld.gov.au/parks/fitzroy-island/culture.html. See also Dixon, *Words of Our Country*, 1–2, 43–44, 90–95, 106–8; Galvin, "Selected Bibliography of the Djabugay/Tjapukai/Djabuganjdji Language and People Held in the AIATSIS Library," Australian Institute of Aboriginal and Torres Strait Islander Studies.
21. Dore Bryant, November 6, 1900, newspaper clippings, ABM MLMSS 4503, add-on 1822, Box 14 (69), Mitchell Library.
22. Jacobs, *White Mother to a Dark Race*.
23. Craig, "Social Impact of the State," 51.
24. Halse, "Reverend Ernest Gribble," 169–70.
25. Dixon, *Searching for Aboriginal Languages*, 269–71.
26. See Stanner, "The Dreaming," in *White Man Got No Dreaming*. For another discussion, see Myers, *Pintupi Country, Pintupi Self*. For a more critical appraisal of its history, see Wolfe, "On Being Woken Up."
27. Dixon, *Words of Our Country*, 113–17, 83–86.
28. E. R. Gribble to Dr. Roth, July 14, 1900, (1) AIATSIS, MS 1515/9.
29. Gribble, "Mission Methods," *Argus*, May 28, 1910, 9; Gribble diary, October 10, 1892; E. Gribble, *Forty Years*, 84. These attitudes toward intermarriage with aliens were also shared by W. E. H. Roth. See Halse, *Terribly Wild Man*, 50–53; excerpt from *Mission News*, ca. 1906, in A/04889, QSA; see also A/70007, QSA; *Missionary Notes* 16, no. 7, 116; *Aboriginal News*, June 15, 1907.

30. *Aboriginal News*, April 15, 1907, extracted from *Trinity Times*.
31. *Aboriginal News*, April 15, 1907.
32. E. Gribble, *Despised Race*, 146. Gribble attributes this as a "Goonjanji song," which would now be transcribed as "Gunggandji" or "Kongkandji."
33. Gribble diary, October 31, 1892.
34. Gribble diary, October 15, 1892.
35. Gribble diary, February 19, 1893.
36. Gribble diary, October 15, 1892.
37. Gribble diary, October 17, 1893.
38. Gribble diary, March 27, 1893.
39. Gribble diary, October 15, 1892.
40. Gribble diary, November 3, 1892.
41. Gribble diary, November 6, 1892.
42. J. Gribble, *Dark Deeds in a Sunny Land*; J. Gribble, *Black but Comely*. Gribble also introduced new "disciplines" for himself—for example, giving up pipe smoking; Gribble diary, November 1, 1892.
43. Gribble diary, November 22, 1892.
44. Gribble diary, October 29, 1892, January 17, 1893, and March 7, 1906. The March 7 entry is from Box 5(69).
45. Australian Board of Missions, *Yarrabah: Church of England Mission*.
46. Sandow's exercises were used as a "drill": Gribble diary, January 26, 1904, Box 5(69).
47. Gribble diary, January 21, 1893.
48. Gribble diary, January 21, 1893.
49. Gribble diary, January 21, 1893 (emphasis in original).
50. Halse, *Terribly Wild Man*, 36–37.
51. Australian Board of Missions, "General Rules," in *Yarrabah: Church of England Mission*.
52. Australian Board of Missions, *Yarrabah: Church of England Mission*.
53. Ada Pickles was included in one such list from 1907: Gribble diary, Memoranda 1907, Box 5(69).
54. Hector had "severely handled" his wife, Dinah. Gribble gave him "a good hiding for his treatment of his wife was brutal. Poor boy he seems very penitent and preached at night for some time": Gribble diary, September 10, 1906, Box 5(69).
55. Gribble, *Argus*, May 28, 1910, 9.
56. Keen, *Knowledge and Secrecy*, 300, chap. 6, 7. Although writing of Yolgnu, this applies for much of northern Australia.
57. The term *budi-L* means "put down, put away, marry"; *Warra* means the wrong way. There were two moieties—*gurraminya*, the summertime moiety, and *gurragulu/gurrabana*, the wintertime moiety—and each person was expected to marry someone from another moiety. Dixon, *Words of Our Country*, 251, 276, 150; McKnight, *Of Marriage, Violence and Sorcery*.
58. *Aboriginal News*, June 11, 1910.

59. As will be discussed in the final chapter, Queenslanders looked to the forced removals of the Cherokees and other American Indians as a segregation model to follow — in order to remove the danger of violence and sexual intermixing.
60. Australian Board of Missions, *Yarrabah: Church of England Mission*.
61. *Missionary Notes* 17, no. 9, 150.
62. Australian Board of Missions, *Yarrabah: Church of England Mission*.
63. *Aboriginal News*, April 27, 1909; *Missionary Notes*, 16, no. 7, 115; *Missionary Notes*, 16, no. 8, 123–24; *Aboriginal News*, February 15, 1907. In some ways, it should be noted, Yarrabah was way ahead of other missions. A council, run by "King Menmuny," presided over matters of law and decided on punishment of genders against moral codes. While Gribble presided as chair, the elected members made the decisions. There must have been internal community endorsement of principles. *Missionary Notes*, 15, no. 1, 3–5.
64. This tradition continued. Menmuny's granddaughter Lorna Schrieber recalls her father, Albert's story and her own honor, based upon the British royal wedding ceremony of Queen Elizabeth II; Thomson, *Reaching Back*, 69.
65. I was unable to verify the name of Menmuny's mother. Jordan, *Hidden Voices*, 34.
66. Craig argues the complexity of John Menmuny Barlow's clan and land affiliations; Craig, "Social Impact of the State," ix.
67. "John Barlow (Menmuny)," in E. Gribble, *Forty Years*, opposite 25.
68. *Missionary Notes*, February 15, 1900.
69. Halse, *Terribly Wild Man*, 20–21.
70. Not only was the bride attended by eight bridesmaids, she wore a crown on her head and the *Aboriginal News* reported, "To mark the special character of the event the bride was attended by eight bridesmaids, who in white dresses trimmed with ribbons of various colours with wreaths of flowers & fern on their heads looked fit for any royal wedding. Good wishes from every body were given to the young royal couple." Thomson, *Reaching Back*, 69–70.
71. Schrieber in Thomson, *Reaching Back*, 69.
72. Dixon, *Grammar of Yidin*, 26.
73. Halse, *Terribly Wild Man*.
74. *Aboriginal News*, July 31, 1909.
75. The closest word to this in Yarrabah dialects is *juja*, which means "backbone": Dixon, *Words of Our Country*, 291.
76. Hollingsworth interview, June 1, 2000.
77. Thomson, *Reaching Back*, 81, 85–86.
78. Such a policy was in dramatic contrast to Roth's, Cecil Cook's, and Neville's later policy in the Northern Territory and Western Australia, which encouraged marriage of light-skinned women to white men to breed out color.
79. Craig, "Social Impact of the State," 70.
80. Hollingsworth interview, June 1, 2000.
81. Thomson, *Reaching Back*, 81–86; Craig, "Social Impact of the State," 62.

82. *Missionary Notes* 17, no. 9, 151.
83. "Aboriginal Concert a Brilliant Success a Big and Enthusiastic Audience," *Morning Post*, August 14, 1903, 7.
84. J. B. Gribble cites Harriet Beecher Stowe and the implications of the slave trade on the first page of *Dark Deeds in a Sunny Land*. Gribble argues that a slave system of labor operated on the Western Australian frontier, with chains and women "owned" by their masters for whatever purposes they desired. See also David Pilgrim, "The Picaninny Caricature," October 2000, edited 2012, Jim Crow Museum of Racist Memorabilia, Ferris State University, http://www.ferris.edu/jimcrow/picaninny/; G. Davis, *Dance, Pickaninnies, Dance!*
85. I use this song name because it is historically accurate. I do not endorse the terminology, which is offensive. "Ten Little Indians" is a comic song written in 1868 by Septimus Winner of Philadelphia. English songwriter Frank Green adapted it for use in a Victorian minstrel show, giving it new lyrics and changing "Indians" to "Niggers."
86. "Aboriginal Concert a Brilliant Success a Big and Enthusiastic Audience," *Morning Post*, August 14, 1903, 7.
87. "Aboriginal Concert a Brilliant Success a Big and Enthusiastic Audience," *Morning Post*, August 14, 1903, 7. Also quoted in Australian Board of Missions, *Yarrabah: Church of England Mission*, 3–11.
88. Early anthropologists assumed this was organized by males, but Diane Bell and others demonstrated women's key role in this aspect of social organization: D. Bell, *Daughters of the Dreaming*.
89. Halse, *Terribly Wild Man*, 28–29. See Keen, *Knowledge and Secrecy*, 295.
90. Walter Roth compiled brief notes on various northern marriage ceremonies. Roth described this subject as an "interesting position" and "the peculiar method of copulation in vogue throughout all these tribes." Roth, "*Ethnological Studies*, 179, fig. 433, plate XXIV, 177–78. Although Gribble does not mention such rites, male introcision (permanent opening up of the penile portion of the urethra) and cutting of the perineum in females were reported by Roth to be commonplace around 1900. While such practices may have been widely accepted, some individuals may have been keen to escape such ceremonies. See Roth, "Marriage Ceremonies and Infant Life"; Roth, *Ethnological Studies*.
91. Thomson, *Reaching Back*, 75–77.
92. *Missionary Notes* 16, no. 7, 116. On the history of Melanesian and Asian labor in Queensland, see McGrath, "Exile into Bondage"; R. Evans, Saunders, and Cronin, *Race Relations in Colonial Queensland*.
93. *ABM Review*, December 15, 1910, 182.
94. Halse, *Terribly Wild Man*, 50.
95. Halse, *Terribly Wild Man*, 78.
96. Mission residents were normally provided only with flour, sugar, and tea and were expected to find local supplies of fish, dugong, and turtle. There were many complaints

about food, although a diversity of tropical fruits was being grown: guavas, cassava, bananas, coconuts, and so forth. Apparently it was not enough for the population. The tropical reef fish available in the region are sought after in many parts of the world. Nonetheless, Europeans were attuned to eating unavailable meats such as lamb and beef. For various reasons, including the impositions of new industries and the availability of mission rations, Aboriginal people were not traveling as much to reap a more widely balanced diet.

97. *ABM Review*, August 15, 1910, 103.
98. Australian Board of Missions, "General Rules," in *Yarrabah: Church of England Mission*.
99. Interview with Thomas Allen in Hume, "Them Days," 11 (emphasis added).
100. Hume, "Them Days"; Hume, "Yarrabah, Christian Phoenix."
101. Craig, "Social Impact of the State," 62.
102. *ABM Review*, December 15, 1910, 184; Finlayson, "Don't Depend on Me," 115–16. After being freed of mission constraints, Yarrabah residents eventually transformed weddings into huge events in the social calendar. By the 1970s, "rag-time" described a long-bygone era. The increasingly autonomous community now organized everything themselves, with every wedding a white wedding with a great get-together and a lavish feast. Yarrabah wedding festivities became the way everyone experienced a sense of belonging and learned about their extended family. Hollingsworth interview, June 1, 2000; Thomson, *Reaching Back*, 85–86.
103. Gribble said Pearson had "fallen into sin," "it is a most serious affair." Halse, "Reverend Ernest Gribble," 184.
104. Halse, *Terribly Wild Man*, 76–77.
105. Gribble diary, October 17, 1901; Halse, "Reverend Ernest Gribble," 191, 184–85.
106. *Aboriginal News*, March 15, 1908.
107. Halse, *Terribly Wild Man*, 82; O. Miller, "K'gari, Mrs. Fraser and Butchulla Oral Tradition." See also E. Gribble, *Problem of the Australian Aboriginal*, 56–57.
108. Halse, *Terribly Wild Man*, 82–84.
109. E. Gribble, *Forty Years*, 162; Gribble diary, January 23, 27, 29, 1906, all in Box 5(69). "The Queensland Cyclone," *Advertiser*, January 31, 1906, 7.
110. E. Gribble, *Problem of the Australian Aboriginal*, iv.
111. E. Gribble, *Despised Race*, opposite 54.
112. Gribble diary, January 10, 13, 23, 29, 1906, all in Box 5(69). E. Gribble, *Forty Years*, 162.
113. Gribble diary, December 21, 14, 1907, Box 5(69).
114. In early 1908 the *Aboriginal News* reported, "Mrs Reeves has permanently left the Mission after many years work." *Aboriginal News*, March 15, 1908. Thanks to Kate Ellinghaus for providing a copy of Ethel's wedding certificate. See also Halse, "Sex at Yarrabah," in "Reverend Ernest Gribble," 172–210.
115. The ABM cited the wedding certificate of Ethel Reeves and Fred Wondunna, dated December 30, 1907; Australian Board of Missions, "ABM Committee Minutes," February 6, 1908, Box 35(69), MLMSS 4503, add-on 1822, Mitchell Library.

116. Australian Board of Missions, "ABM Committee Minutes," February 11, 1908, Box 35(69), MLMSS 4503, add-on 1822, Mitchell Library.
117. E. Gribble, *Forty Years*; Thomson, *Reaching Back*, 14.
118. "Half-Caste Jeannie," *Morning Post*, January 1, 1901, 5; Halse, *Terribly Wild Man*, 52–55.
119. Gribble newspaper clippings, *Cairns Daily Argus*, n.d., ABM MLMSS 4503, add-on 1822 14 (69). See also Aboriginal Protector's Office, personal files, QSA.
120. *Aboriginal News*, June 15, 1907, extracted from *Trinity Times*, November 21, 1906.
121. "Half-Caste Jeannie," *Morning Post*, January 1, 1901, 5.
122. D. J. Murphy, "Givens, Thomas (1864–1928)," *Australian Dictionary of Biography Online*, http://adb.anu.edu.au/biography/givens-thomas-6395; Halse, *Terribly Wild Man*, 54 (emphasis in original).
123. *Aboriginal News*, June 1908.
124. During the scandal over Jeannie's removal to the mission, newspapers reported her age to be "around 13"; from this we can approximate that Jeannie was nineteen years younger than Gribble. "Jeannie the Half Caste," *Morning Post*, September 25, 1901, 3.
125. *Aboriginal News*, June 15, 1908.
126. *Aboriginal News*, March 15, 1908, 3; Halse, *Terribly Wild Man*, 86.
127. Halse, *Terribly Wild Man*, 85.
128. Halse, *Terribly Wild Man*, 91.
129. *Aboriginal News*, July 15, 1907.
130. *Aboriginal News*, March 15, 1908.
131. *Aboriginal News*, July 31, 1909; E. Gribble, *Despised Race*.
132. *Aboriginal News*, July 15, 1907.
133. Halse, "Reverend Ernest Gribble," 187.
134. "Half-Caste Jeannie," *Morning Post*, January 1, 1901, 5.
135. Halse, "Reverend Ernest Gribble," 92, 191. See *Aboriginal News*, March 15 and July 15, 1908.
136. Hollingsworth interview, June 1, 2000; Thomson, *Reaching Back*.
137. Halse, "Reverend Ernest Gribble," 194.
138. *Aboriginal News*, September 8, 1908.
139. Halse, *Terribly Wild Man*, 92.
140. *Aboriginal News*, September 30, 1908; Mackett, "Yarrabah Baptisms 1891–1927," MS3234, Australian Institute of Aboriginal and Torres Strait Islander Studies Library.
141. Interview with May Smith, in Halse, *Terribly Wild Man*, 88.
142. Halse, "Reverend Ernest Gribble," 202.
143. See Australian Board of Missions, "ABM Committee Minutes," July 9, 1909, Box 35(69), MLMSS 4503, add-on 1822, Mitchell Library; *Aboriginal News* 5, no. 27, 1910.
144. *Aboriginal News*, January 1, 1910; Australian Board of Missions, "ABM Committee Minutes," July 9, 1909, Box 35(69), MLMSS 4503, add-on 1822, Mitchell Library; *Aboriginal News* 5, no. 27, 1910.
145. *Aboriginal News*, January 1, 1910; Halse, *Terribly Wild Man*, 91–92.

146. Churches tend to be more lenient toward scandal than heresy. On heresy, see Vsiwanathan, *Outside the Fold*.
147. Dixon, *Words of Our Country*, 237.
148. Some Gribble descendants told historian Henry Reynolds that he and Christine Halse had got it all wrong—that Ernest had never had such an illicit love. While the diverse evidence appears strong, we need to allow for different possibilities.
149. Interview with Elva Sands in Halse, "Reverend Ernest Gribble," 201.
150. Hollingsworth interview, June 1, 2000. Via a Yarrabah intermediary, I inquired of other descendants whether they wished to participate in an interview, but I was informed that they were not eager to revisit this history. Out of respect for their position, I did not pursue this further.
151. Excerpt from *Mission News*, [1906], A/04889, QSA. See also A/70007, QSA.
152. *Aboriginal News*, July 31, 1909.

3. SOCRATES, CHEROKEE SOVEREIGNTY, AND REGULATION OF WHITE MEN

1. Socrates, "Intermarriages." See also Socrates, "Strictures on the Report of the Joint Committee."
2. Young, "Exercise of Sovereignty." The Choctaws also introduced a constitution in 1826 that included laws pertaining to marriage, polygamy, infanticide, and wills. See Kidwell, *Choctaws in Oklahoma*; "Choctaws," *Cherokee Phoenix* 11, no. 8 (May 27, 1829), 2.
3. Yarbrough, *Race and the Cherokee Nation*; Miles, *Ties That Bind*; Perdue, *Cherokee Women*; J. Brooks, *Captives and Cousins*; Yarbrough and Holland, *Crossing Waters, Crossing Worlds*; S. Slater and Yarbrough, *Gender and Sexuality*.
4. See Thornton, *Cherokees*.
5. Here I draw upon William Cronin's discussion in *Changes in the Land*, as cited in J. Brooks, *Captives and Cousins*, 68.
6. John Locke was most influential; Ketcham, *James Madison*, 294–95.
7. Socrates, "Intermarriages."
8. Socrates, "Intermarriages" (emphasis in original).
9. Socrates, "Intermarriages."
10. While most Georgians were concerned only about increasing their own property rights, others were more humanely inclined toward Indians, fearing that if left unchecked, the rapacious actions of whites might see them punished by God. See Young, "Exercise of Sovereignty."
11. Socrates, "Intermarriages."
12. Socrates, "Strictures on the Report of the Joint Committee." See also Socrates, "Mr. Boudinott Editor Cherokee Phoenix"; Socrates, "Intermarriages."
13. Socrates, "Intermarriages."
14. The population figure is taken from a census performed by the National Committee in 1825. See John Ridge to the Hon. Albert Gallatin, March 10, 1826, in Sturtevant, "John Ridge on Cherokee Civilization." See also Smithers, *Cherokee Diaspora*, 100.

15. McLoughlin, *Cherokees and Missionaries*, 268–69. See also Thornton, *Cherokees*.
16. Thornton, *Cherokees*, 50; McLoughlin, *Cherokees and Missionaries*; McLoughlin, *Cherokee Renascence*. See also Perdue, *Cherokee Women*, 74–83; Sturtevant, "John Ridge on Cherokee Civilization"; Corman, "Reading, Writing and Removal," 190–91.
17. McLoughlin, *Cherokee Ghost Dance*, 228.
18. For a discussion of the 1825 census, see McLoughlin, *Cherokee Ghost Dance*, 218–26.
19. See J. Hoffman, *Gender and Sovereignty*; Calloway, *Crown and Camulet*; Blackhawk, *Violence over the Land*; Shinoda, *Re-examining Sovereignty*; Moreton-Robinson, *Sovereign Subjects*; Keller, Lissitzyn, and Mann, *Creation of Rights of Sovereignty*. Pateman and Mills, *Contract and Domination*, attempts to analyze contract theory in terms of colonialism but its most incisive findings reflect more upon recent than historical events.
20. Cherokee Nation, *Laws of the Cherokee Nation*, 10, 38. See also Strickland, *Fire and the Spirits*; Yarbrough, "Legislating Women's Sexuality"; Weierman, "A Wicked and Mischievous Connection," in *One Nation, One Blood*, 34–61; Berger, "After Pocahontas"; Yarbrough, *Race and the Cherokee Nation*; McLoughlin, *Cherokees and Missionaries*.
21. Acts 17:26.
22. For a sustained discussion of this issue, see Sturm, *Blood Politics*.
23. Sulu's story is still given primacy at the Museum of the Cherokee Indian, Cherokee, North Carolina, https://www.cherokeemuseum.org. See also Perdue, *Cherokee Women*, 13–15.
24. 1 Corinthians 7:32–34.
25. Schmidt, Wilkins, and Buttrick quoted in McLoughlin, *Cherokees and Missionaries*, 187–88.
26. Sturtevant, "John Ridge on Cherokee Civilization," 88.
27. Sturtevant, "John Ridge on Cherokee Civilization," 88.
28. Sturm, *Blood Politics*, 225. Cherokees of different descent and belief have conflicting ideas about racial and cultural mixing, sense of peoplehood, and cultural and racial "essence."
29. Perdue, *Cherokee Women*, 147: in 1825 "the council severely compromised matrilineality when it extended Cherokee citizenship to the children of Cherokee men and white women, living in the Cherokee Nation as man and wife" and "entitled to all the immunities and privileges enjoyed by the citizens descending from the Cherokee race, by the mother's side." Shoemaker states, "The Cherokees disavowed their matrilineal past when they formed a constitutional government in 1827." Shoemaker, *American Indian Population Recovery*, 64. See also Miles, "Circular Reasoning."
30. Sturm, *Blood Politics*, 55.
31. "Constitution of the Cherokee Nation: July 1827," *Cherokee Phoenix* 1, no.1 (February 21, 1828), 1–2 (emphasis added). See also Cherokee Nation, *Laws of the Cherokee Nation*, 118–30.
32. Persico "Early Nineteenth-Century Cherokee Political Organisation," 108; Cherokee Nation, *Laws of the Cherokee Nation*. While an earlier constitution was adopted in 1823,

Cherokee Nation, *Laws of the Cherokee Nation*, gives 1827 for the date of constitution. John Ross was president of the National Committee, 1819–26. From 1826, Lewis Ross was president until John Ross reassumed the position in 1829. Elijah Hicks and Joseph Vann also played senior roles on the committee during the 1840s. See Cherokee Nation, *Laws of the Cherokee Nation*; Miles, *House on Diamond Hill*.

33. Socrates, "Intermarriages." While Smithers argues that Socrates implied that African Americans were included in his opinions on intermarriage, Yarbrough disagrees: see Smithers, *Cherokee Diaspora*, 100; Yarbrough, *Race and the Cherokee Nation*, 36–37.
34. Socrates, "Strictures on the Report of the Joint Committee."
35. Vattel's *Law of Nations* remains one of the most influential texts on modern sovereignty and is frequently used even today to sort out Indigenous entitlements in New World colonies such as Australia and the United States. See also Cumfer, *Separate Peoples, One Land*, 42–44.
36. Shinoda, *Re-examining Sovereignty*, 37–36. See also Cott, *Public Vows*.
37. Pavlich, "On the Subject of Sovereigns," in Barbour and Pavlich *After Sovereignty*, 27. The "liberal populist conception of sovereignty" defines the sovereign as administrator of the will of people. Barbour and Pavlich, *After Sovereignty*, 4. Mill, Locke, Rousseau, and other liberal theorists refer to human autonomy, the independence of private individuals, and human rights as matters for constitutions. For gendered insights into sovereignty and empire, see Ballantyne and Burton, *Moving Subjects*; Ballantyne and Burton, *Bodies in Contact*; Levine, *Gender and Empire*; F. Cooper and Stoler, *Tensions of Empire*; Stoler, *Haunted by Empire*; Moreton-Robinson, *Sovereign Subjects*.
38. "Washington and the Cherokees," *Cherokee Phoenix* 1, no. 5 (March 20, 1828), 1–2.
39. George Washington, "Talk to the Cherokee Nation," August 29, 1796, Miller Center, University of Virginia, http://millercenter.org/president/speeches/detail/3941.
40. Ford, *Settler Sovereignty*, 3–13.
41. "New Echota State Park," Roadside Georgia, http://roadsidegeorgia.com/site/new_echota.html.
42. Perdue, *Cherokee Women*, 24–25. Perdue quotes Cephas Washburn, a missionary observer in 1819. See also W. Anderson, Brown, and Rogers, *Payne-Butrick Papers*.
43. See Hudson, *Southeastern Indians*; Perdue, *Cherokee Women*; McLoughlin, *Cherokee Renascence*; Mooney, *Myths of the Cherokee*.
44. McLoughlin, *Cherokees and Christianity*, 149–50. Yarbrough, *Race and the Cherokee Nation*, 12, 27.
45. Springplace diary, October 13, 1815, paraphrased in McLoughlin, *Cherokee Renascence*, 176. See also Saunt, "Telling Stories," 678.
46. Return J. Meigs to Henry Dearborn, August 4, 1805; and Return J. Meigs to Chiefs Chulio and Sour Mush, March 14, 1808, in McLoughlin, *Cherokee Renascence*, 70.
47. McLoughlin, *Cherokee Renascence*, 178.
48. McLoughlin, *Cherokee Renascence*, 178, 180. McLoughlin argues, "The well-to-do were becoming secularists who relied on their own wits and skills; the poor relied upon the

supernatural powers of the spirit world" (178). While McLoughlin's insight is accurate in some ways, it perhaps underemphasizes the value of spiritual connection and cultural richness for Cherokee people. For a reconsideration of the power of such historical interpretation, see Chakrabarty, *Provincializing Europe*; Hokari, *Gurindji Journey*. In Chakrabarty's terms, a subaltern logic of historical causation effectively "provincialises": it unsettles Europe as world center.

49. Exhibition on display at the Museum of the Cherokee Indian, Cherokee NC, April 12, 1998. See also Perdue, *Cherokee Women*, index. Despite the groom now becoming part of the wife's matrilineal clan, it was polygamy rather than polygyny that was acceptable. Perdue, "Selu Meets Eve," in *Cherokee Women*, 159–84. Hogeveen discusses quests for alternative conclusions; Hogeveen, "Specters of Colonialism," in Barbour and Pavlich, *After Sovereignty*, 125.
50. Saunt, "Telling Stories," 678.
51. Saunt, "Telling Stories," 678–79.
52. Return J. Meigs to Henry Dearborn, August 4, 1805; Return J. Meigs to Chiefs Chulio and Sour Mush, March 14, 1808, in McLoughlin, *Cherokee Renascence*, 70.
53. Hatley, *Dividing Paths*, 236.
54. Sturm, *Blood Politics*, 16.
55. Yarbrough, *Race and the Cherokee Nation*, 11.
56. See Cumfer, *Separate Peoples, One Land*.
57. "General Council," *Cherokee Phoenix* 2, no. 28 (October 21, 1829), 3.
58. John Ridge, "Indian Address" in Peyer, *American Indian Nonfiction*, 121.
59. Cherokee Nation, *Laws of the Cherokee Nation*, 10; Murchison, "Intermarried-Whites in the Cherokee Nation."
60. Cherokee Nation, *Laws of the Cherokee Nation*, 10.
61. Cherokee Nation, *Laws of the Cherokee Nation*, 10.
62. Cherokee Nation, *Laws of the Cherokee Nation*, 10.
63. Cherokee Nation, *Laws of the Cherokee Nation*, 10.
64. "Constitution of the Cherokee Nation, July 1827," *Cherokee Phoenix* 1, no. 1 (February 21, 1828): 1–2.
65. See Cott, *Public Vows*, 1–4, 9–28, 56–65.
66. Hudson cited in Boulware, *Deconstructing the Cherokee Nation*, 16.
67. Boulware, *Deconstructing the Cherokee Nation*, 10–11.
68. Boulware, *Deconstructing the Cherokee Nation*, 30–32.
69. Before 1824 the Office of Indian Affairs came under the purview of the U.S. Department of War.
70. Cherokee Nation v. Georgia 30 U.S. 1 (1831), Justia, https://supreme.justia.com/cases/federal/us/30/1/case.html; McLoughlin, *Cherokee Renascence*, 443–44; D. Wilkins and Lomawaima, *Uneven Ground*; Yarbrough, "Legislating Women's Sexuality."
71. The *Cherokee Phoenix* reprinted Washington's and Jefferson's speeches; "Washington and the Cherokees, 1796," *Cherokee Phoenix* 1, no. 5 (March 20, 1828): 1–2. See also

Perdue, *Cherokee Women*; Johnston, *Cherokee Women in Crisis*; Yarbrough, *Race and the Cherokee Nation*.

72. Asserting their superiority and greater power in official negotiations, the Cherokees referred to the Choctaws as "little brothers." For a valuable discussion of Native American imperial-like contests for power, see Hämäläinen, *Comanche Empire*.

73. "Washington and the Cherokees, 1796," *Cherokee Phoenix* 1, no. 5 (March 20, 1828): 1–2.

74. Young, "Exercise of Sovereignty," 47.

75. See Calloway, *White People, Indians, and Highlanders*.

76. Perdue, *Cherokee Women*, 81.

77. McLoughlin, *Cherokee Renascence*, 39. Note that what is now Princeton University was then called the College of New Jersey, Princeton. See Axtell, *Making of Princeton University*.

78. McLoughlin, *Cherokee Renascence*, 39, 42.

79. McLoughlin, *Cherokee Renascence*, 47–48.

80. Quoted in Perdue, *Cherokee Women*, 147; and McLoughlin, *Cherokee Renascence*, 70–71.

81. McLoughlin, *Cherokees and Missionaries*, 175; McLoughlin, *Cherokees and Christianity*, 265.

82. Thornton, *Cherokees*, 53. Slaves from nearby states cannily used Cherokee territory as an escape route, which led to additional tensions with neighbors. By the same token, Cherokee slaves also escaped into other states.

83. Bataille and Laurie, *Native American Women*, 331.

84. Yarbrough, "Legislating Women's Sexuality"; Yarbrough, *Race and the Cherokee Nation*. The Cherokee Committee feared that social intermixing could cause Cherokee status to deteriorate even further.

85. McLoughlin, *Cherokee Renascence*, 358. The "American race" or Indigenous Americans were often seen as equal in the early nineteenth-century Enlightenment period. By the 1850s, a more hierarchical notion of color, race, and superiority prevailed in the United States. See Shoemaker, "How the Indians Got to Be Red."

86. Cherokee Nation, *Laws of the Cherokee Nation*, 38.

87. Gordon-Reed, *Hemingses of Monticello*.

88. Requests for slaves to assist households appeared from time to time in the ABCFM papers relating to the Cherokee missions in the South. Evarts and others, correspondence, in ABCFM Archives, Houghton Library; Miles, *Ties That Bind*, 65; McLoughlin and Conser, "Cherokees in Transition."

89. Cott, *Public Vows*, 61–63. See also Lewis, "Republican Wife."

90. John Ridge to Gallatin, March 10 [February 27], 1826, in Sturtevant, "John Ridge on Cherokee Civilization," 81. See also Konkle, *Writing Indian Nations*, 58; Minges, *Slavery in the Cherokee Nation*, 36.

91. See Miles, *Ties That Bind*; Sturm, *Blood Politics*, 59–60; W. Anderson, Brown, and Rogers, *Payne-Butrick Papers*, 106–9.

92. See Yarbrough, *Race and the Cherokee Nation*, 36–37, 50, 58; Weierman, *One Nation, One Blood*, 54; Smithers, *Cherokee Diaspora*, 103.
93. Cherokee Nation, *Laws of the Cherokee Nation*, 131–32.
94. Perdue, *Cherokee Women*, 43.
95. "Matrimony," *Cherokee Phoenix* 1, no. 3 (March 6, 1828): 3. It was not until the 1840s and 1850s that white women in most states of the United States became entitled to retain property in marriage.
96. Sturm, *Blood Politics*, 54.
97. "Washington and the Cherokees, 1796," *Cherokee Phoenix* 1, no. 5 (March 20, 1828): 1–2. See also Perdue, *Cherokee Women*, 111.
98. R. Anderson, *Memoir of Catharine Brown*, 96.
99. Yarbrough, *Race and the Cherokee Nation*, 52–65. Yarbrough extends the intermarriage story to the 1850s, when more extensive legislation was introduced, noting the paternalistic nature of marriage interventions in which male lawmakers restricted women's marital choices.
100. Under contemporary law of the early nineteenth century, Anglo-American and British wives were treated as the property of the husband and had no property rights themselves. Upon marriage, the wife's own property assets became her husband's, who was at liberty to dispose of them. Salmon, *Women and the Law of Property*.
101. Cherokee Nation, *Laws of the Cherokee Nation*, 10 (emphasis added).
102. John Ridge to Gallatin, March 10 [February 27], 1826, in Sturtevant, "John Ridge on Cherokee Civilization," 83.
103. John Ridge to Gallatin, March 10 [February 27], 1826, in Sturtevant, "John Ridge on Cherokee Civilization," 84.
104. Cherokee Nation, *Laws of the Cherokee Nation*, 142–43.
105. Shyrock and Smail, *Deep History*; Smail, "In the Grip of Sacred History."
106. Boudinot [IV], *Star in the West*. This is the Euro-American Boudinot, president of the Bible Society.
107. Wollstonecraft, *Vindication of the Rights of Woman*, 87; Barker-Benfield, *Abigail and John Adams*, 425–26.
108. Cott, *Public Vows*, 79.
109. Cott, *Public Vows*.
110. Many Cherokees, Choctaws, and others cherished their appellation as "civilized tribes," and the notion of being "civilized" demanded relatively stable categories. Yet to these peoples, "civilized" did not imply cultural absorption nor did it suggest loss of face, or betrayal or selling out of their polity. Both Cherokee traditionalists and progressive factions believed in Cherokee sovereignty and were following anticolonial political agendas. See also Cumfer, *Separate Peoples, One Land*, 231–36.
111. Cott, *Public Vows*, 11, 59. The preamble to the 1827 Cherokee Constitution acknowledges the "goodness of the sovereign Ruler of the Universe," imploring "*his* aid and direction" to guide the government. "Constitution of the Cherokee Nation: July 1827,"

Cherokee Phoenix 1, no.1 (February 21, 1828): 1–2. Such a higher power is also implored by Socrates in "Strictures on the Report of the Joint Committee."

112. See Holmes, *Shelley on Love*; Plato, *Symposium*.
113. Shelley, "Women as Property," in Holmes, *Shelley on Love*, 64. See also Wollstonecraft, *Vindication of the Rights of Woman*. Cherokee views coincided with environmentalist understandings from contemporary natural scientists: "The brothers *from this side* of the sea were originally *white* as those from the other side, but they did not take the same care to protect themselves against the sun." Saunt, "Telling Stories," 678.
114. Irving, "Miscellaneous Traits of Indian Character."
115. For details about the Great Seal of the United States committees, see "Original Design of the Great Seal of the United States," 1782, *Our Documents: 100 Milestone Documents from the National Archives*, U.S. National Archives, http://www.ourdocuments.gov/doc.php?flash=true&doc=5. See also "Third Great Seal Committee — May 1782," GreatSeal.com, http://greatseal.com/committees/thirdcomm/index.html.
116. The Great Seal dropped the burnt-earth meaning of the phoenix but included the arrows of Indian warfare. "Original Design of the Great Seal of the United States," 1782, *Our Documents: 100 Milestone Documents from the National Archives*, U.S. National Archives, http://www.ourdocuments.gov/doc.php?flash=true&doc=5.
117. Bibliophile Society, *Romance of Mary W. Shelley*; de Baillou, *John Howard Payne*, 4–5; Harrison, *John Howard Payne*. Again, there is a story of Payne falling in love with Mary Harden, a general's daughter from Athens, Georgia. He stayed at their home on his way to the Cherokee country. Neither ever married.
118. John Howard Payne, quoted in Perdue, *Cherokee Women*, 44.
119. Irving, "Miscellaneous Traits of Indian Character," March 6, 1828. See also Irving, "Miscellaneous Traits of Indian Character," March 13 and March 20, 1828.
120. Miles, "Circular Reasoning."
121. Sturtevant, "John Ridge on Cherokee Civilization," 79–80.
122. Sturtevant, "John Ridge on Cherokee Civilization," 85. This letter from John Ridge is also interesting for what it leaves out. Although not mentioning the specifics of intermarriages with white women or white men, he makes an important comment about intermarriage at the end of his letter. Anglo-American commentators, he remarked, including the benevolent Albert Gallatin, stereotyped Indian women as "slaves and beasts of burden," either failing to understand or intentionally ignorant of their cultural and material power.
123. Although only twenty-three years old, Ridge accepted his role as a literate bilingual man of speaking to Anglo-Americans on behalf of Cherokee men and women, revealing how the authority of Cherokee elders was changing in response to white demands to negotiate in English and otherwise think along English lines.
124. Sturtevant, "John Ridge on Cherokee Civilization," 85.
125. Waterhunter, "The Wedding," *Cherokee Phoenix* 1, no. 13 (May 21, 1828): 2.
126. *Cherokee Phoenix*, quoted in Corman, "Reading, Writing and Removal," 199.

127. Ellinghaus, *Taking Assimilation to Heart*; Ellinghaus, "Taking Assimilation to Heart."
128. John Ridge to Gallatin, March 10 [February 27], 1826, in Sturtevant, "John Ridge on Cherokee Civilization."
129. See Block, *Rape and Sexual Power*.
130. John Ridge to Gallatin, March 10 [February 27], 1826, in Sturtevant, "John Ridge on Cherokee Civilization," 82.
131. Teuton, *Cherokee Stories*, 42.
132. Perdue, *Cherokee Women*, 159–84; Hutchins, "Rattlesnakes in the Garden." A number of Cherokee artists and storytellers depict powerful mythical creatures that are serpents, snakes, or hybrid snake-like monsters. Teuton, *Cherokee Stories*.
133. Authoritative leaders managed to get into the Christian boarding schools to preach a segregationist message that rejected the white immigrants' values as evil and argued for segregation for their own "good society." See McLoughlin, *Cherokee Renascence*.
134. Yarbrough, "Legislating Women's Sexuality"; Persico "Early Nineteenth-Century Cherokee Political Organisation," 95. The Cherokee National Council was established in 1817.
135. Socrates, "Strictures on the Report of the Joint Committee."
136. De Ville, "Sovereignty without Sovereignty," in Barbour and Pavlich, *After Sovereignty*, 58–59, 61–63. Derrida has written on the "purity" or finality of the signature as compared with the iterative speech event, which was not final and subject to repetition.
137. Laws and punishments were founded on gender and race. See Yarbrough, "Legislating Women's Sexuality."
138. On Georgian debates, see U.S. Congress, *Report of the Select Committee*.
139. See Cumfer, *Separate Peoples, One Land*, 180–81, 188–89, 197.
140. "General Council of the Cherokee Nation," *Cherokee Phoenix* 1, no. 37 (November 12, 1828): 1–2.
141. "General Council," *Cherokee Phoenix* 2, no. 28 (October 21, 1829): 3 (emphasis added).
142. Lake and Reynolds, *Drawing the Global Color Line*.
143. See Sturm, *Blood Politics*. The Cherokees have been attempting to control citizenship through race or blood quantum ever since.
144. Boudinot quoted in Peyer, "Elias Boudinot and the Cherokee Betrayal," in *Tutor'd Mind*, 127–30 (emphasis in original).
145. See Barker-Benfield, *Culture of Sensibility*; Barker-Benfield, *Abigail and John Adams*.
146. Barbour and Pavlich, *After Sovereignty*, 6.
147. Plato, *Phaedrus*.
148. Socrates, "Strictures on the Report of the Joint Committee."
149. Hine and Faragher, *American West*, 176.
150. Cherokee Nation v. Georgia (1831); Peters, *Case of the Cherokee Nation*, 2.
151. See *Brainerd Journal*, November 11–12, 1824, 18.3.1, vol. 2, ABCFM Archives, Houghton Library. See also McLoughlin, *Cherokee Renascence*, 369.

4. JOHN ROSS AND MARY BRYAN STAPLER

1. Cited in Perdue, *"Mixed Blood" Indians*, 94–95; see also McLoughlin, *Cherokee Renascence*, 70. After 1825 such wives and children had some protection under new Cherokee laws, which assured their citizenship, but they did not necessarily gain full cultural rights. Although Ross may have backed the changes, political developments further complicated Cherokee attitudes toward intermarriage. According to the historian of the Cherokees Theda Perdue, because of the uncertain status of any children born into their matrilineal society, his opposition was not racial but cultural. Whether the categories of race and culture can be entirely separated is a moot point.
2. See Denson, "The Long and Intimate Connection" in *Demanding the Cherokee Nation*, 15–52, quote on 32. The spelling "connexion" is drawn from the Vaill collection of letters.
3. Perdue, *"Mixed Blood" Indians*, 94; Ann Paine, Notebook 2, December 20, 1820, ABCFM Archives, Houghton Library.
4. Mary's middle name was sometimes spelled "Brian" or "Bryant."
5. Perdue, *Cherokee Women*, 150.
6. Ross to Sarah F. Stapler, April 2, 1842, in J. Ross, *Papers*, 2:119.
7. Mary to Ross, July 14, 1844, in J. Ross, *Papers*, 2:220–21.
8. T. Wilkins, *Cherokee Tragedy*, 205; Moulton, *John Ross*, 6.
9. Some have suggested the bird was an egret; however, the exact species is obscure. See, for example, Fradin, *Trail of Tears*, 23.
10. For example, Ross used the name in correspondence with McKenney: Ross to Thomas L. McKenney, August 25, 1844, in J. Ross, *Papers*, 2:241. For its use in correspondence with Mary, see Ross to Mary B. Stapler, June 16, 1844, in J. Ross, *Papers*, 2:208–9.
11. Ross and Payne were released November 16, 1835. Moulton, *John Ross*, 69. See also Hine and Faragher, *American West*, 177.
12. Worcester and Butler were jailed in 1831, released March 3, 1832. Moulton, *John Ross*, 45–46.
13. McLoughlin, *Cherokees and Missionaries*, 307.
14. McLoughlin, *Cherokees and Missionaries*, 307.
15. Keel, *Cherokee Archaeology*; Mooney, *Myths of the Cherokee*.
16. McLoughlin, *Cherokees and Missionaries*, 306–7.
17. Hine and Faragher, *American West*, 177.
18. Hine and Faragher, *American West*, 177–78; Thornton, *Cherokees*, 74–76. Although the figure of four thousand deaths is accepted by most recent scholars, there are difficulties with accurate measurement. See also Lumpkin, *Removal of the Cherokee Indians*; Emmet Starr, *History of the Cherokee Indians*.
19. Moulton, *John Ross*, 12–13.
20. Woodward, *The Cherokees*, 176, 217. See also Perdue and Green, *Cherokee Nation and the Trail of Tears*.
21. Ross's ongoing task was to work with a U.S. political system that had backtracked on previously recognized treaties and its own federal court rulings on Cherokee sovereignty.

22. Ross to Elizabeth Milligan, September 5, 1841, in J. Ross, *Papers*, 2:101.
23. Ross to Elizabeth Milligan, September 5, 1841, in J. Ross, *Papers*, 2:101.
24. McKenney and Hall, *History of the Indian Tribes*, 310, refers to Ross as "a leader of his people in their exodus from the land of their nativity to a new country, and from the savage state to that of civilisation." However, McLoughlin states that he may have been "like Moses." McLoughlin, *Cherokees and Missionaries*, 349.
25. All three Cherokee delegations were present in 1844. Moulton, *John Ross*, 56–57.
26. Moulton, *John Ross*, 113, 116, 126.
27. As travel was too dangerous, Ross was advised to seek safety in a nearby fort, but he was disinclined to leave his stately home unprotected. Moulton lists the threat against Ross's life as coming from Stand Watie and the letter warning him as being from Mrs. (Delight Sargeant) Boudinot. The narrative is derived from letters between General Arbuckle and Ross and a statement from T. C. Hindman in the Ross papers. Moulton states that Arbuckle recommended Ross should enter Fort Garrison, but on the advice of his friends, he instead stationed two hundred guards around his home. Moulton, *John Ross*, 113; J. Ross, *Papers*, 1:717–18.
28. Moulton, *John Ross*, 128–29; Ross to Elizabeth Milligan, September 19, 1842, in J. Ross, *Papers*, 2:148.
29. McLoughlin, *Cherokees and Missionaries*, 349.
30. T. Wilkins, *Cherokee Tragedy*, 205.
31. McKenney and Hall, *History of the Indian Tribes*, 310.
32. Moulton, *John Ross*, 6.
33. Moulton, *John Ross*, 155.
34. Quatie's child Susan married Ross's nephew William Shorey Coodey. Moulton, *John Ross*, 13; A. Ross, "Murder of Elias Boudinot."
35. For example, Ross to William P. Ross, August 19, 1841, in J. Ross, *Papers*, 2:96–97. Ross's only daughter, Jane, born in 1821 and some five years older than Mary, had attended the Moravian Female Academy in Salem, North Carolina. John found time to shepherd a new Cherokee diaspora in the "civilized" parts of the United States. J. Ross, *Papers* 1:4; Smithers, *Cherokee Diaspora*.
36. Ross to Araminta, May 8, 1841, in J. Ross, *Papers*, 2:84.
37. J. Ross, *Papers*, 2:203, 235–36.
38. Mary B. and Sarah F. Stapler to "Most Esteemed Uncle" [John Ross], to [and 23], 1844; and Mary to "My dearest Friend" [John Ross], August 6, 1844, in J. Ross, *Papers*, 2:203, 236.
39. Ross to Sarah F. Stapler, April 2, 1842, in J. Ross, *Papers*, 2:118–19.
40. Mary to John, August 10, 1841, in J. Ross, *Papers*, 2:94–95; Prucha, "Thomas L. McKenney"; Viola, *Thomas Lorraine McKenney*.
41. Mary B. Stapler and Sarah F. Stapler to Ross, August 10, 1841, in J. Ross, *Papers*, 2:94–95 (emphasis in original).
42. Ross to Mary B. Stapler, June 27, 1844, in J. Ross, *Papers*, 2:212–14. Ossian's writings were also very popular at the time.

43. Mary B. Stapler and Sarah F. Stapler to Ross, August 10, 1841, in J. Ross, *Papers*, 2:94–95.
44. Kvasnicka and Viola, *Commissioners of Indian Affairs*, 1–2; Viola, *Thomas Lorraine McKenney*.
45. Viola, *Thomas Lorraine McKenney*; J. Ross, *Papers*, 2:743
46. Viola, *Thomas Lorraine McKenney*; Remini, *Andrew Jackson & His Indian Wars*, 214–51; Tyrrell, *Transnational Nation*, 74–75; *Philadelphia Inquirer*, March 21, 1843, 2; *Philadelphia Inquirer*, July 24, 1843, 2; "The Indians and Col. McKenny's Plan for Their Protection," *National Aegis*, November 1, 1843, 2; Weierman, *One Nation, One Blood*, 51–52.
47. Ross to Mary B. Stapler, June 16, 1844, in J. Ross, *Papers*, 2:209 (emphasis in original). By June 1844 Ross was writing to Mary under his Cherokee totemic name, Kooweskoowe.
48. Nanohetahee Richard Taylor to John Lowrey, John Walker, Major Ridge, Richard Taylor, Ross, and Cheucunsenee, January 10–11, 1816, in J. Ross, *Papers*, 1:22.
49. McKenney's troubles finding employment have sometimes been attributed to his "thinking too much" of the Indians at a time of Jacksonian hostility. It was more complicated than this and was due to other political enmities and legacies, especially his backing of Calhoun rather than the successful presidential nominee, Jackson. McKenney and Hall, *History of the Indian Tribes*; McKenney, *Memoirs*.
50. Mary B. Stapler and Sarah F. Stapler to Ross, August 10, 1841, in J. Ross, *Papers*, 2:94–95.
51. Mary B. Stapler and Sarah F. Stapler to Ross, August 10, 1841, in J. Ross, *Papers*, 2:94–95. Reverend Kummer was a tutor at the Bethlehem School for Ladies from 1815; from 1826 he was the principal of Linden Hall. Mombert, *Authentic History of Lancaster County*, 458, 468. See also C. O. Zigenfuss, "Borough History of Bethlehem," U.S. GenWeb Archives, http://files.usgwarchives.net/pa/northampton/history/local/davis/davis22.txt.
52. John Ross to Sarah F. Stapler, April 2, 1842, in J. Ross, *Papers*, 2:118–19. The Brandywine River meets the Christine River at Wilmington. There is a Stapler Park in Wilmington, Delaware, near Pennsylvania Avenue. The Quaker meeting hall was in the locality known as Quaker Hills today. The Delaware Historical Society holds listings of the Stapler family and details of membership of the Quaker meetinghouses. Mary Bryan Stapler was buried in Wilmington and Brandywine Cemetery, Wilmington, Delaware. An early railway line linked Wilmington, Baltimore, and Philadelphia from 1837. Munroe, *History of Delaware*; Smiley, *History of Wilmington*.
53. Elizabeth Kornhauser, "All Nature Is New to Art," in Johns, Sayers, Kornhauser, and Ellis, *New Worlds from Old*, 71–77.
54. McLoughlin, *Cherokee Renascence*; McLoughlin, *Cherokees and Missionaries*.
55. See the letters of Mary in J. Ross, *Papers*.
56. P. Deloria, *Playing Indian*; Green, "Pocahontas Perplex"; Berkhofer, *White Man's Indian*.
57. Hale's and Morse's works were published in the 1810s; see Saunt, "Telling Stories."
58. Ross to Sarah F. Stapler, April 2, 1842, in J. Ross, *Papers*, 2:118 (emphasis in original).

59. Cott, *Bonds of Womanhood*.
60. Lewis Ross, John's brother, warned him to only travel with friends and to be on guard. Lewis Ross to John, January 3, 1840, in J. Ross, *Papers*, 2:4–5.
61. Mary B. Stapler to Ross, August 1, 1844, in J. Ross, *Papers*, 2:231.
62. Ross to John Howard Payne, January 22, 1840, in J. Ross, *Papers*, 2:5–6. See also Harrison, *Life and Writing of John Howard Payne*. The lyrics were written for a play staged in London, England, but Payne was an actor already well known in the United States. Patriotic American audiences made the song their own.
63. Mary B. Stapler to Ross, May 3, 1844, in J. Ross, *Papers*, 2:197.
64. Charvat, "American Romanticism and the Depression of 1837."
65. Emerson, "Letter to Martin Van Buren," in Filler and Guttmann, *Removal of the Cherokee Nation*, 94–97.
66. McCalman, *Oxford Companion to the Romantic Age*.
67. Mary B. Stapler to John, May 22, 1844, in J. Ross, *Papers*, 2:202.
68. Mary B. Stapler and Sarah F. Stapler to Ross, May 22 [and 23], 1844, in J. Ross, *Papers*, 2:203.
69. E. Jane Ross to Ross, June 8, 1844, in J. Ross, *Papers*, 2:206
70. E. Jane Ross to Ross, June 8, 1844; Ross to Mary Connelly, September 12, 1841; Ross to E. Jane Ross, June 18, 1844; Mary Connelly to Ross, May 30, 1844, in J. Ross, *Papers*, 2:206, 103–4, 210–11, 197. Eliza and Mary stayed friends and Mary B. Stapler Ross asked after her in 1865, referring to her as "our good kind friend." Mary B. Ross to Ross, January 10, 1865, in J. Ross, *Papers*, 2:617. Had she ever given up on John?
71. Ross to E. Jane Ross, June 8, 1844, in J. Ross, *Papers*, 2:207.
72. Ross to Mary B. Stapler, August 13 [and 14], 1844; Mary B. Stapler to Ross, June 16, 1844, in J. Ross, *Papers*, 2:237–38, 208.
73. Ross to Mary B. Stapler, August 13 [and 14], 1844, in J. Ross, *Papers*, 2:237; "Clay Clubs," *Portland Advertiser*, August 3, 1844; *Eastern Argus*, August 8, 1844; *Portland Directory*, 296.
74. Ross to Mary B. Stapler, August 13 [and 14], 1844, in J. Ross, *Papers*, 2:237.
75. Ross to Mary B. Stapler, June 27, [June 30, and July 1], 1844, in J. Ross, *Papers*, 2:212–13 (emphasis added).
76. McKenney *Memoirs*, 109–12, 116–20.
77. Ross to Mary B. Stapler, June 16, 1844, in J. Ross, *Papers*, 2:208 (emphasis in original).
78. Ross to Mary B. Stapler, June 27, [June 30, and July 1] 1844, in J. Ross, *Papers*, 2:212.
79. Ross to Mary B. Stapler, May 9, 1844, in J. Ross, *Papers*, 2:200.
80. Ross to Mary B. Stapler, June 16, 1844, in J. Ross, *Papers*, 2:209. "Sachem" was the term for chief and spiritual leader used in earlier contact literature and now applied as a pan-Indian category.
81. Exhibition on display at the Museum of the Cherokee Indian, Cherokee, North Carolina, April 12, 1998. By now even the traditionalists among the Cherokees had replaced "soft dressed buffalo skins" with other fabrics—buffalo being too difficult to obtain

anyway. Indeed, the Cherokees had great flair for adapting French and English fashion to their own tastes in stylish original outfits. The New Echota Historic Site and Museum, Calhoun, Georgia, displays depictions of various stunning fashion ensembles. See Cherokee portraits in McKenney and Hall, *History of the Indian Tribes*.

82. McKenney and Hall, *History of the Indian Tribes*.
83. William P. Ross to Ross, August 2, 1842, in J. Ross, *Papers*, 2:144.
84. Bibliophile Society, *Romance of Mary W. Shelley*.
85. Mary B. Stapler to Ross, July 14, 1844, in J. Ross, *Papers*, 2:220–21. Mary did not follow the stanzas of the publication. The poem actually ends with "I only know we loved in vain — I only feel — Farewell! Farewell!" Moore, *Works of Lord Byron*, 211.
86. Moore, *Works of Lord Byron*, 97–98.
87. Ross to Mary B. Stapler, July 25, 1844, in J. Ross, *Papers*, 2:228–29.
88. Ross to Mary B. Stapler, June 27, [June 30, and July 1], 1844, in J. Ross, *Papers*, 2:214 (emphasis in original).
89. Mary B. Stapler to Ross, July 28, 1844, in J. Ross, *Papers*, 2:229–30. For Ross and Mary's correspondence over this period, see J. Ross, *Papers*, 2:202–42.
90. Ross to Mary B. Stapler, June 27, [June 30, and July 1], 1844, in J. Ross, *Papers*, 2:212–14.
91. Ross to Mary B. Stapler, May 9, 1844, in J. Ross, *Papers*, 2:199.
92. *Daily Argus*, August 17, 1844.
93. Please note that some texts use the spelling "Dolly" and some "Dolley." I have settled on the most common spelling, Dolley, as recognized by Holly C. Shulman. See David Sewell, "Dolley Madison Digital Edition: 300 New Documents," University of Virginia Press blog, April 24, 2013, http://www.upress.virginia.edu/2013/04/24/dolley-madison-digital-edition-300-new-documents/.
94. Ross [signed Kooweskoowe] to Mary B. Stapler, June 16, 1844, in J. Ross, *Papers*, 2:208–9 (emphasis in original).
95. Ross to Mary B. Stapler, August 28, 1844, in J. Ross, *Papers*, 2:242.
96. Ross to Mary B. Stapler, May 9, 1844, in J. Ross, *Papers*, 2:199.
97. Mary B. Stapler to Ross, June 26, 1844, in J. Ross, *Papers*, 211–12.
98. Ross to Mary B. Stapler, July 27 [and August 1–2], 1844, in J. Ross, *Papers*, 2:232 (emphasis in original).
99. Perdue, *Cherokee Women*, 150, 154.
100. Mary B. Stapler and Sarah F. Stapler to Ross, May 22 [and 23], 1844, in J. Ross, *Papers*, 2:203.
101. Ross to Mary B. Stapler, July 27 [and August 1–2], 1844, in J. Ross, *Papers*, 2:232–33.
102. Ross to Mary B. Stapler, July 27 [and August 1–2], 1844, in J. Ross, *Papers*, 2:233.
103. McKenney, *Memoirs*, 118–19.
104. McKenney, *Memoirs*, 117. Green, "Pocahontas Perplex," discusses the tragic motif of the jilted Indian lover and his or her tendency to jump off cliffs.
105. Ross to Mary B. Stapler, June 27, [June 30, and July 1], 1844, in J. Ross, *Papers*, 2:212.
106. Ross to Mary B. Stapler, July 27 [and August 1–2], 1844, in J. Ross, *Papers*, 2:232–33.

107. Sarah F. Stapler to Ross, August 17, 1844, in J. Ross, *Papers*, 2:240.
108. Ross to John Stapler, August 14, 1844, in J. Ross, *Papers*, 2:238–39. John Stapler Sr. died in the Indian Territory and is buried at Tahlequah on the summit of the Ross family burial grounds. Ross to Maria B. Stapler, January 18, 1861, in J. Ross, *Papers*, 2:455.
109. Sarah F. Stapler to Ross, August 17, 1844, in J. Ross, *Papers*, 2:240 (emphasis in original).
110. Mary B. Stapler to Ross, August 26, 1844, in J. Ross, *Papers*, 2:241.
111. This letter was not found, but Mary responded to Ross at the end of August and it appears that his previous letter was relatively recent.
112. Mary B. Stapler to Ross, August 28, 1844, in J. Ross, *Papers*, 2:242.
113. Ross to Thomas L. McKenney, August 25, 1844, in J. Ross, *Papers*, 2:240–41.
114. Ross to Thomas L. McKenney, August 25, 1844, in J. Ross, *Papers*, 2:240–41. See also Lyons, *Sex among the Rabble*.
115. In *John Ross*, Moulton mistakenly has McKenney at the ceremony; he was invited but unable to attend. Gary Moulton and I have discussed the matter and he notes this was an error. Ross to McKenney, July 3, 1844; Ross to McKenney, September 6, 1844, in J. Ross, *Papers*, 2:214–15, 243–44; Gary Moulton, personal communication, August 20, 2010.
116. Ross to Thomas L. McKenney, August 25, 1844, in J. Ross, *Papers*, 2:240–41.
117. Ross to Thomas L. McKenney, August 25, 1844, in J. Ross, *Papers*, 2:241.
118. This recalls John Demos's telling in *Unredeemed Captive* of a kidnapped white wife who did not wish to leave her Indian husband or family.
119. Mary B. Stapler to Ross, August 6, 1844; Mary B. Stapler to Ross, August 1844, in J. Ross, *Papers*, 2:236–37.
120. Ross to Mary B. Stapler, July 27 [and August 1–2], 1844; Mary B. Stapler to Ross, August 13, 1844; Ross to Mary B. Stapler, August 13 [and 14], 1844, in J. Ross, *Papers*, 2:232–33, 236–37, 237–38.
121. Ross to Mary B. Stapler, July 27 [and August 1–2], 1844, in J. Ross, *Papers*, 2:232–33. Similarly, Ross had spoken of "consummation" [*sic*] of negotiations with President Tyler. Ross to Sarah Stapler, April 2, 1842, in J. Ross, *Papers*, 2:119.
122. "Correspondence Commercial Advertiser," *Spectator*, August 7, 1844, 4.
123. "2 September 1844," folder 5326.290, Ross Collection, Gilcrease Museum.
124. Nanohetahee (X) and Richard Taylor to John Lowrey, John Walker, Major Ridge, Richard Taylor, Ross, and Cheucunsenee, January 10 [and 11], 1816, in J. Ross, *Papers*, 2:22–23.
125. Ford, *Settler Sovereignty*.
126. McLoughlin, *Cherokees and Missionaries*, 9–10.
127. McLoughlin, *Cherokees and Missionaries*, 348–49, 350–51.
128. Ross to Mary B. Stapler, June 27 [June 30 and July 1], 1844, in J. Ross, *Papers*, 2:213–14. Ross also mentions attending church services, rehearses what he heard, and renders something of a pious sermon himself. Ross's pious oratory is cited in letter excerpts in McKenney and Hall, *History of the Indian Tribes*, 323; McLoughlin, *Cherokees and Missionaries*, 348–49.

129. Westcott, *History of Philadelphia*.
130. Ross to Thomas L. McKenney, September 6, 1844, in J. Ross, *Papers*, 2:243.
131. Weems, *Life of William Penn*, 149.
132. Kenny, *Peaceable Kingdom Lost*, 1–3; Moulton, *John Ross*, 7; Richter, "Onas, the Long Knife."
133. Quoted in McKenney and Hall, *History of the Indian Tribes*, 323; Denson, *Demanding the Cherokee Nation*, 25. See also Austen, "Marrying Red."
134. Penn, *Essays on the Present Crisis*; Andrew, *From Revivals to Removal*. See various issues of the *Cherokee Phoenix* for Evarts's use of the pen name.
135. Unfortunately the original Penn was not particularly inspired when it came to the rights of white women, including widows, to property. Salmon, *Women and the Law of Property*, 163–66.
136. See Nash, *First City*.
137. Kenny, *Peaceable Kingdom Lost*, 1–3.
138. "History of Philadelphia," in *Pennsylvania Almanac*, 470–74. McElroy, *McElroy's Philadelphia City Directory*, 363, lists "Hartwell H.J. (Washington House) Chestnut above 7th." Stevick, *Imagining Philadelphia*; Dorsey, *Reforming Men and Women*.
139. The exact site is a matter of some dispute. Famous representations of the meeting and treaty signing include Quaker artist Edward Hicks's painting *Peaceable Kingdom* and Benjamin West's *Penn's Treaty with the Indians at Shackamxon*. See Kenny, *Peaceable Kingdom Lost*, 15, frontispiece. For an image of the hotel where John and Mary were married, see Julio Rae, 700 block chestnut Street, north side, eastern portion, *Philadelphia Pictorial Directory and Panoramic Advertiser*, 1851, in *Places in Time: Historical Documentation of Place in Greater Philadelphia*, Bryn Mawr College, http://www.brynmawr.edu/iconog/panos/r7ne11A.jpg.
140. See Ross to Mary B. Stapler, July 19, 1844; Ross to John G. Kummer, April 25, 1842, in J. Ross, *Papers*, 2:228, 121. The latter letter is stamped "Washington House 223 Chestnut St. Philadelphia."
141. William P. Ross to Ross, May 23, 1842, in J. Ross, *Papers*, 2:124–25. Viola refers to the "Chestnut Street boarding house." Viola, *Thomas Lorraine McKenney*, 281.
142. Rae panorama of 700 block chestnut Street, north side, eastern portion, in *Places in Time*, http://www.brynmawr.edu/iconog/panos/r7ne11A.jpg; Wright, *First Wall Street*.
143. Quoted in S. Warner, *Private City*, 83. For photos of Philadelphia fashions, see S. A. and A. F. Ward, "Philadelphia Fashions, Spring and Summer 1844," Flickr photostream, Library Company of Philadelphia, http://www.flickr.com/photos/library-company-of-philadelphia/4679164183/.
144. Jeff Cohen, personal communication, ca. 2010.
145. The Cherokees held the first president in special regard. Their chiefs had put much effort into making up political ground with him, and they had studied the details of his letters and addresses.

146. Peter Van Allen, "President's House Exhibit at Washington's Residence Opens in Phila.," *Philadelphia Business Journal*, December 15, 2010; Edward Lawler Jr., "A Brief History of the President's House in Philadelphia," updated May 2010, USHistory.org, http://www.ushistory.org/presidentshouse/history/briefhistory.htm.
147. Washington quoted in Oberg, *Dominion and Civility*, 1.
148. John Tyler to Ross, David Vann, and John Benge, September 20, 1841, in J. Ross, *Papers*, 2:104–5. John Tyler was the tenth president of the United States, April 6, 1841, to March 3, 1845.
149. *Pennsylvania Inquirer and National Gazette*, September 3, 1844.
150. "Marriage Extraordinary," *Public Ledger*, September 5, 1844, 5. See also "Marriage Extraordinary," *Sun*, September 6, 1844, 2; "Marriage of Ross," *Spectator*, September 7, 1844, 1.
151. Ross John to Thomas L. McKenney, September 6, 1844, in J. Ross, *Papers*, 2:243.
152. John Tyler to Ross, David Vann, and John Benge, September 20, 1841, in J. Ross, *Papers*, 2:104–5.
153. Ross to Sarah F. Stapler, April 2; Ross to Thomas L. McKenney, July 3, 1844, in J. Ross, *Papers*, 2:118–19, 214.
154. Perdue, *Cherokee Women*; Johnston, *Cherokee Women in Crisis*; Yarbrough, *Race and the Cherokee Nation*.
155. Moulton, *John Ross*, 6–7.
156. See Saunt, "Telling Stories"; Stoler, *Along the Archival Grain*.
157. Mary B. Stapler to Ross, July 27 [and August 1–2], 1844, in J. Ross, *Papers*, 2:232–33.
158. Mary B. Stapler to Ross, July 14, 1844, in J. Ross, *Papers*, 2:221.
159. Mary B. Stapler to Ross, August 10, 1841, in J. Ross, *Papers*, 2:94–95.
160. Ross to Mary B. Stapler, May 9, 1844, in J. Ross, *Papers*, 2:199.
161. Renee Harvey, Gilcrease librarian, personal communication, August 20, 2010. The collection was sold to the Gilcrease Museum by Mrs. Pyburn, a descendent of John Ross.
162. [Dolley Madison], "The Burning of Washington: August 23, 1814," Amy Ridenour's blog, National Center for Public Policy Research, http://www.nationalcenter.org/WashingtonBurning1814.html. Other witnesses, and more recently, historians, have disputed the story, but Dolley Madison's letter to her sister the day before is fairly convincing. Whether it was she who saved the portrait or ordered it to be saved, what is most relevant is the way this "saving" of a symbol of the republic's heritage—the portrait of its first president—had gathered such cherished significance.
163. Cutts, *Memoirs and Letters of Dolly Madison*.
164. Jefferson, 1808, quoted in McLoughlin, *Cherokee Renascence*, 33 (emphasis added).

5. HUSBANDS UNDER SURVEILLANCE

1. ADP (Aboriginal district protector), September 2, 1901, Queensland Parliamentary Papers.
2. Kidd, *Way We Civilise*; R. Evans, *History of Queensland*; Fitzgerald, *Made in Queensland*.

3. Quoted in R. Evans, Saunders, and Cronin, *Race Relations in Colonial Queensland*, 106–7.
4. Weaver, *Great Land Rush*.
5. Reynolds and Loos, "Aboriginal Resistance in Queensland"; R. Evans, *History of Queensland*; Evans, "The Country Has Another Past," in Peters-Little, Curthoys, and Docker, *Passionate Histories*; McGregor, *Imagined Destinies*; McGregor, *Indifferent Inclusion*; W. Anderson, *Cultivation of Whiteness*; Ørsted-Jensen, *Frontier History Revisited*.
6. ADP (Aboriginal district protector), September 2, 1901, Queensland Parliamentary Papers; Roth to Under Secretary, September 2, 1901; and Roth to Under Secretary, September 18, 1901, A/58764, QSA.
7. Queensland, "An Act to Amend and Consolidate the Laws Affecting the Solemnization of Marriage," A/69514, QSA. A published synopsis of the Marriage Act was also provided. See also Queensland Statutes, Queensland Parliament, 1889.
8. The British act declared this as "any authority competent to make laws for any of Her Majesty's possessions abroad." Colonial Marriages Act (28 & 29 Vic. C64), June 29, 1865, included in POL/J17, QSA.
9. Queensland, "An Act to Amend and Consolidate the Laws Affecting the Solemnization of Marriage," A/69514, QSA.
10. Synopsis of the Marriage Act, A/69514, QSA.
11. Aboriginals Protection and Restriction of the Sale of Opium Act, 1897; Kidd, *Way We Civilise*.
12. McGregor, *Imagined Destinies*, xx–xxi, 5–6.
13. For an overview of relations between the Chinese and Kuku-Yalanji, see C. Anderson and Mitchell, "Kubara." Slurs about racial "inter-breeding" and opium-trading slurs became entwined in legislative and police targeting of Asians. Only two years before this act, the opium trade was legal in Queensland and numerous social groups used opium recreationally and medicinally. Asian settlers and Pacific Islander workers had already been prohibited from competing with white men in labor and business. By preventing Asian access to Aboriginal labor and banning sexual and longer-term, marriage-style partnerships, the Aborigines Act further authorized Asian economic disadvantage.
14. The patient courtship of Jack Akbar, an Afghan, and Lallie of Linden, Western Australia, led to a life of police and family harassment. See Tonkin and Landon, *Jackson's Track*. Aborigines of mixed descent ran into trouble with restrictions on intermarriage. See Camfoo, *Love against the Law*; Probyn-Rapsey, "Uplifting White Men."
15. That the Queensland act did not prohibit white women from marrying Aboriginal men was probably not widely known, for occasionally a young woman or her guardian still sought permission to marry a man of Aboriginal descent. For a U.S. perspective, see Hodes, *White Women, Black Men*.
16. Missionary and humanitarian accounts of colonizer "vices" reflected their sexual prudery; they viewed interracial sex as causing race degradation. A nasty class of exploiters guilty

of rapaciousness and vice certainly existed. The bureaucratic window of the Marriages Files held by the Queensland State Archives permits glimpses into private emotions, including the love of several non-Aboriginal men for their Aboriginal wives. We hear directly from the men who wanted to be husbands and even from those who hoped to continue as responsible fathers.

17. Gilmore, *Gender and Jim Crow*; Klarman, *From Jim Crow to Civil Rights*.
18. Haskins and Maynard, "Sex, Race and Power"; Ellinghaus, "Margins of Acceptability"; Reed, "White Girl," 9.
19. Lake, "Frontier Feminism."
20. Cott, *Public Vows*, 65.
21. Markus, *Australian Race Relations*, chap. 4 and 5; Saunders, "The Black Scourge," in R. Evans, Saunders, and Cronin, *Race Relations in Colonial Queensland*.
22. Lake and Reynolds, *Drawing the Global Color Line*, 78, 144, 147, 164, 183, 187, 225, 233.
23. The Queensland Aboriginal population had already gained experience dealing with male newcomers from many parts of the world. Asian visitors known as Macassans from the Celebes had long preceded the British, with Aboriginal people along the far northern coasts of Arnhem Land and the Gulf of Carpentaria cooperating with their trepang and *beche de mer* trade. From the sixteenth or seventeenth century, a couple of centuries prior to British arrival, they moored on Australia's far northern beaches, planted rice and tamarind trees, arranged for Aboriginal labor and wives, and exchanged and left behind stories, words, dances, and descendants. See Stephenson, *Outsiders Within*; Ganter, *Mixed Relations*; Reekie, *On the Edge*, 18; McDonald, *Marriage in Australia*, 134.
24. Saunders, *Workers in Bondage*.
25. Reid, *Nest of Hornets*.
26. L. Moore and Williams, *True Story of Jimmy Governor*, 17–19, 27.
27. Markus, *Australian Race Relations*, 86, 73, 72. By 1860, 583 of 681 Chinese women residing in Cairns were prostitutes. Many were sold to brothel owners. Bolton, *Thousand Miles Away*; May, *Topsawyers*. For Western Australia, see J. Ryan, *Ancestors*; Hurtado, *Intimate Frontiers*, 91; Levine, *Gender and Empire*.
28. Couples were sometimes targeted for police harassment on other grounds. Vagrancy and suspicion of carrying opium were common reasons for detention, especially of Chinese men. See HOM J36, QSA.
29. For a similar situation in the Northern Territory, see McGrath, *Born in the Cattle*; Jebb and Haebich, "Across the Great Divide," in Saunders and Evans, *Gender Relations in Australia*. See also Henningham, "Picking up Colonial Experience."
30. Nash, "Hidden History of Mestizo America"; Castaneda, "Engendering the History of Alta California."
31. Moreton-Robinson, *Whitening Race*; Dyer, *White*; W. Anderson, *Cultivation of Whiteness*, 73–94; Bashford, *Imperial Hygiene*.
32. Painter, *History of White People*; Moreton-Robinson, *Whitening Race*.

33. McDougall and Davidson, *Roth Family*, 23, 267; Khan, *Catalogue of the Roth Collection*.
34. Thorpe, "Archibald Meston and Aboriginal Legislation," 54.
35. Ørsted-Jensen, *Frontier History Revisited*; Reynolds and Loos, "Aboriginal Resistance in Queensland."
36. Thorpe, "Archibald Meston and Aboriginal Legislation."
37. A. Meston to Under Secretary, Home Secretary, July 7, 1900, A/58764, QSA (emphasis in original).
38. Quoted in R. Evans, Saunders, and Cronin, *Race Relations in Colonial Queensland*, 108 (emphasis in original). This "law" was refuted by the 1920s, leading to Cecil Cook's policy to "breed out the color." See Duvall and Nerad, "Suddenly and Shockingly Black."
39. Newspapers and popular fiction were the main sources of information.
40. The term "half-caste" had already been used in New South Wales legislation during the 1830s. McCorquodale, *Aborigines and the Law*.
41. Wolfe, "Nation and MiscegeNation."
42. W. Anderson, *Cultivation of Whiteness*; McGregor, *Indifferent Inclusion*.
43. Quoted in R. Evans, Saunders, and Cronin, *Race Relations in Colonial Queensland*, 108.
44. Roth, "Report of the Northern Protector of the Aboriginals," A/589/2, QSA; McDougall and Davidson, *Roth Family*.
45. Registrar General to Under Secretary, March 4, 1901; and Registrar General to Under Secretary, September 26, 1901, A/58764, QSA. See also Kidd, *Way We Civilise*.
46. Meston to Under Secretary, August 21, 1903, A/58929, QSA.
47. J. Nicol, Seymour River, to the Protector of Aborigines Townsville, May 15, 1902, A/58929, QSA.
48. Rev. B. Bryant to Inspector Meldrum, Protector of Aborigines Townsville, May 17, 1902, A/58929, QSA. Getting the man's name wrong probably indicates that he was not a regular churchgoer.
49. Quoted in R. Evans, Saunders, and Cronin, *Race Relations in Colonial Queensland*, 108.
50. Hannah, "Constituting Marriage," 28.
51. "Marriage of Half Caste and Aboriginal Women — 1901," A/58764, QSA.
52. "Report of Northern Protector 1900," COL/142, 4884/01, QSA. For various cases, see A/58764, QSA.
53. J. Bradley to Inspector Graham, December 10, 1898, POL/J16, QSA.
54. J. Bradley to Inspector Graham, December 10, 1898, POL/J16, QSA.
55. Archibald Meston, Permit to Marry, August 4, 1903; and Rice to Sub Inspector Breene, July 13, 1903, A/58929, QSA.
56. Leary Acting Sergeant Memo, June 29, 1903; and John Greer to Sub Inspector Breene, July 13, 1903, A/58929, QSA.
57. Meston to Under Secretary, August 21, 1903, A/58929, QSA.

58. Meston to Under Secretary, August 21, 1903, A/58929, QSA.
59. John Baker to the Curator, Mogumber Mission, September 24, 1941, MN993 460/39, QSA; CNA to Sergeant Gravestock, December 9, 1941, MN993 460/39, QSA; CPA to Mitchell, October 31, 1929, WAA, ACC 653 342/25, QSA.
60. Const. James Hayes to Inspector of Police, November 22, 1903, A/58764, QSA.
61. See Report on Constable Creedy v. Ah Kow, October 20, 1906; Lee Chew statement, February 22, 1912; and various correspondence in A/45206, QSA.
62. See Report on Constable Creedy v. Ah Kow, October 20, 1906; Lee Chew statement, February 22, 1912; and various correspondence in A/45206, QSA.
63. P. Bowen, Sub Inspector, October 20, 1906, A/45206, QSA.
64. The lists of those granted permission to marry suggest that the apparently higher rate of approvals for non-Anglo men may have stemmed from the higher proportions of Asian and Pacific Islander men actually living with Aboriginal women in longer-term unions. However, I did not see complete lists of all those who applied. (Fearing white racial degradation, it is possible that protectors were just as keen if not keener to prevent hybrid whites being born as other admixtures.) As restrictions upon Asian men's employment of Aborigines denied them white men's main excuse for having these women on their premises, permission to marry was essential to avoiding other charges. Greater police surveillance and fear of deportation meant that Asian men had more reason to fear disobeying the cohabitation laws.
65. See "Tables and Graphs," in Hannah, "Constituting Marriage."
66. "The 'Sultan of Frazer's Island': A Cruel Monster," *Patriot*, [June 1902], A/58929, QSA.
67. For information on the brolga, see P. Slater, Slater, and Slater, *Slater Field Guide*, 50; Simpson, Day, and Trusler, *Field Guide*; Morcombe, *Field Guide*; "Brolga," Our Wildlife Factsheet, September 2010, Department of Sustainability and Environment, http://www.depi.vic.gov.au/__data/assets/pdf_file/0008/205883/Brolga.pdf.
68. "The 'Sultan of Frazer's Island': A Cruel Monster," *Patriot*, [June 1902], A/58929, QSA.
69. It did not lead to a changed policy, however, and another female protector, Mary McKeown, was working in 1908. Cole, Haskins, and Paisley, *Uncommon Ground*.
70. McDougall and Davidson, *Roth Family*, 267, 23; Barrie Reynolds, "Roth, Walter Edmund," *Australian Dictionary of Biography Online*, http://adb.anu.edu.au/biography/roth-walter-edmund-8280.
71. Roth to Under Secretary Home Department, September 18, 1901, A1/58764, QSA; this document summarizes discussion in other correspondence.
72. Roth, *Ethnological Studies*, 179, fig. 433, plate XXIV.
73. Walter E. Roth to Bishop White, June 19, 1904, A/58850, QSA.
74. Hamilton to Hon. Minister for Lands, June 14, 1904, A/58850, QSA, 3.
75. Roth wrote a range of glowing letters and annual reports regarding Gribble's Yarrabah Mission. For example, Roth to Under Secretary, October 9, 1905, A/58850, QSA.
76. Roth to Under Secretary, February 27, 1903, A/58850, QSA, 2.
77. Burton, *Venus Oceanica*.

78. Roth to Under Secretary, September 18, 1901, A/58764, QSA. See also various discussions in POL/J16, QSA.
79. For example, Registrar General to Under Secretary, March 4, 1901, and accompanying files, A/58764, QSA.
80. "Marriage of Half Caste and Aboriginal Women, 1901," A/58764, QSA; "Report of Northern Protector 1900," COL/142, 4884/01, QSA.
81. Foxton memorandum, August 27, 1902, A1/58764, QSA. Curiously, the wording of the act does allow for other acts to override it, but for some reason it appears that the Aboriginals Protection Act was viewed as of lesser status than the Marriage Act.
82. See Levine, *Prostitution, Race and Politics*, 10, 21, 183, 226.
83. Colonial Marriages Act (28 & 29 Vic. C64), June 29, 1865, included in POL/J17, QSA.
84. Hughes, Registrar General, to Under Secretary, March 4, 1901, A/58764, QSA.
85. Walter Edmund Roth to Under Secretary, June 1, 1902, A1/58764, QSA.

6. CONSENT AND ABORIGINAL WIVES

1. Constable James Hayes to Inspector of Police, November 22, 1903, A/58764, QSA (emphasis added).
2. Aboriginal Australians talk of their "law" in the singular — "the law" — and of a "law man" or "law woman" with gravitas. Elkin used the term "men of high degree" to indicate the high levels of attainment of certain individuals who had been "through the law" — an educational and ritual knowledge system. The term "elders" is also used interchangeably as a term of respect, although "law man" generally indicates a more elevated status and superior level of knowledge. Elkin, *Aboriginal Men of High Degree*.
3. While the term "dreaming stories" has its own history and is much debated among academics, many Aboriginal people use it for their much-valued cultural stories that explain the creation of the landscape and the correct behaviors of people on it. Stanner, "The Dreaming," in *White Man Got No Dreaming*. For a critical interrogation of "dreaming" in western representations, see Wolfe, "Should the Subaltern Dream?" Despite Wolfe's arguments, it is important to note that many Aboriginal people do speak about revelations through dreams and deploy the English word in what they consider an apt translation.
4. The Queensland State Archives has a protocol for vetting use of Aboriginal Protection Board records with the assistance of an Aboriginal liaison unit.
5. Levine, *British Empire*; Levine, *Gender and Empire*.
6. Hannah, "Constituting Marriage"; Henningham, "Picking up Colonial Experience.". The dialogic nature of "middle ground" marriages is discussed in Zastoupil, "Intimacy and Colonial Knowledge."
7. Delbridge, *Macquarie Dictionary*, 405.
8. *Merriam-Webster.com*, s.v. "constitution," http://www.merriam-webster.com/dictionary/constitution.

9. While the files do not indicate that all women were asked whether they consented, it is difficult to know whether this was a flaw in the written reports or indicative of actual practice.
10. Westermarck, *History of Human Marriage*; Crawley, *Mystic Rose*. Even prior to British arrival, the British believed that "New Holland" Aborigines were brutish in their practices, that they practiced "loose intercourse of sexes" guided by "impulse" in a "natural state of society, in which human species live promiscuously" without "permanent union." See Grant, "Origin of Marriage," in *Essays on the Origin of Society*, 191–94. For a comparative perspective, see Gunlög Maria Fur, "The Struggle for Civilised Marriages in Early Modern Sweden and Colonial North America," in Grimshaw and McGregor, *Collisions of Cultures and Identities*, 40–63. See also Konishi, *Aboriginal Male*, 73–76; McGrath, "Modern Stone-Age Slavery."
11. Roth, "Marriage Ceremonies and Infant Life," 7.
12. Roth, "Marriage Ceremonies and Infant Life," 3.
13. McKnight, *Of Marriage, Violence and Sorcery*, 25, 55, 74.
14. Roth, "Marriage Ceremonies and Infant Life," 11.
15. McKnight, *Of Marriage, Violence and Sorcery*, xv.
16. D. Turner, *Australian Aboriginal Social Organization*, 60–63; McKnight, *Going the Whiteman's Way*, 60–61.
17. McKnight, *Going the Whiteman's Way*, 23, 74; Roth, "Marriage Ceremonies and Infant Life," 9.
18. McKnight, *Going the Whiteman's Way*; McKnight, *Of Marriage, Violence and Sorcery*.
19. McKnight, *Of Marriage, Violence and Sorcery*, xxi, 175, 186–87, 210.
20. For a study of northeastern Queensland tribes and boundaries, see Dixon, "Tribes, Languages and Other Boundaries."
21. Hiatt, *Arguments about Aborigines*.
22. McKnight, *Of Marriage, Violence and Sorcery*, 55.
23. McGrath, *Born in the Cattle*.
24. Lawrie interview; McGrath, *Born in the Cattle*; McKnight, *Of Marriage, Violence and Sorcery*, 55; Rose, *Dingo Makes Us Human*; Dixon, *Words of Our Country*; Roth quoted in N. Peterson, *Tribes and Boundaries in Australia*, 213.
25. Hokari, *Gurindji Journey*; Hokari, *Radikaru ōraru hisutorī*; Rose, *Dingo Makes Us Human*.
26. Circular Memo, April 4, 1901, A/58764, QSA (emphasis in original).
27. Queensland, "An Act to Amend and Consolidate the Laws Affecting the Solemnization of Marriage," 28, no. 15, and "The Marriage Act of 1864 and Synopsis of the Marriage Act 28 no. 15 in connection with the celebration of Marriages in Queensland," A/69514, QSA.
28. "Marriage of Half Caste and Aboriginal Women–1901," A/58764, QSA; "Report of Northern Protector 1900," COL/142; 4884/01, QSA.

29. McKnight, *Going the Whiteman's Way*; McKnight, *Of Marriage, Violence and Sorcery*.
30. Clive Moore, "Good-Bye, Queensland, Good-Bye, White Australia; Good-Bye Christians," *New Federalist*, December 4, 2000, 22–29.
31. *Rockhampton (QLD) Morning Bulletin*, June 4, 1902 (emphasis added). See also A/58764, QSA.
32. "Marriage of Half Caste and Aboriginal Women–1901," A/58764, QSA; "Report of Northern Protector 1900," COL/142, 4884/01, QSA; Crown Solicitor, Memorandum, January 14, 2007, A/589/2, QSA; Richard Howard to Under Secretary, Home Secretary's Office, January 7, 1907, A/589/2, QSA.
33. Walter E. Roth to Undersecretary, January 21, 1901, A/58764, QSA.
34. Law Reform Commission of Western Australia, *Aboriginal Customary Laws*, 8.
35. W. E. Roth to Under Secretary, September 18, 1901, A/58764, QSA (emphasis in original).
36. A. Meston to Under Secretary of Lands, September 5, 1903, A/58929, QSA.
37. The Commonwealth Franchise Act extended the vote to all residents, "except for lunatics and certain classes of criminals." However, Asians, Africans, and Australian Aborigines were excluded. McGrath, "Beneath the Skin."
38. Lake, "Marriage as Bondage."
39. A. Meston to Under Secretary of Lands, September 5, 1903; newspaper clipping, *Patriot* [June 1902], both in A/58929, QSA.
40. Various correspondence, A/58929, QSA; "The Central Aboriginals: Removals to Durundur," *Rockhampton Morning Bulletin*, June 4, 1902.
41. Constable David Twaddle of Maytown, October 8, 1906; Report on Constable Creedy v. Ah Kow, October 20, 1906; Lee Chew Statement, February 22, 1912; various correspondence, all in A/45206, QSA.
42. Magee to Police Inspector, February 23, 1912, A/45206, QSA.
43. P. Bowen, Sub Inspector, October 20, 1906, A/45206, QSA.
44. Crown Solicitor, Memorandum, January 1, 1907; Richard Howard to Under Secretary, Home Secretary's Office, January 7, 1907, both in A/589/2, QSA. See also Henningham, "Picking up Colonial Experience," 63.
45. Various correspondence, A/58766, QSA. Personal names are not used here for privacy reasons.
46. Roth, "Marriage Ceremonies and Infant Life," 3.
47. Fowler, *Concise Oxford Dictionary*, 851.
48. Nygh, *Butterworths Concise Australian Legal Dictionary*, 86–87.
49. Stockwood, *A Bartholmew Fairing for Parentes*.
50. Bufford, *Discourse against Unequal Marriages*.
51. Jalland, *Women, Marriage and Politics*.
52. Nash interview.
53. Shellam, *Shaking Hands on the Fringe*, underlines the empowering aspects of traveling on British sailing craft and journeys to new "country."
54. Dixon, "Tribes, Languages and Other Boundaries."

55. "Eelemarni, The Story of Leo and Leva," source listing, Australian Screen Online, http://aso.gov.au/titles/documentaries/eelemarni/availability/. The film tells the story of the marriage moieties between the Githrabaul and Ngarakbaul people of northern New South Wales between Casino, Kyogle, and Mt. Warning and Tweed Heads, Brunswick Heads, and Byron Bay on the coast. Thanks to Katherine Aigner for this information.
56. Dixon, *Words of Our Country*, 213, 231.
57. Roth quoted in N. Peterson, *Tribes and Boundaries in Australia*, 213.
58. Rose, *Dingo Makes Us Human*, chap. 8.
59. Hokari, *Gurindji Journey*; Rose, *Dingo Makes Us Human*.
60. Extensive newspaper clippings and correspondence, A/45206, QSA.
61. McGrath, "Modern Stone-Age Slavery"; Hokari, *Gurindji Journey*.
62. Durham to Protector Aborigines, June 1, 1904, A/45206, QSA.
63. The Australian Citizenship Act introduced in 1948 entitled all Australian-born people to citizenship; however, in reality, Aboriginal people still lacked many rights. After a 1967 referendum, there was wider acceptance of their citizenship entitlements; however, state governments continued to impede these by other means, often via excessive police surveillance and imprisonment. Davidson, *From Subject to citizen*; Chesterman and Galligan, *Citizens without Rights*; N. Peterson and Sanders, *Citizenship and Indigenous Australians*; Attwood and Markus, *1967 Referendum*; Taffe, *Black and White Together*; Attwood, *Struggle for Aboriginal Rights*.
64. Reynolds, *Nowhere People*; Mary Anne Jebb and Anna Haebich, "Across the Great Divide: Gender Relations on Australian Frontiers," in Saunders and Evans, *Gender Relations in Australia*, 20–35.
65. CRS A/58766, QSA. South Australia introduced the Married Women's Property Act in 1883 and other colonies followed. Married Women's Property Acts 1890–1897, amended to 1908 (54 Vic. No. 9). In the United States, the changes commenced in 1839, pertaining to slaves, and in 1839 and in 1848 for personal property and real estate. See also Cott, *Public Vows*, 52–54.
66. CRS A/58766, QSA. Administrators stated that they generally "did not interfere" with Aboriginal women legally married to non-Aborigines. While some stated that such a woman was no longer governed under the act, other administrators were confused about her legal status and whether the Aboriginal act still applied to her.
67. Kinnane, *Shadow Lines*, frontispiece.
68. For these stories, see Rajkowski, *Linden Girl*; Camfoo, *Love against the Law*.
69. Lee Chew statement, February 22, 1912; Report on Constable Creedy v. Ah Kow, October 20, 1906; and various correspondence in A/45206, QSA.
70. On the "metis" as "laboratories of modernity," see Ann Laura Stoler, "Sexual Affronts and Racial Frontiers: European Identities and the Cultural Politics of Exclusion in Colonial Southeast Asia," in F. Cooper and Stoler, *Tensions of Empire*, 226–27.
71. See Ellinghaus, *Taking Assimilation to Heart*.

7. POLYGAMY'S NEW WORLDS

1. Grieves, "Aboriginal Spirituality"; Grieves, "We Are Survivors." For a contemporary take on these themes, see J. Bell, "Persistence of Aboriginal Kinship and Marriage Rules."
2. Attwood, *Telling the Truth*; Axtell, *The European and the Indian*; Axtell, *Natives and Newcomers*.
3. Carter, *Importance of Being Monogamous*.
4. Perdue, *Cherokee Women*, 5, 43–44; Yarbrough, *Race and the Cherokee Nation*, 27–28.
5. Grimshaw, "Women and the Family in Australian History — A Reply"; Grimshaw, "Women and the Family in Australian History"; Grimshaw, McConville, and McEwen, *Families in Colonial Australia*. See also Grimshaw, Lake, McGrath, and Quartly, *Creating a Nation*; De Cruz, *Family Law, Sex and Society*, 115; Halley, "Behind the Law of Marriage."
6. Hokari, *Gurindji Journey*.
7. McLoughlin, *Cherokee Renascence*, 13. See also Fogelson, "On the 'Petticoat Government'"; Yarbrough, *Race and the Cherokee Nation*, chaps. 1–2.
8. Yarbrough, "Legislating Women's Sexuality," 396.
9. Moreton-Robinson, *Talkin' Up to the White Woman*; D. Bell, *Daughters of the Dreaming*.
10. McGrath, *Born in the Cattle*; Levine, *Prostitution, Race and Politics*; Levine, *Gender and Empire*; Bashford, *Imperial Hygiene*.
11. McKnight, *Of Marriage, Violence and Sorcery*, 23, 25, 41; Dewar, *"Black War" in Arnhem Land*. The word "loan" is often used for women in a temporary-stay situation, along with "loan wives," but I find this analogous to seeing the woman as property. In Australian Aboriginal societies, exchange relationships were more complex. There has been a parallel debate about women being property under western patriarchal law and about wives being property akin to slaves.
12. Dewar, *"Black War" in Arnhem Land*; Egan, *Justice All Their Own*; Australia, "Board of Enquiry Concerning the Killing of Natives in Central Australia by Police Parties and Others and Concerning Other Matters, 1929," unpublished report, Australian Institute of Aboriginal and Torres Strait Islander Studies Library.
13. Reynolds, *Forgotten War*.
14. McGrath, *Born in the Cattle*; Grimshaw, Lake, McGrath, and Quartly. *Creating a Nation*, 131–50.
15. Cott, *Public Vows*, 22–23.
16. Perdue, *Cherokee Women*, 146, 99, 179.
17. D. Bell, *Daughters of the Dreaming*; Perdue, *Cherokee Women*, 44, 175.
18. Perdue, *Cherokee Women*, 146.
19. Yarbrough, *Race and the Cherokee Nation*, 27–28. Despite an excellent Cherokee archive having been accumulated, on some matters of earlier practices, scholars often have to rely on the accounts of amateur observers and ethnographers for key insights.
20. Cott, *Public Vows*, 26–27. Jedidiah was the father of Samuel Morse, mentioned by John Ross, and a friend of Dolley Madison's. Samuel sped up America's, then the world's, communications in the 1840s.

21. Gordon, *Mormon Question*, 56; Rifkin, *When Did Indians Become Straight?*, 163–70; Cott, *Public Vows*, 73, 74, 114, 120, 139.
22. "Indian Polygamy Revelation," excerpt from H. Michael Marquardt, *The Joseph Smith Revelations Text and Commentary*, 374–76, Utah Lighthouse Ministry, http://www.utlm.org/onlineresources/indianpolygamyrevelation.htm.
23. *Book of Mormon*, quoted in Hyde, *Empires, Nations, and Families*, 458.
24. B. Hardy and Erickson, "Regeneration; Now and Evermore!"; Nichols, *Prostitution, Polygamy, and Power*; Burgett, "On the Mormon Question." See also Castaneda, "Comparative Frontiers," 294. Anne Hyde also discusses national responses to Mormon polygamy and Native American policies in *Empires, Nations, and Families*, 361, 452–58.
25. Hyde, *Empires, Nations, and Families*, 458.
26. Cott, *Public Vows*, 74.
27. Westermarck, *History of Human Marriage*; Crawley, *Mystic Rose*; Gardner, *Gathering for God*, 191–94.
28. McGrath, "Modern Stone-Age Slavery."
29. For a comprehensive discussion of status in marriage, see Halley, "Behind the Law of Marriage."
30. *Philadelphia Inquirer*, March 21, 1843, 2; *Philadelphia Inquirer*, July 24, 1843, 2.
31. McGrath, "Being Annie Oakley"; McGrath, "Playing Colonial." See Lake, "Frontier Feminism"; Cole, Haskins, and Paisley, *Uncommon Ground*, 2005.
32. Holland and Brooks, *Rethinking the Racial Moment*; Holland, "Whatever her race," 142–51.
33. McGrath, *Born in the Cattle*; Lake, "Frontier Feminism."
34. Bennett, *Australian Aborigine as a Human Being*.
35. Holland, "Whatever her race," 130–31.
36. Jacobs, *White Mother to a Dark Race*; Lake, "Marriage as Bondage"; Cole, Haskins, and Paisley, *Uncommon Ground*; Haskins, *Matrons and Maids*; Holland, "Whatever her race."
37. *Smiths Weekly*, September 24, 1921; *Smiths Weekly*, November 13, 1920, 9.
38. Stoler, *Race and the Education of Desire*; Foucault, *History of Sexuality*.
39. Plane, *Colonial Intimacies*, 67.
40. Plane, *Colonial Intimacies*, 177.
41. Plane, *Colonial Intimacies*, 8; E. Gribble, *Forty Years*.
42. Plane, *Colonial Intimacies*, 41, 8–9, 67.
43. R. White, *Middle Ground*, 502.
44. R. White, *Middle Ground*, 508; Edmunds, *Shawnee Prophet*, 39 (emphasis added).
45. For example, see Miles, *Ties That Bind*, 45, 36.
46. This theme is also developed in the film *Ten Canoes*.
47. For a good general introduction to Aboriginal thought and culture, see Broome, *Aboriginal Australians*. For cultural practices, see Berndt and Berndt, *World of the First Australians*. On marriage, see McKnight, *Of Marriage, Violence and Sorcery*; Rose, *Dingo Makes Us Human*, 30.

48. See Carter, *Importance of Being Monogamous*, for a comprehensive discussion of polygamy as it pertained to Aboriginal peoples in Canada; for missionary attitudes toward polygamy, see 129–34, 194–99, 214–16.
49. Yarbrough, "Legislating Women's Sexuality"; Yarbrough, *Race and the Cherokee Nation*, esp. 9–13. Yarbrough valuably discusses the insights allowed by statutory law in understanding a distillation of cherished values, at least regarding those with hegemonic power. Yarbrough, *Race and the Cherokee Nation*, 13.
50. McLoughlin, *Cherokee Renascence*; Perdue and Green, *Cherokee Nation and the Trail of Tears*.
51. Yarbrough, *Race and the Cherokee Nation*, 27–28; McLoughlin, *Cherokees and Christianity*, 21–22.
52. Murchison, "Intermarried Whites in the Cherokee Nation," 300. The legislation was signed by J. Ross, Path Killer, and Chas Hicks.
53. Sturtevant, "John Ridge on Cherokee Civilization," 85.
54. Cited in Perdue, *Cherokee Editor*, 82.
55. Perdue, *Cherokee Editor*, 82; Yarbrough, *Race and the Cherokee Nation*, 29.
56. Yarbrough, "Legislating Women's Sexuality," 397–98.
57. Yarbrough discusses the case of Sam Dent, who killed his Deer clan wife. Yarbrough, *Race and the Cherokee Nation*, 26. As noted in chapter 3, when the Cherokee Nation insisted that white men legally marry their Cherokee marital partners in a monogamous, Christian ceremony, this intervention was intended to regulate white intruders so that they would fulfill marital duties.
58. Cherokee Nation, *Laws of the Cherokee Nation*; Yarbrough, *Race and the Cherokee Nation*, 29–30, 57.
59. Sturtevant, "John Ridge on Cherokee Civilization," 85.
60. Cited in Perdue, *Cherokee Editor*, 75.
61. Yarbrough, "Legislating Women's Sexuality," 396, discusses evidence of controversies over out-marriage by Cherokee men and women.
62. "Aboriginals I have Known—John Menmunie—King of Yarrabah," Papers of J. B. Gribble, Australian Board of Missions, Box G15, MLMSS 4503, Series 22/1, Mitchell Library; Halse, *Terribly Wild Man*, 152.
63. *ABM Review*, December 15, 1910, 184; Finlayson, "Don't Depend on Me," 115–16.
64. Gribble did confide in like-minded men like Walter Roth and some churchmen.
65. Note that Gribble's newspaper-cutting book was entitled "Some Marriage Stories."
66. For example, see Trudinger, "Language(s) of Love."
67. "Bishop F X Gsell," Diocese of Darwin, http://www.darwin.catholic.org.au/our-story/bishop-gsell.htm.
68. Bennett, *Australian Aborigine as a Human Being*; Holland, "Whatever her race."
69. *Smiths Weekly*, October 21, 1922.
70. *Smiths Weekly*, July 30, 1921, 17.
71. McGrath, *Born in the Cattle*, chap. 4. Some of the ongoing sexual and racial tensions were exposed over the Moree swimming pool incident recounted in Curthoys, *Freedom Ride*.

72. Grieves, "We Are Survivors."
73. The same pattern applied in other states with restrictive legislation against cohabitation and intermarriage. See McGrath, *Born in the Cattle*.
74. Yarbrough, *Race and the Cherokee Nation*, 27, 30–31.
75. Yarbrough, "Legislating Women's Sexuality," 388.
76. Plane, *Colonial Intimacies*, 180.

8. ENTWINED SOVEREIGNTIES AND THE GREAT UNWEDDING

1. See Van Kirk, *Many Tender Ties*, 36, 155–57; Faragher, "Custom of the Country"; Schlissel, Ruíz, and Monk, *Western Women*; Jacqueline Peterson, "Women Dreaming: The Religiopsychology of Indian-White Marriages and the Rise of a Metís Culture," in Schlissel, Ruíz, and Monk, *Western Women*; J. Peterson and Brown, *New Peoples*; J. Peterson, "People in Between"; J. Brooks, *Confounding the Color Line*; Shoemaker, *Negotiators of Change*; Hine and Faragher, *American West*.
2. Connecticut State Library, Indians, second series, 1666–1820: Mohegan petitions.
3. Weaver, *Great Land Rush*. For a psychoanalytic discussion of global colonialism, see W. Anderson, Jenson, and Keller, *Unconscious Dominions*.
4. Conforti, *Jonathan Edwards*; Conforti, *Imagining New England*; Healy, *Forgetting Aborigines*.
5. Government subsidies were provided to the Queensland sugar plantations to replace "colored labor."
6. T. Wilkins, *Cherokee Tragedy*; Perdue and Green, *Cherokee Nation and the Trail of Tears*.
7. Andrew Jackson, "Indian Removal and the General Good," in Filler and Guttmann, *Removal of the Cherokee Nation*, 49, 51; *Johnson v. McIntosh*, cited in Wolfe, "Corpus Nullius," 133.
8. Ross to Thomas L. McKenney, August 25, 1844, in J. Ross, *Papers*, 2:241.
9. "The Indians and Col. McKenny's Plan for their Protection," *National Aegis*, November 1, 1843, 2; Weierman, *One Nation, One Blood*, 51–52.
10. Curthoys, "Expulsion, Exodus and Exile"; Tyrrell, "American Exceptionalism."
11. Lake and Reynolds, *Drawing the Global Color Line*.
12. This colony instigated a military strategy known as the Black Line, designed to corner all Aboriginal residents in order to oust them from the mainland and relocate them to a smaller island. *Hobart Town Gazette*, December 1, 1826; Jorgen Jorgenson to magistrate Thomas Anstey, June 8, 1829, available through the Tasmanian Archive and Heritage Office, Colonial Secretary's Office, 1/7578/320. Information supplied by Lyndall Ryan. Tasmania became a focus of genocide debates. See L. Ryan, *Tasmanian Aborigines*.
13. L. Russell, *A Little Bird Told Me*; McGrath, *Contested Ground*; L. Ryan, *Tasmanian Aborigines*.
14. *Aboriginal News*, April 15, 1907.
15. Blake, *Dumping Ground*; Kidd, *Way We Civilise*.
16. Yarbrough, "Legislating Women's Sexuality"; Yarbrough, *Race and the Cherokee Nation*.

17. For a fuller discussion of the Aboriginal protector Cecil Cook's views, see Probyn-Rapsey, "Uplifting White Men"; on science and race, see Smithers, *Science, Sexuality and Race*; W. Anderson, *Cultivation of Whiteness*.
18. Pascoe, *What Comes Naturally*, 94.
19. For a study of entwined families on the western frontier of the United States, see Hyde, *Empires, Nations, and Families*.
20. Despite Aboriginal people being under strict surveillance on reserves, the Aboriginals Protection Act did not stipulate special permission for Aboriginal marriages.
21. Ravenscroft, *Postcolonial Eye*; McGrath, *Born in the Cattle*, chap. 4.
22. Hartog, *Man and Wife in America*, 16–17; Cott, *Public Vows*. In *Provincializing Europe*, Chakrabarty invites us to reflect upon cultural perspectives of historical causation. In *Gurindji Journey*, Hokari calls for "cross-culturalizing" history. In "Categories," Shoemaker argues the problem of categories, indicating how use of language materials will open the way for a creative new scholarship. "Categories," in Shoemaker, *Clearing a Path*, 51–74. See also Nabokov, *Forest of Time*.
23. McGrath, "Modern Stone-Age Slavery."
24. D. Allen, *We the People*.
25. Wolfe, "Settler Colonialism"; Wolfe, "Land, Labor, and Difference"; Stoler, *Race and the Education of Desire*, 8; Stoler, *Along the Archival Grain*, 143; F. Cooper and Stoler, *Tensions of Empire*, 199. When domestic arrangements linked to public order, Cooper and Stoler refer to the "stretch between the public institutions of the colonial state and the intimate reaches of people's lives." F. Cooper and Stoler, *Tensions of Empire*, vii. Wolfe, "Nation and MiscegeNation"; Edmonds, *Urbanizing Frontiers*, 16; Kidd, *Way We Civilise*.
26. See Denson, *Demanding the Cherokee Nation*; McLoughlin and Conser, "Cherokees in Transition"; Wolfe, "Corpus Nullius"; Perdue and Green, *Cherokee Nation and the Trail of Tears*.
27. Perkins, *Bastard Like Me*; Tovey, *Little Black Bastard*.
28. Yarbrough, *Race and the Cherokee Nation*; Miles, *Ties That Bind*; Perdue, *Cherokee Women*; J. Brooks, *Captives and Cousins*; Yarbrough and Holland, *Crossing Waters, Crossing Worlds*; S. Slater and Yarbrough, *Gender and Sexuality*. This theme is discussed in chapter 3.
29. Meanwhile, through marriage, certain men of the Cherokee elite asserted their parity with white men.
30. For more on comparative policies, see Ellinghaus, *Taking Assimilation to Heart*. For more on race in Cherokee society in the mid- to late nineteenth century, see Yarbrough, *Race and the Cherokee Nation*; Yarbrough, "Legislating Women's Sexuality."
31. Probyn-Rapsey, "Uplifting White Men."
32. A good example of this is explored in Curthoys, *Freedom Ride*.
33. Future studies need to consider the impacts of the reserve and reservation systems, which affected income and sustenance and prevented engagement in landownership and the open economy.

34. In a landmark autobiographical account published during Australia's Bicentenary (of the first British settlement), Sally Morgan drew national attention to the topic with *My Place*. Since then there have been claims made by numerous families, including the Bancrofts, Hancocks, Tullys, and others. See also Read, Peters-Little, and Haebich, *Indigenous Biography and Autobiography*.
35. In New South Wales, children were taken from families on the basis of Aboriginality. In Queensland, they were more likely to be sent as a group to reserves; however, children of mixed descent often had different experiences and were sought after as domestic servants. The Northern Territory introduced a more racially based policy for children with lighter skin. See McGrath, *Contested Ground*; Read, *Rape of the Soul*; Jacobs, *White Mother to a Dark Race*; Haebich, *Broken Circles*.
36. Jacobs, *White Mother to a Dark Race*; Haebich, *Broken Circles*; Edwards and Read, *Lost Children*; Kidd, *Way We Civilise*.
37. Eve Serico/Fesl, "Beyond Survival," Unpublished typescript in author's possession, 16. See also Kinnane, *Shadow Lines*; Camfoo, *Love against the Law*; Rajkowski, *Linden Girl*.
38. For more discussion of the act, see Kidd, *Way We Civilise*. Kidd also kindly provided me with a summary of changing legislation. See also Blake, *Dumping Ground*.
39. See Aboriginals Protection Act, Queensland, 1901; Blake, *Dumping Ground*.
40. Hannah, "Constituting Marriage." See Ellinghaus, "Absorbing the Aboriginal Problem"; Haskins and Maynard, "Sex, Race and Power."
41. "Cabinet Contentions — Strange Romance of a Black Gin. Curious Capers of the Member for Cook. Copious Correspondence and Collect Wires," newspaper cuttings, QSA. This article contains a transcription of a letter from Robert Baird to Hamilton MLA, Bloomfield River, July 11, 1901. See "The Lizzie Johnston Case," *Brisbane Courier*, November 21, 1902.
42. Via traveling performers and publishing, such popular music circulated globally. Richard Waterhouse traced the circulation of African American "blackface" in Australia. Waterhouse, *From Minstrel Show to Vaudeville*. See Ravenscroft, *Postcolonial Eye*; Bellanta, *Larrikins*.

EPILOGUE

1. Harriett to Parents, July 17, 1926, Willie Stewart White Papers, University of North Carolina.
2. Harriett to H. Vaill, January 5, 1827, Box 1, MS 519, Vaill Collection (emphasis added). The "he" is questionable but seems to be the only viable possibility.
3. Harriett to Mrs. Turner, July 17, 1826, White Papers.
4. Harriett to Parents, July 17, 1826, White Papers.
5. B. Gold to Rev. Hermann Vaill, November 21, 1827, Box 1, MS 519, Vaill Collection.
6. Perdue, *Cherokee Editor*, 36.
7. Quoted in Gaul, *To Marry an Indian*, 55, 27.

8. Hermann Vaill to sister Mary, August 2, 1825; Brinsmade to Hermann Vaill, July 14, 1825; Mary to H. Vaill and Sister, July 14, 1825; Brinsmade to My dear sister, June 29, 1825; all in Box 1, MS 519, Vaill Collection.
9. B. Gold to Rev. Hermann Vaill, November 21, 1827, Box 1, MS 519, Vaill Collection.
10. Elias Boudinot to brothers and sisters, September 14, 1829, Box 1, MS 519, Vaill Collection.
11. Harriett to Herman and Flora Gold Vaill, March 29, 1832, Box 1, MS 519, Vaill Collection (emphasis in original); cited in Gaul, *To Marry an Indian*, 55.
12. Harriett to Herman and Flora Gold Vaill, March 29, 1832, Box 1, MS 519, Vaill Collection; cited in Gaul, *To Marry an Indian*, 55.
13. Harriett to Hermann and Flora, October 29, [1832], Box 1, MS 519, Vaill Collection (emphasis added). Although this letter appears in 1829, its chronology suggests that it must be from 1832.
14. Harriett to Hermann Vaill and Flora, October 29, 1832, Box 1, MS 519, Vaill Collection. The name "William Penn," was no doubt a historical statement about reconciliation and good colonizing practice; it was also the nom de plume of lawyer Jeremiah Evarts when writing for the Boudinot-edited *Cherokee Phoenix*.
15. Harriett to Hermann Vaill and Flora, October 29, 1832, Box 1, MS 519, Vaill Collection.
16. Wallace, *Philadelphia Reports*, 16:132–33. See also "Old Families — Boudinot Family," Historical Society of Pennsylvania.
17. Her death is attributed to illness a few months after a stillbirth. However, Frank was three months old when she died; her lived until 1864. He became a captain of the New York Mounted Rifles, fighting for the Union cause. Various letters from Frank are reproduced in Dale, *Cherokee Cavaliers*.
18. Elias Boudinot to Job Swift Gold, October 26, 1836, Box 1, MS 519, Vaill Collection.
19. Elias Boudinot to My Dear Father and Mother, August 16, 1836, in Gaul, *To Marry an Indian*, 183–84.
20. Elias Boudinot to My dear Mother and father, May 20, 1837, Box 1, MS 519, Vaill Collection; cited in Gaul, *To Marry an Indian*, 65, 199.
21. Gaul, *To Marry an Indian*, 199.
22. Moulton, *John Ross*, 113.
23. Elias C. Boudinot, *Remarks on Behalf of the Bill*; Elias C. Boudinot, *Memorial*. After their mother died, the children went to live with aunts and uncles in New England. Strongly identifying as Cherokee, however, most returned to fight for recognition and their entitlements in their own nation. Having a white mother made it harder for them. Their tribal status was always suspect.
24. Parins, *Elias Cornelius Boudinot*. Elias's granddaughter Mary Brinsmade Church became the family historian, researching and preserving the valuable letters about the marriage controversy; Church, *Elias Boudinot*; J. Ross, *Papers*, 2:717.
25. E. Gribble, *Forty Years*, 7.
26. Gribble, "Views of Missionary Life," MLMSS 4503, add-on 1822, Box 16(69), Mitchell Library.

27. Halse, *Terribly Wild Man*, 178.
28. E. Gribble, *Despised Race*, 25–26. The Mitchell Library also holds a draft manuscript: Gribble, "A Despised Race," MLMSS 4503, add-on 1822, Box 12(69).
29. Hokari, "Cross-Culturalizing History." A range of related articles may be found on Being Connected with Hokari Minoru, www.hokariminoru.org. See also Cato, *Mister Maloga*.
30. Austin-Broos, "Narratives of the Encounter at Ntaria"; Christine Halse, "Gribble, Ernest Richard Bulmer (Ernie) (1868–1957)," *Australian Dictionary of Biography Online*, http://adb.anu.edu.au/biography/gribble-ernest-richard-bulmer-ernie-10367; Halse, "Reverend Ernest Gribble."
31. Halse, "Gribble, Ernest Richard Bulmer," *Australian Dictionary of Biography Online*.
32. See various entries in Gribble's diary for 1908, including back pages, in Box 3(69), MLMSS 4503, add-on 1822, Mitchell Library; Halse, "Reverend Ernest Gribble," 195; Halse, *Terribly Wild Man*, 86–87.
33. Thomson, *Reaching Back*, 100–101.
34. An award-winning Australian novel was based on Curry's story. Astley, *Multiple Effects of Rainshadow*. Thanks to Paul Turnbull for sharing his interview with Peter Pryor and other insights. Joanne Watson has investigated this further. Watson, *Palm Island*; Watson, "Becoming Bwgcolman"; Joanne Watson, "Curry, Robert Henry (Bob) (1885–1930)," *Australian Dictionary of Biography Online*, http://adb.anu.edu.au/biography/curry-robert-henry-bob-12874.
35. Gribble, "Views of Missionary Life," MLMSS 4503, add-on 1822, Box 16(69), Mitchell Library.
36. Hollingsworth interview, May 2000; Gribble, "Views of Missionary Work," MLMSS 4503, add-on 1822, Box 16(69), Mitchell Library.
37. Ellinghaus, *Taking Assimilation to Heart*, 163–65; Halse, *Terribly Wild Man*, 84.
38. Schaffer, *In the Wake of First Contact*; Fraser, *Narrative of the Capture, Sufferings, and Miraculous Escape of Mrs. Eliza Fraser*; Darian-Smith, Poignant and Schaffer, *Captive Lives*.
39. "Miller, Olga Eunice (1920–2003)," Australian Women's Register, http://www.womenaustralia.info/biogs/PR00345b.htm. See also O. Miller, "K'gari, Mrs. Fraser, and Butchulla Oral Tradition," 35, 34–36.
40. Moulton, *John Ross*, 181.
41. Mary to John, June 4, 1864, in J. Ross, *Papers*, 2: 582–83.
42. Moulton, *John Ross*, 181.
43. John Ross to Sarah Stapler, March 25, 1860, in J. Ross, *Papers*, 2:436–37; John to Mary B. Ross and Sarah F. Stapler, March 23, 1860, in J. Ross, *Papers*, 2:435–36.
44. Mary to My Dear Husband, June 2, 1864, in J. Ross, *Papers*, 2:583–84.
45. Apess, *Son of the Forest*.
46. Ross to Mary, June 4, 1865, in J. Ross, *Papers*, 2:643.
47. John to Mary Ross, June 6, 1864, in J. Ross, *Papers*, 2:583. By this date the family had begun to use the spelling "Brian," which also appears on Annie's gravestone.

48. Ross to Mary B. Stapler, June 27, [June 30, and July 1], 1844, in J. Ross, *Papers*, 2:214.
49. Last Will and Testament of John Ross, in J. Ross, *Papers*, 2:681–82.
50. J. Ross, *Papers*, appendices; "Mary Brian Stapler Ross," Find a Grave.com, http://www.findagrave.com/cgi-bin/fg.cgi?page=gr&GRid=9438456.
51. From the 2011 Australian census, commentators conclude that the better-off people identifying as Aboriginal are of mixed descent. *Australian*, June 22, 2012; N. Peterson and Taylor, "Aboriginal Intermarriage and Economic Status"; Heard, Birrell, and Khoo, "Intermarriage between Indigenous and Non-indigenous Australians"; Khoo, Birrell, and Heard, "Intermarriage by Birthplace and Ancestry in Australia." See also Thornton, "Tribal Membership Requirements"; Shoemaker, *American Indian Population Recovery*, 63–64, 66, 87–88; Spickard, *Mixed Blood*.

BIBLIOGRAPHY

NOTE: Relevant digital sources are cited in endnotes.

UNPUBLISHED SOURCES

American Board of Commissioners for Foreign Missions (ABCFM) Archives, Houghton Library, Harvard University
    Missions to the North American Indians. ABC 18.3–18.8.
    Paine, Anna. Notebook 2, Candidate Department, ABC 6, vol. 11.
Australian Institute of Aboriginal and Torres Strait Islander Studies (AIATSIS) Library, Canberra
    Australia. "Board of Enquiry Concerning the Killing of Natives in Central Australia by Police Parties and Others and Concerning Other Matters, 1929." Unpublished report, National Library of Australia.
    Gribble, Ernest R. Collected papers, 1892–1957. MS1515.
    Gribble, Ernest R. Register of Baptisms, Yarrabah Bellenden, Kerr Aboriginal Mission. MS3234.
Connecticut State Library, Hartford
    Indians, second series, 1666–1820: Mohegan petitions; 2 vols. and index.
Gilcrease Museum, Tulsa OK
    Ross Collection. Folder 5326.290.
Mitchell Library, Sydney
    Australian Board of Missions: additional documents. MLMSS 4503, add-on 1822, boxes 1–35(69).
Museum of the Cherokee Indian, Cherokee NC
    List of students attending the Foreign Mission School, Cornwall CT, January 1820. 1987.042.001.
Princeton University Rare Books and Special Collections Library

Queensland State Archives (QSA)
>Correspondence, Aboriginal and Torres Strait Islander, 1901–1938. Series 18090.
Correspondence and other files relating to the Office of the Chief Protector:
A/45206; A/58764; A/58766; A/58850; A/58892; A/58929; A/69514; COL/142, 4884/01; MN 993 460/39; POL/J16; POL/J19; WAA, ACC 653 342/25.
General Correspondence of the Chief Protector, 1900–1909. Series 18091.
Personal Files, Office of the Chief Protector of Aboriginals, 1902–1978. Series 4429.

Rutgers University Libraries, Special Collections and University Archives

Stirling Memorial Library, Yale
>Vaill, Herman Landon, Collection. MS 519.

Tasmanian Archive and Heritage Office
>Colonial Secretary's Office. 1/7578/320.

University of North Carolina, Special Collections
>White, Willie Stewart, Collection.

Genealogical and various files held in:
>Cornwall Historical Society, Cornwall CT.
Delaware Historical Society, Wilmington.
Historical Society of Pennsylvania, Philadelphia.
Library Company of Philadelphia.
Maine Historical Society, Portland.
Newberry Library.
Oklahoma Genealogical Society, Oklahoma City.
University of North Carolina Library.
University of Oklahoma Western History Collections, records of the Cherokee Nation and related papers.

Brumby, Les and Daphne. Interview by author. May 30 2000. In author's possession.

Cott, Nancy. Interview by author. 2000. In author's possession.

Duncan, Barbara, and other Cherokee curators. Discussion with author. April 12, December 4, 1998, Museum of Cherokee Indian. Author's notes.

Gordon-Reed, Annette. Interview by author. May 2001. In author's possession.

Hollingsworth, Charmaine. Interview by author. May 2000, June 1, 2000. In author's possession.

Lawrie, Amy. Interview by author. July 17, 1978. In author's possession.

Nash, David. Interview by author. October 2005. In author's possession.

Serico/Fesl, Eve. "Beyond Survival." Unpublished typescript in author's possession.

PUBLISHED SOURCES

ABM Review. 1910. Serial publication of the Anglican Church of Australia, Australian Board of Missions.

Aboriginal News. 1906–10. Newsletter from the Church of England mission to Australian Aboriginals. Published Yarrabah: E. R. Gribble.

Allen, Danielle. *We the People*. New York: Norton, 2014.
Anderson, Benedict. *Imagined Communities: Reflections on the Origin and Spread of Nationalism*. London: Verso, 1991.
Anderson, Christopher, and Norman Mitchell. "Kubara: A Kuku-Yalanji View of the Chinese in North Queensland." *Aboriginal History* 5, no. 1 (1981): 21–38.
Anderson, Rufus. *Memoir of Catharine Brown: A Christian Indian*. 2nd ed. Boston: Crocker and Brewster, 1825.
Anderson, Warwick. *The Cultivation of Whiteness: Science, Health and Racial Destiny in Australia*. Carlton VIC: Melbourne University Publishing, 2006.
Anderson, Warwick, Deborah Jenson, and Richard Keller, eds., *Unconscious Dominions: Psychoanalysis, Colonial Trauma, and Global Sovereignty*. Durham NC: Duke University Press, 2011.
Anderson, William L., Jane L. Brown, and Ann F. Rogers, eds. *The Payne-Butrick Papers*. Lincoln: University of Nebraska Press, 2010.
Andrew, John. *From Revivals to Removal: Jeremiah Evarts, the Cherokee Nation, and the Search for the Soul of America*. Athens: University of Georgia Press, 1992.
Anthony, Katherine. *Dolly Madison, Her Life and Times*. Garden City NY: Doubleday, 1949.
Apess, William. *A Son of the Forest: The Experience of William Apes, a Native of the Forest*. New York: Apes, 1831.
Armitage, David. *The Declaration of Independence: A Global History*. Cambridge MA: Harvard University Press, 2008.
———. "What's the Big Idea? Intellectual History and the Longue Durée." *History of European Ideas* 38, no. 4 (2012): 493–507.
Aslanian, Sebouh David, Joyce E. Chaplin, Ann McGrath, and Kristin Mann. "How Size Matters: The Question of Scale in History." AHR Conversation. *American Historical Review* 118, no. 5 (December 2013): 1431–72.
Astley, Thea. *The Multiple Effects of Rainshadow*. Ringwood VIC: Penguin, 1996.
Attwood, Bain. *The Struggle for Aboriginal Rights: A Documentary History*. St. Leonards NSW: Allen & Unwin, 1999.
———. *Telling the Truth about Aboriginal History*. Sydney: Allen & Unwin, 2005.
Attwood, Bain, and Andrew Markus. *The 1967 Referendum: Race, Power and the Australian Constitution*. Canberra: Aboriginal Studies Press, 2007.
Austen, Barbara. "Marrying Red: Indian/White Relations and the Case of Elias Boudinot and Harriet Gold." *Connecticut History* 45 (Fall 2006): 256–60.
Austin-Broos, Dianne. "Narratives of the Encounter at Ntaria." In "Aboriginal Histories, Aboriginal Myths," edited by J. Beckett. Special issue, *Oceania* 65, no. 2 (December 1994): 131–150. Reprinted in *Aboriginal Australians and Christian Missions: Ethnographic Historical Studies*, edited by Tony Swain and Deborah Bird Rose. Bedford Park: Australian Association for the Study of Religions, 1988.
Australian Board of Missions. *Missionary Notes* no. 18, June 1896; no. 14, March 1910.

———. *Yarrabah: Church of England Mission: Rules and Regulations*. Sydney: Australian Board of Missions, 1899.
———. *Yarrabah: Mission to the Aborigines*. Sydney: Australian Board of Missions, W. A. Pepperday, 1903.
Australian Human Rights Commission. *Bringing them Home Report*. Canberra: Australian Government Printer, 1997.
Axtell, James. *The European and the Indian: Essays in the Ethnohistory of Colonial North America*. Oxford: Oxford University Press, 1991.
———. *The Making of Princeton University*. Princeton NJ: Princeton University Press, 2006.
———. *Natives and Newcomers: The Cultural Origins of North America*. New York: Oxford University Press, 2000.
Ballantyne, Tony, and Antoinette Burton. *Bodies in Contact: Rethinking Colonial Encounters in World History*. Durham NC: Duke University Press, 2005.
———. *Moving Subjects: Gender, Mobility, and Intimacy in an Age of Global Empire*. Urbana: University of Illinois Press, 2009.
Barbour, Charles, and George Pavlich, eds. *After Sovereignty: On the Question of Political Beginnings*. Abingdon UK: Routledge, 2010.
Bardaglio, Peter Winthrop. *Reconstructing the Household: Families, Sex and the Law in the Nineteenth Century*. Chapel Hill: University of North Carolina Press, 1995.
Barker, Joanne, ed. *Sovereignty Matters: Locations of Contestation and Possibility in Indigenous Struggles for Self-Determination*. Lincoln: University of Nebraska Press, 2005.
Barker-Benfield, G. J. *Abigail and John Adams: The Americanization of Sensibility*. Chicago: University of Chicago Press, 2010.
Barker-Benfield, G. J. *The Culture of Sensibility: Sex and Society in Eighteenth-Century Britain*. Chicago: University of Chicago Press, 1992.
Bashford, Alison. *Imperial Hygiene: A Critical History of Colonialism, Nationalism and Public Health*. New York: Palgrave Macmillan, 2004.
Bataille, Gretchen M., and Lisa Laurie, eds. *Native American Women: A Biographical Dictionary*. New York: Routledge, 2001.
Bell, Diane. *Daughters of the Dreaming*. Melbourne: Spinifex, 2002.
Bell, Jeanie. "The Persistence of Aboriginal Kinship and Marriage Rules in Australia: Adapting Traditional Ways into Modern Practices." *Journal of the European Association for Studies of Australia* 4, no. 1 (2013): 65–75.
Bellanta, Melissa. *Larrikins: A History*. St. Lucia: University of Queensland Press, 2012.
Belmessous, Saliha. "Assimilation and Racialism in Seventeenth- and Eighteenth-Century French Colonial Policy." *American Historical Review* 110, no. 2 (April 2005): 322–49.
Bennett, M. M. *The Australian Aborigine as a Human Being*. London: Alston Rivers, 1930.
Ben-Porath, Sigal R., and Rogers M. Smith, eds. *Varieties of Sovereignty and Citizenship*. Philadelphia: University of Pennsylvania Press, 2013.

Berger, Bethany Ruth. "After Pocahontas: Indian Women and the Law, 1830 to 1934." *American Indian Law Review* 21, no. 1 (1997): 1–61.
Berkhofer, Robert F. *The White Man's Indian: Images of the American Indian from Columbus to the Present*. New York: Vintage Books, 1978.
Berndt, Ronald, and Catherine Berndt. *The World of the First Australians: An Introduction to the Traditional Life of the Australian Aborigines*. Sydney: Ure Smith, 1964.
Bibliophile Society. *The Romance of Mary W. Shelley, John Howard Payne and Washington Irving*. Boston: Bibliophile Society, 1907.
Blackhawk, Ned. *Violence over the Land: Indians and Empires in the Early American West*. Cambridge MA: Harvard University Press, 2006.
Blake, Thom. *A Dumping Ground: A History of the Cherbourg Settlement*. St. Lucia: University of Queensland, 2001.
Block, Sharon. *Rape and Sexual Power in Early America*. Chapel Hill: University of North Carolina Press, 2006.
Bolton, G. C. *A Thousand Miles Away: A History of North Queensland to 1920*. Brisbane: Australian National University Press, 1972.
Bottoms, Timothy. *The Conspiracy of Silence*. Crows Nest NSW: Allen & Unwin, 2013.
Boudinot, Elias [IV]. *A Star in the West; or, A Humble Attempt to Discover the Long Lost Ten Tribes of Israel*. Trenton NJ: D. Fenton, S. Hutchinson and J. Dunham, 1816.
Boudinot, Elias [Cherokee]. *An Address to the Whites Delivered in the First Presbyterian Church, 26 May 1826, by Elias Boudinott, a Cherokee Indian*. Philadelphia: William F. Geddes, 1826.
———. *Letters and Other Papers Relating to Cherokee Affairs: Being in Reply to Sundry Publications Authorized by John Ross*. Athens GA, 1837.
Boudinot, Elias C. *Memorial of Elias C. Boudinot, a Cherokee Indian to the Senate and House of Representatives of the United States*. Washington DC, 1870.
———. *Remarks of Elias C. Boudinot of the Cherokee Nation on Behalf of the Bill to Organize the Territory of Oklahoma before the House Committee on Territories, May 13, 1874*. Washington DC: Printers and Stereotypers, 1874.
Boulware, Tyler. *Deconstructing the Cherokee Nation: Town, Region, and Nation among Eighteenth-Century Cherokees*. Gainesville: University Press of Florida, 2011.
Bouvier, Virginia Marie. *Women and the Conquest of California, 1542–1840: Codes of Silence*. Tucson: University of Arizona Press, 2001.
Boyd, George A. *Elias Boudinot: Patriot and Statesman, 1740–1821*. Princeton NJ: Princeton University Press, 1952.
Bredbenner, Candice Lewis. *A Nationality of Her Own: Women, Marriage and the Law of Citizenship*. Berkeley: University of California Press, 1998.
Briscoe, Gordon. *Racial Folly: A Twentieth-Century Aboriginal Family*. Canberra: ANU E Press, 2010.
Brook, Heather Jane. "The Conjugal Body Politic: Governing Marriage and Marriage-Like Relationships in Australia." PhD thesis, Australian National University, 1999.

Brooks, James F., ed. *Captives and Cousins: Slavery, Kinship, and Community in the Southwest Borderlands*. Chapel Hill: University of North Carolina Press, 2002.

———. *Confounding the Color Line: The Indian-Black Experience in North America*. Lincoln: University of Nebraska Press, 2002.

Brooks, Lisa. *The Common Pot: The Recovery of Native Space in the Northeast*. Minneapolis: University of Minnesota Press, 2008.

Broome, Richard. *Aboriginal Australians: Black Responses to White Dominance, 1788–1994*. St. Leonards NSW: Allen & Unwin, 2010.

Brown, Jennifer S. H. *Strangers in Blood: Fur-Trade Company Families in Indian Country*. Vancouver: University of British Columbia Press, 1980.

Bruyneel, K. *The Third Space of Sovereignty: The Postcolonial Politics of U.S.-Indigenous Relations*. Minneapolis: University of Minnesota Press, 2007.

Bufford, Samuel. *A Discourse against Unequal Marriages: Viz, against old persons marrying with young, against persons marrying without the consent, against persons marrying without their own consent*. London: Printed for Dan Browne, 1696.

Bulletin (Sydney).1894.

Burgett, Bruce. "On the Mormon Question: Race, Sex and Polygamy in the 1850s and the 1900s." *American Quarterly* 57, no. 1 (January 2005): 40–61.

Burnstein, Richard B. *The Wisdom of John and Abigail Adams*. New York: Metro Books, 2002.

Burton, R. *Venus Oceanica: Anthropological Studies in the Sex Life of the South Sea Natives*. New York: Oceanica Research, 1935.

Calloway, Colin G. *Crown and Camulet: British-Indian Relations, 1783–1815*. Norman: University of Oklahoma Press, 1987.

———. *New Worlds for All: Indians, Europeans and the Remaking of Early America*. Baltimore: Johns Hopkins University Press, 1997.

———. *White People, Indians, and Highlanders: Tribal Peoples and Colonial Encounters in Scotland and America*. Oxford: Oxford University Press, 2010.

Camfoo, Tex. *Love against the Law: The Auto-biographies of Tex and Nelly Camfoo*. Edited by Gillian Cowlishaw. Canberra: Aboriginal Studies Press, 2000.

Carter, Sarah. *The Importance of Being Monogamous: Marriage and Nation Building in Western Canada to 1915*. Edmonton: University of Alberta Press, 2008.

Castaneda, Antonia. "Comparative Frontiers: The Migration of Women to Alta California and New Zealand." In *Western Women: Their Land, Their Lives*, edited by Lillian Schlissel, Vicki L. Ruiz, and Janice Monk, 283–301. Albuquerque: University of New Mexico Press, 1988.

———. "Engendering the History of Alta California, 1769–1848: Gender, Sexuality, and the Family." *California History* 76, nos. 2–3 (1997): 230–59.

Cato, Nancy. *Mister Maloga*. St. Lucia: University of Queensland, 1976.

Cave, Alfred. *The Pequot War*. Amherst: University of Massachusetts Press, 1996.

Chakrabarty, Dipesh. *Habitations of Modernity: Essays in the Wake of Subaltern Studies*. Chicago: Chicago University Press, 2002.

———. "The Muddle of Modernity." *American Historical Review* 116, no. 3 (June 2011): 663–75.

———. *Provincializing Europe: Postcolonial Thought and Historical Difference*. Princeton NJ: Princeton University Press, 2000.

Charvat, William. "American Romanticism and the Depression of 1837." *Science and Society* 2, no. 1 (Winter 1937): 67–82.

Cherokee Nation. *Laws of the Cherokee Nation Adopted by the Council at Various Periods: Printed for the Benefit of the Nation*. Tahlequah OK: Cherokee Advocate Office, 1852.

Cherokee Phoenix (New Echota GA). 1828–31.

Chesterman, John. *Civil Rights: How Indigenous Australians Won Formal Equality*. St. Lucia: University of Queensland Press, 2005.

Chesterman, John, and Brian Galligan. *Citizens without Rights: Aborigines and Australian Citizenship*. Cambridge: Cambridge University Press, 1997.

Church, Mary Brinsmade. *Elias Boudinot: An Account of His Life*. Town History Papers of the Woman's Club of Washington, 1913. Available at Alice Robertson Collection, series 2: Correspondence, box 1, folder 9, McFarlin Library, University of Tulsa, http://www.lib.utulsa.edu/digital/robertson/Series_II/pdf/AR2_01_09_108.pdf.

Child, Lydia M. *Hobomok: A Tale of Early Times*. Boston: Cummings, Hilliard, 1824.

———. *Hobomok and Other Writings on Indians*. Edited by Carolyn L. Karcher. New Brunswick NJ: Rutgers University Press, 1997.

Cole, Anna, Victoria Haskins, and Fiona Paisley. *Uncommon Ground: White Women in Aboriginal History*. Canberra: Aboriginal Studies Press for AIATSIS, 2005.

Conforti, Joseph. *Imagining New England: Explorations of Regional Identity from the Pilgrims to the Mid-twentieth Century*. Chapel Hill: University of North Carolina Press, 2001.

———. *Jonathan Edwards, Religious Tradition, and American Culture*. Chapel Hill: University of North Carolina Press, 1995.

Conn, Steven. *History's Shadow: Native Americans and Historical Consciousness in the Nineteenth Century*. Chicago: University of Chicago Press, 2005.

Cooper, Frederick, and Ann L. Stoler, eds. *Tensions of Empire: Colonial Cultures in a Bourgeois World*. Berkeley: University of California Press, 1997.

Cooper, Thomas. *Strictures Addressed to James Madison on the Celebrated Report of William H. Crawford: Recommending the Intermarriage of Americans with the Indian Tribes*. Philadelphia: Jasper Harding, 1824.

Corman, Catherine Ann. "Reading, Writing and Removal: Native American Literacies, 1824–1835." PhD thesis, Yale University, 1998.

Cott, Nancy F. *The Bonds of Womanhood: "Woman's Sphere" in New England, 1780–1835*. New Haven CT: Yale University Press, 1977.

———. DeVane Lecture Series papers, Yale University, New Haven CT, January 21, 28, 1998.

———. "Passionlessness: An Interpretation of Victorian Sexual Ideology, 1790–1850." *Signs* 4, no. 2 (1978): 219–36.

———. *Public Vows: A History of Marriage and Nation*. Cambridge MA: Harvard University Press, 2000.

Craig, Daniel. "The Social Impact of the State on an Aboriginal Reserve in Queensland, Australia." PhD thesis, University of California, Berkeley, 1980.

Crawley, Ernest. *The Mystic Rose: A Study of Primitive Marriage and of Primitive Thought in Its Bearing on Marriage*. New York: Boni and Liveright, 1927.

Cumfer, Cynthia. *Separate Peoples, One Land: The Minds of Cherokees, Blacks, and Whites on the Tennessee Frontier*. Chapel Hill: University of North Carolina Press, 2007.

Curthoys, Ann. "Expulsion, Exodus and Exile in White Australian Historical Mythology." *Journal of Australian Studies* 23, no. 61 (1999): 1–19.

———. *Freedom Ride: A Freedom Rider Remembers*. Crows Nest NSW: Allen & Unwin, 2003.

Curthoys, Ann, and Ann Genovese. *Rights and Redemption: History, Law and Indigenous People*. Sydney: University of New South Wales Press, 2008.

Curthoys, Ann, and Ann McGrath, eds. *Writing Histories: Imagination and Narration*. Monash Publications in History. Melbourne: School of Historical Studies, Monash University, 2000.

———. *How to Write History That People Want to Read*. Sydney: University of New South Wales Press, 2009.

Cutts, Lucia B., ed. *Memoirs and Letters of Dolly Madison, Wife of James Madison, President of the United States*. Port Washington NY: Kennikat Press, 1971.

Daggett, Hermann. *An Inauguration Address Delivered at the Opening of the Foreign Mission School, May 6, 1818*. New Haven CT: Nathan Whiting, agent of the Foreign Mission School, 1819.

Dale, Edward Everett. *Cherokee Cavaliers: Forty Years of Cherokee History as Told in the Correspondence of the Ridge-Waite-Boudinot Family*. Norman: University of Oklahoma Press, 1939.

Darian-Smith, Kate, Roslyn Poignant, and Kay Schaffer. *Captive Lives: Australian Captivity Narratives*. London: Sir Robert Menzies Centre for Australian Studies, University of London, 1993.

Davidson, Alastair. *From Subject to Citizen: Australian Citizenship in the Twentieth Century*. Cambridge: Cambridge University Press, 1997.

Davis, Gussie. *Dance, Pickaninnies, Dance!* New York: Hitchcock, 1895.

Davis, James F. *Who Is Black?: One Nation's Definition*. University Park: Pennsylvania State University Press, 1991.

de Baillou, Clemens, ed. *John Howard Payne to His Countrymen*. Athens: University of Georgia Press, 1961.

De Cruz, Peter. *Family Law, Sex and Society: A Comparative Study of Family Law*. New York: Routledge, 2009.

De Heer, Rolf, dir. *Ten Canoes*. Australia: Palace Films, 2006.

Delbridge, Arthur, ed. *The Macquarie Dictionary*. St. Leonards NSW: Macquarie Library, 1981.

Deloria, Philip J. *Playing Indian*. New Haven CT: Yale University Press, 1998.
Deloria, Vine, Jr., and Clifford M. Lytle. *The Nations Within: The Past and Future of American Indian Sovereignty*. New York: Pantheon, 1984.
Demos, John. *Circles and Lines: The Shape of Life in Early America*. Cambridge MA: Harvard University Press, 2004.
———. *A Little Commonwealth: Family Life in Plymouth Colony*. New York: Oxford University Press, 1970.
———. *The Unredeemed Captive: A Family Story from Early America*. New York: Alfred Knopf, 1994.
Dening, Greg. *Performances*. Carlton VIC: Melbourne University Press, 1996.
Den Ouden, Amy E. *Beyond Conquest: Native Peoples and the Struggle for History in New England*. Lincoln: University of Nebraska Press, 2005.
———. *The Unredeemed Captive*. New York: Vintage, 1995.
Denson, Andrew. *Demanding the Cherokee Nation: Indian Autonomy and American Culture, 1830–1900*. Lincoln: University of Nebraska Press, 2004.
Department of Natural Resources and Mines. *Guide to Compiling a Connection Report for Native Title Claims in Queensland*. Brisbane: Queensland Government, 2013. Available at http://www.nrw.qld.gov.au/nativetitle/pdf/connection_guide.pdf.
Dewar, Mickey. *The "Black War" in Arnhem Land: Missionaries and the Yolngu, 1908–1940*. Darwin: North Australian Research Unit, Australian National University, 1992.
Divine, Robert A., T. H. Breen, R. Hall Williams, George Frederickson, Randy Roberts, Ariela Gross, and H. W. Brands. *America, Past and Present*. New York: HarperCollins, 1991.
Dixon, Robert. *A Grammar of Yidin*. Cambridge: Cambridge University Press, 1977.
———. *Searching for Aboriginal Languages: Memoirs of a Field Worker*. St. Lucia: University of Queensland, 1984.
———. "Tribes, Languages and Other Boundaries in Northeast Queensland." In *Tribes and Boundaries in Australia*, edited by Nicholas Peterson, 207–38. Canberra: Australian Institute of Aboriginal Studies, 1976.
———. *Words of Our Country: Stories, Place Names and Vocabulary in Yidiny, the Aboriginal Language of the Cairns-Yarrabah Region*. St. Lucia: University of Queensland, 1991.
Dorsey, Bruce. *Reforming Men and Women: Gender in the Antebellum City*. Ithaca NY: Cornell University Press, 2002.
Dru Stanley, Amy. *From Bondage to Contract: Wage Labor, Marriage and the Market in the Era of Slave Emancipation*. Cambridge: Cambridge University Press, 1998.
DuVal, Kathleen. "Indian Intermarriage and Métissage in Colonial Louisiana." *William and Mary Quarterly* 65 (April 2008): 267–304.
Duvall, Michael J., and Julie Cary Nerad. "'Suddenly and Shockingly Black': The Atavistic Child in Turn-into-the-Twentieth-Century American Fiction." *African American Review* 41, no. 1 (Spring 2007): 51–66.

Dwight, Edwin. *Memoirs of Henry Obookiah: A native of Owhyhee and a member of the Foreign Mission School, who died at Cornwall, Connecticut, February 17, 1818, aged 26 years*. New Haven CT: Nathaniel Whiting, 1819.
Dyer, Richard. *White*. London: Routledge, 1997.
Ebersole, Gary L. *Captured by Texts: Puritan to Postmodern Images of Indian Captivity*. Charlottesville: University Press of Virginia, 1995.
Edmunds, David R. *The Shawnee Prophet*. Lincoln: University of Nebraska Press, 1983.
Edwards, Coral, and Peter Read, eds. *The Lost Children: Thirteen Australians Taken from their Aboriginal Families Tell of the Struggle to Find Their Natural Parents*. Sydney: Doubleday, 1989.
Egan, Ted. *Justice All Their Own*. Carlton South VIC: Melbourne University Press, 1996.
Elkin, A. P. *Aboriginal Men of High Degree*. St. Lucia: University of Queensland Press, 1977.
Ellinghaus, Katherine. "Absorbing the Aboriginal Problem: Controlling Interracial Marriage in Australia in the Late 19th and Early 20th century." *Aboriginal History* 27 (2003): 183–207.
———. "Margins of Acceptability: Class, Education, and Interracial Marriage in Australia and North America." *Frontiers: A Journal of Women's Studies* 23, no. 3 (2002): 55–75.
———. *Taking Assimilation to Heart: Marriages of White Women and Indigenous Men in the United States and Australia, 1887–1937*. Lincoln: University of Nebraska Press, 2006.
———. "Taking Assimilation to Heart: Marriages of White Women and Indigenous Men in Australia and North America, 1870s–1930s." PhD thesis, University of Melbourne, 2001.
Evans, Julie, Ann Genovese, Alexander Reilly, and Patrick Wolfe, eds. *Sovereignty: Frontiers of Possibility*. Honolulu: University of Hawai'i Press, 2013.
Evans, Raymond. *A History of Queensland*. Cambridge: Cambridge University Press, 2006.
Evans, Raymond, Kay Saunders, and Kathryn Cronin. *Race Relations in Colonial Queensland*. St. Lucia: University of Queensland Press, 1988.
Faragher, John Mack. "The Custom of the Country." In *Western Women: Their Land, Their Lives*, edited by Lillian Schlissel, Vicki L. Ruiz, and Janice Monk, 119–225. Albuquerque: University of New Mexico Press, 1988.
Fiege, Mark. *Republic of Nature: An Environmental History of the United States*. Seattle: University of Washington Press, 2012.
Filler, Louis, and Allen Guttmann, eds. *The Removal of the Cherokee Nation: Manifest Destiny or National Dishonor?* Boston: D. C. Heath, 1962.
Finlayson, Julie. "Don't Depend on Me: Autonomy and Dependence in an Aboriginal Community in North Queensland." PhD thesis, Australian National University, 1991.

Fisher, Linford D. *The Indian Great Awakening: Religion and the Shaping of Native Cultures in Early America*. New York: Oxford University Press, 2012.

Fitzgerald, Ross. *Made in Queensland: A New History*. St. Lucia: University of Queensland Press, 2009.

Fitzmaurice, Andrew. "The Genealogy of Terra Nullius." *Australian Historical Studies*, 38, no. 129 (2007): 1–15.

Fixico, Donald. *Call for Change: The Medicine Way of American Indian History*. Lincoln: University of Nebraska Press, 2013.

Fogelson, Raymond D. "On the 'Petticoat Government' of the Eighteenth-Century Cherokee." In *Personality and the Cultural Construction of Society*, edited by David K. Jordan and Marc J. Swartz, 161–81. Tuscaloosa: University of Alabama Press, 1990.

Ford, Lisa. *Settler Sovereignty: Jurisdiction and Indigenous People in America and Australia, 1788–1836*. Cambridge MA: Harvard University Press, 2010.

Ford, Lisa, and Tim Rowse, eds. *Between Indigenous and Settler Governance*. New York: Routledge, 2013.

Foreman, Carolyn T. "The Foreign Mission School at Cornwall, Connecticut." *Chronicles of Oklahoma* 7, no. 3 (September 1929): 242–59.

Foster, Stephen. "A Connecticut Separate Church: Strict Congregationalism in Cornwall, 1780–1809." *New England Quarterly* 39, no. 3 (September 1966): 309–33.

Foucault, Michel. *The History of Sexuality*. New York: Vintage Books, 1980.

Fowler, H. W., ed. *The Concise Oxford Dictionary of Current English: Based on the Oxford English Dictionary and Its Supplements*. Oxford: Clarendon Press, 1933.

Fradin, Dennis B. *The Trail of Tears*. New York: Marshall Cavendish Benchmark, 2007.

Fraser, E. *Narrative of the Capture, Sufferings, and Miraculous Escape of Mrs. Eliza Fraser, Wife of the Late Captain Samuel Fraser, Commander of the Ship Sterling Castle*. New York: Charles S. Webb, 1837.

Fur, Gunlög Maria. *A Nation of Women: Gender and Colonial Encounters among the Delaware Indians*. Philadelphia: University of Pennsylvania Press, 2009.

Gabriel, Ralph. *Elias Boudinot, Cherokee, and His America*. Norman: University of Oklahoma Press, 1941.

Gammage, Bill. *The Biggest Estate on Earth: How Aborigines Made Australia*. Sydney: Allen & Unwin, 2012.

Gannett, Michael R. *The Distribution of the Common Land of Cornwall, Connecticut, 1733–1887*. Cornwall CT: Cornwall Historical Society, 1880.

Ganter, Regina. *Mixed Relations: Asian-Aboriginal Contact in North Australia*. Crawley: University of Western Australia Press, 2006.

Gardner, Helen. *Gathering for God: George Brown in Oceania*. Dunedin: Otago University Press, 2006.

Gaul, Theresa Strouth, ed. *To Marry an Indian: The Marriage of Harriett Gold and Elias Boudinot in Letters, 1823–1839*. Chapel Hill: University of North Carolina Press, 2005.

Gilmore, Glenda Elizabeth. *Gender and Jim Crow: Women and the Politics of White Supremacy in North Carolina, 1896–1920*. Chapel Hill: University of North Carolina Press, 1996.

Gitlin, Jay. "Private Diplomacy to Private Property: States, Tribes, and Nations in the Early National Period." *Diplomatic History* 22, no. 1 (1998): 85–99.

Gold, Theodore S. *Historical Records of the Town of Cornwall, Litchfield County, Connecticut*. Hartford CT: Press of the Case, Lockwood and Brainard Co., 1877.

Goodman, David. *Gold Seeking: Victoria and California in the 1850s*. St. Leonards NSW: Allen & Unwin, 1994.

Goodwin, Gary C. *Cherokees in Transition: A Study of Changing Culture and Environment Prior to 1775*. Chicago: University of Chicago, Department of Geography, 1977.

Gordon, Sarah Barringer. *The Mormon Question: Polygamy and Constitutional Conflict in Nineteenth-Century America*. Chapel Hill: University of North Carolina Press, 2002.

Gordon-Reed, Annette. *The Hemingses of Monticello: An American Family*. New York: W. W. Norton, 2008.

———. *Thomas Jefferson and Sally Hemings: An American Controversy*. Charlottesville: University Press of Virginia, 1997.

Govor, E. V. *My Dark Brother: The Story of the Illins, a Russian-Aboriginal Family*. Sydney: University of New South Wales Press, 2000.

Grafton, Anthony. *Bring Out Your Dead: The Past as Revelation*. Cambridge MA: Harvard University Press, 2001.

Grant, James. *Essays on the Origin of Society, Language, Property, Government, Jurisdiction, Contracts and Marriage*. London: Printed by B. Millian for G. G. J. Robinson, J. Robinson, and C. Elliot, 1785.

Graybill, Andrew. *The Red and the White: A Family Saga of the American West*. New York: Liveright, 2013.

Green, Rayna. "The Pocahontas Perplex: The Image of Indian Women in American Culture." *Massachusetts Review* 16, no. 4 (Autumn 1975): 698–714.

Greer, Allan. "Commons and Enclosure in the Colonization of North America." *American Historical Review* 117, no. 2 (2012): 365–86.

Gribble, Ernest R. *A Despised Race: The Vanishing Aboriginals in Australia*. Sydney: Australian Board of Missions, 1933.

———. *Forty Years with the Aborigines*. Sydney: Angus and Robertson, 1930.

———. "Mission Methods." *Argus*, May 28, 1910.

———. *The Problem of the Australian Aboriginal*. Sydney: Angus and Robertson, 1932.

Gribble, John B. *Black but Comely; or, Glimpses of Aboriginal Life in Australia*. London: Morgan & Scott, ca. 1884.

———. *Dark Deeds in a Sunny Land; or, Blacks and Whites in North-West Australia*. Perth: University of Western Australia Press, 1987.

Grieves, Victoria. "Aboriginal Spirituality: Aboriginal Philosophy: The Basis of Aboriginal Social and Emotional Wellbeing." Discussion Paper Series No. 9 Casuarina NT: Cooperative Research Centre for Aboriginal Health, 2009. https://www.lowitja.org.au/sites/default/files/docs/DP9-Aboriginal-Spirituality.pdf.

———. "We Are Survivors: The Persistence of Life and Hope in Aboriginal Marriage, Family and Kinship Practices." *Journal of the European Association for Studies of Australia* 4, no. 1 (2013): 1–5.

Griffiths, Tom. "The Poetics and Practicalities of Writing." In *Writing Histories: Imagination and Narration*, edited by Ann Curthoys and Ann McGrath, 1–13. Melbourne: School of Historical Studies, Monash University, 2000.

Grimshaw, Patricia. "Interracial Marriages and Colonial Regimes in Victoria and Aotearoa/New Zealand." *Frontiers: A Journal of Women's Studies* 23, no. 3 (2002): 12–28.

———. *Paths of Duty: American Missionary Wives in Nineteenth-Century Hawaii*. Honolulu: University of Hawaii Press, 1989.

———. "Women and the Family in Australian History." In *Women, Class and History: Feminist Perspectives on Australia, 1788–1978*, edited by Elizabeth Windschuttle, 37–52. Sydney: Fontana/Collins, 1980.

———. "Women and the Family in Australian History: A Reply to 'The Real Matilda.'" *Historical Studies* 18 (1979): 412–21.

Grimshaw, Patricia, Marilyn Lake, Ann McGrath, and Marian Quartly. *Creating a Nation, 1788–1990*. Ringwood VIC: McPhee Gribble, 1994.

Grimshaw, Patricia, Chris McConville, and Ellen McEwan. *Families in Colonial Australia*. Sydney: Allen & Unwin, 1985.

Grimshaw, Patricia, and Russell McGregor, eds. *Collisions of Cultures and Identities: Settlers and Indigenous Peoples*. Melbourne: RMIT, 2007.

Gutiérrez, Ramón. *When Jesus Came, the Corn Mothers Went Away: Marriage, Sexuality, and Power in New Mexico, 1500–1846*. Stanford CA: Stanford University Press, 1991.

Haebich, Anna. *Broken Circles: Fragmenting Indigenous Families, 1800–2000*. Freemantle WA: Fremantle Arts Centre Press, 2000.

Haag, Oliver. "From the Margins to the Mainstream: Towards a History of Published Indigenous Australian Autobiographies and Biographies." In *Indigenous Biography and Autobiography*, edited by Peter Read, Frances Peters-Little, and Anna Haebich. Aboriginal History Monograph 17. Acton ACT: ANU E Press and Aboriginal History, 2008.

Halley, Janet E. "Behind the Law of Marriage," pt. 1, "From Status/Contract to the Marriage System" *Unbound: Harvard Journal of the Legal Left* 6, no. 1 (2010): n.p.

Halliburton, R. *Red over Black: Black Slavery among the Cherokee Indians*. Westport CT: Greenwood Press, 1977.

Halse, Christine. "The Reverend Ernest Gribble and Race Relations in Northern Australia." PhD thesis, University of Queensland, 1992.

———. *A Terribly Wild Man*. Sydney: Allen & Unwin, 2002.

Hämäläinen, Pekka. *The Comanche Empire*. New Haven CT: Yale University Press, 2009.

Hämäläinen, Pekka and Samuel Truett. "On Borderlands." *Journal of American History* 98, no. 2 (2011): 338–61.

Hannah, Mark. "Constituting Marriage: Indigenous and Inter-cultural Marriage and Power of 'Protectors.'" PhD thesis, Australian National University, 2005.

Harrison, Gabriel. *John Howard Payne, Dramatist, Poet, Actor and Author of "Home Sweet Home": His Life and Writings*. Philadelphia: J. B. Lippincott, 1885.

———. *The Life and Writing of John Howard Payne*. Albany NY: J. Munsell, 1875.

Hardy, B. Cameron, and Dan Erickson. "'Regeneration; Now and Evermore!': Mormon Polygamy and the Physical Rehabilitation of Humankind." *Journal of the History of Sexuality* 10, no. 1 (January 2001): 40–61.

Hardy, Frank. *The Unlucky Australians*. Melbourne: Nelson, 1968.

Hartog, Hendrik. *Man and Wife in America: A History*. Cambridge MA: Harvard University Press, 2000.

Haskins, Victoria. *Matrons and Maids: Regulating Indian Domestic Service in Tucson, 1914–1934*. Tucson: University of Arizona Press, 2012.

Haskins, Victoria, and John Maynard. "Sex, Race and Power: Aboriginal Men and White Women in Australian History." *Australian Historical Studies* 37, no. 126 (October 2005): 191–216.

Hatley, M. Thomas. *The Dividing Paths: Cherokees and South Carolinians through the Era of Revolution*. New York: Oxford University Press, 1993.

Hay, Denys. "The Use of the Term 'Great Britain' in the Middle Ages." *Proceedings of the Society of Antiquaries of Scotland* 89 (1955–56): 55–66.

Haywood, Claire, dir. *A Frontier Conversation*. Civic Square, ACT: Ronin Films, 2006.

Healy, C. *Forgetting Aborigines*. Sydney: University of New South Wales Press, 2008.

Heard, Genevieve, Bob Birrell, and Siew-Ean Khoo. "Intermarriage between Indigenous and Non-indigenous Australians." *People and Place* 17, no. 1 (2009): 1–14.

Heiss, Anita. *Am I Black Enough for You?* Honolulu: University of Hawai'i Press, 2012.

Henningham, Nicki. "Picking up Colonial Experience: White Men, Sexuality and Marriage in North Queensland, 1890–1910." In *Raiding Clio's Closet: Postgraduate Presentations in History*, edited by Martin Crotty and Doug Scobie, 89–104. Melbourne: Department of History, University of Melbourne, 1997.

Hiatt, L. R. *Arguments about Aboriginies: Australia and the Evolution of Social Anthropology*. Cambridge: Cambridge University Press, 1996.

Hine, Robert V., and John M. Faragher. *The American West: A New Interpretive History*. New Haven CT: Yale University Press, 2000.

Hirst, John. "The Pioneer Legend." *Historical Studies* 18, no. 71 (October 1978): 316–37.

———. *The Sentimental Nation: The Making of the Australian Commonwealth*. Melbourne: Oxford University Press, 2000.

Hodes, Martha. "Four Episodes in Re-creating a Life." *Rethinking History: The Journal of Theory and Practice* 10, no. 2 (June 2006): 277–90.

———. "Reflections upon Being a Scholar and Writer." *Rethinking History: The Journal of Theory and Practice* 14, no. 1 (2010): 47–53.

———. *The Sea Captain's Wife: A True Story of Love, Race and War in the Nineteenth Century*. New York: W. W. Norton, 2006.

———, ed. *Sex, Love, Race: Crossing Boundaries in North American History*. New York: New York University Press, 1999.

———. *White Women, Black Men: Illicit Sex in the Nineteenth-Century South*. New Haven CT: Yale University Press, 1997.

Hoffman, John. *Gender and Sovereignty: Feminism, the State and International Relations*. New York: Palgrave, 2001.

Hoffman, Ronald, Mechal Sobel, and Fredrika J. Teute, eds. *Through a Glass Darkly: Reflections on Personal Identity in Early America*. Chapel Hill: University of North Carolina Press, 1997.

Hokari, Minoru. "Cross-Culturalizing History: Journey to the Gurindji Way of Historical Practice." PhD thesis, Australian National University, 2001.

———. *Gurindji Journey: A Japanese Historian in the Outback*. Honolulu: University of Hawaii Press, 2011.

———. *Radikaru ōraru hisutorī: Ōsutoraria senjūmin Aborijini no rekishi jissen*. Tokyo: Ochanomizu Shobō, 2004.

Holland, Alison. "'Whatever her race, a woman is not a chattel': Mary Montgomery Bennett." In *Uncommon Ground: White Women in Aboriginal History*, edited by Anna Cole, Victoria Haskins, and Fiona Paisley, 129–52. Canberra: Aboriginal Studies Press for AIATSIS, 2005.

Holland, Alison, and Barbara Brooks, eds. *Rethinking the Racial Moment*. Newcastle, UK: Cambridge Scholars, 2011.

Holmes, Richard. *Shelley on Love: An Anthology*. London: Wildwood House, 1980.

Hoxie, Frederick. *This Indian Country: American Indian Political Activists and the Place They Made*. New York: Penguin Press, 2012.

Hoxie, Frederick, Ronald Hoffman, and Peter Albert, eds. *Native Americans and the Early Republic*. Charlottesville: University Press of Virginia, 1999.

Huber, Margaret, ed. *Museums and Memory*. Knoxville TN: Newfound Press, 2011.

Hudson, Charles M. *The Southeastern Indians*. Knoxville: University of Tennessee Press, 1976.

Huggins, Jackie. "Always Was Always Will Be." *Australian Historical Studies* 25, no. 100 (1993): 459–64.

Huggins, Jackie, and Thom Blake. "Protection or Persecution? Gender Relations in the Era of Racial Segregation.'" In *Gender Relations in Australia: Domination and Negotiation*, edited by K. Saunders and R. Evans, 42–58. Sydney: Harcourt Brace Jovanovich, 1992.

Huggins, Rita, and Jackie Huggins. *Auntie Rita*. Canberra: Aboriginal Studies Press, 1994.

Hume, Lynne. "Them Days: Life on an Aboriginal Reserve, 1892–1960." *Aboriginal History* 15, no. 2 (1991): 4–21.

———. "Yarrabah, Christian Phoenix: Christianity and Social Change on an Australian Aboriginal Reserve." PhD thesis, University of Queensland, 1989.

Hurtado, Albert L. *Intimate Frontiers: Sex, Gender and Culture in Old California*. Albuquerque: University of New Mexico Press, 1999.

Hutchins, Zachary McLeod. "Rattlesnakes in the Garden: The Fascinating Serpents of the Early, Edenic Republic," *Early American Studies: An Interdisciplinary Journal* 9, no. 3 (2011): 677–715.

Hyde, Ann. *Empires, Nations, and Families: A History of the North American West, 1800–1860*. Lincoln: University of Nebraska Press, 2011.

Ifekwunigwe, Jayne O., ed. *"Mixed Race" Studies: A Reader*. London: Routledge, 2004.

Irving, Washington. "Miscellaneous Traits of Indian Character." *Cherokee Phoenix* 1, no. 3 (March 6, 1828): 4; 1, no. 4 (March 13, 1828): 4; 1, no. 5 (March 20, 1828): 5.

Jacobs, Margaret D., "Western History: What's Gender Got to Do With It?" *Western Historical Quarterly* 42, no. 3 (Autumn 2011): 297–304.

———. *White Mother to a Dark Race: Settler Colonialism, Maternalism, and the Removal of Indigenous Children in the American West and Australia, 1880–1940*. Lincoln: University of Nebraska Press, 2009.

Jalland, Patricia. *Women, Marriage and Politics, 1860–1914*. Oxford: Oxford University Press, 1988.

Johansen, Bruce Elliott, and Barry Pritzker, eds. *Encyclopedia of American Indian History*. Santa Barbara CA: ABC-Clio, 2007.

Johns, Elizabeth, Andrew Sayers, Elizabeth M. Kornhauser, and Amy Ellis. *New Worlds from Old: 19th-Century Australian and American Landscapes*. Canberra: National Gallery of Australia, 1998.

Johnson, Kevin R., ed. *Mixed Race America and the Law: A Reader*. New York: New York University Press, 2003.

Johnston, Carolyn R. *Cherokee Women in Crisis: Trail of Tears, Civil War, and Allotment, 1838–1907*. Tuscaloosa: University of Alabama Press, 2003.

Jones, Jacqueline. *A Dreadful Deceit: The Myth of Race from the Colonial Era to Obama's America*. New York: Basic Books, 2013.

Jones, Rod. *Billy Sunday*. New York: Henry Holt, 1996.

Jordan, Ann. *Hidden Voices: Working Creatively with Conflict*. College Station TX: Virtualbookworm, 2006.

Keel, Bennie C. *Cherokee Archaeology: A Study of the Appalachian Summit*. Knoxville: University of Tennessee Press, 1976.

Keegan, Kristen Noble, and William F. Keegan, eds. *The Archaeology of Connecticut: The Human Era, 11,000 Years Ago to the Present*. Storrs CT: Bibliopola Press, 1999.

Keen, Ian. *Knowledge and Secrecy in an Aboriginal Religion: Yolngu of North-East Arnhem Land*. Melbourne: Oxford University Press, 1994.

Keller, Arthur S., Oliver J. Lissitzyn, and Frederick J. Mann. *Creation of Rights of Sovereignty through Symbolic Acts, 1400–1800*. New York: Columbia University Press, 1938.

Kennedy, Randall. *Interracial Intimacies: Sex, Marriage, Identity and Adoption.* New York: Pantheon, 2002.
Kenny, Kevin. *Peaceable Kingdom Lost: The Paxton Boys and the Destruction of William Penn's Holy Experiment.* Oxford: Oxford University Press, 2009.
Kenslea, Timothy. *The Sedgwicks in Love: Courtship, Engagement, and Marriage in the Early Republic.* Boston: Northeastern University Press, 2006.
Ketcham, Ralph L. *James Madison: A Biography.* New York: Macmillan, 1971.
Khan, Kate. *Catalogue of the Roth Collection of Aboriginal Artefacts from North Queensland.* Vol. 3. Technical Reports of the Australian Museum, no. 17. Sydney South NSW: Australian Museum, 2003.
Khoo, Siew-Ean, Bob Birrell, and Genevieve Heard. "Intermarriage by Birthplace and Ancestry in Australia." *People and Place* 17, no. 1 (2009): 15–27.
Kidd, Rosalind. *The Way We Civilise: Aboriginal Affairs — The Untold Story.* St. Lucia: University of Queensland Press, 1997.
Kidwell, Clara S. *The Choctaws in Oklahoma: From Tribe to Nation, 1855–1970.* Norman: University of Oklahoma Press, 2007.
Kiernan, Ben. *Blood and Soil.* New Haven CT: Yale University Press, 2007.
King, Duane H. *The Cherokee Indian Nation: A Troubled History.* Knoxville: University of Tennessee Press, 1979.
Kinnane, Stephen. *Shadow Lines.* Fremantle WA: Fremantle Arts Centre Press, 2003.
Kinney, James. *Amalgamation! Race, Sex and Rhetoric in the Nineteenth-Century American Novel.* Westport CT: Greenwood Press, 1985.
Klarman, Michael J. *From Jim Crow to Civil Rights: The Supreme Court and the Struggle for Racial Equality.* Oxford: Oxford University Press, 2004.
Klein, Kerwin Lee. *Frontiers of the Historical Imagination.* Berkeley: University of California Press, 1997.
Konishi, Shino. *The Aboriginal Male in the Enlightenment World.* London: Pickering and Chatto, 2012.
Konkle, Maureen. *Writing Indian Nations: Native Intellectuals and the Politics of Historiography, 1827–1863.* Chapel Hill: University of North Carolina Press, 2003.
Kvasnicka, Robert M., and Herman J. Viola, eds. *The Commissioners of Indian Affairs, 1824–1977.* Lincoln: University of Nebraska Press, 1979.
A Lady. *Catharine Brown the Converted Cherokee: A Missionary Drama, Founded on Fact.* New Haven CT: Converse Printer, 1819.
Lake, Marilyn. "'The brightness of eyes and quiet assurance which seem to say American': Alfred Deakin's Identification with Republican Manhood." *Australian Historical Studies* 38, no. 129 (2007): 32–51.
———. "Frontier Feminism and the Marauding White Man." *Journal of Australian Studies* 20, no. 49 (1996): 12–20.
———. "Marriage as Bondage: The Anomaly of the Citizen Wife." *Australian Historical Studies* 29, no. 112 (1999): 116–29.

Lake, Marilyn, and Henry Reynolds. *Drawing the Global Color Line: White Men's Countries and the Question of Racial Equality*. Carlton VIC: Melbourne University Press, 2008.

La Nauze, John Andrew. *Alfred Deakin: A Biography*. Carlton VIC: Melbourne University Press, 1965.

Laurie, Arthur, and Ann McGrath. "I Was a Drover Once Myself: Amy Laurie of Kununurra." In *Fighters and Singers: The Lives of Some Australian Aboriginal Women*, edited by Isobel White, Diane Barwick, and Betty Meehan., 76–90. Sydney: George Allen & Unwin, 1985.

Law Reform Commission of Western Australia. *Aboriginal Customary Laws: The Interaction of Western Australian Law with Aboriginal Law and Culture: Final Report*. Perth: Law Reform Commission of Western Australia, 2006.

Leneman, Leah. "The Scottish Case That Led to Hardwicke's Marriage Act." *Law and History Review* 17, no. 1 (1999): 161–69.

Levine, Philippa. *The British Empire: Sunrise to Sunset*. New York: Pearson Longman, 2007.

———. *Gender and Empire*. Oxford: Oxford University Press, 2004.

———. *Prostitution, Race and Politics: Policing Venereal Disease in the British Empire*. New York: Routledge, 2003.

Lewis, Jan. "The Republican Wife: Virtue and Seduction in the Early Republic." *William and Mary Quarterly* 44, no. 4 (October 1987): 689–721.

Limerick, Patricia Nelson. "Going West and Ending Up Global." *Western Historical Quarterly* 32 (Spring 2001): 5–23.

———. "Turnerians All: The Dream of a Helpful History in an Intelligible World." *American Historical Review* 100, no. 3 (1995): 697–716.

Littlefield, Daniel F. *The Cherokee Freedmen: From Emancipation to American Citizenship*. Westport CT: Greenwood Press, 1978.

Litwack, Leon F. *North of Slavery: The Negro in the Free States, 1790–1860*. Chicago: University of Chicago Press, 1961.

Lumpkin, Wilson. *The Removal of the Cherokee Indians from Georgia*. New York: Dodd, Mead, 1907.

Lyons, Clare A. *Sex among the Rabble: An Intimate History of Gender and Power in the Age of Revolution, Philadelphia, 1730–1830*. Chapel Hill: University of North Carolina Press, 2006.

MacFarlane, Ingereth, and Mark Hannah, eds. *Transgressions: Critical Australian Indigenous Histories*. Aboriginal History Monograph series, 16. Canberra: ANU E Press and Aboriginal History, 2007

MacIntyre, Stuart, and Anna Clark. *The History Wars*. Carlton VIC: Melbourne University Press, 2006.

Macmillan, Ken. *Sovereignty and Possession in the English New World*. New York: Cambridge University Press, 2006.

Mandell, Daniel R. *Tribe, Race, History: Native Americans in Southern New England, 1780–1880*. Baltimore: Johns Hopkins University Press, 2008.
Marini, Stephen. "Hymnody as History: Early Evangelical Hymns and the Recovery of American Popular Religion." *Church History* 71, no.2 (2002): 273–306.
Markus, Andrew. *Australian Race Relations: 1788–1993*. St. Leonards NSW: Allen & Unwin, 1994.
Martin, Joel W. "Crisscrossing Projects of Sovereignty and Conversion: Cherokee Christians and New England Missionaries during the 1820s." In *Native Americans, Christianity and the Reshaping of the American Religious Landscape*, edited by Joel W. Martin and Mark A. Nicholas, 67–92. Chapel Hill: University of North Carolina Press, 2010.
Martin, Joel W., and Mark A. Nicholas, eds., *Native Americans, Christianity and the Reshaping of the American Religious Landscape*. Chapel Hill: University of North Carolina Press, 2010.
May, Catherine. *Topsawyers: The Chinese in Cairns, 1870–1920*. Townsville QLD: James Cook University History Department, 1984.
Maynard, John. *Fight for Liberty and Freedom: The Origins of Australian Aboriginal Activism*. Canberra: Aboriginal Studies Press, 2007.
———. *True Light and Shade: An Aboriginal Perspective of Joseph Lycett's Art*. Canberra: National Library of Australia, 2014.
McCalman, Iain, ed. *An Oxford Companion to the Romantic Age: British Culture, 1776–1832*. Oxford: Oxford University Press, 1999.
McCarthy, Conor. *Marriage in Medieval England: Law, Literature and Practice*. Rochester NY: Boydell Press, 2004.
McClintock, Anne. *Imperial Leather: Race, Gender and Sexuality in the Colonial Contest*. New York: Routledge, 1995.
McCorquodale, John. *Aborigines and the Law: A Digest*. Canberra: Aboriginal Studies Press, 1987.
McDonald, Peter F. *Marriage in Australia: Age at First Marriage and Proportions Marrying, 1860–1971*. Canberra: Australian National University, 1974.
McDougall, Russell, and Iain Davidson. *The Roth Family: Anthropology and Colonial Administration*. Walnut Creek CA: Left Coast Press, 2008.
McElroy, A. *McElroy's Philadelphia City Directory: 1844*. Philadelphia: A. McElroy, 1844.
McGrath, Ann. "Being Annie Oakley: Modern Girls, New World Woman." *Frontiers: A Journal of Women's Studies* 28, nos. 1 and 2 (2007): 203–31.
———. "Beneath the Skin: Australian Citizenship, Rights and Aboriginal Women." *Journal of Australian Studies*, no. 37 (June 2003): 99–114.
———. *Born in the Cattle: Aborigines in Cattle Country*. Sydney: Allen & Unwin, 1987. Also available as an ACLS e-book.
———, ed. *Contested Ground: Australian Aborigines under the British Crown*. St. Leonards NSW: Allen & Unwin, 1995.

———. "Exile into Bondage: An Analysis of Asiatic Indenture in Colonial Queensland." BA (honors) thesis, University of Queensland, 1976.

———. "Marriage, Citizenship and Nation." Paper presented at the International Federation of Research in Women's History Conference, Melbourne, 1998.

———. "'Modern Stone-Age Slavery': Images of Aboriginal Labour and Sexuality." *Labour History*, no. 64 (November 1995): 30–51.

———. "Negotiating Entanglement: The Story of Harriette Gold and Elias Boudinot." In *Sexuality in Early America: A Conference*. Philadelphia: McNeil Center for Early American Studies; Williamsburg VA: Omohundro Institute for Early American Culture, 2002.

———. "Playing Colonial: Cowgirls, Cowboys and Indians in Australia and North America." *Journal of Colonialism and Colonial History* 2, no. 1 (2001): 1–19.

———. "Taking Charge of the Offspring of Mixed Frontier Unions." In *Antipodean Childhoods: Growing Up in Australia and New Zealand*, edited by Helga Ramsey-Kurz and Ulla Ratheiser, 47–67. Newcastle, UK: Cambridge Scholars, 2010.

———. "White Brides: Images of Marriage across Colonising Boundaries." *Frontiers: A Journal of Women's Studies* 23, no. 2 (Spring 2002): 76–108.

McGrath, Ann., and Mary Anne Jebb, eds. *Long History, Deep Time: Deepening Histories of Place*. Canberra: ANU Press, 2015.

McGregor, Russell. "'Breed out the Colour,' or the Importance of Being White." *Australian Historical Studies* 33, no. 120 (2002): 286–302.

———. *Imagined Destinies: Aboriginal Australians and the Doomed Race Theory*. Carlton VIC: Melbourne University Press, 1997.

———. *Indifferent Inclusion: Aboriginal People and the Australian Nation*. Canberra: Aboriginal Studies Press, 2011.

McKenney, Thomas L. *Memoirs, Official and Personal: With Sketches of Travels among the Northern and Southern Indians*. New York: Paine and Burgess, 1846.

McKenney, Thomas L., and James Hall. *History of the Indian Tribes of North America: With Biographical Sketches and Anecdotes of the Principal Chiefs*. Vol. 3. Philadelphia: D. Rice, 1872.

McKnight, David. *Going the Whiteman's Way: Kinship and Marriage among Australian Aborigines*. Aldershot, UK: Ashgate, 2004.

———. *Of Marriage, Violence and Sorcery: The Quest for Power in Northern Queensland*. Aldershot, UK: Ashgate, 2005.

McLoughlin, William G. *The Cherokee Ghost Dance: Essays on the Southeastern Indians, 1789–1861*. Macon GA: Mercer, 1984.

———. *Cherokee Renascence in the New Republic*. Princeton NJ: Princeton University Press, 1986.

———. *The Cherokees and Christianity, 1794–1870: Essays on Acculturation and Cultural Persistence*. Edited by Walter H. Conser Jr. Athens: University of Georgia Press, 2008.

———. *Cherokees and Missionaries, 1789–1839*. New Haven CT: Yale University Press, 1984.

———. *Revival, Awakenings, and Reform: An Essay on Religion and Social Change in America, 1607–1977*. Chicago: University of Chicago Press, 1978.

McLoughlin, William G., and Walter H. Conser Jr. "The Cherokees in Transition: A Statistical Analysis of the Federal Cherokee Census of 1835." *Journal of American History* 64, no. 3 (December 1977): 678–703.

Meggitt, Mervyn J. *Desert People: A Study of the Walbiri Aborigines of Central Australia*. Sydney: Angus and Robertson, 1974.

Melish, Joanne P. *Disowning Slavery: Gradual Emancipation and "Race" in New England, 1780–1860*. Ithaca NY: Cornell University Press, 1998.

Mellor, Doreen, and Anna Haebich, eds. *Many Voices: Reflections on Experiences of Indigenous Child Separation*. Canberra: National Library of Australia, 2002.

Meriwether, Robert L., ed. *The Papers of John C. Calhoun*. Columbia: University of South Carolina Press for the South Caroliniana Society, 1959.

Merrell, James H. *The Indians' New World: Catawbas and Their Neighbors from European Contact through the Era of Removal*. Chapel Hill: University of North Carolina Press, 1989.

Miles, Tiya. "Circular Reasoning: Recentering Cherokee Women in the Antiremoval Campaigns." *American Quarterly* 61, no 2 (June 2009): 221–43.

———. *The House on Diamond Hill: A Cherokee Plantation Story*. Chapel Hill: University of North Carolina Press, 2010.

———. *Ties That Bind: The Story of an Afro-Cherokee Family in Slavery and Freedom*. Berkeley: University of California Press, 2005.

Miller, Martha. *The Needle's Eye: Women and Work in the Age of Revolution*. Amherst: University of Massachusetts Press, 2006.

Miller, Olga. "K'gari, Mrs. Fraser and Butchulla Oral Tradition." In *Constructions of Colonialism: Perspectives on Eliza Fraser's Shipwreck*, edited by Ian J. McNiven, Lynette Russell, and Kay Schaffer, 28–36. London: Leicester University Press, 1998.

Milner, Clyde A., Walter Nugent, Elliot West, Karen R. Merrill, Philip J. Deloria, and Richard White. "A Historian Who Has Changed Our Thinking: A Roundtable on the Work of Richard White." *Western Historical Quarterly* 33, no. 2 (2002): 137–57.

Minges, Patrick N. *Slavery in the Cherokee Nation: The Keetoowah Society and the Defining of a People, 1855–1876*. New York: Routledge, 2003.

Mombert, Jacob I. *An Authentic History of Lancaster County, in the State of Pennsylvania*. Lancaster PA: J. E. Barr, 1869.

Mooney, James. *Myths of the Cherokee*. New York: Johnson Reprint, 1970.

Moore, Clive. *Kanaka: A History of Melanesian Mackay*. Port Moresby: Institute of Papua New Guinea Studies, 1985.

Moore, Laurie, and Stephan Williams. *The True Story of Jimmy Governor*. Sydney: Allen & Unwin, 2001.

Moore, Thomas. *Works of Lord Byron: With His Letters and Journals and His Life.* Vol. 7. London: J. Murray, 1832.

Moran, Rachel, *Interracial Intimacy: The Regulation of Race and Romance.* Chicago: University of Chicago Press, 2001.

Morcombe, Michael. *Field Guide to Australian Birds.* Archerfield QLD: Steve Parish, 2000.

Moreton-Robinson, Aileen, ed. *Sovereign Subjects: Indigenous Sovereignty Matters.* Sydney: Allen & Unwin, 2007.

———. *Talkin' Up to the White Woman: Aboriginal Women and Feminism.* St. Lucia: University of Queensland Press, 2000.

———. *Whitening Race: Essays in Social and Cultural Criticism.* Canberra: Aboriginal Studies Press, 2004.

Morgan, Sally. *My Place.* Fremantle WA: Fremantle Arts Centre Press, 1988.

Morse, Jedidiah. *A Report to the Secretary of War of the United States, on Indian Affairs.* New Haven CT: Davis and Force, 1822.

Morse, Samuel F. B. *His Letters and Journals.* Vol. 1. Boston: Houghton Mifflin, 1914.

Moulton, Gary E. *John Ross: Cherokee Chief.* Athens: University of Georgia Press, 1978.

Munroe, John A. *History of Delaware.* Newark: University of Delaware Press, 1984.

Murchison, A. H. "Intermarried-Whites in the Cherokee Nation between the Years 1865 and 1887." *Chronicles of Oklahoma* 6, no. 3 (September 1928): 229–326.

Murphy, Lucy Eldersveld. *A Gathering of Rivers: Indians, Métis, and Mining in the Western Great Lakes, 1737–1832.* Lincoln: University of Nebraska Press, 2000.

Myers, Fred. *Pintupi Country, Pintupi Self: Sentiment, Place, and Politics among Western Desert Aborigines.* Washington DC: Smithsonian Institution Press; Canberra: Australian Institute of Aboriginal Studies, 1986.

Nabokov, Peter. *A Forest of Time: American Indian Ways of History.* New York: Cambridge University Press, 2002.

Nakata, Martin N. *Disciplining the Savages: Savaging the Disciplines.* Canberra: Aboriginal Studies Press, 2007.

Namias, June. *White Captives: Gender and Ethnicity on the American Frontier.* Chapel Hill: University of North Carolina, 1993.

Nash, Gary B. *First City: Philadelphia and the Forgiving of Historical Memory.* Philadelphia: University of Pennsylvania Press, 2006.

———. "The Hidden History of Mestizo America." *Journal of American History* 82, no. 3 (December 1995): 941–64.

Nash, Gary B., Charlotte Crabtree, and Ross E. Dunn. *History on Trial: Culture Wars and the Teaching of the Past.* New York: Vintage Books, 2000.

Nichols, Jeffrey D. *Prostitution, Polygamy, and Power: Salt Lake City, 1847–1918.* Urbana: University of Illinois Press, 2002.

Nygh, Peter Butt, ed. *Butterworths Concise Australian Legal Dictionary.* Sydney: Butterworths, 2004.

Oberg, Michael L. *Dominion and Civility: English Imperialism and Native America, 1585–1685*. Ithaca NY: Cornell University Press, 1999.
O'Brien, Jean. *Firsting and Lasting: Writing Indians Out of Existence in New England*. Minneapolis: University of Minnesota Press, 2010.
One Hundreth Anniversary of the Mariners' Church of Philadelphia. 1919.
Ørsted-Jensen, Robert. *Frontier History Revisited: Colonial Queensland and the "History War."* Brisbane: Lux Mundi, 2011.
Painter, Nell Irvin. *The History of White People*. New York: Norton, 2010.
Parins, James W. *Elias Cornelius Boudinot: A Life on the Cherokee Border*. Lincoln: University of Nebraska Press, 2005.
Pascoe, Peggy. "Race, Gender and Intercultural Relations: The Case of Interracial Marriage." *Frontiers: A Journal of Women's Studies* 12, no. 1 (1991), 5–18.
———. *What Comes Naturally: Miscegenation Law and the Making of Race in America*. Oxford: Oxford University Press, 2009.
Pateman, Carole. *Contract and Domination*. Cambridge: Polity, 2007.
———. *The Sexual Contract*. Cambridge: Polity, 1988.
Pateman, Carole, and Charles W. Mills. *Contract and Domination*. Cambridge: Polity, 2007.
Pemberton, Jo-Anne. *Sovereignty: Interpretations*. Basingstoke, UK: Palgrave Macmillan, 2009.
Penn, William. *Essays on the Present Crisis in the Condition of the American Indians*. Attributed to Jeremiah Evarts. Philadelphia: T. Kite, 1830.
Pennsylvania Almanac. 1844–48.
Perdue, Theda, ed. *Cherokee Editor: The Writings of Elias Boudinot*. Athens: University of Georgia Press, 1996.
———. *Cherokee Women: Gender and Culture Change, 1700–1835*. Lincoln: University of Nebraska Press, 1998.
———. *"Mixed Blood" Indians: Racial Construction in the Early South*. Athens: University of George Press, 2003.
———. *Slavery and the Evolution of Cherokee Society, 1540–1866*. Knoxville: University of Tennessee Press, 1979.
Perdue, Theda, and Michael D. Green. *The Cherokee Nation and the Trail of Tears*. Penguin Library of American Indian History. New York: Viking, 2007.
Perkins, Charles. *A Bastard Like Me*. Sydney: Ure Smith, 1975.
Persico, Richard V., Jr. "Early Nineteenth-Century Cherokee Political Organisation." In *The Cherokee Indian Nation: A Troubled History*, edited by Duane H. King, 92–109. Knoxville: University of Tennessee Press, 1979.
Peters, Richard. *The Case of the Cherokee Nation against the State of Georgia: Argued and Determined at the Supreme Court of the United States, January Term 1831*. Philadelphia: J. Grigg, 1831.
Peters-Little, Frances, Ann Curthoys, and John Docker, eds. *Passionate Histories: Myth, Memory and Indigenous Australia*. Canberra: ANU E Press, 2010.

Peterson, Jacqueline. "The People in Between: Indian-White Marriage and the Genesis of a Métis Society and Culture in the Great Lakes Region, 1680–1830." PhD thesis, University of Illinois, 1981.
Peterson, Jacqueline, and Jennifer S. H. Brown. *The New Peoples: Being and Becoming Métis in North America.* Winnipeg: University of Manitoba Press, 1985.
Peterson, Nicolas, ed. *Tribes and Boundaries in Australia.* Canberra: Australian Institute of Aboriginal Studies, 1976.
Peterson, Nicholas, and Will Sanders. *Citizenship and Indigenous Australians: Changing Conceptions and Possibilities.* Cambridge: Cambridge University Press, 1998.
Peterson, Nicholas, and J. Taylor. "Aboriginal Intermarriage and Economic Status in Western New South Wales." *People and Place* 10, no. 4 (2002): 11–16.
Peyer, Bernd C. *American Indian Nonfiction: An Anthology of Writings, 1760s-1930s.* Norman: University of Oklahoma Press, 2007.
———. *The Tutor'd Mind: Indian Missionary-Writers in Antebellum America.* Amherst: University of Massachusetts Press, 1997.
Plane, Ann Marie *Colonial Intimacies: Indian Marriage in Early New England.* Ithaca NY: Cornell University Press, 2000.
———. "Legitimacies, Indian Identities, and the Law: The Politics of Sex and the Creation of History in Colonial New England." *Law and Social Inquiry* 23, no. 1 (1998): 55–77.
Plato. *The Phaedrus.* Translated by C. J. Rowe. Adelaide: University of Adelaide, 2008.
———. *The Symposium.* Translated by Benjamin Jowett. Adelaide: University of Adelaide Library, 2008.
Poirier, Sylvie. *A World of Relationships: Itineraries, Dreams, and Events in the Australian Western Desert.* Toronto: University of Toronto Press, 2005.
Poor Sarah; or, Religion Exemplified in the Life and Death of an Indian Woman. Translated into Cherokee by Elias Boudinot. Mountpleasant OH: Elisha Bates, 1823.
Portland Directory. Portland ME, 1844.
Povinelli, Elizabeth A. *The Cunning of Recognition: Indigenous Alterities and the Making of Australian Multiculturalism.* Durham NC: Duke University Press, 2002.
———. *The Empire of Love: Toward a Theory of Intimacy, Genealogy, and Carnality.* Durham NC: Duke University Press, 2006.
Pratt, Mary Louise. *Imperial Eyes.* Routledge: London, 1992.
Probyn-Rapsey, Fiona. "Uplifting White Men: Maintenance, Marriage and Whiteness in Queensland, 1900–1910." *Postcolonial Studies* 12, no. 1 (2008): 89–106.
Prucha, Frances Paul. *The Great Father: The United States Government and the American Indians.* Lincoln: University of Nebraska Press, 1995.
———. "Thomas L. McKenney and the New York Indian Board." *Mississippi Valley Historical Review* 48, no 4 (March 1962): 635–55.
Rajkowski, Pamela. *Linden Girl: A Story of Outlawed Lives.* Nedlands: University of Western Australia Press, 1995.

Randall, Bob. *Brown Skin Baby (They Take 'Im Away)*. Australia: Australian Broadcasting Commission, 1970.
Ravenscroft, Alison. *The Postcolonial Eye: White Australian Desire and the Visual Field of Race*. Surrey, UK: Ashgate, 2012.
Read, Peter. *A Rape of the Soul So Profound*. St. Leonards NSW: Allen & Unwin, 1999.
Read, Peter, Frances Peters-Little, and Ann Haebich, eds. *Indigenous Biography and Autobiography*. Aboriginal History Monograph 17. Acton ACT: ANU E Press and Aboriginal History, 2008.
Reed, Liz. "White Girl 'Gone Off with the Blacks.'" *Hecate* 28, no. 1 (2002): 9–22.
Reekie, Gail, ed. *On the Edge: Women's Experiences of Queensland*. St. Lucia: University of Queensland Press, 1994.
Reid, Gordon. *Nest of Hornets: The Massacres of the Fraser Family at Hornet Bank Station, Central Queensland*. Melbourne: Queensland University Press, 1982.
Remini, Robert V. *Andrew Jackson and His Indian Wars*. New York: Viking, 2001.
Reynolds, Henry. *The Forgotten War*. Sydney: New South Publishing, 2013.
———. *The Law of the Land*. Ringwood VIC: Penguin, 1992.
———. *Nowhere People*. Camberwell VIC: Penguin, 2005.
———. *The Other Side of the Frontier: Aboriginal Resistance to the European Invasion of Australia*. Sydney: University of New South Wales Press, 2006.
———. *This Whispering in Our Hearts*. St. Leonards NSW: Allen and Unwin, 1998.
Reynolds, Henry, and Noel Loos. "Aboriginal Resistance in Queensland." *Australian Journal of Politics & History* 22, no. 2 (April 1976): 214–26.
Richter, Daniel K. "Onas, the Long Knife: Pennsylvanians and Indians, 1783–1794." In *Native Americans and the Early Republic*, edited by Frederick Hoxie, Ronald Hoffman, and Peter Albert, 125–61. Charlottesville: University Press of Virginia, 1999.
Rifkin, Mark. *When Did Indians Become Straight? Kinship, the History of Sexuality, and Native Sovereignty*. New York: Oxford, 2011.
Rigney, Lester-Irabinna. "Indigenous Australian Views on Knowledge Production and Indigenist Research." In *Indigenous Peoples' Wisdom and Power: Affirming Our Knowledge through Narratives*, edited by Julian E. Kunnie and Normalungelo I. Goduka, 32–50. Burlington VT: Ashgate, 2006.
Robert, Dana L. *American Women in Mission: A Social History of Their Thought and Practice*. Macon GA: Mercer University Press, 1996.
Roberts, Tony. *Frontier Justice: A History of the Gulf Country to 1900*. St. Lucia: University of Queensland Press, 2005.
Rose, Deborah Bird. *Country of the Heart: An Indigenous Australian Homeland*. Canberra: Aboriginal Studies Press for AIATSIS, 2002.
———. *Dingo Makes Us Human: Life and Land in an Australian Aboriginal Culture*. Oakleigh, UK: Cambridge University Press, 2000.
Ross, Allen. "The Murder of Elias Boudinot." *Chronicles of Oklahoma* 12, no. 1 (March 1934): 19–24.

Ross, John. *The Papers of Chief John Ross*. Edited by Gary E. Moulton. Norman: University of Oklahoma Press, 1985.
Roth, Walter E. *Ethnological Studies among the North-West-Central Queensland Aborigines*. Brisbane: Queensland Government Printer, 1897.
———. "Marriage Ceremonies and Infant Life." North Queensland Ethnography Bulletin no. 16. *Records of the Australian Museum* 7, no. 1 (1908): 1–17.
Rothman, Ellen K. *Hands and Hearts: A History of Courtship in America*. Cambridge MA: Harvard University Press, 1987.
Russell, Howard S. *Indian New England before the Mayflower*. Hanover NH: University Press of New England, 1980.
Russell, Lynette Wendy, ed. *Colonial Frontiers: Indigenous-European Encounters in Settler Societies*. Manchester: Manchester University Press, 2001.
———. *A Little Bird Told Me: Family Secrets, Necessary Lies*. Crows Nest NSW: Allen & Unwin, 2002.
Ryan, Jane. *Ancestors: Chinese in Colonial Australia*. Fremantle WA: Fremantle Arts Centre Press, 1995.
Ryan, Lyndall. *Tasmanian Aborigines: A History since 1803*. Crows Nest NSW: Allen & Unwin, 2012.
Ryan, Mary P. *Cradle of the Middle Class: The Family in Oneida County, New York, 1790–1865*. Cambridge: Cambridge University Press, 1981.
Ryan, Susan M. *The Grammar of Good Intentions: Race and the Antebellum Culture of Benevolence*. Ithaca NY: Cornell University Press, 2003.
Saks, Eva. "Representing Miscegenation Law." *Raritan* 8 (Fall 1989), 39–69.
Salesa, Damon. *Racial Crossings: Race, Intermarriage, and the Victorian British Empire*. Oxford: Oxford University Press, 2011.
Salmon, Marylyn. *Women and the Law of Property in Early America*. Chapel Hill: University of North Carolina Press, 1986.
Saunders, Kay. *Indentured Labour in the British Empire, 1834–1920*. London: Croom Helm, 1984.
———. *Workers in Bondage: The Origins and Bases of Unfree Labour in Queensland, 1824–1916*. St. Lucia: University of Queensland Press, 1982.
Saunders, Kay, and Raymond Evans. *Gender Relations in Australia: Domination and Negotiation*. Sydney: Harcourt Brace Jovanovich, 1992.
Saunt, Claudio. "Telling Stories: The Political Uses of Myth and History in the Cherokee and Creek Nations." *Journal of American History* 93, no. 3 (2006): 673–97.
Schaffer, Kay. *In the Wake of First Contact: The Eliza Fraser Stories*. Cambridge: Cambridge University Press 1995.
Scharff, Virginia. *The Women Jefferson Loved*. New York: Harper, 2011.
Schlissel, Lillian, Vicki L. Ruíz, and Janice J. Monk, eds. *Western Women: Their Land, Their Lives*. Albuquerque: University of New Mexico Press, 1988.
Schmidt, Ryan W. "American Indian Identity and Blood Quantum in the 21st Century: A Critical Review." *Journal of Anthropology* 2011 (2011), doi:10.1155/2011/549521.

Schoelwer, Susan. "The Absent Other: Women in the Land and Art of Mountain Men." In *Discovered Lands, Invented Pasts: Transforming Visions of the American West*. Edited by Jules David Prown, Nancy K. Anderson, William Cronon, Brian W. Dippie, Martha A. Sandweiss, Susan P. Schoelwer, and Howard R. Lamar, 135–66. New Haven CT: Yale University Press, 1992.

Schreiner, Samuel A., Jr. *The Passionate Beechers: A Family Saga of Sanctity and Scandal That Changed America*. Hoboken NJ: John Wiley and Sons, 2003.

Schreir, Jesse T. "Indian or Freedman?: Enrollment, Race and Identity in the Choctaw Nation, 1896–1907." *Western Historical Quarterly* 42, no. 4 (Winter 2011): 458–97.

Scott, Joan. "Unanswered Questions." *American Historical Review* 113, no. 5 (2008): 1422–30.

Shellam, Tiffany. *Shaking Hands on the Fringe: Negotiating the Aboriginal World at King George's Sound*. Crawley: University of Western Australia Press, 2009.

Shields, David. *Civil Tongues and Polite Letters in British America*. Chapel Hill: University of North Carolina Press, 1997.

Shinoda, Hideaki. *Re-examining Sovereignty: From Classical Theory to the Global Age*. Basingstoke, UK: Macmillan, 2000.

Shoemaker, Nancy. *American Indian Population Recovery in the Twentieth Century*. Albuquerque: University of New Mexico Press, 1999.

———, ed. *Clearing a Path: Theorizing the Past in Native American Studies*. New York: Routledge, 2002.

———. "How the Indians Got to Be Red." *American Historical Review* 102, no. 3 (June 1997): 625–44.

———, ed. *Negotiators of Change: Historical Perspectives on Native American Women*. New York: Routledge, 1995.

Shyrock, Andrew, and Daniel Lord Smail. *Deep History: The Architecture of Past and Present*. Berkeley: University of California Press, 2011.

Silver, Peter. *Our Savage Neighbours: How Indian War Transformed Early America*. New York: Norton, 2008.

Simpson, Ken, Nicolas Day, and Peter Trusler, eds. *Field Guide to the Birds of Australia*. 5th ed. Ringwood VIC: Viking, 1996.

Slater, Peter, Pat Slater, and Raoul Slater. *The Slater Field Guide to Australian Birds*. Dee Why NSW: Rigby, 1986.

Slater, Sandra, and Fay A. Yarbrough. *Gender and Sexuality in Indigenous North America, 1400–1850*. Columbia: University of South Carolina Press, 2011.

Sleeper-Smith, Susan. *Indian Women and French Men: Rethinking Cultural Encounter in the Western Great Lakes*. Amherst: University of Massachusetts Press, 2011.

Sleeper-Smith, Susan, Richard White, Philip J. Deloria, Heidi Bohaker, Brett Rushforth, and Catherine Desbarats. "Forum: The Middle Ground Revisited." *William and Mary Quarterly* 63, no. 1 (January 2006): 3–96.

Smail, Daniel Lord. "In the Grip of Sacred History." *American Historical Review* 110, no. 5 (2005): 1336–61.

———. *On Deep History and the Brain*. Berkeley: University of California Press, 2007.
Smiley, F. T. *History of Wilmington: The Commercial, Social, and Religious Growth of the City during the Past Century*. Wilmington: F.T. Smiley, 1894.
Smith, Andrea. *Conquest: Sexual Violence and American Indian Genocide*. Cambridge MA: South End Press, 2005.
Smith, Daniel S. "Parental Power and Marriage Patterns: An Analysis of Historical Trends in Hingham, Massachusetts." *Journal of Marriage and the Family* 35, no. 3 (August 1973): 419–28.
Smith, Daniel S., and Michael S. Hindus. "Premarital Pregnancy in America, 1640–1971: An Overview and Interpretation." *Journal of Interdisciplinary History* 5, no. 4 (Spring 1975): 537–70.
Smith, Linda Tuhiwai. *Decolonizing Methodologies: Research and Indigenous Peoples*. Dunedin: University of Otago Press, 1999.
Smithers, Gregory. *Cherokee Diaspora: A History of Indigenous Identity*. New Haven CT: Yale University Press, 2015.
———. *Science, Sexuality and Race in the United States and Australia, 1780s-1890s*. New York: Routledge, 2009.
Smith-Rosenberg, Carroll. "Captured Subjects/Savage Others: Violently Engendering the New American." *Gender and History* 5, no. 2 (Summer 1993): 177–95.
———. "The Female World of Love and Ritual: Relations between Women in Nineteenth-Century America." *Signs* 1, no 1 (Autumn 1975): 1–29.
Snow, Dean R. *The Archaeology of New England*. New York: Academic Press, 1980.
Socrates [pseud.]. "Intermarriages." *Cherokee Phoenix* 1, no. 6 (March 27, 1828): 2.
———. "Mr. Boudinott Editor Cherokee Phoenix." *Cherokee Phoenix* 3, no. 12 (July 10, 1830): 3.
———. "Strictures on the Report of the Joint Committee." *Cherokee Phoenix* 1, no. 6 (March 27, 1828): 2.
Spickard, Paul R. *Mixed Blood: Intermarriage and Ethnic Identity in Twentieth-Century America*. Madison: University of Wisconsin Press, 1989.
Stanner, W. E. H. *White Man Got No Dreaming*. Canberra: Australian National University Press, 1979.
Starr, Edward C. *A History of Cornwall, Connecticut, a Typical New England Town*. New Haven CT: Tuttle, Morehouse & Taylor, 1926.
Starr, Emmet. *History of the Cherokee Indians and Their Legends and Folklore*. Oklahoma City: Warden, 1979.
Stephenson, Peta. *The Outsiders Within: Telling Australia's Indigenous-Asian Story*. Sydney: University of New South Wales Press, 2007.
Stevick, Philip. *Imagining Philadelphia: Travelers' Views of the City from 1800 to the Present*. Philadelphia: University of Pennsylvania Press, 1996.
Stockwood, John. *A Bartholmew Fairing for Parentes: To bestow upon their sonnes and daughters, and for one friend to give unto another*. London: Printed by John Wolfe, for John Harrison the younger, 1589.

Stoler, Ann L. *Along the Archival Grain: Epistemic Anxieties and Colonial Common Sense.* Princeton NJ: Princeton University Press, 2009.

———, ed. *Haunted by Empire: Geographies of Intimacy in North American History.* Durham NC: Duke University Press, 2006.

———. *Race and the Education of Desire: Foucault's "History of Sexuality" and the Colonial Order of Things.* Durham NC: Duke University Press, 1995.

———. "Sexual Affronts and Racial Frontiers: National Identity, 'Mixed Bloods' and the Cultural Genealogies of Europeans in Colonial Southeast Asia." CSST working paper, University of Michigan, 1991.

———. "Tense and Tender Ties: The Politics of Comparison in North American History and (Post) Colonial Studies." Round Table on Empires and Intimacies: Lessons from (Post) Colonial Studies. *Journal of American History* 88, no. 3 (2001): 829–65.

Strickland, Rennard. *Fire and the Spirits: Cherokee Law from Clan to Court.* Norman: University of Oklahoma Press, 1975.

Sturm, Circe. *Blood Politics: Race, Culture, and Identity in the Cherokee Nation of Oklahoma.* Berkeley: University of California Press, 2002.

Sturtevant, William C. "John Ridge on Cherokee Civilization in 1826." *Journal of Cherokee Studies* 6 (Fall 1981): 79–91.

Sweet, John W. *Bodies Politic: Negotiating Race in the American North, 1730–1830.* Philadelphia: University of Pennsylvania Press, 2006.

Taffe, Sue. *Black and White Together: The Federal Council for the Advancement of Aborigines and Torres Strait Islanders, 1958–1973.* St. Lucia: University of Queensland Press, 2005.

Teuton, Christopher B. *Cherokee Stories of the Turtle Island Liars' Club.* Chapel Hill: University of North Carolina Press, 2012.

Thelen, David. "Of Audiences, Borderlands, and Comparisons: Toward the Internationalization of American History." *Journal of American History* 79, no. 2 (September 1992): 432–62.

Thomson, Judy. *Reaching Back: Queensland Aboriginal People Recall the Early Days at Yarrabah Mission.* Canberra: Aboriginal Studies Press, 1989.

Thornton, Russell. *The Cherokees: A Population History.* Lincoln: University of Nebraska Press, 1900.

———. "Tribal Membership Requirements and the Demography of 'Old' and 'New' Native Americans." *Population Research and Policy Review* 16, nos. 1 and 2 (April 1997): 33–42.

Thorpe, William. "Archibald Meston and Aboriginal Legislation in Colonial Queensland." *Historical Studies* 21, no. 82 (April 1984): 52–67.

Tilton, Robert. *Pocahontas: The Evolution of an American Narrative.* Cambridge: Cambridge University Press, 1994.

Tonkin, Daryl, and Carolyn Landon. *Jackson's Track: Memoir of a Dreamtime.* Melbourne: Viking, 1999.

Tovey, Noel. *Little Black Bastard: A Story of Survival.* Sydney: Hodder Headline Australia, 2005.
Trudinger, David. "The Language(s) of Love: JRB Love and Contesting Tongues at Ernabella Mission Station, 1940–46." *Aboriginal History* 31 (2007): 27–44.
Turner, David H. *Australian Aboriginal Social Organization.* Canberra: Australian Institute of Aboriginal Studies, 1981.
Turner, Frederick Jackson. *The Frontier in American History.* Huntington NY: R. E. Kreiger, 1986.
Tyrrell, Ian R. "American Exceptionalism in an Age of International History." *American Historical Review* 96, no. 4 (October 1991): 1031–55.
———. "Reflections on the Transnational Turn in United States History: Theory and Practice." *Journal of Global History* 4, no. 3 (2009): 453–74.
———. *Transnational Nation: United States History in Global Perspective since 1789.* Basingstoke, UK: Palgrave Macmillan, 2007.
———. *True Gardens of the Gods: Californian-Australian Environmental Reform, 1860–1930.* Berkeley: University of California Press, 1999.
U.S. Congress. *Report of the Select Committee of the House of Representatives, to Which Were Referred the Messages of the President U.S. of the 5th and 8th of February, and 2d March, 1827.* Washington DC: Gales & Seaton, 1827.
Van Kirk, Sylvia. *Many Tender Ties: Women in Fur-Trade Society, 1670–1870.* Norman: University of Oklahoma Press, 1983.
Van Toorn, Penny. *Writing Never Arrives Naked: Early Aboriginal Cultures of Writing in Australia.* Canberra: Aboriginal Studies Press, 2006.
Vardoulakis, Dimitris. *Sovereignty and Its Other: Towards the Dejustification of Violence.* New York: Fordham University Press, 2013.
Vattel, Emer de. *The Law of Nations; or, Principles of the Law of Nature Applied to the Conduct and Affairs of Nations and Sovereigns.* London: G. G. and J. Robinson, 1797.
Veracini, Lorenzo. *Settler Colonialism: A Theoretical Overview.* New York: Palgrave Macmillan, 2010.
Viola, Herman J. *Thomas Lorraine McKenney: Architect of America's Early Indian Policy, 1816–1830.* Chicago: Swallow Press, 1974.
Vsiwanathan, Gauri. *Outside the Fold: Conversion, Modernity, and Belief.* Princeton NJ: Princeton University Press, 1998.
Walker, Robert S. *Torchlight to the Cherokees: The Brainerd Mission.* New York: Macmillan, 1931.
Wallace, Henry E. *Philadelphia Reports.* Philadelphia: J. B. Hunter, 1887.
Wanhalla, Angela. *In/Visible Sight: The Mixed-Descent Families of Southern New Zealand.* Wellington: Bridget Williams Books, 2009.
———. *Matters of the Heart: A History of Interracial Marriage in New Zealand.* Auckland: Auckland University Press, 2013.

Ware, Susan, ed. *New Viewpoints in Women's History: Working Papers from the Schlesinger Library 50th Anniversary Conference.* Cambridge MA: Schlesinger Library, 1994.

Warner, Michael. *The Letters of the Republic: Publication and the Public Sphere in Eighteenth-Century America.* Cambridge MA: Harvard University Press, 1982.

Warner, Sam B. *The Private City: Philadelphia in Three Periods of Its Growth.* Philadelphia: University of Pennsylvania Press, 1987.

Waterhouse, Richard. *From Minstrel Show to Vaudeville.* Kensington: University of New South Wales Press, 1990.

Watson, Joanne. "Becoming Bwgcolman: Exile and Survival on Palm Island Reserve, 1918 to the Present." PhD thesis, University of Queensland, 1994.

——— . *Palm Island: Through a Long Lens.* Canberra: Aboriginal Studies Press, 2010.

Weatherford, Jack. *Native Roots: How the Indians Enriched America.* New York: Fawcett Books, 1991.

Weaver, John C. *The Great Land Rush and the Making of the Modern World, 1650–1900.* Montreal: McGill-Queen's University Press, 2003.

Webber, Jeremy, and Colin M. McLeod, eds. *Between Consenting Peoples: Political Community and the Meaning of Consent.* Vancouver: UBC Press, 2010.

Weems, W. L. *The Life of William Penn, the Settler of Pennsylvania.* Philadelphia: Uriah Hunt, 1829.

Weierman, Karen Woods, *One Nation, One Blood: Interracial Marriage in American Fiction, Scandal and Law, 1820–1870.* Amherst: University of Massachusetts Press, 2005.

Wesley, John, and Charles Wesley. *Hymns and Sacred Poems.* Philadelphia: A. Bradford, 1743.

Westcott, Thompson. *A History of Philadelphia, from the Time of the First Settlements on the Delaware to the Consolidation of the City and Districts in 1854.* Philadelphia: Dispatch, 1867.

Westermarck, Edward. *The History of Human Marriage.* London: Macmillan, 1901.

White, Gilbert. *Thirty Years in Tropical Australia.* London: Society for Promoting Christian Knowledge, 1918.

White, Richard. *The Middle Ground: Indians, Empires, and Republics in the Great Lakes Region, 1650–1815.* Cambridge: Cambridge University Press, 1991.

Wigginton, Caroline. "A Late Night Vindication: Annis Boudinot Stockton's Reading of Mary Wollstonecraft's *A Vindication of the Rights of Woman*." *Legacy* 25, no. 2 (2008): 225–38.

Wilkins, David E., and K. Tsianina Lomawaima. *Uneven Ground: American Indian Sovereignty and Federal Law.* Norman: University of Oklahoma Press, 2001.

Wilkins, Thurman. *Cherokee Tragedy: The Story of the Ridge Family and of the Decimation of a People.* New York: Macmillan, 1970.

Wirt, William. *Opinion on the Right of the State of Georgia to Extend Her Laws over the Cherokee Nation.* New Echota, Cherokee Nation: Phoenix, 1830.

Witgen, Michael J. *An Infinity of Nations: How the Native New World Shaped Early North America*. Philadelphia: University of Pennsylvania Press, 2012.

Wolfe, Patrick. "Corpus Nullius: The Exception of Indians and Other Aliens in U.S. Constitutional Discourse." *Postcolonial Studies* 10, no. 2 (2007): 127–51.

———. "Land, Labor, and Difference: Elementary Structures of Race." *American Historical Review* 106, no. 3 (June 2001): 866–905.

———. "Nation and MiscegeNation: Discursive Continuity in the Post-Mabo Era." *Social Analysis* 34 (October 1994): 94–152.

———. "On Being Woken Up: The Dreamtime in Anthropology and in Australian Settler Culture." *Comparative Studies in Society and History* 33, no. 2 (April 1991): 197–224.

———. "Settler Colonialism and the Elimination of the Native." *Journal of Genocide Research* 8, no. 4 (2006): 387–409.

———. "Should the Subaltern Dream? Australian Aborigines and the Problem of Ethnographic Ventriloquism." In *Cultures of Scholarship*, edited by S. Humphreys, 57–96. Ann Arbor: University of Michigan Press, 1997.

Wollstonecraft, Mary. *A Vindication of the Rights of Woman*. Adelaide: University of Adelaide, 2008.

Woods, Karen M. "Law Making: A 'Wicked and Mischievous Connection': The Origins of Indian-White Miscegenation Law." *Legal Studies Forum* 23, no. 37 (1999): 37–70.

Woodward, Grace S. *The Cherokees*. Norman: University of Oklahoma Press, 1963.

Wright, Robert E. *The First Wall Street: Chestnut Street, Philadelphia, and the Birth of American Finance*. Chicago: University of Chicago Press, 2005.

Yarbrough, Fay A. "Legislating Women's Sexuality: Cherokee Marriage Laws in the Nineteenth Century." *Journal of Social History* 38, no. 2 (Winter 2004): 385–406.

———. *Race and the Cherokee Nation: Sovereignty in the Nineteenth Century*. Philadelphia: University of Pennsylvania Press, 2008.

Yarbrough, Fay A., and Sharon P. Holland, eds. *Crossing Waters, Crossing Worlds: The African Diaspora in Indian Country*. Durham NC: Duke University Press, 2006.

Young, Mary. "The Exercise of Sovereignty in Cherokee Georgia." *Journal of the Early Republic* 10, no. 1 (Spring 1990): 43–63.

Zastoupil, Lynn. "Intimacy and Colonial Knowledge." *Journal of Colonialism and Colonial History* 3, no. 2 (Fall 2002).

INDEX

ABCFM (American Board of Commissioners for Foreign Missions), 40, 77, 95, 154
ABM (Australian Board of Missions), 95, 133, 141–42
Aboriginal marriage laws: consent in, 312–13; elders in, 443n2; enforcement of, 253, 328–29; and kinship, 112–13, 252, 294–95, 297–98, 299–302, 318–19; and landscape, 294–95; outsiders' impact on, 301; punishments under, 301–2, 328–29; and social order, 112–13; state recognition of, 302–7; transmission of, 101–2, 252; Yarrabah mission's impact on, 119–20, 127. *See also* Aboriginals Protection Act (APA)
Aboriginal men: images of, *93*; intermarriage to white women, 259; obligations as husbands, 301–2; opposing intermarriage, xxii–xxiii, 315; state recognition of rights, 303–7, 320
Aboriginal News, 134, 135
Aboriginal societies: ancestral stories of, 98–99; benefits of mission life, 116; birthing rituals, 121–23; child betrothal in, 108–9; citizenship status, 446n63; concept of illegitimacy in, 361; decimation of, 19; economic changes, 91, 260–61; enacting sovereignty, 12–13; and frontier violence, 91–94; governance systems, 21, 117; hiding identity, xxii; historical occupation, 260; images of, *92, 93, 269*; impact of colonialism on, 91, 95–96, 102, 315–16; impact of segregation on, 364–67; importance of landscape to, 21, 100–102, 121–23, 294–95, 399n45; initiation rites, 420n90; land rights, 102, 398n37; marriage in, 126, 127, 264, 299–302, 314, 326; and polygamy, 108–9, 301, 337–38; pre-British contact, 440n23; precontact economy of, 417n11; premarital pregnancy in, 129; Roth's nude photographs, 284–85; sexual joking in, 334–36, 344; social organization, 29, 403n115; women's status in, 311, 447n11. *See also* Aboriginal marriage laws; Aboriginals Protection Act (APA); kinship

489

INDEX

Aboriginals Protection Act (APA), 10; archives generated by, 252–53, 295; and Asian men, 257, 273–74, 275–78, 439n13, 442n64; child removal under, 99; consent required by, 296; contested power of, 288–89; context of, 256–57; determining husbandly suitability, 270–75, 277–78; exemptions from, 309–11; goals of, 94, 251, 267, 307; impact on Aboriginal women, 316, 317; impact on sovereignty, 316; implementation of, 251, 257–58, 270–75, 277–78, 319–20; introduction of, xxi, 94; mixed-decent children under, 362; opposition to, 259–60, 275–78, 287–88, 290–91; segregation philosophy, 269–70; undermining Aboriginal law, 302–3; unintended marriage incentive, 270; vilification of protectors, 278–87

Aboriginal women: advantages of intermarriage for, 309–11, 317; under the APA, 257–58, 270–75, 316, 317; and Chinese men, 273–74, 275–78, 291; and consent, xxii, 293–94, 296–98, 313, 314–15, 318–19, 321; cross-cultural negotiations of, 320–22; forced removal of, 129–30; impact of colonialism on, 23; marriage arrangements for, 300–302, 313–15; married to Aboriginal men, 311; and Pacific Islander men, 273–74, 291; social status of, 311, 447n11; views of marriage, 304–5, 307–8; and white men, xxii, 262–63, 344–45, 358; at Yarrabah, 105

Ada (Aboriginal woman), 275
Adair, William Penn, *378*
Adams, John Quincy, 340
An Address to the Whites (Boudinot), 84–85, 340
African Americans: Cherokee laws regarding, 164–65, 172–77, 188; in Cherokee social order, 17, 163, 164–65, 172–73, 366; citizenship of, 17, 172–73; intermarriage with whites, 16–17, 258–59; in New England, 51–52; and segregation policies, xx

Ah Chin, 274
Ah Kow, 276
Akbar, Jack, 318, 439n14
Algonquins, 9–10, 25, 252, 325, 337
Ambrym, Willie, 97, 106
American Bible Society, 65, 108
American Board of Commissioners for Foreign Missions (ABCFM), 40, 77, 95, 154
American Constitution, 4, 16, 149, 157, 236, 246
American Eagle (newspaper), 41, 78
Anderson, Rufus, 54
APA (Aboriginals Protection Act). *See* Aboriginals Protection Act (APA)
Apess, Pequot William, 390
Aranda framework, 299–300
Argyle, Jessie, 318
Asian men: Aboriginal classification of, 301; under the APA, 257, 273–74, 275–78; arrivals of, 90; coerced labor of, 400n66; demographics, 263; images of, *255, 277, 310*; under White Australia policy, 291
assimilation, 4, 28, 68, 171, 184–85, 202, 225, 322, 372
atavism, 267
Australia: assertion of sovereignty, 11; citizenship status of Aborigines, 446n63; compared to New Zealand, 400n70; history of colonialism in, 18–21, 90, 401n75; maps of, *x, xxxii, 86, 122*; practice of polygamy in, 325–26; recognition of Aboriginal rights, 398n37; reinvented histories of, xx–xxii; relation to U.S., 14–15; significance of floods in, 313; violence in, 91–94, 253–54, 262

INDEX

Australian Board of Missions (ABM), 95, 132–33, 136, 139, 141–42
Australian Citizenship Act (1948), 446n63

Baker, Joanne, 12
band (Yarrabah mission), *108, 109*
Beecher, Catharine, 183
Beecher, Lyman, 40, 55–56, 65, 69, 83, 406n20
Bennett, Mary Montgomery, 334
Bindam (Aboriginal woman), 100
Bing, Tony, 274
Black but Comely (Gribble), 98
The Black Predecessor (cartoon), *335*
"blood" concept, 5, 27, 154, 268, 274–75. *See also* kinship
Booger dance, 162
Boudinot, Annis, 63–64
Boudinot, Caroline Matilda Rogers Fields, *377*
Boudinot, Delight Sargent, 205, 374, 375
Boudinot, Eleanor Susan, 373, *376*
Boudinot, Elias (Buck Watie): advocacy work of, 84–85, 190, 191–92, 233, 370–71; ancestry of, 50–51, 170, 410n99; appearance of, 78, 79–80, 410n110; assassination of, 204–5, 374–75; boundaries crossed by, 67–68; children of, 371, 373–74, 375; church's marriage bann, 39–40, 55–56, 69–70; community supporters of, 77–78; courtship of, 45, 69–74; effigy burning, 35–39, 56–57; elite status of, 411n118; Gold family's response to, 44–50, 51, 52–55, 350; and Harriett's death, 374; images of, *37, 372*, 410n110; impact of controversy on, 374; journey to Cornwall, 61–63, 66–67; missing love letters of, 69–74; name change of, 66–67, 182, 236, 405n3; on polygamy, 340; previous names of, 61–62; significance of marriage, 56, 81–84; and Socrates, 164; on the Treaty Party, 196–97, 200; wedding of, 78
Boudinot, Elias IV, 63–67, 180, 182, 236, 411n119
Boudinot, Elias Cornelius, 373, 375, *376, 378*
Boudinot, Frank Brinsmade, 374, *376*, 453n17
Boudinot, Frank Josiah, 372
Boudinot, Hannah (née Stockton), 63–65
Boudinot, Harriett (née Gold): anti-colonial journey of, 371–72; boundaries crossed by, 67, 74, 81–84; Cherokees' welcome of, 369–70; children of, 233, 371, 373–74, 375; church's marriage bann, 39–40, 55–56, 69–70; community supporters of, 77–78; courtship of, 45, 69–74; death of, 374, 453n17; effigy burning, 35–39, 56–57; family's response to engagement, 42–50, 51, 52–55, 350; images of, *36, 372*; impact of controversy on, 371, 374; missing love letters of, 69–74; rationale for marriage, 80; values of, 57–58; wedding of, 78
Boudinot, Mary Harriett, 373, *376*
Boudinot, Sarah Parkhill, 373
Boudinot, William Penn, 233, 372, 373–74, 375, *376, 377*
Bowen (Australian subinspector), 277
Bradley (Australian constable), 274
Brinsmade, Daniel, 45–46, 51, 55
Brinsmade, Mary (née Gold), 45–46, 56–57, 58, 371
brolga (bird), 278–79
Brooks, Fred, 329
Brown, Catharine, 54, 178–79, 413n158
Bryant, B., 272
Buchanun, William, 275
Buckley (Australian constable), 274

INDEX

Bufford, Samuel, 312
Bunce, Isaiah, 41, 56, 78, 407n50
bundling practice, 412n140
Bunyan, John, 83
Butler, Elizur, 197
Buttrick, Daniel S., 79, 154
Byron, Lord (George Gordon), 181–82, 217, 221

Calhoun, John C., 63
Calvinism, 40–41, 73
Cameron, Milton, *387*
Camfoo, Nelly, 318
Cape Cottage (ME), 218–19
captivity narratives, 74–75, 220–21, 228–29, 241, 384
cartoons, *xvii, 280, 334, 335,* 343–44
Casey (Australian constable), 276, 309
census (Cherokee), 153
Charles II (king of England), 233
Cherokee Constitution, 155–56, 167, 178–79, 424n32, 428n111
Cherokee Council, 156, 167, 173, 177, 178–79, 339
Cherokee marriage laws: impact on citizenship, 177; introduction of, 153; mixed views on, 185–86; regulating white men, 150, 156–57, 164–67, 186–92; slaves addressed in, 164–65, 172–77, 188; and sovereignty, 147, 156–58, 170, 186–92; women's rights in, 179–80
Cherokee men: on equality with whites, 78–81; in matrilineal systems, 178; opposing intermarriage, 314, 337; property rights of, 187; stereotypes of, 76–77; views on polygamy, 336; and white women, 154–56. *See also* Boudinot, Elias; Ross, John
Cherokee Nation: African Americans in, 164–65, 172–77, 366; challenges to sovereignty, 80, 147–49, 157–59, 167–70, 192; citizenship in, 225, 366, 431n1; colonizing compact, 26–27, 236–37, 247; concept of illegitimacy in, 361; demographics, 152–53; educating youth, 41, 61–63; forced removal west, 196–97, 240, 353–54, 364–67; governance structure, 148–49, 158, 168; impact of intermarriage on, 167; in Indian Territory, 202, 204–5, 240; intermixed ancestries, 50; literacy's impact on, 72; maps of, *34, 146, 354*; matrilineal social structure, 27, 74, 154, 167–68, 424n29; modernization of, 21, 68–69, 78–80, 82, 148–49, 183–85; negotiations for restitution, 229; ontologies of, 13, 27; opposition to intermarriage in, 314, 337; polygamy in, 167, 331, 338–41, 346–47; under President Tyler, 239–40; responses to colonialism, 161–63; slavery in, 153, 163, 165, 167, 172–77; sovereignty campaigns, 10–11, 20, 61, 182–83, 192; sovereignty of, 12, 152–55, 360; understandings of marriage, 326, 327; U.S. recognition of, 10–11, 20, 21, 168, 195, 360; weddings, 159–60, 184; welcoming Harriett Gold, 369–70
Cherokee Nation v. Georgia, 168, 415n187
Cherokee Phoenix (newspaper), 147, 150–52, 176, 178, 181–83, 183–84
Cherokee women: colonialism's impact on, 23, 328; erosion of power, 167, 177–81, 361; historical intermarriage, 170–72; in matrilineal system, 361; political power of, 178–79; property rights of, 163, 179–80; restrictions on intermarriage, 150, 156–57, 165–67, 358, 361; role in assimilation, 184–85
Chew, Lee, 276, 309, 319
Child, Lydia Maria, 75, 333

child betrothal, 108–9
children (mixed-race): activism as adults, 385; forced removal of, 99, 362, 363–64, 452n35; and inheritance, 361–63; and legitimacy, 360–61; living arrangements, 264; perceived threats of, 267–68
Children of John and Mary Ross (Waugh), 388
Chinese men: Aboriginal classification of, 301; under the APA, 257, 273–74, 275–78; arrivals of, 90; coerced labor of, 400n66; demographics, 263; images of, *255, 277, 310*; under White Australia policy, 291
Choctaws, 41, 69, 169, 423n2
Chong Choy, 276–77
Christianity: Cherokees' adoption of, 180; equality in, 78–81, 153–54; motives for conversion to, 120; pilgrimages in, 82–83; on polygamy, 112, 330–31, 337; on Queensland's marriage laws, 288–89; reinventing history through, 162
citizenship: of Aboriginal people, 310, 446n63; of African Americans, 16–17, 172–73; in the Cherokee Nation, 155–56, 177, 225, 366, 431n1; gendered concepts of, 26; and legitimacy, 360–61; marriage's impact on, 240
civilization: Cherokee understanding of, 428n110; marriage's role in, 112, 183–85, 356–57; and polygamy, 340–41; relation to colonialism, 271; slavery in, 175
Clark, Emily, 274
Clark, Janie (Janey, Jeannie, Jane) (née Forbes), 133–40, 375, 378–81, *382*, 383
Clark, Jeannie (née Forbes), 133–40, 375, 378–81, *382*, 383
Clark, Nola, 139, 143–44, 375–76, 378–81, *380*, 383

Clark, Steve, *382*
Clark, Willie, 138, 139–40, 378–81, *382*, 383
Coghlan, T. A., 268
cohabitation. *See* interracial sexual relationships
Cohen, Jeff, 236
College of New Jersey, 63
Colonial Intimacies (Plane), 336–37
colonialism: Cherokees' negotiation of, 161–63, 186–87; concept of legitimacy in, 359–61; conflicting ethics of, 51, 82–84; impact on Cherokee Nation, 185; impact on Indigenous sovereignty, 315–16; intermarriage's impact on, 1–4, 8–9, 22, 80–81, 350–52, 358–59, 392–93; intimate frontiers in, 24–25, 231; middle grounds of, 24, 25; monogamy's role in, 330, 331; new worlds created by, 2–3; perfect sovereignty under, 356–58; and polygamy, 325–26, 336–37, 343–48; power dynamics of, 22; reinvented histories of, xx–xxii, 23, 57, 74–77, 235; in the republic period, 21–22; role of marriage law in, 10, 295–96; sovereignty enacted in, 11–12, 240–41; transnational ground of, 6; violence during, 91–94, 262, 297, 303–4, 329; white identities created in, 15; William Penn's version of, 233–34
Colonial Marriages Act (1865), 10, 255, 289, 397n31
colonizing compact, 26–27, 66, 158, 169, 175–76
Commonwealth Franchise Act, 445n37
Conforti, Joseph, 57
Congregational Church (Cornwall), 39–41, 55–56, 67–68
Coniston Massacre, 329
Connecticut Assembly, 59
Connelly, Mary, 218

consent: Aboriginal kinship-based, 314–15, 318–19; Aboriginal women's understanding of, 319, 321–22; and colonization, 26; required under APA, 302–3, 306–7; significance of, 293; various conceptions of, 312–13
constitution, defined, 295–96
convicts, 10, 15, 20, 90
Cook, Cecil, 19
Cooper, James Fenimore, 65, 85
Cornwall (CT), 38–39, 57, 58–60, 78–79, 350
Cott, Nancy, 7, 180, 330, 399n55
"country" concept, 13, 113–14, 123, 294–95, 399n45
Cowlishaw, Gillian, 318
Crawford, William H., 17, 52, 79, 356, 400n61
Crawley, Ernest, 297, 332
Creedy (Australian constable), 276
Curry, Robert, 381

Daggett, Hermann, 67
Dark Deeds in a Sunny Land (Gribble), 98, 420n84
Davis, George Barber, 153
Deakin, Alfred, 18
Delawares, 233
Deloria, Philip, 214–15
Discourse against Unequal Marriages (Bufford), 312
divorce, 178, 304–5, 326, 342
Dixon, Robert, 314
Dodson, Annie Bryan (née Ross), 387, *388*, 390, 391
Dodson, Leonidas, 391
Dolly (Aboriginal woman), 276, 309, 319
doomed-race theory, 104, 355, 404n121
Douglas, Orson, 230, 231, 235
dreaming (Aboriginal concept), 101, 294, 313–14, 443n3

Durham, H. R., 316
Dwight, Timothy, 40

Edouart, Auguste, 210
Edwards, Jonathan, 406n21
"Eelemarni" (marriage story), 314, 446n55
effigy burnings, 35, 38–39, 56–57
Elk, Chief, 162
Ellinghaus, Kat, 184
Emerson, Ralph Waldo, 217
England, 20–21, 288–89, 312
equality, 78–81, 228–29
eugenics, 19, 270, 275
Evarts, Jeremiah, 79, 234, 453n14

Fesl, Eve (née Serico), xxiii–xxiv, 364
Fields, Matilda Rogers, 372
Fields, Richard, *378*
Fitzroy Island (Kobahra), 99, 121, *122*, 139–40, 383
floods (Aboriginal concept), 313
Ford, Lisa, 4, 158–59
Foreign Mission School (Cornwall), 40–42, 45, 56, 61–63, 68, 407n50
Foucault, Michel, 158, 336
Foxton, Justin, 288–89
Fraser family, 262
Fraser Island, 384–85
Freeman, Bill, 272–73
Frodsham, George, 141
frontier violence. *See* violence

Gabriel, Ralph, 76
Gallatin, Albert, 183
Gambold, Anna, 72
gender: in Aboriginal governance, 117, 118; in Aboriginal marriages, 126; and captivity narratives, 75; in Cherokee social order, 163; in Christian teachings, 40, 77; and colonialism, 23, 328; divisions of labor, 169; feminism's impact on,

333–34; and marriage, 25–26, 180–81; in marriage laws, 179–80, 402n103; and sexuality, 47–48
Georgia, 148, 157, 168–69, 170, 192, 196, 200, 423n10; map of, *146*
Georgia, Cherokee Nation v., 168, 415n187
Georgia, Worcester v., 168, 197, 415n187
Ghost Dance movement, 161
Gilmore, Glenda, 367–68
Givens, Thomas, 134
Glackens, Louis M., xvii
Godwin, Mary Wollstonecraft, 181–82
"going to water" ceremony, 159–60
Gold, Benjamin, 44, 45, 55, 56–57, 370–71, 374
Gold, Eleanor, 44, 45, 55, 56–57, 370–71, 374, 376
Gold, Harriett. *See* Boudinot, Harriett (née Gold)
Gold, Stephen, 35, 39, 42–44, 54–55, 57, 72, 350
Gold, Theodore, 405n13
Goon Goo (Chinese man), 251, 254, 284
Gordon-Reed, Annette, 173–74
Governor, Ethel, 24
Governor, Jimmie, 24, 262
Grant, Eva, 281
Green, Rayna, 214–15
Green Corn festival, 13, 160, 206
Greenough, F. W., 43
Gribble, Bert, 130
Gribble, Emilie Julie (née Wriede), 109–10, 134, 135, 136–37
Gribble, Ernest: Aboriginal classification of, 119–20, 142; alliance with Menmuny, 117–18; archival files on, 94–95; arrival at Yarrabah, 106; attraction to Aboriginal women, 105; birth of, 97; and brother Bert, 130; connection to Aboriginal peoples, 102; control over Aboriginal marriages, 119–21, 357; and daughter Nola, 139, 375–76, 383; death of, 383; and Ethel's marriage, 131–33; grave of, *387*; images of, *96, 380, 385, 386*; importance of weddings to, 87, 125–28; legacy of, 89, 144; love affair with Jeannie, 133, 135–40, 143, 377–78, 381, 383, 423n148; marriage of, 109–10, 136–37; mission-building work of, 98–99, 100, 107–8; musical performances, 124–25; opposition to intermarriage, 103, 141–42; on Palm Island, 381–83; past secrets of, 107; on polygamy, 108–9, 341–42; punishments administered by, 111–12, 120–21, 418n54; removal from Yarrabah, 139, 140–41; segregation policies of, 95, 103–5, 355; sexual policing of, 110–12
Gribble, Ethel. *See* Wondunna, Ethel (née Gribble)
Gribble, Illa, 100, 125, 128, 139
Gribble, John Brown, 87, 91, 97–98, 106, 417n14, 420n84
Gribble, Mary Ann (née Bulmer), 97, 100, 127, 128, 136, 139
Grimshaw, Patricia, 327
Gsell, F. X., 342–43
Gunggandji people, 98, 100, 123, 129
Gurindji walk-off (1960s), xxiii, 315

Hall, James, 208
Hamilton (Australian politician), 284–85
hand-holding symbolism, 230–31
Hartog, Hendrik, 402n103
Hemings, Sally, 16–17, 246
Henley, Elizabeth Brown, 201–2, 204, 236
Henley, Susan, 201
Higgins, Bradley, *387*
The History of Human Marriage (Westermarck), 297, 332–33
History of the Indian Tribes of North America (McKenney and Hall), 208

INDEX

Hobomok (Child), 75, 333
Hollingsworth, Charmaine, 143
"Home Sweet Home" (song), 216, 367
Hornet Bank Massacre, 329
Howard, Richard, 310
Humpherson, Edith, 281

identity: in the Cherokee Nation, 27, 154; and colonialism, 15; impact of forced removal on, 366–67; marriage's impact on, 3–4, 80–84; role of land in, 294–95
illegitimacy, 121, 143, 349, 360–61
imperialism. *See* colonialism
Indian Removal Act (1830), 196, 353–54
"The Indian Song, Sarah and John" (poem), 76, 414n159
Indian Territory, 201, 204, 240, 353–54
inheritance, 362–63
International Indian Council (Tahlequah), 239
interracial marriage: advantages for Aboriginal women, 309–11, 317; advocated by founding fathers, 16–18, 52, 399n59; allegiance shifts, 171; and Cherokee sovereignty, 147–50, 152–55; as colonial middle grounds, 24–25, 358–59; contradictory attitudes toward, 15–16; gendered limits, 17–18, 52, 68, 74–77, 81; impact of forced removal on, 364–67; impact on colonialism, 1–4, 8–9, 22, 80–81, 350–52, 358–59, 392–93; impact on identity, 3–4; impact on sovereignty, 2–3, 9–10, 245–46, 350–52, 356–59, 392–93; Indigenous opposition to, 314, 337; and legitimacy issues, 360–61; and polygamy, 339–40, 343; reasons for secrecy, xii, xxi–xxii, 6, 362–63, 366, 367–68; and slavery, 173; as test of the American republic, 81–84; transnational significance of, 1–4, 244–45;

247. *See also* Aboriginals Protection Act (APA); marriage laws
interracial sexual relationships: Aboriginal humor regarding, 334–36; in Aboriginal kinship systems, 103; impacts on colonialism, 22, 392–93; and legitimacy issues, 360–61; mixed understandings of, xxii, 328; potential power through, 336; Queensland's regulation of, 257–58; reasons for secrecy, xx, xxi, 94, 142–43, 344–45, 366–68, 376–78, 381; restricted at Yarrabah, 110, 342
Irving, Washington, 181, 182

Jackson (Aboriginal man), 310–11
Jackson, Andrew, 148, 192, 196, 353–54
Jackson, W. H., 274
Jacky (Aboriginal man), 309, 319
Jacobs, Margaret, 364
jarralyku (floodout), 313
Jefferson, Thomas: advocating intermarriage, 16–17, 52, 79, 247, 356, 357, 399n59; Cherokee students' visit with, 62; compact with the Cherokees, 169, 237; in Philadelphia, 234; and Sally Hemings, 173–74, 246
Jemison, Mary, 75
Jinnie (Aboriginal girl), 130
Joe (author's grandfather), xxi
Johnstone, Lizzie, *132*, 367
journey routes, 13, 100–101, 123, 366
Jumbo (Aboriginal man), 275

Karpa Creek outstation, *124*
Katchewan, Pompo, 97
Kendall, Henry, 125
Kidwell, Clara Sue, xi, xiii, *xviii*
King Philip's War, 58–59
Kinnane, Edward, 318
Kinnane, Stephen, 318

496

INDEX

kinship: Aboriginal classificatory rules, 103, 142, 299–300; in Aboriginal societies, 27, 314, 318–19; APA's undermining of, 302–3; classification of outsiders, 301; marriage laws regulating, 9, 112–13, 294–95, 299–302; obligations under Aboriginal law, 119; Yarrabah mission's impact on, 119–20. *See also* matrilineal systems; patrilineal systems

Kitty (Aboriginal woman), 251, 254, 284

Kobahra Island (Fitzroy Island), 99, 121, *122*, 139–40, 383

Kooweskoowe. *See* Ross, John

L., Lizzie (Aboriginal woman), 309–10

labor trade, 18–19, 20, 90–91, 260–61, 400n66

landscapes, 100–102, 121, 294–95, 399n45

"The Last of His Tribe" (Kendall), 125

The Last of the Mohicans (Cooper), 85

Laurie, Amy, xxii

Law of Nations (Vattel), 157, 424n35

Leftwich, Madge, *380*

legitimacy, 359–61

Levy, Grace, 217–18, 221

Levy, Sandra, 387

Linnay (Aboriginal man), 308

literacy, 72

Lizzie L. (Aboriginal woman), 309–10

Lomawaima, K. Tsianina, 20

Loomis, Deacon, 54

Madison, Dolly: and the first telegram, 223; images of, *xvi, 224*; as political wife, xvii, 62, 234, 240; and the Quakers, 231; Ross-Stapler wedding flowers, xiii, xiv, 246–47, 391; and Washington's portrait, 438n162

Madison, James, 62, 231, 234, 236, 246

maps: of Australia, *x, xxxii, 86, 122*; of the Cherokee Nation, *36, 146, 354*; of Georgia, *146*; of Queensland, *86*; of Yarrabah mission, *122*

Maria (Aboriginal woman), 277

Mariner's Church, 231, 232, 235

marriage: in Aboriginal societies, 264, 299–302; connections through, 27, 56, 63–64, 299–302, 312–15, 338; consent in, 48, 293, 312–15; feminism's impact on, 180–81, 333–34; impacts on women, 80, 180–81; as performance of sovereignty, 2; personal nature of, 290; role in civilization, 112, 183–85, 356–57; role in nationalism, 3, 7–9, 399n55; and social order, 9–10; suitability requirements, 79–80; symbolism of, 56, 230–31, 247; varying conceptions of, 326–27. *See also* interracial marriage

marriage banns, 39–40, 55–56, 69–70

marriage ceremonies. *See* wedding ceremonies

marriage laws, 9–10, 255–56, 288–89, 326–27, 344–45, 359–61. *See also* Aboriginal marriage laws; Aboriginals Protection Act (APA); Cherokee marriage laws

Marshall, John, 168, 192, 353, 415n187

masculinity: APA as threat to, 259–60, 285–87, 305–6; and the captivity narrative, 75, 228–29; in colonialism, 23, 320, 328; intermarriage's impact on, 56, 241, 244; and marital consent, 297–98

Massey, Winnie, *380*

Matbar, Lallie, 318

matrilineal systems: changes to Cherokees', 154, 155–56, 167, 178–80, 361, 424n29; in the Cherokee Nation, 177–78; and identity, 27, 154; polygamy in, 331; property rights under, 179–80, 346, 361–62; role in social order, 27–28, 154

Mawe, Albert, *101*

McCrea, Jane, 75

McDonald, James Lawrence, 225–26

497

McKenney, Thomas L.: Cape Cottage home, 218–19; and Dolley Madison, 246–47; and James McDonald, 225–26; and John Ross, 211, 212–13, 227–28, 238, 353; in Philadelphia, 235; political work of, 212–13, 240, 333; troubles finding employment, 433n49; writings of, 208

McLoughlin, William, 161, 232

Meigs, Annie Stapler, 372

Meigs, Return J., 68, 153, 161, 171

Memoir of Catharine Brown (Anderson), 54

men. *See* Aboriginal men; Cherokee men; white men

Menmuny (Gunggandji elder), 89, *101*, 109, 117–18, 120, 130, 341–42

Menmuny Museum, 87–89

Meston, Alexander, *282*

Meston, Archibald: background of, 266–67; cartoon of, *280*; as chief protector, 265, 269–75, 303, 304, 307–8, 357; images of, *266, 269, 283*; son of, 282; vilification of, 278–81

Metacom (Wampanoag leader), 59

Miantonomo (Mohegan man), 59

Miller, Alfred Jacob, xiii, xix

Miller, Olga, 385

Milligan, Elizabeth, 203, 205–6

Minnie (Aboriginal woman), 304, 308, 319

missionaries, 40–42, 77, 330–31, 408n64. *See also* Gribble, Ernest; Yarrabah mission

Missionary News, 114

Mitchell, Pat, 368

Mohegans, 10, 58–60, 350

monogamy: in Christianity, 110–12, 330; in colonialism, 16, 236, 325–26; and inheritance, 362–63; modern ideas of, 7; at Yarrabah mission, 103, 110–12, 125, 143

Monroe, James, 52, 61, 63, 79

Montesquieu, Baron de, 16, 330

Moravian Female Academy, 194, 209

Mormon Church, 331–32

Morrill, Justin, 332

Morse, Jedidiah, 331, 408n77

Morse, Samuel, 223

Moulton, Gary, 201, 206

Murragun outstation, *123*

The Mystic Rose (Crawley), 297, 332–33

naming practices, 236, 373, 411n122

Nan-ye-hi (Nancy Ward), 172–73, 182

Narragansetts, 336–37

nation, concept of, 3

"Native American movement" (anti-Irish uprising), 234–35

Native Americans: in captivity narratives, 74–75, 228–29, 241; enacting sovereignty, 12–14; impacts of colonialism on, 398n38; and legitimacy, 360–61; status of, 17; stereotypes of, 76–77, 214–15, 220–21, 226, 238, 389–90; views on polygamy, 336; William Penn's treatment of, 233–34. *See also* Cherokee Nation

Native Police force, 93, *123, 277,* 297

Nelly (Aboriginal woman), 276

New Echota Treaty (1835), 196, 200

New Zealand, 11–12, 19, 400n70

Nicol, J., 272

Nina (Aboriginal woman), 279

Nora (Aboriginal woman), 130, 341–42

Northrup, Sarah. *See* Ridge, Sarah (née Northrup)

Northrup family, 71, 79

Oakley, Annie, 334

Occam, Samson, 59

Olsen, Evelyn, 364–65

Olsen, John, 364–65

Oo-wat-ie (Elias's father), 50–51, 61, 170
Operation Sovereign Borders, 398n35
opium trade, 439n13
Opukaha'ia (Pacific Islander), 40
outstation settlements, 124

Pacific Islander men, 90–91, 261, 273–74, 291, 301, 400n66
Paine, Ann, 193
Palm Island, 121, 381–83
Parkes, Henry, 18
Pascoe, Peggy, 357
Pateman, Carole, 25–26
patrilineal systems, 81, 178, 338, 360, 361–62, 363
Payne, John Howard, 181–82, 196–97, 216, 221, 367, 429n117
Pearson (white missionary), 106, 130
Penn, William, 233–34, 235, 437n135
Pennsylvania Inquirer and National Gazette (newspaper), 237
Pequot War, 58
Perdue, Theda, 155, 185, 330–31, 424n29, 431n1
perfect sovereignty, 4, 28, 158, 351, 356–58, 368, 392
Pettit, James, 339
Philadelphia (PA), 233–35
phoenix, 163, 182
Pickles, Ada, 139–40, 143, 378
Pilgrim's Progress (Bunyan), 83
Pitt, Myra, 143, 378, *382*, 383
Plane, Ann Marie, 336
plural marriage. *See* polygamy
police (Queensland), 274–77, 287–88, 297, 303–4, 329
polyandry, 326, 345
polygamy: in Aboriginal societies, 108–9, 301, 309–11, 318–19, 336, 337–38; advantages of, 330; and colonialism, 325–26, 330–31, 345–48; connections created through, 338; defined, 326; frontier forms of, 343–45; as against modernity, 338–41; in the Mormon Church, 331–32; in Native American societies, 167, 331, 336–37, 338–41, 346–47
polygyny, 326, 345
Poor Sarah (missionary tract), 76, 413n158
Povinelli, Elizabeth, 15
premarital pregnancy, 121, 129–30
Princeton University, 63
property ownership rights: of Aboriginal societies, 102; in the Cherokee Nation, 154, 163, 179–80, 187; impact of forced removal on, 365–67; and interracial marriage, 362–63; and marriage prospects, 80; of married white women, 428n95, 428n100; and slavery, 173; and sovereignty, 4, 148, 157–58
Pryor, Peter, 381
Public Ledger (newspaper), 238

Quakers, 231–32
Queensland: colonization of, 21; demographics, 262, 263; gender imbalance in, 262; government surveillance archives, 252–53; labor economy of, 260–61; lack of borders in, 263–65; map of, *86*; segregation policies of, 269–70, 354–56, 419n59; significance of floods in, 313; violence in, 91–94, 253–54, 262
Queensland Marriage Act (1865), 10, 255–56, 288–89, 397n31

race: classifications, 77, 155, 268; and colonialism, 28; degeneration fears, 18, 261; and marriage roles, 48; and religion, 60
ragtime weddings, 128–30
Rajkowski, Pam, 318
Reading, Maisie, 378
Red Jacket, Chief, *159*
Reece, Susanna, 50, 61

INDEX

Reeves, William, 131–32
"The Reign of Dolly Madison" (cartoon), *xvii*
religious revivals, 60
reservations and reserves, 353–56, 364–67. *See also* Indian Territory
Reynolds, Henry, 423n148
Ridge, John: advocacy work of, 79, 155, 183, 185, 429n123; ancestry of, 50; assassination of, 204–5, 375, 409n98; and the Cherokee Socrates, 164; controversy over marriage, 41–42, 49, 153, 154; at Cornwall's mission school, 61; image of, *43*; on intermarriage, 79, 155, 429n122; meeting Sarah, 406n23; and the New Echota Treaty, 196–97, 200; on polygamy, 340; on relations with slaves, 176; on women's rights, 179, 183
Ridge, John Rollin, *376, 378*
Ridge, Major, *42*, 161, 174, 204–5, 375
Ridge, Sarah (née Northrup): controversy over marriage, 41–42, 49, 153; meeting John, 406n23; significance of marriage, 79; stereotypes of, 76; as a widow, 187–88, 205, 409n98
Robinson, Aileen Moreton, 12
Rocky Island, *122*, 139
romanticism, 149, 181–82, 217, 221, 243
Rose Cottage, *175*, 241, 387
Ross, Annie Bryan, 387, *388*, 390, 391
Ross, Caroline C. (née Lazalear), 391
Ross, Eliza Jane, 211, 218, 238
Ross, George Washington, 236
Ross, John: archival files of, xii–xiii, 243; background of, 206–7; and the Cherokee Constitution, 424n32; and Cherokee political tensions, 204–5; children of, 387, 388; courtship letters of, 194, 195–96, *198, 199*, 211–12, 213–14, 215–20, 241–45; death of, 390; death threat against, 432n27; diplomatic work of, 202, 236, 239–40, 389, 431n21; first marriage of, 201–2; first meeting Mary, 194, 206, 209; images of, *207, 208, 210, 239, 244, 379*; impact of William Penn on, 233–34; marital boundaries crossed, 240–41, 243–46, 353; marriage negotiations, 222–29; names of, 195; opposition to intermarriage, 172, 193–94; opposition to removal west, 196–97, 200, 240; religious views of, 232; romanticizing mixed marriage, 220–22; Rose Cottage, 175, 385–89; search for second wife, 202–3, 205–6; slaves of, 174, 175; wedding certificate, *xv*, 230–31; wedding flowers, xiii, *xiv*, 246–47; wedding of, 235, 237–38
Ross, John Junior, 387, *388*, 391
Ross, Mary Bryan (née Stapler): archival files on, 243; background of, 209–11; boundary crossing of, 240–41, 243–46, 353; children of, 387, 388; courtship letters of, 194, 195–96, *198, 199*, 211–12, 213–14, 215–20, 241–45; death of, 390; first meeting John, 194, 206, 209; images of, *242, 244*; impact of William Penn on, 233–34; in Indian Territory, 385–89; marriage certificate, *xv*; marriage negotiations, 222–29; romanticizing mixed marriage, 220–22; use of stereotypes, 389–90; wedding certificate, 230–31; wedding flowers, xiii, *xiv*, 246–47; wedding of, 235, 237–38
Ross, Quatie, 201–2, 204, 236
Ross, William P., 221
Roth, Vincent, 281
Roth, Walter E.: background of, 265–66; as chief protector, 265, 270–73, 287–89, 303, 306, 307, 357; and Ernest Gribble, 105, 127; ethnographic work of, 266, 284–85, 298–99, 303, 314, 420n90; images of, *266, 286*; vilification of, 281–87

Rules and Regulations (Gribble), 110–11, 114, 128–29

Saladin (Spanish conquistador), 170
same-nation marriage, 18, 103–4, 111–12, 125, 357–58
Sands, Elva, 143
Sargent, Delight, 205, 374, 375
Saunt, Claudio, 162
Schermerhorn, John F., 200
Schrieber, Lorna, 118, 128
scientific racism, 257, 270
Scott, Joan, 9
segregation policies: African Americans in, xx; in Australia, 269–70, 354–56, 419n59; Gribble's support of, 95, 103–5, 355; impact on Aboriginal societies, 364–67; in the United States, 353–54, 355–56
Selu (Cherokee corn mother), 13, 154, 159–61, 162, 173, 190–91
Sequoyah, 68, *189*
Serico, Nurdon, xxiii–xxiv
Shaw, Frances Prowse, 279–81, 282
Shaw, Leonard, 171
Shawnees, 337
Shelley, Percy Bysshe, 181–82, 190
Shinoda, Hideaki, 157
Simpson, Cuthbert, *88*
Simpson, Joe, 272
Simpson, Mathilda, *88*
slavery: in the British Empire, 18; in the Cherokee Nation, 153, 163, 165, 167, 172–77; escape routes, 427n82; opposition to, 411n119; and religion, 60; in the United States, 16–17, 51–52, 173–75, 180, 352. *See also* labor
Smith, Bill, 272–73
Smith, Joseph, 332
Smith, Mae, 378
Smith, Marion, xi–xii
Smiths Weekly (magazine), 343–44

social order: in Aboriginal societies, 29, 112–13, 403n115, 447n11; African Americans in, 17, 163, 164–65, 172–73, 366; colonialism's impact on, 81, 162–63; and marriage, 9–10, 81; in matrilineal systems, 27–28, 154; slavery in, 173–77; women in, 180–82
Socrates (Cherokee), 147, 149–50, 152, 156–57, 163–64, 177, 186, 191
Socrates (Greek), 150, 190–91
A Son of the Forest (Apess), 390
sovereignty: and Aboriginal marriage laws, 294–95; challenges to Cherokee, 147–49, 157–59, 167–70; Cherokees' assertion of, 152–55, 186–92; colonialism's impact on, 315–16, 356–58; concept of legitimacy in, 359–61; defined, 11; enactments of, 11–14, 240–41; impact of forced removal on, 364–67; impact of intermarriage on, 2–3, 9–10, 245–46, 350–52, 356–59, 392–93; and land ownership, 4; reinvention of, 367
The Spirit of the Pilgrims (Beecher), 83
"squaw" stereotype, 76, 226
St. Alban's Church (Yarrabah), *104*
Stanley, John Mix, 239
Stapler, John, Sr., 209–11, 212, 225, 226–27, 238, 387
Stapler, Mary Bryan. *See* Ross, Mary Bryan (née Stapler)
Stapler, Sarah, 209, 211, 215, 219, 222, 225, 226–27, 387, 389
A Star in the West (Boudinot), 65
state biopower, 158
stereotypes: of captive white women, 74–75, 220–21, 228–29, 241; and Indian wealth, 238; of Indigenous consent, 297; of Indigenous savagery, 4; of perceived backwardness, 76–77; "squaw" stereotype, 226; the "white man's Indian," 214–15, 389–90

INDEX

Stirling Castle (ship), 384
St. Ledger, Mary, 279
Stockton, Richard, 63
Stockwood, John, 312
Stoler, Ann Laura, 8
Stowe, Harriet Beecher, 406n20
Stuart, Gilbert, xvi
Sturm, Circe, 155–56
Supreme Court (U.S.), 168–69, 197, 415n187

Mr T (Aboriginal man), 304, 308, 319
Tahseekeyarkey (Cherokee man), 176
Tasmania, 95, 354–55
Taylor, Eunice Wadsworth, 73
Taylor, John, 232
Tecumsah (Shawnee man), 337
telegraphs, 223
"Ten Little Niggers" (song), 125, 420n85
Tenskwatawa (Shawnee man), 337
terra nullius concept, 20, 316
Tiger (Aboriginal man), 276
Topsey (Aboriginal woman), 274
Toulmin, Ada, 281
Trail of Tears, 200–201, 202, *354*
The Trapper's Bride (painting), xiii–xviii, xix
treaties, 12, 21, 196, 200, 239–40
Treaty of New Echota (1835), 196, 200
Trucaninni (Tasmanian woman), 95, 355, 404n121
Turner, Frederick Jackson, 23
Tuskaroras, 228
Tyler, John, 237, 239–40
Tyson, James, 97

Uncas (Algonquin man), 59, 397n30
United States: founding fathers' visions for, 16–18; maps of, *34*; national symbol of, 182; practice of polygamy in, 325–26; recognition of Cherokee Nation, 10–11, 20, 21, 195, 360; relation to Australia, 14–15; slavery in, 16–17, 51–52, 173–75, 180, 352, 411n119, 427n82; and sovereignty, 11; women's social status in, 180–83
unity metaphor, 78–81

Vaill, Flora (née Gold), 55, 58, 72
Vaill, Hermann, 44–45, 46–50, 49, 51, 55, 74, 80, 350
Van Buren, Martin, 217
Van Diemen's Land, 95, 354–55
Vann, David, 164, *166*
Vann, James, 174
Vann, Joseph, 164
Vann House, *165*
Vattel, Emer de, 157, 180, 424n35
Victoria, Queen, 21, 255, 289
A Vindication of the Rights of Woman (Wollstonecraft), 180
violence: and Aboriginal law, 303–4, 328–29; and Australian colonialism, 91–94, 253–54, 262; under colonialism, 8; in the gold fields, 18–19; J. B. Gribble's exposure of, 97–98; and New England colonialism, 58–60; and sovereignty, 359

wampum, 58–59
Ward, Bryan, 173
Ward, Joseph, 224
Ward, Nancy, 172–73, 182
Ward, Russell, 23
Warlpiri language, 313
Washburn, Cephas, 159–60
Washington, George, 62–63, 66, *159*, 232, 234, 236–37, 354, 437n145
Washington House Hotel (Philadelphia), 235–36
Watie, Buck. *See* Boudinot, Elias
Watie, Saladin, *378*

Watie, Stand, 375, 432n27
Waugh, Samuel Bell, 242, 388
wedding ceremonies: Aboriginal rituals in, 311; in the Cherokee Nation, 159–60, 184; Gribble's focus on, 87, 118; performative nature of, 7; at Yarrabah, 125–28, 421n102
wedding certificate, *xv*, 230–31
Westermarck, Edward, 297, 332
White, Bishop, 285
White, Richard, 25
White Australia policy, 19, 256, 258, 291
white men: Aboriginal classification of, 301; under Aboriginal law, 302, 328–29; and Aboriginal women, 262–63, 265, 320, 358; under the APA, 257–58, 271–73; challenges to Cherokee sovereignty, 147–48; under Cherokee law, 150, 156–57, 165–67, 177, 179–80; and Cherokee women, 170–72, 339–40, 358; gendered role in colonialism, 23; opposing intermarriage, 17–18; opposing the APA, 259–69, 278–79, 285–87, 290–91, 304; reasons for secrecy, 265, 344–45, 362–63; views of marriage, 344–45. *See also* gender; Gribble, Ernest; masculinity
white women: in Aboriginal protection work, 279, 364; appropriate values of, 57–58; and black men, 174–75, 258–59; in captivity narratives, 74–75, 241; changing rights of, 307–8; involvement in Aboriginal protection, 281; marital rights of, 428n95, 428n100; marriage's impact on, 225, 240; marriage to Aboriginal men, 259, 439n15; marriage to Cherokee men, 74–77, 154–56, 241; reasons for secrecy, 362–63; in religious teachings, 40, 47–48; reproductive expectations of, 77; status in Cherokee law, 187, 431n1. *See also* Boudinot, Harriett (née Gold); Ross, Mary Bryan (née Stapler)
Wild Australia (traveling show), 267, *268*
Wild Rose (Nancy Ward), 172–73, 182
Wilkins, David E., 20
Wolfe, Patrick, 3
Wollstonecraft, Mary, 180, 181, 333
Wondunna, Ethel (née Gribble), 100, 125, 128, 131–33, 367, 383–85
Wondunna, Fred, 131–33, 383–85
Worcester, Samuel, 40, 197
Worcester v. Georgia, 168, 197, 415n187
Wright, Charles John, 141
"wrong-way" marriage, 113, 119, 300, 418n57
Wrotham Park station, 315

Yarbrough, Fay A., 331, 428n99
Yarrabah Court, 113
Yarrabah mission, *89, 105, 135*; advantages of, 116, 117; building of, 100, 107–8; diet of, 420n96; goals of, 98; governance of, 113–14, 116–18, 419n63; Gribble Point image, *386*; Gribble's impact on, 142–43, 144, 342; Gribble's removal from, 140–41; Jeannie's role at, 134–36; landscape of, 95; map of, *122*; married couples at, *111*, 114–16; mission classrooms, *96*; musical band, *108, 109*; outstations, *123, 124*; punishments administered in, 120–21; ragtime weddings at, 128–30; segregation policy of, 103–5; sexual policing in, 110–12; shipwreck, *90*; St. Alban's Church, *104*; wedding ceremonies at, 125–28, 421n102
Yidinjdji people, 98–99, 142–43, 260

IN THE BORDERLANDS AND
TRANSCULTURAL STUDIES SERIES

How the West Was Drawn: Mapping, Indians, and the Construction of the Tran-Mississippi West
David Bernstein

Chiricahua and Janos: Communities of Violence in the Southwestern Borderlands, 1680-1880
Lance R. Blyth

The Borderland of Fear: Vincennes, Prophetstown, and the Invasion of the Miami Homeland
Patrick Bottiger

Captives: How Stolen People Changed the World
Catherine M. Cameron

Transnational Crossroads: Remapping the Americas and the Pacific
edited by Camilla Fojas and Rudy P. Guevarra Jr.

Conquering Sickness: Race, Health, and Colonization in the Texas Borderlands
Mark Allan Goldberg

Globalizing Borderlands Studies in Europe and North America
edited and with an introduction by John W. I. Lee and Michael North

Illicit Love: Interracial Sex and Marriage in the United States and Australia
Ann McGrath

The Limits of Liberty: Mobility and the Makin g of the Eastern U.S.-Mexico Border
James David Nicholas

Native Diasporas: Indigenous Identities and Settler Colonialism in the Americas
edited by Gregory D. Smithers and Brooke N. Newman

The Southern Exodus to Mexico: Migration across the Borderlands after the American Civil War
Todd W. Wahlstrom

To order or obtain more information on these or other University of Nebraska Press titles, visit nebraskapress.unl.edu.

OTHER WORKS BY ANN MCGRATH

Long History, Deep Time:
Deepening Histories of Place, ed.
Ann McGrath and Mary Anne Jebb
(Canberra: ANU Press, 2015)

How to Write History That People Want to
Read, by Ann Curthoys and Ann McGrath
(New York: Palgrave Macmillan, 2011)

Proof & Truth: The Humanist as
Expert, ed. Iain McCalman and Ann
McGrath (Canberra: Australian
Academy of the Humanities, 2003)

Writing Histories: Imagination and
Narration, ed. Ann Curthoys and Ann
McGrath (Melbourne: School of Historical
Studies, Monash University, 2000)

Contested Ground: Australian Aborigines
under the British Crown, ed. Ann McGrath
(St. Leonards NSW: Allen & Unwin, 1995)

Creating a Nation, 1788–1990, by
Patricia Grimshaw, Marilyn Lake,
Ann McGrath, and Marian Quartly
(Ringwood VIC: McPhee Gribble, 1994)

Born in the Cattle: Aborigines in
Cattle Country, by Ann McGrath
(Sydney: Allen & Unwin, 1987);
also available as an ACLS e-book

www.ingramcontent.com/pod-product-compliance
Lightning Source LLC
Chambersburg PA
CBHW030558230426
43661CB00053B/1770